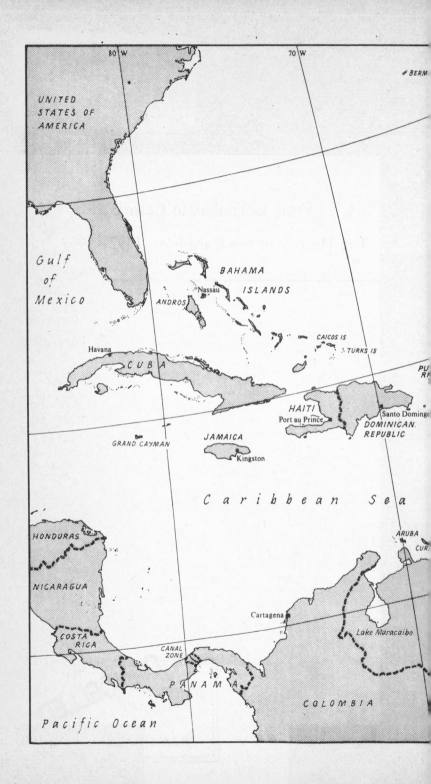

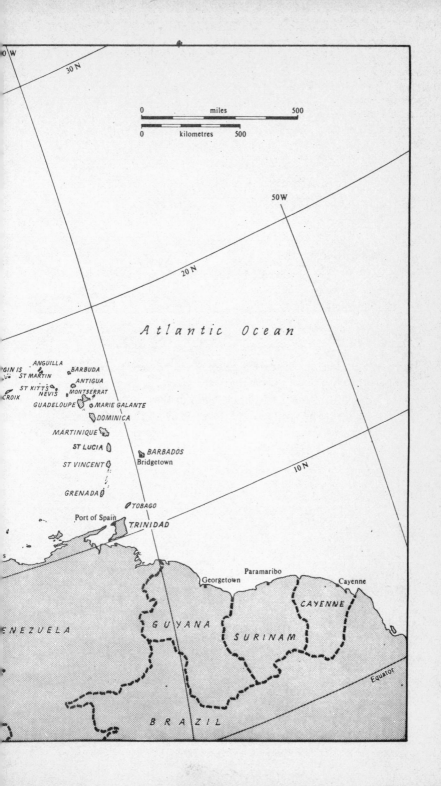

Books by the same author

History of the People of Trinidad and Tobago
Capitalism and Slavery
British Historians and the West Indies
Inward Hunger: The Education of a Prime Minister

From Columbus to Castro: The History of the Caribbean 1492—1969

ERIC WILLIAMS

ANDRE DEUTSCH

First published in 1970 by
André Deutsch Limited
Fifth impression 1978

First paperback edition September 1983

From Columbus to Castro:
The History of the Caribbean 1492–1969
Copyright © 1970 Eric Williams
All rights reserved

Printed in Great Britain by
The Thetford Press Limited
Thetford Norfolk

ISBN 0 233 97656 6

For permission to reproduce copyright material as illustrations in
this book the author and publisher acknowledge their thanks to: the
Corporation of Birmingham for plate 15; Keystone Press Agency
Ltd for plate 28; Radio Times Hulton Picture Library for plate 12;
the Trustees of the British Museum for plates 1, 2, 3, 4, 5, 7, 9, 10, 13,
14, 16, 26, 27; United Press International (UK) for plate 29; the
West India Committee Library for plates 8, 11, 18, 19, 20, 21, 22, 23,
24, 25.

TO THE PEOPLE'S NATIONAL MOVEMENT OF
TRINIDAD AND TOBAGO

'Great is the P.N.M. and it will prevail'

Contents

Illustrations

Introduction

For over four and a half centuries the West Indies have been the pawns of Europe and America. Across the West Indian stage the great characters, political and intellectual, of the Western World strut and fret their hour—Louis XIV and Bonaparte, Chatham and Pitt, Castlereagh and Canning, John Stuart Mill and Carlyle, Clarkson and the Abbé Raynal, Victor Schoelcher and José Marti, Jefferson and Adams, Joseph Chamberlain and Theodore Roosevelt, the *ancien régime* and the Revolution of 1789, Gladstone and Disraeli, Cobden and Bright, Russell and Palmerston, the mercantilists and the Manchester School. The beet sugar industry of Prussia, slave labour from Africa, contract labour from India and China, Christianity, Hinduism and Islam—all have left their mark on our West Indian society. Of the West Indies more than of most geographical areas it is possible to say that we are one world.

But in intellectual, as in political matters the Caribbean is a geographical expression. There is no history of the Caribbean area as a whole. Indeed, histories worthy of the name exist for only a few of the Caribbean territories.

After more than four and a half centuries of metropolitan

control, shared among several countries of Europe and America, all that we can boast of is a few monographs, the product of a metropolitan scholarship that has been fragmented, irregular, sporadic, and often pathetically inaccurate and prejudiced. Few 'colonials' have to date extended their nationalism to the cultural field and dedicated themselves to the task of writing—or rewriting, where necessary—their own history.

The present work is designed to fill this gap and to correct this deficiency. Its scope is the entire West Indian area, including the Guianas—whether their connections have been or are British or French, Spanish or American, Dutch or Danish, or whether they have discarded or are about to discard the alien rule of previous centuries.

Its goal is the cultural integration of the entire area, a synthesis of existing knowledge, as the essential foundation of the great need of our time, closer collaboration among the various countries of the Caribbean, with their common heritage of subordination to and dictation by outside interests.

The book was begun some eighteen years ago, but pressures of one sort or another have militated against its completion. Its publication at this moment is particularly timely in the context of the resolute attempt now being made by West Indians themselves to prevent the further fragmentation of the area and present a united front to the outside world.

Eric Williams   Port-of-Spain, Trinidad   October 10, 1969

Chapter One

Westward Ho!

The decisive landmark in the history of the fifteenth century, representing the transition from the Middle Ages to the modern era, was the Portuguese exploration and conquest of the West African coastline.

Up to 1415, when the Portuguese attacked and captured the Moorish stronghold of Ceuta in North Africa, the world, as known to and by the Europeans, was virtually limited to the world known to the Phoenicians, Greeks and Carthaginians. It embraced Europe, Asia Minor and North Africa—though Alexander the Great and the Roman legions had left behind memories of India, and Ethiopian civilisation was known to the Greeks. But the *Travels* of Marco Polo in the thirteenth century whetted the appetite with their descriptions of the Kingdom of Prester John, the empire of the Grand Khan, and the gold of Java and India.

With their conquest of Ceuta, the Portuguese set out on their discovery and exploration of the West African Coast. In 1435 they reached Senegal, in 1443 Cape Bojador, in 1446 Sierra Leone, in 1455 Guinea, and in 1481 the Congo. They stood poised for that superb achievement of Vasco da Gama, the rounding of the Cape of Good Hope, which opened the way to India.

That was Europe's dream in the fifteenth century, that was Europe's ambition—to reach India and the East. The Crusades had disrupted the normal overland connections, while the Italian maritime States of Venice and Genoa, sitting astride the sea routes, charged heavy tolls. The search for a westward route to India which dominated the fifteenth century had its roots in severely practical considerations. The Estates General of France in 1484 complained that in four years two previous Popes had drained France of more than two millions in gold.

The practical urge to discovery and expansion was also based on a much greater store of theoretical knowledge than had previously been available. The medieval view that the earth was flat could not withstand the Renaissance outlook which had developed renewed interest in a knowledge of geography from the study of Ptolemy, Strabo and Greek geographers who had speculated on the possibility of more easily reaching the Far East by a western voyage from the Pillars of Hercules. In the thirteenth century Roger Bacon's scientific method with its subordination of philosophy to mathematics led him to speculate as to the distribution of land and ocean over the globe, to hazard the view that a few days' sail westward from Spain would lead to eastern Asia, and to anticipate instruments for navigation, the automobile and the crane. The end of the fifteenth century witnessed the scientific method of Leonardo da Vinci, the representative man of the Renaissance, who anticipated the discovery of the law of gravity, designed the first submarine, and clearly foresaw the aeroplane.

By 1474 Columbus, even then planning his historic voyage, was assured by the great Italian geographer, Pablo Toscanelli, that his intentions were sound: 'The voyage you wish to undertake is not as difficult as people think; on the contrary, the ship's course is certain ...'

The course was certain if only because the necessary scientific and technological developments were available. Europe had already discovered or borrowed, and learned how to utilise, three decisive innovations which, unknown to or unutilised by the ancients, changed the whole face of the then known world. The first of these was printing; the second was gunpowder; and the third was the magnet.

But there were reasons other than technological. The political climate in the fifteenth century was congenial to discovery and overseas expansion.

In the first place the nation state had emerged. The feudal barons had been reduced in power by a combination of three causes—they killed each other off in their wars (in England, in the Wars of the Roses); they were more easily controlled by the national sovereigns like the Tudors in England and Ferdinand and Isabella in Spain; and, thirdly, they were defeated by the rising power of the townsmen, by such bourgeois leaders as Artevelde in Flanders and Marcel in France, in such decisive battles as Courtrai in Flanders and Morgarten in Switzerland.

The nation state had emerged also in revolt against foreign domination. If English Kings could still waste their substance at Crécy and Agincourt in the attempt to maintain their claim to rule over a part of France, French nationalism was symbolised by Joan of Arc. Portugal established its independence of Spain and Spain established its independence of the Moors. It was in 1492 that the last Moorish Kingdom, Granada, surrendered to the centralising monarchy of Ferdinand and Isabella, and the Moorish King, Abu Abdullah, threw himself on the clemency and generosity of the victors. Spain was accordingly ready to emulate in the West the Portuguese triumphs in Africa.

The national sovereign was thus the symbol of the Church triumphant, and the crusading zeal bottled up by the failure of the Crusades and the fall of Constantinople to the Turks in 1453 found an outlet in discovery and overseas expansion. Azurara, the Portuguese chronicler of the conquest of Guinea, justified the conquest in 1453 on the ground that the Africans became 'as good and true Christians as if they had directly descended, from the beginning of the dispensation of Christ, from those who were first baptised'. The challenge to the Roman Catholic Church by first Wycliffe, then Hus, then Luther gave Protestantism too its place in the world sun. The foundation was laid for the association of the churches with imperialism; and if Ximenes in Spain, Wolsey in England, Richelieu and Mazarin in France represented the Church's service to the nation state, in the new colonial areas the vocation of Holy Orders involved not merely serving the Church but also serving the State.

Economic considerations reinforced the political, the scientific and the religious urge to discover a new world.

The Venetian commercial hegemony in the Mediterranean and the Hanseatic League in the Baltic anticipated in their way the development of the world market. Venice in the fifteenth century was a city of shopkeepers. The financial transactions of the Lombards heralded the rise of high finance. The cloth industry of Flanders prepared the way for large scale production which by 1450 was a reality in England. Jack of Newbury, called 'the clothier', had 200 looms in one room, employing altogether close to 800 workers.

The old feudal order was being uprooted in the countryside, and the manorial system was being superseded in the fifteenth century by the enclosure of lands for sheep pastures, the basis of the woollen industry. This was the case particularly in England but it also took place in Spain, leaving the peasantry landless, sending them into the towns, converting them into vagrants and highwaymen suitable for transportation, by fair or foul means, to any new colonial areas.

The changing economic pattern in the fifteenth century had two further characteristics of great and direct relevance for the adventure of Columbus. The first was that, in the Mediterranean, Europe had developed on a large scale the sugar industry learned from India and the Middle East. Important centres of production were Sicily and Cyprus, and the large plantation and large factory had evolved.

The second characteristic was the European experience with colonial labour, based firstly on the Moorish domination of Spain and secondly on the Portuguese conquest of West Africa—to the point where the Portuguese verb 'to work' became 'to work like a Moor'. On the island of St. Thomas off the coast of Guinea the Portuguese developed a sugar industry based on the large plantation operated by Negro slave labour.

Thus on August 3, 1492, when Columbus set out from Palos in Spain for the Canary Islands as his first stop in his voyage to the New World in three small ships totalling some 400 tons and with a crew of about 100 men, his equipment included the European wanderlust, a powerful economic impulse, the requisite technical aids, a dominant crusading motive, all backed by the necessary political organisation. Above all he took with him the knowledge that Africa was a capacious reservoir of labour which could become (as Gilberto Freyre of Brazil has described the Negro) 'the white man's greatest and most plastic collaborator in the task of agrarian colonisation'.

Chapter Two

Christopher Columbus and the Discovery of the West Indies

Every schoolchild now knows that Columbus did not 'discover' America. There is sufficient evidence available today of the immigration of the Vikings via Greenland in the North, while it is thought that Africans had direct contact with South America before Columbus sailed for 'the Indies' in 1492.

Columbus' achievement lies in the fact that his planned voyage was successful and that he was able over a decade to come and go, between Europe and the Caribbean, as if he was travelling up and down the Mediterranean. After ten weeks his expedition sighted the Bahamas on October 12, 1492. The island, called by the native inhabitants Guanahani, was taken possession of by Columbus in the name of the King and Queen of Spain and christened San Salvador. From the Bahamas Columbus proceeded to Cuba and Hispaniola before returning to Spain. On subsequent voyages he discovered most of the Caribbean archipelago and the northern coast of South America.

Columbus was convinced that he had realised his lifelong dream and that he had reached Asia by sailing west. He had steeped himself in his youth in the extensive geographical literature that the age had made available, had even learned Latin for this

18

purpose, and he had in particular been profoundly impressed with the opinion of the Greek philosopher, Aristotle, that 'between the end of Spain and the beginning of India the sea was small and navigable in a few days'. He had made Marco Polo's account of China virtually his Bible.

In recent years the view has been expounded that Columbus had no design of sailing west in order to reach the East, and that he set out merely to discover new lands in the west, whose existence was suspected midway between Europe and Asia, which the Portuguese denominated 'Antilha' and the sailors of Bristol 'Brazil'. However, the fact remains that the idea that he had reached Asia became a veritable obsession with Columbus, who carried with him letters from the Sovereigns of Spain to the Great Khan. Making the wish the father to the thought, he repeatedly misinterpreted and unconsciously distorted the information he received from the natives, whose language he could not understand, and who could not understand his. He called them 'Indians', an appellation which has survived to this day to describe the aborigines of the New World, and the islands of the 'West Indies'.

Informed by them of an island which they called Cuba, and of a region they called Cibao in the island he baptised Hispaniola, he insisted on saying that they were corruptions of Cipango, · Marco Polo's name for Japan. He actually sent a Jewish interpreter on an expedition to the Great Khan, thought that he was not far from the oriental cities of Guinsay and Zaitun described by Marco Polo, and repeated in his Journal of his voyage stories which originated with Marco Polo, of islands without men, people without hair, and inhabitants born with tails. Such was his fixation that he required officers and sailors on his second voyage to take a solemn oath that they had no doubt that Cuba—which the cartographer on the expedition plainly depicted some years later as an island—was mainland, the beginning of the Indies, and the terminus of all those who desired to come from Spain to the new parts of the world. But for this *idée fixe*, which he carried to his grave, Columbus might well have discovered Florida, Mexico and Yucatan, which were left to those who followed in his wake.

Contemporaries openly scoffed at his belief that he had reached Asia. But Columbus remained unshaken even when, in 1499, the

King of Portugal exultantly announced that the real Indies had
been reached by Vasco da Gama, and when, in the following
year, another Portuguese navigator, Cabral, following in the course
of da Gama, was driven by the current to Brazil, thus discovering
America for the second time, and was thus able to confirm that
there was an entire hemisphere in the west blocking the road to
India. Columbus' mistaken scientific notions were further distorted
in the last years of his life by a vein of religious mysticism, in
which he appeared to himself as 'the messenger of the new heaven
and the new earth', who had discovered 'the earthly paradise'.

Standing on the very threshold of the modern age of commerce
and imperialism, Columbus' vision was focused on the past. He
was the last of the medieval crusaders. The chief significance of
the New World, in his eyes, was the opportunity it afforded of
bringing multitudes into the Catholic faith. On his return from
his first voyage, he ended his narrative of his exploits to the
Sovereigns with the assurance that 'God had reserved for the
Spanish monarchs, not only all the treasures of the New World,
but a still greater treasure of inestimable value, in the infinite
number of souls destined to be brought over into the bosom of
the Christian Church'. He vowed to the Sovereigns that his
personal profits from the first voyage would be used for the
recapture of Jerusalem from the Saracens. In a letter to the Pope,
in February, 1502, he explained that it had been his plan to pay
for 100,000 infantry and 10,000 cavalry for the reconquest of
Jerusalem, and he gave assurance that the profits of his fourth
and final voyage, which he was about to undertake, would be
appropriated for the guarding of the Holy Sepulchre when it had
been recaptured.

Columbus had stipulated before his departure, and the
Sovereigns had agreed, that he would be appointed Admiral and
Viceroy over all the lands he might discover, the former honour
being transmissible to his heirs and successors in perpetuity; that
he should recommend the names of three persons for each
office in the new territories, from which the Sovereigns were to
choose one; and that he should receive ten per cent of the profits
and have the privilege of supplying one-eighth of the cargo, in
return for which he was to receive a further one-eighth of the
profits. The humble Genoese mariner, son of an obscure woollen

weaver, became, by the discovery of the New World, Admiral Don Christopher Columbus, a grandee of Spain. On his return from his memorable voyage, the King and Queen received him with a splendour befitting his exploits. Seated on the throne, surrounded by courtiers, knights, and an immense throng, they held out their hands for him to kiss, refused to allow him to kneel, and desired him to be seated in their presence, the highest honour to which a grandee could aspire.

The Spaniards' hatred of Columbus as a foreigner, their jealousy of his perquisites, quarrels among his own followers, and opposition to his methods of rule combined to bring about his downfall. The standard of revolt was raised against him in Hispaniola. He filed charges against his enemies, and they replied with counter-charges. The Sovereigns thereupon appointed a new governor in 1499, who on arrival in Hispaniola, after a one-sided hearing, clapped Columbus and his brother in irons and sent them back to Spain. Columbus' bitter disillusionment was expressed in a letter he wrote to a noble lady, formerly the nurse of Prince John. If he had stolen the Indies from the altar of St. Peter (he wrote) and given them to the Moors, greater enmity could not be shown to him in Spain. The governor had treated him worse than a pirate or merchant. He continued bitterly in what is the first imperialist assertion of special non-European treatment of colonial areas:

'They judge me over there as they would a governor who had gone to Sicily, or to a city or town placed under regular government, and where the laws can be observed in their entirety without fear of ruining everything; and I am greatly injured thereby. I ought to be judged as a captain who went from Spain to the Indies to conquer a numerous and warlike people, whose customs and religion are very contrary to ours; who live in rocks and mountains, without fixed settlements, and not like ourselves; and where, by the divine will, I have placed under the domination of the King and Queen, our sovereigns, another world, through which Spain, which was reckoned a poor country, has become the richest. I ought to be judged as a captain who for such a long time up to this day has borne arms without laying them aside for an hour ... or otherwise I receive great injury; because in the Indies ... there is neither town nor settlement.'

The King and Queen ordered Columbus' release, and assured him that their instructions had been exceeded and that his property and rights would be restored to him. But Columbus never recovered his former position of authority, and he steadily

lost his monopolistic control of western exploration. His fourth
and final voyage in 1502 was the last flicker of a dying candle.
He died at Valladolid on May 20, 1506, in total obscurity. In
the following year, the final injustice was perpetrated. A German
professor of geography christened the New World which
Columbus had discovered. He named it 'America', after a
Florentine adventurer, Amerigo Vespucci, who reached the New
World only in 1499, but who, by his writings, which were widely
reprinted and read all over Europe, succeeded in conveying the
impression that he eclipsed Columbus. Columbus' name was not
commemorated in the world he had discovered until the early
nineteenth century, when the independent republic of Colombia
in South America was named after him.

Chapter Three

Gold and Sugar

'I was attentive, and took trouble to ascertain if there was gold.' Thus did Columbus record in his Journal on October 13, the day after he landed in the Bahamas.

Columbus' voyage was the first gold-rush in the history of the modern world. The agreement signed with the Spanish Sovereigns before his departure specifically mentioned gold and silver in the clause relating to Columbus' share in the profits. Once land had been sighted, and Columbus noticed gold rings in the noses of the inhabitants of the Bahamas, his voyage became a search for gold mines. 'Without doubt,' he wrote in his Journal on November 12, 'there is in these lands a vast quantity of gold, and the Indians I have on board do not speak without reason when they say that in these islands there are places where they dig out gold, and wear it on their necks, ears, arms and legs, the rings being very large.' He returned to Spain trusting that the settlement he left behind in Hispaniola would obtain a ton of gold by barter and discover mines before his return to the island. In a letter to his patron and friend, Luis de Santangel, in 1493, he assured him that there were many mines of metal in Cuba, great mines of gold in Hispaniola, and incalculable gold in another island.

Gold brought the West Indies face to face, not for the last time, with monopoly. In Europe in the Middle Ages mines were a royal monopoly. In 1501, therefore, Ferdinand and Isabella forbade anyone to seek or operate mines without their permission. They were concerned almost exclusively with mines of gold and silver. Despite the existence of mines of iron and copper in the New World, the colonies imported iron and most of their copper from Spain, though a few copper mines were worked in Cuba and Hispaniola. In 1504 all Spaniards generally received permission to operate mines, on condition that their claims were registered, and provided that they took an oath to bring all the produce to the royal smeltery to be assayed, taxed, and stamped. Not until 1584 were the mines declared to be the property of those who discovered them, able to be freely sold or disposed of.

The monarchy received royalties from those who developed the mines. In Spain these amounted to two-thirds. Fixed originally at one-half in the colonies, they were eventually reduced to one-fifth.

By 1500, according to Columbus, individuals in Hispaniola were collecting 110, 120, as many as 250 *castellanos* a day. The collection of from twenty to fifty *castellanos* was considered a good day's work, and he added: 'It is the general opinion, that if even the whole population of Castile were to flock there, however lazy a person might be, he would not gain less than one or two *castellanos* a day; and it is to be considered that this is only the beginning.'

Columbus was wrong. It was the end, not the beginning. Hispaniola, in reality, had little gold, and the early exhaustion of its deposits by the primitive methods of the time sent the Spaniards up and down the Caribbean seeking new deposits. It was gold which determined the location of Spanish settlements, which led to their concentration on the Greater Antilles and to their neglect of the Lesser Antilles, except those which had strategic significance for the protection of the trade routes. It was gold also which ultimately drew them to the mainland—'May God take me to Peru!' was the universal cry in Puerto Rico in 1534—and which brought about their subordination of North America generally in preference for Central America and the western coast of South America.

A Spanish historian, writing in 1587, stated that the treasure which entered Spain from the New World was sufficient to 'pave the streets of Seville with blocks of gold and silver'. Estimates of this treasure vary widely, and it is thus impossible to verify the accuracy of the statement. But the royal income from the Indies amounted to 8,000 ducats in 1503, nearly 59,000 in 1509, about 90,000 in 1512, and about 120,000 in 1518. Mexico was not conquered until 1519, nor Peru until 1526. Thus the gold obtained up to 1518 came almost exclusively from the Caribbean. With the conquest of Mexico and Peru, Spanish revenues skyrocketed. They were nearly 320,000 ducats in 1535. The fleet of 1538 brought nearly one million ducats, the fleet of 1543 over half a million, another fleet in 1551 over a million and a half. In the years 1557–1559, over three and a half million ducats were received by the royal treasury, and, in the single year 1587, nearly six and a half million. During the entire period, 1503–1590, Spanish revenues from the Indies amounted to over 58 million ducats, or an annual average of over 660,000. In 1608 the annual revenue was reckoned at two million ducats from the New World, and the fleet of 1626 brought over two and a half million.

By that time, of course, the Caribbean colonies were no longer producers of the precious metals. The Spanish Caribbean colonies turned to sugar. On his second voyage, in 1493, together with livestock, vegetables, wheat, barley, vine and fruit trees, oranges, lemons, melons, and other plants, Columbus included, on his stop at the Canary Islands, the greatest gift of the Old World to the New—the sugar cane.

The cane introduced by Columbus came to be known as the 'creole' variety. This remained the dominant variety until the introduction of the Otaheite cane in the middle of the eighteenth century. An enthusiastic description in 1518 described 'fields of sugar cane that are wonderful to see, the cane as thick as a man's wrist, and as tall as the height of two men of medium stature'.

Hispaniola became the cradle of the Caribbean sugar economy. In a memorandum for his Sovereigns on January 30, 1494, Columbus wrote enthusiastically of the future of the industry in Hispaniola, and compared it with that of Andalusia and Sicily.

But cane cultivation was one thing, the production of sugar another. The one was a question of agriculture and largely one of labour, the other of industry, capital and technology. The former demanded chiefly the labourer, the latter required the capitalist and the technician.

The first method used for extracting the juice of the cane, in or about the year 1506, was to crush the cane with primitive wooden instruments. These can still be seen in many parts of the West Indies today. However valuable or useful the resultant syrup, it was not sugar. Some method had to be devised for crushing large quantities of the raw material and producing in the mass a standardised product which could be shipped in bags or casks to the waiting world market. It is alleged that the technical competence required was provided largely by Jews.

The first sugar mill was established in Hispaniola in 1516 by Gonzalo de Vedosa. Called by the Spaniards a *trapiche*, it was a horse-powered mill, in which horses—oxen or slaves were sometimes substituted—turned a main wheel by moving steadily around the machine. Not long after, an important technological revolution was initiated by the substitution of water power for human or animal power. The water-powered mill was called by the Spaniards an *ingenio*. During the first century of the industry, *trapiche* and *ingenio* existed side by side, the *trapiche* more expensive by virtue of the horses or oxen required, the *ingenio* limited to areas with an abundant supply of water.

The *ingenio* was twice as efficient as the *trapiche*. In Brazil, where similar technological differences existed, it was estimated that the capacity of a *trapiche* was 25–35 cartloads of cane every twenty-four hours to produce 840 pounds of sugar, while a hydraulic mill could grind 40–50 cartloads of cane and extract between 1,120 and 1,960 pounds of sugar during the same period.

Thus the twentieth-century Caribbean giant began as a pigmy in the sixteenth. In modern terms, the *trapiche* produced less than nine hundredweight of sugar per day. Yet from the very beginning sugar was an industry for the big capitalist. Gonzalo Fernando de Oviedo, in his *General and Natural History of the Indies*, composed in 1546, one of the first histories of the Caribbean, has left us an invaluable account of the sugar industry. Each *ingenio* required a capital investment of ten or twelve thousand gold ducats, and fifteen thousand was not unknown. It employed a labour force of from 80 to 120 workers, as compared with the 30 to 40 of the *trapiche*. A herd of 3,000 cattle was needed to feed the workers. Carts were required to haul the cane to the mill and bring in wood for fuel, and trained technicians were wanted to make the sugar.

The profits were correspondingly large. One particular *ingenio*, according to Oviedo, was worth over 50,000 gold ducats, and it yielded its owner an annual income of 6,000. 'It is a fact,' wrote the historian, 'that the owner of an unencumbered and well-equipped *ingenio* has a fine and rich property, and one that brings in a great profit and return to its owner ... there is no island or kingdom among Christians or pagans where there is anything like this industry of sugar.' At the time that Oviedo wrote, Hispaniola had twenty *ingenios* and four *trapiches*, and each *ingenio* in 1552 was yielding an annual profit of ten thousand ducats.

Capital was scarce in sixteenth-century Spain. The wealth from the Indies was dissipated in war and power politics, while the Catholic Church's ban on interest tended to restrict commercial loans. Would-be entrepreneurs fell back, therefore, on state aid, and from its birth the Caribbean sugar industry was characterised by subsidies from and protection by the state. Loans were made by the Spanish Government to those wishing to set up *ingenios*; a moratorium was imposed on debts of the sugar planters; the tithe to the Church was reduced by one-half; sugar experts were sent out by the metropolitan government; machinery and materials for the construction and operation of sugar mills were exempted from import duties; the attachment, seizure or sale of mills for debt were prohibited by law.

The sugar industry spread from Hispaniola to Jamaica, Puerto Rico and Cuba. Its development was gradual but steady. By 1523 there were thirty *ingenios* in Jamaica; five years later, there were ten in Puerto Rico, producing approximately 170 long tons. Exports from Hispaniola in 1542 amounted to 1,200 long tons. During the second half of the sixteenth century Cuba's exports amounted to an annual average of about 460 long tons. Such was the importance of the industry that Las Casas could write: 'this island of Hispaniola contains 40 or 50 sugar *ingenios*, and could have 200, which are more valuable and advantageous to the human race than all the silver, gold and pearls of England'.

Three concomitants of sugar production soon manifested themselves. The first was the tendency to amalgamate factories. By 1617, the total production of Bayamon and Santiago in Cuba amounted to a little over 300 long tons, produced in 37 *trapiches*, twenty-six in Santiago and eleven in Bayamon, or about eight tons per factory. One planter in Santiago owned five *trapiches*; five planters in Santiago and two in Bayamon owned two each. One-half of all the mills were thus owned by eight planters in the two districts.

The second was the tendency to grow sugar for export and to import food. The early settlers took over the subsistence economy of the Indians, which lacked domestic animals, and which was based on the production of corn, potatoes and cassava, from the last of which they made a sort of bread. The Indians also grew tobacco, cotton and tropical fruits, such as pineapples and bananas. Their tools were primitive, made for the most part of stone, as they were ignorant of the use of metals. So backward was their system of cultivation that it was estimated that one Spaniard, utilising the inefficient methods characteristic of feudal Europe, produced as much as thirty Indians. In the early years of the conquest, the Spaniards expanded these crops, and added to them livestock and crops introduced from Spain.

But by the middle of the sixteenth century Las Casas struck the first note of alarm which has since characterised Caribbean economy. He specifically attributed to the expansion and profitableness of the sugar industry the Spaniards' lack of interest in local production of bread and failure to produce more wheat than all Italy or Spain, and their preference for imports. With two casks of flour imported from Castile, he lamented, at a cost of ten *castellanos*, they had enough to eat for a year, and would not bother about sowing and setting up mills for producing bread. 'If in this island,' he concluded, 'there is no bread or not so much bread, not more wheat or better bread than in all parts of the world, there is no other cause than this.'

The third concomitant of early Caribbean sugar production was the problem of the world market. From Cuba the sugar cane was transplanted to the continental possessions. In 1531

Cortes in Mexico possessed three *ingenios*, which produced very fine sugar. Production increased to such a point that, in a few years, it was sufficient to meet the local demand, while, by the middle of the century, sugar was being exported from Mexico to Peru and even to Spain. Mills were shortly after established in Peru, and exports to Spain began in 1560. The Caribbean planters faced competition not only from their compatriots on the main-land, but also from the Portuguese in Brazil. An account of that country in 1584 stated that there were 66 plantations, producing annually 2,230 long tons of sugar, and giving employment to forty ships; the mills were inadequate for the supply of cane and the ships for the trade in sugar.

Overshadowing all these questions, however, was the crucial problem of labour.

Chapter Four

White Capital and Coloured Labour

It has been said of the Spanish conquistadors that first they fell on their knees, and then they fell on the aborigines. They brought to the New World an economic and social heritage in which slavery and serfdom were constituent elements. The thirteenth-century code of *Las Siete Partidas,* rooted in the ancient Code of Justinian, recognised slavery as an integral part of the Spanish economy. It divided men into three categories—free men, slaves and freedmen. It acknowledged three types of slaves: prisoners of war as enemies of the Catholic faith; children of slaves; freemen who had voluntarily surrendered their freedom. The code prescribed certain rights for the slave: his owner could not kill him or ill-treat him to the point of suffering; he had the right to his holding with the consent of his owner; and he had the right to marriage and manumission even against the will of the owner. Permeated with a liberal spirit, the code insisted that 'it is a rule of law that all judges should help liberty, because liberty is natural, and because not only man, but all other animals, love it'.

Like the economy of medieval Europe in general, the Spanish economy also recognised serfdom or villeinage, whereby the grant of land by an overlord carried with it the privilege of labour by

the tenants of the land, in a quantity and of a nature prescribed
by custom.

Columbus had sailed to Guinea in the Portuguese merchant
marine, and had acquired a personal experience of the slave
trade. His long residence in Portugal and his years in Spain had
given him also a familiarity with slavery and with Negro slavery.
On his arrival in the West Indies, therefore, he naturally turned
his attention to instituting both a slave trade and slavery. Gold,
as the Spaniards recognised, did not grow on trees. They needed
labour. The discoverer of gold and the introducer of sugar tried
also to provide the solution to the labour problem.

On his very first encounter with the Indians, on October 12,
1492, he recorded ominously in his Journal: 'They should be good
servants and intelligent, for I observed that they quickly took in
what was said to them.' He considered them timid and unwarlike.
Ignorant of Spanish weapons, ten thousand of them would not
stand up before ten Spaniards, and he was of the opinion that,
with the small force at his disposal, he could overrun all the
islands without opposition. 'So that,' he continued, 'they are good
to be ordered about, to work and sow, and do all that may be
necessary.' There was some doubt in his mind, however, as to
whether they should be kept in captivity in the West Indies or
transported to Castile. He decided to take a few over to Spain
to teach them the language. He deliberately included women in
their number, explaining that the Portuguese had been unsuccessful in similar efforts with Negroes from Guinea because
they had taken males only, but that the Indians, having their
women with them, would be inclined to perform what they
were required to do, whilst the women would also teach the
Spaniards their language.

As the years went by, Columbus more and more adopted the
view that the real riches of the West Indies lay in their Indian
population. He saw in the cannibalism of the Caribs a pretext for
their enslavement. He described them as 'a wild people fit for
any work, well proportioned, and very intelligent, and who, when
they have got rid of their cruel habits to which they have been
accustomed, will be better than any other kind of slaves'. On his
third voyage in 1498, he shipped six hundred Indians back to
Spain. The slave trade in the Caribbean thus began as outward

and not inward cargoes, taking the form of Indians transported from the West Indies to Spain rather than of Negroes transported from West Africa to the Caribbean.

In the meantime, however, the Pope had enjoined on the Spanish Sovereigns the duty of treating the Indians kindly and converting them to Catholicism. The Sovereigns thereupon issued a royal decree whereby those Indians who accepted Spanish sovereignty and submitted to it without resistance were considered subjects of the Crown, and as such could not be reduced to slavery. The decree left the road open to the enslavement of those who resisted; the legal basis for slavery became the infamous Requisition, read out by a notary to natives who did not understand Spanish. The others were to be treated as free men and employed for wages.

By 1495 the Spaniards were engaged in open warfare with the Indians. Naked, armed only with bows and arrows, the Indians were no match for the Spanish crossbows, knives, artillery, cavalry, and the dogs trained by the Spaniards to hunt them down. Thoroughly terrorised, the Indians were subjected to the payment of a tribute, amounting to from one-half to two-thirds of an ounce of gold every three months in the case of those who lived near the mines, and twenty-five pounds of cotton for those who did not. The Indians, in despair, fled to the mountains, abandoned all cultivation, and preferred to starve to death. One of their chiefs offered to put an enormous tract of land under cultivation for grain if only Columbus would not demand gold. Columbus refused, but agreed to reduce the tribute by one-half. Even this was too much. Whilst Columbus, and Las Casas after him, grossly exaggerated the numbers of the Indian population, there is no doubt that the population of Hispaniola was reduced by at least two-thirds as a result of the war and the imposition of the tribute. Vain attempts were made to increase the population by encouraging a slave trade from the 'useless' islands of the Bahamas.

Two years later Columbus was faced with insurgents in his own ranks, who demanded as their price grants of land. Columbus allotted them the lands of the Indians, which carried with them the enforced labour of the natives. Thus originated the system of *repartimientos* or *encomiendas*, and Spanish feudalism was transplanted to the Caribbean. The Spanish Crown, torn between the desire to satisfy the colonials' need for labour and the desire to protect the Indians as far as possible, agreed to the *encomienda* system on condition that the Indians were treated as free men, not servants, and that the grantee of an *encomienda* instructed them in the Catholic faith. The allocation was, in theory, of a personal character, temporary, revocable, and subject to supervision by the authorities. It was Spain's sixteenth-century version of 'the white man's burden'.

At first labour in the mines was restricted to a term of from six to eight months. But the *encomienda* tended inevitably, more and more, to lose its temporary character and become permanent. At the beginning there were enough Indians to satisfy the demand. But it was in the colonial's interest to obtain as much as he could from his labourers in the shortest possible time. The King of Spain, in 1512, tried to deal with the problem by limiting the hours of labour for the Indians, regulating their food and shelter, and providing for the nomination of inspectors. As the inspectors were themselves possessed of *encomiendas*, the code remained a dead letter.

The results are to be seen in the best estimates that have been prepared of the trend of population in Hispaniola. These place the population in 1492 at between 200,000 and 300,000. By 1508 the number was reduced to 60,000; in 1510, it was 46,000; in 1512, 20,000; in 1514, 14,000. In 1548 Oviedo doubted whether five hundred Indians of pure stock remained. In 1570 only two villages survived of those about whom Columbus had assured his Sovereigns, less than eighty years before, that 'there is no better nor gentler people in the world'.

They died, but they died with dignity and fortitude, these first colonial rebels against imperialism. The story is told of the Indian chief in Hispaniola, Hatuey, who fled before the invaders to Cuba. Captured in Cuba, he was ordered as an encouragement to the others to be burnt alive. At the stake a Franciscan friar exhorted him to take pity upon his soul, and not expose it to eternal damnation, when he might procure it the happiness of dwelling in Paradise for ever. Hatuey inquired whether any Spaniards were in Paradise. The friar assured him that only the good ones were. Hatuey is then supposed to have replied: 'The best are good for nothing, and I will not go where there is a chance of meeting one of them.'

The decimation of the Indians is imperishably associated with the humanitarian effort of a Spanish priest, Bartolomé de las Casas, to arrest the horror and protect the survivors. Scion of an old French family which had been established in Seville from the middle of the thirteenth century, Las Casas was born in 1474. A graduate of the University of Salamanca in the field of law, served for a time in his student days by a little Indian slave boy, he decided to adopt the career *par excellence* of that period and to take Holy Orders. He went to Hispaniola with Governor Ovando in 1502, and ten years later, on the call of the Governor of Cuba, migrated to that island. Like his compatriots, clerical and secular, he was given a grant of land, one of the best, with the Indians that went along with it. A humane 'trustee', he nevertheless employed Indian labour, under the euphemism then in vogue, in agriculture and mining.

But, while preparing his sermon one year for the Feast of Pentecost, he happened casually on Chapter 34 of Ecclesiastes, in which he read that the offering is stained which makes sacrifices of injustice, that he who offers sacrifice of the goods of the poor is like one who kills a child in the presence of its father. Las Casas was profoundly moved. Convinced of the injustice meted out to the Indians, he determined to renounce his lands and workers, informed the Governor of his views, preached passionately against the *encomiendas*, and became thereafter the 'apostle of the Indies'. In 1516 the Spanish Government appointed him Protector of the Indians, in the West Indies as well as on the continent. He took his duties seriously, and promptly declared war on the *encomienda*.

Such was the feeling aroused in the colonies, that the Emperor Charles V summoned him to a conference in Spain in 1519. His speech on the occasion ranks as one of the finest episodes in Caribbean history. His views, he informed the Emperor, were based not on what he had read in histories, but on what, as 'one of the oldest immigrants to the Indies', he had seen with his own eyes—'cruelties more atrocious and unnatural than any recorded of untutored and savage barbarians'. The only reason that, in his view, could be assigned for them was 'the greed and thirst for gold of our countrymen'. He assured the Emperor that, 'the spiritual interests of your soul excepted, nothing is of greater importance to your majesty than the finding of a remedy for these evils. For not one of your European kingdoms or all of them together equal in vastness and greatness your transatlantic possessions.' Eschewing all personal rewards or favours, he ended his speech with these words: 'Sire, it therefore behoves your majesty that you banish, at the beginning of your reign, that gigantically tyrannical system, which, horrible alike in the sight of God and man, is the ruin of the majority of mankind.'

As a Catholic bishop, Las Casas spoke with authority. But, with the progress of the discoveries, the dice became more heavily loaded against humanitarianism. In 1537 a papal bull defined and proclaimed that 'Indians or any other people' discovered by Catholics must in no way be deprived of their liberty or possessions and enslaved; if enslaved, their slavery must be considered null and void. Las Casas' influence was more directly responsible for the New Laws for the good treatment and preservation of the Indians, issued by Charles V on November 20, 1542. These laws represented the fruit of forty years of assiduous labour on the part of Las Casas for an enlightened policy towards the Indians. They enjoined very special care by the courts for the good treatment and preservation of the Indians, and stated categorically that the Indians were not to be enslaved on any pretext of war, rebellion, barter, or for any other cause. All enslaved Indians were to be set at liberty. For the future the Indians were to carry only such loads as did not endanger their lives and health, and such work was under no circumstances to be forced upon them. No free Indian was to be employed in the pearl fishery against his will, and slaves employed therein were to be protected. If deaths were inevitable, the fisheries must cease: 'for, as is reasonable, we value much more highly the preservation of lives than the profit which may come to us from the pearls'. Holders of *encomiendas* found guilty of ill-treating the Indians were to be deprived of them. Indians were henceforward to be subjected only to a moderate tribute, while those in the West Indies were specifically exempted from oppression by tribute or services 'in excess of what is due from Spaniards who reside in the said islands'.

The New Laws gave rise to such a storm of protest in the colonies that the Emperor abrogated them in the following year. The colonials, like Pizarro, had 'come to take their gold', not to civilise the aborigines. Defeated, Las Casas took to historical writing. He wrote an impassioned pamphlet, *Very Brief Account of the Destruction of the Indies*, in which he charged that fifteen millions had perished as a result of the cruelty of the Spaniards. Published in 1552, at a time when Catholic Spain was widely hated as the centre of Popish power, the pamphlet was translated into the chief European languages. During the sixteenth and seventeenth centuries, it went through three Italian editions, three Latin, four English, six French, eight German, and eighteen Dutch. But the pen, mighty as it was, could neither correct nor repair the damage done by the sword.

It is fashionable to accuse Las Casas of gross exaggeration and to condemn him for the propagation of an indictment of Spain which failed to take into account the equally nefarious activities of other nations.

Las Casas may have been guilty of exaggerating the horrors. To his eternal honour he left it to others to be guilty of exaggerating the advantages. Diatribe though it may be, the *Very Brief Account* is one of the noteworthy documents of the doctrine of trusteeship more honoured in the breach than the observance in the history of the Caribbean as well as of other areas, and Las Casas ranks with the eighteenth-century Englishman, Thomas Clarkson, and the nineteenth-century Frenchman, Victor Schoelcher, in his defence of the rights of man in the Caribbean.

He engaged in a bitter and vigorous battle of the books with the renowned jurist, Sepulveda, about the nature of the Indians. The Indians, asserted Sepulveda, were 'little men', as different from Spaniards as monkeys are from men. The happiest people in the world if only they knew God, was the ringing reply of Las Casas, who added that all the peoples of the world are men. In one of his finest passages he stated: 'No nation exists today, nor could exist, no matter how barbarous, fierce, or depraved its customs may be, which may not be attracted and converted to all political virtues and to all the humanity of domestic, political, and rational men.'

Las Casas refused to sacrifice the welfare of the Indians to the

greed of the Spaniards. He consented, however, to sacrifice the
well-being of the Negroes to the preservation of the Indians. What
he gave to humanity with one hand, he took away with the
other.

The significance of Spain's Indian policy lies in the fact that
it provided an instruction for Spain's successors in the Caribbean
which they were not slow to better. It marked an indelible stamp
of degradation on labour in the Caribbean. And it served as the
basis for the later, more extensive, and more comprehensive
treatment of the Negro.

In order to protect the Indians from the excessive labour imposed on them, Las Casas accepted the solution proposed by the
Dominican monks in an approach to the King in 1511, to the
effect that, 'as the labour of one Negro was more valuable than
that of four Indians, every effort should be made to bring to
Hispaniola many Negroes from Guinea'. The rationalisation of
Negro slavery and the Negro slave trade had begun.

But the Spanish Government turned first, not to the Negro,
but to the white man for the solution of the labour problem
raised by the disappearance of the Indians. This white emigration
to the West Indies was carefully supervised. A few months after
the discovery, the Sovereigns prohibited emigration without their
express permission, under pain of death and confiscation of goods.
Columbus' voyage had been financed not by the Spanish Government, but by Queen Isabella of Castile, a Spanish feudal
principality, which, wedded to Aragon, the principality of King
Ferdinand, had brought into being the unitary state of Spain. The
coat of arms allowed to Columbus as a part of his aggrandisement
after the voyage read: 'To Castile and Leon Columbus gave a
new world.' The New World was thus looked upon as the private
preserve of Isabella, and at the beginning only her 'subjects' of
Castile were given permission to go there.

Economic realities, however, triumphed over the feudal out-.
look. The colonies needed labour, if the Spanish Sovereigns were
to get gold. Four expedients were available, as far as white labour
was concerned.

The first was convict labour. In June 1497, on the occasion of
Columbus' third voyage, a general order was issued to all justices
in Spain authorising the transportation to Hispaniola of criminals

—with the exception of heretics, traitors, counterfeiters and sodomites—in commutation of death or prison sentences. This expedient appears not to have been repeated, and there seems to have been no straining of the law in Spain, as there was in seventeenth-century England, to make the punishment fit the colonial need of labour.

The second expedient was white slaves. In 1504 permission was given for the transportation of five white slaves, and in 1512 of two more to Puerto Rico. In the latter year orders were given that white Christian female slaves should be sent to the Caribbean to become wives of the colonials, as they would be preferable to Indian women. In 1532 twenty Spaniards received licences to take white slaves to the West Indies. The available evidence would seem to indicate that these slaves were generally women, and that the supply, as one would expect, was limited. The white indentured servant, generally male, of British and French colonial policy in the Caribbean had no place in Spanish efforts to cope with the population problem.

The third source of immigrant labour was foreigners. Columbus had recommended to the Sovereigns after his first voyage that no foreigners should be admitted into the West Indies, making a reservation in favour of Catholics. The Spanish Government was inclined to favour the total restriction of all foreigners. But, with the accession of the Emperor Charles V in 1519, Spain became a part of a heterogeneous empire which included Italians, Flemings and Germans. The Emperor's outlook was continental rather than peninsular, and in 1526 all his subjects were accorded permission to go to the Indies, 'since it was reasonable after such vast territories had been discovered that they should be peopled with Christians'.

But no large-scale emigration resulted from the imperial decree. Occasional licences were granted to individual foreigners, but the first substantial immigration of non-Spaniards did not take place before 1565, when the Spanish Government authorised the admission into Hispaniola of one hundred and fifty Portuguese, one third of whom were to be married, with their wives and children. Apart from this, Spanish policy remained exclusive, jealous of possible contamination by non-Catholics, and the wholesale deportation by Cromwell in the seventeenth century of

Irish Catholics and Scottish and English political non-conformists had no parallel in Spanish policy.

Convicts, white slaves and foreigners having proved inadequate to the need, the sole alternative of the Spanish Government was to relax the barriers against Spaniards other than Castilians and actively to encourage and promote free Spanish emigration. In 1511 the ban on non-Castilians was lifted. In 1518 emigrants were promised a free passage, free grants of land, implements, livestock and plants, maintenance for a year after arrival in the New World, and exemption from all taxes and payments, except the tithe to the Church, for twenty years. Premiums were offered for the best husbandry—two hundred dollars for the first who produced twelve pounds of silk, one hundred and fifty for the first who gathered ten pounds of spices, one hundred for the first fifteen hundredweight of wood, and sixty-five for the first hundredweight of hulled rice.

In 1498 Columbus drew a picture of these Spanish emigrants; there is perhaps some exaggeration in it, as a result of the troubles he was then experiencing in Hispaniola. According to him, those who had come as miners, labourers and scullions would not go a furlong from their houses, unless they were borne on palanquins. The West Indian colonial society had begun. The Spaniards came to understand that law of colonial society stated centuries later by an English professor, Herman Merivale, that, in countries where slavery existed, or forced native labour was available, no white man was industrious, as typified by the picture of the Brazilian sugar planter who went out escorted by a slave girl, whose duty it was to light the cigar to put into his mouth, or the Surinam slave owner on his way to church followed by the slave girl with a cushion for him to kneel on. Two years later Columbus wrote more fully:

'... in the island of Hispaniola there are few who are not vagabonds, and not one with a wife and children... such an abandoned race, who neither fear God, the King, nor the Queen, and are wholly given up to wickedness and violence... there are not five among them all, who would not be ready to collect all they could, and depart at a moment's notice. It would be advisable to have Castilians, and also to know who and what they are; and that the country should be peopled by respectable persons ... Now that so much gold is found, there is a difference of opinion whether it is not more profitable to go about robbing, than to go to the mines. They will as readily pay 100 *castellanos* for a woman as for a farm; and it is now very common to see dealers going prowling about for girls of nine and ten years of age; now, women of all ages are in request.'

Another account, about the middle of the sixteenth century, stated that the white labourers who had been brought to Hispaniola were barbers, tailors and other useless people, who soon sold the livestock which the King had given to them, would not work, and populated only the hospitals and the cemeteries. It reads exactly like accounts of 'free' emigration to the French colonies in the seventeenth century, or to Trinidad in the nineteenth.

It is, perhaps, in the light of these strictures that we must see the royal decree of 1528, by which every Spaniard in Puerto Rico was ordered to marry within two years, on pain of losing his grant of Indians. In the middle of the century, the former rigid supervision of Spanish emigrants was restored. An emigration permit was once more required. One explanation is that it was an effort to protect the colonies from being overrun by adventurers anxious only to get rich quickly, and not content with food and clothing, which every moderately industrious man was assured of. Finally, in 1584, the Spanish Government declared that no person would be permitted to go to the West Indies unless he could present authentic information with respect to his morals and good behaviour.

White immigration, however, even in the period of mobility, was of little avail as a solution of the labour problem of the West Indies. Spanish settlement followed not the flag but gold, and the discovery of or search for gold on the mainland led to a steady depopulation of the islands. Between 1492 and 1511 the Greater Antilles had all been settled—that is, settlements existed in every island. The first continental colony was established in 1511 in Darien. Then followed the conquest of Mexico. Thereafter came the long tale of Spanish occupations and annexations: Panama and Costa Rica in 1519; Nicaragua in 1522; Guatemala in 1523; Honduras in 1524; Ecuador in 1525; Peru in 1526; Venezuela and Yucatan in 1527; Florida in 1528. The depopulation of the Antilles, where there was little gold, was inevitable. In 1526 the King decreed that no resident of the Caribbean, wnatever his station in life, was to emigrate to the other islands or to the continent, under pain of death and confiscation of property.

But the exodus continued. Before the great emigration Hispaniola had 14,000 Castilians. In 1574 the number was reduced to five hundred households. Puerto Rico's second town was founded in 1510; the third not before 1646. Jamaica in the sixteenth century had only two towns. The conquest of Cuba was begun in 1511. The first town was founded in the next year, the second in 1513, five others in 1514 and 1515. Santiago de Cuba, at one time almost as populous as Hispaniola's capital, was reduced to thirty households in 1574. In 1620, the total population of Cuba was less than seven thousand. The Governor of Trinidad in 1593 claimed that he had only seventy white men to oppose six thousand Indians.

Spain's limited population could not possibly supply the demands made on all its extensive colonial possessions, for both gold and sugar. In the search for gold in the Caribbean the Indians had been liquidated, though, more numerous on the mainland, they were still available there. For the production of sugar in the Caribbean another reservoir of labour was therefore required.

The Spaniards did not have far to look. The Negro slave trade, in the hands of the Portuguese, was more than half a century old when the sixteenth century began, and the Spaniards were already accustomed to purchase Negro slaves in the Portuguese slave markets. The Portuguese monopoly of the Guinea trade was a severe handicap to Spain. For this reason, and also because of the constant anxiety to keep the colonies immune from heresy, the Spanish Government turned to the Negro slaves in Spain, who had been converted to Catholicism. The Negro slave trade was initiated by the King on September 3, 1501, in a letter to the Governor of Hispaniola, in which he said: 'In view of our earnest desire for the conversion of the Indians to our Holy Catholic Faith, and seeing that, if persons suspect in the Faith went there, such conversion might be impeded, we cannot consent to the immigration of Moors, heretics, Jews, re-converts, or persons newly converted to our Holy Faith, unless they are Negro or other slaves who have been born in the power of Christians who are our subjects and nationals and carry our express permission.' The Spanish slave trade thus began as a trade not from West Africa to the West Indies, but from Spain, and it thus excluded all non-Christian slaves and Christian slaves born in the power of non-Spaniards.

But there were simply not enough Negro slaves born in the power of Christian Spaniards. The planters and miners in the colonies gave economics priority over religion, and desired a Negro slave trade from Guinea, freed from its religious integument; they regarded the Negroes, as Columbus had regarded the Indians, as having no religion, and, therefore, free from the taint of idolatry or heresy.

What became a torrent in the seventeenth, eighteenth and nineteenth centuries began as a rivulet in the sixteenth. The slaves were virtually sent out by the King's command, in small numbers. Thus seventeen were sent in 1505 to work in the copper mines of Hispaniola, and a few months later the King promised to send a hundred. In 1510, an order for fifty slaves was issued. The Negroes, however, died as rapidly as the Indians, to everyone's surprise. 'I cannot understand how so many Negroes have died,' wrote the King in 1511 to an official in Hispaniola; 'take good care of them.'

Unlike the mortality of the Indians, however, Negro mortality meant merely obtaining more Negroes from where the original ones had been procured. The introductions steadily increased. In 1517 the first *asiento*, or contract, was arranged for the importation of four thousand Negroes in eight years into the West Indies. In 1523 the King ordered the provision of another four thousand into all the Spanish dominions, of which fifteen hundred were to go to Hispaniola, five hundred to Puerto Rico, and three hundred each to Cuba and Jamaica. In 1528 Cuba requested a further seven hundred. In the same year a contract was signed with two Germans for the importation of four thousand slaves into the Caribbean colonies in four years. According to Las Casas, thirty thousand were imported into Hispaniola alone by 1540, and more than a hundred thousand into all the Spanish dominions. Prices tended to rise so sharply that an attempt was made in 1556 to stabilise them—the tariff for the West Indian islands was a hundred ducats per slave. But this decree was revoked five years later. In 1552 slaves were being imported into Hispaniola at the rate of two thousand a year. In addition to the legal trade, a contraband trade of considerable proportions developed by the end of the sixteenth century.

Thus did Las Casas and the planters come to terms. At daggers drawn over the labour of the Indian, they saw eye to eye on the labour of the Negro. At loggerheads over the Indian question, they were reconciled on the Negro question. Justice to the Indians was purchased at the price of injustice to the Africans. The belligerent Protector of the Indians became a benevolent promoter of Negro slavery and the slave trade, though he was responsible for the initiation of neither. In 1531, fifteen years after he had been appointed Protector of the Indians, he appealed to the Spanish Government for the despatch of five or six hundred Negroes to the West Indies, emphasising that one of the most important reasons for the backwardness of Hispaniola was the failure to accord to all and sundry the freedom to import Negroes.

Las Casas had seen the light on the Indian question, renounced his *encomienda*, and poured out his frustration in his *Very Brief Account*. He owned no Negro slaves himself. But he saw the light very late on that issue, never became Protector of the Negroes, and his repentance was a lame acknowledgement of error. 'In the old days,' he wrote in his *History of the Indies*, 'before there were any *ingenios*, we used to think in this island that, if a Negro were not hanged, he would never die, because we had never seen one die of illness, and we were sure that, like oranges, they had found their habitat, this island being more natural to them than Guinea. But after they were put to work in the *ingenios*, on account of the excessive labour they had to endure, and the drinks they take made from cane syrup, death and pestilence were the result, and many of them died.' He admitted that the Spanish purchasers of the slaves were the real cause of the outrages committed in the slave trade in Africa, that the reasons which he had urged against the servitude of the Indians were equally valid against the slavery of the Africans, and apologised for an 'indiscretion' committed under the impression that the Negro slaves were justly captured in war.

These were faint damns compared with the thunder of the denunciations against the oppressors of the Indians. But they represent the first small voice of the abolitionist sentiment. A few of Las Casas' colleagues developed the theme. In 1587 Tomas Mercado published a book openly opposed to the slave trade, which, he stated, was notoriously founded in deceit, robbery and force. Emphasising the mortality in the Middle Passage, he added: 'One would never end one's narrative of the treatment meted out to the survivors.' In 1573 Bartolomé de Albornoz attacked slavery itself. Facing squarely the conventional argument, originated by the Spaniards and developed by the British, French and the planters of the United States, that the slaves were better off in the West Indies where they were baptised and converted to Catholicism, Albornoz denied that the law of Christ authorised the liberty of the soul at the price of the slavery of the body. Such an attack on religion could not be tolerated. The Holy See put the book on the Index and banned further editions, and Albornoz' abolitionist sentiments were suppressed.

In 1610, the American Jesuit, Alonso de Sandoval, continued the attack. Stressing the fraud and injustice which surrounded the slave trade, he published statements tending to show the uneasy conscience of the slave traders. His ideas were warmly supported by many enlightened teachers in the New World. Thus encouraged, Sandoval proceeded to deplore slavery as a misfortune, and wrote words which were a striking contrast to what was to become the practice of the coming age: 'Among human possessions, none is more valuable and beautiful than liberty... All the gold in the world and all the goods of the earth are not a sufficient price for human liberty... God created man free... Slavery is not only exile, but also subjection, hunger, sorrow, nakedness, insult, prison, perpetual persecution, and, in short, is a Pandora's box of all the evils.'

It was the voice of Cassandra. These abstract sentiments, creditable though they were to those who expressed them, ran counter to the economic necessities of the age. It was more than three centuries after the suppression of Albornoz' attack on slavery that slavery was abolished in Cuba and so banished from the Caribbean. In the sixteenth century the Negro had been brought to the Caribbean to stay, to perpetuate, wherever he was allowed to do so, his tribal African customs—such as the *coumbite* and the voodoo of Haiti, the arts of the Bush Negro of Surinam, the shango and the *susu* of Trinidad—to produce a civilisation in the Caribbean in which, as Freyre says of Brazil, 'it was Europe reigning without governing; it was Africa that governed'. By the middle of the sixteenth century the ethnological change that had taken place in the Caribbean in a mere fifty years—despite the small number of Negroes introduced when compared with the statistics of later periods—was so striking that the Spanish historian, Herrera, in his *History of the Indies*, was able to write of Hispaniola: 'There are so many Negroes in this island, as a result of the sugar factories, that the land seems an effigy or an image of Ethiopia itself.'

Chapter Five

Spanish Colonialism

Monopoly was the core of the political system, economic organisation and social structure in the Europe of Columbus' day. Therefore, inevitably, monopoly became the core of the Spanish colonial system in the Caribbean. The Caribbean colonies became a royal monopoly and the Caribbean Sea became *mare clausum*, the closed sea, closed to all but Spanish trade, Spanish government, Spanish religion, Spanish nationals.

The European nations of the day were as much concerned with the adverse trade balance, the disparity between imports and exports, as is our own generation. In their view the difference represented a drain on the country's bullion, its stock of the precious metals, gold and silver. As pertinaciously as in our day, therefore, each state sought to strengthen itself by increasing its stock of gold and silver, by encouraging its exports and reducing its imports.

The drain of bullion became the *bête noire* of European statesmen for three centuries. From the Spanish angle, it is clearly brought out in the report of the *Cortes* to Philip II in 1593. The report states:

'The *Cortes* of Vallodolid in the year 1586 petitioned Your Majesty not to allow the further importation into the Kingdom of candles, glassware, jewelry, knives and similar articles; these things useless to human life come from abroad to be exchanged for gold, as though the Spaniards were Indians ... The general remote cause of our want of money is the great excess of this Kingdom in consuming the commodities of foreign countries, which prove to us discommodities, in hindering us of so much treasure, which otherwise would be brought in, in lieu of those toys ...'

Among the articles which aroused the wrath of the Spanish legislators were the wines of France, the Rhine and the Levant, the lawns and cambrics of Hainault, the silks of Italy, the spices of the East Indies, and, curiously enough—the sugar and tobacco of the West Indies. 'All which,' concluded the legislators, 'are of no necessity unto us and yet are bought with ready money.'

It was in this atmosphere that Spain's colonial system evolved. There were two aspects to the system, the one purely commercial, the other political: both designed to achieve the same end, the development of the Spanish colonies as the exclusive preserve of Spain. The emergence of the Caribbean as the appendage or satellite of European imperialism, its resources being drained away from domestic development to metropolitan aggrandisement, had begun.

The Spanish commercial monopoly was based in the first place on the designation of a single port through which all trade with the Caribbean, inward and outward, had to pass. In 1493 Cadiz, as Columbus had recommended, was designated the sole port of entry and departure for ships trading with the West Indies. All persons and goods accompanying the expedition had to be registered before a Crown agent; on arrival in the West Indies, they were checked against the original register, and any surplus confiscated to the Crown. A custom house was erected for the receipt of the royal merchandise, and every commercial transaction had to be recorded in the presence of three royal representatives.

This system of state trading, or, to be more precise, royal monopoly, however, was of short duration, and the trade with the Caribbean was thrown open in 1495 to all subjects of Castile. It continued, nevertheless, to be concentrated in the single port of Cadiz, in order to facilitate that supervision of every detail of trade and navigation which was the aim of the Crown. All ships had to register in Cadiz, sail from that port, and return thither on the homeward voyage. One tenth of the tonnage was reserved for the Crown, without payment of freight, and one tenth of everything secured in the Caribbean belonged to the King, with the exception of gold in Hispaniola, where the proportion was one-third, and later one-fifth.

As a result of the great increase of trade with the West Indies, the Crown in 1503 determined to create a *Casa de Contratación*, a House of Trade, for its regulation and encouragement. The restriction of the trade to a single Spanish port was reaffirmed. But Cadiz, despite its superior facilities, lost its monopoly to Seville, the wealthiest and most populous city of Castile.

This House of Trade consisted of three royal officials, a treasurer, a comptroller and a business manager, who resided in Seville and met daily to transact business. A chief pilot was added a few years later, the first to hold this office being Amerigo Vespucci. The beginning of a school of navigation then appeared, the earliest and most important in modern Europe, together with a postmaster general, secretaries and legal advisers. Through the house all merchandise for and from the New World had to pass. It was responsible for the despatch of ships to the New World, and supervised, licensed and registered all emigrants to these parts. It was the watchdog over the laws relative to navigation, commerce and emigration. It was the government's adviser on economic conditions and policy in the colonies, and collected the duties on commodities imported from the New World. The necessary judicial functions in the fields of its competence were assigned to it, in both civil and criminal matters, sentences involving death and mutilation being, however, subject to review by the political arm of the Spanish colonial system.

In each of the colonies a branch of the House was established, in charge of officials of the Royal Treasury. These colonial houses, situated in the capital or the most important seaport, were at one and the same time a custom house and a commercial warehouse. To diminish the work of the House in Seville, a judge appointed by the King was set up in Cadiz to permit the loading and unloading in that port of ships trading with the New World. The innovation gave rise to much friction and jealousy between the two cities and the officials concerned, but by the early seventeenth century it had become customary to reserve approximately one quarter of all outward cargoes for the Cadiz merchants. A merchant guild was authorised in Seville to settle all civil suits between its members engaged in trade with the New World.

The Spanish commercial monopoly was thus a tale of two cities. Apart from the inflexibility of the system, there was little, either in geography, industry or maritime enterprise, to warrant the privileged position of Seville or Cadiz over other Spanish ports. When, with the accession of Charles V, Spanish interests became subordinate to those of the Hapsburg empire, sailings to the New World were authorised from a number of other ports, Corunna, Bayona, Aviles, Laredo, Bilbao, San Sebastian, Cartagena and Malaga, on condition that the ships returned to Seville. This relaxation of the monopoly seems, however, to have remained only on paper, and the monopoly of Seville was maintained until 1717 when, by a curious irony, the roles of Seville and Cadiz were reversed. Cadiz became the seat of the board of trade, and the agency was transferred to Seville. Spanish trade with the New World thus remained wedded to its original principle, concentration in a single Spanish port, until 1789, nearly three centuries after the discovery of the West Indies, when the trade was declared free.

Monopoly meant not only a designated port but also prescribed sailings. At the beginning of the sixteenth century, the trade between the New World and Seville was based on the despatch of an annual fleet from Seville to Hispaniola, whence the goods were trans-shipped to the other colonies. The return cargoes similarly assembled in Hispaniola, whence they sailed to Seville. With the conquest of Mexico and Peru and the increase of nautical knowledge of both the Atlantic and the Caribbean, a new system of routes was established. Two organised fleets sailed from Seville, at first separately, later together, as the seas became more and more unsafe from pirates. Thereby, however, the very piracy the system was designed to prevent was facilitated. A tax on imports and exports was levied to defray the cost of the convoy; the tax averaged about two and a half per cent, but was occasionally as high as seven per cent. Total expenditures for the convoys were high. They amounted to nearly 30,000 ducats for the fleet of 1559, over 100,000 for the fleet of 1555.

The fleets, on leaving Seville, sailed for the Canary Islands and the Lesser Antilles, entering the Caribbean between the Virgin Islands and Puerto Rico. The first, the *flota*, then made for Vera Cruz in Mexico, stopping at Puerto Rico, Hispaniola and Cuba on the way. The other, the *galleones*, was bound for Cartagena on the mainland. On arrival in Cartagena, news was sent to Porto Bello and Lima, and from Lima the Southern Armada sailed for Panama with its cargo of precious silver. From Panama the silver proceeded to Porto Bello by caravan, to coincide with the arrival of the *galleones* for the great fair of Porto Bello. After the fair the *galleones* returned to Cartagena for the return cargo, and both *galleones* and *flota* met in Havana for the return voyage to Seville through the Bahama Channel. It has been estimated that in the sixteenth century the combined size of the two fleets amounted to about 10,000 tons.

The West Indian islands were served by supplementary ships, whose number and tonnage were fixed by law, sailing each year in the fleets. From two to six ships each were assigned to Hispaniola and Havana in Cuba, two to Puerto Rico, one to Jamaica and Santiago de Cuba combined, and one to Trinidad.

Some idea of the effect of the system on the Spanish overseas possessions may be obtained from statistics of shipping for the years 1506–1555. The total number of outgoing vessels was 2,824, or fifty-six a year; the number of incoming was 1,976, or thirty-nine a year. The highest outgoing number was 101 in 1549, the lowest three in 1554; the highest incoming was eighty-four in 1551, the lowest ten in 1510, 1516 and 1524. These statistics refer to trade with all the New World possessions, including the West Indies. Statistics for the West Indies indicate that, during the years 1548–1555, a total of seventy-four ships sailed for Hispaniola, two to Havana, twelve to Puerto Rico. Returning vessels numbered 159 from San Domingo and three from Monte Christi, the two chief towns in Hispaniola, two from Santiago de Cuba, seventeen from Havana, thirty from Puerto Rico and three from Jamaica. Hispaniola thus enjoyed pre-eminence in the Spanish Caribbean empire, and Puerto Rico ranked above Cuba and Jamaica.

Spanish monopoly of trade with the New World was designed to achieve two principal objects—first, to prevent the drain of American gold and silver to foreign countries; secondly, to reserve the profits to the King and his subjects. Spanish monopoly consisted of an attempt to reserve to itself exclusively the supply of European commodities to the colonies, not necessarily of Spanish commodities, and colonial production, especially the precious metals. This policy was consistent with the promotion of agriculture and even industry in the colonies. In this respect, more than in any other, the Spanish colonial system differed from the system established later by Spain's rivals, England and France. Spain's monopoly was a monopoly of trade and navigation. The English and French monopolies were monopolies of production as well.

Thus, in 1516, the inhabitants of Cuba were allowed to build and own vessels for trade with other Spanish settlements. By the end of the sixteenth century Havana had become the chief shipbuilding centre in the Caribbean. It would appear, however, that the production of cordage, tackle and hardware was prohibited in the colonies, and the industry suffered accordingly. An edict in 1545 directed the encouragement of the cultivation of hemp and flax. The manufacture of silk, cotton and woollen textiles was permitted in Mexico and Peru. Attempts were made to acclimatise in the New World the domestic animals, cereals, vegetables and fruits of Spain. Serious efforts were made to grow wheat.

The Spanish colonial system was content to foster in the colonies the most important metropolitan industries. For example, whereas, in 1503, the production of wine was prohibited in Hispaniola, in 1519 the House of Trade was instructed to send with every ship sailing for the island a number of vines to be planted there. No opposition was placed in the way of the cultivation of olives and grapes in Peru, though after 1569 the local authorities were instructed to prevent further plantings, and by the end of the century suggestions were made forbidding altogether the production of wine in Peru. But the remedies adopted were the prohibition of an extension of the industry and of export to territories which could be supplied by Spain, and the imposition of a tax on wine produced and bottled locally.

The *Cortes* of 1584 urged that the colonies should produce their own manufactures, and in that year factories for the making of silks in Mexico were specifically authorised. The cloth industry in Peru was officially recognised by a decree of 1565, though after 1569 an unsuccessful effort was made to prohibit the production of finer cloths which competed with those of Spain. In 1595

it was ordered that no new factories were to be established, but
the vested interests involved were already too powerful, and the
industry continued to expand. Colonial industry had reached such
a point in 1584, in the form chiefly of wine and wool, that the
fleets of that year were alleged to have lost trade to an annual
sum of 200,000 ducats.

The nature of the Spanish colonial monopoly is best exemplified by the case of tobacco in the province of Caracas in 1607.
The Spanish Government banned its cultivation for ten years. The
reason was not that Venezuelan tobacco competed with a metropolitan product, but rather that the trade was monopolised by
the Dutch. The Spanish monarchy, rather than have its trading
monopoly infringed, preferred to destroy the economic basis of
the colony. The Spaniard cut off his nose to spite his face. But
what was involved was not colonial production but colonial trade.
The Spanish colonial system was not strict mercantilism; it looked
askance not on the growth of industry in the colonies but on
contraband trade between the colonies and foreigners.

The commercial system was in effect the transplantation to the
Caribbean of the medieval European system. Its annual fleets were
the marine version of the caravan. Its annual fairs were purely
European in origin. The system had important consequences for the
Caribbean. It marked the supremacy of Cuba over Hispaniola,
and established the strategic significance of Havana, 'the key of
the Indies'. It led to the subordination of the other Antilles,
Puerto Rico and Jamaica, and to the virtual desertion of the
northern coast of Hispaniola and the southern coast of Cuba.
Caribbean production and population were concentrated in the
vicinity of the trade routes. The necessity of protecting these
routes and their cargoes involved fortifications and military pre-
paredness. Whilst this led to the booms attendant on the construction of military bases, it served also to strengthen the
militaristic aspect of government—from this period, for example,
the governor of Cuba was usually a military man.

Whilst Spain preached the doctrine of monopoly, in practice it
was necessary for her to make concessions to reality. Neither
Spanish production nor Spanish shipping was adequate to take
care of colonial needs, and in the vital point of the slave trade
Spain was particularly vulnerable. The asientists were frequently

Genoese, with whom Spain had developed close commercial ties in the Middle Ages—of this tie Christopher Columbus was a notable example. Special concessions were also frequently made to the Portuguese, colonial rivals of Spain though they were, and the commercial ties between the two countries became closer from 1580 to 1640 when Portugal was under Spanish rule.

Germans received special concessions also as Spain became merged in the vast Hapsburg empire, whose ruler became dependent on German financiers. The sixteenth century was the great age of German high finance, especially of Jacob Fugger, 'the glory of all Germany', whose *News-Letters* did full justice to the importance of Spanish trade with the New World to the world economy. In 1525 the Welsers of Augsburg, another powerful German house of bankers, were put on an equal footing with Spanish traders in the New World. On this basis they established factories in Seville and Hispaniola. In 1528 the Welsers, in alliance with the Ehingers of Constance, concluded agreements with the Emperor for the transportation of fifty German miners to instruct the colonials in the New World, for the supply of four thousand Negro slaves to the New World within four years, and for the conquest and colonisation of Venezuela. Ambrosius Ehinger, a German, was appointed governor of Venezuela. But the German colonial venture proved abortive, no German settlements were established in Venezuela, and the Welsers soon withdrew from direct participation in undertakings in the New World, and restricted themselves to indirect participation in the form of loans to the Emperor. Germany lost her stake in the New World, and it was not until 1895 that German interest in Venezuela was revived. Then, however, it was too late.

Yet another European country was able to participate, through its inclusion in the Hapsburg empire, in the wealth of the New World. Spanish possession of the Netherlands, reduced with Dutch independence in 1580 to Belgium only, made Antwerp the financial capital of the sixteenth-century world, and its famous Bourse 'a small world wherein all parts of the great world are united'. For the rest, the merchants of Seville were reduced to the position of agents for French, English, Portuguese, German and Dutch merchants, from whom they obtained five-sixths of the cargoes needed for the *flota* and *galleones*. Especially through

Antwerp, Spain's colonial imports percolated through Europe, adding to the Spanish balance of trade.

The Spanish Government reaped a rich harvest from its New World possessions. For each licence to introduce slaves, there was a charge of two ducats. On arrival in the New World, the slave cargo, like all incoming merchandise, had to pay an import duty of seven and a half per cent, an old Moorish duty, the *almojarifazgo*, which survived the disappearance of the Moors. The *asientos* brought in immediate returns, of which the Spanish Government seemed always in need—for example, an *asiento* of 1536 for the importation of four thousand slaves into the New World in four years was granted in return for the sum of 26,000 ducats. In 1543, an export tax of two and a half per cent was levied in Seville, and the colonial import duty reduced to five per cent, thus transferring one-third of the revenue to the metropolis. At the same time, an import duty of five per cent plus a sales tax of ten per cent were levied at Seville on goods from the New World, all going to the Crown. In 1566 the *almojarifazgo* was increased to five per cent in Seville and ten per cent in the colonies, with a further two and a half per cent export duty in colonial ports. The duties exacted in the New World were based not upon values in Spain, but upon prices in the New World, and all intercolonial trade, except in wheat, flour and vegetables between ports in the same province, was subject to a five per cent import duty and a two and a half per cent export tax.

Yet the wealth from the New World was inadequate for the insatiable needs of the empire. At a conservative estimate, the Emperor Charles V, at his abdication, left a national deficit of about twenty million ducats. He owed two million to the Fuggers for Spain alone, and some five million to other similar houses.

What the *Casa de Contratación* was in the field of commerce, the *Consejo de las Indias*, the Council of the Indies, was in the field of politics. Formally established in 1524, it continued the supervision which the King had entrusted first to Columbus and then informally to various people from the time of the discovery. It consisted of a president, eight councillors, a fiscal or prosecutor on behalf of the Crown, two secretaries and other minor officials, including a professor of mathematics and a cosmographer-chronicler. All its members were nominated by the King, and the

Council was heavily weighted at the beginning on the clerical side, reflecting the dominant role of the clergy in the political life of the age.

The Council met thrice weekly, resided at the royal court, and the Emperor might preside at any time over its sessions. It had legislative power, and enjoyed supreme and exclusive jurisdiction over the Indies in political matters. All important questions were referred to it, either by the Crown or by the local authorities, and it was the Council's function to investigate, assess and make recommendations on the charges frequently brought against the highest colonial officials. It prepared the laws and ordinances regulating the government of the colonies, giving legal form to the principles enunciated by the Crown. Its chief responsibility lay in supervising the execution of those laws. It corresponded with the local officials in the colonies, proposed candidates for vacant posts, determined the territorial boundaries of the colonies, and was entrusted with the supervision of the laws relating to the treatment of the Indians. It was the highest court of appeal in suits arising in the New World.

The Government was represented in the colonies by the royal bureaucracy and the military representatives. The Treasury officials were independent of the governor, and were designated 'royal officials'. For the rest, the policy was one of strict assimilation to the laws of Castile. The governor was all powerful. Beside him was the Church, which, however, was subordinate to the State and abrogated its European privilege of sanctuary. Apart from this renunciation, there was no limit on its powers. It received large grants of land, on which it used Indian serf or Negro slave labour. From 1510 the tithe was made compulsory in all the colonies, imposing a severe burden on the infant agricultural economy. The 'dead hand' of the Church brought vast areas under clerical control. By 1620 the King of Spain could complain that the convents in Lima covered more ground than all the rest of the city. With the Church came the Inquisition, the Index, and the control of education. What the Church lost in Europe with the Protestant Reformation, it more than gained in the New World through discovery.

All the organs of the colonial system, *Casa de Contratación, Consejo de las Indias*, governor and royal bureaucracy representing the absolute monarchy, were designed to assure the same end, Spain's exclusive monopoly of the New World. The inherent weaknesses of the Spanish economy inevitably placed the emphasis on the negative aspect of this goal, the prohibition of contraband trade. In slaves, manufactured goods, and colonial exports, contraband assumed significant proportions in the sixteenth century. The number of royal decrees against the importation of Moorish, Jewish, Berber or other heretic slaves bears mute witness to the prevalence of contraband on the very morrow of the discovery. According to an official in Hispaniola in 1552, for every hundred slaves entered legally, two hundred entered clandestinely, to avoid payment of the duties. Precautions and decrees were useless, for the very officials were frequently involved in the contraband trade.

West Indian history, conceived in monopoly, was reared in smuggling. Contraband became the chief industry of one of Cuba's oldest towns, Bayamon. At the beginning of the seventeenth century the governor of the island decided to make an example. Almost the entire town was arrested, including municipal officials, military men, and churchmen. Heavy sentences, including the death penalty and confiscation of property, were imposed. Feeling in the town ran high, the judge was virtually besieged, and was forced to remain six months in the city, not daring to leave, because a large body of citizens was lying in wait for him on its outskirts. Eventually, when even the governor joined in petitioning the King for clemency, a general amnesty was granted in 1607. But, to prevent recidivism, and to deal more effectively with the contraband menace in the future, Cuba was divided into two jurisdictions. The supreme authority in military matters was entrusted to the Governor of Havana; in all other matters, the jurisdiction of Santiago de Cuba was virtually independent.

The assimilation to the system of Castile resulted in a colonial society which maintained all the social distinctions prevalent in feudal Spain. Some part of Columbus' troubles in the early days was due to his insistence that the Spanish noblemen work with their hands. The class structure was reflected in the grants of land. The plebeian, the peon, received a *peonia*, a modest grant of land, together with gifts of wheat, corn and cattle. The noblemen, the *caballero*, received a *caballeria* (which has since become

the standard Cuban measure) approximately thirty-three acres.
The *caballeria* was equivalent to five *peonias*.

Whilst the Spanish Government did not object to intermarriage
in the early period, from the very beginning purity of blood was
an essential prerequisite of the exercise of all public functions.
Thus originated the familiar saying, that a Spaniard could do anything in Cuba except have a Spanish son. The children were
creoles, with a presumption—frequently not unwarranted—of
mixed blood. The supremacy of peninsulars over creoles was
emphasised at every turn. Despite the Spanish Government's concern with higher education, as evidenced on the continent by the
establishment of the Universities of Mexico and Lima, and in the
Caribbean by those of Santo Domingo and Havana—in this respect
also sharply distinguishing Spanish colonial policy from English
and French—injury was added to insult by that attitude typified
by the Viceroy of Peru in his reply to a colonial delegation requesting political privileges: 'Learn to read, write and say your
prayers, for that is as much as any American ought to know.'

Chapter Six

Colonial Nationalism

Colonialism as developed and enforced by Spain in her Caribbean colonies gave rise to a fundamental conflict between metropolitan and colonial interests. The colonial movement took two forms—the disaffection of the white colonials, the revolt of the coloured colonials. The entire history of the Caribbean has revolved around the possibility that these two elements would coalesce against metropolitan oppression and jointly demand colonial independence.

First, the white colonials. The colonial system worked great hardship on the colonies. The Bishop of Cuba complained in 1556 that the sacrifice of the Mass could sometimes not be performed because of lack of wine; that as a result of the *flota* system, prices had skyrocketed; and that people were daily leaving the island. By the early part of the seventeenth century, scarcity was so pronounced that, in all the large towns of Hispaniola, Mass on Sundays and holy days was said before daylight, so that those who could not appear decently clad might be concealed by the darkness.

The Spanish monopoly, in accordance with the economic practices of all the rising nation states of the age, was designed to further metropolitan, not colonial, interests. The colonials fought against it from the very beginning. The irrepressible conflict between these interests was sharply brought out in 1527 in the reply of the colonials of Cubagua to Luis Lampunano, son of a count, who had been granted by the Crown the exclusive right, for six years, of using a machine for pearl fishing off Cubagua. The colonials sent him back with the bold answer: 'That the Emperor, too liberal of what was not his own, had not the right to dispose of the oysters which live at the bottom of the sea!'

The colonials also attacked the other rights claimed by the King of Spain. First in importance was the attack on the monopoly of Seville and a demand for free trade. The first colonial protest involved, significantly, the trade in sugar. On August 20, 1520, the royal officials in Hispaniola, on behalf of the sugar planters, requested that permission be granted for sugar to be taken from Hispaniola to all parts of the King's dominions, without any obligation to go to Seville. 'If not,' they continued, 'the inhabitants say that everything will be wasted in the fleets, and few will be encouraged to pursue this industry, because there is little despatch in Seville.' In 1540 the Bishop of Santo Domingo and the Court of Hispaniola again took up the cudgels on behalf of the planters. In a letter to the Emperor, they alleged that ships could not leave Seville in bad weather, whilst they could from the Canary Islands to the advantage of the colonies. They added that, as the West Indian colonies were dependent to a large extent on the sugar industry, no restrictions should be placed on it by requiring the transport of sugar to Spain only via Seville, as the ships were insufficient and charged high freight rates. They concluded that the abrogation of the Seville monopoly would be advantageous to the colonies.

The planters were not appeased by the opening of a branch of the House of Trade in Cadiz. The city of Santo Domingo emphasised that one reason for the high prices in the colonies was the requirement that all ships engaged in colonial trade had to be registered in Seville, and that it would be very advantageous if permission were given to all ships to leave from any port in Spain for Hispaniola, without the obligation of registration. The Spanish authorities ignored the petition.

The planters, always ready in the West Indies to defend their interests, were dissatisfied even with free trade with Spain. In April 1518, the proctors elected by the cities and towns of Hispaniola met in conference. They agreed to petition the King, *inter alia*, for general freedom of trade between all the ports of Spain and the New World, even for foreigners, on condition that the duties were paid; for exemption for the products of Hispaniola from export duties in the island and import duties in Spain; and for abolition of all duties on intercolonial trade. The voice of the colonial planters ran directly counter to the voice of the Spanish Government.

The planters were not anti-monopoly. They wanted monopoly as much as the Spanish King, but monopoly in their interests. There was one aspect of monopoly which the colonials not only accepted but advocated and wished to reinforce. That was the colonial monopoly of the Spanish sugar market. The *bête noire* of the Spanish colonials was Brazil. The sixteenth-century struggle for the control of the world sugar market was waged between Spain and Portugal. The Bishop of Santo Domingo and the Judge of Hispaniola pleaded the cause of the planters in 1540. They urged that the importation of sugar from 'other kingdoms of Spain' should be prohibited, and that permission to take sugar to Spain should be conceded to all the ports of the King of Spain's dominions, or at least to Flanders. The Council of the Indies was favourably disposed, but in the following year the Emperor was content to request the Council to take advice on the matter and give him its views on the question of prohibiting sugar imports from Portugal.

Next in importance to the Seville monopoly from the colonial standpoint was the monopoly of the slave trade. The planters opposed the system of licences and *asientos*, and advocated free trade. They opposed also the religious limitations with which the Spanish Government had originally hemmed in the slave trade. In 1517 the Geronimite Fathers in Hispaniola begged the Spanish Government to issue general licences for the importation of slaves from West Africa into the West Indies: 'We beg you to grant this, and to grant it soon, because these people are driving us crazy about it and in our opinion they are right.' They were not the last people to be driven almost out of their minds by the question of slavery.

A year later the Fathers went further. They urged that permission should be granted for the fitting out of ships to the Cape Verde Islands and Guinea, either from Hispaniola itself or by anyone in any part of the Spanish dominions. Ten years later Cuba asked for the same facility, permission to fit out ships for Guinea. In 1519 the Court of Hispaniola recommended that, in order to facilitate the introduction of the largest possible number of Negroes in the shortest possible time, an *asiento* should be made with the King of Portugal. In 1536 the request for a Portuguese *asiento* was repeated. In 1527 certain planters in Hispaniola submitted to the Emperor a project regarding population, in which they urged that each planter should be allowed to introduce one hundred male slaves and one hundred females. The planters complained regularly of the high prices charged by the asientists.

The planters attacked yet a third feature of the Spanish monopoly—the exclusion of foreigners. With the mainland and gold daily drawing away their white settlers, it was perhaps more obvious to them than to the metropolitan government that economics came before politics. An official in Hispaniola, in a letter to the Spanish Government in 1518, indicated the necessity of permitting immigration 'from all parts of the world', excluding only Moors, Jews and those reconverted to the Faith. The conference of proctors in Hispaniola in the same year petitioned for freedom for all foreign immigrants, except French and Genoese. Two years later the island asked for immigrants from any nation.

When, in 1535, the Spanish Government decided to expel the few Portuguese who had settled in Hispaniola, the authorities of the island informed the Council of the Indies that some of the Portuguese planters were married, and that there were in the island more than two hundred Portuguese bachelors who were sugar technicians, labourers, carpenters, ironmongers, and in other occupations which were generally very useful in the towns. They concluded:

'If you order to the contrary, your instructions will be carried out, although to deport them will be a great disadvantage to the country, which suffers from underpopulation, because of the new discoveries and the lack of Indians: we want not only Portuguese, but, indeed, population.'

More forthright, the municipality of Santo Domingo wrote to the Emperor to say that the Portuguese agent for the German asientists was a useful person whose loss would be felt, and it advised the Emperor bluntly to reconsider the matter and not to give ear to 'interested persons'.

The colonials also protested against the heavy duties and charges imposed on them. Hispaniola petitioned against the introduction of the tithe into the colonies. The tithe, a ten per cent tax imposed for the building of churches, and payable in kind, was very burdensome to the infant sugar industry, not only in its quantity, but also because the producer had to pay at a specified place, often at a great distance. In 1518 the same colony urged its reduction to one-thirtieth. The Spanish Government refused, but eventually conceded in 1539 a reduction to five per cent for muscovado sugar and four per cent for refined sugar and molasses. The taxes and duties on colonial produce, in the colonies and on importation into Spain, were so heavy that, in 1546, the Spanish Government was warned that Hispaniola was in danger of being totally ruined.

Two more general indications may be given of the temper of the colonials. In 1532 the Court of Hispaniola sent a petition to the Spanish Government requesting general freedom to introduce Negroes on payment solely of the *almojarifazgo*; immigration of white workers from Spain; permission for Portuguese immigrants; state aid for experiments in the cultivation of wheat and production of wine; general licence to take sugar and other products not only to Flanders but to other ports, without the necessity of entering or leaving from Seville (which was the factor most responsible for the destruction of the islands); and exemption from the *almojarifazgo* on imports of building materials for houses and sugar mills. On May 27, 1558, the Dean and Council of Santo Domingo wrote to the Emperor complaining of the rapid depopulation of the island. Their letter concluded:

'We are dying of hunger for lack of Negroes and cultivators of the soil. As ships arrive only in the *flota*, years pass without provisions coming from Spain, and we lack bread, wine, ham, oil, clothes...When they do come, prices are exorbitant, and if we ask for credit, they hide the merchandise.'

For the rest, the colonials contented themselves with ignoring the law where it was opposed to their interests. 'Let it be obeyed but not enforced,' was the formula for the reception of unpopular decrees from Spain, and distance and official venality did the rest.

Colonial nationalism was not restricted to economic matters. Of fundamental significance was the emergence in the first half of the sixteenth century in the Spanish Caribbean colonies of a vigorous tendency to some measure of local autonomy, in opposition to the centralisation policy of the Spanish monarchy. It did not constitute, it is true, a robust emergence of that democratic spirit which had characterised the medieval communes of Flanders, France, England and Switzerland, and even of Castile in Spain, until it was beaten down by Charles V at the battle of Villalar in 1521. It was not, it is true, a movement for colonial democracy. But it was the first step. In 1507 the towns in Hispaniola sent delegates to Spain to petition the King for the privileges possessed by municipalities in the metropolitan country. The petition was granted. Conventions of proctors or delegates of the towns met from time to time to take common action—a sort of embryo *Cortes* or Parliament. The Governor of Cuba was forced to bow to the demand for a municipal council elected by the settlers. It was the practice of the governor or his deputy to be present at sessions of the council. In 1525 the Council of Santiago de Cuba refused to admit the acting governor, accusing him of restricting its liberty and of trying to impose his views on it. It followed up this action by protesting to the Emperor against the practice of the governor of appointing in the various towns deputies who deprived the municipal officials of their functions. The Emperor viewed both the Council's action and its protest in a favourable light.

The leader of the colonial opposition in Cuba was Manuel de Rojas, a former mayor of Bayamon and Santiago de Cuba, who acted as governor of the island for a brief period after the sudden death of Governor Velasquez in 1524. Rojas' policy was that the municipal council should be a genuine representation of the inhabitants of the island, and that independence was a necessary prerequisite of its function, the protection of local interests. Consequently, he opposed the election of individuals who held official posts under the Crown. In the early years of the councils, the mayors had been appointed by the aldermen, not by the settlers. The elections gave rise to frauds and complaints, because the governors put pressure on the councils in favour of their candidates. Rojas took the view that the mayors must be chosen by the votes of all the people, and a royal decree in 1529 supported him.

The high-water mark of Rojas' influence and the democratic spirit was reached in 1528, when a conference of proctors was convened in Santiago de Cuba. The conference, wishing to assure its independence and popular character for the future, petitioned the Emperor that each town should have its proctor, with the right to form a council as it pleased, in order to seek and procure the common good of the settlers, and to meet with other proctors as necessary to petition the Emperor. These proctors should be elected annually by popular vote. They asked for a royal decree for the governor's guidance, and concluded: 'We, the proctors, are vassals of the King, and as our conference has a public clerk, it does not appear to us that there is any need for us to give an account to any other judge.' The Council of the Indies decided in favour of the conference. The proctors were thereafter to be elected by popular vote, and the governor was instructed to abstain from demanding that he should be informed of any matter respecting which the proctors wished to maintain reserve.

The popular spirit in Cuba, however, was weakened by municipal decadence in Castile and the general decay of the Cuban economy under the double impact of the Spanish colonial system and the chaos caused by revolts of the Indians. A new system of electing the mayors was eventually adopted, whereby the settlers chose two members of the council, the aldermen two, and the governor one. The five names were put into an urn, from which two were drawn. The first to be drawn was mayor, the second deputy mayor. In 1536 re-election was prohibited for two years. The resolutions of the sessions of the conference of proctors in 1542 reveal the change that had come over Cuba and the subordination of political to economic questions:

'The island is well off in Spaniards, natives and Negroes, but it is in great need: the mines are very weak; the Indians very few. Please order the payment for Indians at one-tenth, for slaves at one-fifteenth; here the chief urgency is Negroes ... We beg permission for each planter to bring four Negroes, free of all duties ... Permission should be given for the introduction of Indian slaves without payment of duty, as elsewhere ... The roads are impassable from some towns to others, because some have no roads at all ... Very few ships come from Castile ... some used to come from the Canary Islands... The two German smelters are not adequate for smelting all the copper... We beg that more be allowed to come...'

In the political field the proctors petitioned against the ban on re-election of the mayors; the number of settlers had so diminished that there was a lack of 'worthy persons'. Finally, they asked for funds for the permanent maintenance of a squadron of Indians to pursue rebel slaves.

The last conference of proctors was held in Santiago de Cuba on March 5, 1550. Thereafter the democratic and municipal spirit steadily declined. External attack and internal revolt combined to place all real power in the hands of the governor. The municipal organisations survived, but their original spirit was distorted. They became small oligarchies appointed *ex officio* and for life. They became positions of prestige which could be bought. Finally in 1629, the municipal councils lost their most important function and power, which they had assumed and exercised for almost a century, that of granting land. Metropolitan absolutism seemed firmly in the saddle, and the democratic and autonomous spirit effectively squashed.

It was not until the Cuban War of Independence in 1868, three centuries later, that the white colonials really understood that they could not oppose metropolitan colonialism on the basis of black slavery. They would have to choose—either to remain satellites of the metropolitan power or to seek colonial independence on the basis of political freedom.

In the sixteenth century they made their choice. They needed Negro slavery as they saw it; therefore they needed Spanish power as protection against the Negro slaves. The coloured colonials recognised their enemy—the colonial planter whose position as slaveowner was based on metropolitan law.

The revolt of the coloured colonials took the form, inevitably, of revolts against slavery. If the Spanish slave code gave academic recognition to the fact that slavery is contrary to reason and naturally abhorrent to man, the slaves, on the slave ships themselves and immediately on their arrival in the Caribbean, fought unceasingly for their freedom. The Spanish colonies were kept in a state of permanent revolution, however sporadic, unorganised, and ill-timed may have been the revolts of the slaves.

The centre of disaffection was Hispaniola, the chief island of

Spain's Caribbean empire. Two years after the inauguration of the
Negro slave trade to the Caribbean in 1503, the Governor of the
island urged the Spanish Government to suspend the traffic, on the
ground that the Negroes ran away, made common cause with the
Amerindians, and taught them bad habits. The trade was accordingly suspended, because the Queen thought that it impeded her
cherished aim of converting the Amerindians. But the suspension
was of short duration, and the apprehension and danger of slave
revolts became a normal feature of Spanish Caribbean society.

The Spanish Government experimented with various expedients.
It prohibited the importation of male slaves, or it specified a
proportion of female slaves, or it sought to encourage marriage
among the slaves, or it specified a ratio of one to three in terms
of Negro slaves and free white men, or it even, as with the
Emperor Charles V, sought to limit the Negro population of the
New World countries to a maximum of one quarter of the white
population.

The results were a slave revolt in Hispaniola in 1522 and
another in Puerto Rico in 1527. Thereupon the Spanish Government sought to prohibit the importation of Negroes from various
warlike tribes. For example, in September 1532, importations
from a certain area were banned, 'because this caste of Negroes,
proud, disobedient, rebellious and incorrigible, was the cause
of the revolts and deaths of Christians which have taken place
in Puerto Rico and other islands'.

But the revolts continued throughout the Spanish dominions.
A conspiracy was discovered in New Spain in 1537. The Negroes
elected a king, planned to kill all the Spaniards, and were joined
by the Indians. The Viceroy was so alarmed that he urged the
suspension of the introduction of the slaves he had previously
requested. Another revolt broke out in Honduras in 1548, yet
another in New Spain in 1612, the latter inspiring such terror that
processions in Mexico City in Holy Week were banned and the
churches closed on Holy Thursday. In the Caribbean, Negro
slaves joined French pirates in their sack of Havana in 1538, and
in the same year kept Santiago de Cuba in such a state of panic
that no one dared to leave his house.

Open revolt was not the only weapon of the slaves in their
fight against slavery. The more usual response was flight. They

ran away to the mountains, where they led a subsistence economy based on the traditional African pattern. They became *cimarrones*, the Maroons, as they were later called in the British islands. As early as 1521 the Spanish Government tried to reduce this ever-present danger by prohibiting the inclusion of Negroes in the voyages of discovery and conquest, as this facilitated their running away. Local companies, *rancheadores*, were formed in the islands to hunt down fugitive slaves.

The increasing severity of sixteenth-century legislation against runaways bears eloquent testimony to the widespread nature of the practice. Rewards were offered for information leading to the recapture of fugitives, dogs were specially trained for the task, and the death penalty was decreed in 1574 for free mulattoes or Negroes inciting slaves to flight, the penalty being reduced to banishment in the case of Spaniards. Assistance to runaways incurred the same penalty as flight itself in the case of Negroes or mulattoes, plus confiscation of half their property if they were free, and perpetual banishment in the case of Spaniards. The runaway, if caught, received fifty lashes for an absence of more than four days, one hundred for an absence of more than eight; if he was absent less than four months, the punishment was two hundred lashes for the first offence, banishment for the second; absenteeism exceeding six months was punished by hanging.

Church joined hands with State, and the Inquisition regarded an attempt to escape from slavery as apostasy, to be expiated, if the attempt was successful, by the burning of the runaway in effigy. The repressive measures became harsher as the slaves showed themselves indifferent to punishment in this world and damnation in the next. In 1610 it was proposed in Havana that one ear or the nose of all recaptured fugitives should be cut off, so that they might be recognised if any subsequent attempt was made. In 1619 the King decreed that the ordinary process of the law was not necessary in the case of runaways or rebels.

The gravity of the problem is indicated by the fact that, towards the middle of the sixteenth century, the Maroons in Hispaniola were estimated to number seven thousand, whereas the white male population barely exceeded one thousand. The local authorities, unable to subdue the Maroons, offered in 1545 to allow them to live in peace and even to send them clergymen to instruct them in the Christian religion, on condition that they left the whites alone. The Maroons replied that such was their desire, but that they did not trust the word of the Spaniards. The Court of the Island complained in 1546 that, as a result of the example set by the Maroons, the planters dared not give orders to their slaves except in the gentlest terms. The Maroon leader, Diego de Campo, was feared throughout the country. He defeated troops sent against him, burned sugar mills, and abducted slaves. Eventually he was caught, whereupon, pleading to be spared, he offered to lead expeditions against his former followers and colleagues. Such was his reputation that his offer was accepted. Only then did the Spaniards breathe freely and the Maroon danger diminish for a time. The price of slavery for the white colonials was eternal colonialism.

Chapter Seven

The Cockpit of Europe

Gold, sugar, slaves, this Caribbean trinity represented an enormous accession of wealth and power. Not surprisingly, Spain's imperialist rivals insisted on their share. The Caribbean islands began their association with modern society as the pawn of European power politics, the cockpit of Europe, the arena of Europe's wars hot and cold.

This imperialist rivalry was anticipated even before the voyage of Columbus. A resident of Portugal, Columbus first sought Portuguese sponsorship for his projected voyage of discovery. The Portuguese Crown rejected him. The exploration of the African coastline, culminating in the voyage of Bartholomew Diaz to the Cape of Good Hope in 1486, had brought the circumnavigation of Africa and the discovery of the Cape route to India within their reach. The Portuguese saw no point in supporting a man whom they regarded as a boastful adventurer with a crack-brained scheme designed to achieve a purpose—a new route to India—which seemed already assured.

Columbus then approached the Italian republic of Genoa, where he was born, and Venice. He found, however, similar vested interests in his path, concerned with keeping Oriental trade in its existing overland channels via the Mediterranean, from which both republics benefited considerably.

Columbus turned, therefore, to the younger nations, which had no such vested interests in the question, and which were interested in any project tending to break down existing monopolies which belonged to others: Spain, England and France. Shrewdly playing off one against the other, he himself went to Spain, whilst he sent his brother to the Court of Henry VII of England. Spain's decision was delayed by the war against the Moors, but, with the conquest of Granada, the last Moorish stronghold, the Sovereigns of Spain reached an agreement with Columbus. When his brother arrived with an invitation to visit England, it was too late.

Portugal's apprehension and jealousy were soon manifested. On leaving the Canary Islands, Columbus evaded three Portuguese vessels which, in his opinion, had been sent to intercept him. On his return from his successful voyage, he encountered Portuguese unfriendliness in the Azores, and when he landed near Lisbon after a severe storm he had encountered, the King of Portugal sent for him. At the meeting the King expressed the view that Columbus' voyage violated the monopoly of Guinea he had received from the Pope, and Portuguese hostility was not diminished by Columbus' delusion that he had reached Asia. As the story goes, however, the King refused to agree to a suggestion from some of his courtiers that a quarrel should be picked with Columbus and that the discoverer be slain on the spot.

Columbus assured the Sovereigns of Spain that the countries he had discovered were as much theirs as their kingdom of Castile. The Sovereigns, taking no chances, hastened to secure confirmation of the annexations by the traditional method of the period, a bull from the Pope, who happened to be a Spaniard, Alexander VI. Portuguese monopoly of Guinea rested on a series of discoveries, sanctioned by papal bulls granting to the King of Portugal all land discovered south of Cape Bojador. By a treaty of 1480 Spain had conceded to Portugal all the islands discovered or to be discovered from the Canaries southward in the region of Guinea. Some compromise and delimitation of the respective claims of the two governments were necessary if a clash was to be avoided between the two imperialist powers. The natural arbiter where two Catholic powers were concerned in that period was the Pope.

In a bull issued in 1493, the Pope confirmed the existing rights of Portugal and established those of Spain by drawing an imaginary line from north to south, one hundred leagues west of the Azores and the Cape Verde Islands. East of this line was the Portuguese sphere of influence; west, the Spanish. Dissatisfied because no mention was made of India, the Spanish Government persuaded the Pope to issue another bull, in September, 1493, in which Spain was accorded full rights to hold such lands as it might discover to the south and west 'and eastern regions and to India'. Columbus' hope of reaching India by sailing west thus received papal recognition.

The Portuguese Government was not satisfied with this line of demarcation. The two powers thereupon entered upon direct negotiations, which culminated in the Treaty of Tordesillas, on June 7, 1494. This treaty fixed the line at 370 leagues west of the Cape Verde Islands. By this rectification, Brazil became Portuguese.

Caribbean history, conceived in international rivalry, was reared and nurtured in an environment of power politics. The Pope enjoined his partition on all men and nations, as follows: 'Let no person, therefore, presume to infringe, or, with rash boldness, to contravene, this page of our commendation, exhortation, requisition, donation, concession, assignation, constitution, deputation, decree, mandate, inhibition, and will. For if any person does, he will incur the indignation of Almighty God, and the blessed apostles Peter and Paul.'

But the Pope had no divisions. On March 5, 1496, Henry VII issued a patent to another sailor, John Cabot, to undertake a voyage of discovery. The date has been called the birthday of the British Empire. Whilst no concrete results were obtained, the patent is of significance. It omitted the words 'Southern Seas', thus giving tacit recognition to Spanish and Portuguese discoveries and, to that extent, to the papal document. But its very issuance rejected any interpretation of a partition of the entire world between Spain and Portugal, and was a warning that the English Government regarded ownership as based at least on discovery. What had not been discovered was open to all. Francis I, King of France, in a celebrated protest, made explicit what was implicit in Henry VII's charter to Cabot. 'The sun shines for me as for others,' he said. 'I should very much like to see the clause in Adam's will that excludes me from a share of the world.' God, he added, had not created those lands for Spaniards only.

While England concentrated in the main on a north-east passage to Asia, France sent out expeditions which reached the St. Lawrence, Florida and Brazil. As the Protestant Reformation reduced the Pope's 'divisions', and Europe moved closer to the wars of religion, Protestantism and nationalism saw in the Spanish monopoly of the New World the chief bulwark of Catholicism in Europe and the sinews of Spain's military strength. Protestant England and Catholic France became the chief enemies of Spain; they were soon to be joined by Protestant Holland, when it succeeded in declaring its independence from Spain.

England became the spokesman for the newcomers against Spanish pretensions to a monopoly of the entire New World based on the papal partition. Sir William Cecil (later Lord Burleigh), the Elizabethan statesman, told the Spanish Ambassador to England in 1562 that 'the Pope had no right to partition the world and to give and take kingdoms to whomsoever he pleased'. The British Government countered Spanish claims with the doctrine of effective occupation. In 1580 it rejected the Spanish pretension to a monopoly, 'either because of donations from the Pope or because of occupations touching here and there upon those coasts, building cottages, and giving names to a few places ... by the law of nations such occupations could not hinder other princes from freely navigating those seas and transporting colonies to those parts where the Spanish did not actually inhabit; ... prescription without possession availed nothing.' Queen Elizabeth herself forcefully enunciated the doctrine of freedom of the seas: 'The use of the sea and air is common to all; neither can any title to the ocean belong to any people or private man.'

The stake involved was enormous: the entire treasure and empire of the New World, and not only of the West Indies. On September 26, 1583, the treasure fleet from the New World brought a shipment of fifteen million pesos in bullion, after leaving a million behind in Havana because the ships were too heavily laden. 'This is a pretty penny,' concluded one announcement, 'which will give new life to commerce.'

England, France and Holland, however, also desired new life for their commerce. Three policies were available to the newcomers. The first was piracy and buccaneering—knight-errantry, as a British historian whimsically describes it. The first and most obvious method of challenging Adam's will was to take from his self-appointed heir. Columbus met French pirates on his first voyage, and, on his return from his third voyage, had to take a different route to avoid a French fleet which was awaiting him. The Spaniards were wont to speak of 'Lutheran corsairs'. But Catholic Frenchmen had no scruples about preying on the treasure of another Catholic state. In 1522 a Florentine buccaneer, Verrazanno, in the service of the King of France, captured three Spanish vessels, two laden with Mexican treasure, and the third with sugar, pearls and hides from Hispaniola. He made presents therefrom to the King of France, who, in amazement, exclaimed: 'The Emperor can carry on the war against me by means of the riches he draws from the West Indies alone!'

Piracy thereafter lost its individual and occasional character and became an essential feature of national policy on the part of Spain's enemies in Europe. The pirates, directly or indirectly backed by their governments, lay in wait for the treasure fleets, attacked isolated ships, and even carried their depredations to the Spanish dominions, where they besieged cities, held them to ransom and plundered them. The undeclared war in the Caribbean, in the sixteenth-century phrase, 'no peace beyond the line,' was enshrined in the Treaty of Cateau-Cambrésis of 1559 between France and Spain: 'west of the prime meridian and south of the Tropic of Cancer ... violence by either party to the other side shall not be regarded as in contravention of the treaties.'

The incarnation of this phase of Caribbean history is Sir Francis Drake. Born in Devonshire, of a father who was both a strong 'Reformation man' and a kinsman of seamen, bred and reared among ships and sailors, Drake personified the Elizabethan age, its growing sense of nationalism, its confidence in 'this scepter'd isle ... this precious stone set in the silver sea', and its antagonism to Spanish absolutism and Catholicism. To Drake his attacks on Spain were as dear in the sight of Heaven as they

notoriously were in the sight of his Queen; he regarded them as
a crusade, a war against idolatry.

But the material aspects of his crusade were not lost upon him.
'I have brought you,' he said to his men before Nombre de Dios
in 1572, 'to the Treasure-House of the World. Blame nobody
but yourselves if you go away empty.' His famous message to
the Spanish Governor of the town, that he had come 'to reap
some of your harvest which you get out of the earth and send
into Spain to trouble all the earth', typified national policy. Drake
assured Queen Elizabeth that, though the whole world were the
King of Spain's garden, it was hers to pluck the fruit thereof.
The Queen participated in his famous and grandiose expedition to
Spain's multi-million dollar empire in the New World, which
yielded a dividend of forty-seven pounds on every pound invested. 'It was such a cooling to King Philip', said someone in
Europe, 'as never happened to him since he was king of Spain.'

The danger was obvious. The Spanish Ambassador to England
urged his King to issue orders 'that no foreign ship should be
spared in either the Spanish or Portuguese Indies, but that every
one should be sent to the bottom . . . This will be the only way to
prevent the English and French from going to those parts to
plunder; for at present there is hardly an Englishman who is not
talking of undertaking the voyage, so encouraged are they by
Drake's return.' But it was Drake whom the Spaniards feared
most. They were apprehensive that he would capture the entire
treasure fleet, which, as the Venetian Ambassador at Madrid
reported, would mean the ruin of half Spain, while a mere delay
would cause the bankruptcy of many merchants in Seville. Drake,
however, missed the fleet by a few hours, 'the reason best known
to God,' as he stated philosophically. But Spain was in a panic.
The Bank of Seville broke; the Bank of Venice was in despair;
and the King of Spain, regarded as a bankrupt, was unable to
raise a loan of half a million ducats.

England's destruction of the Spanish Armada in 1588—in
which Drake, leaving his game of bowls, played the leading role
—did much more than save England from invasion. It signified
the supremacy of British over Spanish sea power, and the lesson
was underlined by Drake's daring exploit of 'singeing the King
of Spain's beard' in the very harbour of Cadiz itself. The Pope

mocked that Elizabeth's distaff was keener than Philip's sword. Drake became a legend, a devil whose name kept colonial children quiet, and the luckless admiral of the Spanish Armada was tormented by urchins who cried under his window, 'Drake is coming, Drake is coming'. But more than all this, the significance of Drake for Caribbean history lies in his words to Lord Burleigh on July 28, 1586: 'There is a very great gap opened, very little to the liking of the King of Spain.'

The second policy pursued by Spain's rivals was that of contraband trade, which showed up the holes in Spain's commercial system as Drake had found the chinks in Spain's armour. The exemplar in this field was another Englishman, Sir John Hawkins, a kinsman of Drake. Sailing to Guinea in 1562 in violation of the Portuguese monopoly, he initiated the English slave trade by obtaining a cargo of three hundred slaves, partly by the sword, as he confessed, partly by other means. Taking the slaves to the West Indies, he trespassed on the Spanish monopoly, and disposed of two-thirds of his cargo in Hispaniola to the eager planters for hides. Either through audacity or stupidity, Hawkins left the remainder with the authorities as a deposit, and sent half the consignment of hides to Cadiz in Spanish ships in the care of a partner. The cargo was confiscated in Spain, Hawkins' partner narrowly escaped the Inquisition, and the slaves left in Hispaniola were forfeited. Hawkins protested in vain.

But the incident indicated that the Spanish monopoly could be whittled away by contraband trade as well as sapped by military means. Contraband became the continuation of war by other means. The Dutch, independent in 1580, were quick to learn the lesson. So ubiquitous did they become in the Caribbean that the Spanish Governor of Venezuela recommended that they should be kept out by poisoning the neighbouring salt pans to which they were in the habit of resorting.

Drake and Hawkins revealed that Spain was unable to defend its empire and monopoly. The attention of Spain's rivals was thereby directed to their third policy, that of encroaching on Spain's territorial monopoly, establishing colonies of their own even in the southern seas, in defiance of the papal injunction, and from there penetrating more easily the paper walls of the Spanish colonial system. The wish of an obscure clerk in the

British Treasury, Richard Eden, was about to be fulfilled, that 'that rich treasury called PERULARIA', the bullion warehouse of Seville, should be brought to the Tower of London.

Using as their yardstick the doctrine of effective occupation rather than mere declarations of sovereignty, the newcomers directed their attention in the main to three easily accessible regions which Spain had neglected and over which its suzerainty was merely nominal. These areas were the Lesser Antilles, Guiana and North America.

The intellectual exponent of this phase of inter-imperialist rivalry was an obscure English clergyman, Richard Hakluyt, a man of wide vision and discernment, whose imagination had been fired by accounts of the voyages of discovery, the industrious editing of which has been his chief claim to fame, and which has been commemorated by the establishment of the distinguished society which bears his name. Hakluyt was, in the deepest sense of the word, an imperialist, and he looked upon colonies as a cure for the ills, particularly the economic ills, of the state.

Hakluyt set himself the task of stimulating the English to colonial activity and of bolstering national pride. Delving into old and rare documents going back to the remote past of Tacitus and the Venerable Bede, he insisted that England had, from the beginning, played an honourable part in trade and discovery. In fact, he argued, England's exploits were more daring than those of Spain and Portugal. These two nations had had the writers of antiquity to guide them, who had guessed at the existence of the New World, and their voyages of discovery had been launched with their own towns and islands to succour them, the Canaries and the Azores for example. England, on the other hand, had turned to the stern and uncouth North Seas, 'altogether destitute of such clear lights and inducements', to lands which, unlike the Spanish and Portuguese voyages, were barred with ice, mist or darkness. Hakluyt was forced to concede that English enterprise had not met 'with the like golden success, nor with such deductions of Colonies, nor attaining of conquests'. This it was necessary to correct.

'But now', he wrote in his preface to the famous book he published in 1589, *The Principal Navigations, Voyages, Traffiques and Discoveries of the English Nation*, 'it is high time for us to weigh our anchor, to hoist up our sails, to get clear of these boisterous, frosty and misty seas, and with all speed to direct our course for the middle, lightsome, temperate, and warm Atlantic Ocean, over which the Spaniards and Portuguese have made so many pleasant, prosperous and golden voyages.' Hakluyt spared neither time nor energy in, and subordinated all opportunities for private gain and preferment to unlocking and disseminating Spain's secrets, obtaining and translating Spanish documents ('as may any way avail us or annoy them') describing all the chief rivers, ports, towns, cities and provinces of the West Indies, providing all the necessary information so that Queen Elizabeth 'shall by God's assistance, in short space, work many great and unlooked for effects, increase her dominions, enrich her coffers, and reduce many Pagans to the faith of Christ'.

Hakluyt objectively appraised the possibilities. 'The time approacheth,' he concluded, 'and now is, that we of England may share and part stakes (if we will ourselves) both with the Spaniard and the Portuguese in part of America and other regions as yet undiscovered.' A staunch supporter of Raleigh's expedition to Virginia in 1584, Hakluyt envisaged that 'this western voyage will yield unto us all the commodities of Europe, Africa and Asia, as far as we were wont to travel, and supply the wants of all our decayed trades'. The Governor of Virginia assured him that the new colony would produce wines, oils, flax, resins, pitch, frankincense, currants and sugar—whatever England was in the habit of obtaining from Spain, France, Italy and the East.

The influence and personality of Hakluyt played a role not to be minimised in the orientation of British policy. An ardent advocate of the improvement of navigation, he urged the establishment of a readership in the art of seamanship either at London or at Bristol. He advocated investigation into the causes and cure of tropical diseases. No ivory tower intellectual and propagandist, he was himself a shareholder in many of the colonising and commercial ventures of the period. By his editing of *The Principal Navigations* and, above all, by his *Discourse of Western Planting*, which he wrote in 1584 and presented to Queen Elizabeth, Hakluyt was able, by the time of his death in 1616, to exercise more influence over the minds of his countrymen and over the development of the British colonial empire than all his contem-

poraries combined. Before his time, British policy, like earlier
Spanish policy, had not gone beyond concern with gold—taking
Spanish gold, as Drake had done, or seeking new mines of gold,
as Raleigh sought in Guiana. With Hakluyt imperialism was
substituted for buccaneering, agriculture supplanted gold,
mercantilism superseded bullionism.

In this inter-imperialist rivalry the dominant commercial considerations were reinforced by powerful political and religious
motives. Spain, lord of the New World monopoly, was the centre
of the Counter-Reformation in Europe. Spain's wealth from the
Indies represented the mainstay of Catholic strength in Europe.
Spain's armies and Spanish hegemony in Europe were financed
by Spain's mines and trade in the Caribbean and America. It became, therefore, a matter of vital policy for the Protestant powers
to sap Spanish strength and drain Spanish resources by diver-
sionary expeditions over the ocean. Gaspard de Coligny, for example, Admiral of France and the leader of the French
Protestants, strongly advocated the policy of attacking Spain in
the Indies in order to weaken her in Europe. The battlefield of
the Wars of Religion was not only Germany but also the Caribbean.

Big business and imperialism associate a country with strange
bedfellows. There emerged a *de facto* Protestant alliance between
England and the Netherlands, supported to a considerable extent
by Catholic France, against Spain. The struggle, on the part of
England with its increasingly parliamentary government and the
Netherlands, whose citizens were revolted colonials, had over-
tones of a 'democratic' struggle against absolutism. Virginia, said
Sir Thomas Dale, its Governor, on his return to England in
1616, 'being inhabited by His Majesty's subjects will put such a
bit into our ancient enemy's mouth as will curb his haughtiness
of Monarchy.'

But it was to the Caribbean that the European challenge, following Spanish policy, was chiefly directed. Sir Walter Raleigh made
several attempts to colonise Guiana. A hundred years later than
Columbus, he was as much obsessed with gold as Columbus had
been. He longed to discover 'a better Indies for her Majesty than
the King of Spain hath any'. This meant gold, for Spanish wealth
and strength came not 'from the trades of sacks and Seville
oranges, nor from aught else that either Spain, Portugal, or any

of his other provinces produce; it is his Indian gold that endangereth and disturbeth all the nations of Europe'.

This was, no doubt, true. But Raleigh was in essence a *conquistador* after his time. In his opinion, 'where there is store of gold it is in effect needless to remember other commodities for trade'. Guiana, he was convinced, had gold, 'a country that hath yet her maidenhead, never sacked, turned, nor wrought', and he looked to the establishment in London of 'a Contraction-House of more receipt for Guiana than there is now in Seville for the West Indies'. This was the first, but not the last, occasion on which Guiana was considered as offering a solution of the problems posed in the West Indies.

Partly owing to the influence of Hakluyt, England had become too sophisticated to take Raleigh seriously. He was released from imprisonment to make a final attempt to locate the gold of Guiana, in the very year of Hakluyt's death, and, as a result of his failure, he was executed two years later. It was to permanent settlements in the Caribbean that England and the other European nations turned. In an effort to reinforce one of the expeditions to Guiana, the English made their first attempt to settle in the West Indies, in St. Lucia, in 1605.

But the settlement was a failure as a result of the hostility of the Carib Indians. A similar attempt to settle in Grenada four years later failed for the same reason. The Dutch landed on the barren rock of St. Eustatius in 1600, and the Dutch West India Company was established in 1621. In 1623 the English landed in St. Kitts, and in 1625 in Barbados. In the latter year the French also landed in St. Kitts. The two nations decided to partition the island between themselves. In 1624 the British House of Commons considered a project for the formation of a West India Association regulated and established by Act of Parliament, along the lines of similar companies organised in the past for trade with the Levant, Russia, and the East Indies. Sir Benjamin Rudyerd strongly supported the project as the best way 'to cut the King of Spain at the root and seek to impeach or supplant him in the West Indies'. The struggle over Adam's will was about to enter a new phase. The will itself was to be challenged.

What did the new nations propose to do with their new Caribbean colonies? The Spaniards had made no bones about their policy. They wanted gold, they wanted sugar, they wanted both reserved to Spain. If they could get both only by enslaving the Amerindians and transporting enslaved Africans, they were prepared to enslave.

The European intellectuals of the day were outraged. The Englishman, Sir Thomas More, in his *Utopia* opposing the substitution of livestock for agriculture which depopulated the English countryside, launched an attack on Spain's policy. His Utopians held the gold and silver adored by the Spaniards 'in reproach and infamy', using them for making chamber pots, fetters and chains. But his Utopia, where property was held in common, where there were neither rich nor poor, where time was devoted principally to intellectual pursuits, was based on slaves—or 'bondmen', as More euphemistically called them.

Las Casas, in his turn, presented a picture of the noble savage and of Hispaniola, the cradle of Spanish imperialism, as the true Elysian fields of the ancients. This was the line followed by the celebrated French essayist, Michel de Montaigne, who condemned the Spaniards for their destruction of Amerindian civilisation and turning 'the richest and most beautiful part of the world upside-down for the traffic of pearls and pepper!' Francis Bacon, after Hakluyt, took a more positive approach. In his essay 'On Plantations' he set out his ideas of colonisation. He envisaged not an economy based on mining, export crops, and slavery, but a self-sufficient society of small farmers producing principally food crops. Bacon was particularly hostile to the mining economy, and he advocated free trade in respect of colonial produce. Never even mentioning slaves, Bacon proposed the emigration of free artisans —gardeners, ploughmen, smiths, carpenters, joiners, fishermen, with a few druggists, surgeons, cooks and bakers.

Europe, however, was not impressed by its intellectuals. 'The design in general is to gain an interest in that part of the West Indies in the possession of the Spaniard, for the effecting whereof we shall not tie you up to a method by any particular instructions.' Thus did Oliver Cromwell, Protector of England, launch in 1655 the expedition to the West Indies which he called his 'Western Design'. The pattern, however, was not English but European.

The British from their original bases in Barbados and the central portion of St. Kitts, had proceeded to Nevis, Antigua and

Montserrat before Cromwell's acquisition of Jamaica.

From St. Kitts, where they occupied the two extremities, the French moved to Martinique and Guadeloupe, St. Bartholomew and St. Martin which, abandoned by the Spaniards, they partitioned with Holland in the same year. After driving out the Caribs, the French occupied Grenada and laid claim to St. Lucia. In the same year, 1650, France took possession of St. Croix, driving out the Spaniards who had expelled the English, who had in their turn removed the Dutch with whom they had at first shared possession. Tobago was ceded to France by the Dutch in 1678, and after many vicissitudes, France also secured a part of Guiana, known as Cayenne. By the Treaty of Ryswick, in 1697, Spain confirmed French occupation of its long established settlement in Hispaniola, 'the most beautiful and fertile part of the West Indies and perhaps of the world', which became Saint-Domingue.

The English and French governments, unable to agree as to the disposition of Dominica and St. Vincent, signed a treaty with the Caribs in 1660 by which the latter were left in possession.

The Dutch, traders first, last and always, occupied St. Eustatius and Saba. By The Treaty of Breda, in 1667, they ceded New Amsterdam (New York) to England in exchange for Surinam.

The Danes made their first permanent Caribbean settlement on St. Thomas and a few years later laid claim to St. John.

The race to secure a place in the Caribbean sun was joined by the German state of Brandenburg-Prussia. The Elector, Frederick William I, listened readily to proposals of a Dutchman, Benjamin Raule, to set up a Brandenburg company to trade with Guinea and the West Indies. In 1680 a Prussian naval expedition was sent to the Caribbean to prey on Spanish shipping. The expedition suffered from the handicap that Prussia possessed no harbour in the Caribbean, and accomplished no more than the capture of a few small vessels. In 1684 Raule unsuccessfully tried to buy either St. Vincent or St. Croix, but France was the stumbling block. Thereupon he turned to Denmark, and, in the following year, a treaty was signed by the two governments whereby, while St. Thomas remained Danish, the Brandenburgers received a plantation sufficient to employ two hundred Negroes, free from taxes for the first three years. Difficulties with the Danes led the

Brandenburgers to continue the search for their own territory. They tried to secure Crab Island, which was subject to occasional raids by the Spaniards from Puerto Rico, but the Danes refused to withdraw their claims to it. Negotiations in 1687 to secure Tobago failed owing to Dutch opposition. Eventually, in 1689, Brandenburg took possession of the rocky islet of St. Peter in the Virgin Islands. Upon this rock Prussia sought to build a Caribbean empire. It was *ersatz* for the vast western design of the Welsers in the preceding century.

One European country was unsuccessful in its bid for a share in Adam's inheritance. That country was Sweden, temporarily raised in the seventeenth century by the military achievements of Gustavus Adolphus in the wars of religion, to the status of a great power. The stimulus to Swedish colonial expansion, as in the case of Brandenburg-Prussia, came from a Dutchman, Willem Usselincx, who had played an important role in the founding of the Dutch West India Company, but who, disgruntled with the results, offered his services first to Denmark and then to Sweden. In 1624 the King of Sweden directed Usselincx to establish a general company for trade with Asia, Africa and America. Financial difficulties delayed inauguration until 1627. The company founded a settlement on the banks of the Delaware. In 1647 another company, the Swedish African company, was organised to establish a trade with Guinea. The entire scheme was a failure. The Dutch looked upon the Swedes as rivals, and both the Delaware settlement and the forts in West Africa fell to the Dutch in a war between the two countries. Sweden had to wait until the following century to obtain a share in the slave trade and a colony in the West Indies—part of the small French island of St. Bartholomew.

Spain had to face not only the assaults of her European rivals but also the attacks of European pirates. Men of all nationalities and faiths, united by the fact that the majority were fugitives from justice, their only industry was war on the Spaniard. Called buccaneers, from the Indian word *boucan* (a wooden gridiron made of several sticks placed upon four forks upon which they broiled hogs) they constituted an unorganised group of men who acknowledged no leadership except on their raids, when they chose the most expert as their leader, a Morgan or a L'Olonnais.

Of no fixed abode, they concentrated in the neighbourhood of the wild cattle, used sheds covered with leaves as protection from the rain, wore only a pair of trousers and a shirt, and slept in sacks to keep off the insects. They looked, said a French observer after seeing some who had returned from hunting wild cattle, like 'the butcher's vilest servants, who have been eight days in the slaughter-house without washing themselves'. Brave, well-armed, fairly numerous, operating from Tortuga, off the coast of Hispaniola, their *mission civilisatrice* was to constitute a terror to the Spaniards and a valuable auxiliary to Spain's rivals.

The raids of the buccaneers contributed materially to the weakening of Spain by depriving her of a great store of the precious metals. Their plunder, however, served no constructive economic purpose, such as, we may be sure, Drake's did; the historian of this phase of Caribbean history tells us that they spent 'with huge prodigality what others had gained with no small labour and toil'. The capture of Maracaibo in 1666 yielded a plunder of 260,000 'pieces of eight', the buccaneers even carrying away the ornaments of the church, its bells and paintings, to consecrate, they said, that part of their booty to building a church in Tortuga. Morgan stormed Porto Bello two years later, obtaining a booty of a quarter of a million 'pieces of eight'. His address to his men is reminiscent of the spirit of Sir Francis Drake: 'If our number is small, our hearts are great; and the fewer persons we are, the more union, and the better shares we shall have in the spoil!' Trinidad was plundered in 1673, yielding a booty of 100,000 'pieces of eight'. In 1683 buccaneers captured Vera Cruz, the richest city in the New World, gaining possession of more than six million dollars. So profitable and popular was the profession that even women participated; the sex of Mary Read and Anne Bonny, captured in 1721, was only revealed when they declared that they were pregnant.

Buccaneering ultimately became a nuisance to the governments which fostered and connived at it, but the buccaneers were not reluctant to flout the wishes of even their own governments. When war between France and Spain was brought to an end by the Treaty of Aix-la-Chapelle in 1668, the buccaneers claimed that they were not bound by the provisions of the treaty, as they had not signed it or participated in the negotiations. By the Treaty of

Madrid, in 1670, England and Spain agreed to forbear from pillage, to revoke all commissions for this end, and to punish those who contravened the treaty. Shortly after, the French Government decided also to suppress the buccaneers because they interfered with ships of all nations. In Saint-Domingue the buccaneers were persuaded to change over to tobacco cultivation. England set a buccaneer to catch a buccaneer: Morgan was raised to the dignity of Sir Henry Morgan, Deputy Governor of Jamaica.

If they could not get at the Spaniards in the colonies, the European buccaneers attacked them on the way home. The Spaniards were harried by large-scale national attacks by their rivals on the Spanish treasure fleets. In 1628 Admiral Piet Heyn of Holland achieved what had been Drake's dearest ambition: he captured the entire Spanish treasure fleet off Cuba and unloaded its cargo on Cuban soil. The Dutch booty consisted of 177,357 pounds of silver; 135 pounds of gold; 37,375 hides; 2,270 chests of indigo; 7,961 pieces of logwood; 735 chests of cochineal; 235 chests of sugar; together with pearls and spices. It fetched fifteen million guilders, and the Dutch West India Company declared a dividend of fifty per cent.

The audacity of the blow, combined with the severity of the loss, was a torture to Spain, and businessmen shuddered. The general of the fleet was executed after five years' imprisonment, while the admiral ended his days in a penal settlement in Africa. On the other hand Heyn became a national hero, and was appointed Lieutenant-Admiral of Holland, second only to the Admiral-General, who was the head of the state, the Prince of Orange. All Holland rushed to pay homage to Heyn. 'Look how these people rave,' he said, 'because I have brought home so great a treasure. But before, when I had hard fighting to do and performed far greater deeds than this, they scarcely turned round to look at me.'

Twenty-seven years later, Holland's success was duplicated by England, and Admiral Blake accomplished what Heyn had done before him. Cromwell's western design, territorially a failure, was a financial success. Blake captured the treasure fleet outside Cadiz; the captain's ship alone carried two million pesos in bullion. Cromwell was among those who witnessed with satisfaction the long procession as the booty was conducted with befitting splendour through the streets of London. Two years later Blake, learning that the Spanish treasure fleet had put in for safety into the Canaries, and its treasure, amounting to ten and a half million pesos, disembarked, attacked the fleet and destroyed it in Santa Cruz harbour. The bullion remained useless to Spain in the Canary hills.

By the end of the seventeenth century, amid all the confusion in the Caribbean, one fact stood out with startling clarity— Adam's will had been proved a forgery. Spain's territorial monopoly had been whittled down to Cuba, Puerto Rico, the eastern two-thirds of Hispaniola, and Trinidad. In 1648 Holland was granted, by the Treaty of Munster, one of the King of Spain's 'two eyes'—freedom of trade with the Spanish colonies. By the Treaty of Madrid, in 1670, Spain recognised England's annexations in the Caribbean, thus dumping the papal injunction of 1493 into the wastepaper basket. By the Truce of Ratisbon, in 1684, France and Spain agreed to peace both in Europe and beyond the Line, thus ending the legal fiction of the preceding century.

The stage was now set for the struggle between Adam's new heirs, with Spain the bystander. By 1674, England was beginning to take the view that it was to her interest to preserve the Spanish empire in the Caribbean, and that the real enemy was France. England's policy was, in the words of a French writer, to 'portugalise' Spain, as Portugal was brought, by a treaty of 1703, into a relationship with England whereby Portugal ruled but England traded. The conflict loomed between Britain and France for the Spanish inheritance. France was fully alive to the prospect. On September 30, 1678, the French Minister of Marine, Colbert, wrote to the Governor of Guadeloupe as follows, in much the same tone as Queen Elizabeth had sent instructions to Sir Francis Drake a century before:

'The King ordered me to write to you these lines on a very important matter which must be kept very secret. Peace being made with Spain in Europe, but not in other parts of the world, it may be true that some day his Majesty will take the resolution to trouble the great and free commerce that the Spaniards have in the West Indies. In order to put yourself in a position to execute his Majesty's orders, he wishes you to pay particular care during your voyage to know surely and exactly the precise times of the departure of the *flotas* and the galleons from the coast of Spain; the precise navigation they pursue; what route they keep; what

islands or mainland they touch at; what is the fighting force of the galleons;
if they are in a state to fight; and the number of the King's ships that
ought to be armed to undertake an enterprise against them.'

'God has committed the Indies to the trust of the Spaniards that
all nations might partake of the riches of the new world; it is
even necessary that all Europe should contribute towards supplying . . . that vast empire with their manufactures and merchandises.'
Thus spoke the Foreign Minister of Spain to the British
Ambassador in the early years of the eighteenth century. The
Ambassador was not a child. The unprecedented liberality concealed a galling humiliation. Spain, the cynosure of all eyes in
the sixteenth century, was the sick man of Europe in the
eighteenth. Had the Ambassador remonstrated, he would have
objected to the 'all Europe'. There was not room enough in the
Caribbean for all Europe. There was not even room enough for
Britain and France. Since neither would renounce, and neither
would agree to share, war was inevitable. The Anglo-French
struggle for the right to minister to the sick man's needs and to be
designated his sole heir constituted the dominant factor in
eighteenth century politics in Europe and the Caribbean.

The French soon saw a less clumsy method than that envisaged
by Colbert for laying hands on the Spanish inheritance. The
Spanish brides of Kings Louis XIII and XIV of France in the
seventeenth century had explicitly renounced all hereditary rights
on the Spanish succession. But, at the end of the century, King
Charles II of Spain, an idiot and a chronic invalid, was still child-
less, and the question of the Spanish Succession became an apple
of discord among the chancelleries of Europe.

The British and the Dutch, the leading maritime powers, feared
that the Spanish crown would fall either to France or to Austria.
The former would mean a vast Franco-Spanish empire dominating
Europe and America. The latter would spell a recrudescence of
the sixteenth-century Hapsburg empire. It was a choice between
the frying pan and the fire. They began, therefore, to work out with
France a treaty of partition of the very Spanish dominions which
had been developed only as a result of the Pope's earlier partition two hundred years before. The King of Spain, concerned
solely with the maintenance of the integrity of the Spanish
dominions, made a will in 1698 in which he declared the Electoral

Prince of Bavaria his sole heir. Nothing so little became the young Prince's life as his leaving it; he died, unceremoniously and injudiciously, less than three months later. The official cause of his death, smallpox, was received with scepticism in many quarters.

Frustrated, the sick man defied prognostications of his imminent demise and made a new will, which was opened immediately after his death on November 1, 1700. The King had declared his sole heir Duke Philip of Anjou, grandson of Louis XIV of France. Louis XIV stood pledged to a partition treaty with England and Holland whereby the Spanish colonies and Netherlands would go to the second son of the Hapsburg Emperor, on condition that they were never to pass into the hands of the Austrian line of the Hapsburg, and the Spanish possessions in Italy to the son of Louis XIV. What was Louis XIV to do? He had signed a treaty renouncing the throne of Spain for any of his immediate family, but the King of Spain, sane, in his own right, had declared a French prince his heir. Louis XIV made his momentous decision before a full meeting of his court, in the presence of the Spanish Ambassador. 'Gentlemen,' he said, pointing to his grandson, 'you see here the King of Spain. His descent called him to this Crown; the deceased King so ordered it by his testament; the whole nation desired it, and earnestly entreated me to give my assent; such was the will of Heaven; I have fulfilled it with joy.' Turning to his grandson, he said: 'Be a good Spaniard; that is now your first duty; but remember that you are born a Frenchman, and maintain unity between the two nations; this is the way to make them happy and to preserve the peace of Europe.'

Louis XIV was wrong. The 'Family Compact', as it came to be called, between the two countries, later solemnised by a formal treaty, may have been the way to make France and Spain happy, but it disturbed the peace of Europe for a century. 'The Pyrenees have ceased to exist,' was the private and exultant comment of Louis XIV. It was a challenge to Britain and Holland, themselves united by a personal union of two crowns. They decided to bury their long-standing commercial hatchet in face of the greater danger that had appeared. More than a century before the statement of George Canning, when faced with a similar predicament in 1823, Britain decided that, if France had Spain, it would not be Spain with the Indies.

The Anglo-French rivalry, begun in 1700, lasted until 1815. Merging with other dynastic and territorial questions in Europe, it was marked by the European campaigns of four of the world's greatest commanders—the Duke of Marlborough, Frederick the Great, Napoleon Bonaparte, and the Duke of Wellington; and, on the naval side, by the exploits of Rodney and Nelson. The vital issue was not who should be king of this country, and who of that, but whether Britain or France should dominate the Spanish colonies and be supreme in the Caribbean. The battlefields were the Spanish Netherlands, the fields of Germany, Italy, Spain and even Russia, Canada and the Caribbean.

But the most important theatre of the war was the Caribbean, the decisive arm the navy and not the army. Jonathan Swift, writing in 1712, wondered how it was that, while some politicians were showing the way to Spain by Flanders, Savoy or Naples, the West Indies never seemed to come into their heads. The Duke of Marlborough was sceptical of what he called sideshows far away, but he dared not oppose the project of sending troops to the West Indies. 'For God's sake,' wrote Horace Walpole, senior, to his brother, Robert, Prime Minister of England, in 1735, 'think of the West Indies. I have hitherto preached in vain; but any misfortune there will hurt you more than any other thing in the world.' Chatham spoke grandiloquently and inaccurately of conquering Canada on the banks of the Elbe. The centre of gravity was the Caribbean; it was there, in the words of Jamaica's leading sugar planter, Alderman William Beckford of London, 'where all our wars must begin and end'.

The long see-saw struggle in the Caribbean is sufficient testimony of the importance attached by both Britain and France to that theatre and all that it represented. There were two aspects to the struggle: the one purely territorial, for additional territory; the other concerning the monopoly of trade with the Spanish colonies.

From the territorial aspect, the West Indian colonies assumed an importance that appears almost incredible today, when one looks at these forgotten, neglected, forlorn dots on the map, specks of dust as de Gaulle dismissed them, the haggard and wrinkled descendants of the prima donnas and box office sensations of two hundred years ago.

Take, for example, the speech of Queen Anne of England to the House of Lords on June 6, 1712: 'The division of the island of St. Christopher's (St. Kitts) between us and the French having been the cause of great inconvenience and damage to my subjects, I have demanded to have an absolute cession made to me of that whole island, and France agrees to this demand.' The acquisition of St. Kitts was one of Britain's greatest gains in the first war for supremacy between the two nations, and the condominium of 1627 was abolished.

St. Kitts, at least, meant sugar. What Crab Island could boast of is not clear, though malice might suggest that there is something in a name. In 1722 the English laid claim to the Danish islands of St. Thomas and St. John, as well as to Crab Island, a constant bone of contention between Denmark and Spain, which had attained international importance in the seventeenth century when Prussia tried to annex it. The Governor of St. Thomas asserted that the British design was, by acquiring St. Thomas and Crab Island, 'so to hem Porto Rico in that they would make themselves masters of it on the first break with Spain'. The eighteenth-century Caribbean islands and islets were the Pacific atolls of the twentieth.

In 1730 Anglo-French hostility flared up anew over the sovereignty of the Windward Islands of St. Lucia, St. Vincent and Dominica. The British claimed 'an undoubted right' to all three, which were associated with the jurisdiction of Barbados. The French asserted 'an incontestable right' to St. Lucia and argued that Dominica and St. Vincent belonged to the Caribs by the treaty of 1660. Both nations agreed to evacuate all the islands until the issue could be determined by negotiations. Foreign bases in the Caribbean have a long, if not a respectable, history.

A good example of the value attached in the eighteenth century to even the most insignificant Caribbean territory is the Anglo-French controversy over Turks Island, today a small dependency of Jamaica, with a population of a few hundred, then as now producing salt. Hardly any eighteenth century statesman could have located it on a map; as the Duke of Newcastle thought that Cape Breton was an island, any of his colleagues might have placed Turks Island somewhere off the coast of Turkey. One of the last links in the Bahama chain of islands, the inconsequential

territory occupied a strategic position at the opening of the
Windward Passage between Cuba and Hispaniola. The Governor
of Saint-Domingue, with the consent of the Governor of the
Spanish part of Hispaniola, who exercised nominal suzerainty
over Turks Island, sent an expedition in 1764 to suppress pirates
who made it their hideout, destroy their settlements, and build
a lighthouse. His motives were, superficially, unimpeachable. The
British, however, claimed the island with an almost incompre-
hensible vehemence. The British Foreign Minister, George Grenville, sent for the French Ambassador, Count de Guerchy, and said
to him:

'Whatever claims you may have, set them up, we will hear them, but
first the island must and shall be restored... When it is restored to His
Britannic Majesty, then, and not till then, will a single word about claims
be heard or admitted. I shall wait nine days for your answer... if I do
not receive your answer at the end of that time, the fleet now lying at
Spithead shall sail directly for the West Indies, to assert the rightful claims
of Britain.'

The French backed down. War over Turks Island was averted.
But not before an even more astonishing idea of its importance
had emanated from the Governor of Saint-Domingue. The suggestion was that a tripartite condominium be established, between
Britain, France and Spain; the co-sovereigns would divide the
saltponds between them, send an equal number of colonists, and
undertake jointly the construction of lighthouses. The Spanish
Government, however, refused to abdicate its sovereignty, and
the British Government thought better of making a mountain out
of a saltpond.

The most dramatic example, however, of Anglo-French rivalry
in the Caribbean was the controversy, at the peace treaty of 1763,
as to whether Britain should restore to France Canada or Guadeloupe, both conquered during the war. The mere equation of the
two areas provokes derision today. Yet the foreign offices of the
two governments were seriously agitated over the issue, and in
England, at least, it gave rise to a violent pamphlet warfare.
Eventually Britain restored Guadeloupe and retained Canada. But
this decision did not mean that Guadeloupe, in the eyes of the
British Government, was less valuable than Canada. In fact,
precisely the opposite was the case. Choiseul, the Foreign Minister

of France, prided himself on a successful diplomatic *coup* by which he had retained a valuable sugar island and given up a vast territory which many Frenchmen derided, as Voltaire did, as 'a few acres of snow'.

This dramatic comparison of the Caribbean and mainland colonies was reinforced by the British restitution to Spain of Cuba, also captured in the war, for Florida. During the War of American Independence, the British Government rated the Caribbean colonies even higher. It was prepared to cede the strategic fortress of Gibraltar to Spain in return for territory in the Caribbean. George III rejected Spanish offers of Oran in return for Gibraltar, and insisted on Puerto Rico instead. The Spaniards baulked at Puerto Rico or Cuba, 'the limbs of Spain', as these two islands were called, and offered West Florida or the Spanish part of Hispaniola in exchange. George III insisted on one of the following equivalents for the fortress: Puerto Rico; Martinique and St. Lucia combined; Guadeloupe and Dominica combined. Formal proposals from the British Government suggested the exchange of Gibraltar for either Puerto Rico or Guadeloupe, St. Lucia and Dominica, or Guadeloupe, Dominica and Trinidad.

The negotiations, which bore no fruit, are particularly significant for the importance they indicate of Puerto Rico, virgin territory virtually, the Cinderella of the Caribbean until 1898. The Spaniards refused to cede the island, no matter what the bribe. On the other hand, the British Parliament would not hear of the cession of Gibraltar. Edmund Burke, the great orator, was the most powerful opponent of the traditional eighteenth century policy towards the Caribbean. He warned the House of Commons in 1782 'against being cheated by the idea of an extensive, rich, and profitable territory being given in exchange for a bare rock. Puerto Rico was in every sense of the word an unclothed territory. All the wealth of Spain had not been equal to its cultivation, and we had a sufficient evidence in our islands of the difficulty and expense of cultivating a territory'.

The second aspect of the Anglo-French struggle concerned not annexations of Caribbean territory but trade with the Spanish colonies. As always, the crucial issue was the trade in Negro slaves, the *asiento* or contract with the Spanish Government for the supply of slaves. The French king of Spain, like a good Spaniard, immediately granted the *asiento* to France, for the introduction of 48,000 slaves in ten years into the Spanish colonies. Britain's victory in the war meant the transfer of the *asiento* from France to her rival, 'the part which we have borne in the prosecution of this war entitling us to some distinction in the terms of peace', as Queen Anne explained to the House of Lords. The British obtained the same privileges as had been conceded to the French, but for the space of thirty years, England was jubilant. The *asiento* clause was the most popular part of the Treaty of Utrecht.

The British, however, obtained yet another valuable privilege by the treaty. This was the right to send one ship a year, of five hundred tons, later increased to six hundred and fifty, to the Spanish colonies with British merchandise. The cargo of the 'annual ship' was to be sold only at the time of the annual fair, and not before the arrival of the Spanish fleets. The goods were to be exempt from all duties. The King of Spain was to have a quarter share in the vessel, and five per cent of the profits on the remaining three-quarters. The long British struggle, for over two centuries, to penetrate the Spanish monopoly, ended in victory for the British.

From the beginning the annual ship contained the seeds of potential trouble. The first sailed from England in July 1717, with a cargo valued at £256,858. During the thirty years for which the concession was granted, only eight annual voyages were undertaken. But there is sufficient evidence to justify the repeated Spanish claim that the ship, unloaded in the day, was secretly refilled at night. The annual ship, the centre of legitimate trade, was thus converted into a depot of contraband trade, a depot in American waters, through which more goods entered the Spanish colonies than were carried in half a dozen galleons. One annual ship, when measured, was found to carry a cargo of 2,117½ tons, exclusive of sixty-five tons of iron. The excess was confiscated by the Spanish authorities. The annual ship carried neither provisions nor water, and was accompanied by sloops from Jamaica, themselves laden with merchandise which was transferred to the ship when it anchored off Porto Bello. It was claimed in England that through the annual ship British goods to the value of

£75,000 sterling were sent to the fair at Porto Bello, and that the trade yielded a profit of 100 per cent.

The smuggling trade which the annual ship facilitated gave rise to many difficulties in the Caribbean. The Spanish coastguard dealt firmly with captured smugglers. One of them was the notorious Captain Jenkins. As the story goes, one of his ears was cut off, and he was told to take it to his King, and tell him that he would be treated in similar fashion if ever the opportunity offered. Jenkins appeared before the House of Commons with his tale. When asked what he thought when he found himself in the hands of such barbarians, he produced his ear and made the memorable reply: 'I recommended my soul to God, and my cause to my country!' The House of Commons stated that it was the un-doubted right of British subjects to sail their ships in any part of the seas of America. The Spaniards countered with the story of a certain noble Spaniard who had been made by an English captain to cut off and devour his nose. His Government took up his cause, though his nose was not available for demonstration. Spain flatly denied the British claim that British subjects had any right to sail to and trade with their West Indian colonies. They protested against the traducing of coastguard activities as in-fractions of commerce and treaties, and pointedly added that the British Government had done nothing to put down smuggling by British subjects. The resultant war, called in the textbooks the War of Jenkins' Ear, settled nothing and left the status quo in the Caribbean unchanged.

The symbol of this period of Caribbean history is the famous British Prime Minister and colonial statesman, William Pitt the elder, Earl of Chatham. He, more than any other Englishman, is responsible for the British tradition which lasted down to the *Entente Cordiale*, that 'France, there's the enemy!'. Chatham's dominating passion is expressed in his computation that British gains were multiplied fourfold by their injury to France. The French, warmly reciprocating his feelings, none the less respected the man; they hailed his resignation from the Cabinet in 1761 as the equivalent of two victories. In a famous speech on January 20, 1775, Chatham described France as a 'vulture hovering over the British Empire, and hungrily watching the prey that she is only waiting for the right moment to pounce upon'. No one in

the eighteenth century appreciated better than Chatham the vast
importance of the West Indian colonies and the danger of the
Family Compact. Out of the Cabinet and in opposition, he
argued—more from parliamentary strategy than from any genuine
disagreement—against the peace treaty of 1763 by which Britain
restored Guadeloupe to France and Cuba to Spain. He wished to
retain Havana, saying that, from the moment of its capture,
'all the riches and treasure of the Indies lay at our feet'. He
condemned the restoration of St. Lucia in the Caribbean and of
Goree in West Africa to France, criticising the British Government for having 'lost sight of the great fundamental principle that
France is chiefly, if not solely, to be dreaded by us in the light of
a maritime and commercial power'.

The activities of other European powers were of lesser significance in the eighteenth century. Denmark strengthened its
claims on St. John by establishing settlements thereon, and increased its Caribbean empire by purchasing St. Croix from France
in 1733. The only other event of importance involving another
European power was the retirement of Brandenburg-Prussia from
the race. There is a note of asperity in the letter of the Great
Elector, Frederick William I, in 1715, announcing the withdrawal: 'The resolution which we have previously made shall remain as it was that we will not divert any more of our means
either in goods or in cash, to this African and American trading
business...' The Welsers had retired from Venezuela, and now
Prussia withdrew from St. Thomas and West Africa.

By 1783, when the war of American Independence came to an
end and put yet another truce to the eighty years of Anglo-
French warfare in the Caribbean, Britain had added Grenada,
St. Vincent and Dominica to its empire. France, however, remained in possession of Saint-Domingue—having settled the
boundary question with Spanish Hispaniola in 1777—Martinique,
and Guadeloupe, their seventeeth century possessions, and had
added St. Lucia and Tobago. The French thus remained in
possession of some of the most valuable West Indian territories,
Cuba excepted. They had lost the war but won the peace.

Chapter Eight

The Poor Whites

The European arrivals in the Lesser Antilles found territories sparsely inhabited, for the most part by the warlike Caribs, who frequently opposed their intrusion. Many an uprising took place, but, by the end of the century, a fairly general pattern had been established; the Caribs were decimated or expelled, removing to Dominica and St. Vincent. What happened to Grenada may be taken as typical of this phase of Caribbean history. The Caribs were literally exterminated by the French, the last group throwing themselves headlong from a precipice, which has since been called *Le Morne des Sauteurs* (Leapers' Hill). Very little effort was made to enslave the indigenous population, though we have accounts of Barbados which speak of Indian slaves imported from the Spanish islands and the mainland, the men to be used as hunters, the women as domestic servants. But the Indian supply, inadequate and unsuitable for the Spaniards in the sixteenth century, could hardly have satisfied the English and French in the seventeenth, especially after the considerable decline of population as a result of the *encomiendas*.

The Europeans turned, therefore, to Europe for white labour, as the Spaniards before them had done. White immigration in the seventeenth century, however, was not free but involuntary. Contemporary opinion in Europe, concerned about the growth of population and unemployment at home, saw in this emigration an advantage not only to the colonies but also to the metropolitan country.

There were three main sources of supply. The first was the indentured servant, the *engagé*, as he was called in France, a man or woman who, in straitened circumstances, agreed to emigrate to the colonies at the expense of another, and to serve for a term, generally three years (hence the popular French description, the *trente-six mois*, the 'thirty-six monthers') occasionally as many as five. At the end of the term the servant was free and generally received a grant of land, from three to five acres. The system became one of the chief means of recruiting labour, skilled as well as unskilled. For example, one Jacques Dubourdieu, a surgeon, entered into an indenture with a merchant on October 29, 1689, by which, in return for his passage, he contracted to work in Guadeloupe for three years. During the first year he received one quarter of the profits, in the second one-third, in the third one-half. His instruments were owned jointly by himself and the merchant.

The system of indenture was open to abuses of three kinds. The first was the treatment of the servants in the West Indies. Du Tertre, the seventeenth-century Catholic historian of the French West Indies, has left us a picture of the conditions under which the *engagés* lived in the French West Indies. He writes:

'They are worked to excess; they are badly fed, and are often obliged to work in company with slaves, which is a greater affliction than the hard labour; there were masters so cruel that they were forbidden to purchase any more; and I knew one at Guadeloupe who had buried more than fifty upon his plantation, whom he had killed by hard work, and neglect when they were sick. This cruelty proceeded from their having them for three years only, which made them spare the Negroes rather than these poor creatures!'

A piteous petition to Parliament in 1659 described the system at work in Barbados—the servants spent their time:

'grinding at the mills and attending the furnaces, or digging in this scorching island; having nothing to feed on (notwithstanding their hard labour) but potato roots, nor to drink, but water with such roots washed

in it, besides the bread and tears of their own afflictions; being bought
and sold still from one planter to another, or attached as horses and beasts
for the debts of their masters, being whipt at the whipping post (as rogues)
for their masters' pleasure, and sleeping in sties worse than hogs in
England.'

The operations of the Danish West India Company in this
respect gave it such a bad reputation among the people of
Denmark 'that they are of the opinion that if they should serve in
the West Indies they would be worse off than if they had served
in Barbary'.

The second abuse to which the system of indenture was open
was the encouragement it gave to kidnapping and enticing people
on false pretences to go to the colonies. This was particularly
true of England, where, in the seventeenth century, kidnapping
became a major problem, especially in the city of Bristol.
Attempts to put a stop to it by legislation proved ineffectual, and
if the practice was no more common than it was, it was due to the
opposition of the masses, who not infrequently used mob violence
on suspected kidnappers.

Ship captains in France, aware of the demand for white servants
on the plantations, began to ply a regular trade. We have an
account, written in 1655 by a Jesuit priest, of their methods:

'They take advantage of the naïveté of many people whom they persuade
that life in the islands is a bed of roses, that the land flows with milk and
honey and that one works little and gains much. They not only deceive
the ignorant . . . but also debauch young children in order to kidnap them.
Some have been mean and knavish enough to entice children aboard their
vessels under various pretexts and force them to go to the islands where
they were sold to masters who fed them poorly and made them work so
excessively and treated them so inhumanely that many of them died in a
short time.'

No compunction was shown about selling one's nationals to a
foreign country. In 1640 two hundred young Frenchmen were
kidnapped, concealed and sold in Barbados for nine hundred
pounds of cotton each, for terms varying from five to seven years.
In 1643 the Dutch sent fifty Portuguese from Brazil to be sold
as slaves in Barbados, but the Governor of the island set them
at liberty, regarding it as an insult that white men and Christians
should be put up for sale.

The third weakness of the system of indenture was that the servants tended to run away when they reached the West Indies. An order of the Governor of St. Thomas in 1672 forbade any person to leave the island without his permission, made those assisting the flight of servants punishable by fines, prohibited the practice of enticing servants away or concealing them, and imposed heavy punishment on servants for absenteeism: a day extra for each week of absence, a week for each month, a month for each year, a year for every seven years, 'and if it is his custom to run away, his master may put him in irons until he is broken of his bad habits'.

The system of white indentured servitude had the full support of the metropolitan governments. The charter of the Company of St. Kitts, organised in 1626 by the French Government, with Cardinal Richelieu, the head of the government, subscribing one-quarter of the capital, specifically authorised it to transport as many whites as it deemed fit to work in the West Indies. In 1671 Colbert required all vessels of 100 tons or more going to the West Indies to carry two cows or two mares, and those of less than 100 tons to carry two indentured servants in place of each cow or mare. An order of the King of France in 1698 required that vessels of 60 tons or less should take three servants, those of 60 to 100, four, those of more than 100, six.

Some idea of the scope of indentured servitude may be obtained from selected statistics. From January, 1637, to June, 1639, more than 600 were sent to the French West Indies from the single port of Honfleur. In 1654, Barbados received 59; in 1655, 157; in 1656, 275; in 1657, 508; in 1658, 461; in 1659, 523; in 1660, 348: a total of 2,331 in seven years. Thereafter, until 1685, the number declined to less than a hundred annually, except in 1667, when the number was 152. It has been estimated that, between 1654 and 1685, ten thousand indentured servants sailed from Bristol alone for all the British colonies, in the Caribbean as well as on the mainland, an average of over three hundred a year; about half of the total went to Virginia.

Protests against the system were rare. Henry Whistler described Barbados as the dunghill whereon England cast forth its rubbish, its rogues and its prostitutes. Josiah Child's characterisation in 1668 of the white indentured servant must have made Francis

Bacon turn in his grave. This is what he wrote in his *New Discourse of Trade*:

'Virginia and Barbados were first peopled by a sort of loose vagrant people, vicious and destitute of means to live at home (being either unfit for labour, or such as could find none to employ themselves about, or had so misbehaved themselves by whoring, thieving, or other debauchery, that none would set them on work) which merchants and masters of ships by their agents (of spirits, as they were called) gathered up about the streets of London, and other places, clothed and transported to be employed upon plantations; and these, I say, were such as, had there been no English foreign plantation in the world, could probably never have lived at home to do service for their country, but must have come to be hanged or starved, or died untimely of some miserable diseases, that proceed from want and vice; or else have sold themselves for soldiers, to be knocked on the head, or starved, in the quarrels of our neighbours...'

But the sugar planter was not too fastidious about his labour. A sugar plantation afforded employment for all sorts of people. A female indentured servant might become a planter's wife, and the Earl of Marlborough in 1660 proposed that women be sent over to the West Indies, the poor maids, with whom few parishes in England were unburdened, being preferred to the women prisoners of Bridewell and Newgate. In France Colbert recommended early marriages and agreed to facilitate these by sending out young girls from the workhouse, specifying that none were to be included who had been shut up for debauchery. The metropolitan government saw eye to eye with the planter on the question. The Lords of Trade and Plantations in England, in 1676, concerned at the general unpopularity of indentured servitude, suggested that the word 'service' should be substituted for 'servitude', which connoted bondage and slavery. The fact, however, was not affected by the substitution.

Besides the white indentured servants, convicts and malefactors provided a second source of white labour. If the existence of a contract gave a semblance of legality to the system of white indentured labour, convict labour was also surrounded with the aura of the law by the commutation of sentences involving death or imprisonment to transportation and servitude in the colonies for a term of years. The crime was extended to fit a punishment which contributed to the solution of the colonial labour problem, and a veritable system in this regard was developed in Bristol,

where magistrates and judges were connected, directly or indirectly, with the Caribbean sugar plantations.

The seventeenth century regarded the transportation of convicts
to the West Indies with equanimity. Planters generally took
the view that an infant settlement would gain more from the
labour of convicts than it would lose by their vices. The attitude
was well expressed by Christopher Jeaffreson, a planter of St.
Kitts:

'For if Newgate and Bridewell should spew out their spawn into these
islands, it would meet with no less encouragement; for no gaol-bird can
be so incorrigible, but there is hope of his conformity here, as well as
of his preferment, which some have happily experimented; insomuch that
all sorts of men are welcome to the public, as well as the private, interests
of the island.'

Such views appealed to metropolitan statesmen, and if white
indentured servitude was dependent largely on private enterprise
and initiative, the State gave benevolent assistance to the provision of convicts. On one occasion Jeaffreson asked for three
hundred malefactors. The Lords of the Committee of Privy
Council agreed readily, even recommending a term of eight years,
that is, double the term of the indentured servant. But here, too,
abuses crept in, and all sorts of bribes and gratuities had to be
passed over, to gaolers, turnkeys, secretaries and judges, whilst
the general unpopularity of labour in the West Indies in the eyes of
the masses was perhaps responsible for the decision that the provision of convicts should be limited to the prisons of London
and Middlesex. Three hundred men could not be condemned in
one or two counties in two or three years' time. This, and the
security insisted upon by the Government, that none of the
convicts should escape or return to England within eight years,
combined to make the system less satisfactory as a solution of
the labour problem than had at first been anticipated. Moreover,
the convicts were poor workers. The Governor of St. Thomas
described the Danish supply as lazy, shiftless louts, vagabonds,
idlers, uncontrollable fellows, whom neither the workhouse nor
the penitentiary in Copenhagen could improve.

The religious and political disturbances which engulfed England
in the seventeenth century afforded yet a third source of white
labour. Nonconformists were deported to the plantations where

they had to perform hard labour. This policy is particularly associated with the name of Cromwell. The few lives saved in the massacre of Drogheda were reserved by him to be sent to Barbados, and thereafter it became his fixed policy to 'barbadoes' his opponents. Seven or eight thousand Scots, taken prisoner at the battle of Worcester in 1651, were sold to the British plantations in the New World. In 1656 Cromwell's Council of State voted that a thousand Irish girls, and as many young men, should be sent to Jamaica, and in the same year Cromwell ordered the Scottish Government to apprehend all known, idle, masterless robbers and vagabonds, male and female, and transport them to the same island. So thoroughly was the Cromwellian policy pursued that the military commander in Jamaica had to appeal to the government for help towards 'a vent for those idle rogues he had secured for the present, some in one country, some in another, being not able to find security for their peaceable demeanour, not fit to live on this side some or other of our plantations'. He added that he could collect two or three hundred at twenty-four hours' notice, and that Jamaica would be well rid of them.

The deportation policy aroused lively apprehensions in the British Parliament during Cromwell's regime. The fortunes of civil war were fickle, and the victors of today might be the deportees of tomorrow. The matter was debated on March 25, 1659, the occasion being the petition, already referred to, of seventy-two Englishmen 'now in slavery in the Barbadoes', having been transported on the ground that they were political prisoners. The petition questioned the authority for their sale and slavery, stressed that their fate might be anyone's else, and affirmed that even the Turks did not sell and enslave their own countrymen. One of the most prominent colonial merchants of the period, Martin Noell, assured the House of Commons that conditions on the plantations were not as bad as the petitioners alleged, that the servants were better off than common husbandmen in England, and that Barbados was 'a place as grateful to you for trade as any part of the world ... not as odious as it is represented'. On the other side of the fence, Mr Boscawen pointed out that, if such conditions were allowed to prevail, 'our lives will be as cheap as those Negroes ... It may be my case. I would have you consider the trade of buying and selling men.' The debate was inconclusive. Its implications went too far.

This system of white labour—indentured servants, convicts and deportees—was rationalised on much the same ground as Negro slavery was later to be. This is how a St. Kitts planter looked upon it:

'It is not the least of their advantages, that, having all things provided for them while they are strangers, at the expiration of their term (which is usually four years, sometimes three), they being well known at first setting up for themselves, their gains are very considerable; so that they may soon grow rich, if they be good husbands. Whereas if they come out upon their own account, they may chance to be fast in prison for debt, before it is known of what trades they are of ... usually such persons, as are volunteers for the West Indies, are under such circumstances, as may reasonably induce them to oblige themselves to an apprenticeship, at least for four years, in hopes of the advantages they may probably make for themselves at the end of the term, during which they are instructed in the nature and customs of the place. It is seldom seen that the ingenious or industrious men fail of raising their fortunes in any part of the Indies, especially here, or where the land is not thoroughly settled. There are now several examples of it to my knowledge—men raised from little or nothing to vast estates ... The white servants are so respected, that if they will not be too refractory, they may live much better than thousands of the poor people in England, during their very servitude, or at least as well.'

Why, asked a Jamaican planter in 1665, should not the King of England send out a family from each parish, not gaolbirds or riotous persons, rotten before they were sent forth, and at best idle and fit only for the mines, but such well-disposed Englishmen as would come, not as indentured servants, but for meat, drink and wages, until they could set up for themselves? Why not indeed?

Where the land is not thoroughly settled, the St. Kitts planter had qualified. The British Caribbean islands, Jamaica excepted, were all very small. Only Jamaica could afford to hold out, as it did in 1661, to prospective white immigrants the inducement of thirty acres of improvable land. As the sugar industry invaded and spread over the others, giving rise to the large plantation, the small farm, the white servant's reward at the end of his term, disappeared, and with it the Caribbean white yeomanry. It then became the custom to give the servant at the end of his term, not land, but three hundred pounds of sugar, worth less than two pounds sterling. The cost of the passage to the employer was about five or six pounds, in addition to which he had to provide food, clothing and shelter. It was hardly worth the servant's while to endure the conditions that have been described for two pounds' value of sugar.

The land of Barbados was thoroughly settled, and the servant did not have the ghost of a chance. On March 23, 1695, the Governor of the island complained that there was no encouragement given to the white servants at the end of their term. They received forty shillings and no inducement to stay in the island. There were, he affirmed, hundreds of servants whose terms had expired, who had not had fresh meat or rum bestowed upon them. 'They are domineered over and used like dogs, and this in time will undoubtedly drive away all the commonalty of the white people and leave the island in a deplorable condition, to be murdered by Negroes or vanquished by an enemy, unless some means be taken to prevent it.' The means recommended by the Governor were that the King should offer rewards which would persuade the servants to stay, and that those who had two acres of land be given the right to vote, so that members of the Assembly 'would sometimes give the poor miserable creatures a little rum and fresh provisions and such things as would be of nourishment to them and make their lives more comfortable, in the hopes of getting their votes'. Caribbean democracy in its infancy may have been no worse than the British democracy of the day, but one could hardly consider the Governor's proposition attractive.

It was thus clear that, by the end of the seventeenth century, the system of white labour, under whatever name, was on its last legs. But the system has its place in Caribbean history. It marked a further stage in the degradation of labour in the Caribbean. The lack of squeamishness shown in the forced labour of whites was a good training for the forced labour of blacks. The transportation of white servants established a precedent for the transportation of Negro slaves. The practice developed and tolerated in the kidnapping of whites laid the foundation for the kidnapping of Negroes. Bristol, Honfleur and other ports turned without difficulty from the servant trade to the slave trade. Barbados, a word of terror to the white servant, became to the

Negro, as a slave trader wrote in 1693, 'a more dreadful apprehension ... than we can have of hell'.

The diminution of the whites and the growing disproportion of the Negroes caused considerable apprehensions in the Caribbean and the metropolitan countries. In 1670, the Jamaica Assembly prescribed a ratio of one white man to every eight Negroes. In French Saint-Domingue, in 1686, the planters were required to keep as many servants as they had slaves. But the supply of servants was simply not adequate to the demand or to the prescription. The islands could not be peopled by force, that is, with white people, as Colbert replied with temper to a request from the French islands for more servants. By 1680 Britain saw in the Negro a means of preventing 'the exhaustion of this Nation of its natural born subjects'. The Negro supply was not only more plentiful, it was also cheaper. A white servant's services for ten years amounted to the price of a Negro slave. Three Negroes worked better than and cost as much as one white man. 'The more they buy,' wrote George Downing, the father of Downing Street, to Governor Winthrop of Massachusetts in 1647 about the Negro slaves in Barbados, 'the better able they are to buy, for in a year and a half they will earn (with God's blessing) as much as they cost'.

The development of the Jamaican sugar economy in the eighteenth century completed the ethnological transformation which had begun in Hispaniola in the sixteenth and continued in Barbados in the seventeenth. As the sugar industry became more and more an undertaking for the large capitalist, it continued to rest more and more upon black labour. The eighteenth century demographic picture of the Caribbean showed a steadily increasing ratio of blacks to whites. In 1698 there was one white to every six Negroes in Jamaica. In 1703 the island had 3,500 white men and 45,000 slaves. In 1778 the whites numbered 18,420, and the slaves 205,261—a ratio of more than eleven Negroes to each white.

In 1698 there were more than eighteen slaves to every white male in Barbados. In 1712 the island had 3,438 white men able to bear arms, and 41,970 slaves—a ratio of 1 to 12. In 1783 the number of whites able to bear arms was 4,361; the slaves numbered 57,434, a ratio of 1 to more than 13.

A similar change took place in the Leeward Islands. In 1707, Antigua had 2,892 whites and 12,892 Negroes—a ratio of 1 to more than 4; in 1774 the population consisted of 2,590 whites and 37,808 Negroes—a ratio of 1 to 15. The white population had declined by fifteen per cent; the Negro population had increased threefold. The English part of St. Kitts had 1,416 whites and 2,861 Negroes in 1707, or two Negroes to every white; the island in 1774, entirely English, had 1,900 whites and 23,462 Negroes, or more than twelve Negroes to every white. The ratio of whites to Negroes in Montserrat changed during the same period from 1 to 2 in 1707 to 1 to nearly 8 in 1774; the white population decreased from 1,545 to 1,300, while the Negro population increased from 3,570 to 10,000. Nevis had more than three Negroes to each white in 1707, ten Negroes to each white in 1774; the white population declined by one-tenth, from 1,104 to 1,000; the Negro population was nearly three times as large, 10,000 in 1774 as compared with 3,676 in 1707. In 1717 the British Virgin Islands had 1,122 whites and 1,509 slaves; in 1774, 1,200 whites and 9,000 slaves.

The change in the racial and social character of the population of Grenada, French until 1763, British thereafter, is brought out in the following table:

Year	Whites	Slaves	Ratio of Whites to Slaves
1700	251	525	1 : 2
1753	1,263	11,991	1 : 9
1763	1,225	12,000	1 : 10
1771	1,661	26,211	1 : 16
1777	1,324	35,118	1 : 27
1783	996	24,620	1 : 25

The development of the sugar industry in Dominica after its annexation by Britain in 1763 is reflected in the racial composition of the population, as follows:

Year	Whites	Slaves	Ratio of Whites to Slaves
1763	1,718	5,872	1 : 3
1766	2,020	8,497	1 : 4
1773	3,350	18,753	1 : 6
1780	1,066	12,713	1 : 12

The domination of the Negro was less rapid in the French

sugar islands. In 1701 Martinique had 6,961 whites and 23,362
Negroes and mulattoes. By 1751 the whites had increased to
12,068, and there were 65,905 Negro slaves and 1,413 free
mulattoes. In 1776, there were 11,619 whites, 71,268 slaves, and
2,892 free Negroes. The ratio of whites to coloured was 1 to
more than 3 in 1701, 1 to more than 6 in 1776. In 1700
Guadeloupe had 3,825 whites and 6,725 slaves, one white to
less than two slaves. In 1779 the whites numbered 13,261 and
the slaves 85,327, or one white to more than six slaves. Saint-
Domingue in 1726 had 30,000 whites and 100,000 slaves and
mulattoes. In 1779 the population amounted to 32,650 whites
and 249,098 slaves.

In 1715 St. Thomas had 155 white men and 3,042 slaves;
in 1754, 139 white men and 3,481 slaves. In 1723, St. John had
123 white men and 677 slaves; in 1739, 208 whites and 1,414
slaves. In 1742 St. Croix had 174 whites and 1,906 slaves; in
1754, 304 whites and 7,566 slaves.

The islands continued their efforts to attract white servants,
for security reasons. They became increasingly apprehensive
about the disproportionate increase of the black population.
Jamaica introduced legislation to attract white immigrants: an
act of 1749 offered to every planter who would introduce a
family, £145, their passage, a grant of twenty acres, with a house,
one Negro slave and £20 in cash. From 1739 to 1752 the island
spent £17,300 in such efforts; between 1749 and 1754, 347
white men, women and children were introduced. The majority,
however, came from the Leeward Islands. The improvement in
the ratio of whites to Negroes in Jamaica was infinitesimal compared with the resulting deterioration of the ratio in the Leeward
Islands. It was robbing Peter to pay Paul.

The islands resorted to yet another expedient—legislation to
compel the planters to maintain a fixed ratio of white servants to
slaves, under penalty of a fine. An act of Jamaica in 1703 required one white man for the first ten Negroes, two for the first
twenty, and one for every twenty thereafter; one white man for
the first sixty head of livestock, another for every hundred after
the first sixty. A fine equivalent to the cost of a servant's maintenance was imposed for each deficiency. The fines were placed
in a special fund to be applied to the passages of other servants.

Nothing happened. By a new law in 1720, the ratio was fixed at one white man for every thirty slaves, and one for every 150 head of livestock, under penalty of a fine of 7s 6d per week. The total yearly fine was fixed at 270s, much less than the cost of maintaining a servant. The planters, therefore, preferred to pay the fine. The Deficiency Law thus became a revenue measure, from which Jamaica collected £151,945 in twenty years from 1721 to 1751, or £7,500 a year. In 1747 the revenue rose to £16,029. Not a single penny of the revenue received from fines was used to import servants.

The extent to which the law of 1720 was evaded can be seen from a consideration of the detailed statistics which are available for the sugar plantations in St. Andrew in 1753. The Pinnock plantation had 280 slaves and 326 head of cattle. It should, therefore, by the law, have had thirteen white servants. In fact, it had sixteen. This was exceptional. Few plantations had their required quota. One plantation had 229 slaves, 220 head of cattle, and seven servants; it should have had ten. Another had 214 slaves, 64 head of cattle, and five servants, instead of eight. Another with 194 slaves and 114 head of cattle had only three servants; it should have had eight. One with 178 slaves and 136 head of cattle should have had seven servants; it had two. So did another with 165 slaves and 201 head of cattle. Where the Pinnock plantation had one white servant for less than eighteen slaves, the ratio increased until, in one case, it was one servant for 82 slaves.

White labour was up against three difficulties. The basic one was that its supply was too inadequate to serve the needs of sugar. The second was that the whites were too expensive. In 1736 it was estimated that it cost fifteen pounds to transport a servant from England to Jamaica, and thirty pounds a year in wages and food after his arrival. The third difficulty was that the sugar latifundia left no scope for the servant at the end of his term. What was he to do? Mercantilism prohibited colonial manufactures, even if sugar would have agreed to them; not until 1781 did Barbados establish a society to encourage spinning and weaving in order to provide useful and suitable employment for the unemployed poor whites. They could not get land. When the French part of St. Kitts was ceded to England, it placed at the disposal of the Crown 20,000 acres or more of sugar land. The governor proposed that the worst lands should be divided into ten-acre plots and distributed free to poor white families, with the obligation of providing an able-bodied man each for the local militia. The interior was to be divided up into 200-acre plantations, which were to be sold to individual families. Each planter was to keep one white servant for every forty acres the first year, and one for every twenty after three years. Absentee capitalists, however, thought otherwise. One English company offered £16,000 for 10,000 acres. As much as eight pounds per acre was offered in certain districts. Eventually the land was sold in 200-acre lots to the highest bidders, and the white servants continued their peregrinations.

The intellectuals took up the issue. Daniel Defoe, in his portraits of Moll Flanders and Colonel Jack, showed that the white servant could make good. Benjamin Franklin in 1751 objected to the 'blackening' of America. 'Why,' he asked, 'increase the sons of Africa by planting them in America, where we have so fair an opportunity, by excluding all blacks and tawnys, of increasing the lovely white and red?' He deplored the reduction of the whites by the competition of the slaves, who had permitted a few families to acquire vast estates, to amass an income for the support of one that might have maintained one hundred, and who tended to 'pejorate' those who used them, by making the white children proud, disgusted with labour, educated in idleness, and unfit to make a living by their own industry. Thomas Jefferson also preferred white servants to Negro slaves. In France Bernardin de Saint-Pierre advocated white labour instead of black. Du Pont de Nemours dismissed with disdain the conventional argument that white men could not work in the West Indian climate. Calculating the expense of owning and keeping a slave for one year at 520 livres, he asked whether, with twenty-five million people in France getting thirty livres a year, it was necessary to do more than announce that there was work available in such and such an island and that embarkation would take place from certain designated ports. The mercantilists disagreed. White labour in the colonies would lead to colonial competition in manufactures, and encourage aspirations to independence. Better, then, black slaves on the plantations.

But the academic side of the question had no real bearing on the issue. The cliché that white labour was unsuited to the tropics need not be taken seriously. It was not taken seriously in those days. The decisive question was a labour supply that was, first, adequate and even in excess of the need; secondly, cheap; thirdly, docile or that could be whipped into docility; finally, that could be degraded to the point which sugar cultivation required. The white servant satisfied none of these desiderata. The Negro slave seemed to satisfy all.

Thus it was sugar which excluded the white labourer from Caribbean agriculture and which made the Caribbean in the eighteenth century even more 'an image or effigy of Ethiopia'. There was room for the white servant or small farmer where the sugar kingdom did not extend. For example, whites have lived for centuries in the Dutch islands of Saba and St. Martin; they were small farmers or fishermen. The white servants left Barbados and went to the British Virgin Islands where, except for Tortola, they raised cotton and provisions and not sugar. In 1717 Anguilla had 96 planters and 824 slaves; each planter had, on an average, less than nine slaves. In Virgin Gorda there were 53 planters and 308 slaves, less than six slaves per planter. In 1756 the same island had 127 white men and 1,204 slaves, a ratio of 1 to 10. Jost van Dyke had 54 white men and 472 slaves. Even Tortola, the largest of the group, had, in that year, 181 white men and 3,864 slaves, about 21 slaves to each white man.

The Spanish territories confirm this picture. In the eighteenth century none was a sugar plantation economy in the sense that we can describe Jamaica or Barbados, Saint-Domingue or Martinique. Consequently they revealed no such disproportion of the Negro slave population as the British and French islands did. Quite the contrary. In 1768 the population of Cuba amounted to 204,155; whites numbered 109,415, slaves, 72,000; free Negroes 22,740. The white population exceeded the coloured. In 1775 Cuba exported 234 tons of sugar. Its chief crop was tobacco; the typical unit of tobacco production was the small farm. No reliable statistics of population are available for Puerto Rico before the census of 1827. In that year whites numbered 162,311; free mulattoes, 100,430; slaves, 34,240; free Negroes 26,857. The total coloured population was 161,527, slightly less than the white.

Only one in five of the coloured population, one in ten of the entire population, was a slave. Puerto Rico's chief crop was coffee, also produced on the small farm. Towards the end of the eighteenth century the Spanish part of Hispaniola had a population of 125,000; 110,000 were free, 15,000 slaves. In 1783 the population of Trinidad consisted of 126 whites, 295 free coloured, 310 slaves, and 2,032 Indians.

Where sugar was king, the white man survived only as owner or overseer. Otherwise, he was superfluous. The Jamaicans considered them lazy, useless and indolent, renegades, loose people, as the Governor described them in 1719. This was only to be expected in a society where discipline and coercion were the decisive characteristics of labour. The British Government continued to send convicts, and the French Government in 1763 decreed that young men of good family who were guilty of 'irregularities' were, to salvage the honour of their families, to be transported to Désirade. The two governments were flogging a dead horse. In 1730 Guadeloupe had only 175 *engagés*, as compared with 600 in 1689. By 1774 indentured servitude was a thing of the past in Jamaica. The economic triumph of sugar meant the demographic domination of the Negro.

Chapter Nine

King Sugar

'It is conceived there is a silvermine in St. Christophers . . . such an enterprise would require a great stock, and an infinite number of slaves. The true Silver-mine of that Island is Sugar.' Thus wrote a historian of the Caribbean islands in the seventeenth century. The British, French, Dutch and Danish acquisitions, profiting by the experience of the Spaniards, turned their attention not to the precious metals but to the sugar industry.

Early agricultural activity in the new European territories, however, emphasised tobacco and cotton. The cultivation of tobacco gave the Caribbean planters their first taste of the capricious world market. The taste was not pleasant. The Council of Virginia protested to the Privy Council in England against tobacco cultivation in the British West Indies, pointing out 'how prejudicial to them are those petty English plantations in the savage islands in the West Indies, by reason of the great quantities of Spanish tobacco they export'. In fact, West Indian tobacco was of poor quality, the Barbados variety being notoriously bad, with an earthy taste. By 1639 the European markets had become so glutted that prices fell alarmingly. Accordingly British and French planters in St. Kitts agreed to cease planting for a year, tried to get the Dutch to collaborate, and turned their attention to cotton and indigo. With the latter they were unsuccessful, while the crowded conditions of the islands made cotton cultivation difficult.

The typical unit of early Caribbean agriculture was the small farm. For example, St. Thomas in 1691 had 101 plantations. Of these eighty-one were cotton plantations. The total population of the island was 389 whites and 555 Negro slaves, of whom 194 were children. The 'plantation' was thus a small farm, with less than four adult Negroes per farm. In 1645, Barbados, with a total arable acreage of less than 100,000 acres, had 18,300 able-bodied white men fit to bear arms, of whom 11,200 were proprietors. There were only 5,680 Negro slaves. The average holding was less than ten acres in size, and there was one Negro slave to approximately seventeen arable acres. With a total area of 166 square miles, the density of population was 217. Thus early had Barbados acquired the reputation which it has never since lost, that of being one of the most densely populated spots on the globe.

Within the space of a decade, this peasant stronghold was transformed into the advanced bastion of the plantation economy. The Dutch, driven out of Brazil, arrived in Barbados, at the time when the tobacco economy was in difficulties, to teach the inhabitants the secrets of sugar cultivation and manufacture. By 1667 the island's eleven thousand small proprietors had dwindled to 745 large plantation owners, the ten-acre holding at 1645 had been displaced by plantations ranging from two hundred to one thousand acres, the average being three hundred, and the less than six thousand slaves had, according to one estimate, increased to the formidable figure of 82,023. Sugar had been enthroned. The ratio of arable acreage to slaves changed from 17 to 1 to approximately 5 to 4.

It was an economic revolution. An account of the island in 1667 reads as follows:

The Barbados crops in 1650, over a twenty month period, were

'The buildings in 1643 were mean, with things only for necessity, but in 1666, plate, jewels and household stuff were estimated at £500,000, their buildings very fair and beautiful, and their houses like castles, their sugar houses and Negroes' huts show themselves from the sea like so many small towns, each defended by its castle.'

worth over three million pounds. Land values were enormously inflated. A plantation of 500 acres which sold for £400 in 1640, fetched £7,000 for a half share in 1648—one thousand pounds down, the remainder in three half-yearly instalments of £2,000 each. The small tobacco farmer was squeezed out. A sugar plantation in the middle of the seventeenth century, comprising eight hundred acres, had at one time been split up among forty proprietors.

Barbados thus replaced Hispaniola as the premier sugar producing colony of the Caribbean. But neither in technology nor in methods of cultivation, nor in yields in field or factory, was any advance made over the sixteenth century. Barbados went through the same stages as Hispaniola had done, from cattle or horse-driven mills to windmills. The new planters encountered the same difficulty as their predecessors in Hispaniola had had to cope with—where water was not available in sufficient quantity, animal-powered mills had to be utilised. With respect to methods of cultivation, the account of a French Jesuit in 1655 indicated that they were primitive and put a premium on manual labour; the planters employed neither oxen nor horses in tilling their lands, but only slaves. The plough was eschewed, and the man with the hoe dominated Caribbean economy.

The English historian, Sir Dalby Thomas, in his account of the rise and growth of the British West Indian colonies, has given us a picture of the sugar industry at the end of the seventeenth century. The typical sugar plantation comprised about one hundred acres, of which forty were planted to cane, forty allowed to lie fallow, and twenty used for pasture, provisions, and as a nursery for canes. The plantation was equipped with a windmill, which turned the great iron rollers, and it had a boiling house, still-house, curing-house, drying house and other buildings for manufacturing the sugar. The labour force amounted to fifty Negro slaves, seven white servants, together with an overseer, a doctor, a farrier and a carter. The plantation had six horses and eight oxen. Land, buildings, slaves, servants and livestock together represented a capital investment of £5,625 sterling. The plantation produced annually 80,000 pounds of sugar—that is, fewer pounds than its gigantic twentieth century counterpart produces tons—about 35 tons, or less than one ton per acre, and twenty hogsheads of 700 pounds each of molasses. After deducting expenses for clothing, wear and tear of tools, and necessary supplies, the sugar and molasses, sold in the West Indies, yielded £540, or an annual profit of nearly ten per cent.

Barbados became the most precious jewel of the British Crown. In 1661 Charles II marked its importance by creating thirteen baronets in the island on the same day, none of them having less than £1,000 a year, and some of them £10,000. At the time the trade of the island employed four hundred ships a year, the cash in the island was estimated at £200,000, and its annual exports to Britain at £350,000. According to a census taken in 1683, there were 358 sugar works in the island.

Barbados became the most precious jewel of the British Crown. the seventeenth century. Christopher Jeaffreson, an Englishman who inherited plantations in St. Kitts, wrote in 1677 of the patience, time and expense required in the perfection of a sugar mill he had embarked upon. But he added that it was then esteemed a great folly for a man to spend his time in planting indigo and tobacco, and that sugar was the only thriving and valuable commodity. The substitution of sugar for tobacco as the currency of the islands, where coin was always scarce, symbolised the change from the old order to the new.

The Dutch, international in outlook, did not limit their pupils to the Barbadians. The expulsion of the Jews from Brazil sent one thousand Dutch to Guadeloupe in 1654 and another three hundred to Martinique. The early French experiments with sugar cultivation and manufacture received a great stimulus from this migration. The sugar production of the French West Indies stood at 5,350 long tons in 1674, and 7,140 in 1682. By 1698 production was two and a half times the figure for 1674, approximately 13,375 tons. An account of the planters in 1664 described them as 'very well established . . . little lords, whereas in former times they were very poor'.

Jamaica, captured in 1655 by the English, also turned its attention to sugar. By 1672 there were seventy sugar works in the island, producing 760 tons of sugar. In the following year, the Governor stated that, granted stable conditions and an adequate supply of labour, in six years Jamaican sugar production would equal that of Barbados; he added that Barbadian sugar cost nearly one-third more than Jamaican. The size of Jamaican plantations is indicated by a survey made in 1670; 200,000 acres had been granted to 717 families, about 280 acres per family.

St. Thomas also paid homage to King Sugar. It is true that in 1691 only five plantations grew sugar, even in part, and that in 1697 there were only seven mills producing brown sugar. But sugar was a very profitable crop. The proceeds from the sugar plantation alone, one of the three plantations owned by the Danish West India Company, amounted to six per cent of the Company's total investment in 1690; in 1699 the percentage rose to eighteen.

The result was the initiation of a fierce struggle in the Caribbean between the rival sugar producers. Barbadian pre-eminence was short-lived. Overcropping in the desire for quick profits soon exhausted the soil. In 1653, a mere seven years after the introduction of the sugar economy, one of the leading sugar planters pointed to the danger which, for three centuries, has been the nightmare of the island: 'This Island of Barbados cannot last in an height of trade three years longer especially for sugar, the wood being almost already spent, and therefore in prudence a place must be presently thought upon, where this great people should find maintenance and employment.'

It was the first call for that vast emigration movement which has placed Barbados among the greatest colonising countries in history. Curiously enough, however, the planters as a body, not for the last time, were hostile to emigration. They opposed English attempts to settle and annex Surinam: 'the sworn enemies of the colony', said one of the Surinam planters in 1663, 'are the Dons of Barbados . . . they use the utmost means to disparage the country'. In that very year the Governor of Barbados stated that the island was 'decaying fast'. Four years later he emphasised that production had declined by one-third, that the land was worn out, and that the inhabitants were ready to desert their plantations. Yet the Barbadians persisted in their antagonism to other settlements. In 1667 the planters of Nevis and the other Leeward Islands petitioned the King for separation of their government from Barbados, alleging that the interest of that island was that 'these Islands be no more settled'. When asked by the Governor of Jamaica in 1683 to contribute to an expedition to suppress piracy in the Leeward Islands, the Barbadians replied irascibly that they would not spend twenty shillings to save the Leeward Islands and Jamaica. To the formidable contributions that sugar has made to contemporary Caribbean pyschology must be added this one, not by any means the least important, that it engendered and nurtured an intercolonial rivalry, an isolationist outlook, a provincialism that is almost a disease, which are among the most striking characteristics, as they are among the most difficult to eradicate, of the twentieth-century West Indian mentality.

The sugar war in the Caribbean was paralleled by a war between the metropolitan countries for the control of the world sugar market. From Portugal and Spain that control passed, with the rise of Barbados, to England. But in 1671 a West Indian petition to Parliament stated that the Brazilian planter could produce sugar 30 per cent cheaper than his English rival. The battle seemed to be going against England, and Dutch and French refining was beginning to undermine England's export trade to the Continent. The danger was serious enough for Sir Dalby Thomas to take its gloomy consequences into account: the supremacy of Holland or France would mean for England a loss similar to what supremacy of England had meant to Portugal, 'no less than the decay of the greatest part of their shipping and the fall of half their revenue'.

The metropolitan struggle for the world sugar market was of decisive significance for the Caribbean economy—it encouraged monoculture. The sugar economy was at first not exclusive. Modyford's plantation in Barbados comprised 500 acres, of which over 200 were in cane, 80 in pasture, 120 in wood, 20 in tobacco, 5 in cotton, 5 in ginger, 70 in provisions, in corn, potatoes, plantains and cassava. Metropolitan policy at first favoured this diversification. In 1656, unable to understand why provisions should have to be sent from England to a place which abounded in all things, Cromwell gave instructions that steps should be taken in Jamaica to sow and plant such crops as would produce bread and other food, and to reduce the heavy expenses attendant on the conquest and occupation of the island. The French West Indies in their early history produced a large proportion of their food supply. A description of colonial life in 1646 spoke of cassava bread being substituted for wheat bread, seacows for beef, lizards for chickens, and the acclimatisation of peas introduced from Italy, Virginia and Angola. The average man's dinner consisted of pea soup and cassava bread, seasoned with red pepper, lemon juice and a small piece of bacon. With the exception of the bacon, the menu consisted of local products.

Twenty years later du Tertre struck the first note of alarm, as Las Casas had done a hundred years before. He said that it was difficult to observe days of abstinence in the colonies, because everyone was occupied with his plantation, and only the well-to-do could afford 'a savage or a Negro' for fishing.

But the metropolitan policy was still inclined to favour and encourage diversification of the economy. In 1664 Colbert wrote to his representative in the French islands:

'Although the planters find more profit in the production of sugar than in that of cotton or indigo, it is necessary to maintain the cultivation of the latter, inasmuch as there is reason to expect that the islands, in proportion as their lands are cleared and put in cultivation, will produce too large a quantity of sugar. Variety in cultivation is more conducive to their welfare.'

He urged the West India Company to try to influence the planters to decrease the amount of land devoted to the cultivation of the sugar cane, to cultivate cotton, indigo and ginger, and to experiment with spices, such as pepper and nutmegs.

Yet Colbert's policy was not consistent. Conflicting economic interests led to confused thinking on the subject then and for the ensuing three centuries. Did he wish to limit sugar production in the islands? He first indicated that it would be advisable. Yet in the very year in which he urged a diminution of the sugar acreage, he informed one of the directors of the Company that 'you can do nothing more advantageous nor which will be more pleasing to me ... than to make the greatest possible efforts for the export of sugar'. Shortly after, he said that the very measures he had recommended were unwise: 'a decrease in the production of sugar meant a decrease in the development of the islands.' Above all, he gave an assurance that there was no danger of colonial overproduction, and that he would 'guarantee ... every means and facility to transport sugar to foreign markets'. As Colbert developed his plans for French sugar refining and the capture of the world sugar market for France, colonial welfare was necessarily subordinated to metropolitan development.

Similar forces were at work in the British West Indies. 'Men are

so intent upon planting sugar,' wrote a correspondent to Governor
Winthrop of Massachusetts in 1647 about Barbados, 'that they
had rather buy food at very dear rates than produce it by labour,
so infinite is the profit of sugar works after once accomplished'.
Monoculture—that is to say, sugar culture—was the order of the
day. Everything was subordinated to it. It was at first thought that
Jamaica, 'the garden of the Indies', might be raised by cocoa to
the splendour to which Barbados had arrived via sugar. In 1690
Sir Dalby Thomas wrote complacently that cocoa was no longer a
commodity of importance in the British West Indies. It had
withered away, 'by some unaccountable cause'. Sir Dalby dismissed as superstition the explanation of the slaves left behind by
the Spaniards, that its cultivation depended on various religious
rites knowi. only to the Spaniards. But he advanced an equally
superstitious explanation—that the Spaniards had wilfully concealed some secret in its cultivation from the slaves, 'lest it might
teach them to set up for themselves, by being able to produce a
commodity of such excellent use for the support of man's life, with
which alone and water some persons have been necessitated to
live ten weeks together, without finding the least diminution of
either health and strength'. The real explanation was very simple
—the preference for the sugar plantation economy over the small
farm, producing cocoa as it had formerly produced tobacco.

The British Government resolved the conflict of interests with
less difficulty. In 1698 a proposal came before Parliament for
prohibiting exports to the West Indies of corn, meal, flour, bread
and biscuit. Parliament rejected the proposal; the prohibition 'may
put the inhabitants there upon planting provisions themselves, instead of sugar-cane, cotton, ginger and indigo; which will be
greatly prejudicial to England, in respect of its navigation and
riches'. No consideration was given as to whether such a prohibition would have been prejudicial to the islands also. The sugar
planters themselves would have rejected it; but monoculture in
the Caribbean was an imperialist injunction. 'Damn your souls,
grow tobacco!' is alleged to have been the reply of an English
Attorney-General in Virginia to a petition of the planters for the
establishment of a college on the grounds that they had souls to
save. 'Damn your foodstuffs, grow sugar!' was imperial policy
in the Caribbean.

The Caribbean sky was sunny; if there were ominous rumblings, they were drowned out by the chorus of Alleluias to the king of crops: 'And he shall reign for ever and ever.' The wealthy West Indian planter began to be seen in England, a visible and tangible symbol of the wealth that was sugar. Barbados maintained a lobby in England from 1670 to look after its interests; they met regularly at a tavern in London. The Jamaican Coffee House, formerly and more appropriately the Jamaica and Guinea Coffee House, came into existence in 1674. The group steadily increased in size. Once he had made his pile, the sugar planter retired to England to live in affluence. Very early the Barbados Assembly complained of the evil effects of absenteeism on the public service of the island. Jamaica tried to compel patentees of offices, at least, to reside in the island. The agent for Barbados in England wrote in 1689:

'By a kind of magnetic force, England draws to it all that is good in the plantations. It is the centre to which all things tend. Nothing but England can we relish or fancy: our hearts are here, where ever our bodies be. If we get a little money, we remit it to England. Where we are a little easy, we desire to live and spend what we have in England. And all that we can reap and rend is brought to England.'

In 1698 it was estimated by one of the economists of the period that the West Indies had sent back annually to England about one hundred of their offspring, with the advantage to England that the fathers went out poor and the children came home rich. British and French experience here diverged from Spanish, where Spaniards settled and made their home in the West Indies. The British and French islands remained destitute of centres of education and learning, the rich planters sending their sons to Eton and Harrow, and Oxford and Cambridge. In 1700 Louis XIV of France refused to grant permission for the erection of a Jesuit college in Martinique: 'Nothing is less necessary than Latin for making good inhabitants, and it may even be said that it is contrary to their interests.' Even some of the planters themselves could not stomach a society which talked, as Baron de Wimpffen learned on his tour of Saint-Domingue, only of the prices of sugar and indigo, the damage done by the latest hurricane, and the wickedness of Negroes. Everything is imported, lamented Père Labat, the Jesuit traveller, except books, and the Guadeloupe poet, Leonard, at the end of the eighteenth century commented on the general absence of books and the limitation of the planters' interests to trade and rural administration.

Here and there a discerning observer, like Sir Dalby Thomas, looking carefully at the imposing edifice, had some doubts of its foundations and showed concern over the 'casualties' which were apt to befall the sugar industry—plagues of ants, excessive drought, susceptibility of canes to fire as a result of 'the malice and drunken rage of angry and desperate runaway Negroes', diseases among horses and cattle, rotting of the canes in unseasonable rains while the slaves and servants 'all stand idle, looking upon their master's decaying fortune', above all, the hurricanes which so often, 'like a fit of an ague, shake the whole islands .

Nature's vagaries were troublesome, but man's seemed worse. The absentee planter was at the mercy of his overseer or attorney in the islands. But there was a still more dangerous fissure in the sugar edifice, and one day an earthquake would topple it to the ground. 'I find', wrote Jeaffreson from St. Kitts to a friend on October 27, 1684, 'that a small estate in England is more valuable than a great one in the Indies, where one does not design to live.'

Two serious proposals were made in the eighteenth century for economic diversification. The first was from the French West Indies, from the pen of Père Labat. He pointed to the possibilities of tea, coffee, pepper, spices, nutmeg, cinnamon, cassia, olives, onions. His vision extended also to industrial development—glassmaking, linen, cultivation of silkworms, sheep-rearing for wool, even so small an industry as the use of goatskins and goat-hair. As Labat advised his compatriots, the first principle of economics was to seek large profits but not to neglect small ones. He emphasised the great use that could be made of porcellanite, called in the islands red cement. The obstacle to this first attempt at economic planning in the islands was the customary nonchalance of the inhabitants, satisfied with gambling and good living. They had, accused Labat, 'no ambition to improve what they found established among them, or to seek something new which could increase their income, do honour to their nation, and be of some advantage to it'.

The second prescription came from the Dutch governor of Essequibo in 1750, Storm Van's Gravesande. He outlined to the

Dutch West India Company a development plan for what later became British Guiana. It was an attack on the obsession with sugar and on 'the obstinacy of our colonists who set their faces against any other undertaking'. He emphasised drugs, rice, coffee, tobacco, sawmills and livestock. But he was fully aware of the obstacles. He wrote:

'The reason why so little has been discovered is that the old settlers through rooted habit and those born in the colony through inborn indifference, so strongly cling to their old way that nothing, not even the most convincing reasoning, can tear them away from it, and nothing in the world can induce them to any new undertaking, there being among them no industrious and enterprising persons.'

The eighteenth century was born in the glory that was sugar. 'The profits of a sugar plantation in any of our West India Colonies,' wrote Adam Smith, in 1776, 'are generally much greater than those of any other cultivation that is known either in Europe or America.' Sugar occupied the place in the eighteenth-century economy that steel occupied in the nineteenth and oil in the twentieth. Sugar was king.

The eighteenth-century sugar plantation was a costly undertaking, which required an increasingly large capital investment for land, buildings, machinery, technologists, labour and livestock. The larger plantation offered the advantage of lower unit costs of production, greater facility for obtaining credit, easier terms on loans, more advantageous freight and insurance rates, higher profits, and a greater accumulation of surplus capital to tide over the vagaries of nature and of man: hurricanes, earthquakes, drought, excessive rain, glutted markets, slave mortality, rebellions and epidemics.

An eighteenth-century planter in Jamaica has left us an account of the process by which the large plantation was created. The general method was to begin with fifteen or twenty slaves, who cleared a piece of land, built huts upon it, and planted food crops. Then the planter brought more land into cultivation, with ginger, cotton and other crops requiring a relatively small supply of labour. As he prospered, he bought more Negroes and more land, and, when the time arrived, by the combined aid of his own resources and credit, he began to establish a sugar plantation.

The eighteenth-century sugar plantation was larger than its predecessor in the seventeenth. A census was made in 1753 of the parish of St. Andrew, the richest of the twenty parishes of Jamaica. The total number of plantations was 154; about one in six was a sugar plantation. The largest, which was also the largest in the island, was that of Philip Pinnock. It comprised 2,872 acres, of which 242, about nine per cent, were in cane, produced 140 hogsheads of sugar (about 112 tons), employed 280 slaves and sixteen white servants, and contained 326 head of cattle. Another large plantation contained 2,434 acres, of which 310, about one-eighth of the acreage, were in cane, produced 230 hogsheads of sugar (about 180 tons), and 34 puncheons of rum a year, employed 229 slaves, seven white servants and 220 head of cattle. There were two other sugar plantations over two thousand acres in size. Twenty-two others were over three hundred acres, generally regarded as the minimum size of a sugar plantation.

The sugar plantation required three times the number of Negroes and livestock needed on a plantation producing crops other than sugar. For sugar cultivation one slave was required for every two acres, as compared with one slave to from five to ten acres of cotton, and one slave to thirty or forty acres of corn. A census of Jamaica in 1774 indicated that there were 680 sugar plantations, with a total of 300,000 acres, 105,000 Negroes, and 65,000 head of livestock. There were 1,498 other estates and farms, with a total of 300,000 acres, 40,000 Negroes, and 71,000 head of livestock. Each sugar plantation on the average had 441 acres, 154 slaves, and 95 head of livestock; each plantation not producing sugar 200 acres, 27 slaves and 47 head of cattle. The sugar plantation thus had two and a half times the acreage, nearly six times the labour force, and double the livestock of a plantation which did not produce sugar (excluding the costly buildings and equipment needed for sugar manufacture).

Much of this labour was totally unproductive, apart from the fact that sugar cultivation involved a long 'dead season', during which the labour required was infinitesimal compared with the needs of the peak period. From twenty to forty domestic servants were not unusual in a single household. The list in one household includes: one butler; two footmen; one coachman; one postillion; one helper; one cook; one assistant; one storekeeper; one waiting maid; three house cleaners; three washerwomen; four seamstresses. Each child in the family had to have its nurse, and each nurse her assistant boy or girl.

In so far as output was concerned, the eighteenth-century sugar plantation was still a dwarf. In 1768 Jamaica had 648 plantations, of which 369 were equipped with cattle mills, 235 with water mills, and 44 with windmills. The total production was 68,160 hogsheads, or a little over 100 hogsheads (80 tons) per mill. The number of Negroes required to produce one hogshead of sugar varied from 1 to 2.5; the island average was 1.66, or about two Negroes to every ton of sugar. Not a single innovation had been made either in technology or cultivation as compared with the preceding century. The eighteenth-century plantation was a version differing only in date from the story begun in Hispaniola in the sixteenth century and continued in Barbados in the seventeenth. Contemporaries estimated that less than one-third of the Jamaican industry was efficient, and that one-seventh of a crop was regularly wasted by neglect and want of foresight. In Jamaica, an Indian name meaning 'the island of springs', the *trapiche* dominated. The French were on the whole more progressive. Grenada, in 1772, had 95 water mills, twelve windmills, and only eighteen mills operated by cattle.

The capital investment required for the establishment of a sugar plantation in the eighteenth century vastly exceeded that of the seventeenth. We have detailed estimates of the cost of a Jamaican plantation of three hundred acres, producing from thirty to fifty hogsheads, that is, from 24 to 40 tons of sugar a year. The land cost three pounds an acre, and a further five pounds an acre to clear it. The buildings for the manufacture of sugar and rum cost £600. The plantation had twelve mules, which cost thirty pounds each, twelve steers, costing fourteen pounds each, and thirty Negroes, costing fifty pounds each. The tools and implements cost fifty pounds, and the 'big house' fifty pounds. The total investment required was £4,923 sterling.

This was a small plantation, the smallest on which it was profitable to produce sugar at a competitive price. For a plantation of the same size, producing double the quantity of sugar, 100 hogsheads, and fifty puncheons of rum (the typical plantation of eighteenth-century Jamaica) the labour force required was 100

Negroes, thirty mules and thirty steers, and the capital investment was £14,029 sterling.

Larger plantations were not uncommon. A plantation of 900 acres—100 in canes, 200 in ratoons, and 100 in young plants—producing 300 hogsheads of sugar, that is, 240 tons, and 150 puncheons of rum, required 300 Negroes, 50 mules, and 80 steers. It was equipped with two cattle mills. The total cost of establishing such a plantation was £39,270 sterling.

Whilst Jamaica forged ahead, Barbados, the jewel of the seventeenth century, lagged behind. In 1736 Barbados produced 22,769 hogsheads of sugar, 17,416 tons. For the years 1740 to 1748 the annual average declined to 13,948 hogsheads, a decline of more than one-third. By 1784 the annual average had fallen to 9,554 hogsheads, forty per cent of the 1736 output. The slave population amounted to 46,362 in 1734, 47,025 in 1748, 57,434 in 1783. Thus the production of one hogshead of sugar required two Negroes in 1736, nearly three in 1748, six in 1783. It was ghastly proof of the inefficiency of slave labour. It was stated in 1717 that thirty acres in sugar required 150 Negroes, fifty to sixty head of cattle and a dozen horses in Barbados, as compared with thirty to forty Negroes and a few horses and cattle in the French Islands. The Governor asserted six years later that one Negro in Martinique cultivated the same amount of ground as well as two in Barbados.

The intensive cultivation of Barbados in the seventeenth century involved a substantial increase per acre in the eighteenth in labour, livestock and equipment. The size of a Barbadian plantation in 1712 was about eighty acres—there were 1,309 plantations, 409 windmills, 76 cattle mills, 24 pot kilns, and 2,471 horses. In 1760 a sugar plantation of 260 acres contained 180 Negroes (about three acres to two slaves), 100 cattle and twelve horses. One of the sugar plantations in the parish of St. Andrew in Jamaica, 300 acres in size, of which 150 were in cane, contained 74 Negroes, less than half the Barbadian number, about one Negro to four acres, and thirty head of cattle, or one-third the number in Barbados. So serious was the problem of soil exhaustion in Barbados that in 1769 attempts were made to import some of the rich soil of Surinam. But wood ants committed such ravages in the vessel that the attempt was never repeated.

Comparison with yet another older British island, Antigua, underlines the superiority of Jamaica. A census in 1720 of the parish of St. Philip indicated that there were 69 proprietors. Two only had plantations from 400 to 480 acres in size, with from 100 to 110 slaves. One other planter had from 300 to 400 acres, three from 250 to 300. Seven had from 50 to 100 slaves. That is, only six plantations had from 250 to 480 acres, and only nine from 50 to 100 slaves. Nearly half the proprietors had from 1 to 25 acres and from one to ten slaves. If they grew sugar, they were what are called in the British West Indies today 'cane farmers'. In 1764 Antigua had three hundred sugar plantations, which employed 25,000 slaves, out of the total of 37,000 in the island. The total capitalisation of the sugar industry was estimated at two million pounds sterling, or about £6,600 each plantation; slightly more than the smallest sugar plantation in Jamaica. The total sugar production of the island was 16,000 hogsheads, slightly more than fifty hogsheads per plantation. The labour force on each plantation averaged a little over eighty; the output per slave was about two-thirds of a hogshead. Antigua's sugar industry was technologically still in the seventeenth century.

In 1775 the British West Indian planters and merchants assessed the total capital investment in the British sugar colonies at sixty million pounds sterling. In 1730 it was estimated that the cost of production of one hogshead of sugar of 1,300 pounds weight, that is, approximately twelve hundredweight, was 185s. At 21s per hundredweight, this fetched in England 220s 6d, leaving the planter a profit of 35s 6d, or a little under 20 per cent on the cost of production. The planters declared this to be the minimum profit at which they could possibly operate. The general average for Jamaica was 10 per cent. Records of one planter showed that a plantation representing a capital investment of £40,000, and requiring annual expenses of £2,000 yielded an average profit of $9\frac{1}{2}$ per cent from 1771 to 1781; in 1774 it was 16 per cent; in 1777, 13 per cent; in 1773, $12\frac{1}{2}$ per cent; in 1779, 11 per cent. The Jamaican planter borrowed capital at 6 per cent interest; he was thus left with a clear 4 per cent profit on the average. Here, again, Jamaica outdistanced its British competitors. In 1737 a Barbados plantation of 1,000 acres, representing a capital investment of £50,000, was making a profit of 2 per cent.

In 1768 profits were estimated at a maximum of 4 per cent in the island. In Antigua they were about the same.

There were two striking characteristics of the eighteenth-century Jamaican sugar economy. The first was that it was associated with a considerable measure of diversification. According to the St. Andrew census of 1753, eight out of ten planters did not grow cane. Of the twenty-six sugar plantations, eighteen raised food crops, the majority on a fairly extensive scale, and almost all maintained large herds of cattle. For example, a 2,000-acre plantation had 190 acres in cane, 200 in food crops, 500 in pen and pasture for 64 head of cattle. Another of 1,500 acres had 60 in cane, 30 in coffee, 10 in ginger, 20 in cotton, 130 in food crops, 1,000 in pen and pasture for 65 cattle. A third of 1,030 acres had 200 in cane, 250 in food crops, 280 in pen and pasture for 136 head of cattle. One of the smallest, 350 acres in size, had 50 in cane, 50 in food crops, 100 in pen and pasture for 25 head of cattle. In 1774 seven out of every ten plantations in the island did not grow cane.

The second characteristic was idle latifundia. The area of Jamaica is about 3,840,000 acres. In 1752 it was estimated that two-fifths were uncultivable, leaving a total of 2,133,336 cultivable acres. Of these 1,500,000 were patented, of which only one-third was in cultivation. Cultivable land not yet taken up amounted to 633,336 acres. Thus the island in 1752 had 500,000 acres in cultivation and 1,633,336 acres of cultivable land lying idle. There were 1,620 planters in 1754; the average plantation was about 1,000 acres. The Governor in that year spoke of the 'overgrown landholder' and of the difficulty of getting land on which to settle. If Barbados had reached its zenith by bringing every acre of cultivable land into cultivation, Jamaica's zenith was reached with three acres of idle cultivable land for every acre in cultivation, whilst for every acre under sugar there was one acre under other crops.

The eighteenth-century sugar economy of Jamaica, therefore, was not incompatible with considerable self-sufficiency. That this was not achieved, that, instead, sugar became 'the wheat or bread' of the British West Indies, as one absentee planter stated with approval in 1747, was due to the planter, who continued the policy initiated in the seventeenth century by the British Government.

The planter, contemptuous of anything but sugar, kept land not used for sugar lying idle. The 2,000-acre plantation referred to above had 1,100 acres in woodland. Another of 1,250 acres had 200 in cane and 800 in woodland. It was a dog-in-the-manger policy. The owner would not use the land, but he would permit no one else to do so. He maintained, as the governor wrote in 1715, 'a sort of barrier against an approaching neighbour'.

The British Government and public, who wanted more sugar and cheaper sugar, stepped in. Why did not the Jamaican planters cultivate sugar on the idle land? The answer is that it was the deliberate policy of the planter to restrict production in order to keep prices at a high level. With a monopoly of the British market, the West Indian planter was determined to maintain monopoly prices and milk the cow dry. The statistics given above indicate that Jamaica might easily have had three times the number of sugar plantations which existed in 1754. The Board of Trade, in 1734, in a representation to the House of Lords, urged that, if the Jamaican Assembly would not or could not act to divest proprietors of their extensive, uncultivated tracts, it would be a proper subject for the consideration of Parliament, in order to facilitate the increase of the white population and the development of agriculture. 'If the Island were improved,' wrote the Governor in 1730, 'there is land uncultivated sufficient to make sugar to serve all Europe.' In 1741 the Governor estimated that two-thirds of the island was uncultivated. In 1752 the Council and Assembly of the island declared that there was room for at least 150 new sugar works producing on an average 1,200 hogsheads of sugar a year, besides molasses, whilst the production of the existing plantations could be increased by one-third if sufficient slaves, livestock and provisions could be obtained at low rates. In the peak year, 1774, Jamaica's exports of sugar to England amounted to just a little over 50,000 tons.

Jamaica could not plead, as Barbados could, soil exhaustion. It was the deliberate policy of a powerful vested interest. It was a struggle between colonial planters and metropolitan refiners. If brown sugar was the money of the plantations, the West Indian planters were determined to get as much as they could out of it. The price of brown sugar at the London Customs House was 24s 10¼d per hundredweight in 1727, 30s 7d in 1743, 42s 5d in

1757. At its lowest it was 17s 10d in 1731; at its highest, 42s 9½d in 1746. At 21s per hundredweight, the planter gained 35s 6d, per hogshead or 3s per hundredweight. When the price doubled, assuming a constant cost of production, the planter's profit per hogshead rose to approximately 20s per hundredweight.

The British Government, refiners and public were furious. The friends of the planters warned them that they were playing a dangerous game. 'If the British plantations cannot, or will not,' one said, 'afford sugar, etc., plenty and cheap enough the French, Dutch and Portuguese do, and will.' An anonymous writer in 1730 urged the government in anger to 'open the sluices of the laws, and let in even the French sugar upon them, till they would serve us at least as cheap as our neighbours are served'. The Council of Trade and Plantations issued a solemn warning in 1739: Jamaica had twice as much land as the Leeward Islands combined, yet the exports of the Leeward Islands exceeded those of Jamaica, 'from whence it would naturally follow that not one half of your lands are at present cultivated, and that Great Britain does not reap half the benefit from your Colony, which she might do if it were fully settled'.

The refiners of London, Westminster, Southwark and Bristol protested to Parliament in 1753 against the 'most intolerable kind of tax' represented by the higher price of British West Indian sugar, and urged Parliament to make it the interest of the planters to produce more raw sugar by increasing the area under cultivation. The petitioners bluntly accused the Jamaicans of finding 'their interest much more in importing small than large quantities of sugar into Great Britain'. In fact, the West Indian crop of 900,000 hundredweight for the average of the years 1748–1751 yielded £1,350,000 at 30s per hundredweight, whereas the crop of 1752, of only 820,000 hundredweight, yielded £1,640,000 at 40s per hundredweight. A supporter of the refiners charged that in twenty years the West Indian sugar monopoly had cost the British people eight million pounds in exorbitant prices, and that the profits of 1759 amounted to £840,000, enough to pay and clothe for one year an army of 40,000 foot soldiers. With such prices prevailing, the masses, as the refiners stated, could not afford to pay for the refining of a raw material which was so dear.

Parliament sidetracked the issue posed by the refiners, who had

themselves recognised that they could not 'set ourselves in competition with the inhabitants of all the sugar colonies, either for
numbers, wealth, or consequence to the public'. No one dared to
challenge King Sugar. The proverbial wealth was not something
that people in England merely heard of in the far off Caribbean.
They saw it in the flesh and rubbed shoulders with it every day.
The absentee sugar planter was a familiar figure in eighteenth-
century England; the glory that was sugar was everywhere in
evidence. Most important of all, the absentees banded together,
bought seats in Parliament, in the fashion of the day, and constituted the most powerful lobby of the century, the West India
Interest. In 1764 the agent for Massachusetts in England reported
that there were fifty or sixty West Indians in Parliament who
could turn the balance any side they pleased.

To be more precise, the West India Interest turned the balance
to their side. If they were determined to restrict cultivation in
Jamaica, the most important British sugar producer, their entire
policy would be defeated if the British market were swamped not
so much by sugar imported from foreign territories, but by sugar
imported from new territories annexed by England. Opposition to
an increase of the British sugar empire was the necessary corollary
to opposition to an increase of Jamaican production. In 1720
the British West Indian planters objected to the annexation of
St. Lucia unless the island was expressly forbidden to grow cane
and instructed to grow cocoa. In 1721 the Board of Trade directed
that Tobago should be settled only if the planters of Barbados
agreed, that its settlement should be so restrained as not to interfere with the produce of the older British West Indian colonies,
and that the new settlers should not plant sugar. The Board recommended cocoa, annatto and indigo. Similar instructions were
issued concerning St. Lucia and St. Vincent. In 1736 the legislature of Barbados passed an act prohibiting the export of clay
for whitening sugar to the Leeward Islands, on the ground that
the planters of the latter were underselling Barbados in sugar and
rum.

It was this constant conflict of interests, between colonies and
metropolitan country, between colony and colony, breeding the
inordinate selfishness and inveterate particularism of the British
West Indian planters, which explains the peace treaty of 1763,

by which Guadeloupe and Cuba were restored to France and
Spain, respectively, and Canada and Florida annexed instead.
'What does a few hats signify,' asked an anonymous writer in
1763, referring to Canada's staple, 'compared with that article of
luxury, sugar?' He reckoned without the West India Interest. It
was that Interest which, through its connections, especially with
Chatham, demanded the restoration of Guadeloupe; they were
willing to permit its annexation only if sugar from the old British
islands was given a preference in the British market. As the Earl
of Hardwicke wrote to the Duke of Newcastle on June 15, 1759:
'They have but one point in view, which is how it may affect
their particular interest; and they wish all colonies destroyed but
that wherein they are particularly interested, in order to raise the
market for their own commodities.' Referring to Chatham's proposal for the capture of Martinique, one British Cabinet Minister
wrote to another: 'I suppose the sugar planters will no more desire
(it) should be retained by us than they did in relation to
Guadeloupe.' As a British writer of 1754 charged, 'The personal
interest of a rich planter at Jamaica is contrary to the interest of
every true Briton, whether in a national or personal light'. Their
great champion was Chatham, who told the House of Commons
in 1759 that 'he should ever consider the colonies as the landed
interest of this Kingdom and it was a barbarism to consider them
otherwise'.

Thus it was that, in 1763, the British Government restored
Guadeloupe, Martinique, Cuba and St. Lucia, and annexed
Dominica, St. Vincent, Grenada and Tobago, a total area of
about 700 square miles. All the islands restored grew sugar then
and grow sugar today; in those annexed the greater part of the
land was too mountainous for sugar cultivation, and it is significant
that none of the four islands today grows sugar. No person was
permitted to purchase more than 300 acres in Dominica or more
than 500 acres in the other islands. Grenada already had, by 1763,
under French occupation, 82 sugar plantations. Tax returns
for slightly more than half of these plantations in that year indicated that only two contained 150 to 200 slaves, three from
100 to 150, twenty-five from 50 to 100; twelve had from 25 to
50, while two had less than 25. Serious competition between
Jamaica and Grenada could hardly be entertained. Yet there was

a curious shortage of capital for these new territories, and in 1772, a bill was introduced into Parliament to encourage foreigners to lend money upon the security of the new plantations, in order to facilitate and expedite cultivation. The older British planters opposed the measure as an 'impolitic innovation'. The mover of the bill, which was eventually passed in an amended form, retorted:

'If the opposers of this Bill mean by public purposes the purpose of keeping up the price of sugar, and by these means to enrich a few old planters at the expense of this nation, I must own that their plan is the more public spirited of the two. Mine is calculated for rendering that commodity more plentiful, and therefore cheaper, by facilitating the cultivation of the newly acquired plantations.'

Another example of the West India Interest in action was provided by the attempt in 1744 to increase the duties on sugar. The West Indians drew up their case against the proposal, sent it to every member of Parliament, and organised committees to interview members. Their aim was 'if possible to get this d——d Bill as much abhorred' as the Excise Scheme of Robert Walpole. The measure to increase the sugar duties, surprisingly, was carried by a small majority. The West Indians, however, succeeded in transferring the extra duty to foreign linens, illustrating, as the parliamentary reporter inserted in his account of the proceedings, 'the difficulties attending the laying a further duty upon sugar from the number and influence of those concerned directly or indirectly in that extensive branch of trade'.

The success of the West India Interest was due to a considerable extent to its cohesion. To protect their interests, the absentee planters in England, in the third decade of the century, formed the Planters Club, maintained by a levy of one penny per hogshead whenever necessary. Similarly, the West India merchants in England organised a society of their own about the same time. The two groups united from time to time to present a common front, until they eventually coalesced. In 1781, the first step towards formal unity was taken with the establishment of a Standing Committee of West India Planters and Merchants.

The West India Interest occupied a prominent position in England in the eighteenth century. Names like Codrington of the Leeward Islands, who gave his valuable library to All Souls Col-

lege, Oxford; Warner, also of the Leeward Islands, the ancestor
of the acknowledged authority on English cricket; the Longs of
Jamaica; the Lascelles of Barbados, who married into the Royal
Family, familiarised England with the wealth and power of sugar.
But the prince of absentees was William Beckford of Jamaica,
whose wealth was symbolised by his imposing country seat, Fonthill Splendens, which he built in Wiltshire. Beckford was the
grandson of Peter Beckford, who, at his death in 1710, was the
richest man in Europe. William and three brothers had seats in
Parliament. William himself became an alderman of the City of
London and Lord Mayor, whose fame is commemorated in a
splendid monument in the Guildhall, erected in his honour as a
tribute to his courage in making a famous plea for freedom of
speech to George III. The speech is graven in letters of gold on
the pedestal of the monument. Beckford was a personal friend and
political crony of Chatham, and he, more than anyone else, was
responsible for the decision in 1763 to restore Guadeloupe to
France.

Beckford defended absenteeism on the ground that 'the climate
of our sugar colonies is so inconvenient for an English constitution, that no man will choose to live there, much less will any man
choose to settle there, without the hopes at least of supporting
his family in a more handsome manner, or saving more money,
than he can do by any business he can expect in England, or in
our plantations upon the continent of America'.

There is nothing disagreeable, however, in the wealth that
radiated from it. The rich absentee planter was the principal
character in a famous play, *The West Indian*, produced in 1771.
The servant philosophises at the splendid reception being prepared for the return of the planter: 'He's very rich, and that's
sufficient. They say he has rum and sugar enough belonging to
him, to make all the water in the Thames into punch.' A picture
of the absentee planters in England in 1765 states:

'Splendour, dress, show, equipage, everything that can create an opinion
of their importance, is exerted to the utmost of their credit. They are
thought rich; and they are so indeed, at the expense of the poor Negroes
who cultivate their lands... an opulent West Indian vies in glare with a
nobleman of the first distinction.'

Absenteeism left the plantations in charge of overseers, had

serious effects on the public service, and left the islands destitute
of the social services. The planters sent their children to England
to be educated; the establishment of schools in the West Indies
was neglected. 'Learning is here at the lowest ebb,' lamented a
historian of Jamaica in 1740; 'there is no public school in the
whole island, neither do they seem fond of the thing; several
large donations have been made for such uses but have never taken
effect. The office of a teacher is looked upon as contemptible ...
A man of any parts or learning that would employ himself in
that business would be despised and starve.' Bishop Berkeley's
grand imperial project of founding a university in Bermuda, to
accomplish, as he said, by private means the public duty neglected
by Britain with respect to the races with which she had come in
contact, was an abortion. George I provided a charter, the
House of Commons voted £20,000 which was never paid, and the
scheme sank into oblivion. A few bequests in the eighteenth
century, out of which arose Codrington's College in Barbados
and Wolmer's Secondary School in Jamaica, the two most important, constituted the educational development in the British
West Indies. In 1783 Barbados had 39 schoolteachers.

The eighteenth-century sugar kingdom continued to suffer
heavily from various casualties: ravages of ants, earthquakes,
fires, hurricanes. The hurricane which was threatening the world
market was worse, however, than any natural visitation which
wiped out Caribbean profits.

Two contestants appeared in the eighteenth century to challenge
the primacy of Jamaica. The first was the French Caribbean
colony of Saint-Domingue. In 1737 it was stated that French
sugar plantations were making a profit of eighteen per cent. In
the middle of the century French sugar was selling in Europe at
half the price at which sugar was being sold in England. British
exports of raw sugar to Europe, 184,609 hundredweight in 1717,
were 63,479 hundredweight a decade later, a decline of three-
fifths. In the war of Jenkins' Ear, the Governor of Jamaica wrote,
in 1748, that unless Saint-Domingue were totally destroyed it
would, on the return of peace, ruin the British sugar colonies by
the quality and cheapness of its production. That is exactly what
happened. 'Was I a refiner,' said a wholesale grocer to a parliamentary committee on the sugar trade in 1781, 'I should certainly

prefer St. Domingo sugar to any other.' All the British sugar colonies, boasted one of the leading planters of Saint-Domingue in 1776, were not equal to Saint-Domingue.

The alternative to destruction was even more dangerous to the British West Indian planters—British annexation of Saint-Domingue. But even that, too, had to be faced. In a scheme proposed to the Duke of Newcastle in 1756 for annexing Saint-Domingue, it was stated that its production was almost equal to that of all the British colonies combined; the writer added that 'therefore if we can take this island we should not only add a large yearly sum to the revenues of the customs, but command all the markets of Europe for sugar, indigo, etc.' The British Government were later to heed the advice, and the British planters, having exorcised the devil of Guadeloupe, had to face the worse devil of Saint-Domingue.

The second enemy was in the East. The Dutch, not content with increasing their sugar imports from Surinam from 4,000 hogsheads in 1700 to nearly 50,000 in 1724, began to develop the sugar industry in Java. Dutch imports of Javanese sugar into Holland were less than 50 tons in 1700. In 1725 they amounted to 2,640 tons, more than one-quarter of the Jamaican exports to England from 1726 to 1727, almost as much as Britain exported to Europe in 1723.

Totally unconcerned, however, the Caribbean planters went their way, serving their one god. In 1774, Nevis exported 3,320 tons of sugar; Montserrat, 2,379; Tortola, nearly 1,700; Tobago, 1,549. Sugar production developed rapidly in the colonies annexed in 1763. In 1774, Dominica exported 2,673 tons; Grenada, 8,968 (more than double its exports in 1763); St. Vincent, 3,129. By 1780 production in St. Croix had reached 11,000 tons. The smallest island was a potential sugar plantation.

The West Indian planter, blind to the competition in the Caribbean and to the enemy in the East, had no suspicions whatsoever of potential attack from two other quarters. The first was the North American mainland. Attempts were made to produce sugar in Louisiana in 1725 and 1762. But winter frosts intervened before the cane was fully ripe, and the enterprise was abandoned. It would not always be so. Thomas Jefferson, in his turn, in 1790, looked to maple sugar, produced by child labour, as a substitute for slave-grown cane.* Holding tight to their British monopoly, the British West Indian planters were losing Europe, and North America, too, was looking for a domestic source of sugar. The North Americans, heavily dependent on their Caribbean trade, were embarking on a course of action which would render them independent of the West Indies which remained dependent on them, thus adding to the clouds on the horizon of the world market.

The second quarter from which a potential attack loomed was beet sugar. In 1747, precisely the year when Beckford called sugar the wheat of the Caribbean, a Prussian chemist, Marggraf, in a communication to the Royal Academy of Science and Literature in Berlin, showed that various kinds of beetroot, the sweet taste of which was already known, contained sugar that could be extracted and crystallised in a fairly simple way. Where the Welsers and the Elector of Brandenburg-Prussia had failed in the attempt to gain for Germany a place in the Caribbean sun, beet sugar indicated that that place was after all unnecessary.

* In a letter to Benjamin Vaughan, dated June 27, 1790. Papers of Jefferson, Princeton, Vol. 16, pp. 578–579.

Chapter Ten

Capitalism and Slavery

'There is nothing which contributes more to the development of the colonies and the cultivation of their soil than the laborious toil of the Negroes.' So reads a decree of King Louis XIV of France, on August 26, 1670. It was the consensus of seventeenth-century European opinion. Negroes became the 'life' of the Caribbean, as George Downing said of Barbados in 1645. The 'very being' of the plantations depended on the supply of Negroes, stated the Company of Royal Adventurers of England trading to Africa to King Charles II in 1663. Without Negroes, said the Spanish Council of the Indies in 1685, the food needed for the support of the whole kingdom would cease to be produced, and America would face absolute ruin. Europe has seldom been as unanimous on any issue as it has been on the value of Negro slave labour.

In 1645, before the introduction of the sugar economy, Barbados had 5,680 Negro slaves, or more than three able-bodied white men to every slave. In 1667, after the introduction of the sugar industry, the island, by one account, contained 82,023 slaves, or nearly ten slaves to every white man fit to bear arms. By 1698 a more accurate estimate of the population gave the figures as 2,330 white males and 42,000 slaves, or a ratio of more than eighteen slaves to every white male.

In Jamaica the ratio of slaves to whites was one to three in 1658, nearly six to one in 1698. There were 1,400 slaves in the former year, 40,000 in the latter. The ratio of slaves and mulattoes to whites increased from more than two to one in Martinique in 1664 to more than three to one in 1701. The coloured population amounted to 2,434 in 1664 and 23,362 in 1701. In Guadeloupe, by 1697, the coloured population outnumbered the whites by more than three to two. In Grenada in 1700 the Negro slaves and mulattoes were more than double the number of whites. In the Leeward Islands and in St. Thomas the whites steadily lost ground.

By 1688 it was estimated that Jamaica required annually 10,000 slaves, the Leeward Islands 6,000, and Barbados 4,000. A contract of October, 1675, with one Jean Oudiette, called for the supply of 800 slaves a year for four years to the French West Indies. Four years later, in 1679, the Senegal Company undertook to supply 2,000 slaves a year for eight years to the French Islands. Between 1680 and 1688 the Royal African Company supplied 46,396 slaves to the British West Indies, an annual average of 5,155.

The Negro slave trade became one of the most important business enterprises of the seventeenth century. In accordance with sixteenth-century precedents its organisation was entrusted to a company which was given the sole right by a particular nation to trade in slaves on the coast of West Africa, erect and maintain the forts necessary for the protection of the trade, and transport and sell the slaves in the West Indies. Individuals, free traders or 'interlopers', as they were called, were excluded. Thus the British incorporated the Company of Royal Adventurers trading to Africa, in 1663, and later replaced this company by the Royal African Company, in 1672, the royal patronage and participation reflecting the importance of the trade and continuing the fashion set by the Spanish monarchy of increasing its revenues thereby. The monopoly of the French slave trade was at first assigned to the French West India Company in 1664, and then transferred, in 1673, to the Senegal Company. The monopoly of the Dutch slave trade was given to the Dutch West India Company, incorporated in 1621. Sweden organised a Guinea Company in

1647. The Danish West India Company, chartered in 1671, with the royal family among its shareholders, was allowed in 1674 to extend its activities to Guinea. Brandenburg established a Brandenburg African Company, and established its first trading post on the coast of West Africa in 1682. The Negro slave trade, begun about 1450 as a Portuguese monopoly, had, by the end of the seventeenth century, become an international free-for-all.

The organisation of the slave trade gave rise to one of the most heated and far-reaching economic polemics of the period. Typical of the argument in favour of the monopoly was a paper in 1680 regarding the Royal African Company of England. The argument, summarised, was as follows: firstly, experience demonstrated that the slave trade could not be carried on without forts on the West African Coast costing £20,000 a year, too heavy a charge for private traders, and it was not practicable to apportion it among them; secondly, the trade was exposed to attack by other nations, and it was the losses from such attacks prior to 1663 which had resulted in the formation of the chartered company; thirdly, the maintenance of forts and warships could not be undertaken by the Company unless it had an exclusive control; fourthly, private traders enslaved all and sundry, even Negroes of high rank, and this led to reprisals on the coast; finally, England's great rival, Holland, was only waiting for the dissolution of the English company to engross the entire trade.

The monopolistic company had to face two opponents: the planter in the colonies and the merchant at home, both of whom combined to advocate free trade. The planters complained of the insufficient quantity, the poor quality, and the high prices of the slaves supplied by the Company; the latter countered by pointing out that the planters were heavily in debt to it, estimated in 1671 at £70,000, and, four years later, at £60,000 for Jamaica alone. The British merchants claimed that free trade would mean the purchase of a larger number of Negroes, which would mean the production of a larger quantity of British goods for the purchase and upkeep of the slaves.

The controversy ended in a victory for free trade. On July 5, 1698, Parliament passed an act abrogating the monopoly of the Royal African Company, and throwing open the trade to all British subjects on payment of a duty of ten per cent *ad valorem* on all goods exported to Africa for the purchase of slaves.

The acrimonious controversy retained no trace of the pseudo-humanitarianism of the Spaniards in the sixteenth century, that Negro slavery was essential to the preservation of the Indians. In its place was a solid economic fact, that Negro slavery was essential to the preservation of the sugar plantations. The considerations were purely economic. The slaves were denominated 'black ivory'. The best slave was, in Spanish parlance, a 'piece of the Indies', a slave 30 to 35 years old, about five feet eleven inches in height, without any physical defect. Adults who were not so tall and children were measured, and the total reduced to 'pieces of the Indies'. A contract in 1676 between the Spaniards and the Portuguese called for the supply of 10,000 'tons' of slaves; to avoid fraud and argument, it was stipulated that three Negroes should be considered the equivalent of one ton. In 1651 the English Guinea Company instructed its agent to load one of its ships with as many Negroes as it could carry, and, in default, to fill up the ship with cattle.

The mortality in the Middle Passage was regarded merely as an unfortunate trading loss, except for the fact that Negroes were more costly than cattle. Losses in fact ran quite high, but such concern as was evinced had to deal merely with profits. In 1659, a Dutch slaver, the *St. Jan*, lost 110 slaves out of a cargo of 219—for every two slaves purchased, one died in transit to the West Indies. In 1678, the *Arthur*, one of the ships of the Royal African Company, suffered a mortality of 88 out of 417 slaves—that is, more than 20 per cent. The *Martha*, another ship, landed 385 in Barbados out of 447 taken on the coast—the mortality amounted to 62, or a little less than 15 per cent. The *Coaster* lost 37 out of 150, a mortality of approximately 25 per cent. The *Hannibal*, in 1694, with a cargo of 700 slaves, buried 320 on the voyage, a mortality of 43 per cent; the Royal African Company lost £10 and the owner of the vessel 10 guineas on each slave, the total loss amounting to £6,560. The losses sustained by these five vessels amounted to 617 out of a total cargo of 1,933, that is, 32 per cent. Three out of every ten slaves perished in the Middle Passage. Hence the note of exasperation in the account of his voyage by the captain of the *Hannibal*:

'No gold-finders can endure so much noisome slavery as they do who carry Negroes; for those have some respite and satisfaction, but we endure twice the misery; and yet by their mortality our voyages are ruin'd, and we pine and fret our selves to death to think we should undergo so much misery, and take so much pains to so little purpose.'

The lamentations of an individual slave trader or sugar planter were drowned out by the seventeenth-century chorus of approbation. Negro slavery and the Negro slave trade fitted beautifully into the economic theory of the age. This theory, known as mercantilism, stated that the wealth of a nation depended upon its possession of bullion, the precious metals. If, however, bullion was not available through possession of the mines, the new doctrine went further than its Spanish predecessor in emphasising that a country could increase its stock by a favourable balance of trade, exporting more than it imported. One of the best and clearest statements of the theory was made by Edward Misselden, in his *Circle of Commerce*, in 1623:

'For as a pair of scales is an invention to show us the weight of things, whereby we may discern the heavy from the light ... so is also the balance of trade an excellent and politique invention to show us the difference of weight in the commerce of one kingdom with another: that is, whether the native commodities exported, and all the foreign commodities imported do balance or over-balance one another in the scale of commerce ... If the native commodities exported do weigh down and exceed in value the foreign commodities imported, it is a rule that never fails that then the kingdom grows rich and prospers in estate and stock: because the over-plus thereof must needs come in in treasure ... But if the foreign commodities imported do exceed in value the native commodities exported, it is a manifest sign that the trade decayeth, and the stock of the kingdom wasteth apace; because the overplus must needs go out in treasure.'

National policy of the leading European nations concentrated on achieving a favourable balance of trade. Colonial possessions were highly prized as a means to this end; they increased the exports of the metropolitan country, prevented the drain of treasure by the purchase of necessary tropical produce, and provided freights for the ships of the metropolis and employment for its sailors.

The combination of the Negro slave trade, Negro slavery and Caribbean sugar production is known as the triangular trade. A ship left the metropolitan country with a cargo of metropolitan goods, which it exchanged on the coast of West Africa for slaves. This constituted the first side of the triangle. The second consisted of the Middle Passage, the voyage from West Africa to the West Indies with the slaves. The triangle was completed by the voyage from the West Indies to the metropolitan country with sugar and other Caribbean products received in exchange for the slaves. As the slave ships were not always adequate for the transportation of the West Indian produce, the triangular trade was supplemented by a direct trade between the metropolitan country and the West Indian islands.

The triangular trade provided a market in West Africa and the West Indies for metropolitan products, thereby increasing metropolitan exports and contributing to full employment at home. The purchase of the slaves on the coast of West Africa and their maintenance in the West Indies gave an enormous stimulus to metropolitan industry and agriculture. For example, the British woollen industry was heavily dependent on the triangular trade. A parliamentary committee of 1695 emphasised that the slave trade was an encouragement to Britain's woollen industry. In addition, wool was required in the West Indies for blankets and clothing for the slaves on the plantations.

Iron, guns and brass also figured prominently in the triangular trade and the ancillary West Indian trade. Iron bars were the trading medium on a large part of the West African coast, and by 1682 Britain was exporting about 10,000 bars of iron a year to Africa. Sugar stoves, iron rollers, nails found a ready market on the West Indian plantations. Brass pans and kettles were customarily included in the slave trader's cargo.

The triangular trade presented an impressive statistical picture. Britain's trade in 1697 may be taken as an illustration.

	Imports £	Exports £
British West Indies	326,536	142,795
North America	279,582	140,129
Africa	6,615	13,435
Antigua	28,209	8,029
Barbados	196,532	77,465
Jamaica	70,000	40,726
Montserrat	14,699	3,532
Nevis	17,096	13,043
Carolina	12,374	5,289

	Imports £	Exports £
New England	26,282	64,468
New York	10,093	4,579
Pennsylvania	3,347	2,997
Virginia and Maryland	227,756	58,796
Total	*1,220,121*	*575,283*

Barbados was the most important single colony in the British Empire, worth almost as much, in its total trade, as the two tobacco colonies of Virginia and Maryland combined, and nearly three times as valuable as Jamaica. The tiny sugar island was more valuable to Britain than Carolina, New England, New York and Pennsylvania together. 'Go ahead, England, Barbados is behind you,' is today a stock joke in the British West Indies of the Barbadian's view of his own importance. Two and a half centuries ago, it was no joke. It was sound politics, based on sound economics. Jamaica's external trade was larger than New England's as far as Britain was concerned; Nevis was more important in the commercial firmament than New York; Antigua surpassed Carolina; Montserrat rated higher than Pennsylvania. Total British trade with Africa was larger than total trade with Pennsylvania, New York and Carolina. In 1697 the triangular trade accounted for nearly ten per cent of total British imports and over four per cent of total British exports. Barbados alone accounted for nearly four per cent of Britain's external trade.

Mercantilists were jubilant. The West Indian colonies were ideal colonies, providing a market, directly as well as indirectly, through the slave trade, for British manufactures and foodstuffs, whilst they supplied sugar and other tropical commodities that would otherwise have had to be imported from foreigners or dispensed with entirely. The West Indies thus contributed to Britain's balance of trade in two ways, by buying Britain's exports and by rendering the expenditure of bullion on foreign tropical imports unnecessary. On the other hand, the mainland colonies, Virginia and Maryland, and, to a lesser extent, Carolina excepted, where the conditions of labour and production duplicated those of the West Indies, were nuisances; they produced the same agricultural commodities as England, gave early evidence of competing with the metropolitan countries in manufactured goods as well, and were rivals in fishing and shipbuilding.

The British economists enthused. Sir Josiah Child in his *New Discourse of Trade* in 1668, wrote:

'The people that evacuate from us to Barbados, and the other West India Plantations ... do commonly work one Englishman to ten or eight Blacks; and if we keep the trade of our said plantations entirely to England, England would have no less inhabitants, but rather an increase of people by such evacuation, because that one Englishman, with the Blacks that work with him, accounting what they eat, use and wear, would make employment for four men in England ... whereas peradventure of ten men that issue from us to New England and Ireland, what we send to or receive from them, doth not employ one man in England.'

In 1690, Sir Dalby Thomas stated that every white man in the West Indies was one hundred and thirty times more valuable to Britain than those who stayed at home:

'Each white man, woman, and child, residing in the sugar plantations, occasions the consumption of more of our native commodities, and manufactures, than ten at home do—beef, pork, salt, fish, butter, cheese, corn, flour, beer, cyder, bridles, coaches, beds, chairs, stools, pictures, clocks, watches; pewter, brass, copper, iron vessels and instruments; sail-cloth and cordage; of which, in their building, shipping, mills, boiling, and distilling-houses, field-labour and domestic uses, they consume infinite quantities.'

Charles Davenant, perhaps the ablest of the seventeenth-century economists, estimated at the end of the century that Britain's total profit from trade amounted to two million pounds. Of this figure the plantation trade accounted for £600,000, and the re-export of plantation produce for £120,000. Trade with Africa, Europe and the Levant brought in another £600,000. The triangular trade thus represented a minimum of 36 per cent of Britain's commercial profits. Davenant added that every individual in the West Indies, white or Negro, was as profitable as seven in England.

What the West Indies had done for Seville in Spain in the sixteenth century, they did for Bristol in England and Bordeaux in France in the seventeenth. Each town became the metropolis of its country's trade with the Caribbean, though neither Bristol nor Bordeaux enjoyed the monopoly that had been granted to Seville. In 1661 only one ship, and that ship a Dutch one, came to Bordeaux from the West Indies. Ten years later twelve ships sailed from that port to the West Indies, and six returned from there. In 1683 the number of sailings to the sugar islands had risen to twenty-six. La Rochelle for a time eclipsed Bordeaux. In 1685 forty-nine ships sailed from that port to the West Indies. Nantes also was intimately connected with West Indian trade; in 1684 twenty-four ships belonging to the port were engaged in West Indian trade.

As a result of the triangular trade Bristol became a city of shopkeepers. It was said in 1685 that there was scarcely a shopkeeper in the city who had not a venture on board some ship bound for Virginia or the West Indies. The port took the lead in the struggle for the abrogation of the Royal African Company's monopoly, and in the first nine years of free trade shipped slaves to the West Indies at the rate of 17,883 a year. In 1700 Bristol had forty-six ships in the West Indian trade.

The basis of this astounding commercial efflorescence was the Negro slaves, 'the strength and sinews of this western world'. In 1662 the Company of Royal Adventurers trading to Africa pointed to the 'profit and honour' that had accrued to British subjects from the slave trade, which King Charles II himself described as that 'beneficial trade . . . so much importing our service, and the enriching of this Our Kingdom'. According to Colbert in France, no commerce in the world produced as many advantages as the slave trade. Benjamin Raule exhorted the Elector of Prussia, on October 26, 1685, not to be left behind in the race: 'Everyone knows that the slave trade is the source of the wealth which the Spaniards wring out of the West Indies, and that whoever knows how to furnish them slaves, will share their wealth. Who can say by how many millions of hard cash the Dutch West India Company has enriched itself in this slave trade!' At the end of the seventeenth century all Europe, and not England only, was impressed with the words of Sir Dalby Thomas: 'The pleasure, glory and grandeur of England has been advanced more by sugar than by any other commodity, wool not excepted.'

The Negro slave trade in the eighteenth century constituted one of the greatest migrations in recorded history. Its volume is indicated in the following table, prepared from various statistics that are available.

Years	Colony	Importation	Average Importation per year
1700–1786	Jamaica	610,000	7,000
1708–1735 & 1747–1766	Barbados	148,821	3,100
1680–1776	Saint-Domingue	800,000	8,247
1720–1729	Antigua	12,278	1,362
1721–1730	St. Kitts	10,358	1,035
1721–1729	Montserrat	3,210	357
1721–1726	Nevis	1,267	253
1767–1773	Dominica	19,194	2,742
1763–1789	Cuba	30,875	1,143
1700–1754	Danish Islands	11,750	214

Average annual importations do not provide a complete picture. In 1774 the importation into Jamaica was 18,448. In fourteen of the years 1702–1775, the annual importation exceeded 10,000. Imports into Saint-Domingue averaged 12,559 in the years 1764–1768; in 1768 they were 15,279. In 1718 Barbados imported 7,126 slaves. During the nine months in which Cuba was under British occupation in 1762, 10,700 slaves were introduced. The British introduced 41,000 slaves in three years into Guadeloupe whilst they were in occupation of the island during the Seven Years' War.

These large importations represented one of the greatest advantages which the slave trade had over other trades. The frightful mortality of the slaves on the plantations made annual increments essential. Consider the case of Saint-Domingue. In 1763 the slave population amounted to 206,539. Imports from 1764 to 1774 numbered 102,474. The slave population in 1776 was 290,000. Thus, despite an importation of over one hundred thousand, without taking into account the annual births, the increase of the slave population in thirteen years was less than 85,000. Taking only importations into consideration, the slave population in 1776 was 19,000 less than the figure of 1763 with the importations added, and the imports for one year are not available.

A much clearer illustration of the mortality is available for Barbados. In 1764 there were 70,706 slaves in the island. Importations to 1783, with no figures available for the years 1779 and 1780, totalled 41,840. The total population, allowing for

neither deaths nor births, should, therefore, have been 112,546
in 1783. Actually, it was 62,258. Thus despite an annual importation for the eighteen years for which statistics are available of
2,324, the population in 1783 was 8,448 less than it was in
1764, or an annual decline of 469. The appalling mortality is
brought out in the following table.

Year	Slaves	Imports	Potential Pop. of next year	Actual Pop. of next year	Decrease	Decrease as % of Imports
1764	70,706	3,936	74,642	72,255	2,387	60
1765	72,255	3,228	75,483	73,651	1,832	57
1766	73,651	4,061	77,712	74,656	3,056	75
1767	74,656	4,154	78,810	76,275	2,535	61
1768	76,275	4,628	80,903	75,658	4,345	90
1769	75,658	6,837	82,495	76,334	6,161	90
1770	76,334	5,825	82,159	75,998	6,171	106
1771	75,998	2,728	78,716	74,485	4,231	155
1764–1771		35,397	106,103	74,206	31,897	90

Thus, after eight years of importations, averaging 4,424 a year,
the population of Barbados was only 3,411 larger. 35,397 slaves
had been imported; 31,897 had disappeared. In 1770 and 1771
the mortality was so high that the importation in those years,
heavy though it was, was not adequate to supply the deficit.
Half the population had had to be renewed in eight years.

In 1703 Jamaica had 45,000 Negroes; in 1778, 205,261, an
average annual increase from all causes of 2,109. Between 1703
and 1775, 469,893 slaves had been imported, an average annual
importation of 6,807. For every additional slave in its population,
Jamaica had had to import three. The total population in 1778,
excluding births and based only on imports, should have been
541,893, and that figure excludes imports for 1776, 1777 and
1778. Allowing 11,000 a year for those three years, the total
population in 1778 should have been 547,893. The actual population in that year was less than forty per cent of the potential total.

Economic development has never been purchased at so high a
price. According to one of the leading planters of Saint-Domingue,
one in every three imported Negroes died in the first three years.
To the mortality on the plantations must be added the mortality
on the slave ships. On the slave ships belonging to the port of

Nantes in France, that mortality varied from 5 per cent in 1746 and 1774 to as high as 34 per cent in 1732. For all the slave cargoes transported by them between 1715 and 1775, the mortality amounted to 16 per cent. Of one hundred Negroes who left the coast of Africa, therefore, only 84 reached the West Indies; one-third of these died in three years. For every 56 Negroes, therefore, on the plantations at the end of three years, 44 had perished.

The slave trade thus represented a wear and tear, a depreciation which no other trade equalled. The loss of an individual planter or trader was insignificant compared with the basic fact that every cargo of slaves, including the quick and the dead, represented so much industrial development and employment, so much employment of ships and sailors, in the metropolitan country. No other commercial undertaking required so large a capital as the slave trade. In addition to the ship, there was its equipment, armament, cargo, its unusually large supply of water and food-stuffs, its abnormally large crew. In 1765 it was estimated that in France the cost of fitting out and arming a vessel for 300 slaves was 242,500 livres. The cargo of a vessel from Nantes in 1757 was valued at 141,500 livres; it purchased 500 slaves. The cargo of the *Prince de Conty*, of 300 tons, was valued at 221,224 livres, with which 800 slaves were purchased.

Large profits were realised from the slave trade. The *King Solomon*, belonging to the Royal African Company, carried a cargo worth £4,252 in 1720. It took on 296 Negroes who were sold in St. Kitts for £9,228. The profit was thus 117 per cent. From 1698 to 1707 the Royal African Company exported from England to Africa goods to the value of £293,740. The Company sold 5,982 Negroes in Barbados for £156,425, an average of £26 per head. It sold 2,178 slaves in Antigua for £80,522, an average of £37 per head. The total number of Negroes imported into the British islands by the Company in these years was 17,760. The sale of 8,160 Negroes in Barbados and Antigua, less than half the total imports into all the islands, thus realised 80 per cent of the total exports from England. Allowing an average price of £26 per head for the remaining 9,600 Negroes, the total amount realised from the sale of the Company's Negroes was £488,107. The profit on the Company's exports was thus 66 per

cent. For every three pounds' worth of merchandise exported
from England, the Company obtained two additional pounds by
way of profit.

The Negroes taken on by the *Prince de Conty* on the coast of
Africa averaged 275 livres each; the survivors of the Middle
Passage fetched 1,300 livres each in Saint-Domingue. In 1700 a
cargo of 238 slaves was purchased by the Danish West Indies
at prices ranging from 90 to 100 rixdollars. In 1753 the wholesale price on the coast of Africa was 100 rixdollars; the retail
price in the Danish West Indies was 150 to 300 rixdollars. In
1724 the Danish West India Company made a profit of 28 per
cent on its slave imports; in 1725, 30 per cent; 70 per cent on
the survivors of a cargo of 1733 despite a mortality in transit of
45 per cent; 50 per cent on a cargo of 1754. It need occasion
no surprise, therefore, that one of the eighteenth-century slave
dealers admitted that, of all the places he had lived in, England,
Ireland, America, Portugal, the West Indies, the Cape Verde
Islands, the Azores, and Africa, it was in Africa that he could
most quickly make his fortune.

The slave trade was central to the triangular trade. It was, in
the words of one British mercantilist, 'the spring and parent
whence the others flow;' 'the first principle and foundation of all
the rest,' echoed another, 'the mainspring of the machine which
sets every wheel in motion'. The slave trade kept the wheels of
metropolitan industry turning; it stimulated navigation and shipbuilding and employed seamen; it raised fishing villages into
flourishing cities; it gave sustenance to new industries based on
the processing of colonial raw materials; it yielded large profits
which were ploughed back into metropolitan industry; and, finally,
it gave rise to an unprecedented commerce in the West Indies
and made the Caribbean territories among the most valuable
colonies the world has ever known.

Examples must suffice. In 1729 the British West Indies
absorbed one-quarter of Britain's iron exports, and Africa, where
the price of a Negro was commonly reckoned at one Birmingham
gun, was one of the most important markets for the British
armaments industry. In 1753 there were 120 sugar refineries in
England—eighty in London, twenty in Bristol. In 1780 the British
West Indies supplied two-thirds of the six and a half million

pounds of raw cotton imported by Britain. Up to 1770 one-third
of Manchester's textile exports went to Africa, one-half to the
West Indian and American colonies. In 1709 the British West
Indies employed one-tenth of all British shipping engaged in
foreign trade. Between 1710 and 1714, 122,000 tons of British
shipping sailed to the West Indies, 112,000 tons to the mainland
colonies. Between 1709 and 1787, British shipping engaged in
foreign trade quadrupled; ships clearing for Africa multiplied
twelve times and the tonnage eleven times.

The triangular trade marked the ascendancy of two additional
European ports in the eighteenth century, Liverpool in England
and Nantes in France, and further contributed to the development
of Bristol and Bordeaux, begun in the seventeenth century. Liverpool's first slave ship, of 30 tons, sailed for Africa in 1709. In
1783 the port had 85 ships, of 12,294 tons, in the trade. Between 1709 and 1783, a total of 2,249 ships, of 240,657 tons,
sailed from Liverpool to Africa—an annual average of 30 ships
and 3,200 tons. The proportion of slave ships to the total shipping of the port was one in a hundred in 1709, one in nine in
1730, one in four in 1763, one in three in 1771. In 1752, 88
Liverpool vessels carried upwards of 24,730 slaves from Africa.
Seven firms, owning 26 vessels, carried 7,030 slaves.

Liverpool's exports to Africa in 1770 read like a census of
British manufactures: beans, brass, beer, textiles, copper, candles,
chairs, cider, cordage, earthenware, gunpowder, glass, haber-
dashery, iron, lead, looking glasses, pewter, pipes, paper, stock-
ings, silver, sugar, salt, kettles.

In 1774 there were eight sugar refineries in Liverpool. Two
distilleries were established in the town for the express purpose
of supplying slave ships. There were many chain and anchor
foundries, and manufacturers of and dealers in iron, copper,
brass and lead in the town. In 1774 there were fifteen roperies.
Half of Liverpool's sailors were engaged in the slave trade, which,
by 1783, was estimated to bring the town a clear annual profit
of £300,000. The slave trade transformed Liverpool from a fishing
village into a great centre of international commerce. The population rose from 5,000 in 1700 to 34,000 in 1773. It was a common
saying in the town that its principal streets had been marked
out by the chains, and the walls of its houses cemented by the

blood, of the African slaves. The red brick Customs House, blazoned with Negro heads, bore mute but eloquent testimony to the origins of Liverpool's rise by 1783 to the position of one of the most famous—or infamous, depending on the point of view—towns in the world of commerce.

What Liverpool was to England, Nantes was to France. Between 1715 and 1775, vessels belonging to the port exported 229,525 slaves from Africa, an annual average of 3,763. In 1751 Nantes ships transported 10,003 Negroes. Slave ships constituted about one-fifth of the total shipping of the port. But the slave trade conditioned all others. The slavers brought back sugar and other tropical produce. The number of sugar refineries declined from fifteen in 1700 to four in 1750. But five textile factories were established by 1769, together with manufactures of jams and sweetmeats dependent on sugar. As in Liverpool, a slave trading aristocracy developed, of big capitalists each owning four or six ships.

The West Indian trade was worth twice as much to eighteenth-century Bristol as the remainder of her other overseas commerce. In the eighties the town had 30 vessels engaged in the slave trade, and 72 in the West Indian trade. Some of its most prominent citizens were engaged in sugar refining. The Baptist Mills of Bristol produced brass manufactures for the slave trade.

As Nantes was the slave trading port *par excellence* of France, Bordeaux was the sugar port. In 1720, Bordeaux had 74 ships, of 6,882 tons, in the West Indian trade; in 1782, 310 ships, of 108,000 tons. In 1749 the town's trade with the West Indies exceeded 27 million livres; in 1771, at its peak, it approximated 171 millions. An enormous stimulus was given to shipbuilding: 14 ships, of 3,640 tons, in 1754; 245 totalling 74,485 tons, between 1763 and 1778. Sugar imports into Bordeaux, less than 10 million livres in 1749, attained the huge figure of 101 millions in 1780. A mere 22 livres of coffee were imported in 1724; in 1771, the figure was 112 millions. Indigo, less than 5 million livres up to 1770, amounted to 22 millions in 1772. Bordeaux, in return, exported codfish from Newfoundland, salted fish from Holland, salted beef from Ireland, flour and wine to the West Indies. There were 26 sugar refineries in the town in 1789. Population rose from 43,000 in 1698 to 110,000 in 1790.

The West Indian basis of Bordeaux' prosperity was symbolised by the aggrandisement of a naturalised Portuguese Jew, Gradis. The founder of the dynasty was David, who became a citizen in 1731. Devoting himself exclusively to West Indian trade, he established a branch in Saint-Domingue, which he entrusted to a brother-in-law, Jacob, and another in Martinique, which was supervised by a nephew. His son, Abraham, became the greatest merchant in eighteenth-century Bordeaux. At the government's order, he supplied Canada in the Seven Years' War, six ships in 1756, fourteen in 1758. He loaned large sums to the State and to the greatest in the land. He died in 1780, leaving a fortune of eight million livres, having lived to hear himself denominated by contemporaries, 'the famous Jew Gradis, King of Bordeaux'.

The remarkable value of the triangular trade can best be presented statistically. As for the seventeenth century, we shall take as an illustration the British West Indies. The table that follows gives British imports from, and British exports to, the several colonies for the year 1773 and the period 1714 to 1773.

Colony	Imports (1773)	Exports (1773)	Imports (1714–1773)	Exports (1714–1773)
Total British	11,406,841	14,763,252	492,146,670	730,962,105
Antigua	112,779	93,323	12,785,262	3,821,726
Barbados	168,682	148,817	14,506,497	7,442,652
Jamaica	1,286,888	683,451	42,259,749	16,844,990
Montserrat	47,911	14,947	3,387,237	537,831
Nevis	39,299	9,181	3,636,504	549,564
St. Kitts	150,512	62,607	13,305,659*	3,181,901*
Tobago	20,453	30,049	49,587†	122,093†
Grenada	445,041	102,761	3,620,504‡	1,179,279‡
St. Vincent	145,619	38,444	672.901	235,665
Dominica	248,868	43,679	1,469,704§	322,294§
Tortola	48,000	26,927	863,931‖	220,038‖
Carolina	456,513	344,859	11,410,480	8,423,588
New England	124,624	527,055	4,134,392	16,934,316
New York	76,246	289,214	1,910,796	11,377,696
Pennsylvania	36,652	426,448	1,115,112	9,627,409
Virginia & Maryland	589,803	328,904	35,158,481	18,391,097
British West Indies	2,830,583	1,270,846	101,264,818	45,389,988
Mainland Colonies	1,420,471	2,375,797	55,552,675	69,903,613
Africa	68,424	662,112	2,407,447	15,235,829

* 1732–1773   † 1764–1773   ‡ 1762–1773   § 1763–1773   ‖ 1748–1773.

Thus Jamaica in the eighteenth century was what Barbados had been in the seventeenth, the most important colony in the British Empire. Its exports to Britain from 1714 to 1773 were three times those of Barbados; its imports from Britain more than double. In these years one-twelfth of total British imports came from Jamaica, nearly one-fortieth of total British exports went to Jamaica. In 1773 one-ninth of total British imports came from the island, one-twenty-second of British exports went to it. Jamaica's exports to Britain were ten times those of New England; the exports to the two colonies were about the same. Jamaica's exports to Britain from 1714 to 1773 were one-fifth larger than those of Virginia and Maryland combined; its imports from Britain about one-tenth less.

From 1714 to 1773 Barbados' exports to Britain were more than one quarter larger than those of Carolina, imports from Britain about one-tenth less. Antigua's exports to Britain were 15 per cent larger than those of Pennsylvania; imports from Britain about two-fifths the figure for that mainland colony. St. Kitts' exports to Britain were seven times the figure for New York; its imports more than one-quarter those of New York. Grenada's exports to Britain in twelve years, 1762–1773, were more than five times as large as Georgia's in forty-two, 1732–1773; Grenada's imports were half as large as those of Georgia.

In 1773 total British imports from the British West Indies amounted to one quarter of total British imports, British exports to the West Indies to about one-eleventh of the total export trade. Imports from the mainland colonies were one-half the West Indian figure; exports less than double. For the years 1714–1773, British imports from the West Indies were one-fifth of the total import trade; from the mainland colonies they were slightly more than half the West Indian figure; from Africa they were half of one per cent. British exports to the West Indies during the period were one-sixteenth of the total export trade; to the mainland, they were one-tenth; to Africa, one-fiftieth. For these sixty years the triangular trade accounted for 21 per cent of British imports; 8 per cent of British exports; and nearly 14 per cent of Britain's total external trade.

The population of the British West Indies in 1787 was 58,353 whites; 7,706 free Negroes; 461,864 slaves—a total of 527,923.

The annual British export of slaves from Africa by 1783 was approximately 34,000. This was the human and social basis of one in every five pounds of British imports, one in every twelve of British exports, and one in every seven of Britain's total trade.

The situation in the French West Indies was essentially similar. In 1715 France's external trade amounted to 175 million livres—imports, 75; exports, 100. West Indian trade accounted for one-sixth of the whole, 30 millions; their imports, of 20 millions, amounted to one-fifth of France's export trade; their exports, 10 millions, constituted one-eighth of France's import trade. In 1776, though France had lost some of the smaller West Indian islands, exports from the French West Indies amounted to 200 million livres, imports to 70 millions, the total external trade of the islands representing more than one-third of total French commerce, which oscillated between 600 and 700 million livres; West Indian trade employed 1,000 ships, outward and inward cargoes in the proportion of 5 to 4. The population of the French West Indies about 1780 amounted to 63,682 whites, 13,429 free Negroes, and 437,738 slaves—a total of 514,849. France's annual export of slaves from Africa was estimated at 20,000.

Magnum est saccharum et prevalebit! Great is sugar, and it will prevail! Mercantilists were jubilant. The colonies, wrote Horace Walpole, were 'the source of all our riches, and preserve the balance of trade in our favour, for I don't know where we have it but by the means of our colonies'. The statistics given above identify the colonies which Walpole had in mind. An annual profit of 7s per head was sufficient to enrich a country, said William Wood; each white man in the colonies brought a profit of over seven pounds, twenty times as much. The Negro slaves, said Postlethwayt, were 'the fundamental prop and support' of the colonies, 'valuable people,' and the British Empire was 'a magnificent superstructure of American commerce and naval power on an African foundation'. Rule Britannia! Britannia rules the waves. For Britons never shall be slaves.

But the sons of France arose to glory. France joined in the homage to the triangular trade. 'What commerce,' asked the Chamber of Commerce of Nantes, 'can be compared to that

which obtains men in exchange for commodities?' Profound
question! The abandonment of the slave trade, continued the
Chamber, would be inevitably followed by the ruin of colonial
commerce; 'whence follows the fact that we have no branch of
trade so precious to the State and so worthy of protection as
the Guinea trade'. The triangular trade was incomparable, the
slave trade precious, and the West Indies perfect colonies. 'The
more colonies differ from the metropolis,' said Nantes, 'the more
perfect they are... Such are the Caribbean colonies: they have
none of our objects of trade; they have others which we lack and
cannot produce.'

But there were discordant notes in the mercantilist harmony.
The first was opposition to the slave trade. In 1774, in Jamaica,
the very centre of Negro slavery, a debating society voted that the
slave trade was not consistent with sound policy, or with the
laws of nature and of morality. In 1776 Thomas Jefferson wrote
into the Declaration of Independence three paragraphs attacking
the King of England for his 'piratical warfare' on the coast of
Africa against people who never offended him, and for his veto
of colonial legislation attempting to prohibit or restrain the slave
trade. The paragraphs were only deleted on the representations
of the states of South Carolina, Georgia and New England.
Two petitions were presented to Parliament, in 1774 and 1776,
for abolition of the slave trade. A third, more important, was
presented in 1783 by the Quakers. The Prime Minister, Lord
North, complimented them on their humanity, but regretted that
abolition was an impossibility, as the slave trade had become
necessary to every nation in Europe. European public opinion
accepted the position stated by Postlethwayt: 'We shall take
things as they are, and reason from them in their present state,
and not from that wherein we could hope them to be.... We
cannot think of giving up the slave-trade, notwithstanding my
good wishes that it could be done.'

The second discordant note was more disturbing. Between 1772
and 1778, Liverpool slave traders were estimated to have lost
£700,000 in the slave trade. By 1788 twelve of the thirty leading
houses which had dominated the trade from 1773 had gone
bankrupt. Slave trading, like sugar production, had its casualties.
A slave trader in 1754, as his supreme defence of the slave

trade, had adumbrated that 'from this trade proceed benefits, far outweighing all, either real or pretended mischiefs and inconveniencies'. If and when the slave trade ceased to be profitable, it would not be so easy to defend it.

The third discordant note came also from the British colonies. The British Government's ambition was to become the slave carriers and sugar suppliers of the whole world. Britain had fought for and obtained the *asiento*. The supply of slaves to foreign nations became an integral part of the British slave trade. Of 497,736 slaves imported in Jamaica between 1702 and 1775, 137,114 had been re-exported, one out of every four. In 1731, imports were 10,079; re-exports, 5,708. From 1775 to 1783, Antigua imported 5,673 slaves and re-exported 1,972, one out of every three. Jamaica resorted to its seventeenth-century policy, an export tax on all Negroes re-exported. In 1774, the Board of Trade, on the representation of the slave traders of London, Liverpool and Bristol, disallowed the law as unjustifiable, improper and prejudicial to British commerce, pointed out that legislative autonomy in the colonies did not extend to the imposition of duties upon British ships and goods or to the prejudice and obstruction of British commerce, and reprimanded the Governor of the island for dereliction of duty in not stopping efforts to 'check and discourage a traffic... beneficial to the nation'.

Chapter Eleven

The Exclusive

'Commerce,' said the French Minister, Colbert, the incarnation of seventeenth-century mercantilism, 'is a perpetual and peaceable war of wit and energy among all nations.' Seventeenth century Caribbean history saw a perpetual war, not always peaceable, between Holland, England and France for Caribbean commerce.

The Dutch, turning their attention to trade rather than plantations, early took the lead. The Dutch West India Company offered the following explanation:

'The expected service for the welfare of our fatherland and the destruction of our hereditary enemy could not be accomplished by the trifling trade with the Indians or the tardy cultivation of uninhabitable regions ... the colonising of such wild and uncultivated countries demands more inhabitants than we can well supply: not so much from lack of population, in which our provinces abound, as from the fact that all who are inclined to do any sort of work here procure enough to eat without any trouble, and are therefore unwilling to go far from here on an uncertainty.'

So successful were the Dutch in their chosen field that, by the middle of the century, of a total of 25,000 ships engaged in the maritime trade of Europe, the Dutch owned 15,000. Called derisively 'sea beggars', they became 'the waggoners of all seas'.

According to the English political scientist, James Harrington, the Dutch sweated more gold than the Spaniards were able to dig; in the words of another contemporary, they sucked honey, like the bee, from all parts. Dutch ships were to be found in every sea and every ocean, and Staten Island and Van Diemen's Land, New Zealand and Tasmania are eloquent testimony of their ubiquitousness and supremacy. Amsterdam, the capital of the Netherlands, built on herrings, sugar and spice, became the Wall Street of the seventeenth century; a 'golden swamp with heaven's plenitude replete, storehouse of east and west, all water and all street', as the national poet, Constantin Huygens, sang in exultation.

Holland became the intellectual and cultural capital of the world. Grotius in international law; Descartes—a Frenchman who made Holland his home—and Spinoza in philosophy; Christian Huygens in science; his father in poetry; Rembrandt, Hals, Vermeer, van Ruysdael and Steen in painting; all combined to make the seventeenth century the golden age of Holland. The visible symbol of this intellectual hegemony over Europe was the University of Leyden; two of its prime material bases were the triangular trade and the trade with the Caribbean sugar colonies.

The Caribbean Sea became virtually a Dutch canal. The new European annexations in the Caribbean, English, French and Danish *de jure*, were *de facto* Dutch. The Dutch stood for free trade rather than monopoly. With the exception of Surinam, where the lure of sugar was corroborated by that Dutch poem in which the father consents to the marriage of his daughter on condition that his prospective son-in-law agreed to spend some time in Surinam before his marriage, their Caribbean possessions were entrepôts and warehouses rather than plantations. It was the Dutch who purchased and transported the tobacco production of the early English and French planters, and provided them in return with the necessary supplies. It was the Dutch who, when tobacco prices fell in the world market, taught the same planters the secrets of cane cultivation and sugar manufacture. It was the Dutch who provided the necessary supply of slaves. The British, French and Spanish planters in the Caribbean in the middle of the seventeenth century were, as the merchants of Flushing said of the French, 'our planters'.

In 1662 the Dutch had from 100 to 120 large vessels engaged in trade with the French West Indies; the total trade of these islands employed 150 vessels, of which only three or four were French. They imported into the islands foodstuffs produced in Germany and goods manufactured in Holland, exported sugar and tobacco to Holland, where, after manufacture, they were re-exported to France. The Dutch were masters not only of the French colonies, but of France itself. In 1646, the French balance of trade with Holland was as follows: imports from Holland, 21,445,520 livres; exports to Holland, 16,701,466 livres. The imports from Holland included sugar to the amount of 1,885,150 livres, together with pepper, cinnamon, nutmeg, mace, ginger—all of which could be produced in the French West Indies—to the value of 3,193,130 livres.

England and France had plucked the fruits of Spain's garden only to put them into a Dutch sack. The war for territory with Spain was thus converted into a war for trade with Holland. 'If they subsist by their trade,' Sir Walter Raleigh had said of the Dutch a generation earlier, 'the disturbance of their trade (which England only can disturb) will also disturb their subsistence.' Raleigh was quite wrong. The French could disturb as well as the English.

The struggle opened with a furious battle of the books between England and Holland. The Dutch position was stated by Grotius, at the request of the Dutch Government, with his *Mare Liberum*, in 1609. This was the official position of the Dutch with respect to free trade. Assailing the papal donation, Grotius claimed, as Queen Elizabeth before him had done, that the sea was incapable of occupation by any one state and was common to the use of all. Every nation, he added, was free to travel to, and to trade with, any other nation.

England, which had used similar language against Spanish claims to monopoly only a few years before, and which was to advance similar claims towards the entire world in the era of free trade in the nineteenth century, countered with Selden's *Mare Clausum* in 1635. For England, the sea was open where Spain was concerned and closed where Holland was concerned. Selden agreed that Spain and Portugal could not support their mono-polistic claims because their naval forces were insufficient, thus shifting the argument from law to force. He cited numerous cases to the contrary to disprove the Dutch claim that the sea is common to the use of all. Admitting that innocent navigation should not be prohibited, he asserted that it could not be claimed as a right. The basis had been laid for the Anglo-French attack on Dutch trade.

The personification of the war against the Dutch commercial monopoly was Jean Baptiste Colbert, born in 1619, descendant of a long line of French merchants and civil servants. His capacity for work soon brought him to the attention of Cardinal Mazarin, who ruled France in the early years of the reign of Louis XIV, until his death in 1661. Colbert rapidly rose in the royal favour. On Mazarin's death he was made Intendant of Finance. Three years later he was made Superintendent of Buildings and Manufactures; in 1665, Controller-General; and in 1669, Minister of the Marine, with jurisdiction over the colonies. In his hands he united all the important branches of administration except that of war. He was the real ruler of France until his death in 1683. Colbert became the architect and the symbol of the seventeenth-century colonial system.

'We must re-establish or create all industries, even those of luxury,' he wrote to Mazarin in 1653; 'establish a protective system in the customs; organise the producers and traders in corporations; ease the fiscal bonds which are harmful to the people; restore to France the marine transport of her productions; develop the colonies and attach them commercially to France; suppress all the intermediaries between France and India; develop the navy to protect the mercantile marine.' It was planned economy on a grand scale. The core was the French colonies in the Caribbean, the 'mortal enemies' the ubiquitous Dutch traders.

In 1494 the Pope had partitioned the world between Spain and Portugal. In 1664 Colbert partitioned it between two French trading companies which he organised as his 'armies' in the war of commerce. The east went to the East India Company, the west to the West India Company. The Pope had proposed, Colbert disposed.

The preamble of the letters-patent of the French East India Company reads as follows:

'The happiness of a people consists not only in a considerable diminution of taxes ... but even more in the maintenance of commerce which
alone can bring into the kingdom an abundance that will serve not as a
means of luxury to the few, but as a blessing to the many. Commerce
stimulates manufactures, by opening markets for their products, and gives
employment to a large number of people of almost every age and sex ...
Oversea commerce is the means. It is certain, both from sound reason
and from the experience of our neighbours, that the profit gained much
outweighs the toil and pain expended therein.'

There were three essential features of the colonial system devised by Colbert. First, the colonies were necessary to the
building up of French trade. Secondly, the colonies were the
exclusive property of the metropolitan country. Thirdly, colonial
interests must be subordinated to those of the metropolitan
country.

With respect to the first essential, the necessity of colonies to
the building up of French trade, Colbert, in a discourse on
manufactures in 1663, discussed the West Indian trade at some
length. He emphasised that the French linen industry might be
aided by opening up markets in the New World, and that Dutch
trade with the French islands amounted to two million livres of
sugar and one million of cotton, tobacco and indigo, all of which
they took to France, together with slaves from Guinea; salt beef
from Ireland, manufactured goods from Holland, which they sold
in the colonies; the trade employed 200 ships and 6,000 seamen.
All that was needed was to transfer this trade from Holland to
France, in order to give France 200 more ships, 6,000 more
French seamen, three million livres in cash, and markets for
French industry and agriculture.

Colbert, therefore, gave the West India Company a monopoly
for forty years of all trade to the West Indies, America and
Africa, and he saw to it that the King and public officials took
shares. When the Company's success turned out to be less than
he had anticipated, Colbert restricted its monopoly to slaves, salt
beef and livestock, and left West Indian trade to the private
trader, provided that he was French. The Company's privileges
were revoked in 1674, but the edict of revocation stressed the
success of Colbert's policy. The French Islands then had a population of 45,000, furnished trade to more than 100 French ships of
50 to 300 tons, provided employment for sailors, pilots, gunners,

carpenters, and other artisans, and offered a ready market for many commodities produced in France.

The second postulate of Colbert's colonial policy was that the colonies were the exclusive property of the metropolitan country. His aim was to exclude the Dutch from French colonial trade, 'even to chase them from the West Indies entirely,' he wrote in 1670 to one of the colonial governors, 'if it can be done without openly violating our treaties, as could be done, for instance, by secretly aiding the Caribs against them in case of a war, or by secretly inciting them to attack the Dutch by furnishing them firearms and ammunition'. The Cato of France, his abiding theme may be expressed in the words, *'Batavia delenda est,'* Holland must be destroyed.

All foreign vessels, but particularly the Dutch, were to be driven out of French colonial ports or confiscated, without exception, and none were to be admitted under any pretext of need for slaves, livestock, equipment for sugar mills, 'however pressing such a need may be,' he emphasised in 1670. The policy thus was not far removed from that of Spain in directing the destruction of the tobacco plantations of Venezuela rather than have the Dutch trade with them. It was the beginnings of the system which the French called with precision *l'exclusif,* 'the exclusive'. The success of Colbert can be gauged from the fact that French ships trading with the Caribbean, which numbered four in 1662, amounted to 205 in 1683. In 1670 Colbert noted with satisfaction that foreigners no longer brought sugar to France.

The third fundamental of Colbertism was the subordination of colonial interests to those of the metropolitan country. The cessation of Dutch trade meant, at the beginning, great hardships for the colonies. The first French ships were like a drop of water on the tongue of a man with a high fever; prices were high; one ship arrived without women's shoes, and they had to go to Mass barefooted. Colbert remained adamant—no concessions. His instructions to the first Intendant of the islands in 1679, emphasising the total exclusion of all foreigners, concluded that they were not to be admitted 'even when the inhabitants are in need of some article of merchandise for their subsistence'. He was well aware that 'the exclusive' involved what he called 'some inconveniences' for the colonies. 'I know very well,' he wrote to one of the governors, 'that these innovations will prove at first somewhat irksome, and that people who do not see beyond the present good or ill prove rather difficult to control, when they are forced to make some real sacrifice, but it is precisely at such times that reason, justice, and, if necessary, force, should be employed to make them submit'.

In the execution of his policy, no detail was too small, no loophole too insignificant, to warrant his personal attention. If ever a man had a system, that man was Colbert. One of the chief articles of the import trade of the French West Indies was salted beef. It was generally obtained from Ireland, the Nantes traders making a profit estimated at 43 per cent. Colbert put his foot down: the West Indies must import French beef. French beef was dearer than Irish, and the supply smaller, everyone insisted. It was pointed out to Colbert that, in order to produce sugar, the slaves must eat, and that salted beef was a staple of the diet of the slaves. Statistics indicated that French beef was not adequate to the demand. Colbert persisted, to the point that one would imagine from his correspondence and instructions on the subject that the French colonial empire was a question of beef. Eventually, in 1680, he had to admit defeat. A royal decree of that year stated that the prohibition of the importation of Irish beef and Madeira wine into the islands was unwise. In view of the small size of the islands, Colbert did not deem it feasible to establish a local supply of beef in the islands.

The two most notorious instances of Colbert's subordination of colonial interests to those of France affected the chief colonial products, tobacco and sugar. Colbert, a rigid mercantilist, forbade tobacco cultivation in Canada on the grounds that it would prove less profitable than other occupations and that it would injure the interests of the West Indies. He also made repeated efforts to discourage its cultivation in France, for similar reasons. But in 1674 he made the sale of all tobacco in France a state monopoly, which was farmed out, and restricted its importation and exportation to certain ports. The planters of Saint-Domingue protested against the monopoly in 1681, on the ground that it tended to lower prices for the raw material and to sacrifice the European market. Colbert immediately renewed the monopoly for the ensuing year. The only concession he made to the colonies was to reaffirm the right of re-exportation of colonial tobacco to foreign countries. The tobacco output of Saint-Domingue declined by one half in a single decade, and the planters turned their attention to sugar.

Tobacco was, however, at best a secondary crop. Sugar was the crop *par excellence* of the Caribbean. As early as 1664, as a campaign in his war with Holland, Colbert projected a sugar refining industry in France. His early plans included refining in the colonies. The tariff of 1665 imposed a duty of twenty-two livres per hundredweight on refined sugar from foreign countries, and four livres on all sugar, raw and refined, from the French colonies. Five years later the colonial duty was reduced by fifty per cent. In 1672 Colbert instructed the Governor of Martinique to make every effort to convince the planters of the advantage to be gained from refining their sugar: 'you know how important it is for the commerce of the islands of America to persuade the planters to refine their sugar themselves and thus to gain a more ready and more assured market for their sugar.' By 1679 two refineries had been established in Martinique and three in Guadeloupe. Not satisfied, Colbert wrote in the following year to the Intendant, who consulted him on the matter: 'You should work to increase by every means the number of refineries.'

The planters really required little persuasion. They were well aware of the advantages. Their raw sugar lost about one-quarter of its weight in the transport, the refined nothing. Refined sugar fetched five times the price of raw sugar. Refining provided a livelihood for the 'poor whites'. From the metropolitan standpoint, higher incomes in the island meant larger purchases of French goods.

The French refiners, however, were not impressed. They protested against colonial refining. They already represented a substantial vested interest in France. By 1683 there were twenty-nine refineries in France, consuming 17,700,000 pounds of sugar. There were no fewer than eight in Rouen, four in La Rochelle, three each in Nantes and Bordeaux, two each in Dunkerque, Orléans and Marseilles, one each in Dieppe, Saumur, Angers, Tours and Toulouse. In contrast there were only five refineries in the colonies, refining three million pounds of raw sugar.

But Colbertism emphasised metropolitan interests rather than colonial. Colbert sided with the metropolitan refiners. In 1682 the duty on colonial refined sugar was raised to eight livres, as compared with two on raw sugar. In 1684 the establishment of new refineries was prohibited in the West Indies. The reason was stated very frankly, though the facts alleged were inaccurate:

'... the king has been informed that the planters of the French islands and colonies of America ... having devoted themselves almost entirely to the plantation and cultivation of sugar-cane, have established a large number of refineries in the said islands; that almost all of the sugar produced is being refined there; and that consequently the refineries established in France have almost ceased work and that men and refiners employed in them who have no other means of gaining a livelihood are leaving the kingdom ...'

Colonial refining, however, continued despite the ban. In 1698 Martinique alone had eighteen refineries. In that year, accordingly, the French duty on colonial raw sugar was reduced by fifty per cent, to one livre, whilst the duty on colonial refined sugar was raised to 22 livres, the same duty imposed on all foreign sugar. The colonial sugar refining industry was strangled. Colbertism thus ousted not only the Dutch from the refining trade, but also the French sugar planters.

Colbert's system differed from the British only in its more thorough organisation. The essential principles of 'the exclusive' were contained in the English Navigation Acts of the middle of the seventeenth century, and the Dutch had to fight a war on two fronts. The Navigation Acts restricted colonial trade to English ships manned by crews three-quarters of whom were English, and with an English captain. The chief colonial products— enumerated commodities, as they were called—could be carried from the colonies only in such ships and only to the metropolitan country. The Dutch protested to the British Government in 1652 against this legislation which was aimed openly at them. The Council of State of England rejected the protest, and refused to recede from the principle enunciated by the Navigation Acts, that the colonies, established at English expense, 'are and ought to be subordinate to and dependent upon England ... and hath ever ... been, and ought to be, subject to such laws, orders and regulations as are or shall be made by the Parliament of England'.

The interests of the British West Indies were subordinated to

English interests, as the interests of the French West Indies were subordinated to those of France. The refiners of England protested against refining in the British colonies. England supported them as France supported the French refiners. The matter came before Parliament in 1671, at the very period when Colbert was urging the increase of colonial refineries. Colonial refined sugar in England was then charged three to four times the duty levied on brown sugar, on the basis that four pounds of brown sugar were needed to make one pound of refined. If this was 'inconvenient' to the colonial planters, said Sir Robert Carr, 'surely it is much more convenient to England, for that by this means our plantations come to need thrice as much cask: we have also employment for thrice as much shipping for bringing the sugar hither; and we do gain also here in England the great trade of sugar-baking, by which a very great stock and number of people are employed here, a great consumption of coals, victuals, and other necessaries for carrying on of this manufacture; his Majesty's revenues by fire, hearths, excise upon beer and ale, increased'. Sir Thomas Clifford added that, if refining was transferred from England to the colonies, it would mean that 'five ships go for the blacks, and not above two, if refined in the plantations; and so you destroy shipping and all that belongs to it; and if you lose this advantage to England, you lose all'. Davenant's pleas at the end of the century for the permission of colonial refining fell on deaf ears. Brown sugar remained the 'money of the plantations'.

The British commercial war with the Dutch ended, however, with the eviction of the Dutch and the entrenchment of the Yankees. New England arose to contest the supremacy of Old England. The mainland colonies in the north (now the United States of America) became the granary of the British West Indies, purveyors of their foodstuffs, livestock and lumber, and purchasers of their sugar and molasses. 'His majesty's colonies in these parts,' wrote the Governor of Barbados in 1667, 'cannot in time of peace prosper, nor in time of war subsist, without a correspondence with the people of New England.' By 1674 the Barbadian planters were fully 'sensible of the great prejudice which will accrue to them' if they lost the New England supply of two indispensable commodities, horses and provisions—power for their mills and food for their slaves. To such an extent had New England, by 1669, become 'the key to the Indies', that a Jamaican planter asked in that year what would become of the New England trade if Jamaica were able to achieve self-sufficiency in foodstuffs.

This was not the only pill that the metropolitan country had to swallow. New England was a competitor not only in the food trade to the West Indies, but also in the slave trade. As early as 1645 New England had initiated its own version of the triangular trade. In that year a New England ship went to the Cape Verde Islands, bought a cargo of slaves, sold them in Barbados for sugar, salt and tobacco, and returned home. New England also traded directly with the West Indies. In 1643, a vessel *The Trial*, took mainland commodities to St. Kitts, where it exchanged them for West Indian products. The trial was successful. Sugar and cotton became very plentiful and cheap in New England. Governor Winthrop of Massachusetts praised God and stressed that this West Indian trade was of considerable assistance in enabling New England to discharge its obligations in England.

Perhaps these considerations played some part in Cromwell's efforts to persuade the New Englanders to migrate to Jamaica, partly to 'enlighten' the island, partly also in their own interest, New England being a 'desert and barren wilderness', and Jamaica a 'land of plenty'. There was a note of exasperation in a representation sent by the Board of Trade in 1699 to the House of Commons with respect to the progress of the woollen manufacture in New England, but the complaint that the New Englanders were not employing themselves 'only in such things as are not the product of this kingdom' applied also to New England's commercial relations with the West Indies and West Africa.

In 1676 English merchants complained to Parliament that New England was fast becoming the great mart and staple of colonial produce. England grumbled, but it was the general view that, if competition was inevitable, it was better to have New England participate in the food trade than compete in manufactured goods. Only a few French planters in Martinique and Guadeloupe discerned vaguely that there was trouble ahead even in New England's trade with the West Indies.

Colbert's system had one significant omission—it made no provision for the by-products of French colonial sugar-syrup and rum, for which no market in France was available. In 1681, therefore, the refiners of Martinique and Guadeloupe proposed that they be allowed to trade these products with the British colonies in North America, in exchange for salt meat and live-stock. They pointed out that, as there was no duty on rum and syrup in France, the revenue would not be diminished; that the income of the planters would be increased because the manu-facture of sugar would be perfected and the by-products would no longer have to be thrown away; that the need of these articles in the British mainland colonies exceeded the supply in the British West Indies; and that, even if the British Government frowned on the trade, 'the English who dwell near Boston will not worry themselves about the prohibitions which the king of England may issue, because they hardly recognise his authority'.

Nearly one hundred years before the Declaration of Independence, the French West Indian planters had formulated the basis of the irrepressible conflict between Britain and America. The French colonial planters anticipated the defiant language of James Otis with respect to the British policy of suppressing the un-lawful trade with the foreign Caribbean colonies by eighty years.

Colbert was loth to exclude the Dutch only to introduce the North Americans. He refused to authorise any modification of 'the exclusive' and rejected the petition of the colonial planters. Instead, he turned his attention to Canada. For the first, but by no means the last, time Canada was held up as a substitute for the mainland colonies as both a market and a source of supplies for the Caribbean territories. The colonial policy of Colbert viewed the French Caribbean colonies as one side of a quad-rilateral, the others being the metropolitan country for manu-factures, West Africa for slaves, and Canada, a temperate zone in the New World, for foodstuffs. That was why he placed his ban on tobacco cultivation in Canada. In 1664 he visualised a trade be-tween the West Indies and Canada, in which Canada, encouraged to build its own ships, would supply staves, hoops and headings for packing sugar, wheat, flour, dry salted eels, codfish and other fish. The Intendant of Canada inaugurated a trade whereby

Canadian vessels carried foodstuffs to the West Indies, exchanged
these for sugar which they took to France, with which in turn they
purchased French merchandise to take back to Canada. Duties on
this intercolonial trade were abolished shortly after Colbert's
death.

But the plan was unsuccessful. Canada provided insufficient
foodstuffs and other articles needed in the West Indies. In
addition, as the actual trade indicated above revealed, Canada
provided too poor a market for West Indian produce; where the
New Englanders took sugar back to New England for local consumption, the Canadians transported it to France. The Yankees,
entrenched in the British West Indies, would one day refuse to
recognise the authority not only of the King of England but also
that of the King of France, and would turn to the French West
Indies. They would find there a sympathetic reception.

There was yet another important aspect of the commercial
warfare in the Caribbean in the seventeenth century. That was
the trade with the Spanish colonies. The Dutch were the first
beneficiaries of Spain's impotence. English and French hostility
to the Dutch, therefore, was not restricted to the trade of their
own colonies. The supply of slaves to the Spanish colonies was
the crucial issue. Charles II tried to get the *asiento* for England,
but failed. In 1670 Colbert asked one of the directors of the
French West India Company to consider carefully what advantage
there would be in supplying slaves to the Spanish islands. But
his exclusivist principles triumphed, and even the Spaniards fell
under his rigid ban on foreigners.

The English were quick to seize the opportunity. In 1625
Parliament had refused to permit Spanish payment in tobacco
for British manufactures; in order to protect Virginia tobacco,
they banned this 'miserable kind of trade' whereby the bullion
that had come in from the West Indian 'fountain' of the Spanish
'cistern' was transformed into a 'a smoky weed'. In 1685 this
decision was reversed, and British colonial governors were
distinctly authorised to admit Spanish vessels into the British
West Indies for the purchase of slaves and British manufactures,
to treat them with civility and even to convoy them on their
departure, to accept Spanish coin and colonial produce in payment, to permit no unnecessary duties or impositions which might

hamper the trade, and to give it every possible encouragement—
on one condition only, that the Spanish vessels did not introduce
goods the product of Europe, Asia or Africa, which might compete
with British manufactures and British trade.

By the end of the seventeenth century this trade with the
Spanish colonies had increased to the point where it employed
annually four thousand tons of British shipping, disposed of
British goods to the value of a million and a half pounds sterling,
and remedied the chronic shortage of specie in the British West
Indies by introducing, particularly into Jamaica and Barbados,
large quantities of bullion, estimated at 150,000 pounds annually.
In addition to the legitimate trade, contraband also flourished. A
Spanish writer, Osorio, writing in the second half of the seventeenth century, states that contraband at Seville amounted to ten
million pesos a year, and that all foreign nations together, by
their contraband trade, secured six times as much of the products
of Spanish America as returned on the Seville fleets. It was the
decline of the Spanish Empire; its fall was delayed until the end
of the nineteenth century.

Herein, again, lay the seed of future international tension. In
1700 Governor Beeston of Jamaica wrote to the Board of Trade
saying that Jamaican trade with the Spanish colonies in drapery
and dry goods was on the decline, as a result of the competition
of the French and Dutch, who were able to undersell the English
by forty per cent. From all appearances, he added, the trade in
flour and provisions would be lost also to the same rivals, unless
some means were found of preventing it.

The seventeenth-century commercial system was dependent on
the political system whereby the colonies were governed. The
British developed a theory of government, the French were content merely with the practice. Harrington in his *Oceana*, in 1656,
typified the spirit of British imperialism. 'To ask whether it be
lawful for a Commonwealth to aspire to the Empire of the World,
it is to ask whether it be lawful for it to do its duty, or to put
the World into a better condition than it was before.' Far in
advance of his age, however, he uttered his well-known prophecy,
that the colonies 'are yet Babes that cannot live without sucking
the breasts of the Mother Cities, but such as I mistake when
they come of age they do not wean themselves'.

The seventeenth century had no time for prophecies. 'Colonies,' wrote Davenant, summing up the thought of the age, 'are a strength to their mother Kingdom, while they are under good discipline, while they are strictly made to observe the fundamental laws of their original country, and while they are kept dependent on it. But otherwise, they are worse than members lopped from the body politic, being indeed like offensive arms wrested from a nation to be turned against it as occasion shall serve.'

But Davenant was unhappy when he descended to particular questions. He was anxious that a declaratory law should be made to the effect that Englishmen had a right to all the laws of England, while they remained in countries subject to the dominion of England, and he realised the wisdom of conceding a large measure of self-government: 'without doubt, it would be a great incitement to their industry, and render them more pertinacious in their defence, upon any invasion which may happen, to find themselves a free people and governed by constitutions of their own making.'

But self-government was not an abstract question. It meant in the colonies particularly the Navigation Laws and 'the exclusive'. Did self-government include fiscal autonomy? Or did it mean no more than it has for so long in the history of the Caribbean, self-government and local constitutions within the framework of the articulate major premise of the metropolitan country with respect to the commercial system? Davenant was silent. But the British Government was not. In 1666 the governors of Barbados protested against the Navigation Laws. Free trade is the life of all colonies, said one. The Navigation Laws will ruin the colonies, said his successor. The Lords of Trade and Plantations ignored the first and censured the second for 'these dangerous principles . . . contrary to the settled laws of the kingdom and the apparent advantage of it'.

Colbert's methods were more direct, less philosophical, and equally effective. He rebuked the Governor of Guadeloupe in 1670: 'I am writing you only a few lines, in response to all the letters which I have been receiving from you for a long time, to tell you that I find them too long, too tedious and of too small importance to spend my time reading them.' To the

Governor of Martinique, he wrote: 'It is really not necessary that you bother yourself with the consideration of the question as to whether it would be more advantageous or not for the company to carry on commerce with the islands to the exclusion of all others. You have nothing to do, in fact, except to attract French vessels which have my passports by the good and just treatment which you accord to them . . .'·

'The world is large,' the British Ambassador to Holland, Sir George Downing, had said to the Dutch in 1661, 'there is trade enough for both, and if there were not, I do not see how it could be made more or more safe by their misunderstanding.' British policy to the Dutch—French policy equally—had disproved the Ambassador's statement. The eighteenth century saw an even fiercer 'misunderstanding' over Caribbean trade, between the British and French, on the one hand, between Old England and New England, on the other and the Caribbean would not be big enough for all three.

'The West Indian colonies are absolutely nothing but commercial establishments.' Thus read the instructions of the French Government to the Governor and Intendant of Martinique, in 1765. 'Where trade is at stake, you must defend it or perish,' supplemented Chatham in England. The two statements constitute the colonial system of the eighteenth century.

The system was a refinement of the seventeenth-century 'exclusive'. West Indian commerce belonged exclusively to the particular metropolitan country concerned. As Storm Van's Gravesande wrote in his letter to the Dutch West India Company on May 24, 1764, 'this should be a hard and fast rule, as immutable as the laws of the Medes and Persians'.

There were two essential characteristics of the exclusive. As stated by the Chamber of Commerce of Nantes, they were: First, the sale of metropolitan products is the first object of commerce; secondly, the colonies have been established for the metropolis, to consume its products, to give employment to its citizens. Put into practice, this philosophy gave rise to a colonial system in which the fundamental details were as follows: First, the colonies must import only metropolitan goods; secondly, the colonies must send their exports only to the metropolitan country; thirdly, colonial trade was a rigid monopoly of metropolitan ships and seamen; finally, the colonies must produce raw materials and not manufactured goods.

These principles, stated the Chamber of Commerce of Bordeaux in June, 1765, had never ceased to proclaim that the colonies had been founded only for the utility of the metropolis. Every departure from them was 'the most monstrous of disorders', a direct attack on the objectives for which they were established. The Chamber asked:

'Can we look without shuddering, at the frightful void that such an appalling reversal of the prohibitive laws would create in our national commerce? Can we behold, without being horrified, the enormous and irreparable detriment to the market for our local produce and to the sale of our manufactured goods resulting therefrom? Can we without a feeling of dismay, watch the decline of our shipping, see the Royal Navy lacking its full complement of sailors whom the shipping would have trained, while all classes of workmen to whom our building and armament works gave employment are loitering idly in our ports, because of unemployment, and perhaps emigrating to foreign countries to seek work and a living which their native land cannot provide; in a word, a crowd of artisans and labourers for whom the business of commerce provides a livelihood, reduced to the last stages of beggary?'

It reads, this doleful picture which the eighteenth century conjured up of any relaxation or deviation from l'exclusif, like a preview of Jules Ferry, the champion of French imperialism a century later. The Chamber of Commerce of Bordeaux concluded two years later: the 'austerity' of the prohibitive laws is the regime which conforms most with the interests of both the colonies and the metropolitan country.

The Chamber of Commerce of Nantes stated categorically in 1762 that the value of the colonies was based purely on the extent to which they enhanced the cultivation, arts and manufactures of the metropolitan country and furnished it with their produce, either for home consumption or for re-export. The Governor of the French West Indies had stated in 1716 that, if the inhabitants enjoyed free trade, and were at liberty to sell their sugar where they pleased, the islands would overflow with money. The Chamber of Commerce of Nantes replied, forty-five years later, that if the exclusive were abandoned, it would be more profitable for a nation to abandon its colonies. 'If the colonists consider themselves a separate people, they may find these

principles too severe, but, when they regard themselves as a part
of the nation, they cannot but find them just.'

The colonial system placed particular emphasis on the prohibition of colonial manufactures. In British North America copper
smelting was prohibited in 1722, the manufacture of hats in
1732, and the Colonial Manufactures Prohibition Act of 1750
sternly forbade the manufacture of bar or pig iron, and provided
for the abolition of colonial slitting-mills, tilt-hammers, and iron
furnaces. Not a nail, not a horseshoe, said Chatham, was to be
manufactured.

Towards this end, the British Government discouraged the
growth of towns in the colonies. In 1714 the English Customs
agreed to the creation of additional ports of entry on the northern
coast of Jamaica, provided that the inhabitants were not thereby
encouraged to reside in the towns and set up manufactures for
their own needs. Such a step, said the Commissioners of Customs,
would discourage British trade and would distract the inhabitants
of the colony from planting and raising sugar, which was more
to the benefit of England.

About the middle of the century the Chamber of Commerce of
Nantes drew attention to the evasion in the colonies of the
prohibition on sugar refining. Without whitening the sugar, the
planters took the brown sugar through the preliminary stages of
refining, and produced a clayed sugar which threatened to replace white sugar in France. The Chamber of Commerce demanded the absolute cessation of this process in all the French
colonies except—for some reason not specified—Martinique. In
1753 the refiners in England made similar complaints of the
British West Indies. They stated that there were seven refining
establishments in Jamaica, five in Antigua, two in St. Kitts, and
several in the other islands. The refiners demanded that the
planters should be restricted to the production of raw sugar for
the British refining industry.

Four significant breaches in the exclusive system were made in
the eighteenth century.

In the Danish Virgin Islands the seventeenth century had witnessed the usual struggle between the monopolistic metropolitan
company and the private trader. The matter was referred to the
Danish Board of Police and Trade in 1716. The chief question

was whether the inhabitants of St. Thomas could be permitted free trade with America and Europe, without thereby violating the monopoly of the Danish West India Company. The Board pointed out that the Company did not supply adequately the needs of the island at reasonable prices, nor did it purchase all the produce of the planters. It concluded that it would be 'un-Christian', in the one case, to deny the planters the chance of making their living in the best way they could, and 'a sin', in the other, that these goods should be lost to commerce. The planters, said the Board, 'ought not to be treated as serfs and slaves of the Company, since they are, indeed, a free people', and the Board recommended free trade with Europe, except with certain ports, Hamburg, Bremen, and with Denmark. Denmark's position in the field of industry and navigation was such that it could not insist on the prohibitions which were imposed in Britain and France.

As a result of a powerful agitation by the West India Interest, the British West Indies were allowed in 1739 to ship sugar direct to European ports south of Cape Finisterre. The West Indian planters estimated that they would thereby gain from fifteen to fifty per cent. The British merchants protested, in vain. A Liverpool petition, for example, stated that the measure would be highly prejudicial in many instances to the interest, manufactures, trade and navigation of Great Britain in general and of Liverpool in particular. The passage of the Sugar Act of 1739 was thus another triumph for the West India Interest.

Little direct trade, however, resulted. Between 1739 and 1753, only forty-eight licences for such trade were granted, and only five were used; the total quantity of sugar shipped was 777 hogsheads, 184 tierces, 253 casks and 126 barrels. Either the British West Indies had only insignificant surpluses after satisfying the needs of the metropolitan market, or they could not compete with cheaper foreign sugar. The real significance of the act lay in its use as a weapon by the planters, if only as a threat, in their struggle against the English sugar trust. Brown sugar, which sold in England for 32s per hundredweight in 1739, rose to 42s 6d by 1757; clayed sugar rose from 38s 6d to 51s 2d during the same period. The West India Interest was strong enough to obtain the participation of colonial-built shipping in this significant breach in the Navigation Laws, on the claim that New England ships could carry freight from the West Indies to Europe 15 to 20 per cent cheaper than the French, and 30 per cent cheaper than the English.

The third breach of the exclusive took place in France. Colbert had had, a century before, to bow to the inescapable and permit Irish salted beef in the French colonies. In 1763 the French colonies received permission to import salted codfish direct, from New England and Newfoundland.

The fourth breach in the exclusive system was the extension of the policy of free ports. This was the essence of the Dutch and Danish systems—the free ports of St. Eustatius, Curaçao and St. Thomas. The French Government extended it in 1771, by giving permission to foreigners to import lumber and livestock in exchange for syrup and rum only into St. Lucia and the Mole Saint Nicholas in Saint-Domingue. What free trade meant to the West Indies is indicated by the development of St. Eustatius, which became 'the Golden Rock' of the Caribbean. A centre of smuggling, with trade hampered neither by duties nor by exclusive mercantilist principles, the island was captured by Rodney in 1781; the value of the property found upon the island was estimated at over three million pounds sterling, exclusive of the shipping in the harbour.

The exclusive had its intellectual defenders. One of the chief was Montesquieu, for whom it was 'an established fact that only the metropolitan country can trade with the colonies, and rightly so, for the aim of their establishment was the extension of commerce, not the foundation of a city or an empire'. The distinguished legal luminary of the age, Sir William Blackstone, echoed Montesquieu. Blackstone based the colonial system either on rights of occupancy or on rights gained by conquest or treaty. Both these rights, in his opinion, were founded upon the law of nature, or at least upon that of nations. The core of the colonial system was the omnicompetence of Parliament: 'What Parliament doth no authority upon earth can undo.' Mercantilist opinion fully endorsed the view stated by Postlethwayt: the duty of the colonies was 'to be immediately dependent on their original parent and to make their interest subservient thereunto'.

Against these views there was the classic denunciation of

imperialism by Jonathan Swift. An Irishman, Swift was the spokesman for the traditional hostility of his countrymen to British
imperialism which had made Ireland the first, chronologically, of
the British plantations. Swift, with the 'savage indignation'
characteristic of all his writings, bitterly satirised European imperialism in *Gulliver's Travels*.

Where Swift emphasised the hypocrisy and brutality of the
first imperialists, Adam Smith denounced them for folly and
injustice. Unlike Swift, he was not content with this, and attacked
the colonial system of his own day. He attacked it at its very
root—the doctrine of mercantilism. He condemned mercantilism
on two grounds—the first, that it was based on monopoly,
on restriction of trade, rather than freedom of trade; the second,
for its prohibition of colonial industry, a prohibition which he
called 'a manifest violation of the most sacred rights of mankind
. . . impertinent badges of slavery imposed upon them, without any
sufficient reason, by the groundless jealousy of the merchants and
manufacturers of the mother country'.

This, it must be emphasised, was in 1776; it could not have
been written in 1676. It marked the graduation of British capitalism from the commercial to the industrial stage. In 1776 Adam
Smith could denounce the whole mercantile system as forcing
capital from trade with neighbouring countries, and from development of British manufacture and agriculture, to trade with distant
countries, from which, he said, Britain derived nothing but loss
and frequent wars. He could do this because colonial trade had
already developed British manufactures and agriculture, because
Britain and France had already drawn the profit from it, and because the wars over the West Indian colonies had already been
fought. Britain's trade statistics in 1773 disproved Adam Smith.
But the West Indies had slipped enough for the most distinguished
economist of the age to turn against them. Adam Smith's was the
voice of doom, proclaiming the end of the exclusive. Damned
by the international economist, it would soon be destroyed by
the American soldier, after which it would be given a third-class
funeral by the Anglo-French politician. What Parliament had done,
Congress would undo.

Chapter Twelve

White Colonials versus Black Colonials

The seventeenth-century British colonies were cradled in revolution. Peopled to a considerable extent by refugees, voluntary or involuntary, from Old England, who sought asylum in a new world where they could practise their faith or entertain their political beliefs unpersecuted (but, if necessary, free to persecute), the colonies early evinced the germs of that spirit which culminated in the independence of the mainland colonies in 1783. The theocratic constitution of Connecticut in 1639, the work of an assembly of all the planters, entirely ignored external authority, abandoned the English common law, and declared the word of God to be the only rule in the colony. Massachusetts flatly denied the legislative power of Parliament, and maintained that 'the laws of the Parliament of England reach no further, nor do the king's writs under the great seal go any further. Our allegiance binds us not to the laws of England any longer than while we live in England'.

The spirit of independence was strengthened by the political upheavals in England, the struggle for power between King and Parliament, and the long period during which Parliament was in abeyance. Virginia, Maryland and Bermuda repudiated Cromwell in 1649, and were followed by Barbados and Antigua in the following year. The Barbadians in 1646 informed the Commission for Plantations in England that they would govern themselves until the two factions in England composed their differences. It must have been a humiliation for the victorious Cromwell.

The colonial spirit, especially in the Caribbean, was fostered by the fact that most of the colonies were in the possession of a single proprietor, to whom an individual island had been given as a grant by the King. Thus, before the inauguration of the French West India Company, the French islands were bought and sold by individual proprietors as the planters were beginning to buy and sell Negro slaves. We are told that de Poincy in Guadeloupe administered justice under a great fig tree, and that de Parquet did the same in Martinique, choosing, however, a calabash tree.

The colonials struggled incessantly against this proprietary regime. In the French colonies it was replaced by the French West India Company—that is, proprietary rule yielded to imperial rule; Colbert replaced the proprietor. We have an amusing account of the transfer of the French part of St. Kitts in 1665. The agent for the Company described the event as follows:

'Having received the key, I opened and shut the doors. I entered and came out again. I went down to the offices, where I had a fire made, and smoked. I drank and I ate. I went into the chapel and had mass performed after the clock struck. I went into the guard-house, and I made the garrison go out, and I made them re-enter, under the authority of the West India Company. I raked the ground, and took up the stones. I cut down the trees by the root, and pulled up the herbs and replanted others; and at last I went upon the terrace, where I had the guns fired, and cried out, "God save the King and the Company!".'

The French West Indies got both King and Company. The British West Indies got the King only. But the latter had another decisive advantage over the former. To secure the support of the planters in Barbados, the proprietor in 1639 summoned a representative assembly for the first time. But the British colonies had to pay a high price for the substitution of the King for the proprietor. The agent of the island of Barbados, sent as a delegate to England to plead for the abolition of the proprietary system, offered a tax on all island produce for the support of a governor and other charges. The planters repudiated this proposal, and contended that their delegate had exceeded his instructions. The British Government remained adamant, and the Barbadians had to agree to an export duty of four and a half per cent on all commodities shipped from the island.

The British West Indians claimed, as Englishmen, the same type of government that England had. In 1652 it was reported that the Barbadians interpreted this literally and entertained 'a design to make this place a free state, and not run any fortune with England either in peace or war'. They demanded the right to elect two members of the British Parliament. In 1668 they petitioned for the vesting of all the former proprietary rights in the inhabitants as a corporate body—in effect, they asked for what would have been called a few years ago Dominion Status.

But the spirit of the planters was brought out most sharply in Jamaica. After a brief period of military rule, the system developed whereby laws were passed by the Governor, Council and Assembly, the laws lasting only for two years unless confirmed by the Crown. The planters argued, 'the governor, being the representative of the crown, his act should bind the crown, and the operation of the laws, thus passed, not be impeded or suspended by waiting for the king's determination upon them'. The British Government tried to take away from the Assembly all powers of initiation and deliberation, particularly in matters of revenue. Jamaica rejected the proposal without equivocation. In 1680 the British Government had to capitulate. The right of the Assembly to make laws with the advice and consent of the Governor and Council was reaffirmed. Such laws, however, were to be agreeable to the laws of England, had to be transmitted to England within three months, and were subject to veto by the Governor and disallowance by the Crown.

The spirit of the West Indian planters was unmistakable in the address of the Grand Jury of Jamaica to King William III in November, 1690. They complained that in the past they had been denied the laws of England, 'which should have been our swords and spears for the defence of our natural rights and privileges', and that their 'task-masters, with an absolute arbitrary power, attended with a tyrannical oppression of all that durst adventure to be honest', had denied them the freedom of electing their own representatives to make laws, being 'resolved themselves to be smiths to forge them'. According to the Governor of Jamaica in 1700, the Jamaican planters in the Assembly believed that 'what the House of Commons could do in England they could do here, and that during their sitting, all power and authority was only in their hands'. The local assemblies proved so difficult that the Governor of the Leeward Islands, in exasperation, recommended —the 'immodest suggestion' had come from Barbados some thirty years earlier—that the West Indian colonies should be annexed to England and given representation in Parliament, in order that he might be delivered from their 'turbulent practices'. It was the first proposal for assimilating the West Indies to the metropolitan country.

The issue between the metropolitan government and the colonies was not an academic one. What was at stake was the Navigation Acts. The difference between dependence and independence was the difference between restricted trade and free trade. The Barbados Assembly in 1651 passed a declaration to the effect that the Navigation Act of the preceding year was prejudicial to the freedom and safety of the inhabitants, and that it would not consider binding the enactments of a Parliament in which the Barbadians were not represented. It was the cry of 'No taxation without representation' one hundred years before James Otis. The Barbadians concluded their manifesto by placing on record their gratitude to the Dutch for the commercial benefits they had received at their hands. With the Governor as their mouthpiece, the planters in 1668 bluntly informed the metropolitan Government that 'whosoever he be that advised his Majesty to restrain and tie up his colonies in point of trade is more a merchant than a good subject'. In 1701 Governor Codrington reported from the Leeward Islands 'so general a conspiracy in people of all ranks and qualities here to elude the Acts of Trade'.

There was a vast difference, however, between words and deeds. The difference was the British Navy. The Navigation Acts remained in force. Colonial opposition was directed to evasion, the English who dwelt near Boston leading the way. The stage was being set for the drama of the eighteenth century, in which, in the tussle between New England and the Navigation Acts, the mainland colonies threw off their allegiance. So serious were the seventeenth-century infractions that the Lords of Trade and Plantations sent out a one-man commission of inquiry in 1676. The commission bore no fruit. Enforcement of the metropolitan legislation depended on colonial concurrence, in a situation where Jamaica and the Bahamas were included for customs purposes within the jurisdiction of the southern mainland colonies, where Barbados was grouped with the Leeward Islands, and where salaries at the customs house were as low as £30 a year for a collector and £75 for a searcher.

The French West Indian colonies, unlike the British, were not satisfied with words. They resorted to deeds. Two incipient revolts in Martinique in 1665 were nipped in the bud by the vigilance and promptness of the Governor, and their ringleaders arrested and imprisoned. The reasons for the revolts were vexation with the exclusion of foreigners from the commerce of the French West Indies and popular hatred of the word 'company'.

The colonial opposition, however, was weakened by the fact that it was not unanimous. The Barbadian planters stated that the Navigation Acts were the work of merchants. The interests of planters and merchants in the colonies were already divergent. The four and a half per cent duty, higher duties on refined sugar, higher duties on raw sugar, bore on the planter, whose costs of production went up and whose profits went down. The merchant's profit was unaffected, depending as it did on the amount of sugar produced, and, particularly, on prices charged for imported commodities. Invariably, the merchants being English and in England, and the planters becoming more and more heavily indebted to them, the struggle became one between metropolitan merchants and Caribbean planters. Hence the voluble protests in the French islands against the French West India Company and in the British islands against the Royal African Company; they were the protests of planters against monopolistic metropolitan merchant companies which supplied the necessary slaves, provided the requisite food supplies and manufactured goods, and took large quantities of colonial staples in exchange.

The conflict of interests was aggravated by the issue of trade with the Spanish colonies. The British relaxation of the Navigation Acts in the interests of Britain contained two implications of danger, or, at the very least, concern for the planters. In the first place, their Spanish rivals were provided by British merchants with the necessary slaves for their plantations. In 1667 the planters of Barbados protested. They claimed that the British slave traders either left the British plantations ill-supplied with slaves, or charged excessive prices for those they supplied, 'whereby the Spanish plantations and commodities must of necessity flourish and rise, and his Majesty's moulder away, and come to nothing'. The British slave traders replied that the planters themselves wished to sell slaves to the Spaniards; that if they did not supply slaves, the Dutch would; and that the slaves were used by the Spaniards not to produce commodities which competed with those of the British West Indies, but in the silver mines and in domestic service.

In 1681 the Jamaica Assembly imposed a tax of £5 on each Negro exported from the island. The Governor, Sir Henry Morgan, agreed to the tax with a warning that it was not to constitute a precedent for the future. The planters contended that the Royal African Company did not supply slaves in sufficient quantity for both national and foreign needs, and that they gave preference to the Spaniards who paid in cash. The Governor of Jamaica gave indirect confirmation of the soundness of this contention in 1682; he said that it was hopeless to think of a sufficient supply of slaves for the Spaniards when the Jamaican planters were in such need of slaves that the last ship which had arrived had more buyers than Negroes. The Assembly complained in 1689 that foreigners were getting the best slaves, and that the Jamaican planters had to be content with the refuse at £22 a head. It proceeded therefore to impose a duty of forty shillings per head on all exported slaves. The Governor vetoed the measure as repugnant to his instructions and as highly prejudicial to both England and Jamaica, 'it being the greatest blow that can be given to trade, which is the life of this place, and I am bound to encourage and protect, and will do it'. In the British scheme of trade and plantations, trade came before plantations.

The British West Indian planters seemed to have been less aware of the second implication of danger in the British policy towards the Spanish colonies—that was, the introduction of non-British tropical produce, sugar in particular, into the British market. Not so the British Parliament. The explanation was the struggle for the world sugar market. The chief competitor was

Brazil. What the English refiners wanted was more raw sugar. If Britain, said the Earl of Sandwich in 1671, could 'become the sole or principal venders of sugar in Europe, the advantages to this kingdom thereby would be more than is needful to enumerate . . .' This British ambition implied either the acquisition of additional sugar colonies or the importation from foreigners of a commodity which the Navigation Acts required the British West Indian planter to ship to England only. The conflict of interests between the metropolitan country and the colonies arising out of both implications was to play an important role in the eighteenth-century history of the Caribbean.

Metropolitan and colonial interests coincided, however, where the black slaves were concerned.

England, France and Holland, unlike Spain, were not directly familiar with the institution of slavery when they annexed their Caribbean possessions. It was necessary for them to prescribe an appropriate code of laws which would give legal sanction to the institution and make provision for the government of the slaves. The most thoroughgoing and systematic attempt in this respect in the seventeenth century was the French *Code Noir,* or Black Code, promulgated in March, 1685, and entitled 'Ordinance concerning the discipline of the Church, and the condition of Slaves in the West Indian Colonies'.

The Code, like the Spanish legislation of the preceding century, was permeated with the spirit of Roman Catholicism. All slaves were to be baptised, only Roman Catholics could have charge of slaves, slaves were not to be worked or to go to market on Sundays or holy days, marriages among them were to be encouraged, consent of father and mother being replaced by consent of the owner. Sexual intercourse between free and slave was penalised by confiscation of slave and children if the master was involved, by fines, and by the stipulation that children followed the status of the mother.

Slaves were forbidden to carry arms or large sticks, and nocturnal assemblies of slaves of different owners were prohibited under any pretext such as weddings. The penalty was flogging and branding for the first offence, and even death for frequent repetition of the offence; owners tolerating such assemblies were fined.

The Code prescribed weekly rations for the slaves—two and a half pots of cassava farine, each weighing two and a half pounds at least, two pounds of salt beef or three of fish. It forbade the substitution of liquor for the subsistence prescribed, or the custom of allowing the slaves certain days of the week to themselves in lieu of rations. Each slave was allowed two suits of clothes a year or four ells of linen. Slaves not clothed and fed by their owners were to lodge complaints with the King's agent. Old and sick slaves were to be fed and maintained by their owners.

The Code forbade the ownership of property by slaves. 'Slaves can possess nothing independent of their masters. All that they may acquire by industry, or through the liberality of other persons, belong in full right to their masters, without the children of such slaves, their fathers, mothers, or their families, or others, pretending any right to the same, either by succession, gift, or otherwise; declaring all gifts, promises, or obligations, made by slaves, to be null and void, and as having been made by persons incapable of acting or contracting and disposing for themselves.' Slaves were forbidden to sell sugar, even with their master's permission; or to sell, publicly or privately, any other kind of produce without that permission.

Owners were held responsible for actions performed by their slaves on their orders. Slaves were declared ineligible for public offices, and could not be witnesses or parties in civil or criminal matters—'in the event of their being called upon as witnesses, their depositions can only serve to assist the judge, without being considered as a presumption or admission of proof'.

Slaves could be prosecuted criminally, without their masters becoming parties. They were subject to the death penalty for striking their master or his wife, and, if the case required it, for ill-treating and striking any free person. Thefts of sheep, goats, hogs, poultry, sugar cane, peas, corn, cassava and other vegetables were punished by flogging by the public executioner and by branding.

The Code paid particular attention to the proneness of the slaves to run away. Absenteeism for one month was punished by cutting off the ears and branding on one shoulder. Absenteeism for the second time in one month was punished by cutting off the buttocks and branding on the other shoulder. For running away the third time, the punishment was death. Manumitted persons who afforded asylum to a fugitive slave were punished by the forfeiture of 3,000 pounds of sugar to the owner of the slave for each day of asylum; other free persons paid a fine of ten livres a day. If a slave was put to death on the denunciation of his owner, the latter received compensation for his value, as assessed by two of the chief inhabitants appointed by the judge, out of a public fund constituted from a levy upon all Negroes liable to duty.

Owners were permitted, 'when they consider their slaves deserve punishment', only to chain them and flog them with rods or cords. Torture and mutilation were prohibited, under penalty of confiscation of the slaves and prosecution of the owner. Owners or drivers who killed a slave under their orders or protection were to be prosecuted criminally.

Slaves were considered movable property, as such liable to mortgage. The same forms were to be observed in the seizure of slaves as of movable property, except that husband, wife and children could not be sold separately, field slaves from 14 to 60 could not be seized for debts unless sold together with the plantation, slaves born during seizure were to be considered a part of the property seized and disposed of accordingly, and in the distribution of the proceeds of the sale of a property seized the price of land and slaves was to be considered as one. Guardians and overseers of plantations were ordered to treat their slaves with humanity; they were not obliged, after their administration, to account for slaves who might have died, or decreased in value from sickness or otherwise. Owners were given the right to free those who had been slaves for over twenty years. Slaves who were their owners' heirs were to be reputed and declared free. Manumitted slaves were to enjoy the same rights, privileges and immunities as persons born free, but they were 'desired to be singularly respectful to their ancient masters, their wives and children'.

Such was the *Code Noir*. It has a great reputation and rightly so. Frequently cited as an example of the milder treatment of Latin masters, it was better than other efforts and did try to bring slavery under the sanction of law. It made the slave a chattel and denied him the most elementary rights of man. Its i's were dotted and t's crossed by supplementary legislation of similar tenor and purport in the seventeenth century. Thus the legislature of Bermuda, in 1691, forbade slaves to plant or cultivate tobacco, corn, potatoes or other provisions, or to raise livestock and poultry, or to make cloth, for their own use or profit, under penalty of a fine for the owners and whipping for the slaves. An act of the legislature of Barbados, in 1688, made slave thefts, even to the value of a shilling, a capital offence, as such thefts (the act explained) put the owners in dread of their lives, 'and being brutish slaves, (they) deserve not, for the baseness of their condition, to be tried by the legal trial of twelve men of their peers or neighbourhood'. Barbados in 1676 banned Negroes from Quaker meetings, and Jamaica, twenty years later, while enjoining baptism of slaves, made it absolutely clear that 'no slave shall be free by becoming Christian'. The Jamaica law was fortified by the courts of England: 'if baptism should be accounted a manumission, it would very much endanger the trade of the plantations, which cannot be carried on without the help and labour of the slaves, for the parsons are bound to baptise them as soon as they can give a reasonable account of the Christian faith; and if that would make free, then few would be slaves.'

'I came here,' said Governor Fénelon of the French West Indies in 1767, 'with all the European prejudices in favour of the necessity of instructing the Negroes in the principles of religion. But sound policy and more powerful considerations of humanity are opposed to this. The safety of the whites demands that the Negroes should be kept in the most profound ignorance. I have reached the conviction that the Negroes must be treated like beasts.' That was the slave system in the eighteenth century.

Its essence was that the slave, as the chattel of his master, was to work only for his master and not on his own account. The maintenance of the slave system and the slave economy demanded the suppression of all initiative or independence on the part of the slave. The Assembly in Jamaica, in 1711, forbade slaves to keep horses, mares, mules, asses or cattle, on penalty of forfeiture of the stock, and prescribed whipping for slaves who sold meat, fish, manufactured articles (except baskets, ropes of bark, and earthen pots), sugar and sugar cane, or hired themselves out to work for another without the permission of their owners. In St.

Lucia, in 1734, slaves were expressly forbidden to sell coffee, with or without their masters' permission; slaves found in possession of coffee were to be arrested and imprisoned. In the following year, the prohibition was extended to the sale of cotton.

In the French West Indies, an ordinance of 1744 forbade trade by slaves in cattle, either on their own account or on that of their masters; three years later it was prescribed that slaves selling poultry, fruit and vegetables in the town markets required a written authority from their masters, under pain of confiscation of the goods and imprisonment of the slaves; in 1763 slaves were forbidden to follow the trade of butcher; in 1765 itinerant vendors were forbidden to hawk their merchandise on plantations and in the towns. An act passed in St. Vincent in 1767 forbade slaves to sell sugar, cotton or rum without their owners' written permission, or to plant sugar, cocoa, coffee, cotton or ginger, under pain of the articles being deemed stolen goods.

To adapt to the West Indies the phraseology employed in twentieth-century Africa, the Caribbean economy was divided into the European sector and the Negro sector; the slave was debarred from the European sector. Even the opportunity of profit from his own slave garden was denied him. His inferior status was symbolised by the law relating to his dress. In 1720 the Governor of St. Lucia ordered all field and domestic slaves, Negro, mulatto or Indian, of both sexes, to wear cheaper linen or old clothes of their owners, domestics being allowed to sport silver necklaces and earrings, according to the quality of their master or mistress.

The second aspect of this policy was to limit the initiative and circumscribe the independence of the free Negroes and mulattoes in the colonies, products of manumission and miscegenation between white master or overseer and black slave. Such intelligent men as Père du Tertre in the seventeenth century and Moreau de Saint Méry in the eighteenth lent themselves to all the colonial absurdities of apartheid. The former asserted that mulattoes, like mules, could not reproduce their kind. The latter solemnly reproduced all the gradations of miscegenation which the planters produced from their game of 'washing their blackamoors white'— that is the planter slept with his daughter and his granddaughter and so on, through all the grades of incest. Thus the 'sacatra' had between 8 and 23 parts of the white; the 'griffe' between 24 and

39; the 'marabou' between 40 and 48; the mulatto between 49 and 70; the quarteroon between 71 and 100; the 'métif' between 101 and 112; the mameluke between 113 and 120; the octoroon between 121 and 124; the mixed-blood between 125 and 128.

Though free, the mulattoes were denied political and social equality with the whites. The French Minister of Marine explained the policy without equivocation in 1766: 'All the Negroes have been transported to the colonies as slaves; slavery has imprinted an ineffaceable brand on their posterity; and, consequently, the descendants of slaves can never enter the class of whites. If ever the time came when they could be considered white, they would, like the whites, claim all positions and dignities, which would be absolutely contrary to the constitutions of the colonies.' A French maxim stated: 'colour is wedded to slavery; nothing can render the slave the equal of his master'.

Thus it was that the French Government, in 1778, renewed the prohibitions against intermarriage between whites and coloured people, for, as the Minister of Marine put it, 'if, by means of such alliances, the whites ended by reaching an understanding with the free people of colour, the colony would easily be able to throw off the King's authority and France would lose one of the most powerful links in its chain of commerce'. In Montserrat a fine of one hundred pounds was inflicted on any minister who married a white person to a Negro. The British colonies legislated against the colonial custom whereby white fathers bequeathed real estate and large sums of money to their mulatto children. In 1762 the Assembly of Jamaica ascertained that property to the amount of between £200,000 and £300,000, including four sugar plantations, had been devised to mulatto children. It passed a law limiting legacies from whites to Negroes or mulattoes to £2,000 in cash; real estate, though bequeathed to Negroes, was to go to the heir at law; Negroes and mulattoes born out of wedlock were incapable of purchasing more than £2,000 in real estate.

Another act of Jamaica in 1733 provided that no one who was not three degrees removed in lineal descent from a Negro ancestor should be allowed to vote. In St. Vincent, in 1767, free Negroes and mulattoes were limited to ownership of eight acres of land, and in no case were to be deemed freeholders—which carried political privileges. The act went further and required all free Negroes and mulattoes 'to choose some master or mistress to live with that their lives and conversations may be known and observed'. The French West Indies excluded Negroes and mulattoes, free or slave, from the professions of medicine and surgery; in 1771 the list was extended to include law, pharmacy and the public service. In 1717, all free people of colour in Jamaica, not possessed of a settlement with ten Negroes, were to have certificates of freedom, and wear a public badge of a blue cross upon the right shoulder. The inferior status of the free people of colour was brought out by the act of St. Vincent of 1767. Any free person of colour striking a white person was to be whipped and imprisoned for six months. Any white person beating a free Negro or mulatto, provided proof thereof was presented to a justice of the peace, was to be bound over.

But the obvious way to control the free people of colour was to limit their number—that is, to put obstacles in the way of manumission. Manumission made little headway in the seventeenth century. In 1686, Martinique, for example, had 11,101 slaves and 314 mulattoes, who, presumably, were free. Twenty-two years before, in 1664, there were 2,416 slaves and 18 mulattoes. In 1671, Guadeloupe had 4,267 slaves and 47 freedmen; in 1697, there were 4,983 slaves and 170 mulattoes. For every free mulatto, there were approximately thirty slaves at the end of the century.

In 1736 the written permission of the Governor and Intendant was required in the French islands. In 1761 people of colour calling themselves free were to present their titles of liberty for verification; those whose titles were defective were to be sold as slaves for the profit of the Crown; and, thereafter, lists of manumitted persons were to be kept. Lawyers and priests were forbidden to accept unverified titles of freedom. In 1739 Barbados required all owners manumitting slaves to give security that the freedmen would not become a public charge. Antigua followed suit in 1761, while St. Vincent in 1767 required a payment of one hundred pounds into the public treasury, the freedman receiving four pounds every six months.

The only exception to this rule was the Spanish colonies, where manumission was much easier, as can be seen from the following table.

Colony	Year	Slaves	Free People of Colour	Ratio of free people of colour to slaves
Jamaica	1787	256,000	4,093	1 : 64
Barbados	1786	62,115	838	1 : 74
Grenada	1785	23,926	1,115	1 : 21
Dominica	1788	14,967	445	1 : 33
Saint-Domingue	1779	249,098	7,055	1 : 35
Martinique	1776	71,268	2,892	1 : 25
Guadeloupe	1779	85,327	1,382	1 : 61
Cuba	1774	44,333	30,847	1 : 1.5
Cuba	1787	50,340	29,217	1 : 1.7
Puerto Rico	1827	34,240	127,287	4 : 1

Thus colour was wedded not to slavery but to sugar. The eighteenth century saw two attempts to recognise the economic rights of Negroes. The first was among the Quakers in Tortola. Following the general Quaker policy of emancipating their slaves, Dr. John Lettsom, a brilliant physician, who, almost single-handed, founded the Royal Humane Society of England, the Royal Seabathing Hospital at Margate, and the Medical Society of London, freed his slaves in Tortola immediately after his arrival in 1767. His example was followed by two other Quakers, Samuel and Mary Nottingham, who manumitted their slaves and gave them their plantation, Long Look, to be enjoyed by them in perpetuity as tenants in common. In 1783 Joshua Steele, the proprietor of three plantations in Barbados, abolished arbitrary punishment, established courts conducted by the Negroes themselves, appointed a jury of the older Negroes for the trial and punishment of all casual offences, and, finally, in 1789, divided his plantations on the feudal system, making the Negroes copy-holders bound to the soil and owing rent and services, which involved tilling Steele's land at specified times each week. The legal innovations soon satisfied Steele's expectations, but they were too revolutionary for Barbadian society. They aroused a storm of antagonism, and Steele's society was disrupted. His death in 1791 put an end to the scheme.

The slave system was based on terror. For the slightest offence the slave could be whipped and put in irons; and only a casuist would see any protection for the slave or limitation of the absolute power of the owner in the regulation, more honoured in the breach than the observance, limiting whippings to thirty-nine lashes at one time or for one offence. In some colonies the murder of a slave was punishable by a fine of one hundred pounds in local currency, about fifty-seven pounds sterling. The Assembly of Antigua passed a law in 1723. The following extract speaks for itself:

'Several cruel persons, to gratify their own humours, against the laws of God and humanity, frequently kill, destroy, or dismember their own and other persons' slaves, and have hitherto gone unpunished, because it is inconsistent with the constitution and government of this island, and would be too great a countenance and encouragement to slaves to resist white persons, to set slaves so far upon an equality with the free inhabitants, as to try those that kill them for their lives; nor is it known or practised in any of the Caribbee islands, that any free person killing a slave is triable for his life.'

Thus was freedom slowly narrowed down from precedent to precedent. The legislature imposed a maximum fine of £300 currency and a minimum of £100 for wilful killing of a slave, with imprisonment until the fine was paid; and a maximum of £100 and a minimum of £20 for dismemberment. The same subordination of the laws of God and humanity to the constitution and the government of the islands was evinced in the case of white persons unlawfully assaulting Negroes. In 1778 a Jamaican planter brought an action against the white overseer of a neighbour who had beaten his watchman. Precedents were cited to show that a white person could be indicted for beating and wounding a slave. The Court upheld this contention. Yet, the account of the case reads, 'the jury, governed probably by the generally received notions of slavery, returned their verdict, *not guilty*'. In 1776 Hilliard d'Auberteuil stated that the slave mortality in Saint-Domingue was due not to sickness but to the tyranny of the owners.

There were four ways of escape open to the slaves. The first was suicide, a powerful weapon, practised both on the slave ships and on the sugar plantations with the deliberate intention of striking at the trader or planter. A note of concern is clear in the instructions of the Royal African Company to one of its captains in 1725 to be careful to keep the slaves fettered and locked up and to take all necessary precautions to prevent them from jumping overboard.

The second way out for the slaves was flight from the plantations. The popularity of this weapon is attested by the severity of eighteenth century legislation. Barbados in 1717 enacted that any Negro who had been a year in the island and absented himself for thirty days should have one of his feet cut off. In 1767 St. Vincent required every slaveowner to search the Negro houses for runaways every fortnight. In 1743 it was decreed in the French West Indies that runaways caught with firearms were to be put to death. Slaves found in town at night, without a permit from their masters—the pass laws of the West Indies—were to be deemed runaways and arrested. The French West Indies prescribed in 1766 thirty lashes and eight days in goal for slaves in whose dwellings runaways were apprehended; St. Vincent, in the following year, prescribed fifty lashes for the first offence, one hundred for the second, one hundred and fifty for the third, for slaves harbouring runaways, and permitted the houses of the slaves to be entered at any time without a warrant to search for runaways.

Heavy penalties were imposed on slaves taking canoes or boats. For, except where extradition treaties were agreed upon—as, for instance, with Denmark in 1767 and with France in 1777, respecting the boundary between Saint-Domingue and Spanish Hispaniola—the Spanish Government refused to surrender foreign runaway Negroes. Thus in 1768 the Governor of Cuba rejected a demand for the surrender of Negroes who had escaped from Jamaica. In 1773, the King of Spain decreed that Negroes who had escaped from British Tobago to Spanish Trinidad were not to be surrendered. They were to be welcomed, treated as 'mercenaries' and not as slaves, and to be employed in public works.

After 1772, a third means of escape was opened to slaves in the British West Indies. The British courts had decided in 1728 that slaves brought to England and Ireland from the West Indies were not free in England; the master retained his property or right in the slave wherever the latter was. The decision was confirmed by the Chief Justice in 1749; if, he said, the slave became free on setting foot on the soil of England, there was no reason why this should not be equally so when the slave set foot in Jamaica or any other English plantation. Through the zeal and

1. Columbus being greeted by the Indians

Both from: Theodore de Bry, *Historia Americae*, 1590–1634

2. Spaniards mining gold

3. Sugar: 'the greatest gift of the Old World to the New'

Both from: Theodore de Bry, *Historia Americae*, 1590–1634

4. A Spanish settlement sacked by the French

5. (*above*) The death of Hatuey. From: Bartolomé de las Casas, *Very Brief Account of the Destruction of the Indies*, 1552

6. (*left*) Bartolomé de las Casas, 1474–1566

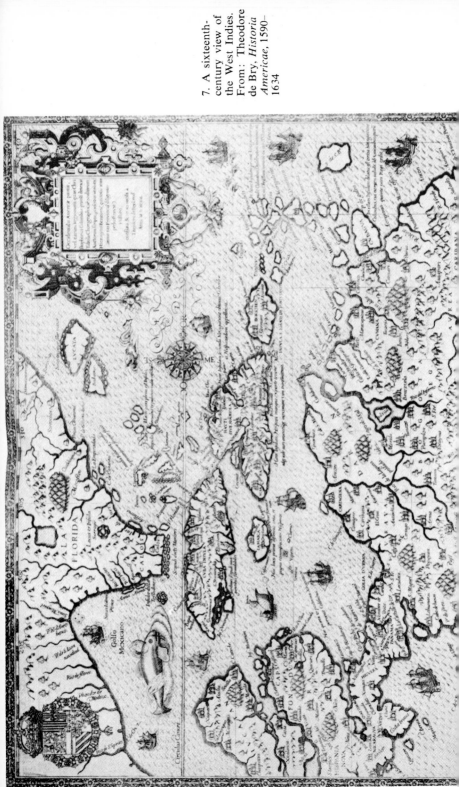

7. A sixteenth-century view of the West Indies. From: Theodore de Bry, *Historia Americae*, 1590–1634

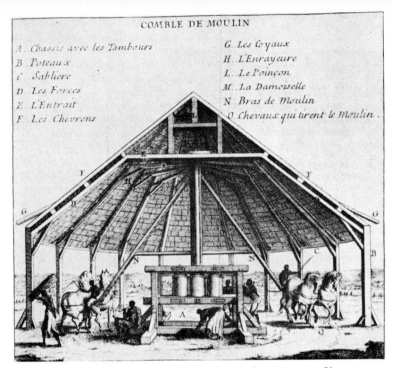

COMBLE DE MOULIN

A. Chassis avec les Tambours
B. Poteaux
C. Sabliere
D. Les Forces
E. L'Entrait
F. Les Chevrons

G. Les Coyaux
H. L'Enrayeure
L. Le Poinçon
M. La Damoiselle
N. Bras de Moulin
O. Chevaux qui tirent le Moulin

8. Cross-section of a *trapiche*. From: Père Labat, *Nouveau Voyage aux Isles de l'Amérique*, 1722

. From: Morgan Godwyn, *The egro's and Indian's Advocate*, 1680

10. From: Sir Dalby Thomas, *An Historical Account of the Rise and Growth of the West-India Collonies*, 1690

THE
Negro's & Indians
ADVOCATE,
Suing for their Admission into the
CHURCH:
OR
PERSUASIVE to the Instructing
and Baptizing of the *Negro's* and
Indians in our Plantations.

SHEWING,

That as the Compliance therewith can prejudice
no Mans just Interest; So the wilful Neglecting
and Opposing of it, is no less than a manifest
Apostacy from the Christian Faith.

To which is added, A brief Account of Religion in *Virginia*.

By MORGAN GODWYN,
Sometime St. of Ch. Ch. Oxon.

Judges 19. 30. And it was so, that all that saw it said, There was
no such deed done nor seen from the day that the Children of Israel
came up out of the Land of Egypt, unto this Day.
Acts 4. 20. We cannot but speak the things which we have seen and heard.

we must answer for our idle Words, how much more for our
silence? St. Augustin.

LONDON, Printed for the Author, by J. D. and are
to be Sold by most Booksellers. 1680.

AN
Historical Account
OF THE
Rise and Growth of the
West-INDIA
COLLONIES,
And of the Great Advantages they
are to *England*, in respect
to Trade.

Licenced According to Order.

LONDON,

Printed for *Jo* Hindmarsh at the *Golden-Ball*, over
against the *Royal-Exchange*. 1690.

11. 'A Negro Festival drawn from the Nature in the Island of St. Vincent.'
From: Brian Edwards, *The History, Civil and Commercial of the British Colonies in the West Indies*, 1794

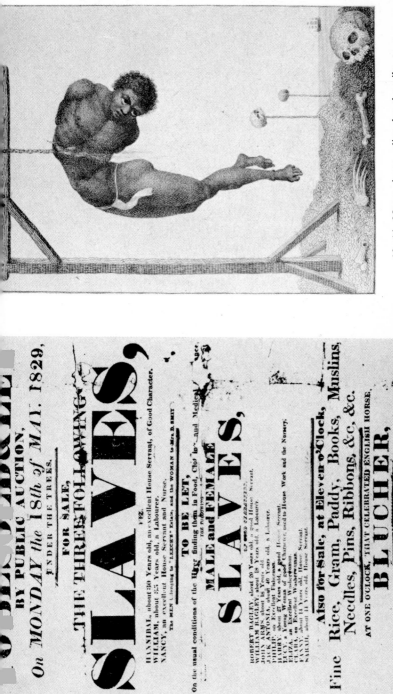

13. 'A Negro hung alive by the ribs to a Gallows.' From: J. G. Stedman, *Narrative of a five years' expedition against the Revolted Negroes of Surinam*, 1796

12. A bill of sale advertising a slave auction posted in the West Indies, 1829

14. Toussaint Louverture, 1743–1803

15. Henri Christophe, 1767–1820

pertinacity of one of the early English humanitarians, Granville Sharp, another test case, involving a Negro, James Somerset, was brought before the Chief Justice, Lord Mansfield, in 1772. Lord Mansfield did his best to avoid giving a decision, and delayed the case three terms; he tried to get the parties to settle the matter out of court, well recognising that about 14,000 slaves and property to the value of £700,000 were involved, and that setting this number 'at once free loose by a solemn opinion, is much disagreeable in the effects it threatens'.

The issue before Mansfield was whether a master who had brought a slave to England in attendance upon him could legally require him to return to slavery in the West Indies, or whether the slave was free as soon as he reached English soil. Since the parties would not agree to an out-of-court settlement, Mansfield was compelled to give a decision. Let justice be done, he said, whatever the consequences. 'So high an act of dominion,' ruled Mansfield, 'must be recognised by the law of the country where it is used. The power of a master over a slave has been extremely different, in different countries. The state of slavery is of such a nature, that it is incapable of being introduced on any reasons, moral or political; but only positive law, which preserves its force long after the reasons, occasion, and time itself from whence it was created, is erased from memory: It's so odious, that nothing can be suffered to support it, but positive law. Whatever inconveniences, therefore, may follow from a decision, I cannot say this case is allowed or approved by the law of England; and therefore the black must be discharged.'

The decision, important though it is, affected, however, only an infinitesimal number of slaves in England, and did not affect the plantations. Every planter, thereafter, knew the consequence of taking domestic servants to England, and it was no easy matter for the slaves to run away from the West Indian plantation to England. Nor did the abolitionists develop, as their colleagues in the United States later, any underground railway to spirit the Negroes away from slavery to freedom in the now pure soil of England.

The final and most popular reply of the slaves to the slave system was revolt. The revolts began on the slave ships. Such evidence as is available suggests a proportion of one slave revolt on every fifteen slave ships from Nantes. In the case of the *Diane*, in 1775, the 244 Negroes on board succeeded in capturing the vessel. In the case of the *Concorde*, all but three of the white crew were killed by the slaves.

The danger of revolt was greater on the plantations, where, in the nature of things, the slaves could not be kept chained and shut up day after day.

Denied the rights of man by State and Church, the Negro slaves in the seventeenth century resorted to the traditional recourse—revolt and flight. A revolt broke out in the French part of St. Kitts in 1639. More than sixty Negroes fled, and built a fort upon the highest part of the mountain, defended by a precipice on one side, and accessible only by one narrow pass. Five hundred men were sent to destroy them. The fort was stormed, and many of the rebels burned alive or quartered. The leader, however, escaped. Pursued by six men, whose muskets jammed, he attacked them sword in hand, and put them to flight. The next day he was shot by other soldiers, his body was quartered, and his limbs hung up in the most frequented places.

Ten years later a revolt, occasioned primarily by cruel treatment, took place in Barbados. The slaves fixed a day for massacring all the whites, but the plot was revealed by one of the slaves. Eighteen of the ringleaders were executed.

In 1656 a general slave insurrection broke out at Capesterre in Guadeloupe. The leaders were two Negroes from Angola. Their plan was to massacre all the white men, and to elect two kings from their number to rule the island. The Negroes in Basse Terre, the other half of the island, were to have joined the revolt; but, natives of another part of West Africa, they were hostile to the Angolans and remained neutral. The Angolans thereupon proceeded alone and for fifteen days continued their depredations. The revolt was eventually subdued, the two 'kings' quartered, several of their followers torn to pieces alive, hanged and flogged.

A revolt broke out in 1679 in Saint-Domingue, another rehearsal for the eighteenth-century denouement. It was headed by a fugitive from the Spanish zone of the island. It was suppressed with the aid of the buccaneers, who stormed the mountain stronghold of the rebels. In 1690 the first slave rebellion of importance broke out in Jamaica. Three hundred slaves on a plantation in the parish of Clarendon broke into the 'big house', seized arms and provisions, and proceeded to an adjoining plantation where they killed the overseer. The militia attacked them, captured two hundred and killed the rest; several of those captured were hanged. In 1692, in the midst of an epidemic, Barbados discovered a conspiracy among the slaves for a general massacre of the whites. Many slaves were tortured and many others executed. It was claimed that the conspiracy was secretly encouraged by the French.

The English conquest of Jamaica had been followed by the flight of most of the Negroes to the interior of the island, whence they continued the struggle against the English troops. The pacification of the island was virtually completed in 1657, when the leader of the main body of the Maroons, Juan de Bolas, surrendered to the English, on terms of pardon and freedom. He was made colonel of a Negro regiment. But not all the Maroons surrendered with Bolas, and their ranks continued to be augmented by runaways from the plantations. The end of the century found the Jamaican militia engaged in open war with the Maroons, who had chosen for their generalissimo a man named Cudjoe.

A revolt broke out in Cuba in 1729, followed by another in 1731, in which the slaves in the copper mines of Santiago took up arms and proclaimed their freedom. They claimed that a royal decree to that effect had been issued in Spain, but that it was being suppressed by the Cuban authorities. The Dean of the Cathedral of Santiago, in a letter to the King, explained the failure of his efforts to apprise the slaves of their error and to make them see reason. 'Although I explained the facts to them several times, I could not make them see their error, for, in addition to their deficient intelligence, they were very anxious for their freedom, and thus they laughed at everything which was opposed to it.' The Dean attributed the revolt to the rigorous treatment to which they had been subjected.

The ball had begun to roll. Here is a table of slave revolts in the eighteenth century:

1733 St. John
1734 Jamaica
1736 Antigua

1737   Guadeloupe
1746   Jamaica
1752   Martinique
1760   Jamaica
1761   Nevis
1763   Surinam
1765   Jamaica
1769   Jamaica
1772   Surinam
1776   Jamaica; Montserrat

The revolt in St. John, the small Danish island, was the reply of the slaves to a slave code promulgated in the previous year. The leader of runaway slaves was to be pinched three times with a red hot iron and then hanged; his followers were to lose a leg each, or, if pardoned by their owners, an ear, and receive 150 lashes. Slaves withholding information of the intention of others to run away were to be burned in the forehead and given 100 lashes; informers received ten dollars for each slave involved in the plot. The penalty for absenteeism for eight days was 150 stripes; for twelve weeks, loss of a leg; for six months, death. Slaves lifting a hand to strike a white person or threatening him with violence were to be pinched and hanged. Torture was permitted in the trial of slaves suspected of crimes. A slave meeting a white person was to step aside, under pain of flogging. Slaves were not to sell provisions without permission of the overseer. Slaves found in the town after nightfall were to be flogged.

In 1733 the population of St. John was 208 whites and 1,087 slaves. The slaves decided to rebel. The rebellion began on November 13, 1733. At the appointed time, slaves delivered fuel at the fort at Coral Bay. Concealed in the bundles of wood were cutlasses and other weapons. The soldiers, unsuspecting, were taken by surprise and the slaves captured the fort. The news of the uprising was kept from the slaves in the neighbouring island of St. Thomas, for fear that they, too, would rise. The slaves held the island for six months, until they were outnumbered by reinforcements of Danes from St. Thomas, Dutch, English, and 400 French soldiers from Martinique. Many of the slaves, refusing to surrender, committed suicide. According to legend, three hundred plunged to their death over a cliff. The Danish officials expressed hope that the bravery and persistence of their French allies, in particular, would be suitably rewarded in high places. Forty-eight of the ninety-two plantations in the island were damaged; on forty-one the buildings were wholly or partly burned. Twenty-seven captured Negroes were tried and executed. The money loss was estimated at 7,005 rixdollars or 'pieces of eight', a considerable sum for so small an island.

The slave revolt in Antigua two years later was a more serious matter than its predecessor in St. John, in that a more valuable island was at stake, and the revolt involved the slaves who were most comfortably off. The revolt was scheduled for October 11, the anniversary of the King's coronation; a grand ball was to have been given in honour of the occasion, and the Negroes planned to blow up the Governor's house, the explosion serving as the signal for a general massacre of the whites. The ball was deferred on account of the death of the Governor's son, and the conspiracy was betrayed by an accomplice. The chief figures in the plot included three waiting men, thirteen carpenters, eight coopers, one coppersmith, one sugar boiler, two masons, one butcher, twenty-six drivers, three coachmen, one head field Negro, one millwright, three fishermen, one wheelwright, one 'obeah man', and three fiddlers—some of the most trusted and valuable slaves. The leader, who called himself King Court, and his two generals, Tomboy and Hercules, were broken on the wheel; so were three others. Six slaves were gibbeted, seventy-seven burned alive, and thirty-six banished.

A commission of inquiry stated that the admission of slaves into 'occupations truly proper only for freemen' was an underlying cause of the insurrection, and it recommended that slaves should be debarred from becoming tradesmen, overseers, drivers, distillers, shopkeepers, hawkers, peddlers, sailors, fiddlers for gain, or from keeping horses or working out for themselves. Tomboy had been a master mason who had been allowed by his master to take Negro apprentices and make what profit he could out of his own and their labour. He paid his owner a fixed sum per month, and it was stated that the remainder of his earnings had been invested in the revolt.

The eighteenth century, before the great slave revolution in

Saint-Domingue in 1791, afforded the slaves two examples of the success of the policy of revolt. The first was the Maroons in Jamaica. The war which began late in the seventeenth century continued until 1739. The Maroons, their ranks swelled by runaways from the plantations, defeated the local militia, Indians from Central America, and regular British soldiers and sailors sent against them. Skilfully led by Cudjoe and two of his brothers, they gave the planters no peace. 'The evil is daily increasing,' the Assembly of the island stated in a plea to the King in 1734, 'and their success has had such influence on our other slaves, that they are continually deserting to them in great numbers; and the insolent behaviour of others gives us but too much cause to fear a general defection.'

There was no alternative but to make peace with the Maroons. The treaty was signed on March 1, 1739. The Maroons were declared free for ever, received an area embracing 1,500 acres, with freedom to plant any crop except sugar; they were to return all fugitive Negroes after the date of the treaty, pledged themselves to join in the future suppression of bands of fugitive slaves, and to assist in the defence of the island against foreign invaders; and they agreed to receive in their territory two white residents. Cudjoe was recognised as commander of the Maroons for life. The Governor of Jamaica tried to make out that the Maroons had been obliged to sue for terms, and that he had empowered the commanders in the field to grant reasonable terms. The subterfuge deceived nobody, least of all the slaves. The British had had to make terms with a band of rebel slaves whom they had been unable to defeat and subdue. The terms represented the erection of a Maroon state within the colony of Jamaica.

What was begun in Jamaica was continued in Surinam, where the jungle was a standing invitation to the discontented. By 1728 the 'Bush Negroes', as the fugitives were called, had become quite formidable in numbers. Expeditions sent against them were unsuccessful. In 1730 the Dutch Government decided to make an example—it inflicted all possible tortures on eleven slaves who had been captured. The slaves endured the tortures without even uttering a sigh. Their colleagues, enraged, redoubled their attacks, and the Dutch had to sue for peace. A treaty of peace was concluded in 1749. The leader of the Bush Negroes, Captain Adoe, was presented by the Governor with a fine large cane, with a silver pommel, on which were engraved the arms of Surinam, as a token of their independence and an earnest of other presents in the future; Adoe returned the compliment by presenting the Governor with a handsome bow and a complete case of arrows, made by his own hands. The other presents never reached Adoe because the detachment of soldiers carrying them was attacked by another party of Negroes, who had not been consulted concerning the treaty of peace. Adoe, thereupon, renewed the war. Six hundred soldiers were sent to Surinam from Holland. Negotiations were eventually resumed, and a peace treaty ultimately signed in 1761.

The spirit of the Bush Negroes is indicated by the language of one of their leaders to the Dutch commissioners:

'We desire you to tell your Governor and your court, that in case they want to raise no new gangs of rebels, they ought to take care that the planters keep a more watchful eye over their own property, and not trust them so frequently in the hands of drunken managers and overseers, who by wrongfully and severely chastising the Negroes, debauching their wives and children, neglecting the sick ... are the ruin of the colony, and wilfully drive to the woods such numbers of stout active people, who by their sweat earn your subsistence, without whose hands your colony must drop to nothing; and to whom at last, in this disgraceful manner, you are glad to come and sue for friendship.'

The treaty required the Dutch to give the Bush Negroes an annual quantity of arms and ammunition. The Bush Negroes, in return, promised to be faithful allies, to deliver up all deserters, and never to appear armed in Paramaribo, the capital, in larger groups than five or six. The treaty of 1761 was naturally an incentive to other slaves on the plantations; by 1772 a new group of rebels had appeared, and the war was resumed, strong reinforcements having been sent from Holland.

The eighteenth century thus saw the passion for freedom among the slaves and the will to fight for it. The Maroons and Bush Negroes were, however, far from demanding or envisaging general emancipation or control of an entire colony. Given a special status within their respective societies, they challenged the slave system for themselves alone. They both undertook to prevent further desertions from the plantations, both were used to help keep the others in slavery. While Jamaica and Surinam were first drafts of the Saint-Domingue story, and Cudjoe and Adoe anticipated Toussaint Louverture and Dessalines, the Saint-Domingue revolution differed fundamentally from the revolts of the Maroons and Bush Negroes in that, ultimately, what was involved was the total abolition of slavery and the independent existence of an entire Negro state.

Chapter Thirteen

Crush the Infamy!

The seventeenth century is an important epoch in the history of the rights of man. It saw a bitter battle of the books, a reflection of the more bitter battle of the armies, regarding the origin and nature of civil government. On the one hand, authoritarian writers like Thomas Hobbes and Robert Filmer in England, and the Catholic clergyman Bossuet in France, pleaded the cause of absolute monarchy and argued for the divine right of kings. On the other hand, John Locke, the Englishman, the apologist of the English Revolution of 1688 against absolute monarchy, stood for the doctrine of natural and inalienable rights, popular sovereignty, limitation of the powers of the executive, and the right of revolution against a tyrannical government. 'I am the State,' said Louis XIV of France. 'Better to reign in hell than serve in heaven,' was the ringing English reply in *Paradise Lost*. 'What I see as white is black if the Church so defines it,' Loyola, the Spanish Jesuit, had preached in the preceding century, launching his doctrine of perfect obedience. The supreme authority in religious matters, replied Spinoza, the Dutch Jew in the seventeenth century, 'is lodged with the individual because it concerns questions of individual right,' and the French atheist, Pascal, preached self-love and the human 'I'.

Negro slavery in the Caribbean provided a good test for these conflicting ideas in Europe. The issue at stake was the legality of the institution of slavery.

The first argument in favour of the legality of slavery was the conventional classical view, which stemmed from the Greeks and Romans, that slavery was the result of war. This was the view of Hobbes, whose all-powerful Leviathan was the only safeguard against the horrors of the state of nature, in which every man's hand was raised against every man, and the life of man was nasty, poor, solitary, brutish and short. But Hobbes went further than this. Not only was slavery the result of war, it was socially desirable. Though he allowed that men are by nature equal, yet 'augmentation of dominion over men being necessary to a man's conservation, it ought to be allowed him'. If Leviathan could have the power over Englishmen that Hobbes advocated, there was nothing to be questioned in the dominion of the sugar planter over Negroes.

Locke agreed with Hobbes' basic thesis with qualifications. Slavery was the result of war, but lawful war; it was 'nothing else but the state of war continued, between a lawful conqueror and a captive . . . he that conquers in an unjust war, can thereby have no title to the subjection and obedience of the conquered . . . captives, taken in a just and lawful war, and such only, are subject to a despotical power'. This was splitting hairs. Were the wars on the coast of West Africa just and lawful? Locke was silent. Did Negro slavery violate the natural and inalienable rights of man—life, liberty and property? Did it infringe Locke's labour theory—because of the fact that the slave's labour was appropriated by the slaveowner for his own use? Locke made the cryptic reply, that 'slavery is so vile and miserable an estate of man, and so directly opposite to the generous temper and courage of our nation, that it is hardly to be conceived that an Englishman, much less a gentleman, should plead for it'. The greatest objection, in the famous phrase of Hobbes, was the practice. At the time that Locke was writing, the prosecution of the slave trade and the utilisation of slave labour had become the distinguishing characteristics of English gentlemen.

The second argument in favour of the legality of slavery was that it was in accord with religion and Christianity. Bossuet in

France regarded any condemnation of slavery as a condemnation
of the Holy Ghost, which, through the mouth of St. Paul, had
ordered slaves to accept their status, and did not make
enfranchisement mandatory. In 1685 the Council of the Indies in
Spain reinforced this general opinion of Catholic theology. Having
obtained the confirmation of theologians and jurists, the Council
expressed, at the request of the King, its opinion on an *asiento*
that was projected with Protestant Holland for the supply of
Negro slaves to the Spanish colonies. The Council emphasised
that the slave trade was lawful where there was no danger of
the Faith being perverted, and that great care had been taken in
the pending contract to safeguard Catholicism, even to the point
of requiring the Dutch asientist to take ten Capuchin monks, at
his expense, to his African factories in order to instruct the
Negroes in the Catholic faith. The Council saw no reason, therefore, for departing from the long-established and general custom
in Castile, America and Portugal, 'without any objection on the
part of his Holiness or ecclesiastical state, but rather with the
tolerance of all of them'. The King, having examined the Council's
memorandum, 'was pleased to decide: It is well'.

The religious argument was reinforced by the consideration
that slavery in the Caribbean was justified where the slaves were
converted to Christianity. Jacques Savary, the intellectual representative of French mercantilism, in his *Parfait Négociant* in
1675, defended the Negro slave trade on the ground that, inhuman though it might appear, the Christian merchants were
enabled by its means to retrieve from a cruel slavery in Africa
people who were idolaters or Muslims, to transport them to a
milder servitude in the West Indies, and to confer upon them
there a knowledge of the true God and the way of salvation by
the teachings of priests and ecclesiastics who took pains to make
them Christians. 'There is reason to believe,' concluded Savary,
'that save for these considerations this trade would not be permitted.' For the 'perfect trader' the 'perfect trade'.

The final argument in support of the legality of slavery was
that slavery was a just retribution for crime. Is it lawful, asked
the Quaker, Richard Baxter, in his *Christian Directory* in 1673,
for a Christian to buy and use a man as a slave? He replied
that there is a slavery to which the criminal may be put by way

of penalty. No man might be so enslaved as to be deprived of those liberties, benefits and comforts, which brotherly love obliges every man to grant to another, except as a just punishment for his crimes; he who deserved it by way of penalty might be penally used; he who stole and could not restore might be forced to work as a servant. Baxter added that 'a *certain degree* of servitude or slavery' was lawful by 'the necessitated consent of the innocent'. The arguments could have been used in support not only of Negro slavery but also of white indentured servitude.

It may be noted here that these seventeenth century arguments in favour of slavery acknowledged, directly or indirectly, that the Negro was a man, and that they were not based on any alleged inferiority—except the implied inferiority of power—of Negroes.

On the other side were the arguments which attacked the legality of slavery and the slave trade. First was the argument that the Negro was a man in the eyes of God.

The French Dominican missionary, du Tertre, the Las Casas of the Negro, was dominated by this spirit of Christian brotherhood. He concluded his treatment of the subject of Negro slavery in his *Histoire Générale des Antilles* in 1671 with an exhortation to the planters to treat their slaves with charity, reasonableness and humanity, because 'these poor wretches are still their brothers by the grace of Baptism, which has made them children of God'. He lamented that the Negroes were treated as horses were in France, wrote feelingly of the punishments inflicted upon them, and anticipated that it would be easier to persuade the rich to renounce their goods than the sugar planters of the Caribbean to abolish 'the shameful commerce, sale and purchase of their fellow men'. If man's toil on earth was God's punishment for his rebellion, then, said du Tertre, the Negro suffered the most rigorous punishment for this revolt.

The same chord of fraternity was struck by Richard Baxter when he descended from the general to the particular. He urged planters to differentiate between men and brutes, and to remember that the slaves were as good as they, reasonable natures, born to as much natural liberty, men who, 'if their sin has enslaved them to you, yet Nature made them your equals'. The slaves had immortal souls, and were equally capable of salvation with their masters. Baxter condemned it as a heinous sin to buy slaves unless it were for the charitable purpose of 'delivering' them; those who had so bought slaves were bound to 'deliver' them: 'make it your chief end,' he exhorted his co-religionists, 'in buying and using slaves, to win them to Christ and save their souls'. Baxter denounced slavery which injured God's interest and service or the slave's salvation. The slaveowners were 'Christ's Trustees', the guardians of the souls of their slaves, and those who kept the slaves from hearing God's word and from becoming Christians, for fear that the slaves would then be free or their value depreciated, 'do openly profess rebellion against God, and contempt of Christ the Redeemer of souls, and indeed they declare that their worldly profit is their treasure and their God'. Not even the veriest cannibals, Baxter asserted, had done 'any thing more cruel or odious than to sell so many souls to the Devil for a little worldly gain'.

It was on these religious grounds that Baxter uttered the most passionate denunciation of the Negro slave trade and Negro slavery that had yet been made:

'To go as pirates and catch up poor Negroes or people of another land, that never forfeited life or liberty, and to make them slaves, and sell them, is one of the worst kinds of thievery in the world; and such persons are to be taken for the common enemies of mankind; and they that buy them and use them as beasts, for their mere commodity, and betray or destroy or neglect their souls, are fitter to be called incarnate devils than Christians, though they be no Christians whom they so abuse.'

But the seventeenth century recognised, despite John Locke, that Caliban was not only a brother in the eyes of God but also a man in the eyes of the world. The Christian brotherhood of du Tertre and Baxter became the egalitarianism of Morgan Godwyn and Thomas Browne. Godwyn, in his *Negro's and Indian's Advocate*, which appeared in 1680, wrote: 'some may perchance object against my spending time in this discourse to prove the Negro's humanity and to shew that neither their complextion nor bondage, descent nor country, can be any impediment thereto'. Godwyn pleaded for mild treatment of the slaves rather than 'this soul-murdering and brutifying-state of bondage'. Godwyn's emphasis was rather on the degradation of the body than on the salvation of the soul.

Sir Thomas Browne, the famous physician and author, wrote objectively and with detachment, in two chapters of his *Pseudodoxia Epidemica* in 1646, about one of the most commonly alleged indications of the inferiority of Negroes, their blackness. He rejected the two generally accepted causes, the heat of the sun and the curse of God on Ham and his posterity. Confessing that the true cause was still a riddle, he advanced the hypotheses that it was due to the 'inward use of certain water', the 'power and efficacy of imagination', 'black jaundice', or 'mutations' like those in animals. He concluded that beauty was determined by opinion, and that the Negroes, content to be black, equated deformity with other colours.

The secular note was struck also by du Tertre. Three factors, in his view, made the toil of the Negroes unbearable—the intense heat of the sun, the irascibility of their overseers, and the most painful and grievous of all, the fruitlessness of their labour; 'for they are well aware that all their sweat is for the profit of their masters, and that if they amassed for the latter mountains of gold, they never would get any part of it, and that, even if they lived for centuries, and worked more than they actually did, they would not derive a cent profit from all their toil'.

Even the seventeenth-century slave trader was not immune from the egalitarian philosophy. In August, 1700, James Barbot, a Frenchman, in his account of his voyage to the Congo, urged the officers on slave ships to adopt a 'gentle humane carriage' towards the unfortunate Negroes, who, though of a different colour and pagans, were men like themselves. There was a practical touch to this advice: 'they ought to do to others as they would be done by in like circumstances, as it may be their turn, if they should have the misfortune to fall into the hands of Algerines or Sallee men, as it has happened to many after such voyages performed'. The sermon from the slaver went unheeded, however.

But the most popular argument in defence of the Negro was neither the religious nor the philosophical, but the literary. The the noble savage, not in the sense that Montaigne had developed it in the preceding century, or in which Rousseau was to develop it in the succeeding, but in the sense of the Negro of high rank seventeenth century saw the beginning of the literary *genre* of unjustly enslaved on the West Indian plantations, the undisputed superior of his white master. The originator of the style was an English novelist, Mrs. Aphra Behn, whose *Oroonoko, The Royal Slave* was published in 1688.

The setting was Surinam, the hero a former Coromantine king in Africa, depicted as a man of real greatness of soul, of refined notions of true honour, capable of the highest passions of love and gallantry, well proportioned, with a nose 'rising and *Roman*, instead of *African* and flat'. If the nose was flat, slavery was more or less justified.

This was the beginning of the practice of singling out the distinguished African from the others. Oroonoko was contemptuous of his countrymen, the field slaves, whom he regarded as 'by nature slaves, poor wretched rogues, fit to be used as Christian tools; dogs, treacherous and cowardly, fit for such masters; and they wanted only to be whipped into the knowledge of the Christian Gods, to be the vilest of all creeping things'. Oroonoko opposed the revolts of the slaves, as did his creator, Mrs. Behn. His hatred was for the slave trade which had enslaved him, the trade by which Negroes were 'bought and sold like apes or monkeys, to be the sport of women, fools and cowards; and the support of rogues and renegades', and he was angered at the thought of having to 'render obedience to such a degenerate race, who have no one human virtue left, to distinguish them from the vilest creatures'.

The real import of the book, however, lies not in its attack on the slave trade but in its satire on civilised Europe. Mrs. Behn's hero was 'as capable even of reigning well, and of governing as wisely, had as great a soul, as politic maxims, and was as sensible of power, as any prince civilised in the most refined schools of humanity and learning, or the most illustrious courts.'

The seventeenth-century intelligentsia were silent on the most important aspect of the Negro slave trade and slavery—the economic. In a case before the English courts in 1677, it was held that 'Negroes being usually bought and sold among merchants, so merchandise, and also being infidels, there might be a property in them ...' Ten years later, another case came before the Courts involving an Amerindian, 'a monster in the Indies,' who had been exhibited in England for profit.

The permanent revolution of the slaves in the Caribbean in the eighteenth century was paralleled by an unceasing battle of the books in Europe and America over the Negro slave. The issue at stake in both theatres, for both slaves and intellectuals, was freedom. As far as the intellectual controversy was concerned, the decisive question was whether the Negro was the inferior of the white man. The intelligentsia approached the question from two angles—the philosophical, the natural rights of man; and the humanitarian, the treatment of the slaves.

On the vital question of the alleged inferiority of the Negro, some of the greatest minds of the eighteenth century were ranged on opposite sides—David Hume, the celebrated philosopher, historian and sceptic, and Thomas Jefferson, the father of American Independence, in favour; Adam Smith, the internationally famous economist, against.

Hume was of the opinion that the Negro was naturally inferior to the white man. In his essay 'Of National Characters', in 1754, he wrote in a footnote: 'there scarcely ever was a civilised nation of that complexion, not even any individual, eminent either in action or speculation. No ingenious manufactures among them, no arts, no sciences...' Not one of the Negro slaves dispersed all over Europe, he added, had indicated any symptoms of ingenuity. Taking the case of a Negro in Jamaica, Francis Williams, who wrote poetry and was pointed to by friends of the Negro as a man of parts and learning, Hume expressed the view that it was likely that he was admired for slender accomplishments, like a parrot who speaks a few words plainly.

Thomas Jefferson's *Notes on Virginia*, published in 1781, gave powerful support to the advocates of Negro inferiority. Describing slavery as a 'great political and moral evil', himself favourably disposed to emancipation, Jefferson regarded the Negro in America as inferior not only to the white man but also to the Amerindian, whose drawings, paintings, carving and oratory proved, in his view, the existence of a germ in their minds which only needed cultivation. But he found the Negro incapable of any thought above the level of plain narration, without even an elementary trait of painting or sculpture. They were gifted with accurate ears for tune and time, but it was yet to be proved whether they were equal to the composition of a more extensive

run of melody, or of complicated harmony. With misery enough
among them, there was no poetry. Phyllis Wheatley's poems he
considered beneath the dignity of criticism. Ignatius Sancho, the
Negro letter writer of England, friend and admirer of Sterne,
was admitted by Jefferson to the first place among those
of his colour who had presented themselves to the public
judgment, but was relegated to the bottom of the column when
compared with European writers. Thus did Jefferson, without
knowing it, dismiss the Benin bronzes, the marvels of Zimbabwe,
Negro music, and the poetry of Aimé Cesaire and Leopold
Sedar Senghor.

The Negroes were equal in memory with the whites, much
inferior in reason, as scarcely one could be found to satisfy
Jefferson's criterion, which was tracing and comprehending the
investigations of Euclid; in imagination they were dull, lacking in
taste, and anomalous. As white slaves in ancient Rome had risen
to the top, it seemed to Jefferson that the distinction between
Negro and white rested not in the condition of the former, but
in nature. He defended the Negro against the charge of immorality
by arguing that the man in whose favour no laws or property
exist, probably feels less bound to respect those made in favour
of others, and he asked the slaveowner whether the religious
precepts against the violation of property were not framed for
him as well as for the slave. Admitting that any conclusion with
respect to Negro inferiority 'would degrade a whole race of men
from the rank in the scale of beings which their Creator may
perhaps have given them', Jefferson concluded that the opinion
that they were inferior to the whites in the faculties of reason
and imagination must be hazarded with great diffidence. But the
differences between the two races, especially that of colour, led
Jefferson to advocate the total removal of the Negroes, after
emancipation, 'beyond the reach of mixture'.

In Europe the vested interests were less diffident. They
approached the problem from the standpoint of their sectional
prejudices and with the narrow perspectives of the slave ship or
the sugar plantation. The slave traders regarded the Negroes as
crafty, fraudulent, born and bred villains, lascivious, addicted
to the worship of snakes, and anthropophagous. To James
Grainger, a doctor in St. Kitts and a poet, who married a sugar

heiress, the slave trade was a business proposition and sugar cultivation a 'pleasing task'. Planter opinion on the Negro was represented by Edward Long's *History of Jamaica*, a classic in the literature of vilification.

To Long the Negroes were a brutish, ignorant, vile, crafty, treacherous, bloody, thievish, mistrustful and superstitious people, addicted to all kinds of lust, ready to promote them in others, incestuous, cruel and vindictive, devourers of human flesh and quaffers of human blood, inconstant, base and cowardly, devoted to every vice that came in their way or was within their reach. Long inquired: 'When we reflect on the nature of these men, and their dissimilarity to the rest of mankind, must we not conclude, that they are of a different species of the same genus?' He concluded that the Negro bore a much closer resemblance to the orang-outang than to the white man. Thus it was that he was able to define slavery as a tacit agreement between master and slave, whereby the slave enjoyed 'a more narrowed degree of liberty than some subjects in Britain, but in several respects a much larger extent than some others'. Slavery, in other words, was liberty with a difference. Long's anthropological adumbrations were obviously not divorced from the substantial profits that he was making from his sugar plantations.

By contrast, Adam Smith's broad historical perspective, the result of his attack on a world-wide economic philosophy, led him to a radically different interpretation of the Negro. In a celebrated passage in this *Theory of Moral Sentiments*, in 1759, he wrote: 'There is not a Negro from the coast of Africa who does not ... possess a degree of magnanimity, which the soul of his sordid master is too often scarce capable of conceiving. Fortune never exerted more cruelly her empire over mankind, than when she subjected those nations of heroes to the refuse of the gaols of Europe ...'

Another English philosopher, not so well known as Hume and Adam Smith, James Beattie, entered the lists in defence of the Negro, in his *Essay on the Nature and Immutability of Truth*, in 1770. Emphasising that civilisation is the work of time, that the inhabitants of Britain and France two thousand years before were as savage as the Negroes of Africa and the Indians of America in the eighteenth century, he denied that Africa had developed no arts or manufactures. Beattie went to the core of the problem raised by Hume:

'It will be readily allowed that the condition of a slave is not favourable to genius of any kind...That a Negro slave, who can neither read nor write, nor speak any European language, who is not permitted to do anything but what his master commands, who has not a single friend on earth, but is universally considered and treated as if he were a species inferior to the human; that such a creature should so distinguish himself among Europeans, as to be talked of through the world for a man of genius, is surely no reasonable expectation. To suppose him of an inferior species, because he does not thus distinguish himself, is just as rational, as to suppose any private European of an inferior species, because he has not raised himself to the condition of royalty.'

The eighteenth-century French philosophers injected into the controversy the democratic slogan of the rights of man, which Locke had scrupulously evaded in the preceding century, and attacked the institution of slavery. Montesquieu, however, became inextricably tangled up in the attempt to reconcile natural equality with the climatic theory, that, in countries where the heat was enervating, slavery was less shocking to reason. Clearly unhappy about the subject—could it have been that, a native son of Bordeaux, his inarticulate major premise was the dependence of the town on the slave system?—Montesquieu could only conclude that, in those countries where slavery was 'based on natural reason', it should be limited to a fixed term and mitigated by legislation favouring the right of the slave to his garden and to purchase his freedom. Montesquieu's dilemma reappeared in England in the historian Robertson, to whom a human being was everywhere the same, whereas in the New World men acquiesced, without a struggle, in the dominion of a superior.

Jean-Jacques Rousseau, for whom nature and liberty were synonymous, found himself in no such difficulty. Time and again, in *Emile*, in *The Social Contract*, in the *Discourse on the Origin of Inequality among Men and Nations*, he returned to the subject of slavery. Rousseau's significance rests on his demolition of the argument, advanced by Grotius, that a man could alienate himself and become the slave of another. To say that a man would gratuitously give up his liberty was, to Rousseau, absurd and inconceivable. Such an act, he said, would be null and void, for to renounce his liberty would be to renounce his rights as a man, the rights of humanity, even his duty as a man. A man, he said in the *Discourse*, might, as he pleased, alienate his possessions, but he could not alienate the essential gifts of nature, life and liberty. Rousseau thus cut away the ground from under the argument of inferiority by refusing to acknowledge any such alienation of individual liberty as would make one man the slave of another. Rousseau's emphasis on the noble savage, his resentment that the privileged few should gorge themselves with superfluities, while the starving multitude are in want of the bare necessities of life, were sufficient to make the chief philospher of the eighteenth century the mortal enemy of the Caribbean slave system.

Diderot, editor of the celebrated *Encyclopaedia*, following Rousseau's doctrine of inalienability, denied that slavery was justified either by conquest or by purchase. 'A man can never be the property of a sovereign,' he wrote, 'or a child the property of a father, a woman the property of a husband, a servant the property of a master, or a Negro the property of a planter.'

To the Marquis de Condorcet, another French philosopher, 'inflexible' justice demanded the destruction of slavery. Condorcet combined the natural rights of Rousseau with the superior Negro of Adam Smith. He begins his *Reflexions sur l'Esclavage des Nègres*, in 1781, with the following address to the slaves:

'My friends: Although I am not of your colour, I have always regarded you as my brothers. Nature has endowed you with the same mind, the same reason, the same virtues as the whites... I know how often your fidelity, your probity, your courage have made your masters blush. If one wished to find a man in the isles of America, it would not be among the people of white skin that one would find him.'

The cry of natural rights was less strident in England than in France, but it was audible. Despite his monumental contempt for the savage man, Dr. Samuel Johnson stood firmly for the natural rights of the Negro. Tom Paine, in his letter on 'African Slavery in America', printed in the *Pennsylvania Journal and Weekly Advertiser* on March 8, 1775, was equally firm. In his *Thoughts upon Slavery*, in 1774, John Wesley, one of the most powerful voices in eighteenth-century England, emphasised that an Angolan had the same natural right as an Englishman: 'It cannot be that either war, or contract, can give any man such a property in another as he has in his sheep and oxen ... Liberty is the right of every human creature, as soon as he breathes the vital air; and no human law can deprive him of that right which he derives from the law of nature.'

The philosophical attack led naturally to the humanitarian. In *Candide*, Voltaire painted the unforgettable picture of the Negro whose hand had been amputated when it was caught in the sugar machinery, and whose leg had been cut off when he tried to escape. Montesquieu uttered his famous gibe: the Negroes could not be men, for, otherwise, the Europeans could not be Christians. Diderot pointed with scorn to the paradox of slavery and Christianity. Rousseau, seeing the wretched slaves changed into beasts of burden, groaned at the thought that he was a man. Helvétius stated that every cask of sugar was tainted with human blood. Wesley, preferring honest poverty to 'all the riches bought by the tears and sweat, and blood of our fellow-creatures', was willing to see the sugar islands uncultivated for ever, even sunk in the sea, rather than cultivated 'at so high a price, as the violation of justice, mercy, and truth'. To Tom Paine, murder, robbery, lewdness and barbarity were not more contrary than the slave trade to the natural dictates of conscience and the feelings of humanity.

It was in literature that the humanitarian note, degenerating at times into mere formalism, at others into sheer sentimentality, was most effective. Defoe, whilst later suggesting methods of invigorating African economy by the slave trade, attacked in his *Reformation of Manners* in 1702 the barter of baubles for the souls of men. The poet Thomson painted a lurid picture of the shark following the slave ship. Chatterton wrote his idyllic *African Eclogues*. Blake wrote of the little black boy whose soul was white. Thomas Day's dying Negro commits suicide, whilst making an earnest address to Heaven. Savage reproached the slave traders. In drama, in Bickerstaff's *The Padlock*, the Negro, Mungo, though no Briton, is a man. Sterne was at his sentimental best—or worst —on the Negro question. He defined slavery as a bitter draught, of which many millions had been made to drink. A friendless Negro girl inspired him with the thought that 'it is by the finest tints, and most insensible gradations, that nature descends from the fairest face about St. James's, to the sootiest complexion in

Africa'. Ignatius Sancho zealously entreated his hero to give half an hour's attention to slavery. With reluctance he observed that England's conduct in Africa and the West Indies had been uniformly wicked; commerce, meant to unite mankind in the blessed chains of brotherly love and to diffuse the riches of the gospel of peace, had been converted into the abominable traffic for slaves, a subject which soured his blood. Boswell's was the only discordant note of the century: to abolish the slave trade, he said, was to shut the gates of mercy on mankind.

The most poignant literary expression was that of the French novelist, Bernardin de Saint-Pierre: 'I do not know whether coffee and sugar are necessary to the happiness of Europe, but I know well that these two vegetables have caused the unhappiness of two regions of the world. America has been depopulated in order to have a soil in which to plant them; Africa is being depopulated in order to have a people to cultivate them.'

The cotton which the ladies wore, the sugar, coffee and chocolate which they used for breakfast, the rouge with which they adorned themselves, they owed all to the unfortunate Negroes. 'You women of sensibility,' he concluded, 'you weep at the tragedies, and what serves for your pleasures is drenched with the tears and dyed with the blood of men!'

The Caribbean sugar planter was mortally wounded by a powerful intellectual attack on the very heart of his empire, slave labour. As early as 1751, Benjamin Franklin, in his 'Observations concerning the Increase of Mankind and the Peopling of Countries', had emphasised that America, with slave labour, could not possibly vie in cheapness of manufactures with Great Britain. The labour of slaves, he added, could never be as cheap in America as the labour of working men in Britain.

The French economists, the Physiocrats, as they were called, carried on Franklin's attack. The Marquis of Mirabeau stressed the backwardness of colonial agriculture and the degradation of labour as a result of slavery. Du Pont de Nemours, editor of the Physiocrat journal, *Ephemerides du Citoyen*, was the Adam Smith of France. He dedicated the journal to a determined anti-slavery policy and to a constant battle against slave labour. His first article was a review of a book on Cochin China, which maintained that free labour in Cochin China sugar plantations was

economically sounder than slave labour. Seven years before Adam
Smith, he emphasised that the slaves had no reason to work
industriously, intelligently and diligently at forced labour. Hence
their productivity was low, and their owners retaliated by driving
them to more continuous and violent labour. The constant war
between slave and master, he stressed, further lessened production,
while free labour would introduce better methods and at least
double production; the wages of the free labourer, compared with
his productivity, would thus be about half as cheap, even though
his initial cost was much more than that of a Negro slave.

Franklin and the Physiocrats prepared the ground for Adam
Smith, the intellectual representative of the new class, the European industrial capitalists. Adam Smith established the fundamental position of the capitalists with respect to freedom of
labour. In his attack on mercantilism, the philosophy and practice
of the commercial bourgeoisie of Europe and America, he denounced slave labour, the fundamental prop and support of
mercantilism, as a reactionary method of production. 'It appears,'
he wrote in his classic, *The Wealth of Nations*, 'from the
experience of all ages and nations, I believe, that the work done
by free men comes cheaper than that performed by slaves.'
Slavery retarded technology; inventions were to be expected, not
from slaves, but from free men. Therefore, more labour was required per unit of work in a slave society than in a free one.
Universal experience demonstrated conclusively, according to
Adam Smith, that 'work done by slaves, though it appears to cost
only their maintenance, is in the end the dearest of any. A person
who can acquire no property can have no other interest than to
eat as much, and to labour as little as possible'. He attacked the
exclusive itself. He wrote: 'The exclusive trade of the mother
countries tends to diminish, or, at least, to keep down below what
they would otherwise rise to, both the enjoyments and industry of
all those nations in general, and of the American colonies in
particular. It is a dead weight upon the action of one of the great
springs which puts into motion a great part of the business of
mankind. By rendering the colony produce dearer in all other
countries, it lessens its consumption, and thereby cramps the
industry of the colonies, and both the enjoyments and the industry
of all other countries which both enjoy less when they pay more

for what they enjoy, and produce less when they get less for what they produce.'

The intellectuals, with rare discernment, realised that the outcome of the controversy would not be determined by the printing press. Savage warned that, one day, 'yoke may yoke, and blood may blood repay'. Dr. Johnson drank toasts to the next slave insurrection in the West Indies. But it was a Frenchman, the Abbé Raynal, who gave the most prophetic warning of the impending storm:

'Where is that great man whom nature owes to her afflicted, oppressed and tormented children? Where is he? He will undoubtedly appear, he will lift up the sacred standard of liberty. The Old World will join its plaudits to those of the New. In all parts the name of the hero, who shall have restored the rights of the human species, will be blest; in all parts trophies will be erected in his glory.'

Where was the Negro Spartacus? He sat, a slave coachman in Saint-Domingue, soon to be known as Toussaint Louverture, reading and re-reading the famous passage of Raynal, soon to raise the sacred standard of liberty and restore the rights of the black race.

Chapter Fourteen

Down with Colonialism!
The American Revolution

By 1776, as George III wrote to Lord North, the mainland colonists had been 'encouraged . . . annually to increase their pretensions to that independency which one state has of another, but which is quite subversive of the obedience which a colony owes to its mother country'. American subversiveness and disobedience had their origin and roots chiefly in the Caribbean.

The germ of the trouble was to be found in the development of the New England merchant marine in the seventeenth century. This early competition with Old England had given New England a footing in both the Caribbean and the triangular trades. By 1700, as we have seen, New England lumber and horses had become essential to British West Indian economy. The British West Indies became more dependent on the mainland in the eighteenth century. They could not carry on their trade, said the Board of Trade in 1709, or even subsist, especially in time of war, without supplies from North America, bread, drink, fish, meat, horses, lumber and staves for casks for their sugar, rum and molasses, timber for their houses and mills. 'Their being,' said a merchant, 'much more their well being, depends almost entirely upon the Continent.'

Two factors combined to make the mainland colonies dissatisfied with this arrangement. The first was the problem of supply and demand as it affected the two areas. The British West Indies could not absorb all the surplus production of the mainland; conversely, the British West Indies could not supply all the sugar and by-products needed by the mainland. With respect to the most important by-product, molasses, mainland and British islands were in open competition for the manufacture of rum. The second factor was that the non-British sugar islands, with an economy similar to that of Jamaica and Barbados, had the same needs and offered the same advantages—with respect to molasses, the French islands, indeed, offered an even greater advantage, as French brandy and wines dominated the metropolitan market and retarded the growth of the rum industry in the sugar islands. The Americans turned, therefore, to the non-British sugar islands.

The obstacle in the way of New England was the exclusive—Colbertism, the Navigation Laws and the Spanish colonial monopoly. If, in 1681, the refiners of Guadeloupe and Martinique had envisaged that the men who dwelt near Boston would not worry about British restrictions, they were guilty of an understatement—the men who dwelt near Boston worried about no restrictions whatsoever, British or non-British. The seventeenth-century struggle against the Dutch free trader became in the eighteenth century a struggle against the Yankee free trader. But whereas the seventeenth-century struggle was one between the metropolitan countries, England and Holland, France and Holland, the eighteenth-century struggle, as far as the British Empire was concerned, was one between the colonial areas, mainland and islands, with the metropolitan government on the side of the islands.

The specific arguments of the West India Interest were that this New England trade, first, enabled the rival sugar planters to develop their own plantations; secondly, afforded a market for the molasses of these rivals which they would not otherwise have; thirdly, reduced in consequence the sale of British plantation produce, especially molasses, which was cheaper in the foreign islands; fourthly, was the means whereby much foreign plantation produce was smuggled into England, thus depressing prices; fifthly, drained the British islands of cash; finally, reduced

North American supplies in British West Indian markets.

The first allegation, that New England supplies facilitated the development of the non-British sugar plantations, was undoubtedly true. It brought sharply into focus one of the chief disabilities with which the Caribbean area has had and still has to contend—the subordination of economics and geography to politics. It was prophetic that the appearance of North America in the Caribbean was marked, almost from the beginning, by a disregard of national boundaries. The validity of the British West Indian argument required, objectively, the expansion of the British West Indian sugar industry—by new annexations, or by cultivation of idle latifundia, or by both means—in order to buy more produce from the North Americans, supply more sugar and molasses to them, and keep their trade within the empire. The conflict between economics and politics could have been averted by subordinating politics to economics. This the British West Indian planter resolutely refused to do. He refused to develop Jamaica, and he refused to permit new annexations. Mainland economic development was to be subordinated to sugar politics. The West India Interest, dominating the English public, bludgeoning the English refiners, wished also to circumscribe the New England farmers and merchants.

The second and third allegations were also correct, that the New England trade afforded a market for foreign plantation produce, which reduced the market for British tropical produce. In 1714 Boston imported from non-British plantations 1,074 hogsheads, 55 barrels and 937 tierces of molasses; 53 hogsheads, 35 barrels and 59 tierces of sugar; 27 hogsheads, 20 barrels and 44 tierces of rum. Total foreign imports into the British Northern Colonies, on which duty was paid, amounted in 1736 to 170 gallons of rum, 2,708 gallons of molasses, and 512 hundredweight of sugar. Duties collected on foreign molasses rose from £79 in 1734 to £2,100 in 1764. Total duties collected in this period amounted to £13,702. At the rate of 6d per gallon, the total importation was thus approximately 548,080 gallons.

From January, 1735 to October, 1752, 2,503 vessels cleared from Jamaica for the Northern Colonies. Of these, 763—one in three—cleared in ballast; of the remainder more than one-half cleared with from one to five hogsheads of sugar or molasses.

Every hogshead of sugar, every gallon of molasses imported into
North America from non-British colonies represented a potential
loss to the British planter. But it was admitted on all sides that
French tropical produce was cheaper than British. In 1730 the
Governor of Barbados stated that molasses, which sold in
Barbados for 9 or 10 pence per gallon, was obtainable at four-
pence in Martinique. Sugar was four or five shillings per hundredweight cheaper. Adding the $4\frac{1}{2}$ per cent duty which all British
sugar exports had to pay, it was possible to deliver French sugar
in the Northern colonies at six or seven shillings per hundredweight cheaper than English sugar.

Moreover, could the British planter supply both Old England
and New? He had been criticised for his failure adequately to
supply Old England with sugar. Rum exports to England were
about 100,000 gallons in 1700, 1,655,922 in 1764, 3,341,020 in
1776, 2,011,861 in 1783. British West Indian sugar exports to
England were 1,288,135 hundredweight in 1763; 1,584,275 hundredweight in 1787. The peak year was 1774, when, 1,962,010
hundredweight were exported. Jamaica exported 22,738 hundredweight to the Northern Colonies in 1750. The total duties collected
on British West Indian sugar exported to the Northern Colonies
from 1745 to 1751, at the rate of 1s 6d per hundredweight on
brown and 5s on white, were £9,891 or £1,413 a year. Assuming
that it was all brown sugar, the average annual exportation was
42,390 hundredweight. It is clear, therefore, that the Northern
trade with the non-British islands was based on the inadequacy
of the supplies from the British plantations, combined with the
cheaper price of non-British produce.

The fourth allegation, that through New England trade foreign
sugar was smuggled into England, need not be taken seriously.
Such importations were in accord with British policy under the
amended Navigation Acts which, in 1681, permitted the exchange
of Negro slaves with the Spaniards in return for sugar. But they
were never large. Between 1699 and 1764 they remained constantly below £20,000, except for 1755, when they were about
£22,500, and 1762, when they were about £58,000. Such importations could hardly have depressed prices. The price of brown sugar
in England was 24s 10d in 1727; it ranged from 32s to 47s in
1760, and from 28s to 49s in 1762.

The fifth West Indian allegation, that New England trade with the foreign plantations drained the British islands of specie, was the most substantial. The New Englander disposed of his produce in the British West Indies for cash, with which he purchased cheaper tropical commodities in the foreign islands. Jamaica's balance of trade with North America showed a maximum importation of £112,825 and a maximum exportation of £29,222. Not for the last time was this unfavourable trade balance with North America and the drain of currency to exercise the minds of metropolitan and local politicians.

The final argument of the West India Interest was that mainland trade with the foreign islands reduced the necessary supplies in British markets, and thus, raised prices. According to the Governor of New York in 1760, after supplying the British West Indian needs, the Northern Colonies had an annual surplus of 100,000 barrels of flour and large quantities of beef, pork and fish. In the years 1771–1773, the Northern Colonies exported the following supplies to the British West Indies:

Boards and timber	76,767,695 feet		
Shingles	59,586,194		
Staves	57,998,661		
Hoops	4,712,005		
Corn	1,204,389 bushels		
Peas and beans	64,006 bushels		
Flour	396,329 barrels	13,099 kegs	
Rice	39,912 barrels	21,777 tierces	
Fish	51,344 hogsheads	47,686 barrels	
	21,500 quintals	3,304 kegs	
Beef and pork	44,782 barrels		
Poultry	2,739 dozen		
Horses	7,130		
Oxen	3,647		
Sheep and hogs	13,815		
Oil	3,189 barrels		
Tar, pitch and turpentine	17,024 barrels		
Masts	157		
Spars	3,074		
Casks	53,857		
Soap and candles	20,475 boxes		
Ox bows and yokes	1,540		
House frames	620		
Iron	399 tons		

In 1755 flour was quoted at 17s per hundredweight in New
York; in 1774–1775 it was selling at from 15s to 25s in Barbados,
from 20s to 30s in the Leeward Islands. Beef, quoted at 50s per
barrel in New York in 1755, sold for 60s to 70s in Barbados in
1774–1775, from 50s to 80s in the Leeward Islands. Corn,
quoted at 2s 3d per bushel in New York in the first year, sold
for 2s 6d to 3s 9d in Barbados, 2s 6d to 6s 3d in Jamaica,
4s to 8s in the Leeward Islands in the second. The West Indies
were learning the lessons of the world market. They were luckier
then than they have been at other times in the relationship between import and export prices. In 1755 brown sugar sold in
England for 34s 3d per hundredweight; in 1774 the price varied
from 27s to 44s per hundredweight.

What did all these allegations amount to? That, in the interest
of the British West Indian sugar planter, the Northern Colonies
should restrict their production and buy in the dearest market.
The British West Indian planter wished to milk the whole empire
dry in order to maintain monopoly prices for his restricted output. Every one was to bow down and worship King Sugar.

The mainland colonies refused. They submitted memoranda to
the Board of Trade regarding the importance of West Indian
trade to their economic development. Thomas Banister, for
example, pointed out in an essay on the trade of New England,
in 1715, that the trade with the foreign colonies provided a market
for small horses which could not otherwise be disposed of,
afforded employment to a great number of ships and sailors,
disposed of much soap, candles, beer, casks, hay, oats, onions,
apples, pork, beef, staves, boards, butter, flour and fish, to the
benefit of both tradesmen and farmers, and had given rise to the
profitable distilling industry.

In 1764 Rhode Island petitioned the Board of Trade, pointing
out that, through this trade, Rhode Island had been able to
establish over thirty distilleries, to export annually 1,800 hogsheads of rum to the slave coast, and to make yearly remittances
to England of £40,000. 'This distillery,' said the colony, 'is the
main hinge upon which the trade of the colony turns, and many
hundreds of persons depend immediately upon it for a subsistence.' The Governor of the colony warned Chatham in 1760,
that, if the trade were stopped, the farmers, who could not sell

their surplus, would 'of course change the manner of their industry, and improvement, and, compelled by necessity, must set about making those things they cannot live without, and now rendered unable to purchase from their Mother Country'. The Governor of New York added another and grimmer warning: 'it is difficult,' he said, 'to prosecute with success against the bent of the people,' and he told Chatham that the New Englanders were 'under the prejudice' that the sugar islands had gained a preference inconsistent with the true interest of England.

One can hardly be surprised, as Banister pointed out, that the mainland colonies should be so desirous of keeping their trade. All the inhabitants echoed his words, that the opposition of the British planters stemmed rather from 'the effect of pique than any public interest'.

The arbiter in the complex conflict of sectional interests was Parliament. It might have paused to reflect as to whether it was more reprehensible for the North Americans to supply the foreign colonies with lumber and livestock than for the British to supply them with slaves; or for the North Americans to take foreign sugar and molasses in payment than for the British to take Spanish sugar; or for the North Americans to smuggle foreign produce into the mainland than for the British to smuggle British produce into the Spanish colonies. It might have occurred to Parliament also that the New England trade was only an illustration of the right of British subjects to sail the seas of America which Parliament itself had enunciated in 1739.

Whatever the cogitations of Parliament on these nuances of international trade in the eighteenth century, it laid it down decisively, according to an American merchant, in the omnicompetence lauded by Blackstone, 'as a fundamental that the Islands were the only useful colonies we had and that the continent was rather a nuisance'. Sugar politics reigned supreme. By the Molasses Act of 1733 and the Sugar Duties Act of 1764, the New England trade with the foreign sugar colonies was subjected to heavy duties, which, by the latter act, were strictly enforced.

Britain sided with the sugar colonies. Chatham, friend of Beckford, the absentee Jamaican planter, condemned the trade as illegal, most pernicious, dangerous and ignominious, subversive of all laws, and highly repugnant to the well-being of England, and he called for exemplary and condign punishment of the culprits. Postlethwayt, the mercantilist propagandist, agreed, adding that it had contributed to reducing the dependency of the mainland colonies, and to alienating their affections from England to France. But Postlethwayt blamed equally the West Indian planters, though it was not in his power, as it was certainly in Chatham's, to make it to the interest of the Americans to respect the laws. He asked why it was, in view of the mainland trade with the French colonies, proper laws had not been enacted to bring more land into cultivation in the British islands, in order to make sugar, rum and molasses as cheap as they were in the French islands. This was in 1757. Six years later, in 1763, the British Government restored Cuba, Martinique and Guadeloupe, and, in the following year, passed the Sugar Duties Act. If the Americans were to remain in the empire, they had to abide by its commercial system.

Much virtue in that 'if'! There was another alternative, which the British Government seemed not to have envisaged, despite the warnings from the colonies—that the Americans would not remain in the empire. Sugar, the darling of mercantilism, led inevitably to the revolution which destroyed mercantilism.

'We know,' resolved the Assembly of Massachusetts in 1771, 'of no Commissioner of H.M. Customs nor of any revenue H.M. has a right to establish in North America: we know and we feel a tribute levied and extorted from those who, if they have property, have a right to the absolute disposal of it...' Massachusetts had repealed the Navigation Acts. James Otis, fulfilling the prophecy of the seventeenth-century planters in Guadeloupe and Martinique, boasted that not even the King of England, encamped on Boston Common at the head of 20,000 men, could enforce obedience to the Sugar Duties Act and provided the slogan—'no taxation without representation'.

Chatham, blind to the real issue, perhaps willing to yield the shadow where he had denied the substance, poured out empty rhetoric in which he failed to the very end to see that he had chosen sugar and could not have North America as well. Rejoicing that America had resisted the Stamp Act, he called upon England to assert her sovereign authority 'in as strong terms as can be devised, and be made to extend to every point of legislation whatsoever; that we may bind their trade, confine their manufactures, and exercise every power whatsoever—except that of taking money out of their pockets without their consent'.

What was at issue was not taking money out of the pockets of the Americans, but preventing them from putting money into their pockets. Chatham, in his shallowness, saw only stamps and was blind to molasses. George III, more realistic than Chatham, understood what was involved. The crux of the matter was that Parliamentary declaration of 1766—that 'the King's Majesty, by and with the advice and consent of Parliament, had, hath, and of right ought to have, full power and authority to make laws and statutes of sufficient force and validity to bind the colonies...in all cases whatsoever'. The mainland colonies rejected the declaration and rebelled. Blows only could decide, as George III recognised.

The American revolution against colonialism met much sympathy among the colonials in the Caribbean, where the same conflict between metropolitan and colonial interests was everywhere in evidence. In 1717 and again in 1723, the Cuban tobacco growers had revolted against Spanish absolutism and mercantilism. St. Eustatius became the first territory in the New World to recognise the independence of the United States. A contingent of troops from Saint-Domingue, mulattoes and Negroes, fought under Lafayette by the side of George Washington.

In the British West Indies also, the North American revolutionaries found support. The stamps were publicly burned, to the accompaniment of shouts of liberty. In 1766 the Jamaica Assembly resolved that it had all the privileges of the House of Commons, and that no instructions from the King or his ministers could abridge or annihilate those privileges. Faced with the threat of the North Americans to stop exports to the islands, the Assembly remonstrated with the British Government on behalf of the mainland. A petition in December, 1774, while professing the conventional loyalty, declared it to be an established principle that no part of His Majesty's dominions could legislate for any other part, and that no law could bind Englishmen which had not received the assent of their representatives. The petition denied the claim that Parliament had a right to legislate for the colonies. Whilst accepting the commercial system, the Assembly demanded that no laws injurious to its constituents should be enacted and forced upon them in the future. The petition concluded with the declaration that colonial dependence upon the metropolitan country was dissolved when the colonials were deprived of equal rights with Englishmen. The Secretary of State for the Colonies voiced public indignation in England by dubbing the conduct of the Jamaica Assembly indecent, and even criminal. The North Americans, on the other hand, extended votes of thanks.

Bermuda went further than this and sent delegates to the Continental Congress. The Assembly of Barbados also viewed the North American case with sympathy. The Bahamas openly supported the mainland colonies. But for the British Navy, it would have been impossible to prevent the British West Indies from joining the Revolution.

The immediate effect of the American Revolution on the Caribbean, especially the British Caribbean territories was economic. On the one hand, the adherence of France and Spain to the cause of the mainland colonies meant the temporary admission of American ships into the French and Spanish colonies. On the other, the mainland ports were closed to British Caribbean produce and exports to the islands were prohibited. 'God only knows,' wrote a planter in Nevis, 'what will become of us. We must either starve or be ruined.' It was worse. The British West Indies starved in the short run and were ruined in the long.

Between 1780 and 1787, fifteen thousand slaves died of famine in Jamaica. By 1788, one hundred slaves had died in Antigua, and about four hundred in Nevis. Between March and September, 1778, over three hundred whites fled from St. Kitts to escape court action for the recovery of debts. Barbados suffered severely from the shortage of supplies. Prices rose steeply, as is indicated in the table below.

Commodity	Colony	Before the War	After the War	
Rice, per cwt.	Barbados	12/6	30/–	(1784)
	Jamaica	13/9 to 20/–	42/6 to 70/–	(1785)
	Leeward Islands	18/– to 24/–	38/– to 41/3	(1785)
Flour, per cwt.	Jamaica	15/– to 20/–	20/– to 50/–	(1785)
	Leeward Islands	20/– to 30/–	30/– to 45/–	(1785)
Beef, per barrel	Barbados	50/–	60/–	(1784)
	Leeward Islands	50/– to 80/–	80/– to 132/–	(1785)
Lumber, per thousand	Barbados	80/–	160/–	(1784)
	Jamaica (pitch pine)	160/– to 240/–	240/– to 600/–	(1785)

Horses, each	Barbados	£20	£30	(1784)
	Leeward Islands	£16.10 to £35	£30 to £70	(1785)
Cattle, each	Barbados	£5 to £7.10	£10	(1784)
	Leeward Islands	£16.10 to £19.16	£20 to £40	(1785)
Red oak staves, per thousand	Jamaica	£6 to £12	£10 to £18	(1785)
	Leeward Islands	£5 to £18	£12 to £15	(1785)
Corn, per bushel	Barbados	2/6	3/9	(1784)
	Jamaica	2/6 to 6/3	7/6	(1785)
	Leeward Islands	4/– to 8/–	8/3 to 10/–	(1785)

The situation was even worse with respect to Caribbean exports, which had to run the gauntlet of hostile navies and privateers. Insurance on vessels for Great Britain rose to 23 per cent. Freight rates soared. British West Indian sugar exports to Great Britain declined from 1,934,080 hundredweight in 1775 to 1,300,056 in 1780; exports of rum from 2,305,789 gallons to 1,617,808; exports of coffee from 5,483,100 pounds to 2,075,600; exports of cocoa from 533,200 pounds to 411,400. From March, 1774 to March, 1775, 354 vessels from the West Indies, with 131,778 casks of sugar, arrived in the port of London; from March, 1777 to March 1778, the number declined to 243, with 76,700 casks. Only 9,554 casks arrived in the year March, 1782 to March, 1783. The price of sugar in England rose from 25s to 39s per hundredweight in 1775 to 50s to 105s in April, 1778. British consumption of sugar declined by 36,000 hogsheads in 1780, compared with the annual average of the six preceding years; in 1781, it was 30,000 less than in 1780. The number of refineries in London dropped from 159 before the war to 125 in 1781. So serious was the situation that, despite the protests of the West India Interest, which was powerful enough to defeat petitions of the refiners for the admission of foreign sugar, the importation of sugar was permitted from British colonies which had passed into French occupation during the war.

To make matters worse for the British West Indian planters, the duty on sugar, which was 6s 3d per hundredweight in 1776 was increased progressively until, by July, 1782, it was 12s 3d, almost double. This was like flaunting a red flag before an enraged bull. The Jamaica Assembly sent a memorial to the King which read: 'Permit us to speak with freedom. You have visited

us, under all our calamities of war and tempest, with an additional
burden of taxes which will drive your faithful subjects from their
land. You must relieve us, or we must abandon the colony.'
Their plea was utterly disregarded.

In 1783 the independence of the mainland colonies was internationally recognised and a new competitor for Adam's inheritance appeared on the scene. The United States view was
explicitly stated by John Quincy Adams, on June 23, 1783: 'The
commerce of the West India Islands is a part of the American
system of commerce. They can neither do without us, nor we
without them. The Creator has placed us upon the globe in such
a situation that we have occasion for each other.' West Indian
dependence on the mainland was not new. But time would show
what both England and the United States would do about the
laws of the Creator. What is more important, however, is that
Adams was referring not to the British West Indies but to all
the West Indian islands. Asked by the Spanish Government in
1782 whether the United States would co-operate with Spain in
suppressing illegal trade by United States citizens with the
Spanish colonies, Robert Livingston, the first Secretary of State
for Foreign Affairs in the new republic, answered emphatically,
No! 'Without a free admission of all kinds of provisions into the
Islands,' he wrote to Benjamin Franklin in 1782, 'our agriculture
will suffer extremely.'

The Caribbean planters dotted the i's and crossed the t's. In
April, 1783, the British West Indian planters and merchants made
representations to the British Government: 'the permission of
American ships, as heretofore, freely to bring the produce of the
dominions of the United States to the sugar colonies, and take
back our produce in return, is so obviously essential, that they
need not adduce any further arguments in support of that proposition'. Did they realise the full implications of the 'as heretofore'
and appreciate that it had led to the Revolution? Perhaps not.

The system of mercantilism hung in the balance. The inveterate
opponent of that system, Adam Smith, pleaded, towards the end
of 1783, for the continuation of economic relations between mainland and islands. Any interruptions, he significantly emphasised,
would hurt the British West Indies more than the United States.
But the year—and the era—ended ominously for the British

West Indies. Lord Sheffield, in a powerful work, *Observations on the Commerce of the United States*, in 1783, demanded the Navigation Laws, the whole Navigation Laws, and nothing but the Navigation Laws: 'The Navigation Act, the basis of our great power at sea, gave us the trade of the world. If we alter that Act, by permitting any state to trade with our islands ... we desert the Navigation Act. and sacrifice the marine of England ...'

West Indian history is indeed nothing but a record of the follies and foibles of mankind. It was the Navigation Act which had caused the American Revolution. Lord Sheffield's ignorance, bliss to himself though it might be, spelled ruin for the British West Indies. That the abandonment of the Navigation Act would sacrifice the marine of England was questioned by Adam Smith and disproved by later statistics. Lord Sheffield did not seem to realise that the enforcement of the Navigation Act would mean the sacrifice of the British West Indies. On its death bed, with the death rattle in its throat, mercantilism would not release its stranglehold on the colonies. It went to its grave with the preservation of metropolitan interests and the subordination of colonial interests embroidered on its shroud.

'The Americans had refused to trade with Great Britain, it was but just that they be not suffered to trade with any other nation.' So ruled Lord North, the British Prime Minister, in 1784. United States commercial relations with the British West Indies came under the ban of the British Navigation Laws. In 1783 orders in council were issued by the British Government regulating the trade between the United States and the British islands. Imports of lumber, livestock, grain, flour, and bread were permitted in British ships; exports of sugar, rum, molasses, coffee, cocoa, ginger and pimento were allowed on payment of duties. United States ships were entirely excluded from the trade, and imports of United States fish and meat were forbidden in the interests of Newfoundland and Ireland, respectively. As a sop to the British West Indies, the British Government held out Canada as a substitute for the United States.

Between 1771 and 1773 Canada had shipped the following supplies to the British West Indies—for the sake of comparison, they are also given as a ratio of the imports from the thirteen colonies which have already been given above:

Commodity	Imports from Canada	*Ratio to Imports from the* 13 Colonies
Boards and timber, feet	232,040	1 : 34
Shingles	185,000	1 : 32
Staves	27,350	1 : 2,120
Hoops	16,250	1 : 290
Corn, bushels	24	1 : 50,182
Peas and beans, bushels	1,017	1 : 63
Flour, barrels	991	1 : 400

The mainland colonies, in the same period, had exported to
the British West Indies 114 hogsheads, seventy-three barrels,
seven quintals and five kegs of fish for every one hogshead,
barrel, quintal and keg, respectively, exported from Canada. To
substitute Canada for the United States, therefore, was tantamount
to increasing the difficulties of the West Indies. But the West
Indians were no longer the cock of the imperial roost. 'It cannot
be surely inferred,' wrote a diehard, Chalmers, 'that 72,000
masters with 400,000 slaves form a community of sufficient bulk
to whose gratifications the interest and even independence of the
nation ought to be sacrificed'. Arthur Young, the champion of the
agricultural interests of England, sided with the government.

The relative importance of supplies from the two areas, despite
the restrictions imposed on United States supplies, is brought
out in the following table of imports in the years immediately
after the independence of the United States:

	Jamaica Imports (July 1783–Feb. 1785)		*Barbados Imports* (Oct. 1784–1785)	
Commodity	U.S.A.	CANADA	U.S.A.	CANADA
Bread and flour, barrels	50,686	10	11,420	551
Rice, barrels	2,241	381	421	–
Corn and peas, bushels	20,832	–	22,187	400
Lumber, thousand feet	1,575,589	99,237	1,974	571
Staves and shingles	2,521,000	unspecified	3,854,000	892,000
Fish, hogsheads	–	2,681	–	1,458
Horses	–	–	595	–

Where 30 ships entered Jamaica from Canada, 253 ships, that

is, British ships, entered from the United States. In Barbados, the numbers were 36 and 89 respectively.

Conversely, the United States, as a market for British West Indian produce, was also more valuable than Canada. Exports of sugar to the United States declined from 47,595 hundredweight in 1784 to 19,921 in 1787, when exports to Canada were 9,891 hundredweight; exports of rum to the United States declined from 2,742,277 gallons in 1784 to 1,620,205 in 1787, when 874,580 gallons were exported to Canada. In 1787, 386 ships cleared from British West Indian ports for the United States, as compared with 215 for Canada.

The Americans, with their long experience, turned to round-about trade—they shipped their products to the Dutch and Danish free ports, whence they were introduced into the British islands at a profit estimated at from 50 to 100 per cent, while Canadian produce could sometimes not be disposed of. As the Governor of St. Vincent wrote in 1785:

'... the Americans find nearly the same demand as formerly, and consequently are only irritated, not injured by the restrictions ... their trade is thrown into a new channel, not destroyed by their separation from the Mother Country, while our natural enemies derive advantage by their Islands becoming deposits for all American goods, and their ports are crowded with their vessels.'

The British West Indians, thereupon, demanded an extension of the free port system. Eventually, in 1787, the British Government forbade the entry of any flour, bread, rice, wheat, other grains and lumber from the foreign West Indies into the British West Indies, except in cases of emergency, for a limited period, and in British ships. So general did the emergency become that, by 1793, the President of the Board of Trade expressed his apprehension that 'every port in our West India islands will apply to be made a free port from a sense of the great advantages to be derived therefrom'.

The United States fully appreciated the importance of the West Indian trade. Access to the West Indies, wrote Jefferson in 1785, was indispensably necessary, and he considered ways and means of forcing open the door that had been closed in his face—for example, by making trade with the United States, which was so valuable to Britain that it was allowed to continue after independence free from all restrictions and discriminations, the price of trade with the West Indies. The British discriminations hit the United States in its most vulnerable spot. If ever the United States had a Navigation Law, wrote Jefferson to Washington in 1788, it should confine exports rather than imports— unlike the European exclusive—to national ships or to ships of nations with whom the United States had treaties. As if American anti-colonialism was no more than European colonialism writ large, though in a different script, Jefferson envisaged the domestic production of sugar from the maple in the United States which would inevitably affect the export trade in the West Indies. But his concern was that the United States needed access not to the British West Indies but to all the West Indian islands, and, not for the last time, envisaged that Europe's troubles would be the United States' opportunity. In a war between Britain and France, France would, in his opinion, have to open up her West Indian ports, whilst he appreciated that the vicinity of the United States to the West Indies was a bridle which, with a small naval force, could be held in the mouths of the most powerful countries of Europe.

For the time being, however, the United States was prepared to negotiate the differences. John Jay was sent to Britain, and, after long wrangling, he was able in 1794, when France and Britain were already at war, and after France had admitted United States ships on the same footing as French ships into the French colonies, to negotiate a treaty. By this treaty United States vessels not exceeding seventy tons were to be allowed to import United States produce and manufactures into the British West Indies for the duration of the war and for two years thereafter, without discriminating duties. On the other hand, these United States vessels were allowed to export West Indian produce to the United States only, the United States pledging itself to prohibit its transportation from either its own harbours or those of the British West Indies to other parts of the world. It was an attempt on the part of the British Government not to help the British West Indies but to reserve to Britain the carrying trade and manufacture of colonial produce. The United States Senate accordingly rejected that article of the treaty which restricted the carrying trade of the country. Trade relations between the United States and the British West Indies remained on their pre-war basis.

It would have been amusing, if so much was not at stake. The British West Indian planters, with metropolitan support, had tried, as the legendary Procrustes had treated those of his guests who were too tall, to lop off superfluous mainland trade in order to make it fit the British West Indian bed. The mainland colonists had refused and seceded. As they were still too long after 1783, the British Government, this time in the face of opposition from the West Indian Governors, merely resorted to the expedient of declaring an emergency and temporarily admitting supplies from the United States from time to time. The following tables indicate the extent of the failure of the British Government's policy:

Imports into St. Vincent, 1794–1805

Commodity	United Kingdom	Canada	USA, British Ships	USA, U.S. Ships
Staves	23,960	129,500	1,122,300	7,025,000
Hoops	3,830,100	141,950	17,000	384,900
Lumber, feet	–	940,500	466,000	32,237,000
Bread & Flour, barrels	16,307	3,384	15,136	67,036
Beef & Pork, barrels	23,588	1,216	443	15,393
Dried Fish, quintals	2,485	110,768	464	28,169
Pickled Fish, barrels	19,949	5,788	1,168	6,405

Imports into St. Lucia, 1803–1806

Flour, barrels	–	–	150	13,096
Bread, barrels	–	–	120	1,115
Corn, bushels	–	500	–	5,269
Codfish, quintals	–	2,713	–	20,322
Pickled Fish, barrels	15	230	–	1,765
Beef, barrels	595	–	–	2,944
Pork, barrels	1,689	–	–	771
Boards, thousands	–	58	–	5,305
Shingles, thousands	–	49	30	7,550

Imports into Tobago, 1805–1807

	Canada	USA
Flour, barrels	73	3,336
Biscuit, barrels	–	224
Cornmeal, bushels	–	3,544
Beef & Pork, barrels	101	1,412
Dried Fish, quintals	796	1,486
Pickled Fish, cwt.	2,751	3,373

Imports into Tobago, 1805–1807 (continued)

	Canada	USA
Lumber, feet	9,027	1,983,170
Staves & Heads	1,567	926,439
Hoops	833	30,093
Shingles	7,000	1,631,798
Value of imports £	7,600	96,786

Lord North had failed. United States trade with the British West Indies could not be stopped. Without it, the islands would have starved. Restrictions, as Adam Smith had warned, did more damage to the British West Indies than they did to the United States. Jay's treaty sought to restrict British West Indian exports to the United States to those for domestic consumption only. The United States, having rejected the treaty, turned to the non-British islands, particularly the French. The following table of United States exports of West Indian produce to European markets tells its own tale of the effect on the British West Indian economy:

Year	Coffee (pounds)	Sugar (pounds)	Year	Coffee (pounds)	Sugar (pounds)
1791	962,977	74,504	1798	49,580,927	51,703,963
1792	2,134,742	1,176,156	1799	31,987,088	78,821,751
1793	17,580,049	4,539,809	1800	38,597,479	56,432,516
1794	33,720,983	20,721,761	1801	45,106,494	97,565,732
1795	47,443,179	21,377,747	1802	36,501,998	61,063,820
1796	62,385,117	34,848,644	1803	10,294,693	23,223,849
1797	44,521,887	38,366,262	1804	48,312,713	74,964,366

Whilst, despite British supremacy of the seas, foreign tropical produce thus continued to find its way into the European market, British West Indian exports to Britain were increasing, but only because of the addition of the foreign territories occupied by the British during the war. In 1783, the British West Indies exported 1,584,275 hundredweight of sugar to Britain; in 1791, 1,808,950 hundredweight; in 1804, 3,125,101 hundredweight. Rum exports, 2,011,861 gallons in 1783, were 2,756,329 in 1804; coffee exports rose from 17,272 hundredweight in 1783 to 328,013 hundredweight in 1804. Total British imports of sugar from all sources were 2,241,921 hundredweight in 1793; 3,397,025 hundredweight in

1804. After allowing for re-exports, British consumption stood at 1,939,640 hundredweight in 1793; 2,670,008 in 1804. The market was glutted, precisely at the time when Bonaparte was about to attack Britain in her most vulnerable spot, her export trade. In 1799, as a result of speculations in sugar following the revolution in Saint-Domingue eighty-two firms in England, the majority connected with West Indian trade, went bankrupt, with engagements totalling two and a half million pounds. A progressive deterioration took place in British West Indian production. After 1800 the sugar planter's profit declined to 2½ and even 1¾ per cent. Between 1785 and 1804 the number of executions on property in the islands amounted to no less than thirty million pounds in local currency.

It was against this background that Adam Smith's powerful attack on the system of mercantilism was renewed. The attack took the form of an attack on the British West Indian monopoly of the British sugar market. Its basis was twofold. First, there was the secession of the mainland colonies. Arthur Young condemned all forms of distant dominion and called the colonies nuisances. 'That great lesson of modern politics,' he wrote with asperity, 'the independency of North America ought to enlarge the horizon of our commercial policy.' Yet the same exploded arguments and fallacies which had been used with reference to the tobacco colonies were being repeated with the sugar colonies. 'This reasoning,' continued Young, 'is not brought to show that the sugar islands are not of consequence; they have been mischievously made of great consequence: but they are not of the consequence their advocates falsely contend for.'

The second attack on the British West Indian monopoly came from a new competitor in the sugar trade, India. The advocates roundly trounced the British West Indies as 'an eternal sponge on the capitals of this country both national and commercial; without their insatiable calls for money ... no cultivation of their sterile rocks (would) have been forced, at such an enormous and unnecessary expense'. Britain, they asserted, was 'ripe for an abolition of monopolies', and they demanded the equalisation of the duties on East and West Indian sugar as an act of justice. The sugar refiners of England, carrying on their traditional struggle with the British West Indian sugar planters, submitted

a petition to Parliament in 1792 blaming the evils of the West
Indian monopoly for the rise in prices and praying for the
admission of foreign sugar in British ships at a preferential tariff
in favour of the British West Indies, and of East Indian sugar
at the same duties as sugar from the British West Indies.

French mercantilism was dead; British mercantilism was dying.
Spanish mercantilism, reading the signs of the times, tried to reform itself. The first step towards free trade was taken by the
abolition of the *asiento* system in 1789 and the concession extended to both Spaniards and foreigners to introduce slaves into
qualified ports in the Spanish West Indies free of all charges for
two years. The concession was renewed in 1791 for a further six
years, and again in 1798 for another six. In 1804 it was extended
for twelve years to Spaniards and six to foreigners. Cuba's imports,
2,285,798 pesos in 1774, rose to 12,319,997 in 1803; exports rose
from 1,197,979 pesos in 1774 to 8,165,735 in 1804. Three-tenths
of the import trade, nearly one-fifth of the export trade represented foreign commerce conducted under foreign flags. The day
of the galleons, the symbols of the haughty Spanish monopoly,
was gone for ever. Cuba's phenomenal development in the nineteenth century was to take place under the banner of free trade
rather than of mercantilism.

Chapter Fifteen

Down with Colonialism and Slavery!
The Haitian Revolution

'Nothing has ever appeared more striking or unaccountable than the difference between the British West Indies and the French.' Thus wrote George Chalmers, in 1784, in his *Opinions on Interesting Subjects of Public Law and Commercial Policy; arising from American Independence.* One of the immediate and most catastrophic consequences of the American Revolution for the British West Indies was that it left them face to face with, and inferior to, their French rivals, once their economic dependence on North America was removed. Their *bête noire* was Saint-Domingue.

The progess of Saint-Domingue from 1783 (the year of the independence of the United States of America) to 1789 (the year of the outbreak of the French Revolution) is one of the most astonishing phenomena in the history of imperialism. Its exports in 1788 amounted to 31,350 tons of clayed sugar, 41,607 tons of brown sugar, 2,806 tons of cotton, 30,425 tons of coffee, 415 tons of indigo; the value amounted to 193 million livres or nearly eight million pounds sterling. The colony contained 800 sugar plantations, 3,000 coffee, nearly 800 cotton, and 2,950 indigo. Saint-Domingue supplied half of Europe with tropical produce. Its exports were one-third more than those of all the British West Indies combined; its commerce employed 1,000 ships and 15,000 French sailors. Saint-Domingue was the world's premier sugar producer, the gem of the Caribbean.

The typical sugar plantation of the period, as described by the able French colonial writer, Moreau de Saint-Méry, required 100 *carreaux* of land, of which two-thirds were planted to cane, 200 slaves, and 100 mules, to produce annually 134 tons of white or clayed sugar. Of the slaves 58 worked in the field, 39 in the factory, and 12 were domestics. The capital investment required for such a plantation was one million livres.

Bryan Edwards, the Jamaican contemporary of Moreau de Saint-Méry, described a typical sugar plantation in Jamaica of the period, producing 160 tons of sugar and 14,300 gallons of rum. Such a plantation required 900 acres of land, of which 300 were in cane, one water-mill or two cattle-mills or one windmill and one cattle-mill, 250 Negroes, 80 steers, and 60 mules. The capital investment required was £30,000 sterling. Comparing the two plantations, it would appear that the Jamaican required more labour and livestock per acre and per ton of sugar, as the Jamaican sugar was not refined.

In 1789 one-third of the Saint-Domingue sugar plantations was yielding an annual profit of twelve per cent, the others eight per cent. The Jamaican average was four per cent. In Barbados the Governor doubted if it was as high as six per cent. In Montserrat the figure was three per cent, in St. Kitts six per cent on the most fertile lands, in Grenada four per cent on the majority of plantations, in Antigua five per cent. Thus it was that Edwards could say that 'a sugar estate, with all its boasted advantages, should sometimes prove a mill-stone about the neck of its unfortunate proprietor, which is dragging him to destruction!', and could consider a farm in England producing an income of $3\frac{1}{2}$ per cent as equal to a sugar plantation in the West Indies yielding double.

The superiority of Saint-Domingue, as that of Barbados and Jamaica before it, was marked by not a single advance in agricultural or industrial technique. In the last decade of the eighteenth century the breadfruit and the Bourbon and Otaheite varieties of cane were introduced into the Caribbean. There agricultural progress was halted. Bryan Edwards lamented the failure of his colleagues to substitute the plough for the hoe; in the words of the Antigua planters, 'nothing has yet been found so completely suited to the disposition of the slaves, and at the same time so efficacious . . . as the hand hoe'. Where the man with the hoe continued to dominate Caribbean agriculture, it was too much to expect the Caribbean sugar planter to adopt the great revolution of eighteenth century science, steam. The primitive and expensive cattle-mill, the *trapiche* of sixteenth century Hispaniola, more than held its own.

The superiority of Saint-Domingue rested on something much simpler, duplicating the history of Barbados and Jamaica. That was the fertility of its soil, before it was exhausted by over-cropping. The same number of Negroes yielded considerably more in Saint-Domingue than in the British islands. The soils of Saint-Domingue, said representatives of the Jamaican sugar industry in 1788, were, beyond all controversy, far more pro-ductive, and required a much smaller proportion of labour, than those of Jamaica. They reckoned the average yield in Saint-Domingue at two and a half hogsheads, two tons, per acre, whereas in Jamaica the average was half a hogshead, eight hundredweight, and in the most productive parish in a favourable year, twelve hundredweight. In Antigua, Grenada and Dominica, the yield varied from half a hogshead to three hogsheads per acre; in Nevis the general average was half a hogshead. The Jamaican sugar representatives estimated that a property, which sold in Saint-Domingue for over £25,000, would probably not have fetched in Jamaica more than £7,000.

As a result, the French planter was able to undersell the British in the European market. Sugar, which cost in Saint-Domingue 36s 4d a hogshead, cost 45s in Jamaica. It was generally estimated that the French could undersell their rivals by from 10 to 20 per cent, one estimate even going as high as 25 per cent. In 1788 the Jamaican planters conceded that they could no longer continue to 'retain in the European market that ascendancy which, we now fear, is irretrievably lost to Britain'. A report prepared by a com-mittee of the Jamaica House of Assembly in 1792 stated that, in the course of twenty years, 177 plantations had been sold for the payment of debts, 55 had been abandoned, and 92 were still in the hands of creditors, while 80,121 executions, amounting to

£22,563,786 sterling, had been deposited in the office of the Provost Marshal.

Adam Smith had argued that one reason for French superiority was that the capital which went to improve the French colonies, particularly Saint-Domingue, was raised almost entirely from the produce of the soil and industry of the planters, whereas he regretted the readiness with which societies of merchants in England bought waste land in the British sugar colonies. Similarly Chalmers compared the British planter, bred in the lap of luxury, owing fifty millions to England, with the French planter, reared in the school of misfortune, revealing the frugality typical of the French, from peer to peasant. This was rhetoric. The French planter was even more heavily in debt than his British rival. French colonial debts were estimated at 20 million livres in 1774, 500 million in 1789. Bordeaux alone invested 100 million livres in Saint-Domingue in five years after the independence of the United States. By the outbreak of the French Revolution, the debts of the French planters were assessed at the value of two years' produce of the islands; such premiums were paid for ready money that, in the purchase of slaves, a discount of 20 per cent was common for cash payments.

The astonishing development of Saint-Domingue had profound effects on the French economy. French imports from the colonies were 185 million livres in 1789, exports to the colonies 78 million. French colonial products re-exported abroad rose from 15 millions in 1715 to 152 millions in 1789. France retained only one-eighth of her sugar imports for domestic consumption. Of 80 millions of French exports to the Baltic in 1789, 55 were colonial produce; of 424 millions exported to Europe, the Levant and America, colonial produce accounted for 152 millions. It was by the re-export of colonial produce, and by it alone, that France maintained a favourable balance of trade with the world.

As Malouet boasted in a speech in the National Assembly on September 29, 1791:

'Every one knows that one million put in circulation in trade can produce 10 to 20 millions in labour. Follow the cask of sugar which goes to pay for copper in Sweden, silk in the Levant, and see how many workers employed to make copper and silk owe their subsistence to that exchange.'

The French colonies, in addition, were the principal market for French manufactures. French colonial imports employed 164,081 tons of shipping, navigated by 33,400 seamen; British West Indian imports 148,176 tons of shipping, navigated by 13,936 seamen. Lord Brougham, the distinguished abolitionist and parliamentarian, concluded:

'Such was the decided superiority of the French over the British colonies before the Revolution. The proportion which the French colony trade bore to the whole French trade was greater than that which the British colony trade bore to the whole British trade... In every view the French American colonies were much more essential to the mother country than the English.'

Barnave, the French parliamentarian, completed the thought of Brougham: '... to relinquish her colonies is therefore to relinquish the naval power of France; in which case the English power will acquire an unrivalled ascendancy in the ocean'.

King Sugar seemed more dazzling than ever, not only in France, but also in England and the United States. Pitt estimated incomes from the West Indies at four million pounds in 1798 as compared with one million from the rest of the world. 'How are the duties, eh, Pitt, how are the duties?' inquired George III on seeing the lavish equipage of an absentee West Indian sugar planter. The opening of the West India Docks in 1800, to accommodate the West Indian sugar ships and relieve the chronic congestion in London, seemed a fitting tribute by the new century to the glory that was sugar.

The independent United States saw two remarkable proofs of that importance of the sugar islands to retain whose trade they had seceded from the British empire. The first was a young man, Alexander Hamilton by name, who, born in Nevis, was working as a mercantile clerk in St. Croix when a dreadful hurricane struck in 1772. Young Hamilton described the disaster in a letter to his father in New York. The letter was alleged to show such talent —it is not so easy to recognise it from a study of the document today—that the lad was awarded a scholarship to King's College in New York. Thus was the United States indebted to the West Indies for its first Secretary of the Treasury and for one of the American classics in political science, the *Federalist*.

The West Indian sugar industry also gave the United States the

very symbol of its independence, the Capitol. It was designed by
a planter in Jost Van Dyke, in the British Virgin Islands, Dr.
William Thornton, a Quaker, who, whilst toying with the idea of
emancipating his slaves and sending them back to Africa, was
more interested in architecture and philology than in sugar. He
had won a competition for a plan for the Philadelphia Library,
founded by Benjamin Franklin, which still stands today though
used for other purposes, and had received a gold medal from the
American Philological Society for his *Cadmus, or a Treatise on
the Elements of Language*, published in Philadelphia in 1793.

Thornton saw, too late, Jefferson's advertisement of a competition for a design of the Capitol. He had an interview with President Washington and presented his own design. Washington gave
him a letter to the Commissioners appointed for the purpose,
urging them to consider Thornton's design. The upshot was that
Thornton's plan was accepted, and the Capitol was erected substantially as he suggested. Washington described Thornton's design
as combining grandeur, simplicity and convenience. According to
Jefferson, it had captivated the eyes and judgment of all; it was
simple, noble, beautiful and excellently arranged.

Jefferson later solicited Thornton's aid for designing the buildings of the University of Virginia, an unsurpassed example of
Georgian architecture. Thornton received a prize of five hundred
dollars and one of the city lots in the city of Washington, D.C.,
became a friend of the President, was appointed one of the three
Commissioners for designing the city, and, from 1802 until 1828,
held the post of first Commissioner of Patents of the United
States. At his death he left a fortune valued at $69,930, including
half a share in a sugar plantation in Tortola containing 120 slaves,
and his valuable papers now form part of the manuscript collection of the Library of Congress.

Saint-Domingue, the West India Docks, the *Federalist* and the
Capitol—it was the brilliant swan-song of mercantilism. For the
net was closing in on the Caribbean sugar industry.

First, there was beet sugar. In 1786 the Frenchman Achard
began to occupy himself with beet cultivation on his estate near
Berlin, in an attempt to translate Marggraf's laboratory demon-
strations into commercial reality. The King of Prussia took a
great interest in beet sugar, and, once convinced of the prospects

of Achard's experiments, he bought a large experimental farm in 1801 and provided Achard with the necessary capital for the erection of a sugar factory. He contributed towards the erection of other factories, and offered premiums to any farmer or manufacturer who succeeded in working up more than twenty tons of beetroot a year. It is alleged that the British Government anonymously offered Achard £30,000 to report that he had failed in his experiments, but that Achard rejected the bribe with contempt.

The second enemy was the United States, in two senses. In 1790 Thomas Jefferson envisaged the production of maple sugar in quantities large enough not only for the domestic demand, but also for export. Jefferson already had the powerful propagandist appeal to which beet sugar would later resort: 'What a blessing,' he wrote, 'to substitute a sugar which requires only the labour of children, for that which is said to render the slavery of the blacks necessary.' Not that Jefferson, a slaveowner himself, had any objection to cane sugar; he regretted the Spanish treaty of 1819 by which the United States had ceded Texas, 'a sugar country sufficient for the supply of the United States'.

But both maple sugar and Texas cane were only possibilities. Louisiana was a reality. In 1794 a Louisiana planter, Etienne de Bore, undertook sugar manufacture in earnest. He bought a supply of cane, planted a large field, engaged a technician and installed the necessary machinery. The day of the test saw a large crowd of onlookers, whose joy broke forth at the sight of crystals in the cooling fluid. Bore received $12,000 for his crop. By 1805 there were 81 sugar plantations in the state. The United States had found a domestic source of sugar which rendered the labour of the Negroes necessary.

The third danger came from India, where the cane was allegedly cultivated by 'free' labour. In April, 1789 its cultivation was recommended by the East India Company. The first shipment reached England in 1791. Imports of Indian sugar increased from 202 tons, valued at £22,345, in that year, to 11,041 tons, valued at £545,937 in 1800. The new development had the full support of Britain's Prime Minister, William Pitt, son of the Earl of Chatham. Pitt's plan was to recapture the European market for British sugar from Saint-Domingue. He turned to India, and the floodgates of propaganda were opened against West Indian slave labour. 'That trade', said one of the protagonists of Indian sugar at a debate of the East India Company's shareholders in 1793, 'with all its valuable appendages, which the French supplanted us in half a century back, and have preserved till almost the hour in which he was speaking, seemed to extend itself towards us and court our embrace'.

The British planters in India promised that they could supply sufficient sugar 'without slavery or oppression of any kind whatever', and expressed regret for the attention paid in the past by Britain and France to the West Indian colonies, but for which 'slavery might have been confined to the malefactor or at least the national reproach of inflicting it on the innocent have rested with the possessors of the mines of Mexico and Peru'.

Pitt's plan, however, was unexpectedly foiled. As sugar was not included in the usual articles imported from India, the duty levied was not that on British West Indian sugar but an *ad valorem* one as on any manufactured article, at the high rate of £37 16s 3d per hundredweight. Competition at this rate was impossible. An application to the Treasury by the Company for the West Indian rate was unsuccessful.

But the principal danger to the British West Indies came from England herself. Urged by his friend Pitt, William Wilberforce launched a campaign in 1787 for the abolition of the slave trade. The British Government appointed a commission of inquiry to investigate closely all aspects of the British West Indian sugar industry, with particular emphasis on the superiority of Saint-Domingue. The Commission soon discovered that Britain was herself, by re-exports of slaves from the British islands, contributing to the development of her rivals. Of the annual British export from Africa of 40,000 slaves, two-thirds were disposed of to foreigners. In Dominica, from 1784 to 1788, total imports amounted to 27,533; re-exports to 15,781, or more than one-half. In Jamaica, from 1784 to 1787, imports were 37,841; re-exports 15,224, or nearly two-fifths. In Grenada, between 1784 and 1792, 44,712 slaves were imported, and 31,210 (seven-tenths) re-exported. Britain, said one of the abolitionists, Rev. James Ramsay, had become the 'honourable slave carriers' of her rivals.

To Pitt, this situation was intolerable. Instead of the slave trade being very advantageous to Great Britain, he said in anger on

April 2, 1792, it was the most destructive that could well be imagined to her interests. He threw himself with fervour into the abolitionist campaign, and opened negotiations for an international abolition which would cut the ground from under Saint-Domingue, and throw the British West Indies into the rubbish heap, whilst Britain got sugar enough to supply all Europe from India. In 1787 he wrote to the special British envoy in France about 'the idea of the two nations agreeing to discontinue the villainous traffic carried on in Africa'. Similar *démarches* were made simultaneously in Spain, Portugal and Holland.

Here, again, Pitt was unsuccessful. The French Government complimented the British on their humanity, but regretted that it could not give up the slave trade. Privately it attributed the British proposal to interested motives in no way connected with humanity and with a determination to ruin Saint-Domingue. The British thereupon directed their propaganda at the French abolitionists and turned to legislation to forbid the export of slaves by British subjects to foreign colonies.

By this time, however, the greatest enemy of all had appeared —the slaves in Saint-Domingue. The worst hell on earth in 1789, Saint-Domingue was absorbing 40,000 slaves a year. British writers, including Adam Smith, wrote about the superior treatment of the slaves by the French, basing their assertions on the defunct *Code Noir*. This was fantastic. The slave mortality in Saint-Domingue was frightful.

Moreau de Saint-Méry cites as a typical case that of a sugar plantation in Léogane, begun in 1750 with 78 creole slaves—that is, they were not fresh importations who died rapidly, but acclimatised slaves. By 1787 the proprietor had purchased 255 other slaves, in addition to which 150 Negroes were born on the plantation during the interim. Notwithstanding this, the plantation contained only 203 Negroes in 1787. This represented a loss, in the thirty-seven years, of nearly four times the original stock. Of the 200 Negroes on his typical plantation, Moreau de Saint-Méry stated that fifteen—seven and a half per cent—must be reckoned as always in the hospital. The mortality was graphic evidence of the treatment inflicted on the slaves. In the midst of the wranglings, conflicts and discussions that the French Revolution engendered in Saint-Domingue, the slaves themselves took the initiative and settled the question of the superiority of Saint-Domingue.

'Saint-Domingue is a second Sodom which will be consumed by the wrath of God.' The Comte d'Ennery's prophecy was partly right and partly wrong. Saint-Domingue was consumed, but the wrath was the wrath of the slaves.

The social structure of Saint-Domingue in 1789 consisted of five classes. The first was the planters, the big whites, described in a saying of the age as *seigneurs*, as compared with the *messieurs* of Martinique and the *bourgeois* of Guadeloupe; they were restless under the exclusive. The second was the royal officials, the representatives of the exclusive, the symbols of the denial of self-governing institutions. Then came the poor whites, the overseers, artisans, professional men, hating the planters above, determined to maintain the bridge that separated them from the men of colour below. The three groups of whites numbered 40,000. Below them came the fourth class, the mulattoes and free Negroes, numbering 28,000, possessing one-third of the real estate and one-fourth of the personal property in the colony, but denied social and political equality with the whites. Finally, there were the 452,000 slaves, many of them only recently arrived from Africa, the foundation on which the prosperity and superiority of Saint-Domingue rested.

Saint-Domingue in 1789 thus had two major characteristics: it was non-selfgoverning; and it was dominated by an aristocracy not only of land but also of the skin.

The French Revolution struck this society like a thunderclap. Its immediate consequences in France were the convening of a National Assembly for the first time in centuries, the power of the Third Estate or bourgeoisie, the limitation of the King's power, the declaration of the rights of man, and the abolition of the feudal system and the ancient privileges of the landed aristocracy. Three questions were immediately posed for Saint-Domingue: first, the rights of the planters; second, the effect of the rights of man on the mulattoes and the slaves; third, the colony's loyalty to the revolutionary regime.

Planters and mulattoes began to lobby and carry on their propaganda in the metropolitan legislature, the former through the Club Massiac, the French counterpart of the West India Interest in England, the latter through the abolitionist society, *Amis des Noirs*, Friends of the Blacks. The issue involved was equality for the mulattoes. No one mentioned the slaves.

The National Assembly moved warily, still dominated, as it then was, by forces that were essentially conservative. In March, 1790, a decree gave the vote in Saint-Domingue to all persons over 25 possessing certain income qualifications. The Abbé Grégoire, a prominent abolitionist, proposed an amendment which would explicitly include the mulattoes. The proposal was not even discussed. Ogé, the young spokesman for the mulattoes, breathed fire and brimstone:

'We will not remain much longer in degradation...We can raise as good soldiers as those of France. Our own arms will render us respectable and independent. Once we are reduced to desperate measures, thousands of men will cross the Atlantic in vain to reduce us to our former condition.'

The prophecy was correct except in one important particular: Ogé was not speaking of the slaves. With British funds, he set out for Saint-Domingue via Britain and the United States, neither of which was upset at the prospect of profound disturbances in the rich French colony. Advised by a friend to launch an immediate uprising of the slaves, Ogé rejected the plan as too radical; property before race. With a handful of followers, he was soon rounded up, tried, and broken on the wheel.

The decree of 1790 left it to the colonial assemblies to determine whether the mulattoes were to be included in the franchise. This meant, in effect, that they were excluded. But the planters were not satisfied with what was implicit. On May 28, 1790, the Assembly of Saint-Marc in Saint-Domingue passed the following resolution:

'No act of the (metropolitan) legislature concerning the internal affairs of Saint-Domingue can be regarded as a definitive law, unless it has been passed by the representatives of the French part of Saint-Domingue. The decrees issued by the National Assembly will not be executed in the French part of Saint-Domingue until they have been consented to by the General Assembly of its representatives.'

In May 1791, the National Assembly arrived at a compromise on the franchise—political and social rights for mulattoes born of free parents. There were about 400 in all in Saint-Domingue. The planters, knowing, in the words of the French proverb, that it is the first step that counts, rejected the compromise. The mulattoes, in their turn, having learned the lesson of Ogé, decided to call out the slaves. Everywhere mulattoes and slaves were victorious. The whites called for a truce, by which the mulattoes were granted full equality with the whites.

By the time the truce had been signed, however, news reached the colony of the reversal by the National Assembly of its earlier decision. By another decree of September 24, 1791, all legislation relating to both slaves and mulattoes was left to the colonial assemblies. The whites thereupon refused to adhere to the truce, and the war was resumed. On April 4, 1792, the National Assembly again reversed itself and conceded to free Negroes and mulattoes the same political rights as the whites. The planters decided that the time had come to throw off their allegiance to France and turned to Britain. Patriotism was all very well in its way, but patriotism and slavery were very much better.

As early as August 10, 1789, less than one month after the fall of the Bastille the British Ambassador in Paris reported that there were rumours that the planters of Saint-Domingue, St. Lucia and Tobago were considering secession from France and allegiance to Britain. On October 29, 1791, the President of the Assembly of Saint-Domingue sent a private communication to Pitt, assuring him that 'all Saint-Domingue' was ready to take the oath of allegiance to Britain on two conditions only—the guarantee of Saint-Domingue's internal regime and permission to trade with the United States. Assuring Pitt that his letter was 'the expression of the general will', he begged him, in the name of humanity as well as for the sake of policy, to accept the offer. Saint-Domingue's example was followed shortly after by Guadeloupe and Martinique, the spokesman for the former declaring that it was the determination of its inhabitants to 'consider themselves no longer a French colony if the present system of government in France continue'.

Pitt, with the investigation by the Privy Council in 1788 in his mind, was well aware of the significance of the offer. He knew, as an anonymous correspondent in Jamaica phrased it, that Saint-Domingue would be 'a noble compensation' for the loss of the thirteen mainland colonies. One Lieutenant-Colonel James Chalmers sent him a communication on December 24, 1792, on the 'vast, vast importance' of Saint-Domingue. Chalmers wrote:

'The advantages of St. Domingo to Great Britain are innumerable—and would give her a monopoly of sugar, indigo, cotton and coffee. This island, for ages, would give such aid and force to industry as would be most happily felt in every part of the empire.'

Chalmers recommended an offensive and defensive alliance with Spain:

'Such friendship for ages might preclude France and America from her New World, and effectually secure the invaluable possessions of Spain. It is indeed better for Europe to see the Spanish and Portuguese colonies dependent than otherwise. Their independence might give such a shock to the commercial, as the anarchy of France has given to the political system.'

But, in an age when declarations of war were still solemnly adhered to, the diplomatic niceties could not be openly violated. Britain and France were officially at peace. Thus Britain could only prepare for the irrepressible conflict. In January, 1793, the Secretary of War, Henry Dundas, sent a private and secret communication to the Governor of Jamaica, introducing four planters of Saint-Domingue and commending them to his care. Dundas wrote:

'It has been distinctly explained to them, that, unless this country is involved in actual hostilities with France, it is impossible for His Majesty, consistently with the line of conduct he had invariably followed, to aid or, in any degree, to countenance any plan of operations affecting the internal concerns of France, either in that country itself or in any of its dependencies. If hostilities do take place, which is highly probable, it will certainly be part of the plan of operations pursued by this country to extend the protection of His Majesty's Government and of the King's Arms to the French West India Colonies, to secure to them the advantage of becoming subject to the Crown of Great Britain, and to preserve by that means as well those islands as the present British colonies from the effect and from the contagion of designs which must lead to their utter subversion.'

The Governor was, therefore, to take no part in the plans of the four planters, but he was free to converse with them on eventual measures, 'supposing that the circumstances should be such as to remove that restraint which is necessarily imposed upon your conduct by the continuance of peace'.

One month later, war was declared between the two countries, and Britain had an opportunity to repay French assistance to the mainland colonies in the American Revolution. Britain accepted the offers of the French West Indian islands. The capitulations signed with the planters of Saint-Domingue guaranteed that the mulattoes would have the privileges enjoyed by their colleagues in the British West Indies—that is, no political equality with the whites; that the laws relative to property and civil rights would be those which had prevailed before 1789—that is, slavery would be maintained; and that Saint-Domingue would be allowed to import from the United States, in American vessels, livestock, grain and lumber—a privilege which, as we have seen, was not accorded to the British West Indies. British troops landed in Saint-Domingue and reinforcements were despatched from Britain.

Thus did the revolution of the mulattoes and slaves in Saint-Domingue lead to the renewal of the eighteenth-century struggle in the Caribbean between Britain and France. During the war Britain captured Trinidad from Spain and what became British Guiana from Holland, and unsuccessfully attacked Spanish Puerto Rico. An assurance was given to the House of Commons that it was a war by Britain not for aggrandisement but for security. Earlier in the century the British Government had been less coy about its intentions. It was perhaps an attempt to conciliate the planters of the British West Indies who could hardly be complacent about the annexation of their leading rival who would now legally be admitted to the British sugar market.

But there was a vastly new element added to the old international antagonism. That element was the slaves, by this time led by Toussaint Louverture. A modern British historian has attempted to justify Pitt's policy by saying that there was, to all appearances, little risk except from the slaves. This is typical of the British genius for understatement. It was the slaves who saved Saint-Domingue for France. As the slaves continued the war against the French planters and British troops, the French revolution, moving more and more to the left, decreed the total abolition of slavery in the French dominions, in 1794. 'Citizens,' cried Danton, 'today the English are riddled! Pitt and his plots are done for!'

The British were attempting to conquer Saint-Domingue and restore the *status quo* before 1789; every Negro and mulatto knew what that meant, slavery for the former, political and social inferiority for the latter. The French Government, which had, in 1792, decreed political equality for the mulattoes, now, in 1794, decreed liberty for the slaves. The British, fighting the old-fashioned eighteenth-century war, ran straight into the revolutionary slogan and more revolutionary fact of 'liberty, equality, fraternity'.

The French Government, hard pressed in Europe, relied entirely on the slaves and mulattoes in Saint-Domingue. It was not disappointed. The British troops were utterly defeated, yellow fever completing what Toussaint Louverture had begun. This is the conclusion reached by Fortescue, the historian of the British army, about the campaign in Saint-Domingue:

'After long and careful thought and study, I have come to the conclusion that the West Indian campaigns, both to Windward and Leeward, which were the essence of Pitt's military policy, cost England in army and navy little fewer than 100,000 men, about one-half of them dead, the remainder permanently unfit for service.'

Britain had captured Martinique, Tobago and St. Lucia, while the British islands of Grenada and St. Vincent were almost in ruins. Fortescue concludes:

'For this England's soldiers had been sacrificed, her treasure squandered, her influence in Europe weakened, her arm for six fateful years fettered, numbed and paralysed ... The secret of England's impotence for the first six years of the war may be said to lie in the two fatal words St. Domingo.'

British greed for sugar had saved the French Revolution in Europe, and Toussaint Louverture had frustrated Pitt's plans. In 1798 the British commander-in-chief, Maitland, decided to evacuate Saint-Domingue and to sign a convention with Toussaint. The latter promised not to attack Jamaica, and Britain pledged herself not to interfere in the internal affairs of Saint-Domingue and to permit entry into designated ports of a quantity of provisions. Maitland was laying a trap for the ruler of France, Napoleon Bonaparte.

Toussaint Louverture stood at the summit of his power. The slave coachman of 1791 had become the victorious general of 1798, the real ruler of Saint-Domingue. Passionately devoted to France, his loyalty was bounded by one fact on which he never wavered or compromised, the abolition of slavery in Saint-Domingue. He trusted France, but it was the trust of a man who had a victorious army behind him. He made this clear in a letter to the Directory, the five men who ruled France, on November 5, 1797:

'Do they (the planters) think that men who have been able to enjoy the blessing of liberty will calmly see it snatched away? But no, the same hand which has broken our chains will not enslave us anew. France will not revoke her principles, she will not withdraw from us the greatest of her benefits ... But if, to re-establish slavery in San Domingo, this was done, then I declare to you it would be to attempt the impossible; we have known how to face dangers to obtain our liberty, we shall know how to brave death to maintain it. This, Citizen Directors, is the morale of the people of San Domingo, those are the principles that they transmit to you by me.'

It was a clear warning to France. Bonaparte decided to ignore it and to rush in where Maitland had feared any longer to tread. The real ruler of France in 1798, intoxicated by his brilliant victories in Italy, dazzled by his vision of a vast French empire which would include Egypt and India, with Louisiana as an American springboard, Bonaparte, the Corsican *parvenu*, who had saved France, was enraged at the Negro *parvenu* who had saved Saint-Domingue. Saint-Domingue was still French, thanks solely to Toussaint; but with a Negro ruler, and with the slaves emancipated, Bonaparte, the self-styled child of the French Revolution, considered the colony useless.

Bonaparte was particularly incensed by a constitution drawn up at Toussaint's direction in 1801. The constitution, naming Toussaint governor of what was still called the French colony of Saint-Domingue, and giving him the right to nominate his successor, was essentially self-governing. Laws were to be made by a Central Assembly on the proposition of the Governor. Once passed they were promulgated by the Governor without reference to France. It was what used to be called until recently Dominion Status. The constitution abolished slavery for all time, and banned colour distinction in the civil service. But it was not democratic as we would use the word today, though it was far ahead of the *ancien régime* in the colony. The Central Assembly was composed of two delegates from each department, who were chosen by the municipal administrations. The members of these administrations were nominated by the Government from a list of at least sixteen persons presented to it.

Toussaint sent a copy of the constitution to Bonaparte, who

had just seized the reins of power by his *coup d'état* of the Eighteenth Brumaire and called himself First Consul, for ratification. Bonaparte wrote to him to say that the constitution, 'whilst including many good things, contains some which are contrary to the dignity and sovereignty of the French people, of which Saint-Domingue is only a part'. Toussaint replied haughtily:

'You say in your letter that Saint-Domingue...is showing a tendency to independence. Why should this not be so? The United States of America did exactly that; and, with the assistance of monarchical France, succeeded ...The high post which I hold is not of my choosing: it has been forced on me by imperious circumstances...You ask me if I desire consideration, honours, riches. Certainly; but not from you. I put my consideration in the respect of my fellow-citizens, my honours in their love, my fortune in their disinterested fidelity. This paltry idea of personal advantages which you hold out to me, does it not give rise to the hope you entertain that I might be induced to betray the cause I have embraced? ...The power which I hold has been as legitimately acquired as your own, and nothing but the expressed wish of the people of San Domingo will force me to give it up.'

When in the course of human events...But Toussaint had no time. Bonaparte set about betraying the principles of the French Revolution, by restoring Saint-Domingue to her ancient dependence and re-establishing the slave trade and slavery. On the pretext of pacifying the country, he sent a formidable expedition, commanded by his brother-in-law, Leclerc, consisting of some of his finest veterans, to depose Toussaint, disarm the Negroes, and restore slavery.

Toussaint was captured by a treachery which he should have foreseen, treated like a criminal, and put on board a warship for France. On the deck of the ship he uttered his memorable prophecy: 'In overthrowing me, you have cut down in San Domingo only the trunk of the tree of liberty. It will spring up again by the roots for they are numerous and deep.' He was imprisoned without trial in a prison high up in the French Alps, where the rigours of the climate and a semi-starvation diet soon had the inevitable effect. On April 27, 1803, he was found sitting by the fireplace, his hands resting on his knees, his head slightly bent, dead. According to one account, the rats had gnawed at his feet. His corpse was thrown into a common grave.

His treacherous capture, incarceration and death had the results that any intelligent man might have anticipated—just as intelligent men anticipated the results of the jailing of twentieth-century colonial leaders in Asia and Africa. His successors, Dessalines and Christophe, continued the struggle to decide, in the words of Leclerc, 'whether Europe will preserve any colonies in the Antilles'. Implicit in Leclerc's statement was the fact that he later made explicit, the restoration of Negro slavery. Leclerc soon realised what he was up against. 'Do not think,' he wrote to the Minister of Marine on August 2, 1802, 'of establishing slavery here for some time.' The restoration of slavery in Guadeloupe tore the veil away from his hypocritical assurances to the people of Saint-Domingue. 'I shall have to wage a war of extermination,' he wrote on September 17, 1802, '... the news of the re-establishment of slavery in Guadeloupe has made me lose a great part of my influence on the blacks.' Nine days later he wrote to Bonaparte: 'The colonists and the men of business think that a decree of the French Government would be sufficient to restore slavery. I cannot say what measures I shall take, I do not know what I shall do ...'

The Negro troops of Dessalines and Christophe were irresistible, and yellow fever no more spared the French soldiers than it spared the British. Fifty thousand Frenchmen perished in Bonaparte's attempt to restore slavery in Saint-Domingue. The French cause was hopeless from the start. Saint-Domingue was the first link in that Bonapartist chain which led to the attacks on the peoples of Spain, Russia and Prussia, and the eventual downfall of Bonaparte. On November 19, 1803, the French army capitulated.

On January 1, 1804, at a meeting of all his generals, at the very spot where Toussaint had been treacherously captured, Dessalines' secretary read out the declaration of independence of the new republic—the second in the New World—which, to remove every vestige of a detested rule, took its ancient Indian name of Haiti and struck out from its flag the white of the French tricolour. The generals abjured for ever allegiance to France, and swore to die rather than live under French domination. Dessalines, entrusted with dictatorial power, assumed the title of Emperor, the very title which Bonaparte was to arrogate to himself in the same year. Mercantilism, which died in Britain's American colonies, was thus damned in France's premier Caribbean colony.

Chapter Sixteen

Colonialism and Slavery after the Haitian Revolution

In 1783 the British Prime Minister, Lord North, in replying to a Quaker petition for the abolition of the slave trade, publicly defended it and stated that its abolition was impossible. Four years later, his successor, William Pitt, was urging his friend, Wilberforce, to sponsor a bill for abolition, and he himself fervently supported the abolition movement.

The first explanation of the change lay in the secession of the thirteen mainland colonies, which reduced the number of slaves in the empire and caused a complete revaluation of the hitherto unquestioned importance of the British West Indies. Dean Josiah Tucker called the colonies millstones round Britain's neck. The abolitionist, Thomas Clarkson, wrote in 1788:

'As long as America was our own, there was no chance that a minister would have attended to the groans of the sons and daughters of Africa, however he might feel for their distress. From the same spot, which was once thus the means of creating an insuperable impediment to the relief of these unfortunate people, our affection, by a wonderful concatenation of events, has been taken off, and a prospect presented to our view, which shows it to be a policy to remove their pain.'

The second explanation was the superiority of Saint-Domingue and the other French colonies, to whose development Britain was herself contributing by the re-export of slaves from the British islands.

The British abolition movement thus had its roots in political and economic considerations. The abolitionists established a society in 1787, which ultimately came to be known as the Anti-Slavery Society. Their leader in Parliament was William Wilberforce, whose position rested on his reputation for saintliness and the fact that he was a good speaker. But the driving force of the abolition movement in its early days was the Prime Minister, William Pitt. With Pitt and Wilberforce there was also Henry Brougham, the great orator, whose book on the colonial policy of the European powers was particularly concerned with the superiority of Saint-Domingue.

Outside Parliament the most prominent of the abolitionists, the brains of the movement, was Thomas Clarkson, who had come into prominence by winning a prize, as a Cambridge graduate, for an essay on the subject, 'Is it lawful to keep men in slavery against their will?' which he later published as one of the abolitionist classics, *An Essay on the Slavery and Commerce of the Human Species, particularly the African*. Clarkson was the director of research of the abolitionist movement, and his other chief work, *Essay on the Impolicy of the African Slave Trade*, was a powerful gun in the propaganda war.

Apart from Clarkson, there were three other writers who had the advantage of first hand experience of West Indian slavery, the Rev. James Ramsay, Zachary Macaulay and James Stephen. Macaulay, the father of the famous nineteenth-century historian, was a key figure in the band of religious sectarians who congregated in Clapham and became known as 'The Saints'; he was, however, personally interested in the development of sugar cultivation in India. Stephen was the father of a son who became more famous as the first Permanent Under Secretary of State for the Colonies and one of the best types of civil servant.

The abolitionists concentrated their attack on the impolicy of the slave system. Their first argument was that the British West Indies had attained a sufficient density of population to render the slave trade unnecessary. Pitt, quoting replies to the Privy Council's questionnaire, stated that, in 1788, the excess of deaths over births in Jamaica was only 1 in 100, that in Barbados the slave population seemed to be increasing, that in St. Kitts the decrease was less than one per cent, that in Dominica births exceeded deaths. Wilberforce, taking up the attack, stated that the decrease of the slave population in Jamaica was $3\frac{1}{2}$ per cent from 1698 to 1730; $2\frac{1}{2}$ per cent from 1730 to 1755; $1\frac{3}{4}$ per cent from 1755 to 1768; one per cent at the utmost from 1768 to 1788. It was calculations of this sort that Mark Twain no doubt had in mind when he said that there were lies, damned lies and statistics. Pitt and Wilberforce used population statistics based on large annual importations from Africa to prove that the population was increasing by natural methods. The whole subsequent history of the Caribbean, as its previous history, exposed the fallacy of their statistics and confirmed that slavery demanded the slave trade, and that, once some form of compulsory, unfree labour was considered essential to sugar cultivation, imports could not be dispensed with.

The second argument of the abolitionists was a popularisation of the thesis of the superiority of free labour propounded by Adam Smith. Arthur Young, the champion of the agricultural revolution in England as Adam Smith was of the industrial, condemned slave labour in sugar cultivation as 'the dearest species of labour' and the least productive of any in the world, and he could think of no system of free labour which would not be cheaper than that of African slaves. It was slavery alone, he said trenchantly, that induced the planters to prefer 'the most preposterous modes of tillage that are known in the world ... the overseers of plantations like the dominion of slaves better than that of cattle'.

Pitt was a good student of Adam Smith, whom he once paid the compliment at a dinner: 'We are all your scholars.' Wherever there was the incentive of honour, credit and fair profit, he declared in an impassioned speech in 1791, there industry would be. 'If you restore to this degraded race the true feelings of men,' he said eloquently in the following year, 'if you take them out from the order of brutes, and place them on a level with the rest of the human species, they will work with that energy which is natural to men, and their labour will be productive, in a thousand ways above what it has yet been; as the labour of a man is always more productive than that of a mere brute.' If a Negro was a free labourer instead of a slave, he added, his productivity would be literally doubled. The Privy Council report of 1789 estimated the ratio of productivity of free to slave labour at three to one.

The third argument of the abolitionists was that the slave trade, so long justified and lauded as the nursery of British seamen and the school of the British Navy, was in reality the grave of the sailors employed in it. According to Clarkson, the slave trade exacted an annual toll of two thousand British sailors, twenty times the mortality in the Newfoundland trade. 'If, therefore,' he said, 'we have any regard to the lives of seamen, we ought to abandon a branch of trade which dissipates the men in so unprofitable a manner.' Wilberforce, with his partiality for statistics, informed the House of Commons in 1791 that, on 350 slave ships, with 12,262 seamen, there were 2,643 deaths in one year, whereas, of 462 ships engaged in the sugar trade, with 7,640 seamen, there were only 118 deaths in seven months.

The abolitionists, in the fourth place, denied that the slave trade was a great source of national wealth, the destruction of which would produce large scale distress. British exports to Africa, valued at an average of £500,000 a year, were regarded by them as 'not of that consequence which may not be made to yield to weighty considerations'. The abolitionists considered it a cause for shame that a single advocate should be found for a trade carried on in a 'shuffling way, at which a Jew pedlar would blush', which amounted merely to the export of cheap cotton goods, trinkets, instruments of torture, bad rum, and firearms, the latter 'for the purposes, doubtless', sneered William Smith, 'of maintaining peace and encouraging civilisation' among the tribes of Africa. The abolitionists concluded, in the words of Ramsay, that 'the African trade is more confined in its utility than is generally imagined and that of late years it has contributed more to the aggrandisement of our rivals than of our national wealth.'

The final argument of the abolitionists represented a complete reversal of the British policy towards the sugar colonies up to 1783, and introduced into the history of the Caribbean what has since proved a spectre of the Caribbean sugar producer, overproduction. One of the advocates of the planters complained to the House of Lords in 1792 that, just at the moment when, with the slave revolution in Saint-Domingue, the British planters could bring their uncultivated lands into cultivation and abandon their exhausted soils, they were told that they could no longer have the slave trade.

It was precisely this new cultivation which the abolitionists wished to restrain. Pitt was particularly concerned with this point. The abolition of the slave trade, he wrote to Wilberforce in 1788, would 'only prevent *further* improvements which *would have taken place*, and not break in upon the advantages at present subsisting'. As Mr Irving of the Customs stated in evidence before a committee of the House of Commons in 1791, the British West Indies produced more sugar and rum than were required for British consumption, and it was unwise to stimulate further a production which could not be carried on within 15 per cent of the price in rival countries. He suggested the growing of food crops and the raising of livestock, and Wilberforce advised the planters to use any additional acreage for the cultivation of cotton and cinnamon.

But the vested interests in England were still powerful. Liverpool took the lead in the struggle. Between 1783 and 1793, 878 Liverpool ships transported 303,737 slaves, whose value was estimated at £15,186,850 sterling. From 1795 to 1804, the Liverpool slave ships numbered 1,099; they transported 323,770 slaves. Thus Liverpool alone transported 627,507 slaves in 1,977 vessels in the period 1783–1804, with the figure for 1794 omitted. This represented an annual average of 94 ships and slightly less than 30,000 slaves.

Far from the slave trade representing no important national interest, as the abolitionists claimed, it was still the basis of Liverpool's position. In the year 1798 alone, Liverpool's slave ships numbered 155, and the slaves transported reached the colossal figure of 57,104. In 1795 one in every four ships in the town was engaged in the slave trade; Liverpool monopolised five-eighths of the British slave trade, and three-sevenths of the European slave trade. Profits were large. The average profit per slave, of the *Lottery*, which shipped 305 in 1802, was £36; of the *Enterprise*, which shipped 392 in 1803, £16; of the *Louisa*, which shipped 326, £26. Taking £26 as the average profit per slave, the slaves transported by Liverpool slave traders during the period represented a profit of over sixteen million pounds.

If the enterprise was a lottery, as was generally said, its profits explain its popularity in the town. A local historian in 1795 wrote:

'This great annual return of wealth may be said to pervade the whole town, increasing the fortunes of the principal adventurers, and contributing to the support of the majority of the inhabitants; almost every man in Liverpool is a merchant, and he who cannot send a bale will send a band-box, it will therefore create little astonishment, that the attractive African meteor has from time to time so dazzled their ideas, that almost every order of people is interested in a Guinea cargo; it is to this influenza that so many ships are seen...'

The writer added that many of these small vessels, importing about one hundred slaves each, were fitted out by attorneys, drapers, ropers, grocers, chandlers, barbers, tailors, and so on; some had one-eighth of a share, some one-fifteenth, some one-thirty-second.

Whatever the abolitionists might say, the Liverpool inhabitants knew on which side their bread was buttered. In 1789 the manufacturers of and dealers in iron, copper, brass and lead, the planters, merchants, mortgagees, annuitants and creditors of the sugar colonies resident in the town, the sailmakers and the bakers, the joiners, shipwrights, ropemakers, coopers, gunmakers, blockmakers, and the Mayor, aldermen, bailiffs and Town Council— this formidable array of vested interests presented no fewer than twelve petitions on a single day, May 20, against abolition of the slave trade, on the ground that it would send forth many as 'solitary wanderers into the world, to seek employment in foreign climes' and lead to general distress in the town.

Support for Liverpool came from other commercial and manufacturing centres in Britain, particularly Bristol and London. The West Indian planters and merchants in Bristol, the principal manufacturers, ship builders, ship owners and traders, petitioned against abolition in 1789. The petitioners stated that the slave and sugar trades constituted three-fifths of Bristol's commerce. Various merchants, ship owners, manufacturers and tradesmen in London, various manufacturers in Birmingham, and manufacturers of African goods in Manchester joined the chorus against abolition.

The House of Lords, the stronghold of the absentee planters and the slave traders, exercised an effective brake on the abolition movement. The Earl of Westmoreland reminded his peers that it was to the slave trade that they owed their seats in it. The Navy was all for slavery. The Duke of Clarence, a member of the Royal Family and a sailor by profession, attacked Wilberforce as either a fanatic or a hypocrite. Earl St. Vincent, who owned slaves in Jamaica, described abolition as 'a damned and cursed doctrine, held only by hypocrites', and expressed the view that plantation life for the Negroes was a veritable paradise compared with their existence in Africa. Rodney opposed the abolitionists. Nelson, who had married a West Indian heiress in Nevis, where tourists are still invited to see the marriage register, unequivocally supported the old order:

'I was bred in the good old school, and taught to appreciate the value of our West Indian possessions, and neither in the field nor in the Senate shall their just rights be infringed, while I have an arm to fight for their defence, or a tongue to launch my voice against the damnable doctrine of Wilberforce and his hypocritical allies.'

It was not only the great victories of the Saints and Trafalgar which explain the erection by the grateful planters of a statue to Rodney in Spanish Town, Jamaica, one to Nelson in Bridgetown, Barbados, the naming of Trafalgar Square in Bridgetown, and the preservation of Nelson's dockyard in Antigua.

Powerful though this opposition was, it is insufficient to explain the failure of the abolitionists for twenty years, from 1787 to 1807, to attain their objective. The real explanation is Saint-Domingue. The moment Pitt and the British Government accepted the offers of the planters in the French colonies, the British abolition movement was doomed. With the acquisition of Saint-Domingue, the British sugar empire would once more be worthwhile. Without the slave trade, Saint-Domingue was useless to that empire. The British Government emphatically assured the planters of Saint-Domingue that both slavery and the slave trade would continue, and that the mulattoes would be kept in their place. Pitt's policy to capture the European market with Indian sugar was unnecessary once he decided to annex Saint-Domingue.

By the same token, abolition by Britain was not only no longer necessary; it was madness.

In 1792, before the beginning of the war with France. Wilberforce recorded ominously in his diary: 'Pitt threw out against slave motion on St. Domingo account.' Pitt continued to speak in support of abolition—he had already committed himself too openly—but his was a perfunctory support. In 1796 he advised Wilberforce to postpone his annual motion; in 1797 he tried to get his friend to accept a compromise—leaving ameliorating measures to the colonial legislatures—and, on Wilberforce's refusal, 'stood stiffly' by him, as Wilberforce records.

The history textbooks tell us that Pitt was afraid that all reform measures would smack of jacobinism and the French Revolution. He might have been. But Pitt could not have Saint-Domingue *and* abolition. Having accepted Saint-Domingue, expending millions in money and thousands of lives in order to secure that ripe West Indian plum, he threw abolition overboard. For precisely the opposite reason, as we have seen, the French Government, before Bonaparte, was converted not only to abolition but even to emancipation.

Thus it was that the British slave trade reached its zenith precisely during the administration of the Prime Minister who had discarded all governmental and family traditions by his forthright support of abolition prior to 1792. British shipping clearing for Africa rose from 19,493 tons in 1793 to 38,966—exactly double—in 1800. The average for the period was 35,000 tons. By the time Dessalines had declared the independence of Haiti, the vested interests involved in the British slave trade had become infinitely more powerful than they had been when the abolition campaign was initiated in 1787.

The extent to which Saint-Domingue changed the abolition picture in Britain is best brought out by the attempt of the abolitionists, in pursuit of what was the most generally acceptable aspect of the early abolition movement, to prevent the exportation of slaves to the conquered colonies of Trinidad and British Guiana. It was in Pitt's power to do this by a simple order in council. It comported with his earlier criticism of the heavy mortality attendant on new cultivation and his desire to restrict West Indian production. Wilberforce urged him to issue the order.

Pitt wavered, hesitated and procrastinated. He eventually offered a compromise with respect to Trinidad—the slave trade would be prohibited, but permission would be extended to transfer slaves from the older islands.

Wilberforce was more concerned with British Guiana, aware of the effects on the old West India islands and of the likely effects of the cultivation to its full extent of this immense region. For this reason he had the support of many West Indian planters. Wilberforce begged and entreated; it would only take half an hour to issue the order in council, he would have to face attacks within his party if the order was not issued. Pitt delayed, and Wilberforce lost his temper. When Pitt did get around to the draft of an order, it was so unsatisfactory that Wilberforce had to implore him not to issue it. Wilberforce kept on calling and writing, writing and calling, to no avail.

To such an extent had Pitt's earlier enthusiasm cooled that, in 1802, he absented himself from the debate on Wilberforce's annual motion. In another year he tried again to get him to defer it; when Wilberforce refused, Pitt was silent in the debate. Yet Pitt himself, in 1804, urged the West Indians to agree to the abolition of the slave trade to the conquered colonies, the very step which he had refused to take. His argument was that the new colonies were rivals of the old, that the sudden and great increase of the Negro population was a danger, and that the West Indies were producing more sugar than could be sold in the world market. The great minister stood self-condemned.

The worst blow for Wilberforce was Pitt's attitude on the question of prohibiting the slave trade in Sierra Leone, where the abolitionists had founded a colony for the transfer of the Negroes in England freed by Lord Mansfield's decision in the Somerset case, and for the beginnings of lawful commerce with Africa. Pitt was simply not interested. In 1799, the abolitionist bill came up for debate. Wilberforce's diary reads: 'shocked to see P. and all the rest opposing bill for limiting from part of African coast, like entire abolition, alas!' When Wilberforce indicated that he wished to answer Pitt's misrepresentations, Pitt had the debate adjourned.

James Stephen accused Pitt of indirect and selfish views, 'Mr Pitt,' he wrote to Wilberforce, 'unhappily for himself, his country and mankind, is not zealous enough in the cause of the Negroes, to contend for them as decisively as he ought, in the cabinet any more than in parliament.' All that Pitt could see was that the British sugar colonies, now reinforced by the new acquisitions, and with Saint-Domingue's former superiority irretrievably gone, were once more the principal sugar producers of the Caribbean. In 1801 Sir F. M. Eden wrote complacently:

'The slave trade (I speak of it only in a commercial view) promises to open new sources of mercantile profit. The demand for Negroes must, for some years to come, be very great; St. Lucia, Martinico, and Trinidad may still be supplied although the "not happier island in the stormy waste", St. Domingo, should continue to be deemed too pure a soil for slaves to dwell in.'

Eden anticipated that, at the end of the war with France, the slave trade would give rise to a greater demand for British manufactures in Africa. In 1792 Pitt had condemned the slave trade as destructive to British interests. In 1804 he was the principal obstacle to abolition. It was abolition itself that had become destructive to British interests.

The cause of humanity, which had seemed so bright in 1789, was further darkened by developments in Cuba, whose potentialities Pitt seemed to have ignored. As a result of a Spanish decree in 1789 conceding free trade in slaves, the island was psychologically ready to step into the gap in the world sugar market created by the slave revolution in Saint-Domingue. Between 1763 and 1789 Cuba had imported 30,875 slaves, an annual average of 1,143; from 1790 to 1804 imports totalled 88,746, an annual average of 5,916; in 1802 no fewer than 13,832 were imported. Cuba's sugar exports rose from 13,910 tons in 1790 to 37,774 in 1802. The slave population of the island rose from 50,340 in 1787 to 138,000 in 1804. The British West Indies, saved from Saint-Domingue, were in danger of succumbing to Cuba. The wheel was coming full circle—beginning with Spain, it was coming back to its starting-point. What the cause of free labour and humanity had gained on the swings in Saint-Domingue, it was about to lose on the roundabouts in Cuba. Denmark's abolition of the slave trade in 1792, to be effective in 1803, was like a pill to cure an earthquake.

The campaign for the abolition of the slave trade was the

signal for a renewal of the traditional battle of the books over the character of the Negro and the nature of slavery. The most remarkable results of the controversy were the views expressed by Thomas Clarkson, the historian of the anti-slavery movement in England, on the Negro and his potentialities. They rank with the finest in modern sociology and anthropology.

Clarkson functioned in the intellectual atmosphere created by Adam Smith, whose doctrines he more or less accepted, especially with regard to the superiority of free labour. But Clarkson was an agitator and a propagandist, not a philosopher; he was an idealist, not an economist. He conveys the impression of a man seeking for a cause to which to consecrate his amazing energy. At the time in which he lived, that cause was the abolition of slavery. He became, as Coleridge later described him, 'the moral steam engine . . . the giant with one idea'.

That idea was, in Clarkson's words, to produce a work which might be useful to injured Africa. The cause was, as he phrased it, the cause of injured innocence. His mind, as he tells us, was over-whelmed by the thought that he might be permitted to become a humble instrument in promoting African liberty. His perspective was simplicity itself. The slave trade was the most monstrous of evils, which began in avarice and was nursed by worldly in-terest; a mere glance was sufficient to affect the heart, to arouse indignation and pity. In his emphatic opinion, the slave trade was contrary to reason, justice, nature, the principles of law and government, the whole doctrine, in short, of natural religion and the revealed voice of God.

It was from this basis that Clarkson approached the question of Negro inferiority and the strictures of Hume on this subject. His views are worth quoting at length:

'Such then is the nature of this servitude that we can hardly expect to find in those, who undergo it, even the glimpse of genius. For if their minds are in a continual state of depression, and if they have no expecta-tions in life to awaken their abilities, and make them eminent, we cannot be surprised if a sullen gloomy stupidity should be the leading mark in their character; or if they should appear inferior to those, who do not only enjoy the invaluable blessings of freedom, but have every prospect before their eyes, that can allure them to exert their faculties. Now, if to these considerations we add, that the wretched Africans are torn from their country in a state of nature, and that in general, as long as their slavery continues, every obstacle is placed in the way of their improvement, we shall have a sufficient answer to any argument that may be drawn from the inferiority of their capacities.'

Clarkson did what Hume and Jefferson had refused to do; he did not argue from the Africans in a state of slavery but went back to their natural habitat, Africa. He drew three conclusions— first, that their abilities were sufficient for their situation; secondly, that they were as great as those of other people in the same state of society; thirdly, that they were as great as those of any civilised people whatsoever, when the degree of the barbarism of the one was compared with the degree of civilisation of the other. His opinion of Phyllis Wheatly and Ignatius Sancho differed from that of Jefferson, and he added that they were only such prodigies as would be produced every day if the Negroes had equal opportunities with the whites. His conclusion is a landmark in the history of the attitude of European and American intellectuals to the Negro:

'If the minds of the Africans were unbroken by slavery; if they had the same expectations in life as other people, and the same opportunities of improvement, they would be equal, in all the various branches of science, to the Europeans, and the argument that states them "to be an inferior link of the chain of nature, and designed for servitude", as far as it depends on the *inferiority of their capacities*, is wholly malevolent and false.'

The measure of Clarkson's towering superiority over even his colleagues in the abolitionist movement is attested by a consideration of one aspect of the abolitionist propaganda which had a powerful popular effect. This aspect was best represented by William Fox's *An Address to the People of Great Britain, on the Propriety of Abstaining from West India Sugar and Rum*. First published in 1791, it ran through several editions. One family, said Fox, could, by such a boycott, prevent the slavery or murder of one fellow-creature; eight families in nineteen and a half years could prevent the slavery or murder of one hundred; while 38,000 families could totally prevent the slave trade. Fox assured the British consumers that, in every pound of sugar, they consumed two ounces of human flesh, and openly recommended the use of East Indian sugar. He deliberately sought to nauseate the British public. Every hogshead of sugar, he said, was impregnated with the sweat of the Negroes, and, as if this was not enough, he added:

'It is well known that the woolly head of the Negro is as fertile in the propagation of a certain domestic insect, as the flaxen locks of the European. Is it, then, any way strange to conceive, that while the labouring slave, perspiring at every pore, with his head as wet as Gideon's first fleece, jumping in the cask with all his might, some of this numerous race who inhabit the capital, may inadvertently lose their hold, and fall in among the sugar; or be carried there with the large drops as they fall from his reeking locks?'

Fox succeeded in his intention, which was compassion for the British consumer rather than for the Caribbean slave.

Clarkson's perspective is best seen by comparing it with the typically narrow vision of the planters and their advocates. To Bryan Edwards, a Jamaican planter, who wrote a history of the British West Indies, slavery and the slave trade, on which his personal fortunes depended, appeared in the following light:

'Moderate labour, unaccompanied with that wretched anxiety to which the poor of England are subject, in making provision for the day that is passing over them, is a state of comparative felicity... men in savage life have no incentive to emulation: persuasion is lost on such men, and compulsion, to a degree, is humanity and charity... a good mind may honestly derive some degree of consolation, in considering that all such of the wretched victims as were slaves in Africa, are, by being sold to the whites, removed to a situation infinitely more desirable, even in its worst state, than that of the best and most favoured slaves in their own country.'

This perspective determined Edwards' analysis of the Negro character. He described the Negroes as of a cowardly, sullen and thievish disposition, the most revengeful and remorseless of tyrants to men and animals when invested with authority. They were promiscuous, licentious and dissolute; the conception of love as a tender attachment to one individual object had no place in African bosoms, and the West Indian Negroes would regard it as the greatest exertion of tyranny and the most cruel of all hardships if compelled to confine themselves to a single connection with the opposite sex. As practical musicians, Edwards had never seen or heard of one who could truly be called a fine performer on any capital instrument. In vocal harmony they displayed neither variety nor compass: 'nature seems in this respect to have dealt more penuriously by them than towards the rest of the human race.'

Another English writer, Henry Bolingbroke, who visited British Guiana in 1797, advanced the view that there was no such thing as slavery at all. This is what he contributed to the controversy:

'From the moment a Negro is for the first time sold by auction, it is preposterous to call him a *slave*. He is become in the strict legal sense of the word a *vassal*. He is ascribed to the soil, and can invoke its nutritious aid, by law, during sickness, famine, or decrepitude. He has climbed a step in human society.'

If, in the course of his ascent, the planter took nine or ten hours of labour every day, it left the 'vassal' with nearly fifteen hours, in addition to board, lodging, clothes, and such luxuries as rum and tobacco. 'What British labourer,' asked Bolingbroke, 'pays for his shelter, his raiment, and his ale-house bill, with the sacrifice of a smaller proportion of his time?' From this standpoint the slave trade, 'the trade which redeems slaves to exalt them into vassals, is a benefit to be encouraged by public premiums. Its continuance is of value to the whole Negro race, and is essential to the further progress of agriculture, in the fertile but unpeopled tropical portions of America'.

The two great British intellectuals of the period treated the Negro question flippantly or unsympathetically. William Cowper has been described as an eager supporter of the anti-slavery movement. This he was not. His *Negro's Complaint* in 1788 is a banal lament of a slave torn from his home, sold for his 'price in paltry gold', but whose mind was 'never to be sold'. His *Charity*, in 1782, strikes the sentimental note with 'the sable warrior, frantic with regret of her he loves, and never can forget'. At best, it was a reply to Bryan Edwards' sneer that true love had no place in an African bosom. The well-known passage in *The Task*, in 1785, is no more convincing. Cowper would not have a slave to till his ground, to carry him, to fan him while he slept, to tremble when he waked. Slaves cannot breathe in England, he said, recalling the Mansfield decision, and he asked: 'We have no slaves at home.—Then why abroad?' There is a touch of levity in his couplet:

'I pity them greatly, but I must be mum,
For how could we do without sugar and rum?'

This was only to be expected from one who confessed that slavery was a subject on which he could ruminate until he felt himself lost in the mazes of speculation.

Cowper claimed that he was among the first in his generation to champion the slave. Wordsworth could have claimed, more accurately, that he was among the first to oppose the slave. Bliss was it in that dawn, he confessed later, referring to the early ebullitions among the British intelligentsia aroused by the French Revolution; to be alive then was very heaven. Even then, however, the subject of slavery had no appeal for him. In *The Prelude* he later expressed his apathy towards the issue at the end of 1792. He wrote:

> '... When to my native Land
> (After a whole year's absence) I return'd
> I found the air yet busy with the stir
> Of a contention which had been rais'd up
> Against the Traffickers in Negro blood,
> An effort, which though baffled, nevertheless
> Had call'd back old forgotten principles
> Dismiss'd from service, had diffus'd some truths
> And more of virtuous feeling through the heart
> Of the English People. And no few of those
> So numerous..............................
> .... were well prepared
> To let that journey sleep awhile, and join
> Whatever other Caravan appear'd
> To travel forward towards Liberty
> With more success. For me that strife had ne'er
> Fasten'd on my affections, nor did now
> Its unsuccessful issue much excite
> My sorrow...........................'

Wordsworth did not join the anti-slavery caravan. His sonnet to the white-robed Negro who was his travelling companion from Calais and that to Toussaint Louverture lack the depth of his finest poetry.

The British poet of the *fin de siècle* who proved the most effective abolitionist was Robert Southey, whose brother wrote a *Chronological History of the West Indies* which he dedicated to the poet. His simple and poignant ballad, in 1798, 'The Sailor who had served in the Slave Trade,' dealt with a sailor found by a minister in Bristol, groaning and praying in a cowhouse. The

sailor had been ordered by the captain of a slave ship to lash a
female Negro slave who had refused to eat. The captain stood by,
cursing whenever the sailor paused because of the woman's cries.
When she was taken down, the woman groaned and moaned, her
voice growing fainter and fainter until she died. No anti-slavery
propaganda was quite so effective as the final stanza of Southey's
ballad:

> 'They flung her overboard, poor wretch,
> She rested from her pain ...
> But when ... O Christ! O blessed God!
> Shall I have rest again!'

The United States attitude to the Negro question was strikingly
illustrated by the refusal of the authorities in Charleston, on
account of his colour, to permit the landing of a young native
of Saint-Domingue, who had fought in the Saint-Domingue
battalion under Lafayette, beside George Washington, and had
saved the Franco-American forces from disaster at the siege of
Savannah in the War of American Independence. Thomas
Jefferson, convinced of the inferiority of the Negro, was apprehensive of the repercussions of the Saint-Domingue slave revolution, which precipitated a slave uprising in his native Virginia.
This made him more than ever determined to remove the Negroes
beyond the reach of mixture with the whites.

Ruling out the possibility of a 'black belt' in the United States
as, firstly, expensive, and, secondly, undesirable to the states in
its vicinity, he looked, in 1801, to Saint-Domingue, conjecturing
that Toussaint Louverture 'might be willing, on many considerations, to receive over that description which would be exiled
for acts deemed criminal by us, but meritorious, perhaps, by
him'. If that failed, then 'back to Africa'. He instructed the
United States Minister to Britain in 1802 to sound out the
possibilities of transporting the Negroes in the United States to
the British abolitionist colony of Sierra Leone. He envisaged that
the expenses of transportation would be heavy, and suggested
that they might be reduced by a form of indenture, which would
encourage those who received their labour to contribute towards
their repatriation, and by permitting the American vessels to
trade with Sierra Leone. Jefferson probably had his tongue in
his cheek when he added that such Negroes as were transported

would be a valuable acquisition to the Sierra Leone settlement, and would be well-calculated to co-operate in the plan of civilisation.

The slave revolution in Saint-Domingue conditioned the attitude to the Negro in France. Necker, the hard-headed Swiss financier, had, before the Revolution, carried on the sentimental protest against treating human beings like brute beasts merely because of a difference in hair or colour. The Revolution changed this. On the one hand, it revived, through Madame de Staël, the noble Negro of Aphra Behn. Her *Mirza*, in 1795, was more perfect than Apollo; his features had, she said, none of the defects of Negroes; a child of his generation, he exuded melancholy. On the other hand, it produced the revulsion typified by Chateaubriand in his *Génie du Christianisme*, in 1802: 'who would still dare,' he asked, 'to plead the cause of the Negroes, after the crimes which they have committed?'

The respectable *London Gazette* dared. On December 12, 1798, it wrote that it was 'a great point gained to the cause of humanity that a Negro domination is in fact constituted and organised in the West Indies under the command of a Negro chief or king (of) the Black Race whom the Christian world to their infamy have been accustomed to degrade'. The *Gazette* was thinking of Maitland's convention with Toussaint: 'every liberal Briton,' it added, 'will feel proud that this country brought about the happy revolution ...' The *Gazette* was discreetly silent as to the British soldiers buried in Saint-Domingue as a result of the happy revolution, and it naturally had nothing to say about the constitution of similar governments in Jamaica and Barbados, where Toussaint's compatriots were still degraded.

And Leclerc, Bonaparte's brother-in-law, also dared. 'We have,' wrote Leclerc to Bonaparte on September 26, 1802, referring to France, 'a false idea of the Negro.' On the following day, he reiterated to Bonaparte, in announcing that he was sending a general to France and asking his brother-in-law to believe what the general would tell him: 'We have in Europe a false idea of the country in which we fight and the men whom we fight against.' Toussaint Louverture, as Raynal had predicted, had restored the rights of the human species. Instead of plaudits, benedictions and trophies, he received a cell and death from Bonaparte. But the slave revolution in Saint-Domingue, the unprecedented feat by which a horde of degraded and vilified beings, who, in the planters' view, passed for men only in the catalogue, were fashioned into an army which humbled the flower of British, French and Spanish militarism, coupled with Toussaint's ascent from slave cabin to the biggest house of Saint-Domingue, had this intellectual consequence —they made the Negro slave trade and slavery morally untenable thereafter anywhere in the world.

The West Indian planters, however, were the last persons whom one would expect to appreciate the lessons of morality. In the British West Indies, as in Saint-Domingue, they presented a united front against all attacks on their system. They were most vociferous on the proposal that the slave trade should be abolished.

They based their opposition on the former sanctions given to the trade by the metropolitan government. 'In every variation of our administration of public affairs,' said their advocate before the House of Lords, 'in every variation of parties, the policy, in respect to that trade, has been the same.' Referring to the idea of abolition as 'the conceits of enthusiasts and visionary people', he declared that the slave trade seemed so intolerable a grievance and so enormous a wickedness that it may well have been thought that the men of the past, if they had the common sense, feelings and justice of men, would have revolted at it, as it was suggested that all reasonable and virtuous persons then ought to revolt. The planters put their faith, not without reason, as we have indicated above, in the House of Lords; the Jamaica House of Assembly stated categorically in 1792: 'the safety of the West Indies not only depends on the slave trade not being abolished, but on a speedy declaration of the House of Lords that they will not suffer the trade to be abolished.'

In 1788 the Governor of Jamaica reported that the proposal for abolition had occasioned great alarm in all ranks of people, who 'conceive the prosperity or ruin of the island to depend upon the issue of a question in which their all is involved'. As the West Indian planters assessed the value of their property at seventy million pounds sterling, the vigour of the opposition is easily imagined. The Jamaica Assembly resolved in 1789 that the slave trade was the great source of every improvement in the West Indies, and that its abolition must, therefore, inevitably diminish the value of all West Indian securities and lead to the ruin of many mortgagees and annuitants. They asserted that, if the worst came to the worst, they would undoubtedly be entitled to compensation for abolition. The Council of Barbados wrote to its agent in London to state that it expected his forcible opposition to the plan of abolition, which it described as pernicious, involving, if successful, the effective ruin of the island. The Antigua Assembly expressed the hope that, 'if it is now thought proper, from motives of more refined humanity', to abolish the slave trade, the justice of Parliament would accord reasonable compensation to the planters.

The planters refused to make a single concession to the abolitionist sentiment. In 1786 the merchants of Kingston stated in a memorial their conviction that the re-export of slaves to the neighbouring islands was a trade of great benefit to Jamaica, and, consequently, to the metropolitan country. The planters openly asserted that it was cheaper to work the slave to death and replace him by another than to keep up the population by breeding; when, in 1804, in pursuance of parliamentary addresses, the governors of the British West Indies were directed to make inquiries as to the births and deaths among the slaves, the Jamaica Assembly maintained a contemptuous silence, whilst a committee of the Council replied that it lacked the necessary documents and could not obtain them.

Their representatives in Parliament claimed that the mortality in the Middle Passage was not as large as the loss in the transportation of British convicts, and argued that abolition would destroy the Newfoundland fisheries, which the slaves supported by consuming that part of the catch which was fit for no other consumption. It was not an amiable trade, said one, but neither was the trade of a butcher an amiable trade, and yet a mutton chop was a good thing. Even the abolitionist colony in Sierra Leone aroused their wrath; at a meeting of the West Indian Planters and Merchants in 1791, it was resolved that the colony, where the abolitionists hoped to raise sugar and cotton, would set a dangerous precedent to foreign nations with African possessions which might prove detrimental to those countries which already possessed colonies in the Caribbean.

It was only the apprehensions of competition from British

Guiana and Trinidad that split the ranks of the West Indian opposition and induced some of the planters to agree to abolition. This self-interest had led some of them to support the bill for the abolition of the foreign slave trade. The slave trade, said Ellis of Jamaica in 1804, ought to be restricted to the old colonies and prohibited in Trinidad, because in the former case the property had been acquired before any idea of abolition was entertained.

The planters claimed that the proposal for abolition was calculated to excite the minds of the slaves. In 1788, before the revolution in Saint-Domingue, the agent for Jamaica asked 'whether it is most probable that they will wait with patience for a tardy event, or whether they will not strike whilst the iron is hot, and by a sudden blow finish the business in the most expeditious and effectual manner, without giving their zealous friends here any further trouble'.

From this argument the Jamaicans proceeded to deny the rights of Parliament to enact legislation for the colonies. The Assembly declared that it was its indispensable duty to maintain the just privileges of the colonials, and pledged itself to oppose, in every constitutional manner, any attempt to deprive them of such rights and privileges. In a report of a committee of the House of Assembly in 1800 the Jamaicans described abolition as a direct violation of the rights of private property to which they were entitled as British subjects, and as an annihilation of that constitution, inherent in the inhabitants, of legislating for themselves on all matters of internal concern, which they had enjoyed for over a century. They concluded with the argument that was to enjoy great vogue in the greater controversy that was to be aroused over emancipation: all legislation relating to the slaves must be left to the colonial legislatures. As the committee of the Jamaica Assembly put it:

'... it is certain that the legislature of Jamaica has done everything possible to be done to render the condition of the slaves therein as favourable as is consistent with their reasonable services, and the safety of the white inhabitants ... The legislature of the island is alone competent to determine on such future measures as may be expedient, further to contribute to this very salutary object, founded on principles of humanity and justice, as well as good policy.'

To men imbued with such ideas, Maitland's convention with

Toussaint Louverture was like the dissolution of the bands of civil society. The Jamaica Assembly described it as a very weak measure, founded on the most mistaken policy, and condemned the intercourse authorised between Toussaint and Jamaica. They inquired:

'What impression then may it not be apprehended will be made on the minds of our slaves, from the example held out by this intercourse? Viewing the measure in all points, the committee are decidedly of opinion, that no possible advantage can be derived to Jamaica by its continuance, but on the contrary, that it is fraught with the most imminent danger to our very existence.'

The Governor of the island, the Earl of Balcarres, himself a slaveowner, hysterically denounced Maitland's right to make a convention for Jamaica; 'it would be thought somewhat odd if the City of London should send over an immense quantity of provisions and clothing for the use of the *sans culotte* army assembled for the purpose of invading England!' The Governor was probably not the least bit impressed by the secret and confidential assurances of the British Home Secretary that the tranquillity and safety of Jamaica were assured by the convention, the direction that he should give the leading planters a right impression of the measure, and the admission that the British Government had 'no alternative but must adopt and maintain the convention to the best of our power'.

The colonial legislation of the period affords the best index of the planters' views on the measures needed on the slavery question. A Bahamas law of 1784 permitted the testimony of free Negroes and mulattoes against whites only in matters of debt where they themselves were involved; in case of crimes such as murder, poisoning, burglary, robbery and rape, slaves 'deserve not, for the baseness of their condition, to be tried by the established laws of England, nor is execution to be delayed ...' The Barbados legislature in 1792 acknowledged that many crimes were committed by slaves because their masters did not allow them time to plant or to provide for themselves. But the safety of the island, according to the legislature, required that the slaves should be punished according to law; the masters were 'not to be countenanced therein at the expense of the public', and the island treasurer was to pay compensation only to the parties injured by the slaves and not to the masters.

By the Jamaica Consolidated Slave Act of the same year, courts were given power to deliver a slave from a master only in case of very atrocious mutilations. The Leeward Islands Melioration Act of 1798 stated that it was improper and ever unnecessary to enforce the celebration of any religious rites, such as marriage, among the slaves, in order to sanctify contracts. In 1802, St. Kitts imposed a tax of £1,000 on the manumission of every slave who had not resided for two years in the island, and half that sum on residents or natives. No slave to whom freedom was bequeathed was to be declared free unless the testator devised the sum of £500, to be paid into the island treasury within six months after his death. If the owner dispensed with the services of a slave, the slave was to be publicly sold, the price being paid into the treasury of the island.

The West Indians were equally on the alert against any attempt to infringe their monopoly of the British sugar market. They were emphatically opposed to the introduction of Indian sugar: they protested that any favour shown to the East Indian traders would violate the unwritten compact between the West Indies and the metropolitan country establishing mutual monopolies in each other's markets. Their advocate in the cabinet, Lord Hawkesbury, the President of the Board of Trade, objected to any relaxation of the high duties levied on Indian sugar, and recommended that the monopolising East India Company should be forbidden to carry on any trade which was not included in its original charter. He suggested that Britain should recapture the European sugar market by permitting the importation of all foreign sugar in British ships, for subsequent re-exportation in a raw or refined state.

Whilst the West Indians were demanding the maintenance of the colonial compact with respect to Indian sugar, they were demanding, with equal vigour, the abolition of that compact with respect to trade with the United States. Their case was stated in a pamphlet in 1784 written by the secretary of the Society of Planters and Merchants:

'To suppose those colonies (Canada) *at all* productive for the purposes of a substantial exportation, is to anticipate the slow effect of many years of that steady and expensive system of encouragement from the Mother-Country, which raised the other North American colonies to independence; and to suppose that at any time their produce can be rendered adequate to the West Indian demand, appears vastly beyond what the climate and other natural disadvantages can ever admit, under any encouragement whatsoever. The truth is, that the Sugar Colonies can alone be supplied with lumber from the Dominions of the United States, and that they cannot either well or cheaply be supplied with many essential articles of provisions from any other country. Flour in particular will not keep in the West Indies, and requires a constant supply by as short a voyage as possible. Even in the voyage from England it frequently grows sour; and livestock of all kinds obviously require a short voyage at a favourable season of the year. Without these supplies, *the cultivation of the Sugar Colonies cannot be carried on . . .'*

The metropolitan events which led up to the Saint-Domingue revolution had their repercussions also in the other French colonies, where there was the same alignment of forces and the same conflict of principles. The colonial assemblies permitted by the metropolis moved very early in the direction of autonomy. They justified this, as did the planter leader in Martinique, Du Buc, by claiming that it was an opposition not to France, but to the scoundrels who had usurped the King's authority, and they passed resolutions of loyalty to the monarchy. Their attitude on the slave question is illustrated by a decree of the Martinique Assembly in 1790 restricting the liberty of the press, in view of 'the danger of too much enlightenment of the inhabitants on their rights in countries where the forgetfulness of these rights has led to the establishment of slavery and where servitude is so inherent in their constitution that they could not exist without it'.

On the proposal of Guadeloupe, a General Congress was held in Martinique early in 1792, with representatives of Martinique, Guadeloupe, St. Lucia and Tobago. This Congress limited the rights granted to the mulattoes by metropolitan decree, and, whilst declaring that the colonies formed a part of the French Empire, indulged in pronounced tendencies to autonomy. Lulled into security for a while by assurances from France that their 'thinking property' (shades of Aristotle!), that is, their slaves, would not be tampered with, the planters eventually followed the Saint-Domingue pattern and offered themselves to Britain. The resolution of the Martinique Assembly, on October 28, 1793, marked the high-water mark of autonomist sentiment: 'The

Colony of Martinique will be considered as a department, independent as to its administration of the French Windward Colonies in America.' Victor Hugues, the Negro representative of the French Government, saved Guadeloupe for France until Bonaparte's restoration of slavery, but Martinique remained in English possession during the war.

The Cuban planters did not at that time find it necessary to resort to treason in order to maintain their system, but they, too, indicated clearly just what the planters of Jamaica had in mind when they asserted their right to pass laws relative to their internal concerns. In 1789 the King of Spain issued a decree in relation to the education, treatment and labour of the slaves. The slaves were to be instructed in the principles of Catholicism; the magistrates were to prescribe the proper clothing and food of the slaves; the slaves were to work from sunrise to sundown, with two hours off for themselves; slave marriages were to be encouraged; punishments were to be limited to twenty-five stripes, with a light instrument which would not cause contusions or effusion of blood; fines were imposed for breaches of the law, which were to be investigated by local officials.

In 1790 the planters of Havana sent representations to the King with respect to the decree. They stated that the regulations regarding food and clothing of the slaves were just, but that, as soon as the slaves understood them, they would adopt an insulting attitude to their masters. To limit the hours of labour from sunrise to sundown would mean that the planters, especially in the busy season, would not be able to operate their sugar factories and would have to abandon them; the slaves worked only during six months of the year, while miners, sailors and soldiers worked the whole year around, and work in the mines was immeasurably greater than work in the sugar factories. The limitation of punishment would make the slaves lose their fear of their masters, loosen the bonds of subordination, and lead to endless complaints on the part of the slaves. The slaveowner, they asserted, was like a paterfamilias, who would give a son twelve or twenty stripes for a slight fault, twenty-five or thirty, or more, if necessary, for a graver one.

Recognising the humanitarianism which had actuated His Majesty, and not prepared to resist it, the planters envisaged melancholy consequences from the decree: the ruin of their plantations, the destitution of their families, the diminution of the royal revenues, the annihilation of the commerce of the island, the abandonment of their lands, the desolation of agriculture, general calamity for the island, and the insurrection of the slaves. In 1804, when Haitian independence was declared, it seemed as if there was only one way of attaining the rights of man in the Caribbean, by a slave revolution from below.

Chapter Seventeen

The Abolition of
the Caribbean Slave System

The slave system was abolished at different times during the nineteenth century throughout the Caribbean. The slave trade, abolished finally by Denmark in 1803, was abolished by Great Britain in 1807. Restored by Bonaparte in 1802, it was abolished by the French Government in 1817. In the same year the Spanish Government signed a treaty with Great Britain whereby it pledged itself to abolition in 1820. Holland proclaimed abolition in 1818, Sweden in 1824. Slavery was abolished in the British colonies in 1833. Sweden followed suit in 1846, France in 1848, Holland in 1863. Slavery was abolished in Puerto Rico in 1873 and in Cuba in 1880.

Certain essential similarities can be discerned in this diversity. We can consider the abolition of the Caribbean slave system under the following five heads: (1) the economic factors involved; (2) the political factors; (3) the humanitarian agitation; (4) international and intercolonial rivalry; (5) the social factors.

(1) The Economic Factors

The establishment and development of the Caribbean slave

system were basically the result, as we have already indicated, of the importance of that system to the economy of the metropolitan governments. Conversely, the abolition of the slave system was basically the result of the fact that the system had lost its former importance, in the nineteenth century, to the metropolitan economy.

The first aspect of this economic revolution was that, on the eve of emancipation in the several Caribbean territories, Cuba excepted, production was either static or declining. The following table indicates the situation in the British West Indies in 1815 and 1833:

Exports	1815	1833	% Change
Sugar, cwt.	3,381,790	3,351,869	−1
Rum, gallon	6,741,668	5,091,821	−25
Cotton, pounds	12,849,411	1,539,984	−88
Coffee, pounds	33,186,700	28,517,813	−14
Cocoa, pounds	1,015,800	2,120,527	+110
Indigo, pounds	29,997	38,560	+29

In the French West Indies sugar production between 1836 and 1848 declined as follows: in Martinique from 25 million kilogrammes to 11.8 million, and in Guadeloupe from 35 million to 12.2. In value the decline was equally serious between 1841 and 1848: from 15.6 million francs to 9.2 million in Martinique, and from 17.5 to 9.8 million in Guadeloupe.

In 1845 Surinam exported 29,787,966 livres of sugar; in 1857, 31,896,993. From 1815 to 1824, St. Croix exported an annual average of 2,540,000 livres of sugar; from 1825 to 1833 an annual average of 2,677,777 livres; from 1834 to 1841 an annual average of 2,625,000 livres.

The British, French, Dutch and Danish colonies thus found themselves on the eve of emancipation in the situation in which a Dutch phrase of the period described Surinam: *Suriname's toelstand is doodstyk krankon*, Surinam is mortally ill.

Their economy was bankrupt. A faithful detail, moaned the Jamaican Assembly in 1805, would have the appearance of a frightful caricature. There were only three topics of conversation in the island: debt, disease and death. Between 1799 and 1807, 65 plantations had been abandoned, 32 were sold under decrees of the Court of Chancery to meet claims against them, and in 1807 suits were pending against 115 others. In 1806 the price of sugar was less than the cost of production, and in 1807 the planter made no profit at all. A House of Commons committee reported in the latter year that the pressure on the British West Indian planter was 'fast approaching to that crisis, that nothing but inevitable ruin can be the consequence, unless some alteration in circumstances takes place'.

With the United States neutral trade in mind, which in 1807 took to Europe 42,122,573 pounds of coffee and 143,136,905 pounds of sugar, whilst Bonaparte's Continental Blockade debarred British produce from Europe, the committee declared that it was 'a matter of evident and imperious necessity to resort to such a system as, by impeding and restricting, and as far as possible preventing the export of the produce of the enemy's colonies from the places of its growth, shall compel the continent to have recourse to the only source of supply, which, in that event, would be open to it'. Thus the salvation of the British West Indies threatened war between Britain and the United States.

In 1832 another committee of the House of Commons reported that considerable distress had existed in the British West Indies for the past ten or twelve years (when there was no international war to be the scapegoat), greatly aggravated within the last three or four. No one, said Lord Redesdale in 1826, would advance a shilling on British West Indian property. The West Indian system was bankrupt. 'If it were not vicious in many respects,' it was written in 1823, 'it is becoming so unprofitable when compared with the expense that for this reason only it must at no distant time be nearly abandoned.'

In St. Croix, in 1841, of 151 plantations, sixteen had passed into the hands of the government because their owners could not repay loans made to them, and sixty others were in the hands of creditors. The inefficiency of slave labour was strikingly demonstrated in Surinam, where, in 1850, it was estimated that 100 slaves furnished 37 days of labour, as compared with 54 put in by 100 free workers.

The principal explanation is that the Caribbean slave economy still lived in the eighteenth century. The small scale of the British West Indian plantation economy is brought out in the table below

of compensation claims made under the British Emancipation Act
of 1833.

Territory	Slaves	Claims	Slaves per Claim
Antigua	23,350	1,082	21
Bahamas	7,734	1,481	5
Barbados	66,638	7,228	9
British Guiana	69,579	3,061	23
British Virgin Islands	4,318	382	11
Dominica	11,664	1,041	11
Grenada	19,009	1,055	18
Jamaica	255,290	16,435	15
Montserrat	5,026	296	17
Nevis	7,225	399	18
St. Kitts	15,667	1,202	13
St. Lucia	10,328	890	11
St. Vincent	18,114	938	20
Tobago	9,078	372	24
Trinidad	17,539	2,356	7
British West Indies	540,559	38,218	14

The British West Indian slave economy was thus based on a
number of slaveowners owning a few slaves each. It is curious
that colonies like Tobago, Montserrat, Nevis, later to become
strongholds of the peasantry, were more truly plantation economies
in 1833 than such conventional colonies as Jamaica and Barbados.
The preponderance of the slaveowners owning less than ten slaves
each is brought out in the following table of unlitigated claims.

Territory	1	2	3-5	6-10	11-25	26-50	51-100	101-151	152-200	201-300	301-500
Grenada	301	128	222	129	76	20	27	45	30	20	4
Dominica	233	124	169	120	87	55	49	23	7	5	–
Montserrat	53	31	33	35	33	7	14	10	7	6	1
Nevis	54	41	67	40	34	14	15	22	9	7	–
St. Kitts	225	113	189	82	43	15	27	29	23	18	2
St. Vincent	211	101	153	102	73	22	31	26	21	22	7
Tobago	105	44	62	27	25	7	25	22	10	12	2

Three in ten of the claims in Grenada and St. Kitts involved
only one slave. Claims involving less than five slaves amounted to
two out of three in Grenada, seven out of ten in St. Kitts, three
out of five in St. Vincent, Dominica and Tobago, one out of two

in Montserrat. Claims involving less than ten slaves amounted to three-quarters of the total in Grenada, Dominica and St. Vincent, four-fifths in St. Kitts. In the combined parishes of St. Catherine, St. Dorothy, St. John, St. Thomas-in-the-Vale, St. Mary, St. Ann, Vere, Clarendon and Manchester in Jamaica, there were 4,059 claims, one quarter of all the claims in the island. Of these, 18 per cent involved one slave; 12 per cent two; 20 per cent three to five; 14 per cent six to ten—in other words, three out of every five claims involved less than ten slaves.

The British West Indies were thus producing for export with an economy geared to subsistence production. Its inevitable difficulties were aggravated by the fact that, in the traditional British West Indian fashion, a considerable proportion of the slaves was non-productive, hangers-on on the 'big house', ministering to the social rather than to the economic aspect of the plantation economy, brushing away flies at dinner and mosquitoes in bed, as Pinckard noted in his travels in 1806. The proportion of domestic slaves is brought out in the following table.

Territory	Total Slaves	Field	Domestic	Domestics as % age of total	Ratio of Domestic to Field
Antigua	23,350	18,421	2,232	9.5	1 : 8
Bahamas	7,734	4,202	2,434	31.5	1 : 2
Barbados	66,638	47,206	12,511	18.8	1 : 4
British Guiana	69,579	57,490	4,871	7.0	1 : 12
British Virgin Is.	4,318	3,088	738	17.0	1 : 4
Dominica	11,664	9,480	1,077	9.0	1 : 9
Grenada	19,009	14,716	1,325	7.0	1 : 11
Jamaica	255,290	187,750	31,966	12.5	1 : 6
Montserrat	5,026	4,070	393	8.0	1 : 10
Nevis	7,225	4,636	1,207	16.5	1 : 4
St. Kitts	15,667	11,350	2,571	16.5	1 : 4
St. Lucia	10,328	8,112	1,451	14.0	1 : 6
St. Vincent	18,114	13,673	2,208	12.0	1 : 6
Tobago	9,078	7,443	632	7.0	1 : 12
Trinidad	17,539	11,824	3,262	18.5	1 : 4
British West Indies	540,559	403,461	68,878	12.75	1 : 6

Thus, of every hundred slaves in the British West Indies and in Jamaica, the most important colony, nearly thirteen were engaged in domestic service; for every hundred slaves producing in the field, nearly seventeen were domestics. This, combined with the large number of slaveowners and the small number of slaves held on an average by each one of them, made the British West Indian slave system in 1833 more like a system of household management than a commercial plantation economy.

The increasing unprofitableness of Caribbean production coincided with its decreasing importance to the metropolitan economies. In 1821 British exports to the British West Indies were £4,704,610; in 1828, £3,726,643; in 1832, £3,813,821. Between 1821 and 1832, therefore, they declined by one-quarter. In 1821 the British West Indies accounted for 11 per cent of total British exports; in 1828, for 7 per cent; in 1832 for less than 6 per cent. Martinique's imports totalled 20,096,100 francs in 1841; 14,153,733 in 1848—a decline of 30 per cent. Guadeloupe's imports declined from 17,365,875 francs in 1841 to 11,980,480 in 1848, a reduction of nearly one-third.

From the metropolitan standpoint the days of mercantilism were over. The West Indies represented shrinking markets, and they produced more expensive sugar which competed with that of better customers of the metropolis. In the case of the British West Indies, the competitors were India and Brazil. In the case of the French West Indies, the conflict was with beet sugar. In 1839 the single town of Lille had a population of 64,186 interested in beet sugar, while Valenciennes had 51,211. 'In a single *arrondissement*,' said Lestiboudois, a propagandist of the French sugar beet industry, 'more people would be affected by the ruin of sugar manufacture than there are whites in our four sugar colonies.' Four departments of France in that year, with 457 beet factories (four-fifths of the French total) producing 32 million kilogrammes of beet sugar (two-thirds of French production) counted 2,800,000 persons, paid 17 million francs in taxes, and represented a territorial revenue of 132 million francs—one-twelfth of the population of France, one-fifteenth of the direct contributions, one-seventh of the national revenue. These departments had thirty-four members in the Chamber of Deputies. The beet sugar interest had replaced the West India Interest.

The beet sugar industry stressed, in addition, that the beet sugar manufacture created more and better customers than cane sugar for metropolitan industry and agriculture. Lestiboudois calculated in 1839 that the food of the Negro slave cost on an average ten centimes a day, whereas the French worker spent 18½ centimes on bread alone. For 3,500 francs one could clothe 150 slaves for a year, at an average of 23 francs each, whereas the most modest calculations put the French workman's expenditure on clothes at nearly 82 francs a year. Did the planters object, asked Dehay, another propagandist, that the cost of the slave in the first instance had been omitted? He replied that the cost of a slave who would serve for a number of years was hardly equal to the cost to the French manufacturer of a single master workman for one year. Thus, concluded Lestiboudois, 'the population employed in the production of indigenous sugar being more numerous, receiving a greater share in the returns and consuming more, contributes more directly to the prosperity of our manufacturers and our agricultural industry than the sugar islands.'

But West Indians learn nothing and profit nothing. The planters talked glibly, as if they were still in the eighteenth century, of their importance to the metropolitan economy. Abolition of the slave trade, said the agent for Jamaica in 1807, would occasion diminished commerce, diminished revenue, and diminished navigation, and in the end would remove the great cornerstone of Britain's prosperity. A West Indian member of Parliament, Henry Goulburn, in 1833 asked the House of Commons to mark the impulse given to trade and agriculture, and to look at the hamlets that had sprung into towns, in consequence of the connection with the colonies. He was greeted with sneers.

With the prospect of French reconquest of Haiti, an association called the Society of the Proprietors of Saint-Domingue was formed. In a pamphlet published in 1820, the Society inquired, as if the French Revolution had been no more than a myth and the Haitian Revolution a nightmare, whether 'the interests of 29 million Frenchmen were to be inconsiderately sacrificed to that of a few thousand Africans or to vain utopias dreamed by imprudent innovators'. As if the clock had stopped in 1763, the pamphlet continued:

'If slavery is a violation of natural law, if in all ages and among all peoples, the best regulated, the most human, this political crime had been inconsiderately tolerated, if the condition of the Negroes destined to be eaten by their compatriots or consigned to death as prisoners is less unfortunate than that which made of them peaceful labourers in Saint-Domingue, there would no doubt have been justification in invoking in their behalf the great principles of liberty and humanity; but it would have been necessary at the same time to prohibit the needs which imperiously press upon us, the luxury which seeks nourishment, the commerce which cannot exist without exchange; it would have been necessary to give to our merchant marine and navy a new orientation or to burn your vessels in your ports; it would have been necessary, in short, to destroy the coactive influence of your colonies on your political system and on the internal movement of your capital, and to make of Frenchmen a new people, without industry and without activity.'

It was a voice from the dead. How, asked Dehay in 1839, could French manufacturers, with a domestic market of 33 million people, be dependent on or at the mercy of a colonial market of 113,961 real consumers and 285,956 slaves, fed on cassava, clothed in cotton trousers, whose annual upkeep did not exceed twenty francs each?

The hostility of metropolitan capitalism in general was reflected in the hostility of particular vested interests. Chief of these was the shipping interest, to which, in the eighteenth century, the sugar colonies were the darlings of the empire. Liverpool itself voted for abolition of the slave trade in 1807. In that year the trade employed only one out of every twenty-four ships in the town engaged in foreign trade. In Britain as a whole it employed one out of every 52 ships, one out of every 23 seamen, and one out of every 80 pounds of the capital invested in external trade.

Liverpool also took the lead in the movement for the abolition of slavery. As a result of the exclusive system, declared the Brazilian Association of Liverpool in 1833, more than two million pounds of British capital were forced into other channels, giving employment to foreign shipping and paying to foreign European States freights, commissions and charges, to the great loss of the British shipowners. Any British minister, said Liverpool's representative in Parliament in the same year, who continued to impose fetters on British commerce, should be impeached. By 1833 Liverpool's economy, which had been based on the transportation of slaves from Africa to produce sugar in the West Indies, was based on the transportation of cotton produced by slaves in the

United States to the textile factories of Manchester.

To Lestiboudois, French West Indian prognostications of the decadence of France's maritime commerce and the inevitable destruction of her marine which would follow emancipation, had no semblance of reality.

Another important vested interest which joined the movement for emancipation was the sugar refiners. The British and French refiners wanted the maximum quantity of raw sugar, which the respective colonies in the Caribbean could not supply. They were thus prepared to jettison all the mercantilist principles and dogmas which had laid the basis of their industry. Were the West Indian interests alone to be regarded, it was asked in 1831 on behalf of the refiners of Preston? Relief from the West Indian monopoly, said William Clay representing the refining district of the Tower Hamlets in 1833, would be cheaply purchased by giving the West Indian planters the compensation that had been proposed. To such an extent had mercantilism been outmoded that even the prospect of Caribbean refining aroused no alarm. The House of Commons committee of 1832 condemned the prohibition of manufacture in any part of the British empire as unjustified, especially the manufacture of their own produce by the cultivators; but it was careful to add that 'a regard for the interests which have grown up under the restrictive system will probably induce the House to relax it very gradually', while it emphasised that, in return, the British refiners should have complete liberty to import non-British sugar.

The refining question raised in Britain one of the most crucial issues in the emancipation controversy. Under the mercantilist arrangement the colonies had a monopoly of the metropolitan market. But, in the war with Bonaparte, the Continental Blockade, and the importation of sugar from colonies occupied by British forces, the British market became overstocked and the price of British West Indian produce went down. The British Government accordingly decided in 1807 that the only solution was that production should be reduced. To this end it abolished the slave trade, which Pitt had failed to do. Were not the planters, asked the Prime Minister, Grenville, 'now distressed by the accumulation of produce on their hands, for which they cannot find a market; and will it not therefore be adding to their distress, and leading the planters on to their ruin, if you suffer the continuation of fresh importations (of slaves)?'

Thus, in the interest of the planters themselves, was introduced for the first time, what has since been a commonplace in Caribbean history—the fact that, whilst world production was increasing by leaps and bounds as a result of all sorts of encouragements, and sugar from all countries was finding its way into the metropolitan market, the Caribbean planters were accused of overproduction. In 1833 the sponsor of the emancipation legislation in Britain, Earl Stanley, affirmed that the West Indian planter was producing sugar to an extent not warranted by the circumstances of the colonies or the demand for sugar in the European markets. British West Indian sugar production, in fact, was actually declining, whilst Britain was making frantic efforts to circumvent the West Indian monopoly and import from Brazil and other places more of the very sugar which the British West Indies were alleged to be overproducing.

The ingenious explanation offered for what would appear to be the height of illogicality was that British West Indian production was in excess of British consumption; the surplus had to be exported to Europe, where it came into competition with the cheaper sugar of Brazil and Cuba which the British imported solely for refining and re-export. Thus, the argument ran, the salvation of the British West Indies depended on their reducing their production to the point where it coincided with British consumption, which would give them a 'real' monopoly. This surplus was estimated at one-quarter of British West Indian production. 'As far as the amount of the production of sugar is concerned,' said Stanley during the emancipation debate, 'I am not quite certain that to some extent a diminution of that production would be matter of regret—I am not quite certain that it might not be for the benefit of the planters and of the colonies themselves, in the end, if that production were to be diminished.'

One hundred years before the Board of Trade had complained that the British West Indian planters were restricting production to maintain prices. Stanley advised them to do precisely that. But in 1733 what was involved was the increase of slave labour; in 1833 its abolition.

Whereas the abolition of the slave system in the British, French,

Dutch and Danish colonies in the Caribbean was a metropolitan measure imposed on recalcitrant colonials, in the Spanish colonies, Cuba and Puerto Rico, it was the metropolitan government which insisted on the system in the face of a powerful colonial opposition. The colonials rested their case chiefly on the economic ground that white, free labour was cheaper than black slave labour. In Cuba it was estimated in 1862 that the sugar production from 490 acres and 74 free workers was equivalent to that from 635 acres worked by 142 slaves. In that year free labour was responsible for one-quarter of Cuba's sugar production and five-sixths of the tobacco. The census figures proved that there was no danger of a shortage of free labour, as follows:

		Free		
Year	Whites	Coloured	Slaves	Total
1817	276,689	119,221	239,694	635,604
1846	425,769	149,226	323,897	898,892
1857	560,161	177,824	372,110	1,110,095
1867	833,157	248,703	344,615	1,426,475

The Cuban situation was aggravated by the fact that the sugar planters, the chief interest concerned with the maintenance of slavery, were not unanimous in desiring its perpetuation and the continuation of the slave trade on which it was based. In 1843 ninety-two planters of Matanzas, one of the chief sugar-producing centres of the island, demanded abolition of the slave trade. In 1866 several slaveowners in the island submitted a memorandum to the metropolitan Senate in which they stated that the consequence of abolition would be 'a reduction of the fabulous profits which the colossal *ingenios* return; at the same time that these fortunes are increased, the small industries, worthy of the most efficacious protection, are impoverished and killed'. As the equipment of sugar manufacture became more costly the price of slaves increased, and as the *ingenio* became larger, fewer and fewer planters could afford the capital investment required. Of the total of 2,000 *ingenios* in 1860, only eight were really monsters. The monsters produced 66,250 tons of sugar, the others 506,800 tons. The average return from 33 acres of cane was 27 tons of sugar in the ordinary *ingenio*, 36 tons with the improved machinery of the monster plantation. The less affluent planters were not indisposed to abolish a system from which they no longer benefited as much as they had done in the past.

The Puerto Rico situation was unique in the Caribbean, in that not only did the white population outnumber the people of colour, but the slaves constituted an infinitesimal part of the total population and free labour predominated during the regime of slavery. The following table has no counterpart in Caribbean history:

Population	1827	1834	1860	1872
Total	323,838	357,086	583,181	618,150
Whites	162,311	188,869	300,430	328,806
Mulattoes	100,430	101,275	241,015 }	257,709 }
Free Negroes	26,857	25,124		
Slaves	34,240	41,818	41,736	31,635
Slaves as % of total	10	12	14	5
Slaves as % of coloured	21	33	16	11

These 31,635 slaves were divided among nearly two thousand owners. Few owners owned more than fifty slaves. Of the total there were only 21,000 between the ages of 15 and 50. Many were domestics; male labourers numbered 11,748. The explanation is that Puerto Rico's was a small farming and diversified economy, based on the cultivation of minor crops rather than plantation staples. In 1830 the total acreage under cultivation amounted to 120,721 cuerdas, divided as follows: starchy vegetables, 40,955; coffee, 17,247; maize, 16,674; rice, 15,290; sugar, 15,242; fruits, 8,301; cotton, 3,170; tobacco, 2,676; other crops, 1,166. There were 70,000 head of cattle in the island, 53,000 horses and mares, 25,000 swine, 347,000 fowl, 7,500 sheep, and 6,000 goats.

Essentially a food-producing colony, with a birth rate of 56 per thousand in 1824, and a density of population of 180 per square mile in 1872, Puerto Rico did not need slavery, had an adequate supply of free labour, and could anticipate no shortage. The island sent delegates to Spain in 1866 to demand the abolition of slavery, not only as a moral necessity, but also as an economic necessity. 'No really acceptable reason,' they stated in their official memorandum, 'can be given for its continuation in Puerto Rico. The general wealth of the island does not need it: its disappearance will not affect any productive element, and the self-interest of the owners must demand the overthrow of that institution.'

Their arguments for the superiority of free labour over slave would have done credit to Adam Smith himself. They deserve to be quoted:

> 'Let all the disadvantages of the one and all the advantages of the other be weighed; let the greater intelligence and interest with which free men work be appreciated, the fidelity and personal responsibility they display, the cheapness of their wages, the stimulus which is awakened in them, let all this be appreciated on the one hand, and then on the other consider the sickness, flights, captures, baptisms, marriages and burials of the slaves, all expenses which fall on the owner; the thefts and judicial proceedings to which they give rise; the absenteeism resulting from punishments, sickness and sometimes also indolence; finally, let the endless and continuous expenses of maintenance, medical care and so many others be added, and it will be seen that, in order to make slave labour cheaper than free, it is necessary for the master to dismiss from his mind every generous sentiment, every notion of justice, and to consider the Negro only and exclusively as a machine for production which, with a minimum of subsistence, can function fourteen hours a day, for four or five years at most.'

If Puerto Rico, by the conventional standards of the final quarter of the nineteenth century, ranked as one of the most backward sectors of Caribbean economy, in intellectual perspective it was head and shoulders above its neighbours.

(2) The Political Factors

The second set of factors in the abolition of the slave system which we are now to consider is the political. This can be treated under two heads—the metropolitan and the colonial.

From the standpoint of metropolitan politics, the abolition of the Caribbean slave system was, on the one hand, a part of that general struggle of the industrial bourgeoisie against the landed aristocracy which began in France with the French Revolution of 1789, advanced in England with the First Reform Bill of 1832, triumphed with the repeal of the English Corn Laws in 1846, and culminated in the victory of the North over the South in the Civil War in the United States. A belated echo of this struggle was the successful Spanish Revolution of 1868 which deposed the monarchy.

On the other hand, the emancipation of the slaves was a part of

the general movement of the European industrial proletariat towards democracy. The centres of the agitation against slavery
were the great industrial towns of Britain and France, with
Manchester, Birmingham, Sheffield and Paris in the lead. 'The
people must emancipate the slaves,' said Joseph Sturge, the
Quaker abolitionist in 1833, 'for the government never will.'
The West Indian slave system depended in Britain upon the
eighteenth-century rotten boroughs and parliamentary venality.
Cobbett, the working-class leader, said that the fruit of slave
labour had long been used to making slaves of the British people.
'God forbid,' said Lord Wynford, an absentee West Indian proprietor, 'that there should be anything like a forcing of the master
to abandon his property in the slave! Once adopt that principle
and there is an end to all property.'

In the elections for the Parliament which passed the First
Reform Bill, slavery in the West Indies was a vital issue. 'I am an
advocate for the abolition of West Indian slavery,' said Brougham
in his campaign in Sheffield, 'and both root and branch I will
tear it up. I have loosened it already, and if you will assist me, I
will brandish it over your heads.' Candidates were quizzed as to
their views on slavery. Negroes were dragged to the election with
golden chains, chimney sweeps being substituted when Negroes
were not available. Half the hustings in the country were decorated
with full-length pictures of white planters flogging Negro women.
The Emancipation Act of 1833 was one of the first measures
passed by the Reformed Parliament.

The organised French working class similarly took up the cause
of the slaves. On January 22, 1844, the workers of Paris petitioned
the Chamber of Deputies for the immediate abolition of slavery,
which they called leprosy, and they protested loudly 'in the name
of the working class, against the upholders of slavery, who dare
to claim... that the condition of French workers is more deplorable than that of the slaves'. Emancipation in France was
the immediate sequel to the French Revolution of 1848, when
barricades were thrown up in the streets of Paris. The emancipation decision was of the simplest: 'French soil cannot support
slavery any longer.' The Provisional Government of the Republic
appointed a commission to prepare, as rapidly as possible, the
act of immediate emancipation in all the French colonies.

The attitude of the Dutch working class towards slavery is brought out by an incident which took place in the new church of Amsterdam, on May 12, 1849, on the occasion of the visit of King William III. An escutcheon was displayed whose glories recalled the glories of Holland. On it there was the motto, in Latin: 'Justice, Piety, Faith.' Below these words someone scrawled the single word: 'Surinam!'

From the standpoint of the Spanish colonials, the abolition of the slave system was an integral part of the struggle for independence in Cuba and autonomy in Puerto Rico. The first war of independence broke out in Cuba in 1868. Cespedes, who raised the standard of revolt, immediately freed the slaves. The Emancipation Decree read:

'The Cuban revolution, while proclaiming the independence of the country, had proclaimed also general liberty, being unable to accept its limitation to only a part of the population. A free Cuba is incompatible with a slave Cuba, and the abolition of Spanish institutions must include and includes of necessity and by virtue of the highest justice the abolition of slavery as the most iniquitous of all.'

Like Lincoln before him, Cespedes understood that no nation could survive half slave and half free. Also like Lincoln, he used emancipation as a powerful political weapon in the struggle. According to the decree, the slaves were freed and drafted into the service of the country. Owners who supported the revolution would be eligible for compensation for their slaves if they so desired; those who opposed it would be ineligible. No one in Europe could sneer, as Samuel Johnson had sneered at the revolutionaries in the thirteen mainland colonies nearly a century before, at Cuban slaveowners uttering the loudest yelps for liberty. The Cuban revolution was able to achieve the moral status which the United States had failed to achieve: it recognised that the Negro was a whole man, and that the political liberty of the whites could not be based on the social subordination of the Negroes.

In Puerto Rico, also, the white population, openly bracketing together dictatorship, monopoly and slavery, placed the rights of the slaves before its own civil liberty. Rafael de Labra, one of the island's representatives in the *Cortes*, quoting Figaro's phrase that 'liberty is not an overseas commodity', challenged the men of the 1868 revolution who had revolted for the imprescriptible rights of men to say that what was truth on one side of the Pyrenees was a lie on the other. 'What example,' asked another representative, Emilio Castelar, 'can we give to Latin America, independent, republican, democratic, when it sees existing in Spanish territories white slavery and Negro slavery, the colonial regime and the slave regime, which the human conscience rejects in indignation?' Referring to the abolition of slavery by the Convention of France in 1794, Castelar, with a knowledge and appreciation of history rare in the protagonists of emancipation, asserted:

'Even though the Convention had committed more crimes than it did, the tears of the pariah redeemed, of the eternal Spartacus emancipated, of the slave made man; those tears which condensed the gratitude of all the future generations and the blessing of all the past generations trampled under the vile heel of slavery, those tears sufficed to wipe out all the stains of blood.'

It was widely suggested in Spain that the settlement of the slavery issue in Puerto Rico should await the outcome of events in Cuba, where the war of independence was in full swing. This was anathema to the Puerto Ricans. Sanroma replied to the *Cortes* in 1873:

'To subordinate the interests of Puerto Rico to those of Cuba is . . . a signal iniquity. I do not admit it; neither from the legal point of view, nor from the political, nor from the historical, nor from the economic can the interests of Puerto Rico be subordinated to those of Cuba . . . When on earth will they leave us of Puerto Rico in peace with their eternal Cuba?'

(3) The Humanitarian Agitation

The humanitarian agitation for the abolition of the slave system is associated particularly with the names of Clarkson, Wilberforce and Fowell Buxton in England, and of Victor Schoelcher in France. It was responsible for two aspects of the abolition struggle —the view that the slave trade was inhuman and its abolition a triumph of humanitarianism, and the policy that emancipation of the slaves must be gradual.

The abolitionists, as they were generally called, sedulously propagated the view that humanitarian considerations were the dominant factor. Wilberforce recorded in his diary with respect to the debates on the abolition of the slave trade in 1807:

'How astonishing is our success, and the eagerness and zeal of the House now, when the members have been so fastidious as scarce to hear a speech about it! Six or eight getting up at once, and the young noblemen especially ...everybody taking me by the hand; and several voting with us for the first time...How popular abolition is, just now. God can turn the hearts of men!'

The British Parliament was at pains to emphasise this interpretation. In the House of Lords objections were raised to the declaration that the slave trade was contrary to justice and humanity on the ground that this was a reflection on the slave traders. An amendment was, therefore, introduced basing abolition on sound policy only. The House of Lords, until recently the obstacle to abolition, voted for the original wording. The amendment, it was felt, would lend colour to the suspicion abroad that Britain, with her colonies well-stocked with slaves, could afford to abolish the slave trade. 'How,' asked the Earl of Lauderdale, 'in thus being supposed to make no sacrifices ourselves, could we call with any effect upon foreign powers to co-operate in the abolition?'

Up to this time the British abolitionists had never supported emancipation. On the day after the abolition of the slave trade, a bill was introduced for the gradual abolition of slavery. Wilberforce rejoiced at its introduction, as it gave him an opportunity to oppose it and show the distinction his party had always made between abolition and emancipation. The abolitionists turned their attention to measures calculated to prevent evasion of the abolition act and secure its enforcement. They introduced a bill for the registration of slaves and another for making the slave trade a felony. In 1814 a suggestion was made that all slaves illicitly imported into the British dominions should immediately be declared free. Wilberforce vetoed it: 'Our object and our universal language was and is, to produce by abolition a disposition to breed instead of buying. This is the great vital principle which would work in every direction, and produce reform everywhere.'

It was not until 1823 that the abolitionists adopted the policy of emancipation, being driven to it, to a considerable extent, by colonial attacks on the missionaries. The policy adopted was one of gradual emancipation. It was stated by Buxton, who had replaced Wilberforce as parliamentary leader, as follows:

'Nothing rash, nothing rapid, nothing abrupt, nothing bearing any feature of violence... (Slavery) will subside; it will decline; it will expire; it will, as it were, burn itself down into its socket and go out... We shall leave it gently to decay—slowly, silently, almost imperceptibly to die away and to be forgotten.'

Under abolitionist pressure the British Government prepared various ameliorating measures, designed to strike a balance between the slaves, on the one hand, and the planters, on the other. The British Government's middle-of-the-road policy of gradualism was explained by the Prime Minister, Canning. There were knots, he said, which could not be suddenly disentangled and must not be cut. What was morally true must not be confused with what was historically false, and, faced with 'conflicting prejudices and extravagances of principle', the Government could not legislate as if it was for a new world, 'the surface of which was totally clear from the obstructions of antecedent claims and obligations'. It was not, nor could it be made, a question merely of right, of humanity, or of morality.

The ameliorating measures were as follows: the abolition of the flogging of female slaves; the prohibition of the whip in the field; the deferment of punishments to a prescribed period after the commission of the offence; the registration of punishments; facilities for compulsory manumission of slaves who could afford the purchase price; acceptance of the evidence of slaves in courts of law; appointment of protectors of slaves; establishment of savings banks for slaves; abolition of Sunday markets and the grant of an alternative day to the slaves for this purpose; a six-day week; a nine-hour day; provision for the religious and moral improvement of the slaves.

The measures were to be introduced forthwith into the crown colonies, British Guiana, Trinidad and St. Lucia, the colonies annexed after the wars with Bonaparte. These had been denied self-governing institutions and the crown legislated by simple orders-in-council. The measures were to be recommended for adoption by the self-governing colonies, with the 'temperate but

authoritative admonition' of the metropolitan government, but
with no direct pressure or intervention unless the colonies re-
sponded with contumacy.

The British abolitionists relied for success upon aristocratic
patronage, parliamentary diplomacy, and private influence with
men in office. They deprecated extreme measures and feared
popular agitation. This conservatism was largely the result of the
leadership of Wilberforce, who was addicted to moderation, compromise and delay. He was a member of the secret committee of
1817 set up to investigate and repress popular discontent, in the
days which foreshadowed the Peterloo Massacre; his house barely
escaped attack by the masses for his support of the corn law
of 1815; he thought parliamentary reform too radical. His policy,
as criticised by one of his ablest lieutenants, Stephen, was 'to
load the shelves of a cabinet minister with laboured memorials,
to haunt him with conferences for years, and at last to be turned
round by the whisper that a governor stands well with great men,
and must not have his toes trod upon'.

With the development of the agitation for parliamentary reform, another type of abolitionist, bolder and more robust in
nature, appeared to demand immediate action. Such a man was
Joseph Sturge. Conservatives and radicals clashed in a meeting
of the Anti-Slavery Society in May, 1830. There had been the
usual resolutions and speeches until Pownwall rose to put his
amendment—immediate emancipation. All was confusion.
Buxton deprecated, Brougham interposed, Wilberforce waved his
hand for silence, but the amendment was eventually carried 'with
a burst of exulting triumph that would have made the falls of
Niagara inaudible at equal distance'.

The outstanding abolitionist of the period was James Stephen
of the Colonial Office, who, from this vantage point, maintained
a watching brief over the slaves and raised the doctrine of trusteeship to a dignity and reality which have never since been equalled.
The following excerpts from two of his official memoranda,
written in 1831 and 1832, reveal the man in action:

'The deprivation of a mansion or an equipage, painful though it may
be, is hardly to be set against the protracted exclusion from those common
advantages of human life under which from the admitted facts of the case
the Slaves are proved to be labouring ... The ultimate end of human

society—the security of life, property and reputation—must be preferred to its subordinate ends—the enjoyment of particular franchises.'

Stephen was the great advocate of crown colony government; his argument, as expressed in a minute of 1841, was that 'popular franchises in the hands of a great body of owners of slaves were the worst instruments of tyranny which were ever yet forged for the oppression of mankind'. A man of tremendous energy and an indefatigable worker, Stephen drafted the Emancipation Act in forty-eight hours, and it was not his fault that it contained concessions by the Secretary of State and amendments to which he was opposed.

The abolitionist policy of gradual emancipation was a failure. In the early years of the abolitionist movement Pitt and Wilberforce had emphasised that the slave population could be maintained without the slave trade. In the eleven years preceding 1832, the slave population of British Guiana declined by 52,000 —a rate at which, by Buxton's calculations, the earth would be depopulated in fifty years. The frightful mortality, the price paid for the extension of sugar cultivation in the colony, was accompanied by an appalling infliction of punishments which amounted in 1829 to over 20,000 a year, or one punishment annually for every third slave, totalling two million lashes. If the workers of Britain had been punished in the same proportion, wrote Stephen, between six and seven million punishments would have been inflicted. British Guiana was a crown colony, where all the ameliorating measures of the abolitionists had been put into effect.

Slavery was abolished in the British colonies in 1833. But it was still gradual emancipation. A system of apprenticeship was instituted, to last until 1840; it was eventually abolished in 1838.

The policy of gradual abolition was adopted also by the French abolitionists and the French Government. In 1832 the tax on manumission was abolished; in the following year the Government suppressed branding and mutilation of slaves, established a general registry of the slaves, and accorded civil rights to free men of colour; in 1836 it revived the early eighteenth-century custom whereby slaves became free on arrival in France. The government measures had the full support of the French Society for the Abolition of Slavery, founded in 1834 as the successor of the *Amis des Noirs*. It was heavily weighted on the side of gradualism. Its president was the Duc de Broglie; one of its two vice-presidents was the economist, Hippolyte Passy; its most distinguished members were the poet, Alphonse de Lamartine, and the political scientist, Alexis de Tocqueville, the famous author of *Democracy in America*.

In 1833 Passy unsuccessfully proposed the freedom of all slave children born after that date and legal provision for manumission at prices fixed by the metropolitan government. A proposal by de Tocqueville in the following year for gradual emancipation in ten years, with compensation to the planters, did not even reach the stage of discussion. In 1840 the government appointed a commission, with the Duc de Broglie as chairman, to study the question. The commission took three years to produce its report, whose vague conclusions satisfied nobody. In 1845 the government made provision for compulsory manumission, limited corporal punishment, and made elementary and religious instruction for the slaves mandatory. The slaves belonging to the State were freed in 1846 and 1847.

At this juncture, with events moving rapidly towards the denouement of the revolution of 1848, the abolitionist leadership passed into the hands of Victor Schoelcher, who was at one and the same time the Clarkson and the Wilberforce of France, the propagandist and political leader. Like Clarkson, a prolific writer and pamphleteer in a cause which he regarded as a crusade, he had travelled widely in slave areas: Mexico, Cuba, the United States and the French West Indies. His most important works are *Slavery of the Negroes and Colonial Legislation*, published in 1833; *French Colonies: Immediate Abolition of Slavery*, in 1842; and *History of Slavery during the last Two Years*, in 1847.

Beginning as a supporter of gradual emancipation, Schoelcher became the intransigent advocate of immediate abolition. Galvanising the entire country into action, with the aid of committees set up in all departments, he presented his 'sixteen points' to the legislature on August 30, 1847. The gospel according to Schoelcher reads as follows:

'Property of man in man is a crime.

'The inadequacy and danger of the so-called preparatory measures adopted are manifest.

'These preparatory measures have not fully been put into force.

'The vices of slavery can be destroyed only by abolishing slavery itself.

'All notions of justice and humanity are lost in a slave society.

'Men are still sold, like cattle, in the colonies.

'There is an annual excess of deaths over births in the slave population.

'The honour of France is compromised by tinkering with a dying institution.

'The example of England has shown the danger of all transitional systems.

'Emancipation in the British West Indies has had satisfactory moral and material results.

'The prolongation of slavery threatens the best interests of the colonies and the security of their inhabitants.

'Abolition, by rehabilitating agricultural labour, will attach the free population to it.

'The owners themselves, at long last, accept emancipation.

'It is more costly to maintain slavery, than to abolish it.

'Barbarous princes have already abolished slavery. (Referring to Tunis and Egypt.)

'Emancipation of the Negroes in the French West Indies will lead to the emancipation of the entire Negro race.

'By virtue of the solidarity which binds all the members of a nation, each of us is partly responsible for the crimes engendered by slavery.'

The advent of the 1848 revolution made the Schoelcher creed the true faith. Appointed Under Secretary of State for the Navy with jurisdiction over the colonies, Schoelcher was designated president of the commission set up to prepare the emancipation legislation. The Commission's report, fundamentally the work of Schoelcher, is one of the most important documents in Caribbean history. It emphasised that slavery was no longer tenable, and that immediate emancipation, without any transition period of apprenticeship, was in accord not only with natural law but also with the best interests of the colonies. It ends with a ringing peroration of the 'eternal example' France was setting to the world:

'The Republic rejects distinctions in the human family. It does not believe that a people glorying in freedom can pass over in silence a whole class of men kept outside the pale of the common rights of humanity. It has taken its principles seriously. It is making reparation to these unfortunate people for the crimes which it committed against their ancestors and the land of their birth by giving them France as their fatherland and all the rights of French citizens as their heritage, thereby bearing witness that it excludes no one from its immortal motto: *"liberty, equality, fraternity"*.'

The policy of gradual emancipation was adopted also by the Danish Government. By a royal decree of 1834, compulsory manumission was established, the right of the slave to his plot of land affirmed, public sale of slaves and the separation of children from their parents prohibited, and steps prescribed to prepare a law on the labour, maintenance and discipline of slaves. Regulations respecting the last-mentioned subject were issued in 1838. In 1836 Sunday labour was forbidden. Schools were started for the moral and religious instruction of the slaves.

But, as the tempo of events in Europe accelerated, the demand for immediate emancipation became more vigorous. In 1846 a deputy in the metropolitan legislature proposed immediate emancipation with compensation. The proposal was passed by a vote of two to one, and the government was directed to prepare a law for complete emancipation. On July 23, 1847 the Danish Government issued a decree, however, abolishing slavery but maintaining the power of the owners until 1859, all children born in the interim being declared free. Slavery was abolished in 1848, and a period of apprenticeship substituted which lasted until 1878.

The Cuban abolitionists were concerned more with the abolition of the slave trade in accordance with the treaty signed with Britain than with the abolition of slavery. But even this was too dangerous under the Spanish regime. The abolitionists were summarily dealt with by the Spanish authorities, who took the view, expressed by the planters, that 'the Negroes come here ready made, the bags of sugar have yet to be made'. Prominent Cubans like José Antonio Saco, the historian, Domingo del Monte, the planter, and Domingo Gener, another intellectual, were exiled or forced to leave the island for writing against the slave trade or endorsing abolitionist petitions. Gaspar Betancourt Cisneros, a rich planter, was severely admonished for being suspected of supporting abolition. Luz y Caballero, the distinguished Cuban philosopher, was hauled before a military commission. Manuel Martinez Serrano was incarcerated without trial and died in prison. The Captain-General of the island refused to see a deputa-tion of planters from Matanzas who wished to protest against the slave trade, tore to pieces another address presented by planters of Havana, replied to a third delegation with menaces. Such was the Cuban environment that Saco wrote that it was better to be branded an independent than a Negrophile.

The establishment of the Spanish Anti-Slavery Society in 1865 did not materially alter the situation. The Government followed the beaten path of gradualism, though the Society itself stood committed to immediate emancipation. In the very years of Cespedes' emancipation proclamation, the Spanish republican government castigated slavery as an outrage to humanity and an affront to Spain; their humanitarianism was limited, however, to the modest proposal that all children born thereafter should be declared free. This so-called 'law of the free stomach' was promulgated in 1870; in addition, freedom was decreed for slaves who had helped the Spanish troops in the civil war in Cuba, for slaves of the State, and for slaves who had reached the age of sixty. Eventually emancipation was proclaimed in 1880. But gradualism triumphed; a period of apprenticeship was instituted which lasted until October 7, 1886.

Spanish paternalism was best illustrated by the case of Puerto Rico. The planters to a man demanded immediate emancipation, with or without compensation. The metropolitan government decreed otherwise. On March 22, 1873 slavery was abolished. But the 31,635 slaves were required to enter into contracts with their owners for a period of not less than three years. If their owners refused to enter into such contracts, they were entered into contracts with other persons or with the government. Three functionaries were appointed protectors of the freedmen. After five years the freedmen were to receive political rights. It was like using a sledge-hammer to kill a fly.

(4) International and Intercolonial Rivalry

International and intercolonial rivalry also played a conspicuous part in the abolition of the Caribbean slave system.

With the British annexation of British Guiana and Trinidad, the planters of the older British colonies resumed their eighteenth-century opposition to new settlements. In the opinion of one of the leaders of the Jamaican plantocracy in 1804, the British slave trade ought to be restricted to the old colonies and prohibited to Trinidad. In 1806 a bill was passed by Parliament to abolish the foreign slave trade and to prohibit the introduction of slaves into British Guiana and Trinidad. As the Government spokesman argued, it was British subjects and British capital which supplied slaves to the rivals of the British planters in Cuba, Hispaniola, Martinique, Guadeloupe. As the colonies were not only the sources of the prosperity but also the foundation of the maritime strength of the European countries, it seemed to him that it was contrary to sound policy that Britain should afford them the means of rivalling her own colonies and of attaining a high degree of commercial prosperity.

The abolition of the British slave trade in 1807 left British Guiana and Trinidad desperately short of labour. Subsequent legislation making the slave trade a felony and requiring a general registry of the slaves in each colony made evasion of the abolition act difficult. But the act contained one loophole—it permitted the slaveowner on his travels to take with him two domestic servants. British Guiana and Trinidad exploited this advantage to the maximum, with the support of speculators in the old colonies. A fraudulent intercolonial trade in domestic slaves soon grew up and attained large proportions. Between 1808 and 1825 a total of 9,250 domestics was imported into British Guiana, and, up to 1821, 3,815 into Trinidad.

Specious arguments were used by Governors and planters alike to justify and encourage this trade. The most popular was that, as crown colonies, without discretion with respect to the ameliorating measures commanded by the metropolitan government, the slaves should be encouraged to migrate from the self-governing colonies. 'If the order in council cannot go to the slaves,' argued the Attorney General of Trinidad, 'the slave might be permitted to come to the order in council in Trinidad'. The poor black wretches, said the Governor of Trinidad, had only six pints of cornmeal per week in islands like Tortola, the most miserable of all the colonies. In Trinidad, on the other hand, he continued, no one starved, a Negro had not only his pig, but half a dozen goats or dogs as well, while the richness and extent of the soil permitted the planters to give the slaves more ground for the cultivation of their own produce. At the same time, so the Governor argued, the richness of the soil diminished the labour of the slaves—an argument which elicited from the Colonial

Office the comment: 'this is not only a *non sequitur*, but I should think a *nusquam sequitur*. Where the soil is rich less labour is required to raise a given amount of produce, but more produce will be raised, not less labour employed.'

It was the superior value of slaves and the greater fertility of the soil of Trinidad and Guiana which formed the background to this intercolonial slave trade. The cost of a slave in Barbados or Antigua was only £35 or £40, in Guiana and Trinidad it was from £80 to £90. In 1813 the relative fertility of British Guiana and Barbados was estimated at four to one in terms of slave output *per capita*. In Guiana it took 200 days' labour to produce 5,000 pounds of sugar; in Barbados 400. In the former no outlay of capital for manure was necessary, in the latter it required one-fourth of the labour of the plantation. A Guiana plantation of 600 slaves produced 800 to 900 hogsheads of sugar in a year; Montserrat, with between 3,000 and 4,000 slaves, exported only 1,500 hogsheads. The canes in Trinidad produced saccharine matter in the proportion of 5 to 2 as compared with the older islands; the average output of sugar was three hogsheads per slave as compared with one in the older islands. The older islands faced the prospect of being denuded of both planters and slaves. Bolingbroke viewed the matter with studied nonchalance. It was a natural consequence to expect 'the total abandonment of the barren islands for the more fertile soil of the continent'. The 'barren islands' were Curaçao, St. Eustatius, Saba, St. Martin, Tortola, Tobago, Grenada, and St. Vincent.

At the beginning of the British campaign for abolition of the slave trade, the Prime Minister, William Pitt, was concerned not only with the abolition of the British slave trade, but also with an international abolition of the slave trade by all the powers connected with its prosecution. The initial reaction to this proposal was unfavourable, and the proposal itself was abandoned when war broke out between Britain and France and British policy concentrated on the annexation of the French colonies in the West Indies.

With the abolition of the slave trade by Britain in 1807, the issue of an international abolition again arose. As matters stood, the British West Indies were deprived of their annual supply of African slaves, whilst their foreign rivals were free to augment their labour supply from this source. The result was that the British West Indian planters, who had for so long opposed British abolition, became now the loudest advocates of the cause of humanity. In 1810, Hibbert of Jamaica looked forward with dread to the end of the war with France, when France would again be in possession of extensive colonies in the West Indies. Marryat of Trinidad said that, in assisting Spain in the contest with Bonaparte, Britain was fighting for liberty with one hand and slavery with the other. Lord Holland, a West Indian proprietor, kept the slave trade before the House of Lords after 1807 as persistently as Wilberforce had kept it before the House of Commons before 1807. He denounced the slave trade as 'a system of manstealing against a poor and inoffensive people', and criticised the Government on the ground that, 'at Paris, at Madrid, and at Rio de Janeiro the cause has been very coldly, or at least very inefficiently, supported, if it has not actually been betrayed'.

An Address to the Prince Regent in 1814, presented by Wilberforce, concerning the total annihilation of the slave trade, was supported and eulogised by the member for Liverpool, a member for Bristol and the most prominent of the West Indian planters. It was Barham, another West Indian, who introduced a bill to make criminal the employment of British capital in the foreign slave trade, and even to make the insurance of ships in a slave trade voyage criminal. The Committee of Correspondence of the Jamaica Assembly stated in 1822 that, so long as the slave trade was permitted to continue to supply foreign colonies, nothing that the British Government might do on behalf of the West Indies would be of any avail.

Among the remedies suggested by the West India Interest in London in 1830 to meet the increasing distress of the colonies was the following: 'to adopt more decisive measures than any that have hitherto been employed, to stop the foreign slave trade; on the effectual suppression of which the prosperity of the British West India Colonies, and the consequent success of the measures of amelioration now in progress in them, ultimately depend.'

The Jamaica Assembly sent two delegates in 1832 to Britain to discuss the question of emancipation. The delegates stated that their great adversary was the prodigious increase of the slave trade. They continued: 'The colonies were easily reconciled to the abolition of a barbarous commerce, which the advanced civilisation of the age no longer permitted to exist; but they have thought and apparently with reason that the philanthropists should not have been satisfied with the extinction of the British trade.'

This criticism did not do justice to the abolitionists. They had never expressed their satisfaction with the abolition of the British slave trade alone. They looked to the peace negotiations in 1815 as a providential opportunity for obtaining an international denunciation and renunciation of the slave trade. They appealed to the virtues, humanity and religious feelings of the restored king of France, Louis XVIII. They hoped that the Pope would be induced to denounce the slave trade, and that this denunciation would have its effect on Catholic countries. They brought to bear on the Government of Britain what the sons of Wilberforce called 'friendly violence'. They whipped up public opinion in England to a point that was unprecedented in English history up to that time. Thus, in thirty-four days from June 27, 1814, no fewer than 772 petitions on the subject, bearing nearly a million signatures, were presented to the House of Commons, and the Government was warned that, at the Congress of Vienna, the British plenipotentiary had to speak for Africa. Not content with this, the abolitionists sent their own spokesman, Thomas Clarkson, to the peace negotiations. Wellington wrote that the people of Britain were ready to go to war for abolition.

How strongly the abolitionists felt about the continuation of the slave trade by foreign powers is seen most clearly in a remarkable memorandum sent by Stephen to Lord Castlereagh in preparation for the congress at Aix-la-Chapelle in 1818. The main theme was the fear of French reconquest of Haiti, formerly Saint-Domingue, which would have exposed the British West Indies to the unequal competition of the years before 1789. Stephen wrote:

'It would be of unspeakable importance to Great Britain if means could be found to induce France to release her claim of sovereignty in Haiti, or, if this cannot be accomplished, at least to prevent her from asserting that claim by war. (If Haitian independence was maintained) Britain might perhaps have, at no far distant period, a West Indian Island worth more to our manufactures than all our sugar colonies collectively, and without any drawback for the expenses of its government and its protection in time of war ... might easily secure this commerce to herself ... and even obtain perhaps a conventional monopoly of it, if this were an object we could inoffensively and decorously pursue. Of course, any appearance of a self-interested purpose would spoil all . . . Reconquest of Haiti would mean restoration of the slave trade. It is politic to consider if the people of England are thus to lose their commerce, their money, and their benevolent hopes, by the moral apostasy of France, and her breach of solemn engagements, they may not add to it the loss of their temper; and whether, at some not far distant crisis, the peace of Europe may not be broken on the slave coast.'

The continued pressure of British West Indian planters and British abolitionists placed a terrific strain upon the British Government. Castlereagh begged Parliament to 'moderate their virtuous feelings, and put their solicitude for Africa under the dominion of reason.' Lord Liverpool confessed to Wilberforce: 'If I were not anxious for the abolition of the slave trade on principle, I must be aware of the embarrassment to which any Government must be exposed from the present state of that question in this country.' He knew very well that vested interests stood in the way and that nothing could be done. But, as he confessed to Wellington in 1814: 'The question of the abolition of the slave trade has become so embarrassing that it would be expedient to purchase it by some sacrifice though it should be refused.'

Fourteen years later, when the prospect of international abolition had become remote, Wellington admitted to the Earl of Aberdeen the effects of the pressure of what someone called the 'whole loads of humbug' which expressed the feelings of the country. Wellington wrote: 'we shall never succeed in abolishing the foreign slave trade. But we must take care to avoid to take any steps which may induce the people of England that we did not do everything in our power to discourage and put it down as soon as possible'.

The British Government did its best. Its plenipotentiary at Vienna was authorised to offer as much as three million pounds to France in return for a promise to abolish the slave trade, and the Government was prepared to offer a West Indian colony in return for immediate abolition. In 1818, they signed a treaty with Spain by which the latter agreed to abolish the slave trade on May 30, 1820, in return for a gift of four hundred thousand pounds. They brought pressure on their old ally, Portugal, to obtain the abolition of the Portuguese slave trade to Brazil. The British

Government, however, had to satisfy not only the humanitarians but also the capitalists, and the two interests were not always identical. No wonder Huskisson of the Board of Trade confessed that slave questions nearly drove him mad.

For example, at the peace negotiations, Britain proposed a boycott of the produce of territories that continued to engage in the slave trade. Wellington was authorised to make this proposal at the Congress of Vienna. He was instructed that, if his proposal was met with the inquiry whether Britain was also prepared to exclude the produce of slave trading countries imported not for consumption but for re-exportation, he was to express his readiness to refer that proposition for immediate consideration to his Government. Wellington's proposal was received in silence, and he observed, as he stated in a letter to Canning, 'those symptoms of disapprobation and dissent which convince me not only that it will not be adopted, but that the suggestion of it is attributed to interested motives not connected with the humane desire of abolishing the slave trade'. Canning, the Prime Minister, summed up the whole question for the Cabinet:

'The proposed refusal to admit Brazilian sugar into the dominions of the Emperors (of Russia and Austria) and the King of Prussia was met (as might be expected) with a smile; which indicated on the part of the continental statesmen a suspicion that there might be something of self-interest in our suggestion for excluding the produce of rival colonies from competition with our own, and their surprise that we should consent to be the carriers of the produce which we would fain dissuade them from consuming.'

The proposal for a boycott was thus unsuccessful. This technique having failed, the British Government resorted to another expedient. Latin American countries were struggling for their independence and looking to the European powers for recognition. In 1822 Canning proposed to Wellington that this recognition should be purchased in the case of Brazil by a frank surrender of the slave trade. But Canning realised that there was the danger that France would recognise Brazil, on condition that the slave trade was continued. As he informed the Cabinet:

'We may come too late with our offer contingent upon its discontinuance, and we shall have missed, and missed irrecoverably, an opportunity of affecting the greatest material good of which human society is now susceptible, and of getting rid of some of the most perplexing discussions with which the counsels of this country are embarrassed.'

He put the dilemma very clearly in two letters to Wilberforce, in October 1822. He wrote:

'You argue against the acknowledgement of Brazil unpurged of Slave Trade ... you are surprised that the Duke of Wellington has not been instructed to say that we will give up the trade with Brazil, (for that is, I am afraid, the amount of giving up the import and re-export of her sugar and cotton), if Austria, Russia and Prussia will prohibit her produce. In fair reasoning, you have a right to be surprised, for we ought to be ready to make sacrifices when we ask them, and I am for making them; but who would dare to promise such a one as this without a full knowledge of the opinion of the commercial part of the nation? ... there are immense British interests engaged in the trade with Brazil, and we must proceed with caution and good heed; and take the commercial as well as moral feelings of the country with us.'

The campaign against the foreign slave trade failed because British capitalism was heavily interested in trade with Latin America, particularly Brazil and Cuba. It could not kill the goose that laid the golden eggs—that is, it could not oppose the introduction of the slaves who produced the sugar and coffee that made possible the purchase of British textiles and provided freights for British ships.

There was a second reason for the failure to secure an international abolition of the slave trade. The authorities in France, Spain and Portugal secretly connived at the slave trade or openly patronised it, irrespective of the treaty obligations to which they had subscribed. This is what a British merchant, who had resided many years in Brazil wrote to Wellington in 1828 about the slave trade:

'The Government *may prohibit* their importations at the *principal* ports ... but I am certain it will *leave it to be understood* at the time that *liberty will be given to land* them on any contiguous part of the coast, because the nation to a man, I am persuaded, will acquiesce in nothing short of this. It was as reasonable to make a treaty with their Government to give up the country altogether. It is by this alone that they subsist, and they are not a race of people to abandon their property to the *caprice of their rulers.'*

The same conditions prevailed in Cuba. British protests against violations of Spain's engagements were well received, the authorities promised redress, but the slave trade increased, and was daily carried on more systematically.

In the eyes of Spanish and Cuban planters, there was one prerequisite of their potential development. That was the Negro slave trade. Thus Cuba's economic development, in the customary Caribbean fashion, began at the very time when the Anti-Slavery Society in England and the *Amis des Noirs* in France were beginning to agitate against the slave trade, and when the Negroes in Saint-Domingue were about to begin their struggle against slavery. Cuba, in 1789, was thus about to take the road which Barbados had travelled in the seventeenth century, Jamaica in the early eighteenth, Saint-Domingue in the late eighteenth. The end of the road for Barbados, Jamaica and Saint-Domingue was the beginning of the trail for Cuba.

But Cuba was faced with a serious problem—Britain launched her campaign for general abolition of the slave trade by all nations. It was as if the Barbadian slave trade in the seventeenth century, and the slave trade to Jamaica and Saint-Domingue in the eighteenth, had been pursued in the face of the hostility and the cruisers of another nation. In part the British policy is to be explained by the popular enthusiasm whipped up by the abolitionists in England. But the fundamental reason, especially after abolition of the slave trade by Britain in 1807, was an attempt to protect the British West Indian planters, denied annual slave imports, from competition with sugar producers like Cuba and Brazil, which continued the slave trade. Britain had a powerful weapon in the struggle as a result of her defence and protection of Spain in the wars with Bonaparte. By the treaty of 1818 the two governments agreed to a mutual right of search of suspected slave ships, and set up two courts, in Sierra Leone and Havana, for the adjudication of captured slaves.

The treaty notwithstanding, the slave trade to Cuba continued after 1820, despite the vigilance of the British cruisers on the coast of Africa. The authorities in Madrid and Havana connived openly at the traffic, from which they received substantial bribes. In 1835, therefore, under British pressure, a new treaty was signed, reiterating the right of search, and stipulating that slaves captured aboard a condemned slave ship were to be freed and placed at the disposal of the government whose cruiser made the capture.

To stiffen its policy, the British Government created a post of Superintendent of Liberated Africans attached to the consulate in Havana, and appointed to it and to the consulate two British abolitionists, R. R. Madden and David Turnbull, respectively. It was war, war without bullets, between Britain and Spain.

Britain steadily lost the war. Between 1790 and 1820, when the slave trade to Cuba was to be legally abolished, 236,599 slaves were imported into the island—about 7,600 a year. The highest importation took place in 1817, the year when the abolition treaty was signed—25,841. In the five years 1816–1820 Cuba, preparing for the worst, imported 95,821, or 19,164 a year. The slave imports after 1820 show the extent of the British defeat. In the forty-five years from 1821 to 1865, Cuba imported 200,354 slaves—an annual average of 4,452. In the year 1837, no fewer than 12,240 slaves were illegally imported. Imports for the years 1836, 1838 and 1840 also topped the ten thousand mark.

The British Commissioners in Havana explained the situation in 1822 to their government. They complained of 'how entirely unproductive of any advantage have been the representations which, upon various occasions, we have made to the chief authority of the island. We have been always well received, and redress, as far as it was practicable, promised; but the illicit slave trade increases, and is daily carried on more systematically'. The war of words became more bitter with the years. Lord Liverpool described the attitude of the Spanish Government as 'sheer perverseness', and Lord Palmerston accused the Cuban authorities of 'determined supineness'. The British Minister in Madrid complained to the Spanish Government in 1839 that 'there has been a too easy leaning to popular prejudices or unfounded apprehensions on the part of the authorities ... on whom the pleadings of interested persons have had more influence, than a respect for the laws of humanity or the dictates of national honour'.

The Spanish and Cuban authorities replied with the countercharge that Britain's scrupulous adherence to the treaties was motivated by hypocrisy and an 'exaggerated philanthropy', which were a cloak for the real aim of destroying Cuba and saving the British West Indies. To a prominent Cuban, 'the wealth and prosperity which the island is so rapidly acquiring ... and above all the painful crisis which the mother country is now suffering—are the true causes which impel the British Government indirectly to accomplish its (Cuba's) destruction.' Britain's philanthropy for 'the children of Senegal', in the opinion of a Spanish official in the island, was really designed to secure a monopoly of sugar production for India, at the expense of 'the children of the Ganges'. A spokesman in the Spanish Parliament refused to permit 'the great Antilla to be despoiled, at the pleasure of the Lords of Jamaica'.

It was time, wrote Cuba's Development Corporation, 'to put an end to the interminable demands of the British Cabinet'. National pride was outraged at treaties considered to have been dictated by the influence of foreign powers. The Spanish Foreign Minister asked the British Minister to Spain in 1841: 'Have the justice, the dignity, the decorum, and the independence of the country ... been properly taken into consideration?' The Royal Patriotic Society of Friends of the Country described the British policy as an attempt to 'infringe ... the right of nations' and the Municipality of Havana protested that war would be preferable.

When the British Government, following a proposal made by Turnbull in 1840, tried to secure acceptance of a plan whereby inquiries would be instituted among the slaves to ascertain the date of their importation, with a view to declaring free immediately those imported after 1820, in violation of the treaty of 1817, the Captain-General of Cuba became almost hysterical. 'The investigation of slavery by the slaves themselves would be a dissolving principle to which I can never consent ... My duty is to concern myself less with the clamour of today than with the justice of tomorrow.'

The French Government adhered to the Treaty of Vienna banning the slave trade. The treaty left implementation to the signatory governments, and stipulated no precise date by which the abolition was to be put into effect. The French Government, under pressure from Britain, from time to time issued threats and bans and prescribed penalties. In 1817 it was decreed that any slave vessel entering a French port was subject to confiscation, and its captain, if he was a Frenchman, barred for ever from the command of any ship; the Negroes on the vessels were to be employed in public works in the colonies. French cruisers were stationed on the coast of Africa in 1818. In 1827 the penalty of banishment was imposed on all those who participated, directly or indirectly, in the slave trade. In 1831 imprisonment of from two to five years was decreed for those fitting out slave vessels.

Yet slaves continued to be landed in large numbers in the colonies, under the very eyes of French warships. When complaints were lodged with French consuls abroad, they pleaded that they had received no instructions. Slave ships were publicly fitted out in French seaports, and shares in the ventures openly sold. In 1820 the British commander on the coast of Africa reported to his government that, in the first six months of that year, he had encountered between 25 and 30 slave ships flying the French flag, and that, in the preceding 14 months, 40,000 slaves had been exported from Africa in French ships.

The British Government, determined to put down the slave trade, argued strongly for the right of cruisers of both nations to search suspected slave ships flying either of the national flags. After much opposition from the French Government, a limited right of search was conceded in 1831, specifying the places where the search might be made, the number of cruisers that might be employed, and the nature of the vessels to which the right appertained. The convention gave rise to an outcry in France, especially as no other nation adhered, the United States in particular categorically refusing. As Secretary of State John Quincy Adams said to the British Ambassador in 1822, the right of search was a greater and more atrocious evil than the slave trade.

French patriotism was wounded to the quick, and saw in the convention nothing but English hypocrisy. On the occasion of a new treaty in 1841, strengthening the terms of the convention, the opposition became more vociferous. The Duc de Fitz-James, in a long speech in the Chamber of Deputies, denounced the treaty as 'the beginning of the execution of a vast, immense plan, conceived more than forty years ago by the British Government, designed to achieve nothing less than to make all Europe dependent on England for its consumption of sugar. India is to be this new source of wealth; India, where sugar cane virtually grows wild and where labour receives wretched wages.'

The Chamber voted by an enormous majority an amendment stating that 'we have confidence that, in agreeing to the repression of the criminal traffic, the Government will be able to preserve from all attack the interests of our commerce and the independence of our flag'. The Government, forced to back down, refused to ratify the treaty.

In 1833, on the occasion of the Emancipation Act, the British Government pledged itself to maintain the British West Indian monopoly of the British sugar market, *so far as it was possible.* It thereby frustrated the intentions of the capitalists to abolish simultaneously both the system of British West Indian slavery and the British West Indian planters' monopoly of the British sugar market. So far as it was possible, the British Government adhered to its pledge after 1833, but it was possible to do this neither very far nor for very long.

The British capitalists redoubled their attacks during and after a serious industrial depression in 1839, in the midst of that working class discontent which gave rise to the Chartist Movement. The capitalists advocated the policy of 'the free breakfast table', and denounced protective duties on food as injustice and folly. They claimed that the Negroes in the West Indies, where apprenticeship had been abolished in 1838, were getting rich, would have nothing but quarto bibles with gilt edges in their chapels, and were being taught to keep gigs and drink champagne by a tax levied upon the British working class. Why, asked *The Times* indignantly in 1846, should it be incumbent upon the nation to keep the West Indian Negro in far greater ease and comfort than its own vast and starving masses, and to give a premium to an inefficient system of management and cultivation? The capitalists demanded that the people of Britain should not be excluded from the benevolent purposes of the abolitionists, and Lord John Russell asseverated in 1841 that the unfortunate working classes of Manchester and Bolton would willingly change places with the Negroes of Jamaica.

The capitalist demand for cheap food, particularly cheap sugar, and for the abolition of the West Indian monopoly and the introduction of free trade raised in a new form the old questions of the slave trade and slavery. They had attacked slavery in the West Indies and supported the campaign of the abolitionists. Their intellectual representatives—for example, Adam Smith and Arthur Young—had stressed the superiority of free labour over slave to the point where they had raised it almost to the dignity of a law of nature. After emancipation in the British West Indies, one would have expected that they would have supported the British West Indian sugar planter against his rivals in Cuba, Brazil and elsewhere, who not only utilised slave labour but still carried on the slave trade. The British capitalists, however, were less concerned with slavery than with monopoly. Their open attack, before 1833, on slavery in the West Indies was converted virtually into an open defence, after 1833, of slavery in Brazil and Cuba.

The British West Indian sugar planter, who had fought to the last ditch to maintain slavery before 1833, adopted a curious line of defence: he attempted to differentiate between free-grown and slave-grown sugar. A mass movement developed in Jamaica for the total suppression of the slave trade. The outstanding champion of the planters was William Ewart Gladstone, who later became Prime Minister of England, and whose family owned extensive sugar plantations in Jamaica and British Guiana.

Gladstone, eloquent as always, begged Parliament not to forego, for the sake of small and paltry pecuniary advantages, the high title and noble character which Britain had earned before the whole world by emancipation. Admitting that the distinction between free-grown and slave-grown produce was not so clear that it could be drawn with uniform and absolute precision, Gladstone urged his colleagues not to draw every inconsistency into the light for the purpose of using it as a plea for further and more monstrous inconsistency, or in order to 'substitute an uniformity in wrong for an inconsistent acknowledgement of what is right'.

Benjamin Disraeli, later to become Gladstone's arch rival, defending the corn monopoly as tenaciously as Gladstone defended the sugar monopoly, joined hands with Gladstone in the common cause. He pleaded in his *Lord George Bentinck* for the West Indian monopoly: 'If the consequence of such a monopoly were a dear article, the increased price must be considered as an amercement for the luxury of a philanthropy not sufficiently informed of the complicated circumstances with which it had to deal.'

The British capitalists were not impressed. They heaped scorn on the rather obvious manoeuvre of the West Indians and protectionists. They argued that the distinction which the West Indians wished to draw was a principle for individual agency, not a rule which could direct international commerce. In their opinion, what was involved was not only 'the free breakfast table', but also, if we may borrow a more modern phrase, 'full employment'. Britain's economy was dependent on one essential commodity which was almost entirely slave-grown—cotton. If the importation of slave-grown cotton were prohibited, a million and a half artisans would be thrown out of employment.

Richard Cobden inquired tartly as to what right a people who were the largest consumers and distributors of cotton goods had to go to Brazil with their ships full of cotton, turn up the whites of their eyes, shed crocodile tears over the Brazilian slaves, and refuse to take slave-grown sugar in return? He poked fun at the whole situation in an imaginary interview between the President of the Board of Trade and the Brazilian Ambassador to England. The Ambassador taunts:

'No religious scruples against sending slave-grown cottons into every country in the world? No religious scruples against eating slave-grown rice? No religious scruples against smoking slave-grown tobacco? No religious scruples against taking slave-grown snuff? ... Am I to understand that the religious scruples of the English people are confined to the article of sugar?'

Under pressure from the abolitionists and West Indian planters, the British Government had tried to repress the slave trade after 1807 by stationing cruisers on the coast of Africa, and to restrain British subjects from participating, however indirectly, in the slave trade. But it was notorious that seven-tenths of the goods used by Brazil in the slave trade were British manufactures, and Liverpool's representative in the House of Commons refused to contradict the accusation that the town's exports to Africa were appropriated to 'some improper purpose'. In 1842 Brougham asserted that, with respect to the development of Brazil and Cuba, 'we must needs adopt the painful conclusion that in great part at least such an ample amount of capital as was required, must have belonged to the rich men of this country'. John Bright, representing a Lancashire constituency, argued eloquently in 1843 against a bill prohibiting the indirect employment of British capital in the slave trade, on the ground that it would be a dead letter, and that the matter should be left to the honourable and moral feelings of individuals.

It was under these circumstances that the British capitalists attacked the whole policy of forcible suppression of the slave trade. They argued that slavery could only be abolished by trusting to the eternal and just principles of free trade; commerce was the great emancipator. Bright called it audacious that justice should be done to Africa at the expense of justice to England, and Cobden reminded Parliament that they had a great deal to do at home, within a stone's throw of the Houses of Parliament, before embarking on a scheme for redeeming from barbarism the whole of Africa. Hutt, Member of Parliament, severely criticised the Government's policy:

'The utmost latitude, one might say licentiousness, of means—public money to any extent—naval armaments watching every shore and every sea where a slave ship could be seen or suspected—courts of special judicature in half of the inter-tropical regions of the globe—diplomatic influence and agency such perhaps as this country never before concentrated on any public object.'

He described the British squadrons on the coast of Africa as a threat to world peace, and Carlyle, the distinguished scholar, denied that the laws of Heaven authorised the British people to keep the whole world in a pother about the slave trade. Palmerston, the great Foreign Minister, roundly condemned in 1845 the Government's policy of sacrificing the commercial interests of the country 'all for the purpose of maintaining a favourite crotchet, based upon hypocritical pretences'. Disraeli and Wellington joined in the campaign against suppression, the latter calling it criminal, 'a breach of the law of nations—a breach of treaties'. Even Gladstone, British first and West Indian second, jumped on the bandwagon: 'it is not an ordinance of Providence', he stated in 1850, 'that the Government of one nation shall correct the morals of another.'

Everything depended on the abolitionists. Cobden stated in 1848:

'I am the representative of a county which was eminent in the slavery movement ... Now, I unhesitatingly assert that nearly all the men who led the agitation for the emancipation of the slaves, and who by their influence on public opinion aided in producing that result, are against these hon. Gentlemen in this House who advocate a differential duty on foreign sugar with a view to put down slavery abroad.'

This was no idle statement. Buxton condemned the slave

squadron. Sturge reorganised the Anti-Slavery Party on purely pacific principles. Wilberforce's son, the Bishop of Oxford, called for 'a preventive policy founded on different and higher principles'. Brougham got into a hopeless tangle in his attempt to differentiate between sugar grown in Brazil by slaves imported from Africa and sugar grown in Louisiana by slaves imported from Virginia. Clarkson opposed suppression on the curious ground that it was only putting money into the pockets of British sailors.

The *coup de grâce* to West Indian hopes was administered by Thomas Babington Macaulay, son of the abolitionist Zachary Macaulay, and later famous as the distinguished historian, Lord Macaulay. In a remarkable speech in 1845 on the question, he stated unambiguously: 'My especial obligations in respect to Negro slavery ceased when slavery ceased in that part of the world for the welfare of which I, as a member of this House, was accountable.' He openly challenged the Government's compromise in 1833 whereby foreign sugar, slave-grown, was imported for refining and re-export, but not for domestic consumption. 'We import the accursed thing; we bond it; we employ our skill and machinery to render it more alluring to the eye and the palate; we export it to Leghorn and Hamburg; we send it to all the coffee houses of Italy and Germany; we pocket a profit on all this; and then we put on a Pharisaical air, and thank God that we are not like those sinful Italians and Germans who have no scruple about swallowing slave-grown sugar.' To prohibit such sugar, said Macaulay, would lead to Germany becoming a Warwickshire and Leipzig another Manchester. 'I will not have two standards of right,' concluded Macaulay, 'I will not have two weights or two measures. I will not blow hot and cold, play fast and loose, strain at a gnat and swallow a camel.'

By 1846, therefore, when the free trade question came up for decision, public opinion in England had undergone the 'disgraceful change' bemoaned by Lord Denman. Disraeli attacked the emancipation movement as 'an ignorant movement... a narrative of ignorance, injustice, blundering, waste, and havoc, not easily paralleled in the history of mankind'. Merivale urged that the system of slavery should be looked at more calmly; it was a great social evil indeed, but an evil differing in degree and quality, not in kind, from many other social evils which they were compelled to tolerate, such as the great inequality of fortunes, pauperism, and the overworking of children. The economist McCulloch reminded England that, without slavery, the tropics could never have been cultivated. The new trend culminated in the publication, in 1849, of Carlyle's notorious *Occasional Discourse upon the Nigger Question*, in which he condemned emancipation as an encouragement to idleness, and asserted that the Negro has 'an indisputable and perpetual *right* to be compelled ... to do competent work for his living'.

The British West Indian planters were less able to withstand this combination of capitalists, abolitionists and intellectuals in 1846 than they had been in 1833, because the Government was no longer on their side. The Repeal of the Corn Laws in 1846 was followed inevitably by the repeal of the sugar duties in the same year; the British West Indian sugar planter could not hope to succeed where the British farmer had failed.

The West Indian planter was able, however, to extract two concessions which helped to soften this new blow. In the first place, he obtained the system of indentured Asian immigration. Secondly, the equalisation of the sugar duties was made gradual, to be completed in 1852. The final introduction of the new system coincided with an event in the West Indies which had symbolic significance. The great fortress of Brimstone Hill in St. Kitts, called familiarly 'the Gibraltar of the West Indies', constructed by slave labour in the heyday of the sugar interest, was evacuated by British troops in 1852. The military bastion became thereafter a tourist attraction.

The end of an era for the British West Indies was the beginning of an epoch for Cuba. When the news of the equalisation of the sugar duties by the British Parliament reached Cuba, the city of Havana was illuminated. The spotlight of Caribbean history was thereafter focused on the long neglected 'jewel of the Indies'.

(5) The Social Factors

Behind the protracted discussions and negotiations which were taking place between the British Government, the capitalists, the humanitarians and the planters, there stood the 540,539 slaves (the number on which compensation was eventually paid in 1838) in the West Indies, excluding Honduras and Bermuda, but including the Bahamas. As Daniel O'Connell, the Irish leader in the House of Commons, asserted in 1832: 'The planter was sitting, dirty and begrimed, over a powder magazine, from which he would not go away, and he was hourly afraid that the slave would apply a torch to it.'

Governor Combermere of Barbados wrote to the Secretary of State for the Colonies in 1819 that, in communities like the West Indies, 'the public mind is ever tremblingly alive to the dangers of insurrection'. The situation in the British West Indies in 1833 was the climax to three centuries of slave revolts in the Caribbean.

The emancipation of the slaves in French Saint-Domingue and their establishment of the independent republic of Haiti, recognised by the Great Powers, elevated the slave revolts from the field of island politics to the sphere of national policy and international diplomacy. Never academic, always to be dreaded, a Negro revolt in the British West Indies in the early nineteenth century, designed to abolish slavery from below, was widely apprehended, both in the West Indies and in Britain. These apprehensions were not unjustified.

In 1808, the year after the abolition of the slave trade, a slave revolt broke out in British Guiana. The ringleaders were the 'drivers, tradesmen, and other most sensible slaves on the estates', in the words of the Governor to the Secretary of State for the Colonies.

Eight years later, it was the turn of Barbados. Those of the slaves who were captured denied that ill treatment was the cause. The commander of the troops wrote to the Governor saying that 'they stoutly maintained, however, that the island belonged to them, and not to white men . . .'

British Guiana went up in flames in 1823, for the second but not the last time. The total slave population involved was 12,000, on fifty plantations. The slaves demanded unconditional emancipation. The Governor tried to reason with them and urged them to go gradually. The slaves listened coldly. As the Governor reported to the Secretary of State for the Colonies: 'These things they said were no comfort to them, God had made them of the same flesh and blood as the whites, they were tired of being slaves

to them, they should be free and they would not work any more.'
The Governor assured them that 'if by peaceful conduct they
deserved His Majesty's favour they would find their lot substantially though gradually improved, but they declared they would
be free.'

British Guiana, its full potentialities arrested by its shortage
of labour, as we have already indicated, was a key colony, one of
the most important sugar producers in the British West Indies.
On hearing the news of the Guiana revolt, the Governor of
Barbados wrote confidentially to the Secretary of State for the
Colonies: 'Now the ball has begun to roll, nobody can say when
or where it is to stop.'

From British Guiana the ball rolled, in the following year, to
Jamaica. While the revolt was localised in the parish of Hanover,
it was significant for the spirit which animated the slaves. As a
group they could only with difficulty be restrained from interfering
with the execution of the ringleaders. In addition, the Governor
wrote that the executed men 'were fully impressed with the belief
that they were entitled to their freedom and that the cause they
had embraced was just and in vindication of their own rights.'
According to one of the men, the revolt had not been subdued,
'the war had only begun'. Another of the leaders, who committed
suicide, admitted before his death that his owner was kind and
indulgent, but defended his action on the ground that freedom
during his lifetime had been withheld only by his master.

Outwardly calm and submissive, the slaves continued restless
as the Parliamentary discussions proceeded. The Governor of
British Guiana wrote as follows to the Secretary of State for the
Colonies on May 5, 1824: 'The spirit of discontent is anything
but extinct, it is alive as it were under its ashes, and the Negro
mind although giving forth no marked indication of mischief to
those not accustomed to observe it, is still agitated, jealous, and
suspicious.' In a second letter to the Secretary of State for the
Colonies on the same day, the Governor cautioned against further
delay, not only for the sake of the intrinsic humanity and policy
of the measure, but also to put an end to expectation and conjecture and to release the slaves from that feverish anxiety which
would continue to agitate them until the question was definitely
settled.

But the policy of amelioration and gradualism continued. In 1831 it was Antigua's turn to revolt, and the Governor of Barbados had to send reinforcements. In Barbados itself the slaves believed that the King had granted emancipation which was withheld by the Governor, and that, in the event of insurrection, the troops had received positive orders not to fire upon the slaves.

The climax came in Jamaica at the end of the year. An 'extensive and destructive' insurrection broke out during the Christmas holidays. The Governor reported that it 'was not occasioned by any sudden grievance or immediate cause of discontent, it had been long concerted and at different periods deferred.' Its leaders, he added, were slaves employed in situations of the greatest confidence, and, accordingly, exempted from hard labour. For men in their position, their motives, in the Governor's view, could have been 'no less strong than those which appear to have actuated them—a desire of effecting their freedom, and in some cases of possessing themselves of the property belonging to their masters'.

The planters put the blame for these disorders on the abolitionists, and attributed the ferment among the slaves to the discussions in Parliament. In a sense, there was some truth in these accusations. The slaves, as the Governor of Trinidad wrote in 1831, had 'an unaccountable facility in obtaining partial and generally distorted information whenever a public document is about to be received which can in any way affect their condition or station'. They imagined that every measure discussed or passed by Parliament—abolition of the slave trade, registration of slaves, policy of amelioration—was their emancipation, and that every new Governor brought out emancipation in his pocket. All over the West Indies they were asking 'why Bacchra no do that King bid him?'

In reality, however, it was not the abolitionists who were responsible for the misapprehensions of the slaves, but the planters themselves. Some of them saw in the revolts an opportunity of embarrassing the British Government by raising up the spectre of Haiti. The Governor of Trinidad wrote as follows to the Secretary of State for the Colonies in 1832:

'... the island, as far as the slaves are concerned, is quite tranquil and very easily could be kept so if such was the desire of those who ought to guide their endeavours in this way ... It would almost appear to be the actuating motives of some leading people here to drive the Government to abandon its principles, even at the risk of exciting the slaves to insurrection.'

A year later, the Governor of Jamaica corroborated this point of view. He wrote:

'There is no doubt that there would be those short sighted enough to enjoy at the moment any disturbance on the part of the Negroes arising from disappointment which these persons despairing of their own prospects would consider as some consolation from its entailing embarrassment on the British Government.'

In the Governor's opinion, the slaves were collectively well-disposed, and the planters' meetings and resolutions were more calculated to disturb them than any casual report that some benefit was intended to them by the British Government which their masters wished to withhold. The Governor of Trinidad, in addressing a planters' deputation in 1833, earnestly recommended the planters not to give way to angry feelings or to discuss the subject of slavery on occasions obviously objectionable.

But the planters showed little restraint. In one instance, when the Governor considered public discussions unwise, the planters printed surreptitiously and circulated some ill-advised resolutions which he had deemed it expedient not to publish in the *Gazette*, owing to the disturbed minds of the slaves. In Barbados the Governor ascribed the false reports of a speedy emancipation of the slaves to the continual discussions of the whites and the evil designs of a few planters. In one instance in British Guiana the slaves were armed and led by a white man, and another circulated a story upon different plantations that the British Government had declared freedom for the slaves and ordered them to arm in their defence.

This, then, was the situation in 1833, ten years after the initiation of the British Government's policy of amelioration. On the one hand, there was suspense, which worked, as the Governor of Barbados pointed out, a 'double cruelty'—it paralysed the planters' efforts and drove the slaves to sullen despair. Nothing could be more mischievous, he warned, than holding out to the slaves from session to session the prospect of their freedom; it was most desirable, he wrote on May 23, 1833, that 'the state of this unhappy people should be early considered and decided on

by the Home Authorities, for the state of delusion they are labouring under renders them obnoxious to their owners and in some
instances increases the unavoidable misery of their condition'.

And, on the other hand, there were the slaves themselves. As a
Jamaican wrote to the Governor in 1832:

'The question will not be left to the arbitrament of a long angry
discussion between the Government and the planter. The slave himself
has been taught that there is a third party, and that party himself. He
knows his strength, and will assert his claim to freedom. Even at this
moment, unawed by the late failure, he discusses the question with a
fixed determination.'

The alternatives, therefore, were clear. Thirty years later the
Tsar of Russia was faced with the same problem with respect to
the emancipation of the serfs: emancipation from above or
emancipation from below. Like the British Government in 1833,
he chose emancipation from above. In the British West Indies,
it was no longer a question of slave rebellions *if*, but slave rebellion *unless* emancipation was decreed. Buxton expressed himself
as follows in Parliament on March 19, 1833: 'He was convinced
that it was absolutely indispensable that this question should be
settled, and further, that if it was not settled in that House, it
would be settled elsewhere, in another and more disastrous
manner.' In introducing the Emancipation Act, Stanley expressed
the same opinion: 'They were compelled to act; for they felt
that take what course they might, it could not be attended with
greater evil than any attempt to uphold the existing state of things.'

In other parts of the Caribbean the issue of emancipation posed
the same alternatives. The sugar planters of Martinique, Guadeloupe and French Guiana had also to reckon with the slaves, and
here, again, French West Indian history paralleled British. The
slave resentment was of long standing. On August 30, 1789, an
ultimatum, signed 'All the Negroes,' was sent to the Governor of
Martinique. It read: 'We know that the King has made us free
and, if there is any resistance to giving us our liberty, we shall
set fire to the whole colony and drown it in blood; only the Governor and the religious houses will be spared.'

Their militant spirit was only strengthened after 1789 by the
events in Haiti. Guadeloupe revolted against the restoration of
slavery in 1802. A revolt broke out in Martinique in 1822. A pam-

phlet published in Paris in 1823, entitled *The Situation of the free people of colour in the French West Indies,* led to prosecutions in Martinique, the deportation of thirty inhabitants to Senegal, and the condemnation of its chief authors, Bissette and two others, to hard labour for life; but the deportation order was revoked by the French Government, and the hard labour sentences commuted to banishment. Another conspiracy was detected in 1824 and stifled before it broke out. In 1831 another revolt broke out; its slogan was the dreaded slogan of Saint-Domingue, 'liberty or death'. In 1833, the day after Christmas, an insurrection broke out in the Grande Anse district, resulting in long trials and several death sentences.

The Emancipation Proclamation of 1848 found the colonies in turmoil, perhaps instigated, it is alleged, by the planters themselves, who saw, in the fear that it engendered, a means of prolonging their privileges—similar allegations had been made in the British colonies. Whites were being massacred in Martinique and plantations burnt; Guadeloupe was in a state of siege; three-quarters of the slaves had left the plantations in Guiana. So serious was the situation that the Governor of Martinique proclaimed emancipation before the metropolitan decree arrived.

The proverbial question being asked in Guadeloupe was: 'What is slavery?' This was the reply given: 'A state of affairs in which the Negro works as little as possible, five days a week, for his master, who dares not remonstrate with him.' The general situation in the French West Indies in 1848 duplicated the situation in the British islands in 1833: emancipation either from above or from below, and emancipation from below was no chimera.

The slave revolution of 1848 in the Danish Virgin Islands was sudden and unexpected. The Governor-General arrived in St. Croix from St. Thomas on July 2, totally unsuspicious of any untoward event. He was awakened at two o'clock in the morning by alarming accounts of a slave revolution. The leader was a man named Buddoe, a native of the British islands, the Toussaint Louverture of St. Croix. Able to read and write, very tactful in his handling of men, ambitious, young and handsome, he was popular with both whites and Negroes, and became the secret organiser of the revolution.

In Frederiksted the houses of the town bailiff, the Police

Assistant and one of the wealthiest merchants were sacked. Most of the whites took refuge on vessels in the harbour. The Negroes demanded immediate emancipation. The commander of the fort remonstrated with them. Their leader replied: 'Massa, we po' negar cannot fight sojer; we no fo' got gun; but we can burn and destroy Santa Cruz if we no fo' get free; and that we go'n do.' The slaves, awaiting the arrival of the Governor-General, who reached Frederiksted at three in the afternoon, delivered an ultimatum to him: freedom by four o'clock, or they would burn the town. The Governor-General capitulated and ordered the Emancipation Proclamation to be read out, as follows:

'1. All unfree in the Danish West India Islands are from today free.

'2. The estate Negroes retain for three months from this date the use of the houses and provision grounds of which they have hitherto been possessed.

'3. Labour is in future to be paid for by agreement, but allowance of food to cease.

'4. The maintenance of the old and infirm, who are not able to work, is, until further determined, to be furnished by the late owners.'

Thus did the slaves of the Danish Virgin Islands emancipate themselves. Not a drop of white blood had been shed, though much property had been destroyed. The revolution, despite the Emancipation Proclamation, was not quelled for three weeks, and then only with the aid of Spanish troops from Puerto Rico and a British warship. Buddoe was banished. On January 8, 1849, he landed in Port-of-Spain, Trinidad. The Governor-General resigned his post, ostensibly on grounds of ill-health, and returned to Denmark to stand trial for negligence, the planters accusing him of sympathy with emancipation. He was acquitted, and on September 22, 1848, the Emancipation Proclamation received the sanction of the Danish Government. Basing their arguments on the actions of the governments of England, France and Sweden, and on the promise of the Dutch Government, the Danish planters demanded compensation for their slaves in a petition to the Danish Parliament in June, 1851.

Chapter Eighteen

The Ordeal of Free Labour

On the eve of emancipation in the British West Indies, in December, 1832, Lord Howick, one of the prime movers in the emancipation movement, wrote a memorandum which contained views that later became the official policy of the British Government. He wrote as follows:

'The great problem to be solved in drawing up any plan for the emancipation of the slaves in our colonies, is to devise some mode of inducing them when relieved from the fear of the driver and his whip, to undergo the regular and continuous labour which is indispensable in carrying on the production of sugar... Their (the planters') inability... to pay liberal wages seems beyond all question; but even if this were otherwise, the experience of other countries warrants the belief, that while land is so easily obtainable as it is at this moment, even liberal wages would fail to purchase the sort of labour which is required for the cultivation and manufacture of sugar... The examples of the western states of America, of Canada, of the Cape of Good Hope, and of the Australian Colonies, may all be cited in order to show that even amongst a population in a much higher state of civilisation than that to which the slaves in the West Indies have attained, the facility of obtaining land effectually prevents the prosecution by voluntary labour of any enterprise requiring the co-operation of many hands. It is impossible therefore to suppose that the slaves (who, though as I believe not more given to idleness than other

men are certainly not less so) would if freed from control be induced
even by high wages to continue to submit to a drudgery which they detest,
while without doing so they could obtain land sufficient for their support
... I think that it would be greatly for the real happiness of the Negroes
themselves, if the facility of acquiring land could be so far restrained
as to prevent them, on the abolition of slavery, from abandoning their
habits of regular industry ... Accordingly it is to the imposition of a considerable tax upon land that I chiefly look for the means of enabling the
planter to continue his business when emancipation shall have taken
place ... '

Thus was the law of the superiority of free labour repealed in
the interest of a single class, and metropolitan legislation reinforced
the colonial tradition of debarring the Negro from land ownership. Slavery was abolished, but the plantation and the plantocracy
remained. The emancipated slaves were to be *adscripti glebae*,
attached to the soil, but to the soil of the sugar plantation, to be
compelled, even against their will, to produce sugar which the
British Government alleged was being overproduced. Thus encouraged, the planters of Barbados suggested that all the provision grounds of the former slaves should be destroyed, to compel
them to work, while their colleagues in British Guiana deliberately
destroyed all the fruit trees, to deprive the emancipated slaves of
a source of subsistence which competed with employment on
the sugar plantation.

As an essential step in the implementation of the policy of
making the Caribbean safe for the sugar plantation, the emancipation legislation, except in the French colonies, imposed a period
of what the British euphemistically called 'apprenticeship', and
the French 'organisation of labour', to stimulate the habit of regular
industry. In the British islands the master was required to provide
food, clothing, lodging, medicine and medical attendance for the
apprentice, or, in lieu of food, adequate provision grounds and
time in which to cultivate them. The apprentice, in turn, was to
live up to the contract, do his work honestly, and refrain from
insolence and insubordination. The supervision of the apprentices
and exclusive jurisdiction over them were entrusted to special
magistrates, not to exceed 100 in number, paid £300 a year by the
British Treasury.

It was, in effect, modified slavery, as Lord Stanley, the sponsor
of the Emancipation Act, felt free to admit in 1848, 'because the

prejudice that then existed exists no longer'. It was precisely for this reason that the Schoelcher Commission, describing it as forced labour and a form of slavery, decisively rejected it:

'The Negroes would find it difficult to understand how they could be free and constrained at one and the same time. The Republic would not wish to take away from them with one hand what it has given with the other; in the colonies as in the metropolis, the day of fictions is over.'

But the fiction was adopted in the Danish Virgin Islands. The Emancipation Proclamation of 1848 had stated that labour was in future to be paid for by agreement, with the cessation of allowances of food. However, less than a month after the proclamation, yearly contracts of labour on the plantations were imposed by the Government. This was followed by a more comprehensive act on January 26, 1849, defining the relations between proprietors and labourers. With respect to the annual contract, the law forbade dismissal on the part of the employer or violation on the part of the labourer during the year, except by mutual agreement before a magistrate, or by an order of a magistrate on just and equitable cause being shown, for example, marriage between man and woman on different plantations. Labourers were divided into first, second and third class, and were to perform the work customary for field labourers. The law reads:

'They shall attend faithfully to their work, and willingly obey the directions given by the employer, or the person appointed by him. No labourer shall presume to dictate what work he or she is to do, or refuse the work he may be ordered to perform, unless expressly engaged for some particular work only. If a labourer thinks himself aggrieved, he shall not therefore leave the work, but in due time apply for redress to the owner of the estate, or to the magistrate.'

A five day week was instituted, beginning at sunrise, ending at sunset, with one hour for breakfast and two hours off at midday. Their remuneration, fixed by law, was as follows: the use of a house or rooms built and repaired by the plantation, but kept in order by the labourers; a provision ground thirty feet square for first and second class labourers; fifteen cents an hour for first class labourers, ten cents for second class, and five cents for third class. Labourers reporting late for work forfeited half a day's wages. Parents were to be fined for keeping children from work. Wilful absenteeism for two or more days during the week, or

habitual absenteeism, or bad work and laziness were punishable
by the magistrate.

Thus was the entire state apparatus arrayed against the
emancipated slaves. With all the available land appropriated by
the plantations, and attached to the soil by the Labour Act, the
freedmen resorted to direct action, in 1878. The labourers in St.
Croix, the only island still producing sugar, revolted against the
legislation of 1849. Many whites were massacred, and much
property destroyed. Again Frederiksted was the centre of the
disturbance, which was led by a woman canefield worker, called
'Queen Mary'. The revolt was subdued with the aid of a French
warship, a United States warship, and troops from St. Thomas
and Puerto Rico, and the Labour Act was repealed.

The restrictions imposed on labour were not applied to capital.
The emancipation legislation in each country made provision for
compensation—compensation to the planters. One powerful voice
was raised in favour of compensation to the slaves—that was
Schoelcher's: 'If France owes compensation for this social state
which it has tolerated and is now suppressing,' wrote his commission, 'it owes it rather to those who have suffered from that
state rather than to those who have profited thereby.' Schoelcher
wished to compensate the victims of slavery.

So also did Sanroma in Puerto Rico. In his remarkable speech
to the *Cortes* on February 17, 1873, he spoke as follows:

'Do you wish a grand measure for the preparation of the slave for
freedom? Give him the compensation money which we reserve for his
owner...Do you know how I look at compensation? As an advance
made to the planter for the benefit of the slave; as a fund for paying
wages to the free worker. In this sense, and in no other, I am prepared
to vote for compensation. As for the planter, do you think it small compensation that he will have a greater facility of white immigration, by
which he can provide himself with workers who are not only more intelligent
but also less expensive? The question of compensation is not as minor as
some think: it is by economic reform that we must complete the social.
Give freedom of trade so as to reduce the cost of living. Give freedom
of credit to obtain cheap money. Give vocational education to make good
workers. This is the grand compensation for the owners.'

Schoelcher and Sanroma were overruled. The metropolitan
governments compensated the beneficiaries of slavery. It was compensation not for the deprivation of liberty but for the expropria-

tion of property. Much has been written about the magnanimity to the planter and not to the slave. No requirement was imposed that the money should be used to finance the necessary rationalisation of the Caribbean sugar economy. The planter was free to dispose of his money as he pleased; the absentee interests for the most part withdrew from the West Indies altogether. What such a requirement would have involved can be estimated from an examination of the share of the compensation—£20 millions sterling in all—which fell to the individual British colonies:

Jamaica	£5,853,976	10	11¾
British Guiana	4,068,809	6	4¼
Barbados	1,659,315	0	9
Trinidad	973,442	18	2
Grenada	570,733	1	7¾
St. Vincent	554,716	7	5
Antigua	415,173	14	1¼
St. Kitts	309,908	5	7¼
St. Lucia	309,658	17	9
Dominica	265,071	9	0
Tobago	226,745	14	10¼
Nevis	145,976	19	7½
Bahamas	118,683	13	11½
Montserrat	100,654	0	10
British Honduras	96,571	9	6
Virgin Islands	70,177	13	2
Bermuda	48,253	18	9
	£15,787,869	2	6

Compensation in the French colonies amounted to 126 million francs, at a rate which amounted to 430 francs per slave in Martinique, 470 in Guadeloupe, and 618 in French Guiana. Compensation in the Danish Virgin Islands amounted to 5,500,000 francs—about two million dollars or 12 pounds sterling per slave. Dutch proposals in 1857 envisaged a compensation of over 16 million florins, to which the emancipated slaves themselves were to contribute; the proposed indemnity was based on a rate of 500 florins for each slave employed in sugar in Surinam, 325 for cocoa and coffee, 700 for domestics, and from 50 to 500 in the islands. In Puerto Rico the compensation amounted to 35 million pesetas. No compensation was paid in Cuba—the Spanish Government could hardly insist on what the planters who had joined the revolution themselves rejected.

Was apprenticeship necessary? Was there any real ground for assuming, with the planters, that emancipation would breed idleness? There are three Caribbean territories where free labour can be judged on its merits—Haiti, Puerto Rico, and the French West Indies, all of which rejected a transitional stage between slavery and freedom.

The Haitian Constitution of 1804, promulgated by Emperor Dessalines, abolished slavery for all time, prohibited the acquisition of landed property by whites, and confiscated all property formerly owned by white Frenchmen. Trouble soon began. In the same year Dessalines complained bitterly that mulatto children of the whites had laid claim to their property 'to the prejudice of my poor Negroes', and he warned both Negroes and mulattoes that 'the property which we conquered with our blood belongs to us all; I intend it to be equitably distributed'. The mulattoes revolted and Dessalines was assassinated.

Towards the end of his reign Christophe, who had been declared king, and who had begun by maintaining large-scale property, increased the number of small proprietors by distributing small plots from the national domain to his veterans. Pétion, the champion of the small farmer, died shortly after he was acclaimed president for life. Boyer was selected to replace Pétion. In 1821 he suspended all alienations of State land. He followed this up by renewing the decrees of Leclerc and Toussaint before him prohibiting the registration of sales of all property of less than 50 *carreaux*. His intention was to force the peasants to cultivate the large plantations by preventing them from setting up as independent proprietors. Boyer agreed in 1825 to the French demand for an indemnity of 150 million francs in six annual instalments, thus imposing on the infant independent state a heavy financial burden which effectively crippled its development of the social services.

The crowning pressure on the small farmer was the rural code of 1826. This code forbade the peasant, under penalty of imprisonment, and in the case of recidivism, hard labour, to travel into the interior without a permit of the landowner or overseer on whose land he was employed; prescribed the number of hours of work; suppressed the labourer's right to leave the fields and migrate to the towns; prohibited workers' associations for the purchase of plantations; required the labourer to be submissive and respectful to the planter or his overseer, under pain of imprisonment.

It was the restoration of slavery, minus the whip. Dessalines' constitution of 1805 had destroyed colour distinctions and prescribed that all Haitians would thereafter be known by the generic name of Blacks. Boyer's rural code revived and stimulated the colour distinctions by which the mulatto regarded himself as the superior of the black man. It was the black worker who was bound to the plantation and restricted to the rural areas. Boyer's rural code made of Haiti two nations and was an evil omen for the black peasantry in the other Caribbean territories where the old plantocracy survived. A peasant revolt in 1846 was drowned in blood by one of Boyer's successors. Haiti remained a country in which, as the peasantry said: 'The rich Negro is a mulatto, the poor mulatto is a Negro.' The Haitian development was aggravated by the fact that, after independence, the country ceased to grow sugar and turned to coffee, which was readily adaptable to the small holding.

According to a census of 1872, there were 31,635 slaves in Puerto Rico out of a total population of 168,150, slightly more than half of whom were white. The remainder were mulattoes and free Negroes. Of the slaves 19,928 were workers; 11,572 were between the ages of twelve and sixty. Did the steady manumission of the more than a quarter of a million mulattoes and free Negroes lead to widespread idleness and the paralysing of Puerto Rico's economic life? The following table of exports supplies the answer:

Year	Sugar quintals	Coffee quintals	Molasses gallons	Tobacco quintals
1869	1,627,451	5,969,020	141,396	28,688
1870	2,025,966	7,293,011	192,645	64,973
1871	2,162,667	7,590,915	210,066	55,240

This could hardly have been possible if the manumitted slaves and free people of colour numbering over 40 per cent of the population in 1872 were idlers. In 1860 there were 8,855 white property owners in the island, 4,563 coloured; there were 3,091 white merchants and 321 coloured; 26 white factory owners and 6 coloured; 891 white small businessmen and 512 coloured; 17,395 white agricultural labourers and 9,642 coloured.

Puerto Rico proved not only that the freed Negro worked in the fields, but, more important, that the white man also did. Cuba, the slave territory *par excellence* of the nineteenth century, reinforced the moral. In 1862, notwithstanding the 292,000 slaves, most of whom worked in sugar, there were 453,000 whites and 103,000 free coloured working in the fields. Free labour was responsible for one-quarter of the sugar production, five-sixths of the tobacco.

The French West Indies provide us with an answer to the problem of whether the Negroes deserted the plantations *en masse* after emancipation, refused to work, and threatened the colonies with economic ruin. No immigrants were introduced into these territories prior to 1854. The following table presents the economic situation of the colonies before and after emancipation in 1848:

	Martinique		Guadeloupe	
	1846	1856	1846	1856
Cultivated hectares	34,530	31,725	44,813	32,204
Sugar	20,232	18,202	14,189	22,549
Coffee	1,856	625	4,736	2,206
Cotton	159	47	1,139	656
Cocoa	592	423	134	122
Tobacco	19	345	10	311
Food crops	11,672	12,081	16,379	6,360
Workers	43,486	43,794	51,522	51,659
Horses	2,293	2,954	3,861	3,385
Asses	152	205	892	430
Mules	5,483	4,460	9,114	4,485
Cattle	16,661	15,094	23,450	8,075
Sheep	13,578	11,145	27,238	8,427
Goats	1,388	3,644	6,142	8,057
Pigs	3,902	9,249	9,023	9,331
Raw sugar, kg.	29,318,175*	30,344,650	30,007,807*	38,180,200†
Imports, francs	22,841,091	28,909,910	21,339,190	22,950,177
Exports, francs	18,323,921	18,636,070	20,420,522	15,823,903
Shipping	673	711‡	847	956
Price of sugar (francs) per 100 kg.	129¼	128⅝		

* 1847   † 1854   ‡ 1857

The French islands were not ruined in 1848, and emancipation did not make the Negroes lazy. Sugar exports increased, whilst the labour force remained the same. Total exports declined in Guadeloupe; but imports increased, proving that the Negroes were consuming no less. The 1849 imports showed a large increase of wine, tobacco, flour, cheese, salted meat, soap and oils, textiles, umbrellas, watches, hats and shoes. The former slave was drinking and smoking, feeding himself better, washing himself more, dressing better, imitating his former master who never went out without an umbrella or went bareheaded or barefooted. A decree of 1723, repealed in 1819, had forbidden the slaves to wear shoes. Freed, they tortured their feet. It might have seemed ridiculous; but it was a pregnant symbol of the death of the old order.

If the acreage under coffee, cotton and cocoa declined, the world market must be blamed. The decline in the number of mules and cattle is in all probability to be attributed to the establishment of central factories and the introduction of steam; contrariwise, the number of goats and pigs, the livestock of the peasants, increased considerably. If the above table shows anything, it is that there was a superabundance of labour. The acreage in cultivation declined by more than one-quarter, whilst the number of workers remained virtually the same.

Thus the emancipated slaves did not desert the plantation. Let it be understood that, if they had, this would have been, in the words of the magnificent defence of the freedmen by Augustin Cochin, only natural:

'What prisoner does not escape when the door of his prison is opened? What bird does not fly away when one opens its cage? What! You expected from an ignorant, unfortunate man, less intelligent than a street arab of Paris, less virtuous than a Regulus, what none of those who speak or write on these matters would certainly not have accepted! You expected that you gave him his freedom so that he should resume, under another purely ideal name, the same toil in the same place, under the same authority; that he would be content to change his name but not his condition, and to receive that blessing, the object of all his dreams, freedom, without any effort to make use of it!'

We can now turn our attention to the territories where apprenticeship was instituted.

On November 18, 1839, the year after the abolition of

apprenticeship in the British West Indies, the Governor of British Guiana announced that six emancipated slaves had bought an abandoned sugar estate, *Northbrook*, for over £2,000, two-thirds in cash, the remainder by a note payable in three weeks. They proposed to plant sugar. As the Governor wrote, it was 'a convincing evidence of confidence in the industry of their brethren, and speaks volumes against the determined idleness of the Negro, which a party here would assert'.

About 150 labourers had bought *Orange Nassau*, a cotton plantation, for nearly £11,000; over £4,000 had been offered for two other plantations. The labourers of five plantations combined to purchase *Plantation Friendship* for £16,000, of which £7,000 was paid in cash, £1,000 was to be paid in one month, and the remainder when all the shareholders had paid their quota of £80 each. This plantation, a cotton plantation, had been sold some years before for £6,000; in 1836 it was sold again for £10,000.

There is other evidence of the industry of the emancipated slaves. In 1842 it was claimed that each could earn in seven hours as much as three English labourers earned in sixteen. If one compared the Negro labourers in British Guiana and Trinidad with the peasantry of Dorsetshire or Wiltshire, was there any justice, thundered Lord Howick in 1845, perhaps reflecting on the failure of his proposal in 1832, in taxing the Dorsetshire or Wiltshire peasant for the benefit of the 'singularly well-off' peasant in the West Indies? Howick was referring to the demand of the planters for the continuation of their monopoly of the home market, though the West Indian peasantry certainly did not participate in the monopoly.

In 1840 Lord John Russell, Secretary of State for the Colonies, in a despatch to the Governor of British Guiana, emphasised that there was nothing either singular or culpable in the preference shown by the emancipated slaves for economic independence:

'None of the most inveterate opponents of our recent measures of emancipation allege that the Negroes have turned robbers, or plunderers, or bloodthirsty insurgents. What appears from their statement is, that they have become shopkeepers, and petty traders, and hucksters, and small freeholders; a blessed change, which Providence has enabled us to accomplish.'

Similar results attended emancipation in the French West Indies. 'Emancipation,' wrote Cochin, 'drove a section of the former slaves to the towns, another towards the unoccupied lands, very few towards the prisons and the poorhouses; it gave rise to artisans and small farmers, some vagabonds, few beggars, few criminals.'

A correspondent of the *New York Times*, William G. Sewell, visited the British West Indies in 1859 to study the effects of emancipation. Two striking conclusions emerge from his study. The first was the material and moral progress of the emancipated slaves. All over the British West Indies he found the ignorant, penniless slaves elevated, as in Jamaica, by their own exertions to the rank of landed proprietors, taxpayers and voters; they had moved, as he said of Trinidad, 'step by step, not downward in the path of idleness and poverty, but upward in the scale of civilisation to positions of greater independence'. There were 50,000 small proprietors in Jamaica. From 1833 to 1858 there had been established in Antigua 67 villages, containing 5,187 houses and 15,644 inhabitants.

The statistical returns for St. Vincent for 1857 indicated that 8,209 persons were living in houses built by themselves since emancipation, that, in the preceding twelve years, 12,000 acres had been brought under cultivation by small farmers, and that there were no paupers in the island. The peasantry of St. Lucia were working more profitably and more willingly under the *métayer* system (sharecropping) than they had worked under the slave system. In Barbados, between 1844 and 1859, the number of small farmers owning less than five acres increased from 1,110 to 3,537. The position of the British West Indian peasantry in 1860 bears out Sewell's conclusion about the Jamaican peasant: it was 'a standing rebuke to those who, wittingly or unwittingly, encourage the vulgar lie that the African cannot possibly be elevated.'

Sewell's second conclusion was that emancipation, far from ruining the British West Indies, actually made a powerful contribution to their economic development. The following table indicates the exports of sugar in pounds weight before and after emancipation in those colonies in which free labour had a fair trial.

Colony	Pre-Emancipation Average	Post-Emancipation
Barbados	32,800,000 (1829–1833)	78,000,000 (1856–1860)
St. Lucia	4,000,000	6,261,875
Antigua	20,580,000 (1820–1832)	26,174,000 (1858)
Dominica	6,000,000 (1820–1832)	6,263,000 (1858)
Nevis	5,000,000 (1820–1832)	4,400,000 (1858)
Montserrat	1,840,000	1,308,000
St. Kitts	12,000,000	10,000,000
Jamaica	90,000 (hogsheads 1828–1835)	28,000 (1859)

Thus, except in Jamaica, free labour on the sugar plantations was not only available, it was also profitable, and in Jamaica production had been declining before emancipation. But the emancipated slaves, as small proprietors, were responsible for a healthy and valuable diversification of British West Indian economy, as is brought out in the following table of exports for Jamaica.

Commodity	1834	1859
Logwood, tons	8,432	14,006
Mahogany, feet	1,936	35,000
Coconuts	none	712,913
Arrowroot, lbs	none	72,023
Beeswax, cwt	none	770
Honey, gallons	none	6,954
Fustic, tons	2,126	2,329

Arrowroot exports from St. Vincent, 60,000 pounds before emancipation, amounted to 1,352,250 pounds in 1857, valued at $750,000.

The import trade statistics suggest similar conclusions with respect to an overall rise of the standard of living. The following table for selected colonies bears this out.

Colony	1820–1832 average £	1858 £
Barbados	600,000 (1822–1832)	840,000 (1856)
Antigua	130,000	266,364
Dominica	62,000	84,906
Nevis	28,000	36,721
Montserrat	18,000	17,844
St. Kitts	60,000	109,000

The British West Indian colonies selected amply bear out Sewell's conclusion with respect to Barbados:

'There is very little doubt, and it cannot be intelligently questioned, that Barbados, under the regime of slavery, never approached her present prosperous conditions; and, in comparing the present with the past, whether that comparison be made in her commercial, mechanical, agricultural, industrial, or educational status, I can come to no other conclusion than that the island offers a striking example of the superior economy of the free system.'

The British West Indian planters would have none of this. As Lord John Russell wrote to the Governor of British Guiana in 1840, they used 'the term "ruin" . . . to designate, not the poverty of the people, not the want of food or raiment, not even the absence of riches or luxury, but simply the decrease of sugar cultivation'. In the period of apprenticeship and the few years immediately following its abolition, British West Indian sugar production, as compared with the last years of slavery, was as follows:

Colony	1835–8 compared with 1831–4 + or − %	1839–42 compared with 1831–4 + or − %
Barbados	+24	−11
St. Kitts	−13	+ 5
Nevis	−40	−48
Montserrat	−50	−41
Jamaica	−15	−52
Dominica	−33	−26
Grenada	−20	−52
St. Lucia	−12	−12
St. Vincent	− 5	−40
Tobago	−36	−47
Trinidad	− 7	−15
British Guiana	+ 9	−62

The sugar planters and their advocates launched a campaign for a fresh supply of labour by immigration. Instead of rationalising their methods of production, the planters remained obstinately wedded to them. They attempted to justify their demand on the wholly untenable ground that the Negro, on whom they had depended for generations, when he was a slave, was unsatisfactory as a free worker. Governor Barkly of British Guiana, in emphasising in 1850 that the emancipated slaves had become proprietors to the extent of one in four of the adult male population, expressed the astonishing opinion that:

'The acquisition of a plot of ground has not been so much the sign of superior intelligence or manly independence, as of unfounded suspicions or a love of uncivilised ease; the freeholders being, I am inclined to think, as a body far less industrious than the older and steadier Negroes; who from confidence in their employers and a desire to work continuously have remained on the plantations.'

The planters said candidly that they had no use for the Negro except as a worker on the sugar plantations. Thus wrote Jules Duval, a well-informed French writer on colonial questions, on December 1, 1859:

'The important matter of immigration is beginning to be settled. The solution seems to have been found, on condition that no account is taken of the former slaves and their descendants, who, left to themselves, without the paternal solicitude of their former masters, are relapsing into barbarism.'

No account was taken of the former slaves. British Guiana in 1850 called for a large influx of immigrants without delay. Two years later the Governor asserted that immigration must long continue to be of first necessity in the colony. Thus it was that Sewell could write:

'While agricultural labour in all the British West Indies is the great *desideratum*, and the cry for immigration is echoed and re-echoed, it is amazing to see how the labour which the planter has within his reach is wasted and frittered away; how the particular population upon which the prosperity of the colonies so utterly depends is neglected; how, by mismanagement and unpardonable blunders of policy, the life of a field labourer has been made so distasteful to the peasant that the possession of half an acre, or the most meagre subsistence and independence, seem to him, in comparison with estate service, the very acme of luxurious enjoyment ... every effort is made to check a spirit of independence, which in the African is counted a heinous crime, but in all other people is regarded as a lofty virtue, and the germ of national courage, enterprise, and progress ... I came to the West Indies imbued with the American idea that African freedom has been a curse to every branch of agricultural and commercial industry. I shall leave these islands overwhelmed with a very opposite conviction ...'

One of the great advantages of the encouragement of a Negro peasantry would have been a greater local production of food and a larger measure of insular self-sufficiency. The British West Indian Royal Commission of 1897 emphasised this point. With respect to Antigua, it noted that the island had imported, in 1896, 8,065 barrels of cornmeal, valued at £3,573, when corn could be grown as cheaply as in any part of the world; 37,157 bushels of corn and grain, valued at £3,296; 637,101 pounds of meat, valued at £6,437; 633,394 pounds of oilmeal and oilcake for manures, valued at £1,423. All of these articles, the Commission asserted, might have been advantageously produced by persons not engaged in the sugar industry.

The Commission therefore made its most famous recommendation:

'It seems to us that no reform affords so good a prospect for the permanent welfare in the future of the West Indies as the settlement of- the labouring population on the land as small peasant proprietors ... It must be recollected that the chief outside influence with which the Governments of certain colonies have to reckon are the representatives of the sugar estates, that these persons are sometimes not interested in anything but sugar, that the establishment of any other industry is often detrimental to their interests, and that under such conditions it is the special duty of Your Majesty's Government to see that the welfare of the general public is not sacrificed to the interests, or supposed interests, of a small but influential minority which has special means of enforcing its wishes and bringing its claims to notice ... The settlement of the labouring population on the land, and the encouragement of the products and forms of cultivation suitable for a class of peasant proprietors formed no part of their policy; such measures were generally believed to be opposed to their interests ... If a different policy had found favour the condition of the West Indies might have been much less serious than it is at present in view of the probable failure of the sugar industry.'

The Commission recommended the growth locally of more of the food that was imported and greater attention to the fruit trade. It further recommended agricultural and industrial education, and a department of economic botany to assist the small proprietors; curiously enough, however, it opposed the establishment of agricultural banks and hesitated to recommend any system of state loans to the small farmer on the ground that it was likely to be mismanaged.

The Commission's major recommendations were as follows:

'A loan of £120,000 to Barbados for the establishment of central factories.

'A grant of £27,000 for ten years for the establishment of minor agricultural industries, improved inter-island communications, and the encouragement of the fruit trade. (The Commission's recommendation could hardly have been described as revolutionary.)

'A grant of £20,000 for five years to the smaller islands to assist them to meet their ordinary expenditure of an obligatory nature.

'A grant of £30,000 to Dominica and St. Vincent for road construction and land settlement.'

There were two reasons why the Commission's recommendations, whose self-sufficiency certainly must have been obvious, had not only not been followed throughout the century, but had been deliberately opposed. The first was stated as far back as 1813 by the Governor of British Guiana, who wrote to the Secretary of State for the Colonies that British Guiana was 'most highly qualified by nature to remedy the principal inconveniences' of the suspension of the food trade with the United States. Corn and rice could be cultivated with certain success and in any quantities, whilst Berbice could raise cattle to any extent with great facility and little expense. 'But unfortunately,' he added, 'these humble paths to certain profit are overlooked by people whose whole attention is absorbed in the expectation of obtaining rapid fortunes by the growth of sugar, coffee or cotton.' Three months later his successor reiterated that Demerara could supply any quantity of cassava flour and maize 'if sufficient inducements could be offered on the payment to direct capital and industry to the channel'.

The obstacle was the mercantile creditor in England, to whom the crops were remitted to give him a commission in addition to his interest. 'The sale of timber, rice and corn, finding a market at the door, or near at hand, would be of no advantage to him, beyond the mere interest of the capital he has at stake.' Bolingbroke wrote lugubriously that, if the cultivation of rice was encouraged by the government, British Guiana could rival South Carolina. Thus it was that Pinckard found 'a well-cultivated garden so extremely rare as to appear quite a novelty'; those who 'court the smiles of fortune, by planting the tropical fields, attend only to the cultivation of sugar, coffee, and cotton, which are often seen growing up to the very doorway, or almost creeping in at the windows of the dwelling, not the smallest spot being reserved for garden, pleasure ground or orchard.'

The second reason was that the sugar planter maintained a tenacious hold over the entire economy. Not only did his backward methods represent a considerable loss in terms of sugar production, but he further penalised the economy by retarding, through his control of idle latifundia, the full potentialities of production of alternative crops. The Jamaican sugar plantations comprised 266,903 acres, of which only 24,785 were in cane— nine out of every 10 acres were lying idle. The eighteenth-century mentality dominated here, as elsewhere. In St. Vincent, 134 holdings covered an area of 42,000 acres, of which 10,000 at the most were beneficially employed. The largest proprietor owned 11,826 acres, of which 1,201 were in cane— nine out of ten acres were immobilised. The principal plantations in Trinidad controlled 66,848 acres, of which 33,845, only half, were in cane.

Faithful to his first love, sugar, the planter made one concession to peasant proprietorship—it could exist if it grew cane. The persistence of the eighteenth-century methods of manufacture, however, militated against the growth of any substantial *colono* class in the British West Indies, exclusively growing cane which it sold to the central factory. What did develop in the British West Indies instead was a class of 'cane farmers', labourers growing cane in small patches and quantities. In Trinidad, in 1896, 62,629 tons of canes were thus purchased, from no fewer than 4,098 farmers—an average of 15 tons per farmer. Quantities as small as four hundredweight were purchased in some cases. To pit the Cuban central against this system was to go from the sublime to the ridiculous.

Equally unsatisfactory, from the standpoint of scientific methods, yields, and introduction of new varieties, was the *métayer* system, the West Indian version of sharecropping. This was particularly prevalent in St. Lucia and Tobago. The proprietor supplied the land, equipment for sugar manufacture, carts and horses, while the *métayer* supplied labour in field and factory. The *métayer* received half of the sugar, the proprietor the other half and the skimmings and molasses. The proprietor not infrequently supplied the hogsheads for the *métayer*'s sugar, the *métayer* being responsible for carting it to the port of shipment. Of the Tobago sugar acreage in 1897, over 90 per cent was cultivated by *métayers*. In Jamaica 5,064 acres in cane were cultivated by small farmers.

The planters were supported by the metropolitan governments. In 1842 a committee of the House of Commons, attributing the decline of British West Indian production to the cheapness of land and high wages, resolved that 'one obvious and most desirable mode of endeavouring to compensate for this diminished supply of labour, is to promote the immigration of a fresh labouring population, to such an extent as to create competition for employment'.

The British Government thereafter made loans to the colonies for immigration purposes and actively supported all colonial efforts to prohibit the growth of a Negro peasantry. In 1865 a number of labourers in one of the parishes of Jamaica, complaining of poverty, drought and unemployment, petitioned Queen Victoria for some of 'Her Land' which they might cultivate on a co-operative basis, so that the rent might be guaranteed. The Queen's reply was as follows:

'THAT THE PROSPERITY of the labouring classes, as well as of all other classes, depends, in Jamaica, and in other countries, upon their working for wages, not uncertainly, or capriciously, but steadily and continuously, at the times when their labour is wanted, and for so long as it is wanted: AND THAT if they would thus use this industry, and thereby render the plantations productive, they would enable the planters to pay them higher wages for the same hours of work than are received by the best field labourers in this country; and, as the cost of the necessaries of life is much less in Jamaica than it is here, they would be enabled, by adding prudence to industry, to lay by an ample provision for sessions of drought and dearth; AND THEY may be assured, that it is from their own industry and prudence, in availing themselves of the means of prospering that are before them, and not from any such schemes as have been suggested to them, that they must look for an improvement in their conditions.'

The abolitionists were curiously vague on this issue. Victor Schoelcher's committee in 1848 condemned 'squatting' and envisaged the introduction, if necessary, of 'new free workers'. In 1843 Henry Brougham supported the idea of indentured immigration from Africa under proper restrictions. Five years later he changed his mind—African immigration could only

degenerate into a revival and extension of the slave trade. In the
same year Buxton contented himself with a statement that the
95,000 immigrants from India introduced in ten years into
Mauritius at a cost of £900,000 had doubled production but left
the colony in a state of ruin and bankruptcy. He implied that
the same would be the result of immigration into the West Indies,
but none of the dynamic humanitarianism of the days before
1833 was visible.

One of the most vigorous of the abolitionists, G. Thompson,
said that the immigrants into Mauritius were indolent, mendicants,
runaways, vagrants, thieves, vagabonds, filthy, diseased, dissolute,
immoral, disgusting, covered with sores; some were priests, some
jugglers, some barbers, some wrestlers, some cooks, some grooms,
some buffoons, some herdsmen, some pedlars, some scullions,
bakers, tailors, confectioners, instead of agricultural labourers,

He added:

'It would be found wherever this system was scrutinised, whether in
India, Africa or Demerara, that these persons were a deeply demoralised
class of human beings... The system of emigration had been false, and
to attempt to carry it out extensively, would only be to create a new
slave trade under false colours, and of a modified description, so as to
injure materially the interests of the colonies, as to their social and moral
condition.'

The fact remains that the men who thundered their denunciations of black slavery in the Caribbean were unable to prevent
a migration of semi-free brown and yellow labour into the area, a
migration which reached enormous proportions and which made a
mockery of the so-called experiment of free labour. The Caribbean
planter, Africa denied to him, was encouraged to turn to India
and China.

Chapter Nineteen

Asian Immigration

In 1814, one of the most prominent planters in Trinidad, William Burnley, proposed, as the best method of improving the colony, the importation of free workers from India on a large scale. 'It may be considered as an axiom,' he wrote, 'that without a change in the materials of which the population of the island is composed, no beneficial alteration in its actual state can be effected.' What was required, said Burnley, was a new race of men, 'healthy and free, with habits and science ready formed, and sufficiently numerous to stand unsupported and distinct from our present population on its immediate arrival.' With a limited population in Trinidad, with the door to African labour closed by the abolition of the slave trade in 1807, Burnley turned his eyes to India.

Supporting Burnley's views, Governor Woodford of Trinidad wrote to the Colonial Office in the same year advocating the introduction of East Indian immigrants to prove or disprove the familiar argument in England, that free labour was cheaper than slave. About the same time Jamaica also advocated the introduction of labour from India.

The Governor of Jamaica, Lord Elgin, on August 5, 1845,

opposed the policy of immigration. This is what he had to say:

> 'I have always considered a reliance on Immigration exclusively, as the only practical and available remedy for the material difficulties of the Colony, to be a serious evil, and averse to its best interests ... It was based on the hypothesis, expressed or understood, that the system of husbandry pursued during slavery was alone suited to tropical cultivation. Its tendency therefore was to discourage agricultural improvement, and to retard the growth of that more intimate sympathy between the enlightened friends of the Planter and the Peasant which I was so desirous to promote.'

In Trinidad, the Governor, Lord Harris, wrote as follows on June 19, 1848:

> 'If it be considered that the chief aim and object of society is to create the largest quantity of produce at the lowest possible price ... it is very doubtful whether on that score immigration will succeed; but taking a higher point of view, and looking to the moral results, a population such as I have described is not improved by an influx of such people as immigrants generally are; the habits which they introduce are commonly pernicious, and morally and socially they tend to deteriorate, if left at liberty ...'

But the planters demanded immigration. The Combined Court of British Guiana asked in 1850 for 'a large influx of immigrants ... without delay'. Two years later the Governor asserted that 'immigration must long continue of first necessity in this colony. Were it checked, cultivation must once more fall off, and improvement languish'. Even Victor Schoelcher, the French humanitarian, had envisaged that immigration of free labour would be necessary after emancipation in the French West Indies.

This was the background to a new wave of immigration in the Caribbean which began in 1838 and ended in 1924. Between 1838 and 1917, no fewer than 238,000 Indians were introduced into British Guiana, 145,000 into Trinidad, 21,500 into Jamaica, 39,000 into Guadeloupe, 34,000 into Surinam, 1,550 into St. Lucia, 1,820 into St. Vincent, 2,570 into Grenada. In 1859, there were 6,748 Indians in Martinique. These are fragmentary statistics, and do not give the whole picture. Yet they are sufficient to show a total introduction of nearly half a million Indians into the Caribbean.

Some idea of the scope of the immigration is afforded by

statistics for various years chosen at random: 1869—12,805; 1873—11,823; 1878—14,371; 1894—10,885. The importations into British Guiana averaged nearly 3,000 a year, into Trinidad about 1,800. Imports into British Guiana were over 9,000 and over 7,000 in 1869, 1873, 1885 and 1894. Trinidad imported over 3,000 in each of the years 1867, 1869, 1872, 1875, 1892, 1905, 1910. Surinam's peak was 1,867 in 1909; in 1908, the figure was 1,674; in 1915, 1,567. The year of highest importation in Jamaica was 1847—2,438 immigrants; in 1912 the number was 1,985, and in 1846, 1,851. In 1862, 1,097 Indians were introduced into Grenada.

India was the principal, not the sole source of immigrant labour. Thousands of Madeirans were introduced into the British West Indies, especially British Guiana. Numbers of Chinese also were introduced; 500 reached Martinique in 1859. 14,002 went to British Guiana between 1853 and 1879.

Guadeloupe's immigration statistics read as follows from 1854 to 1887: Indians, 42,595; Africans, 6,600; Chinese, 500; Madeirans, 413; Europeans, 379; Annamites from Cochin China, 272. In 1894, 500 Japanese were brought in to further complicate the demographic picture.

Cuba, desperately short of labour, put Chinese contract workers to work side by side with Negro slaves—in 1861 there were 34,834 Chinese in Cuba, $2\frac{1}{2}$ per cent of the total population; in 1877, the number had increased to 53,811, or 3 per cent of the total population. Flor de Cuba plantation had 409 Negroes and 170 Chinese; San Martin 452 Negroes and 125 Chinese; Santa Susana 632 Negroes and 200 Chinese. Someone pointed out that the heterogeneity of the Cuban population was being increased as a result. A Cuban planter replied with the Spanish equivalent of 'So what?'

Between 1853 and 1924, over 22,000 workers from the Netherlands Indies, principally Java, were introduced into Surinam. The importation in 1920 was 3,559; in 1919, 2,126; in 1922, 1,975. In addition, numbers of Africans captured on slave ships trading to Cuba and Brazil were introduced into the British West Indies, and the French West Indies recruited indentured African labour on the coast of Africa. In 1859 there were almost six thousand of these African workers in Martinique and Guadeloupe.

The Asian immigration, intrinsically significant, both by virtue
of the numbers introduced and the philosophy underlying their
introduction, assumes greater significance when it is recalled that
it coincided, up to 1865, with the Cuban slave trade in Negroes
which was steadfastly opposed by the British Government, the
British abolitionists, and the British West Indian planters. There
was a difference—philosophical, juridical and social—between 'indentured' or contract labour and slave labour. But more fundamental than this difference was the introduction of labour,
whatever its label, for sugar production. From 1800 to 1865 a total
of 386,437 slaves were introduced into Cuba.

Taking into account the fact that the British slave trade was
not abolished until 1807, and that the French slave trade was
resumed after 1815, the total immigration into the Caribbean in the
nineteenth century, from Africa, Asia and Madeira, was well over
one million people, or about 10,000 a year.

Between 1850 and 1865, Cuba imported 35,600 slaves; during
the same period 41,390 Indians were introduced into British
Guiana, 23,862 into Trinidad, and, from 1854 to 1865, 12,504 into
Guadeloupe. As a result of the slave trade, the coloured population in Cuba, 43 per cent of the total in 1775, rose to 58 per
cent in 1841. As a result of Asian immigration, the East Indians
became the largest racial group in British Guiana, and the second
largest in Trinidad; while East Indians and Javanese combined
completely dominated Surinam.

Only four territories in the Caribbean in the nineteenth century
did not participate in the vast demographic revolution which was
in operation in the area as a whole: independent Haiti, Spanish
Santo Domingo, which became independent in 1844, Spanish
Puerto Rico, and British Barbados. Elsewhere the simple population pattern at the end of the eighteenth century— a few whites
of the metropolitan country, some mulattoes, and a majority of
Negroes—became a heterogeneous mixture which included
Indians, Chinese, Javanese, and Portuguese, with all the infinite
gradations, shadings and mixtures produced by miscegenation.

Was Indian immigration successful, that is, did it achieve its
main purpose of maintaining sugar cultivation at a profitable level
in the Caribbean? The appointment of the Royal Commission of

1897 provides the answer. So does a comparison of British West Indian exports for 1828 and 1895:

Territory	1828 (tons)	1895 (tons)
Antigua	8,848	7,219
Barbados	16,942	32,806
Jamaica	72,198	19,546
Trinidad	13,285	54,622
British Guiana	40,115	101,160
St. Kitts–Nevis	8,369	13,095
Montserrat	1,254	631
St. Lucia	4,162	3,628
St. Vincent	14,403	2,585
Grenada	13,493	nil
Total British West Indies	193,069	235,292

British West Indian sugar exports in 1895 were 21.9 per cent greater than in 1828. The total number of Indians only, introduced up to 1894, was 306,731. British Guiana's production increased two and a half times; Indian importations amounted to 188,177. Trinidad's production increased four times; 99,485 imported Indians made this possible. But the 12,801 Indians introduced into Jamaica could not prevent sugar exports from declining in 1894 to one-quarter of the figure for 1828. The doubling of exports in St. Kitts-Nevis could not possibly be attributed to the 337 Indians introduced in 1861. The number of Indians introduced into St. Vincent was 1,826, yet the sugar exports declined by four-fifths. St. Lucia received 1,525 Indians; sugar exports decreased by less than one-tenth. The number of Indians introduced into Grenada was 2,570— yet the sugar industry disappeared. Montserrat received no Indians; the sugar exports decreased by one-half. Barbados imported no immigrants; sugar exports doubled.

The Asian labourer was not a slave. He was a freeman, and he came to the Caribbean on contract, generally for five years. Thus the Caribbean, which had in the seventeenth century sought in the white indentured servant a substitute for the indigenous Amerindian, turned in the nineteenth to indentured Asians as a substitute for the African slave who had supplanted the white indentured servant.

The contract specified that the Asian labourer was to have a free passage to the West Indies and, if he arrived in the West Indies before 1898, a free return passage at the end of his contract;

those who arrived after 1898 were entitled to half the return passage in the case of males, two-thirds in the case of females. In 1897 in British Guiana it cost £17 to introduce one Indian, £12 10s to repatriate him. The immigrant was guaranteed a fixed wage of 1s 6d a day for a specified number of days in each year. The contract further provided for medical attention during his employment, and housing accommodation at the expense of the employer.

In 1850 the Combined Court of British Guiana protested against the stipulation of a return passage at the expense of the colony. In 1852 the Governor of Trinidad stated that the prospect of returning home at an early period had a tendency to unsettle the immigrants, and he, too, regretted the requirement of a return passage. Up to 1924, the number of Indians who returned home from British Guiana was 67,320, or a proportion of more than one out of every four who had been introduced. In Trinidad, the number who returned was 27,853—about one out of every six who had been introduced.

Thus, of 383,000 Indians introduced into both colonies, 95,173, or more than one-quarter, had returned home by 1924. For every four immigrants, therefore, five free passages had to be found. The two-way traffic reached a point where the number of workers who departed annually exceeded those who were introduced. In 1905, for example, 2,704 Indians came to British Guiana on contract; 2,762 departed. In 1897, arrivals numbered 1,194; departures 1,529. In 1904, 1,314 arrived; 1,625 departed. It was a most expensive method of recruiting labour.

Consequently, the colonies made every effort to induce the indentured workers to renew their contract, or, at least, to remain at the end of their term. With reindenture, they were unsuccessful. Reindentures numbered 6,096 in British Guiana from 1874 to 1895; new arrivals totalled 105,205. For every 100 who came, only six who had served their term agreed to a renewal. In the three years 1903–1905, reindentures aggregated 133 in Surinam, one-tenth of the new arrivals in 1902.

The governments then tried inducements to remain. The chief inducement was a grant of land. Between 1891 and 1913, in British Guiana, a total of 31,917 acres was granted to 844 Indians, as free grants or homestead grants, with restrictions on alienation for a period of ten years. In 1898–1899 the number of acres thus granted was 5,992; in 1903–1904, 95 Indians received grants. In addition, 201 leases, involving 10,957 acres, were issued from 1891 to 1913. The value of landed property held by Indians in British Guiana was assessed at $972,761 in 1911–1912; in that year Indians owned 13,384 head of cattle and 3,022 sheep and goats.

In Surinam, between 1903 and 1911, over 200,000 acres of land were allotted to 31,068 immigrants, either in free use, in lease, or by outright purchase; six out of every ten acres were purchased outright, at a total cost of 589,184 florins. In Trinidad, between 1885 and 1895, a total of 22,916 acres was sold to Indian immigrants; between 1902 and 1912, 4,450 grants, totalling 31,766 acres, were distributed, the Indians paying £72,837 for them, or over two pounds an acre.

Thus, by a curious irony, the sugar planter who, in the seventeenth and eighteenth centuries, refused to grant land to the white indentured servant, who, after emancipation, tried to prevent the purchase of land by the former slaves, found himself obliged in the nineteenth century to grant land to the indentured immigrant in order to reduce the expense of immigrant labour. Indian immigration, designed to compete with the Negro landowners, ended in a competition with European landowners. The Negro peasantry was reinforced by the Indian peasantry.

Once the Indian had received his plot of land, he was no more willing to work uninterruptedly and exclusively on the plantation than the former slave had been. A census of 'free' Indians, that is, of those who had completed their indenture, in Jamaica in 1913 showed that, of the total of 17,380, only 9,163 were agricultural labourers—of these 2,854 or one in every six of the total, were employed in the sugar industry, and 5,323 were workers on banana plantations. Small farmers—growing banana, cane, cassava, coffee, foodcrops, rice and tobacco—numbered 607.

One reason for the expense of indentured labour was that the supply exceeded the economic demand An ordinance in Trinidad stipulated that no plantation could obtain additional indentured immigrants where more than 15 per cent of those in residence had earned less than sixpence per day during the preceding year. The ordinance was first put into force in 1892, whereupon it was found that so many plantations were affected that immigration would cease. Consequently, a special law was passed authorising the introduction of immigrants despite the ordinance. In 1895, of 69 plantations in Trinidad utilising indentured labour, only on ten did the percentage of indentured immigrants earning less than sixpence a day fall below the 15 per cent required by the law; seven of these were cocoa plantations. The percentage on sugar plantations was 43 for Usine Ste. Madeleine, 30 for Caroni, 54 for Waterloo, 35 for Woodford Lodge and Brechin Castle.

Trinidad was not unique in this respect. In British Guiana, in 1912, the average weekly earnings of an indentured immigrant was $1.23 in Demerara and Berbice, $1.14 in Essequibo. The percentage of working days worked by each woman immigrant varied from 31 on Providence Plantation to 84 on Farm Plantation, both owned by the Demerara Company; for men, from 64 on Providence Plantation to 87 on Farm. In Surinam a Commission of the Government of India stated in 1915 that 'the regulation entitling the employer to require six days work weekly is certainly not abused. Apparently four labourers are imported to do work which would be light employment for three.' The male immigrants lost one-third of the working days; the average number of days worked in 1911 was 177. Male earnings amounted to thirteen pence per day worked; female, ninepence.

Indian immigration was not only an expensive, it was also an inefficient form of labour. In French Guiana, in the first six months of 1875, where the indentured immigrants averaged 350 a month, the man-days worked numbered 26,852; the man-days lost in the hospital 26,602; the average number of days worked by each immigrant was twelve per month, while, for every day worked, one day was spent in hospital. In Trinidad, in 1895, for 10,720 Indian immigrants, there were 23,688 admissions to hospitals. Thus each Indian went at least twice a year to the hospital, at the expense of the planter and the government.

This meant, as the Surgeon-General of the Colony stated, a loss of 165,816 man-days of labour, or about £8,000. Whilst the immigrant lost his wages during his hospitalisation, the employer had to maintain him and contribute to the upkeep of the hospital, and he lost also the man's labour during the period. The Manager of the Usine Ste. Madeleine Sugar Company in Trinidad, on the basis of the records of 1,996 indentured immigrants for the years 1892–1895, estimated that only 63 per cent of the 280 contract days were worked; one day in every three was lost to the plantations. Eleven per cent of the time was lost through sickness.

In addition to sickness, much time was lost through desertion and absence without leave. On the Usine Ste. Madeleine, the percentage from the causes was seventeen—that is, one out of every six working days. In British Guiana, of 105,205 immigrants introduced between 1874 and 1895, there were 13,129 desertions: one out of every eight Indians deserted. The total number of convictions of immigrants for offences against employers was 56,084, or more than one conviction for every two immigrants. In British Guiana, in 1913, of a mean adult indentured population of 9,671, there were 361 convictions for absence from work, 277 for habitual idleness, 65 for absence from the plantation without leave, 178 for desertion—a total of 881 convictions for these causes, out of 1,439 immigrants convicted for all breaches of the Immigration Laws. In Jamaica, in 1912–1913, of 4,125 indentured immigrants, there were 184 cases of wilful indolence, 74 of unlawful absence from work, 61 of desertion—a total of 319.

Indian immigration had been advocated, and permitted, on the ground that it was free labour. The nature of the freedom is indicated by the Trinidad Ordinance of 1899 relating to immigration. The law made a nine-hour day mandatory. If the immigrant was found drunk on duty, he was liable to a maximum fine of one pound or maximum imprisonment for fourteen days. For using threatening language to any one in authority on the plantation, negligence, hindering or molesting other immigrants in their work, the maximum penalty was five pounds or two months' imprisonment.

Every immigrant was bound to reside on the plantation on which he was under indenture; he was thus attached to the soil. If found anywhere else, without a ticket of leave or a certificate showing exemption from labour, he could be stopped, without a warrant, by the Protector of Immigrants or any person authorised by him in writing, by a plantation policeman or by the employer or his manager, or overseer, and taken to the nearest police station; if convicted, the penalty was a maximum of seven days imprisonment, with or without hard labour.

Absence without leave carried a maximum fine of two pounds for males, one pound for females. Absence for three days constituted desertion; the employer was then required to apply for a warrant for the apprehension of the deserter and to notify the immigration and police authorities. If the employer or manager failed to prefer charges within fifteen days after the immigrant had become a deserter, he was subject to a maximum fine of five pounds, plus one shilling for each day of default. The penalty for the immigrant, if apprehended, was a maximum fine of five pounds and/or a maximum imprisonment of two months. If indentured labour was free, it was, to paraphrase Carlyle, freedom plus a constable.

Notoriously thrifty, the Indian immigrants were able to accumulate considerable savings and remit large sums to India. In 1833 there were 6,274 Indian depositors in the Government Savings Bank in British Guiana; their deposits amounted to $601,166. In 1911–1912, the number of depositors had increased to 8,214; the deposits amounted to £123,051 or $590,645, In Trinidad, in 1911–1912, savings of Indian immigrants totalled £81,403. In Surinam, in 1912, there were 2,711 depositors, with 265,642 florins to their credit. Between 1891 and 1912, East Indian immigrants in British Guiana remitted £52,975 to India. The average remittance in 1911–1912 was over three pounds. In Trinidad remittances from 1890 to 1912 totalled 20,059, amounting to £65,187.

There was considerable local opposition in the West Indies to the system of indentured labour. The first criticism was that it tended to distract attention from the important question of modernising the methods of production. It continued to emphasise manual labour at the expense of machinery, thereby perpetuating the worst aspect of the slavery regime. In the words of an Englishman, Lechmere Guppy, Mayor of San Fernando, Trinidad's second town, before a Royal Commission in 1889, Indian immigration 'serves only to stereotype and perpetuate the lowest and least profitable mode of agriculture'. Guppy added that no improvement in cane cultivation had been made during his forty-eight years' residence in Trinidad.

The second criticism was that indentured labour perpetuated the degradation of the labour which slavery had begun. Guppy constantly harped on this aspect of the system; in fact, he called indenture 'the new slavery'. One of the worst features of the system was the housing provided for the workers. In Trinidad the separate cottages of slavery gave way to 'barracks'—long-rooms partitioned off, without washing or sanitary facilities. Each family had a single room in the 'barracks'—there was no privacy, morality was impossible.

The Mayor of the capital, Port-of-Spain, Sir Henry Alcazar, added to Guppy's criticism. Like Booker T. Washington in the United States, Alcazar believed that you cannot keep a man down in a ditch without getting into the ditch with him. Alcazar's view of the indentured system, as stated to the Royal Commission of 1897, was as follows:

'On his employer, however, the effect is much more similar to that of slavery, for if one fifth of his bondsmen are set free every year, a fresh fifth at once takes their place, and he has thus permanently about him a large number of his fellow men bound to do his bidding under penalty of imprisonment. In fact, with regard to its effect on the employer, the system is not very different from slavery, with the gaol substituted for the whip. And one of the worst consequences of Indian immigration in Trinidad has been to keep its educated classes at the moral level of slave owners.'

The third criticism was that the entire community was taxed to finance a single industry. The slave trade had been a purely private enterprise; a planter needed the slaves, and he bought them, for cash or on credit. And the planter paid for them. Who paid for the Indian immigrant? On December 2, 1859, a newspaper in Guadeloupe, L'Avenir, stated that the 9,166 immigrants introduced from 1854, from India, Madeira and Africa, had depleted the Immigration Fund. The paper advocated that the cost of immigration in the future should be defrayed partly by the employers of immigrants and partly by a head tax on the entire population.

In the British colonies a percentage of the immigration expenditure was provided out of general revenue. In British Guiana in 1896, about 30 per cent of the expenses were paid from general revenue; the planter paid 70 per cent. The proportion in Trinidad was about the same. In Jamaica the cost of introducing an Indian labourer was £56, of which, at the beginning, the Government

contributed £7 (one-eighth). The bankruptcy of the Immigration
Fund and the need for labour combined in 1876 to induce the
local government to contribute at least £26 to the introduction of
a labourer—nearly one half. The planters protested that this was
not enough. Governor Musgrave wrote sharply to the Secretary of
State for the Colonies:

'By the new scheme, at large sacrifices by the community for this purpose, certain labour, labour secured by indenture for five years, is offered
to the sugar planter, at rates which do not amount to 1s 6d per day; and
under the scheme now proposed, the portion which constituted the 6d is
virtually advanced to the planter by the public, and the repayment divided
over five years. It is my deliberate opinion that if sugar cultivation cannot
be continued at that rate of wages for labour in Jamaica ... the causes of
the failure must be sought elsewhere than in the quarters where they are
alleged to be found ... And yet a section of the planting body, though
I am glad to believe only a small section, protest clamorously that it will
be impossible to carry on the cultivation on such terms as these. And one
is led almost to the conclusion that no system for the future will be
satisfactory to them which does not provide at the public expense for
the payment of the estates weekly wages as well as the whole cost of the
introduction of the immigrant to be employed.'

Indian immigration was thus financed to a considerable extent
by those with whom it was intended that the Indian immigrants
should compete.

The financing of Indian immigration was directly related to the
distribution of political power. As soon as elected members were
introduced into the Assembly of Jamaica—which, from 1865,
had a pure crown colony government with nominated members
only—immigration was temporarily suspended. In Trinidad,
Alcazar, one of the leaders of the movement for a reform of the
crown colony constitution, stated in 1897 that the friends of
Indian immigration congratulated themselves on the failure of a
constitution reform petition on the ground that, with the introduction of an elective element into the legislature, Indian immigration was doomed. Yet, Alcazar added, 'it had not been proposed
to place power in the hands of the working classes, but only in
those of the wealthier middle classes.'

The fourth argument against the indenture system was that it
was unnecessary. In 1890, a prominent Trinidadian, Dr de
Boissierre, took the view that Barbados could supply all the

labour needed. History, he said, 'will pen a terrible indictment of neglect against the administration of the last 30 years for not having organised a system by which this natural and free immigration, involving as it does scarcely any cost, would have been taken advantage of, and efforts made to retain it'. The Barbadian, however, would as soon accept a contract as slavery.

But de Boissierre had a powerful argument. The real paradox of Indian immigration is that it coincided with an even larger wave of Negro emigration. Thousands of labourers, not only from Barbados, but also from Jamaica, emigrated to the Panama Canal, to the banana plantations of Costa Rica, to the United States, and, disproving the argument that the West Indian would not cultivate sugar, to the sugar plantations of Cuba. In 1913, Jamaican emigration totalled 15,096—1,510 to Cuba, 9,728 to Panama, 2,313 to Costa Rica. From 1901 to 1917, the net emigration from Jamaica amounted to 24,643, to which must be added 60,200 West Indians who emigrated to the United States— a total of 84,843.

During the same period the net immigration from India into British Guiana and Trinidad—subtracting repatriates from immigrants—was 24,260. As many Indians came in as West Indians left Jamaica. Remittances received through the Barbadian Post Office in the years 1900, 1901, 1906, 1907, 1909 and 1910 from Barbadians abroad totalled £515,934 in money orders and registered letters; in the year 1910, £93,361 was remitted in money orders alone, £66,162 from the Canal Zone, £15,078 from the United States, and £12,518 from British Colonies.

Thus for every East Indian added to the British West Indian labour force before World War I, three West Indians were subtracted. For every pound sent out of the West Indies by East Indians, four were sent in by Barbadians alone.

One final criticism may be made, in retrospect, of the system of Indian immigration. In 1896 Trinidad spent £51,978 on the immigration department out of a total expenditure of £594,462— more than one-twelfth. The expenditure on education was £38,248. Some portion of the Colony's expenditure on police, £44,006, on prisons, £14,072, and on the medical department, £64,918, must also be added to the expenses of immigration. Add to this the expenditure on the unprofitable railway, £51,910, which ran through the sugar district, competing with road and marine transport, and instituted and maintained at the insistence of the sugar planters, and it will appear that Trinidad paid a very high price indeed for the extension of an industry which, in 1897, was bankrupt.

In 1895–1896, British Guiana's public contributions of one-third to the immigration fund amounted to £41,728 out of a total expenditure of £596,493; the total expenditure on primary and secondary education amounted to £26,509. In addition, the colony paid two-thirds of the medical service for the immigrants. As Jules Duval had written in 1859, immigration as a solution demanded that no account be taken of the former slaves and their descendants.

Chapter Twenty

The West Indian Sugar Economy in the Nineteenth Century

The slave revolution in Saint-Domingue and the annihilation of its sugar industry provided the immediate stimulus to Cuban sugar production. The country forged rapidly ahead, until it became the centre of gravity of the Caribbean in the nineteenth century, as Hispaniola, Barbados, Jamaica and Saint-Domingue had been in their day. Spanish imperialism, born in the bright sunrise of Hispaniola, expired in the brilliant sunset of Cuba.

The progress of the Cuban sugar industry in the nineteenth century, though it was retarded by the wars for independence against Spain—the first, from 1868 to 1878, the second from 1894 to 1898—is brought out in the following table:

Year	Exports (tons)	Year	Production (tons)
1810	33,708	1850	223,145
1820	39,192	1859	536,000
1830	72,635	1868	749,000
1840	113,401	1877	520,000
1847	208,599	1886	731,723
		1894	1,054,214
		1897	212,051

In 1859 there were two thousand plantations, occupying about 290,000 acres of land, and employing 550,000 slaves. The capital investment in land, buildings, slaves and machinery was estimated at 239 million pesos. The sugar produced on the plantations fetched 25 million pesos.

A plantation producing a little over 1,000 tons of sugar in 1859 required about 3,300 acres of land and 150 slaves. The cost of the land was 100,000 pesos, of the buildings 50,000. The plantation was equipped with the latest machinery, costing 55,000 pesos. The carts and tools cost another 15,000; the slaves 105,000. Including interest at 8 per cent, the total capital investment required for a plantation of this size was 351,000 pesos. The annual expenses for technicians, artisans, overseers, medical attention, casks, transport of the sugar to market, etc., were estimated at 36,500 pesos. The sugar, at 17 pesos a box, brought in 102,000 pesos. The net profit was 65,000 pesos, or 18 per cent annually on the capital.

The Cuban sugar industry was based, until 1880, on slave labour. Its expansion thus depended, in the first instance, on precisely the same factor which had determined the expansion of its predecessors. Slave labour in Cuba was vulnerable to the same arguments which Barbados, Jamaica and Saint-Domingue had made familiar. The Cuban planters made no improvements in the sphere of cultivation; they paid no attention to improved varieties of the cane. Their distinct advantage in sugar cultivation was exactly the advantage which Barbados had enjoyed in the seventeenth century—virgin soil. By virtue of its size, Cuba merely had more virgin soil. But the inadequacy of labour retarded the full development of the island. Ten times the size of Jamaica, Cuba in 1859 had only twice the slave population of Jamaica in 1787.

From the factory aspect, however, the Cuban sugar economy was marked by two developments which, together with its virgin soil, ensured its undisputed superiority over its Caribbean rivals. The first was the installation of the latest machinery, the virtual disappearance of the old cattle mills, and the amalgamation of factories. The second was the introduction of the railway, which permitted an extension of the radius of the plantation.

The result of these combined developments was a considerable increase in the output per factory. In 1792 Cuba's exports of 14,600 tons were produced in 473 factories—about 30 tons per factory. In 1802 there were 870 factories, and the exports rose to 40,800 tons—less than 50 tons per factory. The 2,000 factories of 1859 produced 536,000 tons or 268 tons per factory. Production in 1870 amounted to 610,300 tons, from 1,200 factories, over 500 tons per factory. In 1890 production was 625,000 tons, but the number of factories had declined to 470—the average output per factory was 1,330 tons. There were as many factories in 1890 as there had been a century before; production and yield had multiplied nearly forty-three times. The record crop of 1894 was produced in 400 factories, an average of 2,635 tons per factory. In a little over ninety years, therefore, the output per factory had increased more than fiftyfold.

The development was so rapid and astonishing that, by 1857, the Cubans were speaking of 'monster' plantations. They were monsters indeed compared with the eighteenth-century establishments; but, compared with those of the mid-twentieth-century, they were only pygmies. The grandest of the 1857 vintage was *Santa Susana*. It comprised 11,000 acres, of which 1,700 were in cane, employed 866 slaves, about two slaves to each acre, and produced nearly 2,700 tons of sugar—the yield was about $1\frac{3}{4}$ tons of sugar per acre and 3 tons per slave. The *Alava* plantation comprised nearly 5,000 acres, of which over 2,000 were in cane; it employed 600 slaves, or one slave for every three acres in cane, and, in 1858, produced a record of 3,500 tons of sugar—the yield was $1\frac{3}{4}$ tons of sugar per acre and nearly six tons per slave. Two plantations, *Purísima Concepción* and *San Martín*, functioned as a single unit, the cane bring transported by railway from the former to be ground in the large mill of the latter. The former comprised 3,000 acres, of which half were in cane; the latter 7,400 acres, of which one-quarter was in cane. The combined labour force of the two plantations was 989, and the production 5,700 tons—a yield of $1\frac{2}{3}$ tons per acre and nearly six tons per slave. The cost of the two plantations was estimated at $1,600,000. The value of a monster *ingenio* ranged from 100,000 to over one million pesos.

Cuban writers were lyrical. Cuba's soil, wrote Cantero, author of the valuable and profusely illustrated *Los Ingenios de Cuba*, and himself owner of one of the monsters, was 'the favourite of Providence for the important cultivation of the cane because of the nature of its lands fertilised by copious and clear rivers, the state and variations of its benign and humid atmosphere, and above all because of the vivifying warmth of its tropical sun'. It seemed to have taken a long time for the sun to vivify Cuba and the rivers to fertilise its soil, but God moves in a mysterious way, and Cantero evidently thought that it was better to worship sugar late than never. 'The majestic sight of the sun,' he expatiated on one of the monster plantations, 'as it appears over the hills from which it bathes with its gilded rays the emerald fields covered with the transparent dew of the morning, gently stirs the soul elevating it to the sublime Creator of such a splendid picture'.

Words would have failed Cantero had he lived to see the even more portentous developments of the end of the century. In 1893 *Soledad* plantation, owned by United States capital, comprised 12,000 acres, of which 5,000 were in cane, contained 23 miles of private railway, and employed 1,200 men in harvest time. Another United States-owned enterprise, *Santa Teresa*, of 9,000 acres, represented a capital investment of $1,565,000. In 1890 *Central Constancia* was the most important sugar factory in the world. It produced 135,000 bags of sugar, about 19,500 tons. The Cuban crop of 1894 was valued at over $62,100,000. Some thirty million dollars of United States capital were invested in the Cuban sugar industry in 1896.

There were two important corollaries of this enormous development. The first was, with the amalgamation of factories, a tendency to separate the industrial and agricultural aspects of the industry. The old comprehensive appellation, sugar planter, gave way to a new terminology—the *central*, the gigantic mill, and the *colono*, the cane cultivator. By 1887 about two-fifths of the Cuban crop was produced under the *colono* system. The second corollary was a vast stimulus to monoculture. In 1833 Cuba's coffee exports amounted to 64,150,000 pounds weight, produced on 2,067 estates; in 1862, the estates had declined in number to 782, and the exports to five million pounds. A few years later Cuba had to import coffee. It was no accident that the Cuban revolution of 1868 was headed by coffee planters and stockmen of the oldest families of Cuba.

Sugar was king. Allowing for the mathematical differences in yield, output and size of the plantations, there was not a single feature of Cuba's economic development in the nineteenth cᴇ ʰury which was not a replica of Hispaniola's, Barbados', Jamaica's and Saint-Domingue's. The vast wealth produced by sugar in Cuba differed only in volume from that produced elsewhere in the Caribbean in previous centuries. The planters, absentee to a considerable extent, flaunted their wealth in Havana, as their British predecessors had done in London and the French in Paris. The wealth was admittedly imposing. With a due sense of their position, the Cuban planters built houses which they modestly called palaces.

Miguel de Aldama, Havana's richest man, whose income was estimated at three million dollars a year, set out, in his own words, 'to build a little house of simple and elegant architecture ...the best, the only one in Havana in which there would at least be intentions and signs of respect and love for the beauty of Art'. The result was the Aldama Palace. Its halls and rooms were vast, its splendid floors of marble. It had balconies with balustrades of cast iron, and its staircase was wide, with balustrades of bronze. In the courtyard there was a small marble fountain. In the great hall there were two magnificent paintings, the one on the right representing the Pilgrim Fathers in prayer as they landed at Plymouth, the other on the left depicting the disembarkation of Cortes in Mexico. These, together with two beautiful bas-reliefs entitled 'Day' and 'Night', were donated by Aldama to the city of Havana, and are today among the most highly-prized artistic treasures of the Municipality. Some have seen in the Italian neo-classicism of the palace a deliberate gesture of rebellion against the colonial style of architecture; others have been able to discern in its majesty an intention that it should one day serve as the executive mansion of a future Cuban republic. Converted later into a tobacco factory, in which room was found for 450 workers, the palace stands today, a monument to King Sugar.

The royal ambitions of the Cuban sugar planters were strikingly demonstrated by an incident which took place in Trinidad, one of the most fertile areas in Cuba, and one of the chief centres of the sugar industry. Three of the leading planters of this city, Becquer, Iznaga and Borrell, envious of the reputation and magnificence

of Havana, decided to challenge the capital's supremacy. They
planned a competition among themselves to build palaces which
would put those of Havana in the shade. The competition was
soon converted into a personal rivalry between the three grandees.
A rumour arose to the effect that Becquer lacked the funds to
complete his grandiose plan. To disprove the falsity of the allegation, he decided to pave his palace with gold coins. His scheme
was frustrated, however, because the Captain-General of the
island pointed out that it was forbidden to walk on the king's
head, which appeared on the coins. The description of the Brunet
palace in the same city will serve as an indication of the others:
'here there is neither grace, nor coquetry, nor frivolity, but
grandeur'.

The full significance of Cuba's development is brought out by
the following table comparing sugar production in that island with
sugar exports from the British, French, Dutch and Danish
territories, in tons:

Colony	1815	1828	1882	1894
Antigua	8,032	8,848	12,670	12,382
Barbados	8,837	16,942	48,325	50,958
British Guiana	16,520	40,115	124,102	102,502
Dominica	2,205	2,497	3,421	1,050
Grenada	11,594	13,493	1,478	3
Jamaica	79,660	72,198	32,638	19,934
Montserrat	1,225	1,254	2,314	1,801
Nevis	2,761	2,309	}16,664	}16,901
St. Kitts	7,066	6,060		
St. Lucia	3,661	4,162	7,506	4,485
St. Vincent	11,590	14,403	8,175	2,727
Tobago	6,044	6,167	2,518	599
Tortola	1,200	663	–	–
Trinidad	7,682	13,285	55,327	46,869
Total B.W.I.	168,077	202,396	315,138	260,211
Martinique	15,814 (1818)	32,812	47,120	36,353
Guadeloupe	20,792 (1818)	35,244	56,592	43,041
Surinam	5,692 (1816)	11,728 (1825)	5,410 (1885)	8,023 (1895)
Puerto Rico	–	112,000 (1853)	65,000 (1886)	48,500 (1893–4)
St. Croix	20,535 (1812)	10,576 (1830)	8,482 (1880–90) (average)	8,000 (1895–6)
Cuba	39,961	72,635 (1826–30) (average)	595,000*	1,054,214*

* Production figures.

Cuba's exports in 1815 were half those of Jamaica, about two
and a half times those of British Guiana, less than one-quarter of
those of the British West Indies, slightly more than the combined

exports of Martinique and Guadeloupe. By 1828 Cuba's exports equalled those of Jamaica, were four-fifths larger than those of British Guiana, were slightly more than one-third those of the British West Indies, and slightly larger than those of Martinique and Guadeloupe added together. In 1882 Cuba's production was nearly nineteen times the exports of Jamaica, nearly five times those of British Guiana, almost double those of the British West Indies, nearly six times the combined exports of Martinique and Guadeloupe. In 1894 Cuba produced more than fifty times as much as Jamaica exported, ten times as much as British Guiana, four times as much as the British West Indies, more than thirteen times as much as the French West Indies. During the period 1815–1894 Cuba's production nearly tripled. Total British West Indian exports increased by one-half. Total French West Indian exports were twice as large in 1894 as in 1818.

An analysis of the British West Indian figures indicates that even the slight increase recorded during the period was only due to the fact that the normal law of Caribbean sugar production—superior fertility of virgin soil—was at work there as well as in Cuba. The newer colonies, British Guiana and Trinidad, forged ahead of the older settlements. British Guiana produced one-tenth of the British West Indian total in 1815, one-fifth in 1828, two-fifths in 1882 and 1894. In 1815 Trinidad produced nearly one-twentieth of the whole, in 1828 one-fifteenth, in 1882 and 1894 more than one-sixth. During the period, the exports of British Guiana and Trinidad increased more than six times. Jamaica's exports in 1894 were one-quarter of the figure for 1815. Exports in Antigua and Montserrat increased by fifty per cent, in St. Lucia by one-quarter, in St. Kitts-Nevis by three-quarters; on the other hand, there was a considerable decline of exports in Dominica (by one-half), in St. Vincent (by three-quarters), and in Tobago (by nine-tenths), while exports disappeared from Tortola and Grenada. Only in Barbados, where exports increased sixfold, was there an increase of production comparable to developments in Cuba, Trinidad and British Guiana; this is explained partly by the considerable decline of production which had taken place before 1815, and partly by other factors which we shall later examine. During the period the exports of Martinique and Guadeloupe doubled.

The following table indicates the nature of the British West Indian sugar industry around 1897:

Colony	Cane Acres	Sugar Workers	Fac- tories	Plantations over 500 Acres	Brown Sugar	Steam Power
Antigua	15,058	12,279	78	1	77	–
Barbados	74,000	47,045	440	23	432	99
British Guiana	66,908	90,492	64	57	2	64
Dominica	975	–	2	–	–	–
Grenada	1,000	–	2	–	–	–
Jamaica	30,036	39,046	140	137	40	95
St. Kitts–Nevis	22,253	15,682	136	35	135	79
St. Lucia	2,086	2,450	4	–	–	–
Tobago	1,942	5,000	40	15	37	20
Trinidad	33,845	14,092	56	–	7	56
Montserrat	6,000	–	26	–	26	12
Total B.W.I.	254,103	226,086	988			

In 1894 the British West Indies exported 260,211 tons of sugar. This quantity was produced on 254,103 acres, in 988 factories, by 226,086 workers. The yield was slightly more than one ton of sugar per acre and per worker, less than 250 tons of sugar per factory, 240 acres of cane per plantation. Barbados' exports of 50,958 tons, produced by 47,045 workers in 440 factories on 74,000 acres, represented less than one ton per worker, two-thirds of a ton per acre, about two workers for every three acres, and an average output per factory of 115 tons: less than half the British West Indian average, less than half the output of each Cuban factory in 1859. Jamaica's exports of 19,934 tons, produced on 30,036 acres in 140 factories by 39,046 workers, represented an average of two-thirds of a ton per acre, half a ton per worker, three workers for every four acres, and an average output of less than 140 tons. Jamaica's technical level in 1895 was approximately half of that reached by Cuba in 1859. Jamaica's total exports of 1894 represented the output of *Central Constancia* in Cuba. Trinidad's output per factory was 1,200 tons; British Guiana's, representing British West Indian technology at its best, 1,570 tons.

The full extent of British West Indian backwardness can be appreciated when it is realised that the average yield per factory in Cuba in 1894 was more than ten times the average in the British

West Indies; or, to put the case differently, British West Indian exports in that year, produced in 1,046 factories, could have been produced in 100 factories in Cuba. Barbados' exports, produced in 440 factories, could have been produced in twenty Cuban factories; Jamaica's, produced in 140 factories, could have been produced in eight in Cuba. However superior British Guiana and Trinidad might appear as compared with Barbados and Jamaica, the fact of the matter is that the average output in Trinidad was less than half that of Cuba, while in British Guiana it was three-fifths.

The competition between Cuba and the British West Indies was a competition between the eighteenth and nineteenth centuries, and between wind and steam. The *central* of Cuba was as to the windmill of Barbados as the hare to the tortoise. Outside British Guiana and Trinidad, the typical British West Indian factory was still producing muscovado sugar (an indication of poor equipment), and steam was the exception rather than the rule. Modyford and Beckford would have been at home on the British West Indian sugar plantation in Barbados and Jamaica at the end of the nineteenth century. James Watt might never have lived for all the effect his invention had on British West Indian sugar production. An observer of British West Indian society in 1835 had noted that the planters objected to the introduction of steam engines because of the scarcity of firewood. In 1894 about one factory in every five in Barbados was equipped with steam; the others were windmills. In Jamaica one in every four factories utilised water power. The proportion of factories using steam was slightly more than half in Tobago, about three-fifths in St. Kitts-Nevis, slightly less than half in Montserrat. All but one of the factories in Antigua and St. Kitts-Nevis, all but eight of those in Barbados, three-tenths of those in Jamaica, all of Montserrat, one-fifth of Trinidad's produced muscovado sugar. As was said in 1835: 'if the finest geologist of Europe were to . . . state that indications of coal were evident in the formations of the neighbouring mountains . . . no effort would be made to obtain it.'

A similar 'statu-quoitism', to quote a traveller in 1825, prevailed in field methods. 'The people of Jamaica make no novel experiments,' wrote a visitor in 1834; 'they find the sugar planted; and where it is they continue to cultivate it.' He added that they found the hoe the ancient instrument of the husbandman, and they had no desire to substitute the plough. In 1840 a Baptist missionary stated that the old methods were the rule, improvements the exception; the planters looked upon the practical knowledge of the eighteenth century as superior to the experience and science of the nineteenth. Implemental husbandry was virtually unknown in St. Vincent in 1860. The first steam plough was introduced into Antigua in 1863; it was only this 'wonder working implement', as it was described in 1886, that helped the sugar industry of that island to keep going. One of the most enlightened planters of the middle of the century stated that he did not understand why people should want to have canes which yielded twenty tons to the acre when they had good canes which yielded two.

The development of central factories, with their tendency to separate manufacture from agriculture, made no headway. In St. Lucia, it was objected to as involving 'a certain loss of independence and position'; it was rejected elsewhere as involving heavy costs in the transportation of cane. As the planters preferred the man with the hoe, so they remained devoted to the transportation of cane on the heads of workers or the backs of donkeys, and opposed the railway. Barbados continued to use up livestock at a rate which required replenishment of the entire stock every four years. As a result the size of the average plantation was 168 acres in Barbados, 178 acres in Jamaica, 193 acres in Antigua, as compared with 604 acres in Trinidad and 1,045 acres in British Guiana.

The results were catastrophic. In St. Vincent, in 1897, it was estimated that the sugar produced under the existing system was worth £20,400; with a central factory it would have been worth £29,650, an increase of nearly fifty per cent. In Antigua the existing system required 13.37 tons of cane to make one ton of sugar; a central factory would have required ten tons, a saving of one-quarter. Backward methods were costing the island £50,000 to £60,000 a year, representing a loss of about one-half of the total sugar produced. The island chemist of Barbados estimated that the failure to develop central factories represented a loss of six and a quarter pounds sterling per acre and a loss of 43 per cent in total production. An average loss of nearly one ton of sugar per acre was left in the canes after crushing; for every hundred pounds of sucrose in the juice, not more than seventy-five pounds of muscovado sugar were recovered, representing a loss of 25 per cent. If only half the plantations of Barbados had adopted the central factory system, the result would have been to add £250,000, nearly 70 per cent of the exports, to the value of the sugar produced.

What improved methods of manufacture and machinery meant, can be seen from estimates in British Guiana of the percentage of sugar that could be extracted from cane containing 12 per cent of fibre: single crushing, 76 per cent; double crushing (dry), 85 per cent; double crushing (with 12 per cent of dilution), 88 per cent; triple crushing (with 10 per cent of dilution), 90 per cent; diffusion (with 25 per cent of dilution), 94 per cent. So slow were the British West Indian planters in adopting modern methods that, in 1870, the process of diffusion was installed in only one factory in Trinidad, as compared with 52 beet factories in Austria, 36 in Germany, 7 in Poland, 8 in Russia. The British West Indian planters justified their backwardness, in the words of the Antigua planters in 1897, on the ground that the profits derived from muscovado sugar were, until the nineties, so good that 'the proprietors were content, and had no motive for adopting improved machinery'.

One of the primary reasons for this backwardness was the domination of absentee capital. The extent of absenteeism—an old British West Indian vice—is brought out in the following table:

Colony	Absentee Acres	% age of Sugar Acres	Absentee Plantations	% age of Sugar Plantations
Antigua	8,335	55		
Barbados	48,550	66	150	34
British Guiana	44,863	67	35	50
St. Kitts-Nevis			46	33
Trinidad			36	64
Tobago	3,015	11	6	15

Absentee owners controlled nearly 40 per cent of the total number of sugar plantations in Barbados, Trinidad, British Guiana, and St. Kitts-Nevis combined, which were responsible for nearly 84 per cent of total British West Indian exports in 1894.

Absentees controlled nearly two-thirds of the acreage in sugar in
Antigua, Barbados and British Guiana combined, whose combined
exports represented 63 per cent of the British West Indian total
in 1894. The average absentee plantation in Barbados was nearly
300 acres in size, as compared with an island average of 168; in
British Guiana it was 1,281 acres as compared with an overall
average of 1,045.

The way in which the British West Indian sugar industry was
dwarfed by the Cuban is further indicated by the capitalisation of
the industry, as follows:

Colony	Sugar Investment £	Average per Plantation £
Antigua	£500,000	£6,411
Barbados	2,000,000	4,545
British Guiana	10,000,000	156,250
Jamaica	1,167,000	8,335
Trinidad	2,500,000	44,643
Total for 5 Colonies	16,167,000	220,184

The capitalisation of the average factory in the five major sugar-
producing colonies of the British West Indies was thus about
$130,000, less than one-tenth of the investment in *Santa-Teresa* in
Cuba. The average for British Guiana was about $750,000, half
the capital investment in *Santa-Teresa*.

Yet sugar was king in the British West Indies in 1894, as much
as it had ever been in 1794 or 1694. The following table indicates
the dependence of the British West Indian export trade on exports
of sugar and by-products, and the place of sugar in the cultivated
acreage and employment rolls of the colonies:

Colony	% age of Sugar Exports to total exports	% age of Sugar Acreage to total acreage	% age of Workers employed in sugar industry
Antigua	94.5	–	34
Barbados	97	70	25
British Guiana	70.5	19	33
Dominica	15	–	–
Jamaica	18	16	6
Montserrat	62	66	–
St. Kitts-Nevis	96.5	30	36

St. Lucia	74	–	–
St. Vincent	12	–	–
Tobago	35	–	–
Trinidad	57	–	–

The combined British West Indies depended on exports of sugar and by-products for 53 per cent of their total export trade. They had put half of their eggs in one basket, which was carried on the uncertain head of their workers. They had been repeatedly urged by the metropolitan government, in the eighteenth century, to grow sugar and chiefly sugar. They failed to do so when the British market could have absorbed their production. They continued in the nineteenth century, to limit their affections to the circumference of a hogshead, when the British market would not absorb their production.

The Royal Commission of Inquiry, sent out in 1897, had this advice to give to the British West Indies:

'It is never satisfactory for any country to be entirely dependent upon one industry. Such a position is, from the very nature of the case, more or less precarious, and must in the case of the West Indies, result in a preponderating influence in one direction tending to restrict development in other ways ... the cultivation of sugar collects together a larger number of people upon the land than can be employed or supported in the same area by any other form of cultivation. In addition to this it also unfits the people, or at any rate gives them no training, for the management or cultivation of the soil for any other purpose than that of growing cane. The failure therefore of a sugar estate not only leaves destitute a larger number of labourers than can be supported upon the land in other ways, but leaves them also without the knowledge, skill, or habits requisite for making a good use of the land.'

In 1897 the British West Indian sugar industry was bankrupt. Its annihilation threatened to involve the entire community in a common ruin. The British West Indies, as the Governor of British Guiana said of that colony, were 'sitting over a powder magazine ... a spark of disaffection, bred by distress or discontent, might easily be fanned into a flame, which could only be extinguished at a cost of much misery and bloodshed.' The British West Indies were paying the cost not only of the planters' backward methods but also of their refusal to heed the lessons of the world market and of the British market in particular.

Chapter Twenty-One

The Struggle for the
World Sugar Market

While the British West Indies continued to place half their eggs in one basket, and Cuba was providing what seemed to be so impressive a demonstration of the economic advantages of monoculture, that is to say, sugar culture, the world market for sugar was becoming increasingly chaotic. The Caribbean cane sugar industry was engaged in a struggle for survival with two enemies, the spread of cane cultivation in other tropical areas, and beet sugar. By 1897 it was bankrupt—politically in Cuba, economically in the British, French, Dutch and Danish West Indies. It was in a state of coma: its end seemed a mere matter of time.

The early nineteenth century saw a rapid spread of cane sugar cultivation in areas which had appeared as rivals of the Caribbean during the eighteenth century—the eastern territories of India, Mauritius, Java, the Philippines and Réunion, Brazil in South America, Louisiana in the United States. The most dangerous of these competitors appeared to be India. Pitt's plan for the period immediately succeeding the independence of the United States was revived by the East India Company and the British abolitionists in the nineteenth century, and a violent struggle developed in England with a view to abolishing the discriminating duties on

East India sugar which favoured the British West Indian planter. The East Indians claimed that they could produce sugar more cheaply than the British West Indies, and that the British West Indian monopoly was a burden to the British taxpayer, which their propagandists estimated at between one and two million pounds sterling annually in the second decade of the century.

Their second argument was that East Indian sugar, produced equally within the British empire, was unjustly discriminated against. Bengal, they pointed out, had been British longer than most of the British West Indian colonies.

Their third argument, one strongly calculated to appeal to British capitalists, was that the British West Indian monopoly was not justified merely because it had been enjoyed for a length of time. Such a policy, the East Indians argued, would be tantamount to saying that a tax should be levied on canal transport because it had superseded conveyance by wagon, or even that the importation of foreign wines should be prohibited and grapes raised in hothouses. The West Indian claim to a protecting duty because they had invested their capital in the cultivation of sugar appeared to Zachary Macaulay, the abolitionist, 'a claim which might be urged with equal force in the case of *every* improvident speculation'.

All this made no sense to the economists. Satisfied with mercantilist monopoly in 1750, they opposed it in 1822. David Ricardo spoke in the House of Commons on May 17 as reported here:

'The case of the West Indies was precisely similar to that of the corn laws. As in the latter case we were protecting our poor soil of the West Indies from the competition of the rich soil of the East Indies. The mischief in such cases was that there was much human labour thrown away without any equivalent. He fully agreed that there would be the greatest possible injustice in sacrificing the vested interests of the West Indies; but it would be cheaper to purchase our sugar from the East Indies, and to pay a tax directly to the West Indies for the liberty of doing so. We could be gainers by the bargain, because there would be no waste of human labour. As he thought a monopoly was a disadvantage on either side, he saw no reason for opposing the present bill, which approached, to a certain degree, to free trade. We could not too soon return to the sound principle; and if we once arrived at it the House would no longer be tormented with these discussions, and with constant solicitations to sacrifice the public good to the particular interests.'

Of almost equal importance with India, from the viewpoint of the British capitalists, was Brazil, with which Britain had developed, through its long association with Portugal, close commercial relations both before and after its independence in 1822. Both Brazil and India, by their size and population, held out prospects of trade for Britain which the British West Indies could not equal. One of Brazil's mighty rivers, it was said, could hold all the British West Indian islands without its navigation being obstructed, while India could produce enough rum to drown the West Indies.

The British shipowner, the pillar of the British West Indian sugar industry in the eighteenth century, thumbed his fingers at it in the nineteenth. In 1828 trade with India employed 109,000 tons of British shipping, and it was claimed that, if Britain admitted Brazilian sugar, this would require a further 120,000 tons. The British export trade with these areas for the years 1821, 1828 and 1832 was as follows, in pounds sterling:

Year	Total Exports	Exports to India and China	Exports to Brazil
1821	43,113,655	3,639,746	2,114,329
1828	52,019,728	5,827,924	6,055,902
1832	65,025,278	6,377,507	5,298,596

Thus India accounted for seven per cent of Britain's exports in 1821, eleven per cent in 1828, nearly ten per cent in 1832. Brazil, which consumed five per cent of total British exports in 1821, represented nearly twelve per cent in 1828, and eight per cent in 1832. British exports to India increased by three-quarters between 1821 and 1832; to Brazil they were two and a half times as large in the latter year as in the former.

In addition to this increase of production in these areas where the sugar industry dated back to the eighteenth century and beyond, cane sugar cultivation spread to other areas. The most important of these was Hawaii, where the sugar industry was initiated by a Belgian colonisation scheme. In 1837 exports amounted to two tons of sugar and sixty-five barrels of molasses. A reciprocity treaty with the United States followed in 1876. No further indication of its effect need be given than the fact that sugar production increased from 13,000 tons in 1876 to 220,000 tons in 1898. The cane was first planted in Queensland, Australia, in 1864, and the first factory produced 230 tons of sugar in 1868. Sugar cultivation began in Fiji in 1880, and in Natal, South Africa, in 1850.

The growth of the sugar industry in these areas is brought out in the following table, in tons:

Territory	1815	1828	1849	1882	1894
India	6,215 *	6,636 *	–	59,010 (1882–92 average)	36,682 (1892–1904 average)
Mauritius	1,002 *	18,061 *	–	124,357 (1884–5)	136,792 (1893–4)
Java	1,235 (1806)	1,223 (1826)	–	287,443	552,667
Philippines	–	–	22,869 *	148,633 *	191,277 *
Réunion	21 *	12,506 (1829)	–	32,504	37,158
Brazil	75,000 * (1820)	83,000 * (1831)	–	246,769 *	275,000
Louisiana	–	45,178	–	136,167 (1882–3)	317,306 (1894–5)
Hawaii	–	–	282 *	51,000	148,000
Queensland	–	–	–	19,051 (1881–2)	91,712 (1894–5)
Fiji	–	–	–	5,232 * (1883)	23,571 * (1895)
Natal	–	–	–	–	19,369

* Exports. Other figures are production figures.

In addition, other states in the United States produced 8,388 tons in 1894–1895; New South Wales, in Australia, produced 207,771 tons of cane in the same year on 14,204 acres, which, taking the Queensland yield of that year (1.84 tons of sugar per acre) may be estimated at about 26,000 tons; Mozambique produced 1,000 tons in 1898; Egypt 99,423 tons in 1897; Madeira 29,530 tons in 1900; Argentina 160,453 tons in 1896; Peru 109,345 tons in 1897; Guatemala about 9,000 tons at the end of the century. As regards the Chinese sugar industry, 80,124 tons were exported from the port of Swatow in 1897; 13,938 tons from Amoy in 1896; 7,725 tons from Kiungchow in 1897. Cane sugar was also being produced in Cochin China, Venezuela, Ecuador and other parts of Central America.

By 1894, Java produced twice as much as the British West Indies exported. Louisiana's production in that year was one-fifth larger than British West Indian exports. Brazil's production was larger than the exports of the British West Indies. Philippine production was three-quarters of British West Indian exports; Mauritius's one-half; Argentina's seven-tenths. Queensland and Egypt each produced almost as much as British Guiana. The combined production of Java, Louisiana and Brazil was larger than that

of Cuba. Queensland produced more than the French West Indies;
Hawaii as much as the combined exports of the French West
Indies, Puerto Rico, Surinam and St. Croix.

Total world production of cane amounted to 1,340,980 tons in
1859–1860, and 3,531,400 tons in 1894–1895. The Caribbean share
is brought out in the following table:

Territory	1859–1860	1894–1895
Cuba	348,157*	1,054,214
British West Indies	198,600*	260,211
French West Indies	58,173* (1860)	79,394*
Surinam	5,825* (1860)	8,023* (1895)
St. Croix	6,000* (1860)	8,000* (1895–6)
Puerto Rico	70,000 (1860)	48,500 (1893–4)
Caribbean total	686,755	1,458,342
Caribbean as % age of world total	51	41
Cuba as % age of world total	26	30
B.W.I. as % age of world total	15	7
Cuba as % age of Caribbean total	50	75
Increase of world total, %	–	163
Increase of Caribbean total, %	–	112

* Exports.

Superior technology and methods of cultivation were to a large
extent responsible for the development of the cane industry outside of the Caribbean. In 1876 the average output per factory in
Queensland was 117 tons; in 1896–1897, 1,354 tons. In 1893 a
French company built three large factories in Egypt, with a combined production of 30,000 tons at the end of the century. In
1894 the average output in Argentina was 3,100 tons per factory,
the largest factory produced 20,000 tons. The huge Casa Grande
factory dominated Peru's sugar industry. In Lousiana the average
output per factory was 187 tons in 1888, 707 in 1898. In Java
it was 3,971 tons; the yield of sugar per acre rose from 0.809
tons in 1840 to over three in 1896; in 1896 the yield per acre
of cane was thirty tons. Irrigation was begun in Hawaii in 1882;
in 1897 the yield was 5.08 tons of sugar per acre on irrigated
land, 4.35 on non-irrigated.

In some instances this technological progress was due directly
to government encouragement. In 1875 the Brazilian Government
guaranteed seven per cent on capital spent in building sugar factories; in 1889, the state of Pernambuco granted allowances total-

ling £28,125 to forty factories which were to be capable of crushing 200 tons of cane per day, the loans to be paid back after
the third grinding season in twenty annual instalments. Argentina
offered an export premium in 1894. The Queensland Government
passed the unique Sugar Works Guarantee Act in 1893, under
which companies were enabled to borrow money for constructing
factories, provided that the cane was cultivated by white farmers
on their own land with the help of white labour. Australia's sugar
industry was to be a white man's industry. In 1895 the Government
obtained the right to buy shares in these companies, and thus
became a shareholder in the subsidised industry.

The Queensland experiment with white labour, completely refuting the pundits who, then as now, have sought to justify slavery
and the slave trade on the ground that, without Negro labour,
sugar cultivation was impossible, represented the only instance in
which the spread of sugar cultivation in other tropical areas
was not attended with the degradation of labour which characterised the Caribbean sugar industry. In Mauritius and Réunion
the abolition of slavery was followed by the large scale importation of contract labour from India. Indians were also taken to
Fiji and Natal, where they developed the sugar industry. Contract
labour from China and the Philippines underlay the expansion
of the Hawaiian industry. In Brazil slavery was not abolished until
1880. Chinese contract workers were imported into Peru. Slave
labour dominated the Louisiana industry until 1865, after which
the Negro sharecropper replaced the slave. Texas used convict
labour on a large scale for sugar cultivation. The much vaunted
propaganda of the British abolitionists respecting free labour in
India was blown skyhigh when Zachary Macaulay, of all people,
made the following statement with respect to slavery in India:

'They had obtained dominion over countries which had been previously
under the Hindu and Mogul Government. They therefore could not be
blamed if, when they came into possession of those countries, they found
principles acted upon with which, however adverse to their feelings, it
would be unsafe to interfere, without due caution.'

This was in 1823, some sixty years after India had passed into
British control. Forty-eight hours before the abolition of slavery in
the British West Indies, a bill for renewal of the East India Company's charter was discussed; it contained a clause to the effect

that slavery should be abolished in India. The Duke of Wellington, the staunch friend of the West Indian slaveowner, said that the clause was a violent innovation, totally uncalled for, which might provoke insurrection. By 1843 the British Government was still speaking of arresting the progress of slavery in India and checking abuses: an example of this was the prohibition, in the preceding years, of the selling of children into slavery in periods of scarcity. But, even without slavery, no one could say that the cheap labour of the Indian ryot or the teeming millions of Java represented any advance over the system of West Indian production.

The second enemy of the Caribbean sugar producer was beet sugar. In 1859–1860 total world beet production amounted to 451,584 tons, one quarter of the world's total sugar production, slightly more than one-third of the world's total cane production, slightly less than two-thirds of total Caribbean production. In 1894–1895 total world beet production amounted to 4,725,800 tons, more than ten times as much as in 1859; it was three-fifths of the world's total sugar production, one-third more than the world's cane production, three and a quarter times the total Caribbean production. Beet sugar production, one-third more than Cuban production in 1859–1860, was four and a half times as large in 1894–1895; two and a quarter times as much as British West Indian exports in the first year, it was eighteen times as large in the second.

The development of the European beet sugar industry was more dramatic than the striking developments which had taken place in the Caribbean and, in their day, astounded the world. The European beet sugar industry represented the triumph of science and technology. It was the great school of scientific agriculture. Where the Caribbean planter remained dependent on the man with the hoe, the beet cultivator introduced deep ploughing, substituting a plough that went to a depth of ten to eleven inches for the conventional plough which went to only four to six inches. Beet introduced a new element into the agricultural rotation, and the methods it required stimulated a vast increase in the yield of cereals. Well adapted to small holdings, the industry was based on a separation of the agricultural and industrial phases, brought winter employment to the countryside, checked the drift to the towns, and provided an enormous quantity of cattle feed. Pointing to the more than one million unemployed in England, a propagandist for the beet sugar industry asked in 1911: 'Can our Government take a wiser step and find a better remedy for settling the question of the unemployed than by giving the homeless and starving creatures permanent work in a healthy environment by means of an indigenous sugar industry?' By concentrating on producing better varieties, with a greater sugar content, German science was able to reduce the quantity of roots needed to make one ton of sugar from 18 tons in 1836 to 11 in 1868.

The developments in the field were eclipsed by the more spectacular progress in the factory. In 1836 Germany's beet production was produced in 122 factories; the average output per factory was less than twelve tons. In 1866 the largest factory, *Waghausel*, worked 66,000 tons of beet; with 12.60 pounds of beets needed to make one pound of sugar in the country as a whole, this represented an output of over 5,000 tons of sugar. There were 296 factories in that year, which produced 201,240 tons of sugar, an average per factory of 679 tons. In 1896 Germany's record production of 1,821,223 tons was produced in 397 factories, an average of 4,587 tons per factory, three-quarters more than that of Cuba. Barbados had more factories than Germany for a sugar export which was one thirty-sixth of German production. Eleven factories in Germany were needed to produce what Barbados' 440 exported in that year; about four to produce what Jamaica's 140 exported. The average output per factory in Trinidad was slightly more than one-quarter of the German average; in British Guiana about one-third.

Austria-Hungary, with 217 factories in 1896, was only slightly behind Germany; the average output per factory was 4,276 tons. The average in France was 2,024 tons. In 1897 there were nine factories in operation in the United States, representing an average output of 4,170 tons.

Beet sugar manufacture required an enormous investment of capital. The editor of the *Chemical Journal* in England estimated in 1870 that it would require an investment of £13,157 for a factory to handle the roots from 500 acres and produce slightly more than 500 tons of sugar. In 1868 the cost of manufacturing 20,000 tons of beetroot—approximately 1,000 tons of beet sugar —was estimated at £30,630. The thirty beet factories in the United

States in 1899 represented a capital investment of $20,959,000, nearly $700,000 per factory. It was estimated in 1911 that, in order to make Great Britain self-sufficient in sugar, it would require 500 factories, each costing £80,000.

Large profits were made in the beet sugar industry. In 1867–1868 the *Jerxheim* factory, one of the best in Germany, reaped a profit of $39,310 on total costs of production amounting to $101,368. Baruchson, in 1868, estimated that a profit of 25 per cent would be obtained from the manufacture of 20,000 tons of beetroot if 6½ per cent sugar were extracted; if the extraction was 8 per cent, however the profit would increase to 48 per cent. The estimates of the editor of the *Chemical Journal* in 1870 were net profits of £6,490 if 8 per cent of sugar were extracted, and £10,090, if 10 per cent; on the capital investment of £13,157, these rates amounted to 50 and 75 per cent, respectively.

It would appear that this combination of science, technology, capital and profits made beet superior to cane. In reality, this was not so. The decisive advantage which cane enjoyed over beet was its superior sucrose content, a gap which European and American science was able to narrow but not close. According to the report of the Commissioner of Agriculture of the United States for 1869, the product of sugar per acre from the cane in the West Indies was nearly twice that from the beet in Europe, the percentage of saccharine matter being as 18 to 10. According to the West Indian Royal Commission of 1897, the yield per acre was 18 tons of cane in Trinidad and Martinique as compared with 10.7 tons of beet in France and 12.85 tons in Germany. But superior science and technology discounted natural advantages. The extraction of sugar was 12½ per cent in Germany, nearly 11 per cent in France, 9½ per cent in Trinidad, 9 per cent in British Guiana, 7¼ per cent in Martinique. The cost of manufacturing one ton of sugar was as follows:

Beet	Germany	1894	$49.60
	France	1894	50.70
Cane	Trinidad	1896	48.70
	British Guiana	1895	52.48
	Martinique	1893	76.32
	Egypt	1893	44.16
	Queensland	1893	41.90

Thus, despite the superior science and technology of the beet sugar industry, cane was cheaper than beet—though not in the British and French West Indies. The reason why beet threatened to supplant cane in the world market lies in the deliberate encouragement given by the countries concerned to the beet sugar industry, precisely the encouragement which had been given by the metropolitan countries concerned to the Caribbean producers in the seventeenth and eighteenth centuries. Known generally as the bounty system, the policy involved a substantial subsidy on exports which permitted the beet manufacturer to dump sugar on the world market, even below the cost of production, whilst he was assured of a protected domestic market. The very monopoly which had built up the Caribbean was now trained against it. Europe, over which Britain, France, Spain, Holland and Portugal had competed for three hundred years for the privilege of supplying it with sugar, became an exporter of sugar on a large scale. The German premium on exports rose from 21 per cent in 1876 to 60 per cent in 1884. The German excise on the raw material, reduced by a drawback on exportation, declined from 58 million marks in 1881 to 14 million in 1887.

The struggle between beet and cane was in reality a struggle chiefly for the British sugar market. The British West Indies lost their monopoly of that market in 1852, when the protectionist duties on sugar were repealed. It was the high-water mark of Britain's free trade policy. Thereafter Britain's interest was to buy in the cheapest market. The following table indicates the consequences of that policy:

Year	British Imports (tons)	% Beet	% British Cane	% Foreign Cane
1853	1,476,714	14	17	69
1863	2,005,637	23	17	60
1873	2,951,152	38	12	50
1882	3,799,284	47	13	40
1896	£1,526,000	75	10	15

Thus it was neither science, nor technology, nor availability of capital, nor the rate of profit which explained the triumph of beet over cane. It was Britain's free trade policy and her desire for cheap sugar. It was that policy and that desire which gave rise to and stimulated the greatest mockery and the very antithesis of free trade, the bounty system. In 1884 it was estimated that Britain's annual gain from the bounty system was £2,750,000, and that, in the thirteen years preceding 1883, Britain had gained £28 million. British *per capita* consumption increased from 68.7 pounds in 1890 to 83.7 in 1900. The price of ordinary refined sugar fell from 28s per hundredweight in 1882 tc 13s in 1896. Unrefined beet fell from 21s to 10s; unrefined cane from 21s to nearly 11s. The British public, refiners, manufacturers of jams and candies benefited.

That was the decisive factor. In a report to the Board of Trade in 1884, it was stated: 'The obvious conclusion ... would be that even admitting the injury to the complaining interests from the bounty system to be as great as alleged, still the interest of the people of the United Kingdom in cheap sugar preponderates so greatly that that injury, in the interests of the majority, and apart from all question as to the intrinsic objectionableness of any possible remedy, should be disregarded.' Britain must have been grateful that Achard had rejected the bribes it had offered him in an earlier period.

That the question of cheap sugar was the overriding factor in the policy of the British Government is best indicated by the fact that 48 per cent of all the sugar imported into England in 1896 was refined beet sugar. Even the traditional interest in the British refiners was thrown overboard. As was stated in the report to the Board of Trade in 1884, the capital invested in the British refining industry was probably no more than £2,750,000. The refining interest was thus infinitely small compared with that of the consumers.

Even the defenders of the British West Indies in Britain thought less of the West Indies than of British interests. According to Neville Lubbock, in a speech in Bristol on November 8, 1887— what a change in a mere century! —before the British and Colonial Anti-Bounty Association, 'were it not for our bounties there is every reason to believe that sugar could, to a certain extent, be profitably produced in some parts of England'. In 1870 beet sugar was regarded as a possible substitute for the injury inflicted on Ireland by the potato; the Chancellor of the Exchequer, in his budget speech, said that such a step would be one of the greatest blessings that could befall that country.

The British West Indies, with their long practice in crying 'wolf', blamed the bounty system for their difficulties, as if to say that, without bounties, their eighteenth-century fossils could have held their own against German technology. But, emphasised the report to the Board of Trade, 'the gain to the people of the United Kingdom by the present excess reduction of price, according to the calculation of the West India Committee, viz. 5,000,000 £., is more than equal to the whole annual value of the exports of sugar from the West Indies'. The report curiously refrained from adding that it was now more than equal to the whole annual value of Britain's exports to the West Indies. It was mercantilism stood on its head.

The West India Royal Commission of 1897 disagreed. 'The benefit which the British Empire as a whole derives from any lowering of the price of sugar due to the operation of the bounty system is too dearly purchased by the injury which that system imposes on a limited class, namely Your Majesty's West Indian and other subjects dependent on the sugar industry.' The Commission emphasised the certain consequences of the extinction of the British West Indian sugar industry. It contented itself, however, with the modest recommendation that 'the abolition of the bounty system is an object at which Your Majesty's Government should aim, if they should see their way to securing that result, and that the accomplishment of such an end is worth some sacrifice...'

But it did not feel itself in a position to make recommendations of practical value towards securing the abolition of the bounty system. The West Indians recommended the imposition of countervailing duties on bounty-fed beet sugar; the Commission doubted the efficacy and wisdom of such a measure which involved 'the danger, direct and indirect, of departing from what has hitherto been considered to be the settled policy of the United Kingdom'. The West Indians urged the extension of the bounty system to West Indian sugar. The Commission found itself unable to recommend this course, which might so stimulate production as to cause a further fall in price which would neutralise its effect. The West Indies found themselves in the position of a patient suffering from a mortal disease, whose physician propounded all the reasons why he could not perform the operation necessary to restore the patient to health.

The only thing that saved the Caribbean sugar industry was access to the markets of the United States and Canada. The former country, blandly protectionist in its outlook and practice, imposed the countervailing duties which were anathema to the free trade gospel in Britain. By the Dingley tariff of 1897, an additional duty, over and above the fixed duty, was imposed on all bounty-fed sugar, to an amount corresponding with that of the bounty. In effect, therefore, the European governments were paying bounties into the United States Treasury.

United States imports from the Caribbean, in tons, are brought out in the following table:

Year	British West Indies	French West Indies
1853	630	4
1863	3,260	130
1873	30,440	12,173
1883	115,105	33,610

Canadian imports from the Caribbean, in tons, are brought out in the following table; while Canada was still less valuable as a market for British West Indian produce than the United States, the British West Indian producers had forgotten their old grudge and were thankful for small mercies:

Year	British West Indies	Spanish West Indies	French West Indies
1870	7,434	18,885	50
1880	10,746	22,278	94
1883	25,308	18,330	132

In 1876, when there was a sharp reduction by nearly five-sixths of Cuban imports as a result of the war of independence, Canada imported 730 tons from the Danish islands and 803 tons from Surinam.

As far as the United States market was concerned, however, the sugar industry in the Caribbean, Cuba excepted, was merely reprieved, not acquitted. President Hayes declared in a farewell address that he believed that, by 1884, the United States would no longer need foreign sugar. The President was a little ahead of his time. But in 1897 the West Indies could hear the breakers ahead. United States consumption of sugar increased from 282,764 tons in 1861 to 2,499,281 tons in 1897; *per capita* consumption rose from 18 to 78 pounds. In 1865 the United States consumed 14 per cent of the world's total production of sugar; in 1897, 31 per cent. The United States was the second best market in the world for sugar.

Virtually excluded from the British market, the Caribbean sugar industry was beginning to find that the United States market, too, was slipping. In 1865, two per cent of the United States consumption was produced by domestic sources; in 1897, thirteen per cent. The United States had taken stern action against the bounty-fed European sugar. But there was really small solace in this for the Caribbean. The United States objected not to the fact of the bounty but to its beneficiaries. If the United States was to be a market for subsidised sugar, that sugar would be American. In 1889 the State of Iowa exempted from taxation until January 1, 1910, later extended to January 1, 1917, the property of beet sugar manufacturers, including the capital invested and the personal property used in connection with the business. In 1895 Minnesota provided a bounty of one cent per pound on sugar manufactured in that State. In 1897 Michigan offered a bounty of two cents per pound. Nebraska offered a bounty in 1895. In 1897 the State of New York provided for the payment of one cent per pound to sugar manufacturers who paid the grower not less than five dollars per ton for beets.

The Federal Government supported the principle that the bounty began at home. In 1890 a bounty of two cents per pound was provided on domestic sugar testing not less than 90 degrees polariscope test, and 1.75 cents for sugar testing less than 90 degrees but not less than 80 degrees. The bounty was repealed in 1894, and thereafter the domestic sugar industry had to depend on tariff protection. An *ad valorem* duty of 40 per cent was levied in that year, equivalent to one cent per pound on sugar selling for 2.50 cents in the foreign market. In 1897, 96 degree sugar paid 1.685 cents per pound, raw sugar 0.95 cents.

The bankruptcy of the British West Indian sugar industry coincided with the 1896 platform of the Republican Party: 'we condemn the present Administration for not keeping faith with the sugar producers of this country. The Republican party favours *such* protection as will lead to the production on American soil of *all* of the sugar which the American people use, and for which they pay other countries more than $100,000,000 annually.' A leaflet of the American Beet Sugar Industry, circulated widely in the presidential campaign of that year, estimated that the production of the 1,804,866 tons of sugar imported by the United States in 1895 would require 920 factories with a capacity of 350 tons of beet each working day of 24 hours. Each factory would work up the product of 2,000 acres of beet—thus calling for a total acreage of 1,840,000 acres. The industry would give employment to people who would represent a population of 2,500,000. The farmer would receive $4.20 per ton of beets; the farm payroll would be $77,280,000. The labour payroll would amount to $17,599,600. The total annual expenditure for the 920 factories would be $122,496,160.

The development of the beet sugar industry was marked by a powerful propagandist appeal against the cane sugar industry on the ground that cane sugar required slave, 'coolie', contract, or some form of degraded labour, black, brown or yellow, whereas the beet sugar industry was the product of white and free labour. The pattern was first developed in France, in the decade of the thirties. Beet and cane, wrote Lestiboudois, in a memorandum entitled *Des Colonies Sucrières et des Sucreries Indigènes*, read to the Royal Society of Science, Agriculture and the Arts of Lille in 1839, were *chemically* similar but *industrially* dissimilar. Cane production, he said, was based on 'exceptional and barbaric principles'; it regarded the Negroes as 'inert machines for sugar ... beasts of burden to go to market ... animate material property'. In the opinion of another writer in the same year, Dehay, cane cultivation was based on 'antediluvian manners ... (a) social regime antipathetic to our age'.

The moral note enjoyed great vogue in the second half of the nineteenth century, particularly in the United States. Every civilised country, wrote the Commissioner of Agriculture in 1868, had 'exerted itself to secure emancipation from slave-grown cane sugar, and to stop the flow of money to a few colonies. Without the United States as a regular customer, Cuba and Brazil might as well give up growing sugar, and direct their attention to a more healthy occupation.' The Commissioner discreetly refrained from referring to Louisiana, which had fought a civil war for four years to prevent the United States from emancipating itself from its own slave-grown cane sugar. H. T. Oxnard, the president of the American Beet Sugar Association, in hearings before the Ways and Means Committee of the House of Representatives on December 30, 1896, distinguished himself by the vigour of his attack on cheap labour contracts, cheap Asiatic and Hawaiian labour and raw material, and the '24- to 48-cent labour in some cases, and coolie labour in other instances,' which made it impossible for California or Nebraska to compete.

According to a United States official, there was a vast difference, from a moral, civic, or philanthropic standpoint, between beet and cane. A pamphlet of the British Sugar Council pontificated:

'Whenever you see a success of cane sugar production you will notice it is a blight on everything else. You will find the employees in the fields and factory ignorant, degraded, poorly clothed and fed, and with no social advantages whatever. A beet sugar factory presents an entirely different picture. You will find every convenience of a prosperous civilised community, and that it has attracted to itself a busy centre endowed with all modern improvements ... to the district come all the social and educational advantages that accrue to closer association of population.'

Descending from the glittering generalities to the grim realities of beet sugar production, the Commissioner for Agriculture in the United States indicated that wages for men in Germany were $31\frac{1}{2}$ cents a day for carrying beets, and 19 cents for girls for topping and trimming them. That is only what one would expect from the fact that the European beet sugar industry, outside France, was very largely developed on the lands owned by the old feudal aristocracy—55 per cent in the case of Russia, 36 per cent in the case of Austria. One of the chief centres of the German beet sugar industry was Prussia, the home of the Junkers. These were precisely the most backward—from the social standpoint—sectors of European agriculture, where feudalism was not abolished until 1917 and 1918. From the moral, civic, or philanthropic standpoint, beet sugar production did not deserve the encomiums lavished upon it. Nor did it, from the standpoint of wages. In the early twentieth century wages in the beet industry were as follows, in dollars and cents per day:

	FIELD			*FACTORY*
Country	*Men*	*Women*	*Children*	
Russia	25	17½	10	–
Germany	47	28½	23	84
Denmark	36	28½	–	–
Hungary	45	33	25	46
Austria	–	–	–	49
Belgium	–	–	–	57
France	–	–	–	83
Holland	–	–	–	86
Sweden	–	–	–	95
U.S.A.	2.60	–	–	2.99

By 1900, there was a powerful labour movement in England and France. In Germany trade unionism and socialism had grown to such an extent that Bismarck had inaugurated a vast social security programme, to 'dish the Socialists'. Joseph Chamberlain in England was preaching his 'gospel of ransom'. Jules Ferry in France and Cecil Rhodes in England based their imperialistic programme on the fear of civil war and revolution in their respective countries. Thus it will appear that European beet workers, as agricultural workers the world over, occupied the lowest rung of the economic ladder, and that the much-vaunted social superiority of beet over cane was propaganda rather than fact. Much of the labour in the Central European industry was imported from Poland, and the child labour, which Jefferson had envisaged as one of the best features of his dream for maple sugar, was one of the worst characteristics of beet cultivation.

The hollowness of the claims of the beet sugar industry to superior methods of production was finally revealed by a study in 1935 of 946 families in the beet sugar industry in the United States. Two-thirds of the workers were migrants, principally Mexican, a clear demonstration of the revulsion of American labour against conditions in the industry. The study revealed that: (a) the yearly earnings were less than $200 per family for 29 per cent of the families and $600 or more for only 22 per cent; (b) about one-fourth of the children 6–16 years of age were working in the fields; (c) more than half of the working children under 16 worked more than 8 hours per day;

(d) only two out of three children 6–16 years of age were enrolled in school;

(e) half of the children 8–16 and three-quarters of the children 15 years of age that were in school were retarded;

(f) three out of five families received support from relief funds;

(g) the general social picture was one of poor living conditions, inadequate diet, insufficient clothing, poor housing with bad over-crowding, lack of needed medical service for most of the families.

But the Caribbean sugar producer was in no position to reply to this propaganda blast. His method of production was economically backward and socially reactionary. In 1870 the editor of the *Chemical Journal* estimated that the growing of one acre of beet required 46 days of human labour (partly children's) and 14 days of horse labour, whereas one acre of cane in the West Indies required 172 days of human labour.

Chapter Twenty-Two

Nineteenth-Century Colonialism

Where French and Spanish autocracy, as we have seen, extended both to the metropolitan country and the overseas colonies, the British, as a part of the metropolitan movement against autocracy in the seventeenth century, had developed some measure of colonial self-government. The resultant conflict between metropolitan interests and colonial interests had led straight to the American revolution.

That conflict had been rooted in British economic practices, in the attempt to keep the colonies as primary producers within the British common market. The conflict of interests that developed in the West Indian colonies revolved around the new British policy towards the institution of slavery.

The American colonists had raised the issue of no taxation without representation. The Jamaican planters raised the issue of non-interference in the internal affairs of a self-governing colony. On October 31, 1815, the Jamaica House of Assembly passed a number of resolutions protesting against British acts for the suppression of the illegal slave trade and proclaiming that they ought not to be bound by laws or touched by subsidies imposed without their assent.

Their fury exceeded all bounds when Britain emancipated their slaves. In June 1838 the House of Assembly passed the protest, full of pompous verbosity, from which the following extracts are taken:

'Jamaica is dependent on the Crown of England, and she admits the right of the English Parliament to regulate the commerce of the empire, but she rejects, with indignation, its claim to make other laws to govern her . . .

'It is unreasonable and unnatural that one nation should assume to pass laws to bind another nation, of whose customs, wants, constitution, and physical advantages and disadvantages, she is, and must be, profoundly ignorant; and whose distance opposes an insurmountable barrier to the attainment of local information, or to the application of remedies for any sudden emergency. The laws enacted, under such circumstances, by the governing nation, will be a code of blunders, even if passed in good faith; and will be the ridicule or terror of the governed—evaded in days of tranquillity, and, when the governing nation is at war openly defied and resisted . . .

The Parliament of Great Britain are already overwhelmed with business; and being 'without time for examining the Colonial Bills that are submitted to them, they must accede, without inquiry, to all the requisitions of the Colonial Secretary; and although we shall in name live under the enactments of the British Parliament, we shall in fact be governed by a Royal Minister. We dread a system of government which has, notwithstanding so many efforts, failed to pacify Ireland, has just caused a rebellion in the Canadas by its capricious policy, and scarcely escaped a war with the United States.

'The Island of Jamaica never will consent to be ruled by men who have, in their proceedings towards them, invaded the ancient statutes of the realm, and usurped the prerogative of the Crown; who have, although not represented amongst them, imposed on her people taxes and penalties, who have set aside trial by jury, and who have placed in the hands of one man the power of making law, and of dispensing with law, by proclamation.

'The last vestige of slavery was in two years to have been removed; and it is an indiscreet and mischievous zeal which, to hasten its extinction by so brief a space, has marked it by the demolition of our sacred rights . . .

'We, therefore, the members of Assembly, do, for ourselves and for the people of Jamaica, solemnly before God and man, and especially before our fellow subjects and fellow colonists, protest against an Act passed by the British Parliament, intituled, "An Act to amend the Act for the Abolition of Slavery in the British Colonies".

'We protest against the Proclamation of his Excellency the Governor, dated the 1st of June 1838, which declares the said Act to be in force in this island.

'We declare the said Act and Proclamation to be illegal, unconstitutional, and an usurpation of our legislative rights, and of the rights of
our constituents; we declare them to be subversive of English law, threatening to the peace of this and our sister colonies, and dangerous to the
integrity of the empire.'

This was the setting in which the constitutional position of the
West Indian colonies was fought out in the nineteenth century.
Were representative institutions to be entrusted to them; and if
so, on what terms?

The humanitarians loudly opposed the planter democracy. In a
famous minute on September 15, 1841, the Permanent Under-
secretary in the Colonial Office, James Stephen, castigated the
planters and advocated disregard of 'the loudest yelps for liberty'
uttered by slaveowners. Stephen wrote:

'Popular Franchises in the hands of the Masters of a great Body of
Slaves were the worst instruments of tyranny which were ever yet forged
for the oppression of mankind. What the Southern States of America are
Jamaica was. If no Assembly had ever been established in the Island I
doubt whether any wise man would create such an institution even now,
when Slavery is extinct. For still there survive indelible natural distinctions and recollections which divide Society into Castes, and which must
make the legislation of the European more or less unjust and oppressive
towards the African race.'

The French Revolution of 1848 solved the problem by representation in the French Parliament and by universal suffrage,
giving full voting rights to the emancipated slaves. With the
coup d'état of Louis Napoleon in 1851, however, this did not
last long; Bonaparte suppressed the 1848 dispensation, 'less to
divorce the colonial element from the legislative sphere in the
Metropolis than to spare the overseas departments the agitation
of political elections'.

The British, as always, saw the issue of colour—representative
government would mean the domination of the Negroes and
mulattoes. The alternatives were faced with the utmost frankness
by the Secretary of State for the Colonies when it came to decid-
ing the constitutional status of Trinidad, acquired from Spain
in 1797. A constitution patterned on Jamaica or Barbados would
mean planter democracy and would intensify planter opposition
to the slavery policy of the Imperial Parliament. More representative institutions would mean the subordination of British to

foreign elements and of whites to non-whites in a community which, in 1808, numbered 21,478 persons. Of these, two in three were slaves, there were more than two free persons of colour for every white person, British whites were in the minority, out-numbered by French, Spaniards, Corsicans and Germans, and the overwhelming majority of the free people of colour were French. How to deal with this multiracial society? The Secretary of State prescribed the formula in a despatch to the Governor of Trinidad on November 27, 1810, which reads as follows:

'The application of the proprietors, white inhabitants of Trinidad, may be divided into two; the British Constitution as it is understood and sup-posed to be enjoyed by the other West India islands—the British laws under whatever frame of Government His Majesty may be pleased to establish in that Colony.

'With respect to the first of these points, it has undergone the most deliberate consideration in all its different bearings. The question proposed for discussion has no necessary reference to that state of things which has existed for so many years in the old West India Islands but may be stated to amount to this: whether in a new Colony in which the rights of the Crown and Parliament must be admitted on all hands to be entire, it would be advisable to surrender these rights in whole or in part and to establish a system of Government analogous to that of other West India islands.

'Even if the circumstances of Trinidad were in all respects much more nearly the same as those of the other West India Colonies than they unquestionably are, the determination of Government would probably be to negative such a proposition. But it so happens that the circumstances of the Island of Trinidad are in many respects so materially different from those of all the West India Colonies, that supposing the system of Govern-ment established in those Islands to be the best could be afforded them in their situation, it would not follow that the same system could be rendered applicable either in justice or in policy to the Island of Trinidad.

'In all the other West India Islands (with the exception of Dominica, an exception which arises out of recent circumstances) the white inhabitants form the great majority of the free people of the Colony and the political rights and privileges of all descriptions have been enjoyed exclusively by them.

'The class of free people of colour in these Colonies, as far as even their numbers extend, has grown up gradually. They have thereby in some degree been reconciled to the middle situation which they occupy between the whites and the slaves. But in the Island of Trinidad the free people of colour at this time form a very great majority of the free inhabitants of the Island and the question would arise according to the proposed system whether in establishing, for the first time, a popular government in that Colony, we shall exclude that class of people from all political rights and privileges. Such an exclusion we know would be regarded by them as a grievance and it may be doubted how far it would be consistent with the spirit of the capitulation by which their privileges were to be secured and their situation certainly not deteriorated from that which they enjoyed under the Spanish Government.

'In the second place in most of the West India Islands, the great body of proprietors and white inhabitants are British or descendants of British families to whom the British Constitution and the Laws have become familiar; they have been educated or supposed themselves to be educated in the knowledge of them and though the resemblance is certainly not great between the Constitution as it is supposed to exist in our West India Islands and as it is enjoyed in Great Britain, the circumstances above referred to would in some degree account for the attachment of the inhabitants of the Old West India Islands to a system of government in which popular assembly forms a material part.

'But in the Island of Trinidad, the white population consists of a mixture of people of all nations. The greater part of them must be wholly ignorant of the British Constitution and unaccustomed to any frame of government which bears any analogy to it. In the case of Trinidad, therefore, amongst the most numerous class of white inhabitants, there can be no material prejudice either of habit or education in favour of such a system and the partial and exclusive principle on which it is proposed by the white inhabitants to be founded, whereby the largest proportion of the free inhabitants of the Island would be excluded from all participation in its privileges, appears to defeat the object of it and to constitute in point of justice and upon the very principles of the system itself, a decided and insuperable objection against it.

'The question has hitherto been considered as far as it may affect the internal state of the Colony itself. But in addition to these considerations it is material to add that the abolition of the Slave Trade by Parliament imposes upon Government the necessity of keeping within themselves any power which may be material for rendering this measure effectual.

'It is essential for this purpose that in a new Colony the Crown should not divest itself of its power of legislation and that neither the crown nor the parliament should be subject to the embarrassments which on such an occasion might perhaps arise from the conflicting views of the Imperial Parliament and of a subordinate Legislature.

'Under these considerations you may consider it a point determined that it is not advisable to establish within the Island of Trinidad any independent Legislature.

'In reserving to himself the power of legislation, His Majesty will delegate in some degree that power as far as local considerations may render necessary or expedient to the Governor as His Representative whose acts will be always subject to be reviewed, altered or revoked by His Majesty himself.

'In exercising this power for local purposes His Majesty feels the advantage which may arise in a Council selected by the Governor from the most respectable of the inhabitants of the Island, but such a Council must be considered as a Council of advice and not of control. The determination of the Governor, even if it should be contrary to the opinion of such a Council, must be considered as obligatory till such time as His Majesty's pleasure shall be known; the members of the Council may, however, in such cases be allowed to transmit their opinion together with their reasons for His Majesty's consideration.

'The advantages of a government of this description in colonies and remote settlements have been experienced in other instances and furnish the strongest possible inducements for acting upon this principle upon the present occasion.'

Seventy-two years later the British viewpoint had not changed. A Royal Commission of December 1882 which enquired into the public revenues, expenditure, debts and liabilities of Jamaica, Grenada, St. Vincent, Tobago and the Leeward Islands, emphasising the dependence of the islands on British investment and British defence arrangements while non-whites dominated the population, concluded:

'...as the employers and employed will be generally speaking of different races, the Imperial Government will continue to have an ultimate responsibility in the administration of these islands, and must consequently retain an adequate proportion of direct power in the administration.'

The Danes in 1850, after the abolition of slavery, experimented with a half-way house between the autocracy of Spain and the planter democracy of the older British colonies. They permitted the establishment of a Colonial Assembly of 16 elected members —eight for St. Croix, six for St. Thomas, and two for St. John— and four members appointed by the King of Denmark. The right to vote was restricted to those of 25 years of age, who had an annual income of $500 or paid four dollars in taxes or held an office in the colonial service. Members were elected for a six-year term. The Colonial Assembly dealt with municipal accounts and could legislate on municipal affairs—roads, public health, fire services, and the exercise of the different trades. But the King could extend to the colonies the general laws for Denmark with such modifications as might be required in the colonial situation. He could also enact special ordinances, relating to schools and public instruction, relations between employers and workers,

masters and servants, the executive police, the support of the
poor, and the militia.

But there was always the fear that the black and coloured
majority would swamp the white minority by achieving the
property qualifications for the franchise. In any case the middle
of the nineteenth century was probably the least congenial period
in human history for the recognition of the rights of man without
reference to skin or race. It was in 1854 that Gobineau published
his *The Inequality of Human Races*, in which he damned the
Negro race:

> 'The Negroid variety is the lowest, and stands at the foot of the ladder.
> The animal character, that appears in the shape of the pelvis, is stamped
> on the Negro from birth, and foreshadows his destiny. His intellect will
> always move within a very narrow circle ... No Negro race is seen as the
> initiator of a civilisation. Only when it is mixed with some other can it
> be initiated into one.'

Thomas Carlyle in England, the sage of Chelsea, out-Gobineau'd
Gobineau. The year of the Chartists in England and of revolution
in Europe and of John Stuart Mill's *Representative Government*
was too much for the hero worshipper, the admirer of Prussian
militarism. He demanded the regimentation of labour, white and
black, and virtually called for the restoration of slavery in the
West Indies. In his *Occasional Discourse upon the Nigger
Question* in 1849 he exploded at the thought that the democratic
philosophy and the rights of man would be extended to the emancipated slaves (as in fact the French had just extended them).
Sneering at universal suffrage, the greatest happiness principle,
liberty, equality and fraternity in England, he could hardly be
expected to enthuse over them in Jamaica and Barbados. His
vision of society was one in which 'the wisest man' was at the top
and 'the Demerara Nigger' at the bottom, to avoid the situation
where one would have 'the vote of a Demerara Nigger equal and
no more to that of a Chancellor Bacon ... Thus were your minimum producible'.

Where Carlyle had opposed democracy and liberty, Trollope
after him challenged the application of parliamentary democracy
to Jamaica. Visiting Jamaica ten years after Carlyle's *Discourse*,
Trollope was satisfied that the Negro was 'a servile race, fitted by
nature for the hardest physical work, and apparently at present

fitted for little else'. He resented the material improvements among the people of colour which allowed them to vote, sit as magistrates, and become members of the House of Assembly —simply and brutally on grounds of colour. His solution was the abandonment of British parliamentary institutions:

'I do not think that the system does answer in Jamaica...I hold that this system of Lords and Commons is not compatible with the genius of the place...there is not room for machinery so complicated in this island ...with all the love that Englishmen should have for a popular parliamentary representation, I cannot think it adapted to a small colony, even were that colony not from circumstances so peculiarly ill fitted for it as is Jamaica.'

British nineteenth-century democracy was thus tainted by a racial limitation. Self-government was 'only applicable to colonists of the English race', as the Earl of Newcastle said in a speech in the House of Lords on July 26, 1858. Even then, it was not fully applicable, as the Canadians and Sir John Macdonald were to learn, when it came to the Canadian Confederation in 1867, with its British Governor-General responsible to Britain, its veto of Canadian legislation if only through the Judicial Committee of the Privy Council, and its total subordination to the United States by the British Government of vital Canadian external interests.

The age of free trade conduced to the propagation of these racial theories. The Cobdenites wanted no colonies at all and an end to expensive defence commitments. The white man's burden was rejected. Never more shall we sin our fathers' sin, sang Tennyson in reference to American Independence, and Disraeli echoed him in the political arena: 'These wretched colonies will all be independent, too, in a few years, and are millstones round our necks.' They were, he said later, so many 'colonial dead-weights which we do not govern'. If we could acquire the whole of Africa, said the Permanent Under Secretary of the Colonial Office in 1841, it would be but a 'worthless possession', and as far as Cobden was concerned, if France wanted North Africa, it was welcome to it. The West Indian colonies, from the vantage point of the Colonial Office, were nothing but foolish governors, furious assemblies, governors and slaves.

But, as Trollope had emphasised, Jamaica was not Canada. When the irrepressible conflict continued to develop in the United

States, to involve the death of thousands of 'excellent white men', as Carlyle complained, for the sake of the emancipation of 'three million absurd Blacks ... likely to be improved off the face of the earth in a generation or two', Britain was ready for the suppression of democracy in Jamaica, and this was in the very year the American Civil war came to an end, and two years before the much-vaunted Canadian step forward on the road to democracy, the Canadian Confederation.

The emancipated Negroes in Jamaica had deserted the plantations in large numbers: when they were willing to work, their labour was intermittent and the wages, from the planter's point of view, were high. The freedmen, where they could, bought land. where they could not, they squatted on the estates' 'back lands'. They started to grow new crops within their means and competence; whilst the plantation staples declined, exports continued to rise as a result of the agricultural diversification. The clearest index of the rise in social standards was the steady increase in imports and their diversification.

With the spread of wealth, more and more people of colour qualified for the franchise. The absentee planters for the most part pocketed their compensation money and pulled out of the island; so estates were going reasonably cheap for those who could afford to buy them. By the sixties two out of three members of the Assembly were people of colour, and they had as their champion a substantial merchant-planter, George William Gordon.

But Jamaica also had, as so often in the West Indies, a Governor who owed his position solely to Colonial Office patronage, against the background of the reduction of status of the Jamaica post. Equipped neither by intellect nor by temperament to deal with a prickly situation, Edward John Eyre was cut out for trouble.

The trouble started when some of the Negroes in one of the parishes, faced with the difficulties of supplies and markets created by the American Civil War, petitioned Queen Victoria for land in the face of the growing contraction of plantation production. Less than twenty years after the almost incredible British bungling in Ireland which had cut the Irish population in half by deaths and emigration, the Queen's reply* via the Colonial Office was

* Quoted on page 345.

not surprising—work and grow rich, she virtually said, though she did not add that they would become voters.

One thing led to another, riots, court cases, minor disturbances, calling out the militia, shooting and retaliation with stones—and the Jamaica Rebellion of 1865 had begun. Eyre declared martial law, called out the Maroons to help preserve law and order, sent frantically everywhere for reinforcements, arrested Gordon in Kingston and took him to the area where martial law prevailed. Gordon was tried and hanged, and a reign of terror was unleashed on the population for a parallel to which one must go to Saint-Domingue before the victory of the slave revolution.

The British Government appointed a Royal Commission of Enquiry which, notwithstanding some double-talk, found that the punishments inflicted were excessive: the death penalty, invoked on 354 occasions by the courts-martial, was too frequently imposed, the floggings were reckless and even barbarous, the burning of houses was wanton and cruel. The Commission found no proof of Gordon's complicity in the rebellion.

The Governor, in self-defence, argued as follows:

(a) It was the military authorities who suppressed the rebellion.

(b) It was necessary to strike terror into the Negro population.

(c) Negroes cannot be treated like the peasantry of Europe.

(d) The intelligent and reflective portion of the community agreed with him.

(e) He saved a noble colony from anarchy and ruin.

(f) Did no excesses occur in repressing the Indian Mutiny?

The Jamaica Rebellion became a *cause célèbre* in Britain, with intellectuals and politicians taking sides. On the side of the Governor was Thomas Carlyle, and with him were Lord Tennyson, Charles Kingsley, Dickens and Ruskin among the writers, Tyndall, Murchison and Hooker among the scientists. The leader of the opposition was John Stuart Mill, with such University men as Goldwin Smith, Dicey, Thorold Rogers, and T. H. Green, Thomas Hughes of *Tom Brown's School Days* fame, and scientists like Darwin, Huxley, Spencer and Lyell. The radical politicians, John Bright, Edward Foster, Edward Beales, were all against Governor Eyre. So were the remnants of the abolitionists.

After a number of court cases which had the effect of making

Eyre a Tory hero, the case against him for the murder of Gordon was dismissed. But the Irish nationalists did not miss the significance of the British policy, and the coincidence of Eyre's trial with the agitation for the Second Reform Bill of 1867 sharpened the alignment of the political forces—Bright for reform, and Carlyle in his pamphlet *Shooting Niagara: And after?* moving closer to the tendencies we today associate with fascism.

The West Indian sequel to the Jamaica Rebellion was more important than the British political differences which were soon assuaged, Eyre ending up with a pension. On December 1, 1865, the Secretary of State for the Colonies tore up the Jamaica Constitution (as Britain was to do ninety years later in British Guiana). Jamaica became a Crown Colony. The ancient problem of whether in 1810 to bring Trinidad up to Jamaica's level was settled in 1865 by bringing Jamaica down to Trinidad's level. The Secretary of State wrote:

'Where there is no wide basis for constituent and representative power and responsibility to rest upon, there is no eligible alternative but to vest power and responsibility substantially in the Crown. This is done in Trinidad, where the Council consists of six official and six unofficial members, with a casting vote in the Governor. The control which the colonists possess over the proceedings of the Governor and his officers consists in the free exposition of adverse views in debate, and the right of recording protests which the Governor is bound to transmit to the Secretary of State. The ultimate control over the Local and Home Government alike is to be found in the power of appealing to Parliament which is at all times ready to listen to complaints of an undue exercise of authority on the part of the Ministers of the Crown.'

Crown Colony government in Jamaica coincided with efforts, begun by Eyre himself in the minor posts he held before he was inflicted on the Jamaican people, to suppress the ancient self-governing constitutions of the smaller islands. Britain's objective was the oldest of these constitutions in the largest of these smaller islands, Barbados. The technique adopted was a federation of the smaller islands, first mooted in the 1860s by Merivale at Oxford, formerly of the Colonial Office.

The man selected for the assignment was Pope Hennessy, made Governor of Barbados in 1876. Hennessy promptly got into trouble with the powerful Barbadian plantocracy who had as their champion a coloured lawyer, Conrad Reeves, and his demagogic appeals to the population regarding the prospects of migration to the underpopulated smaller islands could only end in trouble.

What Britain wished to achieve was a consolidation of these eighteenth-century anachronisms for more effective defence and to reduce costs by a more efficient centralised administration. The federation was a British-imposed federation in Britain's interests. It was modesty incarnate—a federal police force, a federal penitentiary, a federal lazaretto, a federal lunatic asylum, a federal auditor and a federal Chief Justice.

This federation of policemen and paupers, convicts and lunatics, could hardly be expected to appeal to West Indian nationalist sentiment—if there was any such thing; and it was viewed by the Barbadians as nothing more than imposing on their own slender resources Britain's responsibility for the underdeveloped islands. Extensive disturbances developed in Barbados: 8 Negroes were killed, 30 wounded, and 410 arrested. The Secretary of State was so worried that he instructed the Governor to issue a soothing proclamation. The Secretary of State wrote:

'There is only one thing which, with the information at present before me, I think it desirable to add on the present occasion. The statements as to the advantages or disadvantages of Confederation which have been industriously circulated, appear to have created serious delusions, and I am disposed to think that there would be much advantage in the issue of a brief proclamation, setting forth in distinct terms that Her Majesty's Government desire the people to understand the true facts of the case, that it would be a great mistake to suppose that Confederation could either injure or benefit in any considerable degree the social condition of any class; that beyond, possibly, affording some further facilities for movement among the Islands, and for obtaining employment in a larger field, it could do little to change the condition or prospects of the labouring class, and that of course it could give them no proprietorship or occupation of land in an Island in which every acre has long been disposed of; that all parties must rather look to improved education and the amelioration of the public institutions as the most direct means of removing much of the grievance and distress which has prevailed; while, on the other hand, there has been no reason whatever to suppose that Confederation, if adopted by the Legislature, could affect the financial independence of Barbados or make any other changes in the Island than would without Confederation commend themselves to enlightened public opinion. That, therefore, there being no ground whatever for anticipating any very considerable benefit, injury, or change of any kind, it is quite unjustifiable to discuss this or any other legislative proposal in excited meetings, and that all loyal subjects should look to the proceedings of the Legislature for their guidance and information.'

Barbados was adamant—no Federation. Conrad Reeves made this absolutely clear in a speech in the Assembly in May 1876. He spoke as follows:

'...We do not admit any pretensions in the direction of Crown Colony Government. (Cheers) The question of Confederation has been laid before us, and has been respectfully considered by us. We have declined Confederation, because in the form which it takes in the case of the West India Colonies it means, and can only mean, the surrender by us, in the long run, of our representative form of government which we have enjoyed for 250 years. (Cheers) ...'

Barbados had other ideas. Eight years later the planters were making approaches to the Canadian Government to ascertain whether they could join the Canadian Confederation, which would assure them, so they thought, duty-free entry of their produce and the protected market from bounty-fed beet sugar which Britain refused to consider. How things change in a hundred years! This was the same Barbados which had opposed in 1783 the British substitution of Canada for the independent United States. The proposition, as presented to a former Barbados Governor, Sir Francis Hincks, for the consideration of the Prime Minister, Sir John Macdonald, dated April 23, 1884, was as follows:

'The increasing difficulty of securing a reliable and remunerative market for West Indian Sugar is driving the people of this Colony to seek to improve their position in this respect, and they have begun to look towards Canada, in the belief that their best chance of relief lies in the direction of the Dominion, because of its protective tariff.

'I venture therefore to write you on behalf of many influential persons here who eagerly desire to be informed, to ask you to be good enough to favour them, either in your private capacity, should you so prefer, or as the interpreter of the mind of the Government of Canada, to any extent to which you may feel justified in assuming that function, with your views on the following points:

'1. Would the Dominion of Canada favourably entertain an application from Barbados to be admitted a member of their Confederation?

'2. What, stated in a general way, would be the terms your side would be likely to offer as a basis of negotiation?

'3. In the event of such a negotiation growing out of the present overture might Barbados reckon on the whole weight and influence of the Dominion being exerted along with her own to win the sanction of Her Majesty's Government for the arrangement? ...

'If Canada could receive our sugar and molasses duty free, while charging import duty on all other produce of the same kind, which is of course the advantage we contemplate in this proposal, what would be the nature of the *quid pro quo*?

'It appears to us that there is scarcely an article of consequence imported into this Island from the United States of America which could not be supplied in any quantity that might be required at about the same rate, from the Dominion, for our own use, and for inter-colonial distribution by us through the British West Indies; while as the matter stands at present our imports from the British North American Colonies, including Newfoundland are only of one-fifth the value of commodities reaching us from the States.

'If Barbados were favoured as a member of the Confederation in the markets of the Dominion, we should look to see you expecting as one part of the equivalent that, so far as practicable, a monopoly of our markets should be secured to Canada.'

Similar proposals emanated from the Leeward Islands and from Jamaica where the question was debated in the Legislative Council on October 28, 1884, but defeated by 8 to 1 with the nominated and official members abstaining.

But Canada was not disposed to relieve Britain of its colonial burdens. The question therefore remained, what to do with the West Indies? This was the object of the visit paid to the West Indies in the late eighties by James Anthony Froude, disciple of Carlyle, Regius Professor of Modern History at Oxford. An out-and-out imperialist, Froude was having no nonsense of colonial freedom and parliamentary institutions. Defending slavery, Froude regarded the West Indian Negroes as 'children, and not yet disobedient children'; they were conscious of their own defects, responsive to a guiding hand, and would attach themselves to a rational white employer 'with at least as much fidelity as a spaniel'. The answer, in Froude's eyes, was no representative or responsible government.

'A West Indian self-governed Dominion is possible only with a full Negro vote. If the whites are to combine, so will the blacks. It will be a rule by the blacks and for the blacks. Let a generation or two pass by and carry away with them the old traditions, and an English governor-general will be found presiding over a black council, delivering the speeches made for him by a black prime minister; and how long could this endure? No English gentleman would consent to occupy so absurd a situation ... The two races are not equal and will not blend... Do we, or do we not, intend to retain our West Indian Islands under the sovereignty of the Queen? If we are willing to let them go, the question is settled. But we ought to face the alternative. There is but one form of government under which we can retain these colonies with honour and security to ourselves and with advantage to the Negroes whom we have placed there—the mode of government which succeeds with us so admirably that it is the world's wonder in the East Indies...'

It was colonialism unrepentant. When the Americans took over Puerto Rico from Spain in 1898 and abrogated the self-governing constitution which Spain had conceded the previous year, it was also colonialism unrelieved. Puerto Rico under American rule was governed by an executive council which acted also as the upper house of the legislature. This Council was appointed by the United States President and consisted of a secretary, an attorney general, a treasurer, an auditor, a commissioner of interior, a commissioner of education, together with five other persons of good repute.

There were only two rays of light in the colonial darkness of the nineteenth century. The first was a vague concept of a federation of the Greater Antilles embracing Cuba, Santo Domingo and Puerto Rico. Limited solely to considerations of a common Spanish background, culture and language, the concept was purely intellectual and never got down to any discussion of the economic basis and structure of such a federation.

The second ray of light was the figure of José Martí in the Cuban Civil War. That Cuba should have produced such a philosopher-statesman as Martí, with the support of the Negro general Antonio Maceo, augured well for the future of the Caribbean. Martí constitutes with Washington, Jefferson and Bolivar the great quadrumvirate of the history of the Western Hemisphere, and ranks with Las Casas among the greatest gifts of Spanish civilisation to the Caribbean and the world.

For Martí the crucial question for Cuba was independence. This could not be achieved on the basis of Negro slavery. For Martí emancipation was not so much a political necessity as a moral one. The Cuban republic must be 'of all and for all'. That it should include the Negro he never for a moment questioned. This was easy for him, because of his views of race. Whilst Froude in the British West Indies was frothing his racial inequality, for

Martí there 'is no such thing as race hatred because there are no races'. In his philosophy, 'the soul emanates, equal and eternal, from bodies different in shape and in colour...In the broiling desert as in the Scottish cathedral the virtues and vices of men are the same'. What matters it, he once asked, whether one comes from parents of Moorish blood and white skin? 'Man has no special rights because he belongs to a particular race. It is sufficient to say "man" to comprehend therein all rights...Man is more than white, more than mulatto, more than Negro.' The Negro, he added, 'as Negro, is neither inferior or superior to any man'. His vices, like those of the aboriginal Indian, are the fault of the whites. Thus it was that Martí could describe the act of Negro emancipation as 'the purest, most efficacious and trans-cendental act of the Cuban revolution', and could appreciate that it was as Cubans and not as Negroes that the former slaves aspired to justice and happiness; to 'the independence of man in the independence of the fatherland, to the progress of human liberty in independence'.

Chapter Twenty-Three

Manifest Destiny

On June 3, 1842, J. A. Roebuck, one of the prominent colonial reformers of England, Member of Parliament for Bath, the English health resort which had been frequented by absentee West Indian planters in the eighteenth century, was reported by Hansard as saying in the House of Commons:

'He was prepared to say that if the benefits of the people of England demanded it, he would sacrifice the West-India colonies. Why not? How were those colonies of any benefit to the people of England? A set of barren islands, which were early maintained with the pith and sinews of the people of this country! Jamaica to the bottom of the sea, and all the Antilles after it, rather than the interests of the people should be sacrificed.'

Two years later, on June 30, 1844, he returned to the charge:

'He considered that the West India Islands had been most fatal appendages to this great Empire, they had done us no service—they had been the means of occasioning dreadful wars and fearful commotions—they had put us to immense expense, and had given us nothing in requital. He believed that if, tomorrow, by some accidental vicissitude, these Islands disappeared from the face of the earth, as far as England was concerned, however much she might mourn the loss human nature would sustain, she would not lose one jot of her strength, not one penny of her wealth, not one instrument of her power.'

408

In France, also, the political importance of the sugar colonies was regarded as another memory of the past, as Lestiboudois said, in a memorial on behalf of beet sugar presented to the Royal Society of Science, Agriculture and the Arts of Lille in 1839. Britain and France, which had agreed in the eighteenth century on the incalculable importance of the Caribbean territories, agreed in the nineteenth on their indisputable insignificance.

Towards this revolution in colonial affairs, as far as France was concerned, the independence of Haiti was a powerful contributing factor. For a long time France continued to dream of its reconquest, but it was only a dream. Eventually, in 1825, France agreed to give up all claims to Haiti in return for an indemnity of 150 million francs, payable in five annual instalments. Only Martinique, Guadeloupe and Cayenne remained of the once proud empire in the Caribbean, dreamed of by Colbert, Louis XIV and Bonaparte. In 1877 Sweden, reflecting the general European volte-face, restored St. Bartholomew, the inhabitants of which, with one dissenting, voted for the restoration of French sovereignty.

As a result of the war with Bonaparte, Britain emerged in possession of British Guiana and Trinidad, and confirmed in possession of Tobago, St. Lucia and Grenada, which had constantly changed hands in the eighteenth-century see-saw struggle. Britain was on the alert to any French attempt to reconquer Haiti and to extend her power in the Caribbean. When, in 1822, the vagaries of European politics brought French troops temporarily into Spain, the British Prime Minister, George Canning, uttered his famous words: 'We determined that if France had Spain, it should not be Spain with the Indies. We called the New World into existence to redress the balance of the Old.' The British Government thereby supported the revolutions for independence of the Spanish Colonies in America. But there was little in Canning's words besides rhetoric; there was really not any serious possibility that the French Government would resurrect the western design of Louis XIV.

The United States was the only power interested in the Caribbean in the nineteenth century. In 1811 Jefferson dreamed of an independent federation of all the Caribbean islands, looking upon it as 'an enrapturing prospect into futurity'. When that prospect faded, Jefferson turned his eyes to Cuba. He hoped to get

Bonaparte's consent to the admission of Cuba into the Union, stating in 1814 that that would be the *ne plus ultra* of United States expansion in that direction, while Canada could be expected to fall into the lap of the United States during the first war with Britain. The result, said Jefferson, would be 'such an empire for liberty as she has never surveyed since the creation'.

This was too modest for at least one of Jefferson's colleagues, John Quincy Adams, Secretary of State, and later President of the United States. To Adams the manifest destiny of the United States was to dominate the Western Hemisphere, and the United States should endeavour to familiarise the world with this idea. With respect to the Spanish possessions to the south and the British to the north, Adams said to the Cabinet in 1819:

'It is impossible that centuries shall elapse without finding them annexed to the United States; not that any spirit of encroachment or ambition on our part renders it necessary, but because it is a physical, moral and political absurdity that such fragments of territory, with sovereigns at fifteen hundred (*sic*) miles beyond the sea, worthless and burdensome to their owners, should exist permanently contiguous to a great powerful and rapidly-growing nation... until Europe shall find it a settled geographical element that the United States and North America are identical, any effort on our part to reason the world out of a belief that we are ambitious will have no other effect than to convince them that we add to our ambition hypocrisy.'

A new claimant had arisen for Adam's heritage.

The key territory in the Caribbean from the standpoint of the United States was Cuba. Adams wrote to the United States Minister to Spain, on April 28, 1823:

'There are laws of political as well as physical gravitation and if an apple severed by the tempest from its native tree, cannot choose but fall to the ground, Cuba, forcibly disjoined from its unnatural connection with Spain and incapable of self-support, can gravitate only toward the North American Union, which, by the same law of nature, cannot cast her off from its bosom.'

Adams did not explain why Cuba should have been any more incapable of self-support than Haiti or any of the Spanish mainland colonies which, in that very year, with the benevolent neutrality of the United States, were asserting their claims to independence by force of arms, following the example of the great republic which Adams represented. A powerful school already existed in Cuba which demanded independence.

But Adams had to reckon with the British and French Governments. His letter continued: 'The transfer of Cuba to Great Britain would be an event unpropitious to the interests of the Union. The question both of our right and our power to prevent it, if necessary by force, already obtrudes itself upon our councils.' He regarded the Cuban question as of deeper importance and greater magnitude than any other which had occurred since the independence of the United States.

It was with these ideas in mind that President Monroe, in 1823, made his famous speech to Congress which has come to be known as the Monroe Doctrine. Specifically directed towards the Cuban question, but couched in language sufficiently general to exclude any changes of sovereignty whatsoever in the Western Hemisphere —including Russia, as Adams bluntly informed the Russian Minister—Monroe announced to the world firstly that the United States would regard any attempt by the European powers to extend the colonial system in the New World as dangerous to its peace and safety; secondly, pledged itself not to interfere with the existing colonies; thirdly, with respect to the colonies which had declared their independence, 'could not view any interposition for the purpose of oppressing them, or controlling in any other manner, their destiny, by any European power, in any other light, than as the manifestation of an unfriendly disposition towards the United States'.

On the other hand, Britain would not agree to United States or French annexation of Cuba. 'It may be questioned,' noted George Canning, 'whether any blow, that could be struck by any power in any part of the world, would have a more sensible effect on the interests of this country or the reputation of its government.' The upshot was a sort of gentlemen's agreement between the United States and Britain, to which France subsequently adhered, that the *status quo* should be maintained in Cuba, and the island should remain in Spanish possession. The prestige of the Pope's beneficiary in 1493 had sunk to its nadir.

An uneasy truce was maintained until 1852, with clumsy filibustering attempts from the United States to force the issue. In that year, the British and French Governments, suspicious of United States designs, proposed a convention between the three governments. The essence of the proposed convention was contained in the following article:

'The high contracting parties hereby severally and collectively disclaim now and for hereafter, all intention to obtain possession of the island of Cuba, and they respectively bind themselves to discountenance all attempts to that effect on the part of any power or individuals whatever.'

It fell to the Secretary of State, Edward H. Everett, to reply. He was already familiar with the problem. As United States Minister to Spain in 1825, he had proposed to the President that the United States might peaceably secure the island by offering Spain a considerable loan, with Cuba as security, the United States to obtain complete sovereignty if the loan was not repaid within a stipulated time. Everett's objections to the proposed convention were expressed in a letter of December 1, 1852 to the French Foreign Minister. Reiterating the refusal of his government to see Cuba pass under British or French sovereignty, he compared such a step with French and British reaction to the United States acquiring some important island in the Mediterranean. It was the first official step towards denominating the Caribbean 'the American Mediterranean'.

Everett's objections were as follows. First, the convention would certainly be rejected by the United States Senate. Secondly, the convention would be of no value unless it were lasting; the constitution of the United States did not permit the imposition of a permanent disability on its government. Thirdly, one of the oldest traditions of the United States was an aversion to political alliances with European powers. Fourthly, a more grave objection, the proposed convention, although equal in its terms, would be very unequal in its substance. 'If,' emphasised Everett, 'an island like Cuba, belonging to the Spanish crown, guarded the entrance of the Thames and the Seine, and the United States should propose a convention like this to France and England, those powers would assuredly feel that the disability assumed by ourselves was far less serious than that which we asked them to assume.' Fifthly, the convention could only be transitory, 'sure to be swept away by the irresistible tide of affairs in a new country'. It rested on principles applicable to Europe, where international relations were of great antiquity, but which were not applicable to America, 'which, but lately a waste, is filling up with intense rapidity, and adjusting on natural principles those territorial relations which, on the first discovery of the continent, were in a good degree fortuitous'. Behind the sophistry lay a thinly veiled threat to Europe which went far beyond Cuba. 'It would be as easy,' Everett became more specific, 'to throw a dam from Cape Florida to Cuba, in the hope of stopping the flow of the gulf stream, as to attempt by a compact like this, to fix the fortunes of Cuba "now and for hereafter".'

Everett's sixth objection showed a lack of knowledge of history. It could not be doubted, he insinuated, that both France and England would prefer any change in the condition of Cuba to that which was most to be apprehended, a repetition of the revolution in Saint-Domingue. This was a bogey which, least of all, would terrify England, who had preferred the revolution to French sovereignty; so, for that matter, had the United States itself. Finally, concluded Everett, the proposed convention would only intensify the filibustering attacks from the United States.

'No administration of this government, however strong in the public confidence in other respects, could stand a day under the odium of having stipulated with the great powers of Europe, that in no future time, under no change of circumstances, by no amicable arrangement with Spain, by no act of lawful war (should that calamity unfortunately occur), by no consent of the inhabitants of the island, should they, like the possessions of Spain on the American continent, succeed in rendering themselves independent; in fine, by no overruling necessity of self-preservation should the United States make the acquisition of Cuba.'

The confusion of Cuban independence with annexation by the United States could not obscure the full import of Everett's manifest destiny.

It was with this background that the United States turned its attention to the possibility of purchasing Cuba. It was the beginning of dollar diplomacy. In 1854 the United States Ministers to Britain, France and Spain assembled in Ostend, Belgium, and issued a manifesto, known as the Ostend Manifesto, recommending an immediate and earnest effort to purchase Cuba for a maximum price of $120 million. The old-fashioned school of protocol must have been scandalised. In the same year President Pierce authorised the offer of $100 millon for the island, though he added that he would not have the negotiations fail if an additional 20 or 30 millions were required to effect the sale.

In 1859 the Senate, emphasising that 'the law of our national existence is growth. We cannot, if we would, disobey it,' considered three possible solutions of the difficulty—first, possession by one of the European powers; second, independence; third, annexation by the United States by conquest or negotiation. The Senate rejected the first solution as incompatible with the national safety; it dismissed the second on the ground that independence would be nominal, the precursor to a European protectorate, which could not be tolerated; it recommended the third alternative, annexation by negotiation, as the only practicable course, and as cheaper, in the long run, than conquest.

But Spain obstinately refused to sell, and the Cubans had their own views as to their future status. The United States was not free to intervene directly in the question until 1898.

There were two other parts of Adam's heritage, besides Cuba, which attracted the interest of the United States. The first was the Danish West Indies. Weary of the increasingly heavy burden of these tiny islands in the steadily advancing chaos of the world market, the King of Denmark initiated negotiations for their sale to the United States. He announced the convention to his faithful subjects on October 25, 1867, expressing the hope that 'a mighty impulse, both moral and material, will be given to the happy development of the Islands, under the new sovereignty'.

The King, however, had jumped the gun in an anxiety to abandon islands which was as great as the former anxiety had been to acquire them. The United States Senate refused to ratify the convention. The King of Denmark had to announce the rebuff and inform his subjects that they were still his subjects. In another proclamation on May 7, 1870, he assured them: 'ready as We were to subdue the feelings of our hearts when We thought that duty bade Us so to do, yet We cannot otherwise than feel a satisfaction that circumstances have relieved Us from making a sacrifice which, notwithstanding the advantages held out, would always have been painful to Us.' Denmark had to wait until 1917.

The second area in the Caribbean which seemed manifestly destined to obey Adams' law of political gravitation was the Spanish part of Hispaniola. Declaring itself independent of Spain in 1821, the territory was annexed by Haiti in the following year, and remained under Haitian rule until 1844, when it once more declared itself independent, as the Dominican Republic. The unceasing struggle in the interior and the constant apprehension of a renewed attack from Haiti led the President of the Republic to make overtures to the United States for annexation. President Grant sent out a one-man commission of inquiry which recommended annexation. But again the United States Senate refused to ratify the treaty.

In 1871, pursuant to a resolution of Congress, another commission of inquiry was appointed to report on the desire in the Dominican Republic for annexation. The assistant secretary to this commission, which consisted of three men, was the distinguished Negro abolitionist, Frederick Douglass, who later became United States Minister to Haiti. The Commission reported as follows: 'There is but one chance for that Republic ever to recover its independence—to become, after a proper period of probation, one of a union of states, the freedom and substantial independence of each being guaranteed by the strength of all.' The Commission warned that, if the republic were not annexed, 'it is to lie exhausted and helpless until some strong nation shall seize it and hold it in colonial subjection'. In the very next paragraph the commission stressed that the tobacco trade of the republic was rapidly becoming a German monopoly, and that the number of Germans on the north side of the island exceeded those of any foreign power. But the Senate would not budge, and the United States had to wait until World War I before it could get a foothold.

The commission of inquiry, feeling 'a deep interest in the experiment of self-government which the blacks are trying in Haiti', which it wished all success, made efforts to go beyond its terms of reference, and tried to study Haiti also, desiring to give government and important citizens an opportunity of stating their views, both as to their claims on the Dominican Republic and as to their wishes with respect to any changes that might be brought about in the neighbouring republic. They received no encouragement to pursue these inquiries, and the Haitian Government refused to permit them to explore the interior. The Commission, however, expressed the view that the establishment of a well-regulated, orderly and prosperous state in the Dominican Republic would be hardly less beneficial to Haiti than to its neighbour, would set an example to Haiti, would put an end to the exhausting border warfare between the two countries, and would enable both to devote their energies to the education of their people and the development of their resources. Here, also, the United States had to wait for World War I before it could obtain an opportunity to secure a footing.

That a new star had been added to the Caribbean firmament was strikingly and dramatically brought out in 1895, when a fifty-year-old boundary dispute between British Guiana and Venezuela came to a head. The United States, to whom Venezuela had repeatedly appealed, took the view that the dispute fell within the terms of the Monroe Doctrine, which it interpreted to read that, when a European power had a difference with a South American community, the European power shall consent to refer that controversy to arbitration. The doctrine of manifest destiny was never more sharply stated than it was by Secretary of State Olney:

'Today the United States is practically sovereign on this continent, and its fiat is law upon the subject to which it confines its interposition... Being entitled to resent and resist any sequestration of Venezuelan soil by Great Britain, it is necessarily entitled to know whether such sequestration has occurred or is now going on.'

Olney added that the three thousand miles of ocean—geography had improved since Adams' time—separating Europe and America was a physical fact which made any permanent political union between a European and an American state unnatural and expedient. President Cleveland proposed to Congress the appointment of a United States commission to investigate the facts, after which it would be the duty of the United States 'to resist by every means in its power as a wilful aggression upon its rights and interests, the appropriation by Great Britain of any lands or the exercise of governmental jurisdiction over any territory which, upon investigation, we have determined of right belongs to Venezuela'.

The British Foreign Secretary, Lord Salisbury, dealt incisively with the United States claims. He emphasised, in the first place, that the Monroe Doctrine, whatever the respect felt for it, had no place in international law, which was founded on the general

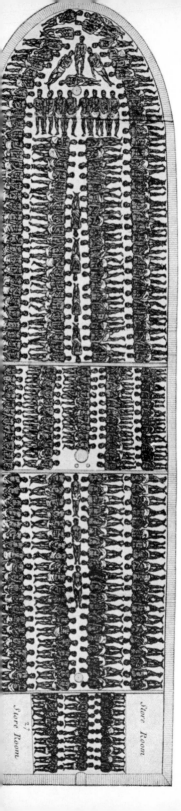

16. (*above*) Thomas Clarkson and, behind,
William Wilberforce

17. (*left*) The plan of a slave ship 'designed
to give the spectator an idea of the sufferings of the Africans in the Middle Passage'.
From: Thomas Clarkson, *The History of
the Rise, Progress, and Accomplishments of
the Abolition of the African Slave-Trade
by the British Parliament*, 1808

18. Holing a Cane-Piece

This sequence of pictures is taken from: William Clark, *Ten Views in the Island of Antigua, in which are represented the Process of Sugar-Making, and the Employment of the Negroes, in the Field, Boiling-House, and Distillery*, 1823

19. Planting the Sugar-Cane

20. Cutting the Sugar-Cane

21. A Mill-Yard

22. Exterior of a Boiling-House

23. Interior of a Boiling-House

24. Interior of a Distillery

25. Exterior of a Distillery

26. Exterior

Views of nineteenth-century Cuban sugar factories. From: J. G. Cantero, *Los Ingenios*, 1857

27. Interior

28. American guard of honour for President Batista of Cuba, 1942

29. Fidel Castro, Prime Minister of Cuba, meets Vice-President Richard Nixon, 1959

30. '1959–1969: Tenth Anniversary of the triumph of the Cuban rebellion'

consent of nations: 'no statesman, however eminent, and no nation, however powerful, are competent to insert into the code of international law a novel principle which was never recognised before, and which has not since been accepted by the Government of any other country.'

In the second place, Salisbury rejected Olney's implications that the union between Great Britain and Canada, between Great Britain and Jamaica and Trinidad, between Great Britain and British Honduras and British Guiana was unnatural and inexpedient, and he emphatically denied the opinion on behalf of the British Government and its American subjects:

'They are not prepared to admit that the interests of the United States are necessarily concerned in every frontier dispute which may arise between any two of the states who possess dominion in the Western Hemisphere; and still less can they accept the doctrine that the United States are entitled to claim that the process of arbitration shall be applied to any demand for the surrender of territory which one of these States may make against another.'

President Cleveland breathed defiance. War between the two nations loomed on the horizon. But in January, 1896, the German Kaiser sent his telegram to President Kruger of the Transvaal congratulating him on the frustration of the Jameson raid. With the Boer War on its hands, and with Joseph Chamberlain as Colonial Secretary flirting with his dream of an alliance of the three great Anglo-Saxon powers, Britain, Germany and the United States, Britain adopted a conciliatory attitude and agreed to arbitration. The decision of the tribunal followed, in the main, the British claim.

The controversy over the Venezuela boundary had a profound psychological effect on the people of the United States and prepared them for new adventures based on a wholly untenable interpretation of a unilateral doctrine which its greatest students in the country could not endorse. The publication of Mahan's history of sea power had helped to give the United States public that taste of empire which, according to the *Washington Post* in 1899, was in the mouth of the people even as the taste of blood in the jungle. The hour was approaching; only the man was needed.

But the man, too, was available—Theodore Roosevelt, Governor of New York, soon to be President of the United States. Cowardice in a race, as in an individual, said Roosevelt at the opening of the Naval War College in Newport in 1897, was the unpardonable sin, and no nation could hold its place in the world unless it stood ready to guard its rights with an armed hand. On February 9, 1898, Roosevelt wrote to a friend:

'I should myself like to shape our foreign policy with a purpose ultimately of driving off this continent every European power. I would begin with Spain, and in the end would take all other European nations, including England.'

With the second war of independence in Cuba; with Olney's curious fears that Cuban independence might lead to a division of the island into two republics, the one white, the other black; with the sugar of Cuba, as the United States Minister to Spain stated to the British Minister in 1897, as vital to the United States as the wheat and cotton of India and Egypt to Great Britain; with all these factors simultaneously bearing upon the problem, the United States followed Roosevelt's prescription and began with the colonies of Spain on April 21, 1898.

Chapter Twenty-Four

The American Mediterranean

A new and more bitter revolution for independence began in Cuba in 1895. Spain was unable to restore order, the non-combatant population was caught between the depredations on both sides, and American commerce and interests suffered heavily. The United States urged Spain to terminate the revolt, but the revolutionaries refused to be satisfied with anything short of independence. The continuing disorders led the United States Government to send the battleship *Maine* to Havana in January, 1898. It exploded shortly after with the loss of two officers and 258 men. The United States, blaming a submarine mine or some external cause, demanded reparation and presented a virtual ultimatum to Spain on March 29, 1898 calling for an immediate armistice. The Spanish Government, blaming an internal explosion, refused. On April 11, 1898, President McKinley, unimpressed by a joint note of the European Great Powers urging further negotiations with Spain, approached the Congress, which passed a joint resolution reading as follows:

'First. That the people of the Island of Cuba are, and of right ought to be, free and independent.
'Second. That it is the duty of the United States to demand, and the

Government of the United States does hereby demand, that the Government of Spain at once relinquish its authority and government in the Island of Cuba and withdraw its land and naval forces from Cuba and Cuban waters.

'Third. That the President of the United States be, and he hereby is, directed and empowered to use the entire land and naval forces in the United States, and to call into the actual service of the United States the militia of the several states, to such extent as may be necessary to carry these resolutions into effect.

'Fourth. That the United States hereby disclaims any disposition or intention to exercise sovereignty, jurisdiction or control over said Island except for the pacification thereof, and asserts its determination, when that is accomplished, to leave the government and control of the Island to its people.'

After three months of war Spain sued for peace, preferring annexation of Cuba by the United States in order to guarantee Spanish life and property and Cuba's external debts to Spain. The United States refused, and the Treaty of Paris, signed on December 10, 1898, provided for the relinquishment of Spanish sovereignty over Cuba, as well as Puerto Rico which was annexed outright by the United States. Thus ended the Papal Donation of 1493 and Spanish power was removed from the Caribbean.

The Military Government established by the United States concentrated on the relief of the starving population, the disarmament of the Cuban revolutionaries and loyalists, the control of yellow fever, and the promulgation of an electoral law as the basis of the election of a convention to frame a constitution. The convention, summoned in 1900, resisted American claims which were clearly and precisely set out in a proviso attached to the Military Appropriation Bill on March 2, 1901, which has come to be known as the Platt Amendment. The Platt Amendment, which was to govern American relations with Cuba down to the advent of Fidel Castro, read as follows:

'I. That the Government of Cuba shall never enter into any treaty or other compact with any foreign power or powers which will impair or tend to impair the independence of Cuba; nor in any manner authorise or permit any foreign power or powers to obtain by colonisation or for military or naval purposes or otherwise lodgement in or control over any portion of said island.

'II. That said Government shall not assume or contract any public debt, to pay the interest upon which, and to make reasonable sinking-fund provision for the ultimate discharge of which, the ordinary revenues of the island, after defraying the current expenses of Government, shall be inadequate.

'III. That the Government of Cuba consents that the United States may exercise the right to intervene for the preservation of Cuban independence, the maintenance of a government adequate for the protection of life, property, and individual liberty, and for discharging the obligations with respect to Cuba imposed by the Treaty of Paris on the United States, now to be assumed and undertaken by the Government of Cuba.

'IV. That all acts of the United States in Cuba during its military occupancy thereof are ratified and validated, and all lawful rights acquired thereunder shall be maintained and protected.

'V. That the Government of Cuba will execute, and, as far as necessary, extend, the plans already devised, or other plans to be mutually agreed upon, for the sanitation of the cities of the island, to the end that a recurrence of epidemic and infectious diseases may be prevented thereby assuring protection to the people and commerce of Cuba, as well as the commerce of the Southern ports of the United States and the people residing therein.

'VI. That the Isle of Pines shall be omitted from the proposed constitutional boundaries of Cuba, the title thereto being left to future adjustment by treaty.

'VII. That to enable the United States to maintain the independence of Cuba, and to protect the people thereof, as well as for its own defence, the Government of Cuba will sell or lease to the United States land necessary for coaling or naval stations at certain specified points, to be agreed upon with the President of the United States.

'VIII. That by way of further assurance the Government of Cuba will embody the foregoing provisions in a permanent treaty with the United States.'

The convention was disinclined to accept the Platt Amendment, taking the view that such demands would deprive the Government of Cuba of all real independence and would pave the way for constant American interference in its internal affairs. The United States made it clear that it would not withdraw from Cuba until the Platt Amendment was accepted, and so the convention backed down. The permanent treaty was signed on May 22, 1903. The United States received in 1903 bases at Guantanamo and Bahia Honda, agreeing to pay an annual rent of $2,000; in 1912 the United States surrendered its right at Bahia Honda in return for an enlarged area at Guantanamo, agreeing to raise the annual rent

to $5,000. Ultimately in 1925 the United States abandoned all
claims to the Isle of Pines which remained under Cuban jurisdiction. The American Government intervened in 1906 when law and
order in Cuba totally broke down, and an American Provisional
Government, under Taft, and later Magoon, was installed from
1906 to 1909.

All this was in accordance with the new interpretation of the
Monroe Doctrine enunciated by Theodore Roosevelt. In its classic
form, the Roosevelt Corollary, as it has come to be known, was
thus stated by Roosevelt in 1904:

'Chronic wrongdoing, or an impotence which results in a general loosening of the ties of civilised society, may in America, as elsewhere, ultimately
require intervention by some civilised nation, and in the Western Hemisphere the adherence of the United States to the Monroe Doctrine may
force the United States, however reluctantly, in flagrant cases of
such wrongdoing or impotence, to the exercise of an international police
power.'

The international policeman carried a big stick. His was the
duty, as President Taft wrote to Secretary Knox in 1909, 'to have
the right to knock their heads together until they should maintain
peace between them'. As stated frankly by Roosevelt himself in
1908 with reference to Venezuela, America had to 'show these
Dagoes that they will have to behave decently'. So Roosevelt just
'took' the Panama Canal while Congress and the South Americans
debated the issue. As Roosevelt himself wrote to Cecil Spring-
Rice of the British Foreign Office in 1904:

'It was a good thing for Egypt and the Sudan, and for the world,
when England took Egypt and the Sudan. It is a good thing for India that
England should control it. And so it is a good thing, a very good thing,
for Cuba and for Panama and for the world that the United States has
acted as it has actually done during the last six years. The people of the
United States and the people of the Isthmus and the rest of mankind will
all be the better because we dig the Panama Canal and keep order in its
neighbourhood. And the politicians and revolutionists at Bogota are entitled to precisely the amount of sympathy we extend to other inefficient
bandits.'

The Caribbean itself was to become America's closed sea,
the American Mediterranean. As Assistant Secretary of State
Loomis stated in 1904:

'... no picture of our future is complete which does not contemplate and comprehend the United States as the dominant power in the Caribbean Sea.'

The need to control the approaches to the Panama Canal did the rest. The new policy was adumbrated by President Taft in his Annual Message to Congress in 1912, as follows:

'The diplomacy of the present administration has sought to respond to the modern idea of commercial intercourse. This policy has been characterised as substituting dollars for bullets.'

The United States was faced with new large British investments in Cuba which from 1909 to 1913 totalled $60 million (French and German about $17 million) as against $35 million from the United States, and with German interests in Haiti and the Dominican Republic related to naval bases and coaling stations. President Wilson was obsessed with his determination 'to teach the South American Republics to elect good men' and Secretary of State Bryan with the opportunities in the Dominican Republic for jobs for 'good deserving Democrats'. The stage was set for American intervention in the Dominican Republic and Haiti.

On February 8, 1907, there was signed at Santo Domingo a convention respecting assistance of the United States in the collection and application of the customs revenues of the Dominican Republic. The pertinent sections of this convention read as follows:

'I. That the President of the United States shall appoint a General Receiver of Dominican Customs, who, with such Assistant Receivers and other employees of the Receivership as shall be appointed by the President of the United States in his discretion, shall collect all the customs duties accruing at the several customs houses of the Dominican Republic until the payment or retirement of any and all bonds issued by the Dominican Government in accordance with the plan and under the limitations as to terms and amounts hereinbefore recited; and said General Receiver shall apply the sums so collected, as follows :
'First, to paying the expenses of the receivership; second, to the payment of interest upon said bonds; third, to the payment of the annual sums provided for amortisation of said bonds including interest upon all bonds in sinking fund; fourth, to the purchase and cancellation or retirement of said bonds as may be directed by the Dominican Government; fifth, the remainder to be paid to the Dominican Government...

'II. The Dominican Government will provide by law for the payment of all customs duties to the General Receiver and his assistants, and will give to them all needful aid and assistance and full protection to the extent of its powers. The Government of the United States will give to the General Receiver and his assistants such protection as it may find to be requisite for the performance of their duties.

'III. Until the Dominican Republic has paid the whole amount of the bonds of the debt its public debt shall not be increased except by previous agreement between the Dominican Government and the United States. A like agreement shall be necessary to modify the import duties, it being an indispensable condition for the modification of such duties that the Dominican Executive demonstrate and that the President of the United States recognise that, on the basis of exportations and importations to the like amount and the like character during the two years preceding that in which it is desired to make such modification, the total net customs receipts would at such altered rate of duties have been for each of such two years in excess of the sum of $2,000,000 United States gold...'

In 1915 the American government occupied the Dominican Republic for fear that the ordinary process of Dominican elections would produce a government not regarded with favour in the United States. The decree of the American Command stated:

'All revenues accruing to the Dominican Government, including revenues hitherto accrued and unpaid—whether from customs duties under the terms of the Treaty concluded on February 8, 1907, the Receivership established by which remains in effect, or from internal revenue—shall be paid to the Military Government herein established which will, in trust for the Republic of Santo Domingo, hold such revenue and will make all the proper legal disbursements therefrom necessary for the administration of the Dominican Government, and for the purposes of the Occupation...'

The Military Government came to an end in 1924.

The Dominican pattern was followed in the case of Haiti with which a treaty was signed by the United States on September 6, 1915, respecting finances, economic development and tranquillity. The Treaty set up a general receivership, associated with a Financial Adviser nominated by the President of the United States. Customs receipts were to be applied to the costs of the Receivership, the salaries and expenses of the Financial Adviser, the interest and sinking fund of the Haitian public debt, and to the maintenance of a constabulary. The Treaty continued:

'Article VIII. The Republic of Haiti shall not increase its public debt except by previous agreement with the President of the United States, and shall not contract any debt or assume any financial obligation unless the ordinary revenues of the Republic available for that purpose, after defraying the expenses of the Government, shall be adequate to pay the interest and provide a sinking fund for the final discharge of such debt.

'Article IX. The Republic of Haiti will not, without a previous agreement with the President of the United States, modify the customs duties in a manner to reduce the revenues therefrom...

'Article X. The Haitian Government obligates itself, for the preservation of domestic peace, the security of individual rights and full observance of the provisions of this treaty, to create without delay an efficient constabulary, urban and rural, composed of native Haitians. This constabulary shall be organised and officered by Americans, appointed by the President of Haiti, upon nomination by the President of the United States...

'Article XI. The Government of Haiti agrees not to surrender any of the territory of the Republic of Haiti by sale, lease, or otherwise, or jurisdiction over such territory, to any foreign government or power, nor to enter into any treaty or contract with any foreign power or powers that will impair or tend to impair the independence of Haiti.'

The American officers of the Haitian constabulary were withdrawn by agreement on August 7, 1933, which provided for the Haitianisation of the constabulary, and the withdrawal of the American marines was to commence on October 1, 1934 and be completed within 30 days. A financial arrangement adjusting the financial guarantees stipulated in 1919 and 1922 limited the number of Americans employed by the Fiscal Representative to 18, and provided further:

'Article XIII. Each year, by January 31st at the latest, the Fiscal Representative shall present a detailed estimate of receipts for the following fiscal year. Except by special agreement, the budget of the Republic shall not exceed the amount of probable ways and means which the Secretary of State for Finance and the Fiscal Representative shall have agreed upon...

'Article XVII. Without the accord of the Fiscal Representative no new financial obligation will be assumed unless the ordinary revenues of the Republic, after defraying the expenses of the Government, shall be adequate to assure the final discharge of such obligations...

'Article XX. The Government of Haiti agrees not to reduce the tariff nor to modify the taxes and internal revenues in such a way as to

reduce the total amount thereof without the accord of the Fiscal Representative...'

United States supremacy in the Caribbean was further underlined when, in 1917, the United States purchased the Virgin
Islands from Denmark for the sum of $25 million, in order to
get possession of the harbour of St. Thomas.

World War II provided the setting for yet a further advance,
this time in the British West Indies. In 1940 the United States
received from Britain 99-year leases of naval bases in Trinidad,
Guyana, Antigua, St. Lucia, Jamaica, the Bahamas—as well as in
Newfoundland and in Bermuda. The difference was that no dollars
were involved—only fifty over-age destroyers for Britain, with its
back to the wall against submarines. How the deal appeared in
United States eyes is brought out in the opinion of Robert Jackson,
the Attorney General, to President Roosevelt on August 27,
1940:

'(b) In consideration it is proposed to transfer to Great Britain the title
and possession of certain over-age ships and obsolescent military materials
now the property of the United States and certain other small patrol
boats which, though nearly completed, are already obsolescent.

'(c) Upon such transfer all obligation of the United States is discharged.
The acquisition consists only of rights, which the United States may
exercise or not at its option; and if exercised, may abandon without consent. The privilege of maintaining such bases is subject only to limitations
necessary to reconcile United States use with the sovereignty retained by
Great Britain. Our Government assumes no responsibility for civil administration of any territory. It makes no promise to erect structures,
or maintain forces at any point. It undertakes no defence of the possessions of any country. In short, it acquires optional bases which may
be developed as Congress appropriates funds therefor, but the United
States does not assume any continuing or future obligation, commitment,
or alliance... The executive agreement obtains an opportunity to establish naval and air bases for the protection of our coastline but it imposes
no obligation upon the Congress to appropriate money to improve the
opportunity...

'I am informed that the destroyers involved here are the survivors of
a fleet of over 100 built at about the same time and under the same
design. During the year 1930, 58 of these were decommissioned with a
view toward scrapping and a corresponding number was recommissioned
as replacements. Usable material and equipment from the 58 vessels removed from the service were transferred to the recommissioned vessels to
recondition and modernise them, and other usable material and equip-

ment were removed and the vessels stripped. They were then stricken from the Naval register, and 50 of them were sold as scrap for prices ranging from $5,260 to $6,800 per vessel, and the remaining 8 were used for such purposes as target vessels, experimental construction tests, and temporary barracks. The surviving destroyers now under consideration have been reconditioned and are in service, but all of them are over-age, most of them by several years.'

Chapter Twenty-Five

The American Sugar Kingdom

Bryan Edwards, the historian of Jamaica at the end of the eighteenth century, had warned that 'the business of sugar planting is a sort of adventure in which the man that engages must engage deeply'. By the end of the nineteenth century the enterprise had become too big for the individual entrepreneur, and the West India Royal Commission of 1897 expressed the opinion that 'under any circumstances that can at present be foreseen, the days of very large or excessive profits from the sugar-cane industry appear to us to have passed away'. The tremendous outlay required for land, labour and machinery exceeded individual capacity, especially in the competition with the beet sugar industry. But the American corporation proved that it was more than ever possible to make the sugar cane industry pay. The age of mass production followed the emergence of American military power and political presence in the Caribbean, and, as Fernando Ortiz of Cuba writes, 'all becomes mass, shapeless, collective and anonymous: the company, the sugar and the syndicate; mass of capitalists, mass of products, mass of workers'.

The West India Royal Commission of 1897 had condemned latifundia and had suggested that experiments be made with the

separation of cane production by small farmers and sugar manufacture in large central factories:

'Where this system can be carried out, it offers many advantages, and
in any of your Majesty's West Indian possessions where a tendency is
shown to adopt it, and the production of sugar is likely to continue, we
think the Government concerned might fairly be expected to encourage it
by providing means of communication between the cane-growing tracts
and the central factories, and by offering every facility for the establishment of cane cultivators on suitable lands.'

The Americans disagreed completely. The powerful Brookings
Institution of Washington, in its comprehensive study entitled
Porto Rico and its Problems in 1930 wrote:

'From a strictly technical standpoint, sugar can be produced more
efficiently and cheaply where both cane growing and sugar manufacturing
are under a single administration... The highest cane and sugar yields
per acre, the best qualities of cane, and the maximum recovery of sugar
per ton of cane, are found in countries where all operations from plowing
the field to bagging the sugar are under one management.'

The period between 1897 and 1930 saw the enormous concentration of latifundia in the Caribbean under the stimulus of
American capital investment. The combined acreage of six plantations operated by the Cuban American Sugar Company totalled
half a million acres; that of the nine plantations of the Cuban
Atlantic Sugar Company 400,000. The Vertientes-Camaguey Company owned or leased over 800,000 acres; the Manati Sugar
Company owned or controlled 237,000 acres of which 29,000
were in cane; the Punta Alegre Company on its three plantations
owned 112,000 acres and leased 43,000—39,000 acres were in
cane. Symbolic of the new age was the United Fruit Company.
The backing for its control of 93,000 acres of cane land in Cuba
was its various properties in the Caribbean, Central and South
America, the Canary Islands, Europe and the United States, totalling at the beginning of 1941 over 3 million acres. Its sugar production in Cuba was part of a huge empire which controlled 65 per
cent of the world's supply of bananas, included a tourist hotel
in Jamaica, embraced its own fleet of cargo and passenger vessels,
and dominated 40 per cent of the entire voting stock of the
International Railways of Central America.

What was true of Cuba under American capital was also true

of Puerto Rico. A law passed in 1900 immediately after the
American occupation prohibiting corporations from acquiring
plantations larger than 500 acres remained a dead letter for
decades. Four large American corporations dominated the sugar
industry which totalled 7,600 farms, 166 over 500 acres. These
166 farms comprised half a million acres or two-thirds of the total
included in sugar-cane farms throughout the island. Plantings
of cane covering more than 500 acres were less than one per cent
of the sugar-cane farms, but comprised 60 per cent of the total
cane acreage and produced 67 per cent of the sugar in 1935. The
four American companies held nearly one-quarter of all the cane
land in the island and nearly one-half of all the land held in
plantations. Central Aguirre owned nearly 25,000 acres and leased
a further 18,000. The holdings of Eastern Sugar Associates totalled
51,000 acres, two-thirds of this owned outright. The Fajardo
Sugar Company owned 30,000 acres and leased 20,000—over
20,000 acres were planted to cane.

The Dominican Republic presented a similar pattern. Two
American companies dominated—South Porto Rico Company and
the West Indies Sugar Corporation. The former owned 150,000
acres of which half were in cane, and the latter 100,000—apart
from a further 123,000 in Cuba.

The key to this American concentration of production was the
railway. In 1899 there were less than 200 miles of railroads in
Puerto Rico. By 1940 there were over 1,000. Nearly two-thirds
of this mileage was owned outright by the sugar plantations and
depended on sugar tonnage for 90 per cent of its business. The
public corporations were dependent only to a lesser extent on
sugar. The most important independent system, the American
Railroad Company, derived 85 per cent of its freight revenues from
sugar. Central Aguirre owned 17 miles of railway, Fajardo 27,
South Porto Rico 50, Eastern Sugar Company 133.

Sugar was equally the life and soul of the Cuban railway
system. In 1938–1939 the railways depended on sugar and its by-
products for 80 per cent of their tonnage and 60 per cent of their
freight revenues. The individual plantations were in addition well-
equipped with their own private systems, and in some instances
dominated the public corporations. Thus the Cuba Company
owned all the stock of the Consolidated Railroads of Cuba, which

extended from Santa Clara to Santiago and served the whole eastern part of the island. They ran through territory which was practically all sugar territory—half of Santa Clara province and the provinces of Camaguey and Oriente. In this region about 70 per cent of Cuba's mills were located, producing 60 per cent of the island's crop. The Cuban-American Company operated 570 miles of railway. Guantanamo Company owned 70 miles and in addition owned 80 per cent of the stock of the Guantanamo Railroad Company. Manati Company owned 176 miles of its own railway and in addition operated the 44 miles of the Ferrocarril de Tunas. The Punta Alegre Corporation owned 228 miles of railway, the Vertientes-Camaguey Company 326.

In addition the American-style sugar plantation owned its own rolling stock on the railways; in many cases its own steamers; its own wharves and warehousing facilities. The scope of its operations can be gauged by the fact that the South Porto Rico Sugar Company found it possible and profitable to grind some of its Dominican cane in its Puerto Rican factories. The West Indies Sugar Corporation owned directly or through subsidiaries warehouses at the port of Santiago in Cuba having a capacity of approximately 100,000 bags of sugar. The same corporation owned the lighters which shipped its sugar from its Dominican factories to the port of San Pedro de Macoris. For the operation of its properties it owned a dairy herd and approximately 21,000 head of cattle. If the large plantation of Cantero's day in 1860 was a monster, the large plantation of 1942 was a colossus.

There were two casualties of this American mode of production. The first was the British West Indian sugar industry. Barbados was typical. The land in plantations totalled 52,000 acres out of a total of 66,000 arable acres. Barbados was therefore a plantation economy. But what sort of plantation was this to compete with the American juggernaut? Of the agricultural holdings, less than 300 were over 20 acres, over 200 were more than 100 acres, and only 9 were over 500 acres in size. British Guiana came closest in the British West Indies to the American pattern of concentration. But even there, the largest plantation, Diamond, was just over 7,000 acres. Three more were over 4,000 acres, while 17 barely had 1,000 acres.

The second casualty of the American system of production

was the *colono* or small cane farmer. It is true that in Trinidad their numbers increased from 3,712 growing 17,500 tons of cane in 1896 to 20,000 growing 375,000 tons of cane (half the island's output) in 1928. But the situation was radically different in Puerto Rico. Nearly 75 per cent of the sugar cane farms in Puerto Rico had less than 10 acres in cane; these farms represented merely 6 per cent of the total acreage in cane. Farms with less than 25 acres in cane were 86 per cent of all sugar farms, but only 12 per cent of the cane area, while they produced 7½ per cent of the total cane. The estimated yield per acre of these 25-acre farms was 20 tons in 1935, as compared with the average of 30 tons for the whole island. A study of 130 *colono* farms ranging from an average acreage in cane of less than 16 for small farms and less than 206 for large, revealed that the average was 30 tons per acre for all, 29 for small farms, 34 for those of middle size, and 30 for the larger farms. If the *colono* held his own in yield, he more than held his own in costs of production. The United States Tariff Commission, in a comparative study of 125 *colono* farms in Puerto Rico harvesting an area of 20,000 acres as against the large plantation, found that *colono* cane cost $4.79 per ton as against $5.60 per ton for plantation cane.

But the *colono* could not withstand the American invasion. Between 1910 and 1935 in Puerto Rico the acreage of farms of 20–99 acres declined 11 per cent, and of farms of 100 to 499 acres nearly 22 per cent. As a Puerto Rican writer pleaded: 'the small *colono* is the romantic figure of individualism in an industry controlled by a handful of corporations or powerful partnerships. While farming to the sugar-cane corporation is merely a manufacturing business, it is a way of living for most *colonos*. The *colonos* constitute an element through whom a better distribution of part of the large income produced by the sugar industry is obtained.'

The large plantation was paralleled by the large factory. Centralisation in the factory paralleled centralisation in the field. Puerto Rican sugar production increased from 60,000 tons in 1898 to over a million in 1934 before the crop restriction programme. In 1898 there were 345 mills in the island, with an average daily capacity of 36 tons of cane each. In 1939 there were 41 modern mills, varying from Guanica with a capacity of 150,000 tons to Pellejas with a capacity of only 1,400; the average for the island was 28,000 tons in 1935. In 1898 each mill in the island ground the cane of only seven producers as compared with an average of 317 producers per mill in 1939. The four American sugar companies produced almost half of the total output in 1935.

American capital accelerated a similar centralisation in the Dominican Republic. The West Indies Sugar Corporation and the South Porto Rico Company together owned six of the 14 mills in that island; the combined production of these six mills represented 75 per cent of Dominican production in 1939–1940. The largest mill, Romana, owned by the South Porto Rico Sugar Company, produced 109,000 tons; Barahona, owned by the West Indies Sugar Corporation, 64,000.

But as centralisation had proceeded furthest in Cuba during the slavery regime, so, stimulated by the flow of American capital, twentieth-century Cuba was well in advance of the other areas. The 2,000 factories in 1860 had been reduced to 158 in the 1930's; where the production was 447,000 tons in 1860, it was over five million in 1925 at the height of the sugar boom and 2,720,000 in 1939 under crop restriction. Production, centered in the western provinces of Havana and Matanzas under the Spaniards, shifted under the Americans to the eastern provinces of Camaguey and Oriente. Of the mills in the thirties, one-fourth were located in Oriente and one-seventh in Camaguey. The Oriente mills produced more than one-third of the total crop, Camaguey's nearly one-third. Together the two provinces produced more than the combined output of the other four provinces. Camaguey, with less than half the number of mills as Santa Clara province, surpassed Santa Clara's output by more than one-fifth.

Of the 158 mills in Cuba, fifty-eight or more than one-third were American-owned. These mills produced 55 per cent of Cuban production. The average per American mill was 157,000 tons of sugar as compared with an average of 104,000 for the whole island; that is to say, the average of the American-owned mill was more than one-half greater than the island average. Even so, the picture of American domination is incomplete. Many American companies controlled more than one mill. Thus the Cuban Atlantic Company owned eight mills which together produced 195,000 tons; the Cuban American Company six mills which had a combined output of 138,000 tons. The mills of the West Indies Sugar Corporation produced 68,000 tons. Cantero's monsters of 1860 made a poor show in comparison with their modern counterparts. Thus Vertientes, with restricted output, produced 71,000 tons in 1939; Stewart 47,000; Moron 46,000; Jaronu 48,000; Delicias 54,000.

Here again the British West Indies could not keep up with the pace set by the Americans. Barbados and Jamaica seemed not to be living in the twentieth century. In 1939 Barbados produced 133,000 tons of sugar in 32 factories, an average of barely 4,000 tons per factory. Greater progress had been made elsewhere. St. Kitts had only one factory, to which all sugar producing areas were connected by a railway encircling the whole island; the normal capacity of the factory was 20,000 tons. Antigua had two factories—the larger produced 19,000 tons in 1929, the smaller 3,500. In 1928 there were 21 factories in British Guiana manufacturing what 64 had done thirty years before. The Trinidad average per factory was 12,800 tons; Trinidad had the largest factory in the British West Indies, the Usine Ste. Madeleine, with a capacity of 41,000 tons in 1939.

Sugar cultivation and manufacture on the scale indicated as a result of American penetration obviously called for a colossal investment of capital which only the United States could afford. The United States Tariff Commission estimated American investment in Cuba in the thirties at $666 million, in the Dominican Republic at $41 million, in Haiti at $10 million. Of these figures sugar represented more than one-third of the Cuban investment, though the money-value declined from $544 million in 1929 to $240 million in 1936. 90 per cent of the American investment in the Dominican Republic was in sugar, over 50 per cent in Haiti. Another estimate put at $30 million the American investment in the sugar industry of Puerto Rico.

The individual American corporation represented a large investment. The Cuban American Sugar Company had a capitalisation of over a million shares in common and preferred stock and total assets of $36 million, of which more than half was in land, buildings, railroad, equipment. The West Indies Sugar Corporation with its interests in Cuba and the Dominican Republic, had a capitalisation of close to a million shares and total assets of nearly $30 million, of which over 60 per cent was in land, buildings, equipment. The Punta Alegre Company, with assets of $19½ million, had over 75 per cent in plants, railroads, land. The Cuban Atlantic Company had assests of $9¾ million; the Manati Sugar Company $8¼ million; the Guantanamo Sugar Company nearly $6 million. Behind the United Fruit Company's sugar operations stood total company assets of $186 million.

The Puerto Rican situation was similar. Central Aguirre Associates, with a capitalisation of over $3½ million in common stock, had total assets of $19½ million, of which half was in plants and properties. The Eastern Sugar Company, with 250,000 shares in common and preferred stock, had total assets of over $13 million, with over 67 per cent in lands and equipment. The Fajardo Sugar Company had a capitalisation of over $6 million and assets of $14½ million, of which nearly half was in plant and properties. The South Porto Rico Company had nearly 750,000 shares of common stock plus $5 million of preferred stock; its total assets amounted to nearly $30 million, of which nearly half represented real property, plant and equipment.

Comparable data for the British West Indies are scarce, but we have sufficient to show that large scale investment was again involved. Where in 1897 the capital invested in the Trinidad sugar industry was estimated at $12 million, an estimate in 1935 put the investment in the British Guiana sugar industry at $26 million on an average of the six-year period 1929 to 1934, and after allowing for depreciation.

Contrary to what the West India Royal Commission had opined in 1897, this large investment yielded large profits. Of Puerto Rico Esteban Bird has written:

'From 1920 to 1935 Central Aguirre, South Porto Rico, and Fajardo Sugar Company have paid cash dividends of practically $50,000,000 and slightly over $10,500,000 in stock dividends or total dividends paid of around $60,500,000. The surplus earnings of these three sugar mills for the same period amount to slightly over $20,500,000. Altogether, therefore, these three companies alone have paid dividends and have accumulated a surplus amounting to over $80,000,000. The average combined annual returns on capital since 1922 has been 19 per cent. During 1928 the average return was as high as 31 per cent but the average return in four years out of the thirteen years period has been over 25 per cent and these companies, on various occasions, have declared stock dividends of 100 per cent and more.'

The Diffies, in their study, *Porto Rico, a Broken Pledge,* stated that the three largest sugar companies paid dividends ranging from 4 to 115 per cent over a period of 20 years. Diffie's figures were challenged by Gayer, Homan and James in their study of the Puerto Rican sugar industry in 1938, who charged him with an inadequate interpretation of stock adjustments. Their own figures speak eloquently enough. Total earnings of the four American companies from 1923 to 1935 averaged 12 per cent upon investors' equity. Deducting the taxes and profits on the Dominican cane of the South Porto Rico Company, the earnings accruing to investors on strictly Puerto Rican operations exceeded 10 per cent. Central Aguirre earned over 12 per cent after income tax deductions; South Porto Rico 11 per cent; Fajardo 7 per cent. In the bonanza year when according to the Diffies, South Porto Rico paid 115 per cent and Fajardo 110 per cent, actual cash dividends were 15 per cent and 40 per cent on par value of stock. It would seem that even with these reduced estimates investors had nothing to squawk about.

Detailed figures published annually in Farr's *Manual of Sugar Companies* confirm this view. From 1919 to 1920 Central Aguirre paid dividends ranging from 5 to 60 per cent. In 1920, on the $20 par value stock, 70 per cent was paid, 37½ per cent in 1921, 30 per cent from 1922 to 1928. In addition an extra cash dividend of 25 per cent was declared in 1923, and 5 per cent in 1927 and 1928, plus an extra stock dividend of 20 per cent in 1925. Dividends from 1929 to 1941 were 7½ per cent, plus extra stock dividend of 5 per cent in 1928 and cash of 5 per cent in 1936 and 1937.

For the six years 1908 to 1913 Fajardo paid average dividends of 7 per cent with 10 per cent in 1908 and 1910. From 1916 to 1921 the dividend increased to 10 per cent, with extra cash dividends of 10 per cent in 1916 and 30 per cent in 1920 and a stock dividend of 70 per cent in the latter year. From 1921 to 1923 the dividend was 5 per cent, from 1923 to 1929 10 per cent. None was paid thereafter until 1935, when 5 per cent was paid. On the new $20 par value stock 7½ per cent was paid in 1936, 20 per cent in 1937 and 1938, 10 per cent in 1939. Between 1923 and 1925 extra cash dividends were paid in addition on the old $100 par value common stock.

The Cuban picture admittedly was different, but after 1938, as a result of the depression and the United States tariff which favoured American capital in the sugar industry of Puerto Rico, the Philippines, Hawaii and the mainland, rather than American capital in Cuba and the Dominican Republic. But the Cuban American Sugar Company paid preferred dividends, except for two years, from 1905 to 1929, averaging 7 per cent from 1915 to 1929; after 1929 payments were irregular. The Cuban Atlantic Sugar Company paid a dividend of 15 per cent in 1937 and 10 per cent in 1940. Vertientes-Camaguey Company paid 4 per cent in 1940 and 1941; the West Indies Sugar Corporation 5 per cent on preferred stock in 1941 and none on common.

These figures tell a sad tale when compared with the dividends of the Amsterdam Trading Company on its sugar, rubber, coffee and other tropical plantations in Java—1924, 40 per cent; 1925, 30 per cent; 1926–1929, 16 per cent; 1930, 15 per cent; 1931–1933, 5 per cent; 1934, 4 per cent; 1935, 8 per cent; 1936, 16 per cent; 1937, 25 per cent; 1938, 17 per cent. They are higher, however, than the average annual profit of slightly over 2 per cent estimated by a British Guiana Commission in 1936 and than the average of 6 per cent reported for the British West Indies. But it must be remembered that the United States Tariff Commission in 1919 had estimated that only 43.3 per cent of the production in Puerto Rico, 48.6 per cent in Hawaii, little or none in Louisiana, and 56.8 per cent in the beet sugar industry would have survived free trade.

The large aggregation of land, buildings, railroads and equipment represented by an American sugar corporation in the twentieth century called for a corresponding concentration of labour. What Cantero would have written had he seen the plantation of the thirties one can only conjecture. Of all the workers in Cuba engaged in sugar production American corporations controlled nearly 60 per cent. The average number of workers per mill in the whole island was 3,200; for American mills it was 5,150. The average per American mill in Camaguey province was 6,880. The Vertientes and Estrella plantations employed 10,000 workers each; Delicias, Manati and Preston 10,500 each. The plantations owned by the Cuban Atlantic Company employed an average of 5,570 workers; the Cuban American Company an average of 5,800; the Punta Alegre Company 5,250.

But the nineteenth century still survived. The gigantic expansion of the Cuban sugar industry after the wars of independence, coupled with the loss of manpower in those wars and the cessation of the Negro slave trade, required the importation of labour. This was true also, though on a much smaller scale, of the Dominican Republic. Both countries turned to the Caribbean islands, those like Haiti and Jamaica, and lesser British areas like St. Kitts and St. Vincent, where the labour supply was overabundant. This importation was called 'swallow' immigration in Cuba; the majority of the workers would come only for the sugar season, after which they would return home. Not all of them, however: Cuba and the Dominican Republic found themselves threatened with a swarm of black alien labourers, on a lower cultural and economic level than the native Cuban or Dominican, white, coloured or black.

Between 1913 and 1924 Cuba received 217,000 labourers from Haiti, Jamaica and Puerto Rico; in the single year 1920, as many as 63,000 from Haiti and Jamaica. In 1931 there were 80,000 Haitians resident in Cuba. The Cuban working class demanded the repatriation of the immigrants, which the planters were less unwilling to concede in the depression. 30,000 Haitians were repatriated in 1936 and 1937. The average annual exodus from Jamaica, largely to Cuba, was 10,000 for the half-century before 1935; in the five years ending in 1935 approximately 31,000 were repatriated at the expense of the British Government. The Dominican Republic resorted to speedier and more drastic methods; a wholesale slaughter of Haitians took place in 1937, straining relations between the two governments to breaking point. But despite the massacre and subsequent repatriation, there were still 60,000 Haitians resident in the Dominican Republic in 1937, and that government resorted to the familiar Latin American practice and insisted that in all employment a certain percentage —fixed at 70 per cent— must be Dominican.

Latifundia, gigantic mill, extensive railroads, large labour force, colossal investment—all added up to monoculture. Sugar was as much king in the first fifty years of the twentieth century as it had ever been in Caribbean history. It was American capital that enthroned sugar in Cuba. From 1902 to 1939 sugar constituted more than 80 per cent of the island's total exports. Less than half in 1902, the proportion was more than nine-tenths in the boom year 1920. There was a corresponding decline in the contribution of the tobacco industry to the economy. Tobacco, the field *par excellence* of small white farmers, represented 40 per cent of Cuba's exports in 1902, only 10 per cent in 1939. For the whole period 1902–1939 the average proportion of tobacco in the total exports was less than 14 per cent.

Under American rule after 1898 sugar regularly constituted more than 50 per cent of the exports of Puerto Rico; in 1939–1940 it represented over 40 per cent of total exports. Coffee had been the staple of Spanish Puerto Rico. American Puerto Rico actually imported coffee. Coffee declined from nearly 5 per cent of total exports in 1920 to less than half of one per cent in 1939. During the same period tobacco exports declined from 20 per cent of the total to slightly more than 5 per cent.

Sugar was the largest single employer, employing about 20 per cent of all workers reporting a gainful occupation. Almost half of all the agricultural labourers over ten years of age worked in some aspect of the sugar industry. This was more than twice the number employed by the next largest industry, coffee, three times the number employed in tobacco, and more than the workers employed in the coffee, tobacco, fruit, dairy and stock-raising industries combined. Whereas 100 acres in sugar provided employment for 46 persons, the same acreage in other crops provided employment for only 31 persons. The acreage in sugar in Puerto Rico increased more than fourfold between 1899 and 1935. In 1899 sugar represented less than 20 per cent of the cultivated land, about 40 per cent in 1940. The value of sugar farms was about 67 per cent of all the farms in the island. From 1926 to 1935 the value of the sugar crop was on the average over five times larger than the tobacco crop and nearly eight times larger than the value of the coffee crop. The value of the sugar cane crop was never below three times as large as the value of the tobacco or the coffee crop during these ten years, while in some years it was 32 times the value of the coffee crop and 45 times the value of the tobacco crop.

For the decade 1929–1938 sugar constituted nearly 67 per cent of the exports of the Dominican Republic. Between 1903 and

1939 the output increased nearly ten times. Under the stimulus of American capital, sugar exports in Haiti increased from an average of 3 per cent of total exports for the decade 1916–1926 to 14 per cent in 1938 and nearly 20 per cent in 1939.

Small as the sugar industry was in the British and French islands, it occupied an equally dominant position in the economy. In the British West Indies 33 per cent of the population of St. Kitts and Antigua was directly employed by the sugar industry, 20 per cent of the population of Barbados, 17 per cent of British Guiana's, 12 per cent of St. Lucia's, 10 per cent of Trinidad's. With the ancillary occupations which have their whole origin in some phase of the sugar industry and its needs, and the families dependent on these sugar workers for support, the Olivier Sugar Commission of 1928 estimated that the extent to which the population of the British West Indies would be affected by the abandonment of sugar was as follows: the entire population of St. Kitts and Antigua, 67 per cent of the population of Barbados, 50 per cent of British Guiana's, 33 per cent of Trinidad's, 25 per cent of St. Lucia's, 10 per cent of Jamaica's. Eighty per cent of the cultivated area in Antigua was planted to cane, 50 per cent in Barbados, 67 per cent in St. Kitts, 33 per cent in British Guiana, 20 per cent in Jamaica, 10 per cent in Trinidad, 67 per cent in Martinique, 50 per cent in Guadeloupe, which depended on sugar and by-products for 60 per cent of its exports.

Little change had taken place between the West India Royal Commission of 1897 and the Olivier Sugar Commission of 1928. Sugar and by-products constituted 97 per cent of total Barbadian exports in 1896 and 95 per cent in 1928. The percentage in Antigua was $94\frac{1}{2}$ per cent in 1896 and 97 per cent in 1928; in St. Kitts-Nevis $96\frac{1}{2}$ per cent in 1896 and 86 per cent in 1928 when Nevis had practically abandoned sugar. In Jamaica it remained the same, 18 per cent. But the percentage declined in these two years in British Guiana from $70\frac{1}{2}$ per cent to 60 per cent; in St. Lucia from 74 to 45; in Trinidad, where oil had been discovered, from 57 to 20; in St. Vincent from 42 to 9.

The 1897 West India Royal Commission had called for agricultural diversification as a matter of the highest policy and the greatest urgency. The Commission recognised that 'the representatives of the sugar industry in the West Indies have had special means of influencing the Governments of the different Colonies, and of putting pressure on the Home Government to secure attention to their views and wishes. Their interests have been to a very great extent limited to the sugar industry, and they have seldom turned their attention to any other cultivation except when the sugar industry ceased to be profitable.' The Commission continued: 'No reform affords so good a prospect for the permanent welfare in the future of the West Indies as the settlement of the labouring population on the land as small peasant proprietors.' The 1928 Commission explained the failure to take action on this recommedation: if the sugar planters 'encouraged action which in their belief, must tend to diminish their labour supply, they would be cutting away the branch upon which they sit'.

By 1928, therefore, precisely nothing had been accomplished. When the largest plantation in British Guiana was once asked about the possibility of land settlement of farmers on some of its lands, the manager wrote in reply:

'We have about 1,000 acres of land uncultivated which will eventually be suitable for growing canes ... We cannot afford to part with any of this land. In fact, we are getting near the end of our tether as regards expansion. The estate is not prepared to lease any portion of these lands to cane-farmers or settlers.'

Even in overcrowded Barbados in 1928 there was much land which was eminently suitable for growing fruit and vegetables, and no doubt these would have been grown 'had it not been deemed to be in the interests of sugar cane cultivation to abstain from encouraging such cultivation'. The Olivier Commission drew attention to the contrast between the prosperity of those colonies in which a peasantry existed and the degradation and squalor of those in which the lower classes were labourers on the sugar plantations.

The 1897 Commission had warned that 'so long as they remain dependent upon sugar their position can never be sound or secure ... Where sugar can be completely, or very largely, re-placed by other industries, the Colonies in question will be in a much sounder position, both politically and economically, when they have ceased to depend wholly, or to a very great extent, upon the continued prosperity of a single industry'. For this reason the Olivier Commission of 1928 refused to recommend the revival of the sugar industry in those places where it had died a natural or artificial death. Elsewhere the situation remained as described by Esteban Bird for Puerto Rico in 1935: 'sugar is everything and everything is sugar; it is the goddess that reigns over practically one-third of the private wealth.' What two students of the situation in Puerto Rico have said was applicable to the whole area: 'A significant change in the economy of the Island through the introduction and commercialisation of new crops is very doubtful under present physical, economic and political conditions.'

Chapter Twenty-Six

Twentieth-Century Colonialism

A land of flattering statistics and distressing realities—Munoz Marin's famous definition of Puerto Rico in the thirties is really a definition of the entire Caribbean area. Lloyd George called the British West Indies the slums of the Empire. Professor Macmillan of South Africa wrote that a social and economic study of the West Indian islands is necessarily a study of poverty. This was the achievement of colonialism in the twentieth century.

The Colonial Secretary of Trinidad and Tobago said, at the height of disturbances in the island in 1937, that 'an industry has no right to pay dividends at all until it pays a fair wage to labour and gives the labourer decent conditions'. He was referring specifically to the 72 cents average daily wage for unskilled labour in the oilfields of Trinidad, while oil companies declared dividends of 45 and 30 per cent, and while the profits for 1935–1936 were four times the wages bill. If oil wages were so low, the situation was far worse in sugar and in agriculture generally. A commission investigating disturbances in Barbados in 1937 repeated the Trinidad Colonial Secretary's warning:

'We have been impressed by the high dividends earned by many trading concerns in the island and the comfortable salaries and bonuses paid to the higher grades of employees in business and agriculture. If the whole community were prosperous and enjoyed a comfortable standard of living, high dividends might be defensible, but when these are only possible on the basis of low wages the time has clearly come for a reconsideration of the fundamental conditions and organisation of industry ... A fundamental change in the division of earnings between the employer and his employees is essential if hatred and bitterness are to be removed from the minds of the majority of employees.'

The Secretary of State placed the following figures for daily wages in the sugar industry before Parliament in 1938 for the unskilled sugar worker: St. Vincent, 28 cents; Antigua, 28–36 cents; Barbados and St. Lucia, 30 cents; Grenada, 30–48 cents; Trinidad, 35; St. Kitts-Nevis, 32–36 cents; Jamaica, 48–60 cents. The minimum wage of a field labourer in the Cuban sugar industry was 80 cents a day. In Puerto Rico average actual weekly earnings in 1935–1936 were $3.75 in the field and $6.78 in the factory. The most common daily wage was in the 75–99 cents a day bracket; this was so for half of the field workers and one-third of the factory workers. This wage in itself represented a substantial increase over the wage paid three years before. Whereas in 1932–1933 40 per cent of the field workers and 10 per cent of the factory workers received less than 75 cents a day, in 1935–1936 only 11 per cent of the field workers and 2 per cent of the factory workers fell below this level. On the Lafayette Plantation, run by the Puerto Rico Reconstruction Administration as a model, a study made by the School of Tropical Medicine indicated an annual income for workers of less than $120. The Administration concluded: 'the sugar industry does not satisfy the requirements of the economic life of the island and should be adjusted in order to meet the needs of the people.'

Sugar set the pattern for the whole agricultural economy. A 1939 study of nearly 6,000 families with over 34,000 members in various coffee, fruit and tobacco regions in Puerto Rico revealed a mean daily wage rate for all areas of 60 cents and an annual income per worker of less than $100 for 60 per cent of the farm labourers investigated, while the remaining 40 per cent earned less than $150. In urban areas the workers were no better off. The Puerto Rican needlework industry, famous for its high quality products, paid wages in 1934 of 12½ cents per hour, while home workers earned less than 4 cents an hour; the industry gave employment to 65,000 persons in factories and homes.

The workers' plight was aggravated by unemployment and underemployment. The sugar industry provides intensive employment during the cutting and grinding season from January to June, which is followed by a 'dead' season when large numbers are out of work. The drop in employment in the 'dead' season is as much as one-half in the field and two-thirds in the factory as compared with the months of peak employment. Gayer and his associates in fact noticed a tendency towards a progressive increase in the swing of seasonal variations, almost certainly to be associated with mechanisation and labour-saving devices. The peak month of the year 1934–1935 showed declines of 16 and 13 per cent respectively, in field payrolls and field workers as compared with the peak month of the year 1927–1928; the corresponding figures for the month of slackest employment were 43 and 45 per cent, respectively.

As a result of this intermittent employment only 60 per cent of full time was actually worked in the field in Puerto Rico and 80 per cent in the factory. A special study of conditions on a sugar-cane plantation found that labourers in sugar cane planting in Puerto Rico worked on an average 34 weeks in the year, only 10 per cent of the unskilled and 40 per cent of the skilled workers finding employment during the whole year. The percentage of workers in the lower wage bracket tended to increase sharply during the 'dead' season. During the peak month 50 per cent of the field workers received 75–99 cents a day, during the 'dead' season 75 per cent. As Gayer and his colleagues wrote: 'Labour income during the slack season consequently is adversely affected in two ways: by the release of large numbers of workers from employment, and by the fact that those workers who remain on the payroll are largely in the lower-income brackets.' In the words of a Puerto Rican scholar, Dr Pico, 'The sugar plantation economy, based on the seasonal employment of thousands of inadequately paid *peones*, does not offer any hope for the amelioration of social and economic conditions; rather it aims to perpetuate the present deplorable situation'.

Coffee, fruit and tobacco workers were not better off. The study in Puerto Rico already referred to states: 'The families affected by unemployment are nearly one-eighth of the total number of gainful workers in the surveyed area. In judging the situation it should be kept in mind that this unemployment occurs among Puerto Rico Reconstruction Administration workers' families and precisely during the months in which the employment rate was highest.'

In Jamaica in 1935 at least 11 per cent of the wage-earning population were continuously unemployed, and it was the considered opinion of the Labour Adviser sent out in 1938 from England to report on labour conditions in the British islands that 'the present prospect (in Kingston) is of a body of some thousands of permanently unemployed maintained by heavy expenditure on what are really relief works'. In 1935 nearly half the wage-earning population of Jamaica obtained only intermittent employment, and both government and private employers adopted the policy of 'rotational employment'—a worker worked for a fortnight and then was discharged to make way for another. In Grenada some employers provided five days' work per week, others no more than two. The average number of days worked per week in Trinidad was four.

In 1928 the sugar planters of the British West Indies tried to impress upon the Olivier Sugar Commission that it was the workers who refused to work; the vicious habit of drinking inferior rum on Sundays was responsible for abstention from work on Mondays, and the labour problem, in the opinion of one witness, could be mitigated by proper attention to the quality of excisable liquor. Other witnesses, however, blamed the old industrial theory, 'still manifestly affecting much of the West Indian estate management, that it is necessary to maintain a constant supply of cheap labour, and that, therefore, no labourer must be too highly paid or given too much employment'. The Commission remarked that there was no difficulty in securing workers in the sugar factories or in the oilfields or bauxite mines, and concluded that 'the field work is conducted upon a fallacious industrial theory that it is better dealt with laxly and without pressure on the lowest subsistence wages, whereas in the factory the economy of full and continuous work is obvious and dominates practice'. In 1930 an Economic Investigation Committee in British Guiana classified the majority of manual workers in the colony as casual workers and declared: 'The policy of the estates has been to maintain, or even to increase slightly, the number of persons employed, *while reducing the total amount paid in wages* and the number of days work per week allotted to each labourer.'

The situation could have been relieved if an active and deliberate policy had been pursued of settling workers on idle agricultural lands and encouraging the diversification of the agricultural economy. But we have already seen that the sugar planters were opposed to this, though it had behind it not only common sense but the force of authority in the form of the recommendations of the Commissions of 1897 and 1928 in the British West Indies.

Yet in an address to the Legislative Council in 1935 the Administrator of St. Vincent could only say that the government was 'studying' the means of extending land settlement. Since 1899 it had been studying it and had purchased 8,250 acres, while the Administrator saw no easy solution of the difficulty. In 1935 more than half of the privately-owned land and most of the best cultivated areas were still owned by some 30 plantations, while of the 2,763 peasants in a population of 55,000, 95 per cent owned holdings of less than 10 acres. In Barbados 75 per cent of the holdings were less than one acre. In Jamaica, more than half of the total area was comprised in 1930 in less than 1,400 properties, each averaging 1,000 acres. The census figures of 1931 in Trinidad and Tobago showed that the proportion of independent cultivators to landless labourers was 1:4, or 8,762 landowners and 38,822 labourers; just over one per cent of the 47,000 persons actively engaged on the land owned half the area under cultivation, comprising units of more than 100 acres. The outstanding example of land settlement in the British colonies was the rice industry of British Guiana, which increased from 29,000 acres in 1926 to 44,000 in 1928 and 62,000 in 1937, enabling the colony to supply to a large extent the needs of the British West Indian islands. As the British Guiana Small Farmers Committee of 1930 warned landlords: 'Sooner or later it will become necessary for the country to pronounce upon the propriety of private owners keeping lands abandoned, unproductive and entirely uncared for, when on the other hand, the economic salvation of the Colony is demanding that all suitable arable lands be put in, and kept under, cultivation.'

The Olivier Sugar Commission paid particular attention to this question of land settlement in 1928 and came up with the following conclusion: 'We must record our considered opinion that it is impossible to expect any sound permanent development of such cultivation unless steps are taken to enable the small cultivators to obtain and possess their land in freehold.' The land offered should be sold in small plots, five or seven acres as the Guiana Small Farmers Committee recommended, with no initial down payment and the cost extended over a number of years at low rates of interest. The land put up for sale should not be the worst land in the country and the question of the suitability of the area for sugar cultivation should not be taken into consideration.

Too often peasant land was inferior land requiring arduous cultivation, in inaccessible places far from railways and markets and lacking roads. The Soil Survey Report of the United States Department of Agriculture drew the following picture of Puerto Rico:

'In many countries similar land would be considered too rough and stony for agriculture, but the population pressure is so great in Puerto Rico that thousands of people are forced into the steep hills in order to raise subsistence crops to supplement the wages received from sugar *centrals*, tobacco ribbing shops, and other industries ... Because of the population pressure, subsistence farmers have been driven to the poorer lands to develop their farms, and a large total area of extremely steep land covered by shallow soils furnishes a meagre living for the people.'

But population pressure was not the only explanation. It was basically the political pressure which the sugar planters and corporations were able to apply. In 1924 the Department of Agriculture of Puerto Rico pointed out that on the whole the resident labourers on the sugar plantations had almost no land of their own while labourers in the coffee and tobacco districts quite generally had an opportunity to raise some food. Of 247,000 workers engaged in Puerto Rican agriculture, less than 20 per cent owned the land that they tilled.

The Secretary of State for the Colonies in England was telling Parliament proudly of £22,988 spent on land settlement in Jamaica in 1937–1938, representing 6,390 acres of land. Just then the Jamaicans rioted. The Government of Jamaica at once decided to spend up to £500,000 on land settlement, and subsequently raised the figure to £650,000. The Puerto Rican law of 1900 limiting farms to a maximum of 500 acres remained unenforced on the statute books, openly violated, trangressors unpunished. Under Governor Tugwell, $7 million were appropriated for the purchase of 200,000 acres of sugar cane land owned by corporations, dividing them into lots of 500 acres or less and selling them on 40-year terms. Up to 1942 not a cent had been spent.

This is the origin of the salt-fish, tinned-milk tradition in the Caribbean. Imports of food were responsible for one-seventh of Haiti's imports, one-fourth of Jamaica's. Jamaica spent over a million dollars on imported fish in 1936 while two of its island dependencies existed on the export of salt to Canada for curing the fish. In a population of nearly two million in Puerto Rico, only 600 professionals derived a regular livelihood from fishing; the annual catch was worth $200,000. The Trinidadian labourer depended on outside sources for 80 per cent of his food. A Barbados Commission reported that in recent years the cultivation of food crops had been so curtailed that the price of locally grown vegetables was often so high as to be beyond the modest means of the labourer, who was thereby reduced to a diet of imported rice and cornmeal. Puerto Rico bought approximately 10 per cent of all food exported by the United States, more than any foreign country except Canada and Britain. It was the second largest market for American wheatgrowers and millers; it bought more rice from the United States than all other countries combined: one-half of the rice exported from the United States and one-fourth of all the rice produced in the United States. It was the third largest customer of United States lard.

Here, again, sugar was everything and everything was sugar. According to the American Chamber of Commerce of Cuba, which believed in exported sugar and imported food, one acre of land planted in sugar cane in the United States reduced United States exports to Cuba from three acres of cotton, and one acre of sugar beet reduced American exports from three acres of corn: 'the decline in our imports of Cuban sugar from 1928 to 1932 was accompanied by a reduction in the Cuban market for

American farm products for more than 800,000 acres of land.' In Puerto Rico the sugar advocates pleaded that an acre of sugar cane would buy, at retail prices, about four acres of sweet potatoes, yams, or white potatoes, about five acres of coffee, about six acres of dried beans, about nine acres of pigeon peas or rice, about twenty-one and a half acres of corn. They argued that the single item of wages paid to sugar workers in growing one acre of sugar cane in 1938 would have bought the crops from two acres planted to any other local food crop; it would have bought three acres of dried beans, four acres of pigeon peas and rice, six acres of corn. They explained that 'the people of Puerto Rico seem to prefer certain food crops obtained from the States'. They paid no attention at all to the effect of the high tariff which prevented Puerto Rico from buying in less expensive markets; the extra cost has been estimated at 75 per cent in the case of rice, 40 per cent for wheat flour, nearly 80 per cent for dried beans, over 24 per cent for codfish. The argument that 'export commodities in Puerto Rico ... generally yield higher incomes per acre than most of the food crops produced for the local market' missed the whole point —higher incomes for whom?

The condition of the worker necessarily reflected these harsh realities of colonialism. Evidence of malnutrition abounded, shocking a medical visitor from the Dutch East Indies who visited Trinidad in 1935. The weekly budget of the Barbadian labourer was less than two dollars; of this food cost him seven cents a day. The Barbadian labourer was fed worse than a gaolbird; he could not afford milk in his tea; said the planters, he did not like milk!

A special study of a small Puerto Rican town revealed a daily expenditure for a family of six of twenty-three cents on food. The Puerto Rican rural labourer had an income of twelve cents a day for all necessities of life—according to Bird, four cents more than the cost of feeding a hog in the United States. Between 67 per cent of the income in the sugar regions and 80 per cent in the coffee, fruit and tobacco districts was spent on food: 'a sure indication,' says one study, 'of the inadequacy of an income of which such a high proportion has to be devoted to mere subsistence.' Most rural families were heavily in debt; the extent of petty larceny in Trinidad, representing mostly thefts of food, was enormous.

Food was not only insufficient, it was deficient—rice and red beans were the staple everywhere, representing a predominance of carbohydrates and an absence of fats and proteins. In Puerto Rican sugar conditions, most people had only black coffee or coffee with milk for breakfast, codfish and vegetables for lunch, rice and beans for dinner. A study of 884 rural families in Haiti revealed that 15 per cent ate only one meal a day, 45 per cent ate two meals, while for those who ate three times a day, lunch consisted of a modest piece of cassava or boiled banana. Over 10 per cent had only black coffee for breakfast, eggs were eaten in the morning by only eight families, in the evening by only seven. Some families went two or three months without meat, others spent between two and four cents a week on fish, fresh or dried. A Haitian soldier got 15 cents a day for food, prisoners 10 cents, inmates of public charitable institutions 6–8 cents. A commission of the Foreign Policy Association sent to investigate the problems of Cuba in 1935 estimated the cost of the food needed by a Cuban adult male for one year at $38, a figure far too high for the income of the majority of labourers.

The daily consumption of fresh milk in Kingston, Jamaica, with its 30,000 children of school age, was one-fifteenth of a quart per head; the Jamaican politicians in the age of colonialism said that the Negroes preferred condensed milk. The average monthly consumption of fresh meat per head of population in the capital was one pound, which included the middle and upper classes. As a committee appointed to consider and report on the question of nutrition in Barbados in 1936 stated: 'The diet of the average worker can be classed at the best only as a maintenance diet, and ... there is no reason to doubt that many households live on the borderland of extreme poverty.'

The results of this deficient diet were devastating. Measurement of 15,500 Puerto Rican labourers, 16 per cent of them coloured, revealed that they were shorter and lighter than American army recruits or American adults. Malaria, hookworm, tuberculosis, venereal diseases, yellow fever killed off the population like flies. An official picture of Trinidad in 1937 described every adult over twenty years of age as affected by deficiency diseases, and the working life of the population reduced by at least one-half: 'a condition of lethargy pervaded the whole community, which was only broken on festive occasions or in times of disorder'. A Rockefeller campaign against hookworm in Dominica was abandoned in the face of the apathy of the local government.

Hookworm, largely a consequence of poor sanitation and the absence of shoes, wrought havoc with the population and was a major factor in reducing efficiency. The percentage of infestation in rural districts in Trinidad varied from 79 to 98; in certain areas of Barbados it was 69, and in Puerto Rico 83. Of the families investigated in Puerto Rico on a sugar plantation, over 40 per cent had no sanitary conveniences of any kind in their homes; the percentage was over 50 in the coffee, fruit and tobacco regions. The investigators on the Lafayette sugar plantation observed that 75 per cent of the children from 1–4 years of age, 60 per cent of the children from 5–9 years, and nearly 50 per cent of the children from 10–14 years did not wear shoes; the percentage wearing shoes in all ages above 15 years fluctuated from 60 to 69, except in the age group 65 years and over in which it was 56.

In the battle between man and mosquito, the mosquito was victorious. The death rate from malaria was enormously high; in Puerto Rico an average of 30,253 cases was reported during 1932–1936. Sugar was again the principal culprit; one of the favourite breeding grounds of the mosquito was irrigated sugar lands. 'Only too frequently,' says a Puerto Rican study, 'houses have been built in places where the soil is very poor, or swampy, so they should not encroach on the sugar cane plantations. The information gathered indicates that more than one-fifth of the houses have swampy surroundings.'

After malaria, tuberculosis. Tuberculosis was the principal cause of death in Puerto Rico for the five-year period 1932–1936, being responsible for 15 per cent of all deaths from all causes, a rate almost unequalled in any part of the world. A comparison with the five rural states in the United States registering the highest death rates from tuberculosis gave these results: the Puerto Rican rate was more than one-half greater than that of Arizona, more than three times New Mexico's and Tennessee's, almost five times Nevada's, seven times the rate of Colorado.

The key to it all was housing. The policy of those responsible, pontificated Trinidad Commissioners in 1937, 'appears to have been influenced by bad traditions,' so bad that they pleaded in Trinidad and British Guiana for the elimination of the old bad words, 'barracks' and 'ranges'—as if the fact would thereby be affected. They described the dwellings in Trinidad as 'indescribable in their lack of elementary needs of decency'; one such barracks had three water-closets 150 yards from the furthest dwelling to serve forty-eight rooms with an estimated population of 226. 'It is hardly too much to say,' they continued, 'that on some of the sugar estates the accommodation provided is in a state of extreme disrepair and thoroughly unhygienic.' But when the question was raised in British Guiana of replacing the filthy, insanitary 'ranges' with simple cottages, the answer was that 'the London directors would not give any money for such a purpose', forcing the Trinidad Commission of 1937 to warn short-sighted directors that 'the claim of the workpeople for the common decencies of home life should be one for primary consideration, and that by maintaining the existing conditions they were providing ground for justifiable discontent'.

This is a description of what the Royal Commission of 1938 saw in Jamaica, where an official survey had put the size of the average room on the plantation at 640 cubic feet, with an average occupancy of $2\frac{1}{2}$ persons; light and ventilation were deficient in half, latrines were bad in nearly three-quarters, almost half needed repair:

'At Orange Bay the Commissioners saw people living in huts the walls of which were bamboo knitted together as closely as human hands were capable; the ceilings were made from dry crisp coconut branches which shifted their positions with every wind. The floor measured 8 feet by 6 feet. The hut was 5 feet high. Two openings served as windows, and a third, stretching from the ground to the roof, was the door. A threadbare curtain divided it into two rooms. It perched perilously on eight concrete slabs, two at each corner. In this hut lived nine people, a man, his wife and seven children. They had no water and no latrine. There were two beds. The parents slept in one, and as many of the children as could hold on in the other. The rest used the floor.'

This was the pattern everywhere. Of 860 families surveyed on the Lafayette sugar plantation in Puerto Rico, there was an average of 3.5 persons per sleeping room. A similar study of families in the coffee, fruit and tobacco regions showed even more serious overcrowding: 5.1 occupants per sleeping room. The furniture in the house of a Haitian peasant was valued at four to fifteen dollars. Less than half of the families studied owned a bed;

only one-quarter owned more than a bed, chairs and a table. The furniture of a Puerto Rican rural family was 'scanty and of the cheapest quality... a few benches, some empty boxes, a small table, one or two cots and a home-made wooden bed is about all that is seen, and in some of them, not even as much as that'. Of these Puerto Rican homes, nearly 90 per cent on the sugar plantations lacked bathing conveniences. To the obvious demand for artesian wells in British Guiana to replace the open unprotected trenches, navigated sometimes by sugar punts, which constituted the water supply of the workers, the planters replied that the workers do not take readily to artesian well water and prefer trench water.

'A faulty diet, heavy parasitic infestation, inadequate housing, poor sanitary conditions, etc., coupled with the weariness resulting from a strenuous work, seem to reduce the rual Puerto Rican worker to a miserable physical condition which becomes more serious with age.' This conclusion of a study of physical measurements of agricultural workers is valid not only for Puerto Rico but also for the entire Caribbean area.

What, then, of the children? With the mother debilitated by hookworm, half-starved and vulnerable to waterborne diseases, the infant mortality rate was staggering. For Trinidad it was 120 per 1,000 live births; for Jamaica 137; for Antigua 171; for St. Kitts 187; for Barbados 217; as compared with 58 in England. For Puerto Rico as a whole it was 126, but for one of the municipalities covered in the sugar-cane plantation survey, it was 144. In Comerio, a small town, 23 per cent of all deaths in 1934 were of infants under one year of age and 43 per cent occurred prior to the fifth year, as compared with 11 and 15 per cent, respectively, for the same age periods in the United States.

Malnutrition was the principal factor. Malnutrition was officially given as the principal cause of $12\frac{1}{2}$ per cent of all deaths under one year for the years 1933–1936 in Dominica. Diseases of the digestive system caused the deaths of 60 per cent of Puerto Rican children under two years of age, clear proof of deficient nutrition. Of the total deaths in Jamaica in 1935, over 33 per cent were of infants under five years of age. An examination of 12,000 schoolchildren in Kingston revealed that 40 per cent were undernourished. Another examination, in St. Thomas in 1937–1938, of

1,360 schoolchildren disclosed that nearly 25 per cent were afflicted with intestinal parasites, 70 per cent had anaemia, and 75 per cent suffered from malnutrition. Of nearly 2,800 schoolchildren examined in Dominica, about half were less than 10 per cent under standard weight, and one-third more than 10 per cent below standard weight for weight and age. Major Wood in 1922 quoted a medical report of March 1918 of an inspection of over 3,000 school children in Georgetown, British Guiana, from 18 schools. Fifty-one per cent suffered from intestinal parasites, 41 per cent from skin diseases, 31 per cent from malnutrition, 25 per cent from filariasis.

The state of the teeth was tragic everywhere. Of nearly 9,000 workers examined in Puerto Rico, almost half had from one to eight teeth missing, and 14 per cent nine or more teeth missing: 'undoubtedly', concludes the report, 'as a result of the lack of economic resources, dentistry work to mend these defects was practically unknown.' Thirty per cent of the schoolchildren in Jamaica's capital had carious teeth. Of 78,000 children in Haiti examined between 1931 and 1937, less than 6 per cent had all their teeth intact, slightly over 12 per cent had clean or passably clean teeth. Of another examination of more than 10,000 children, only 6 per cent used toothbrushes.

Medical men concentrated their services and facilities in the cities. In 1934 nearly half of the doctors in Cuba were resident in Havana; over half the doctors in Haiti were found in Port-au-Prince. Of the municipalities studied in the coffee, fruit and tobacco regions of Puerto Rico, it was said: 'The fact that there are less professional men and, in general, fewer medical facilities in the group of 47 municipalities, is a sure indication that the economic conditions are worse in this part than in the rest of the Island.' The British Labour Adviser in 1938 expressed the emphatic opinion that one of the benefits most needed by the West Indian worker was a cheap health service. The St. Lucia Branch of the British Medical Association opposed this as demoralising to the Negro, who would thereby be given something for nothing. According to the Vice Chairman of the British Royal Commission of 1938, 'Barbados has to thank God for health, not the medical profession'. Even a proposal in 1937 to distribute free to schoolchildren some milk and two biscuits, at an estimated annual gross cost of $35,000, was expected by the Nutrition Committee proposing it 'to be received with derision by many'.

Where there was any ray of hope on the horizon, it related to the sugar industry. A Nutrition Committee in British Guiana, thinking of the working days lost and the cost to plantations of quinine, stated: 'we are strongly of the opinion that a concerted drive against malnutrition in the East Indian and the raising of his nutritional standard of living will result in immeasurable benefit to the sugar industry.' Those who did not want to wait for the millennium from this source simply emigrated—to Panama, Costa Rica, the United States. The average annual remittances sent to Jamaica from overseas reached $600,000. 'Panama money', remitted to Barbados by Barbadians abroad, totalled in 1930 nearly $1,250,000, a sum nearly equal to one-third of the value of Barbadian exports for that year.

But the colonial system was seen at its worst in the neglect and abuse of educational facilities. In 1917 the percentage of illiteracy in Cuba was 46. In the thirties it was over 80 in Haiti, 43 in Trinidad, 60 in British Guiana, 35 in 1935 in Puerto Rico.

The alibi in Trinidad and British Guiana was the objection of the East Indians to the education of their womenfolk. In Puerto Rico it was population pressure. Neither is adequate. The real explanation was the requirements of the sugar industry. In 1926 a committee of the Trinidad Legislative Council considered the restriction of hours of labour. One planter said in evidence: 'Give them some education in the way of reading and writing, but no more. Even then I would say educate only the bright ones; not the whole mass. If you do educate the whole mass of the agricultural population, you will be deliberately ruining the country... Give the bright ones a chance to win as many scholarships as they can; give the others three hours education a day... but if you keep them longer you will never get them to work in the fields. If you want agricultural labourers and not dissatisfaction, you must not keep them longer.' Another planter was asked whether he did not think it would be more satisfactory that children under twelve should be sent to school rather than begin work as soon as they were able, to which he replied that education 'would be of no use to them'. Were the children then to be without education at all? His reply was, 'As long as this is an agricultural country, of what use will education be to them if they had it?'

The conflict between education and sugar, between the rights of the child and the privileges of the sugar planter, was starkly brought out in British Guiana. The Education Ordinance required children to attend school up to the age of 14. But the same ordinance prohibited children from being employed during school hours if below the age of 12. Thus, while the Education Department could prosecute the parent for the non-attendance of a child between the ages of 12 and 14, it could not prosecute the employer for the employment, although the employment was the cause of absence from school. The planters, as always, could make their influence felt in the colonies and in the home country. A special Education Commission, sent out to the colonies from England in 1931, justified child labour:

'We appreciate the argument of those who see in compulsion an instrument for abolishing child labour on the estates. But while accepting the desirability of such abolition we think it is possible to overestimate its extent and its evils. It is for the most part confined to the sugar and, at certain seasons, cotton estates. The conditions are not comparable to those of factory labour under European urban industrial conditions, and we are not convinced that children under 12 years old are necessarily worse off under these conditions than they would be in the overcrowded badly staffed schools which the introduction of compulsion without heavy additional expenditures would perpetuate and extend.'

Why not spend the additional money? In Trinidad in 1931–1932 the expenditure on education per head of population was 6s 10d, as compared with £1 7s 0d per head of population in Huntingdonshire, which corresponded to Grenada, and £1 11s 1d in Bedfordshire, Buckinghamshire, Hertfordshire, which in their combined population corresponded to all the Leeward and Windward Islands taken as a whole. Yet the Trinidad figure was more than double that of Grenada and more than two and a half times that of St. Lucia. Again, according to the Education Commissioners, the average expenditure per child in the English counties was £9 17s 1d, and in the boroughs £10 7s 9d, while in Trinidad the average expenditure was £2 15s 0d, and the average for all the Windward and Leeward Islands £1 5s 8d. Allowing for the difference in the cost of living, the English expenditure per child remained about six times as large as the expenditure in the West

Indies. Yet Trinidad, which spent 10 per cent of its revenue on education in 1934 (as compared with $7\frac{1}{2}$ per cent in 1931), decided, on a recommendation of a committee of the Legislative Council, to restrict expenditures on education, if the financial outlook improved, to $12\frac{1}{2}$ per cent of the revenue; in 1937 the proportion was $9\frac{1}{2}$ per cent.

The result was seen in the enrolment figures all over the area. In 1933 half a million children in Cuba, or well over half the population of school age, were not enrolled in schools. Nearly 67 per cent of the enrolment in the elementary schools was in the first two grades. Enrolment was highest in the provinces of Havana and Matanzas, where sugar was less prominent, and lowest in Camaguey and Oriente, the sugar areas of the island. In 1935 Oriente province could boast of only 16 per cent of the libraries in the island and less than 2 per cent of the volumes. The expenditure on education was $1.49 per capita in 1935, or $13.90 per child enrolled in the elementary schools—less than one-third the sum spent in the poorest state in the United States. Only 5 per cent of the adolescent population in Cuba had an opportunity to continue their education in a public school for more than six years.

In Puerto Rico only 44 per cent of the school population was enrolled, and of this number half were enrolled on half time only. Four out of every five rural schools had facilities for the first three grades only. Slightly more than 25 per cent of the enrolment in 1937–1938 was in grades 4–8. The *per capita* expenditure per child based on current expenses and average daily attendance was $24.21, less than in the poorest states of the United States; yet 40 per cent of the island's budget was assigned to education.

Inadequate in quantity, the education provided was woefully deficient in quality. The elementary school curriculum did not make the necessary distinction between urban and rural needs. A Survey Commission of Teachers College of Columbia University, which visited Puerto Rico in 1925, found that nearly half the school time of the children was devoted to the study of Spanish and English, while Puerto Rico spent 60 per cent more time on the subject of arithmetic than the highly industrialised economy of the United States. The rural school taught no history, civics or music, while nature study, of a very formal type, was valued primarily as a vehicle for training in language. Work in agriculture omitted the chief farming enterprises in Puerto Rico, and such topics as fertilisers, irrigation, rotation and drainage were considered in their general aspect without reference to their local significance. The Education Commission of 1931 in the British West Indies sharply disagreed. It gave prominence to the views of employers as follows:

'What they rightly demand in addition to the training of will and character is the acquisition of a sound and practical knowledge of simple English, that is, ability to understand and use the language for the ordinary purposes of industrial or commercial life, a working knowledge of the simple rules of arithmetic and mensuration, and a sharpening of general intelligence. For vocational training of a specialised kind they see no need... And for practically all other "subjects" they have a profound mistrust as tending to superficiality and diverting attention to inessential, and sometimes unsuitable objects.'

The discrimination against the rural child was quantitative as well as qualitative. According to the Survey Commission, three out of every four rural children in Puerto Rico were on the double enrolment basis—one section attending in the morning, the other in the afternoon. The rural child received no more than half, and probably less, of the instruction afforded to the urban child. The fourth grade rural child was popularly regarded as the equivalent of the third grade urban. Post-primary education in the rural areas was almost completely ignored. In Puerto Rico there was not a single high school in any one of the forty-five rural municipalities with 40 per cent of the population of the island. Secondary school facilities were available chiefly for the one-quarter of Puerto Rico's inhabitants who lived in urban communities, while the remaining three-quarters in the rural districts were almost entirely neglected.

The Haitian situation was much worse. According to Maurice Dartigue, Director of Rural Education: 'In addition to the fact that 85 to 90 per cent of the population of school age lives in rural communities, primary education in the towns received more money from the budget of the Republic than rural education, though the former embraces fewer pupils and far fewer schools, while giving an education far less rich and varied.' Only 10 per cent of the school age population in the rural areas was enrolled. Little attention was paid to girls. One-third of the rural schools were for girls, and enrolment of girls represented only 25 per cent of the total.

The curriculum, especially at the secondary level, was, as a matter of course, based very largely on foreign materials that bore no relation to the daily lives of the pupils or to their environment. The educational system of the Caribbean violated the fundamental principle that education should proceed from the known to the unknown, from the village to the great wide world, from the indigenous plants, animals and insects to the flora and fauna of strange countries, from the economy of the village and household to the economics of the world.

A course of study published for the elementary and junior high schools of the Virgin Islands in the twenties borrowed almost verbatim from the course of study for New Mexico's elementary schools and Utah's junior high schools. Children were taught to sing about 'tripping through the snow to grandfather's house on Thanksgiving Day', this in a Caribbean society where it is often difficult to ascertain the father of the child.

The Puerto Rican curriculum was still further distorted by the fact that the teaching was conducted in a foreign medium. The Survey Commission of 1925 discovered that Puerto Rican elementary schools gave to the study of English the time imperatively needed for instruction in subjects that were wholly neglected. The average child lacked information about health, hygiene, nutrition, the civic conditions and historical development of his people, the scientific and natural world in which he lived, and the economic, political and social conditions of Puerto Rico. After six to eight years of schooling, the Commission concluded, pupils knew about one item in four or five of the types of information that might properly be regarded as the essential knowledge of a person leaving school. The system was utterly wasteful. Twenty-one out of every twenty-five children in the island stayed in school only until the end of the third grade. Neither in reading nor in oral communication could the work done in English in the first three grades reach a point which made it a useful second language. The Commission recommended, therefore, that the teaching of English in all schools be deferred to the fourth grade.

But colonialism intervened. An indispensable part of the United States policy in Puerto Rico, as enunciated by President Franklin Roosevelt, was that 'the coming generation of American citizens in Puerto Rico grow up with complete facility in the English tongue'. So the Puerto Rican schools had to continue to emphasise English. The 1940 census demonstrated the result. Only one in four Puerto Ricans over 10 years of age could speak English, as compared with one in five in 1930. Two out of every five Puerto Ricans in urban areas could speak English, as compared with one in five in rural areas. In 1936 the Detroit Word Recognition Test was given to typical elementary and secondary school children in Puerto Rico in ten representative regions of the urban and rural zones in the island. The results showed that the level attained by third grade urban children in Puerto Rico was slightly below, and the level attained by fourth grade rural children slightly above, that attained by the top group of first grade children in the United States. The results of another test, Detroit Reading Test No. 1, intended for second grade children, showed that second and third grade children in Puerto Rico, at the end of the year, fell below the level reached by the top group of second grade children in the United States at the beginning of the year.

Whilst the Education Commission of 1931 in the British West Indies could not itself stomach the teaching of the Wars of the Roses and the capes of Europe in the elementary schools, teaching based on textbooks unsuitable for West Indian children, the Royal Commission of 1938 went much further and called for

'An end of the illogical and wasteful system which permits the education of a community predominantly engaged in agriculture to be based upon a literary curriculum fitting pupils only for white-collar careers in which opportunities are comparatively limited ... Curricula are on the whole ill-adapted to the needs of the large mass of the population and adhere far too closely to models which have become out of date in the British practice from which they have been blindly copied.'

The secondary school curriculum in the British Caribbean ignored everything West Indian—West Indian history, geography, economics, community organisation and problems. It ignored (except in Trinidad) Spanish, the language of neighbouring South and Central America. Whilst music, art and handiwork were included in the Jamaican law on the subject, they did not figure

prominently; and physical training and organised games were not
included. The British West Indian secondary school was thoroughly
artificial as a result of the system of British external examinations. As analysed by Professor I. L. Kandel, an Englishman, in
terms of Jamaica, 'a secondary education which is organised to
serve the purposes of an external system of examinations is likely
to stress the acquisition, often the unintelligently memorised
acquisition, of certain subjects'. On one notorious occasion Trinidad secondary school students, taking the Cambridge external examination, were asked to write an essay on a day in winter.

What the Education Commissioner of Puerto Rico wrote in his
report in 1943–1944 was valid for the entire Caribbean area:

'The evidence . . . points to the fact that the Puerto Rican school system
is failing to provide sufficient educational opportunities for its potential
citizens . . . The number of illiterates in Puerto Rico is considerable, and
it is doubtful that under present conditions illiteracy will ever be effectively
reduced.'

'Present conditions' again! On the economic side, the introduction and commercialisation of new crops was 'very doubtful under
present physical economic and political conditions'. Now educational change and the elimination of illiteracy 'under present conditions' were equally 'doubtful'. The stage was set for the
emergence of the nationalist movement, the last and rightful
claimant to Adam's will.

Chapter Twenty-Seven

The Colonial Nationalist Movement

The colonial nationalist movement in the Caribbean, like the colonial nationalist movement everywhere, was concerned with the abolition of colonialism. Inevitably in the parcellation of the area and its historical association with different metropolitan countries, the movement took different forms.

(1) The Republics

In Cuba, Haiti and the Dominican Republic, identified as they were with the inter-American system, with the Platt Amendment and Guantanamo Bay in Cuba, and American control of customs and finances in Haiti and the Dominican Republic, anti-colonialism meant anti-Americanism. But the period saw an intensification of American control, personified by totalitarian dictatorships supported by the United States, whose primary concern was order and stability.

The American occupation of Haiti gave rise to the *caco* revolt of 1918. The *cacos* were turbulent peasants. living in the wild mountain country along the northern part of the eastern frontier; professional revolutionaries, they supported the highest bidder in the stakes for the Haitian Presidency. The principal cause of the revolt was the American revival of the Haitian *corvée*, forced labour for a given period on the roads. After two years of military operations, the revolt was suppressed at a cost of some 1,500 Haitian lives. A Committee of the United States Senate was appointed in 1921 to report on the problem. It found 'a failure to develop a definite and constructive policy under the Treaty or to centralise in some degree responsibility for the conduct of American officers and officials', and 'a failure of the Departments in Washington to appreciate the importance of selecting for service in Haiti, whether in civil or military capacities, men who were sympathetic to the Haitians and able to maintain cordial personal and offical relations with them.' The American Marines were withdrawn by Franklin D. Roosevelt as part of the Good Neighbour Policy.

The situation was more discouraging in Cuba, which was in every sense of the term an American colony. The Americans openly supported, in the interest of stability, the dictator Machado who raised no awkward questions of Cuban independence and who was concerned merely with the exile or assassination of hostile labour leaders and the reckless and enormous increase of the public debt, both public and private. America dominated the scene. One American writer has stated that no one could become President of Cuba without the endorsement of the United States. According to another, the American Ambassador in Havana was the most important man in Cuba. A third analyses United States policy as 'putting a veto on revolution, whatever the cause'. The Platt Amendment dominated the relations between the United States and Cuba. On the occasion of a threatened rebellion by a Negro political party, the Independent Party of Colour, the United States sent troops to Cuba. In reply to Cuba's protests Secretary of State Knox stated: 'The United States does not undertake first to consult the Cuban Government if a crisis arises requiring a temporary landing somewhere.' In 1933 Ambassador Sumner Welles identified six desirable characteristics which a Cuban President should possess. These read in part : 'First, his thorough acquaintance with the desires of this Government ... Sixth, his amenability to suggestions or advice which might be made to him by the American Legation.'

A far worse dictator was Rafael Trujillo of the Dominican

Republic who, from 1929 until his assassination on May 30, 1961, organised and established a tyranny on the Latin American pattern which ranks among the most ruthless and efficient in the history of the entire world. He maintained the outward trappings of a democracy—elections, Congress, the courts, etc. But his elections were national farces, in which on one occasion the votes were announced before they were even counted; the Dominican Republic was a one party state. Congress was a nonentity, its members being handpicked, nominated and removed by Trujillo at his pleasure. The dictator's astonishing sexuality, with his partiality for mulatto women and his procurer service in the office of the Presidency, his obsession with titles and decorations, the vulgar adulation which he demanded, his open control of press and radio, the nepotism and family preferment in which he indulged were an international scandal. His international Fair of Peace and Fraternity of the Free World cost the country $30 million, one third of the 1955 budget. In a sense more vivid and comprehensive than Louis XIV, Trujillo was the state. He openly participated in the economic life of the country through his personal and family enterprises. Beginning with monopolies of meat and milk, he eventually came to control production and trade in rice, tobacco, salt, edible oils and sugar, for the last of which he voted himself a 10-year tax exemption. At the close of his career, Crassweller has estimated, he owned 1,500,000 acres of improved land and vast tracts of unimproved property, his factories employed 60,000 workers, his sugar interests were valued at $150 million. The total value of all his holdings at home and abroad has been assessed at $500 million. As Crassweller has concluded: 'The organised and systematic use of every state power in furtherance of Trujillo's private ends was conspicuous.'

The United States watched and condoned all this without batting an eyelid. For, as Franklin D. Roosevelt put it, 'He may be an S.O.B., but he is our S.O.B.' What impressed the United States was Trujillo's repayment of the entire foreign debt, as a result of which the Dominican Republic and the United States signed a treaty on September 24, 1940 ending United States administration of the Dominican customs under the 1924 Convention. The Dominican Congress voted Trujillo the title 'restorer of Financial Independence'.

But it was a different story in terms of Trujillo's foreign relations, where he clashed repeatedly with United States interests.
Trujillo was responsible for the 1937 massacre of between 15,000
and 20,000 Haitians. He entertained repeated designs on Haitian
independence and more than once had puppets in his pay
nominated President of Haiti. He supported Batista in Cuba
against Castro. Trujillo, in league with such other dictators as
Somoza of Nicaragua, was fanatically hostile to the democrats
Figueres of Costa Rica and Betancourt of Venezuela, culminating
in his attempt to get Betancourt assassinated in 1960. This led to
condemnation of him by the Organisation of American States for
aggression and the breaking off of diplomatic relations with the
Dominican Republic by the members of the Inter-American system.
At the end of his career, when even the hitherto docile church
turned against him, Trujillo was on very bad terms with the United
States, was seeking to improve his relations with countries behind the Iron Curtain, and even reached a temporary understanding with Castro. As Crassweller analyses the Caribbean policy of
the United States, it involved 'a central preoccupation, which was
Cuba, and a peripheral distraction, which was Trujillo'.

Trujillo's assassination led to predictable confusion in a country
decimated by dictatorship for more than 30 years. The Americans
feared another Cuba in the hemisphere and intervened massively
in 1965, to the great consternation of the Organisation of American States, in order to prevent a leftist takeover. At the peak
their forces reached 22,000 men. The force was eventually converted on the surface into an O.A.S. force in the face of hostile
world opinion, and since then the Dominican Republic has uncertainly, under President Balaguer, sought to chart a course as a
Latin American democracy.

(2) Association with the Metropolitan Country

Henry Carroll, the special commissioner appointed by the United
States for Puerto Rico in 1898, set out his impressions of Puerto
Rican expectations from annexation as follows:

'They expect under American sovereignty that the wrongs of centuries
will be righted; that they will have an honest and efficient government;
the largest measure of liberty as citizens of the great Republic under the
Constitution; home rule as provided by the Territorial system...and

the general adaptation to the island of all those institutions which have contributed to the prosperity, progress, and happiness of the American people.'

For 300 years Spain had treated Puerto Rico as a military outpost. The Puerto Ricans repeatedly agitated for increased participation in their own government. The single concession accorded to them was the declaration in 1812 that Puerto Rico was an integral part of Spain; its people were declared Spanish citizens with the right to name a deputy in the Spanish *Cortes*. In addition, a provincial assembly of nine members, including the Governor, was created, with limited powers over certain local activities.

The agitation for home rule continued throughout the century and culminated in 1897 in the Charter of Autonomy. Under this charter Puerto Rico continued to send delegates to the *Cortes*, and was accorded an elected Chamber of Representatives and a 15-member Council of Administration (a Senate), eight of whom were elected by Puerto Rico; the remaining seven were nominated by the Governor-General appointed by the crown. The Puerto Rican Legislature had certain powers where the Governor General was concerned; it could pass on all matters of purely insular importance; it could fix the budget and determine tariffs and taxes; its concurrence in commercial treaties concluded by Spain was provided for. But the Governor General retained the power to suspend civil rights and to refer to the Council of Ministers of Spain insular legislation which was in his view detrimental or unconstitutional.

Under the Charter the first Puerto Rican Cabinet was appointed in February 1898, and general elections were held in March. Then came the Spanish-American War in April and the American occupation in June. From that time until now Puerto Rico has been dominated by the question of its political status.

Henry Carroll opted for self-government and home rule. He wrote in 1899:

'The question remains whether, in view of the high rate of illiteracy which exists among them and of their lack of training in the responsibilities of citizenship, it would be safe to entrust them with the power of self-government. The Commissioner had no hesitation in answering this question in the affirmative. Who shall declare what is the requisite measure of capacity for self-government? ... Porto Ricans are surely better pre-

pared than were the people of Mexico, or of the colonies in Central and
South America, which have one after another emancipated themselves
from foreign domination and entered upon the duties and privileges of
self-government... Let Porto Rico have local self-government after the
pattern of our Territories and she will gain by her blunders, just as cities
and states in our own glorious Republic are constantly learning.

'It should be remembered that Porto Rico is not asking for independent
self-government. The people are far from desiring separation from the
U.S. This simplifies the problem and reduces the risk; for what they might
not be able to do if left entirely to their own resources, they may easily
accomplish under the strong protecting hand of the Government of the
U.S....

'The commissioner is convinced by what he saw, heard, and learned
in Porto Rico by contact with all classes, that while many changes and
modifications are desired and are absolutely essential to the future
welfare of the island, the existing institutions and laws, usages, and
customs should not be revolutionised or severely reformed. The customs
and usages and language of a people are not like old vestments, which
may be slid aside at command, but become a part of their life, and are
very dear to them... The attachment to the language has long and strong
roots. It will not do and it is not necessary to take any harsh measures to
sever it... Both Spanish and English may be used side by side for years
to come.'

The American Congress ignored Carroll. They passed the
Foraker Act in 1900 establishing a temporary civil government for
Puerto Rico. Executive authority was vested in the American
Governor and an 11-member executive council, five of whom were
Puerto Ricans, all appointed by the President of the United States.
This council also constituted the Senate of the legislature. Six
of its members were to hold high executive positions. The lower
house comprised thirty-five members elected every two years by all
who qualified as voters on March 1, 1900. The Governor could
veto laws passed by the Legislature, but his veto could be over-
ridden by a two-thirds majority in the insular Legislature. But
Congress in the United States could annul any law passed by the
Puerto Rican Legislature. The President appointed the island's
Supreme Court, the Attorney General, the Commissioner of
Education, and the Auditor.

This was not the self-government the Puerto Rican nationalists
had aspired to. They were only partially satisfied by the change
in 1917 which offered United States citizenship to Puerto Ricans
and promulgated a bill of rights for the island.

In 1937 came the nationalist uprising led by Albizu Campos in Ponce in Puerto Rico. According to Gordon Lewis, the killings in this uprising subsequently played a role in the Puerto Rican political psychology not unlike that of the massacre of Amritsar in the psychology of the Congress Party of India after 1919. The result was the emergence of Muñoz Marin with his Popular Democratic Party which won the 1940 elections on the slogan, 'Land, bread, liberty'. Puerto Rico received an elected governor in 1947; he was given the power to appoint, with the advice and consent of the Puerto Rican Senate, the heads of all executive departments. In 1950 the Puerto Ricans received the right to draw up their own constitution.

The solution adopted by Muñoz Marin was a commonwealth freely associated with the United States. Commonwealth status has been in force since 1952, supported by the majority of voters in election after election, opposed, however, on the one hand, by the Independence Party, wishing to make Puerto Rico another Latin American Republic, whose support has been diminishing, and, on the other hand, by the Statehood Party, wishing to make Puerto Rico a state of the United States of America, whose support has been increasing in recent years. But the obsession with political status remains. As Gordon Lewis writes:

'It remains still an open question as to whether the *Popular* magic will be able permanently to resolve the conflict which in many Puerto Rican hearts burns still between a natural desire for independence and a fear of the hardships that would assuredly lie in its wake...the magic is comparatively helpless to appease the preoccupation with status...the claim that the *estado libre asociado* is the "final solution" to colonialism becomes more and more flat, stale, and unprofitable.'

The recent victory of the Puerto Rican Republican Party in the election for Governor in 1968 suggests that Puerto Rico may now abandon the concept of the associated free state and, like Hawaii and Alaska, proceed to statehood in the American system.

The French West Indies, in their turn, chose in 1946 assimilation as departments of metropolitan France. The popularity of this solution was attested by a popular refrain which indicated that before assimilation they used the jackass, with assimilation they graduated towards the mule, and it was expected that the changes from assimilation would soon lead them to the horse—the symbol of authority and status on the sugar plantation. Enthusiasm for assimilation has become less pronounced with time. As one essayist put it in 1962: 'France is in the air. Fort de France. French Rediffusion. Grand Hotel de France. Read the paper *FRANCE SOIR*. Travel Air France.' It is France everywhere: police, army, priests, department stores, post offices, banks, barracks, churches, motorcars. Recent uprisings in Guadeloupe suggest great disenchantment with assimilation and the future is not clear.

The Dutch colonies, Netherlands Antilles and Surinam, opted for a new relationship with Holland, which became a tripartite kingdom, the overseas sections being consulted on foreign affairs and defence and retaining autonomy in internal matters. But Surinam has recently become restless with this dispensation and serious riots have taken place in Curaçao.

(3) The British Caribbean

If republican America could not do appreciably better than monarchist Spain, the situation in the established British colonies could easily be imagined. World War I gave rise to an increasingly vociferous demand on the part of the middle classes for racial equality in the civil service, democratic institutions, widening of the franchise, constitution reform, and federation of the islands. Representative associations sprang up throughout the islands. As a result of this agitation the Colonial Office sent Major Wood (later Lord Halifax) to visit the colonies in 1921. Wood opposed the idea of federation, recommended the introduction of a minority of middle class elected members into the Legislative Councils on a restricted franchise, and issued a warning to the British Government:

'The whole history of the African population of the West Indies inevitably drives them towards representative institutions fashioned after the British model ... We shall be wise if we avoid the mistake of endeavouring to withhold a concession ultimately inevitable until it has been robbed by delay of most of its usefulness and of all its grace.'

Wood was ignored, as Carroll had been. The tendency in the British Caribbean was to put the clock back rather than forward. The test case, not for the last time, was British Guiana.

Up to 1927 British Guiana was a colony not possessing responsible government with a partly-elected legislature not providing for an official majority. The distinctive feature of its constitution was its division of the legislative power between the Court of Policy and the Combined Court. To the Court of Policy, comprising Governor, seven officials and eight elected unofficial members, and constituted with the Governor's casting vote to secure an official majority, belonged the power of legislation in matters not fiscal. The Combined Court, comprising the Court of Policy and six more elected members known as the Financial Representatives, enjoyed the power of imposing taxes and in practice the right to control the appropriation of public funds. In the Court of Policy the Government was subject to a potential veto inasmuch as, if seven of the elected members abstained from attending, they could prevent the formation of the quorum prescribed. In the Combined Court, on the other hand, and consequently in matters of taxation or matters involving expenditure, the elected members possessed a majority, and the only limitation on their powers was that they could not increase, though they could reduce or reject, any item on the annual estimates which were prepared by the Governor in Executive Council.

This Constitution was considered unsatisfactory, on the ground that, as expressed by a former Governor, there was 'an element of insecurity which cannot fail to serve as a deterrent to prospective investors, but may be gravely prejudicial to our chances of obtaining money in the London market on favourable terms when the time comes to float our loan'. The principal investor, Sir Edward Davson, was more outspoken. As far back as 1907 he had said:

'I do not believe that in any Colony of the Empire the white element should be subject to the coloured, whether it be black, brown or yellow —African, East Indian, or Mongolian. For it may be the blacks today who rule the land; it may be the East Indians tomorrow; it may—who knows?—be the Japanese in the future.'

In his opinion the white officials, the representatives of Imperial rule, should have a permanent majority, as they could be 'guaranteed to take a broader and more impartial view of matters than those whose knowledge of economics, finance or commerce has oft-times not a very deep foundation'.

It was in these circumstances that a commission was sent out
to Guiana in 1927. The commission condemned the constitution
on the ground that the government had never been able to govern.
It reported:

'The practical consequences of this lack of ultimate control are chiefly
to be seen in the financial system of the Colony. This system is prejudicial
to trade, inconducive to sound financial policy, and costly in that it prevents
the Colony's loans from being issued as trustee securities ... At present
the elected members are in the position of a minor who can overrule his
own trustee ... The divorce of responsibility from power, which is so
marked a feature of the constitution, places the elected members as well
as the Government in a false position. The elected members tend to be
placed in the position of a permanent opposition, unrestrained by experience or prospect of office ... The position of the Government, under
such conditions, might in some respects be compared to that of a ministry
without a majority.'

The Commission recommended that the two legislative bodies
should be merged into a single Legislative Council, and suggested
that the time had come to consider on its merits the question of
importing a nominated element into the legislature—which was
done in the following year. Thus British Guiana in 1928 followed
Jamaica in 1865—less, rather than more self-government. The practical result was soon evident. It was only on the recommendation
of the 1927 Commission that income tax was instituted in 1929, in
a colony whose financial position had frequently been described
as highly unsatisfactory. Even then there was no surtax, and the
incidence of income tax was very light; for instance, a married man
with two children paid nothing on an income up to £460, and on
an income of £710 he paid only £5. On the other hand customs
duties were high. In 1936, whereas £507,000 came from import
duties, only £76,000 came from income tax.

And so with the franchise. All that the 1927 Commission could
offer was steps to ensure the secrecy of the ballot and to close
liquor shops on polling day. The qualification for voters was
ownership of a house or land valued at over $480, or an annual
rent of over $96, or an annual income or salary of approximately
$300. No person was allowed to vote unless he could read or
write some language. A local commission was appointed in
1934 to investigate the franchise. The Commission refused to
recommend any lowering of the franchise and especially of the

income qualifications on the ground that it 'would tend to let in persons who by their lack of education (moral as well as mental) would be still more open to extraneous influences and less likely to exercise an independent judgement'. Indeed, they even inclined to an increase of the income qualification, 'in the hope that higher income and salary qualifications would tend to secure a purer electorate by excluding persons of a low educational standard (moral and mental)'.

The situation in the British West Indies was due largely to the fact that trade union organisation did not exist. Take Trinidad, for example. A Trade Union Ordinance was passed in 1932, embodying substantially the provisions of the English Acts of 1871, 1876, 1913 and 1927; but the workers steadily refused to register under this Ordinance, on the advice of the British Trades Union Congress, because it did not provide for peaceful picketing or protect the unions against actions in tort on the lines of the British 1906 Act. A local commission of 1934 commented on the lack of any constituted body which could properly make representations on behalf of the workers. The British commission investigating the oil disturbances of 1937 traced 'the true origin of the disturbances... to the more or less general sense of dissatisfaction for which there was no adequate means of articulation through recognised machinery of collective bargaining'. The commission lamented the fact that before the 1937 strike in the oilfields 'employers generally had been slow to realise the importance of the development of machinery for conciliation or collective bargaining on modern lines, and that indeed their attitude had been the reverse of encouraging'.

The road to revolution had been marked out. The revolution broke out in the years 1935–1938. Consider the chronology of these fateful years. A sugar strike in St. Kitts, 1935; a revolt against an increase of customs duties in St. Vincent, 1935; a coal strike in St. Lucia, 1935; labour disputes on the sugar plantations of British Guiana, 1935; an oil strike, which became a general strike, in Trinidad, 1937; a sympathetic strike in Barbados, 1937; revolt on the sugar plantations in British Guiana, 1937; a sugar strike in St. Lucia, 1937; sugar troubles in Jamaica, 1937; a dockers' strike in Jamaica, 1938. Every British Governor called for warships, marines and aeroplanes; total casualties in the British colonies amounted to 29 dead, 115 wounded.

The working class began to form trade unions everywhere—the Bustamante Industrial Union in Jamaica, the Oilfield Workers Trade Union in Trinidad, the Manpower and Citizens Association in British Guiana. Political parties began to emerge—Manley's People's National Party in Jamaica, Adams' Progressive League in Barbados, the West Indian Nationalist Party in Trinidad. The new nationalist spirit of 1938 can best be gauged by a comparison with the middle-class sentiments which had dominated in 1932.

In 1932, with the British Government sending out a commission to the West Indies to consider closer union of the colonies, a West Indian Conference was called in Dominica to elaborate a constitution based on federation and full elective control of the legislative assemblies. The moving spirits were Cipriani of Trinidad and Rawle of Dominica. The conference foundered on the rock of the franchise. No agreement could be reached on the question of adult suffrage, and the compromise adopted permitted each colony to settle its own franchise qualifications. The British commission itself opposed the idea of federation, endorsed the system of nomination of some councillors, and was emphatic in its opposition to 'the grant of universal suffrage until the present standard of education in the islands has greatly advanced'.

Compare 1938. A Labour Congress of the West Indies and British Guiana met in British Guiana. The demands included: federation; a purely elected legislature elected by universal suffrage, with the Governor enjoying the powers of the king of England in relation to Parliament; nationalisation of the sugar industry; prohibition of plantations larger than fifty acres; co-operative marketing; state ownership of public utilities; social legislation such as old age pensions, national health insurance, unemployment insurance, minimum wage, 44-hour week, workmen's compensation; trade union immunities; free compulsory elementary education.

The nationalist movement was on the march. World War II strengthened the nationalist cause, as the Atlantic Charter was announced and the Four Freedoms enunciated. Universal suffrage came to Jamaica in 1944 and to Trinidad and Tobago in 1946.

The British West Indies proceeded to adapt the relevant British procedures. The ministerial system was introduced, and discussions initiated towards a Federation of the British West Indies. As these discussions were proceeding the British Guiana Constitution was suspended in 1953 on the alleged ground that the party in power was planning to introduce a communist state, whilst in 1956 a recognised democratic party was born in Trinidad and Tobago, the People's National Movement.

The Federation of the West Indies, inaugurated in 1958, collapsed in 1962 with the secession of Jamaica. Its failure was due to the two rival conceptions, Jamaica's weak central government and Trinidad's strong central power. Since that time Jamaica, Trinidad and Tobago, Guyana (the former British Guiana) and Barbados have achieved independence, in that order. The smaller islands have become Associated States of Britain, with Britain responsible for defence and external affairs, but this has given rise to great discontent in the islands and the future must bring some change—in the direction either of a federation of the smaller islands or of the unitary state that has been proposed since 1962 by Trinidad and Tobago. In 1967 Trinidad and Tobago followed by Barbados joined the Organisation of American States. Efforts were made in the several territories to create a Caribbean Free Trade Area, which came into effect on May 1, 1968, with headquarters in Guyana. The questions of a regional air carrier and a Caribbean Development Bank* are now under consideration; Belize (British Honduras), Bahamas, the Dominican Republic and Haiti have shown interest in the new grouping. The next steps are a common external tariff and harmonisation of fiscal incentives. Centrifugal forces, however, are still at work: Anguilla has 'seceded' from the Associated State of St. Kitts-Nevis. After an invasion by Britain derided by the whole world, it has been agreed that a Caribbean Commission is now to consider the matter and make recommendations. Rumblings of secessionist discontent have come from Barbuda in its relations with Antigua. A secessionist rebellion broke out early in 1969 in the Rupununi in Guyana, where it is alleged to be connected with the Venezuela-Guyana boundary dispute which has been resurrected by Venezuela.

The nationalist movement is in the saddle everywhere. Its greatest victories have been the return of the naval base of Chaguaramas

* Inaugurated on January 31, 1970.

in Trinidad by the Americans and the abolition by Venezuela
of the 33⅓ per cent surtax on West Indian products.

(4) Economic and Social Progress

The colonial nationalist movement in the Caribbean, in its
struggle against colonialism, necessarily has had to pay the greatest
attention to economic and social improvements to provide a
better life for its citizens and raise their standard of living.
We shall take the British Caribbean and Puerto Rico as our
examples.

The first major move has been tax reform, to provide the
governments with the financial capacity to carry out their reform
proposals. The countries with mineral resources have here been
better placed than those that are primarily agricultural—Jamaica
and Guyana with bauxite, Trinidad and Tobago with petroleum.
Trinidad and Tobago's prospects for the future have been recently
enhanced by the discovery offshore on the east coast of significant
quantities of sulphur-free crude oil and natural gas.

The second concern has been with the increasing population,
the result of indiscriminate and excessive importations in the
colonial past. Almost all governments have instituted family planning programmes as a long-term measure to reduce the cost of the
growing social services. Short-term measures have been directed
to relentless efforts to provide more jobs—by industrial development on a large scale particularly in Puerto Rico which, as part
of the United States customs area, can attract United States capital
by labour cost differentials; by agricultural diversification to reduce
the dependence on monoculture, produce more of the food cur-
rently imported, and so improve the balance of payments position,
particularly in Guyana with its rice which now has a Caribbean
market, and in Trinidad and Tobago with milk, pork and poultry
as well as vegetables and ground provisions, all on the basis of a
large programme of agrarian reform and the distribution of small
farms; by developing the tourist trade, especially in Jamaica,
Puerto Rico, Barbados and Antigua and by attracting, as in Montserrat, the 'second home' type of wealthy tourist; and by heroic
efforts to secure a reasonable position for their basic sugar industry,

Puerto Rico in the American market, and the British Caribbean in the British market by the Commonwealth Sugar Agreement, fortified by the recent adoption of a reasonable International Sugar Agreement.

But this development in industry, agriculture, sugar and tourism requires foreign investment, which results in the perpetuation of the old colonial economy anathema to those who would like to see emerge a native Caribbean identity. Trinidad and Tobago has gone furthest in this direction by establishing national companies for petroleum and sugar, encouraging joint ventures with foreign investors either by the government or by local capitalists, prohibiting the further sale of land to foreigners and substituting long leases, rejecting the establishment of casinos and the alienation of beaches to private investors, and taking a government share in the mass media of radio and television and in telecommunications as the first step towards ultimate national ownership. Where aid comes in from international rather than private foreign sources, there are technical assistance agreements with Canada, the facilities of the International Bank for Reconstruction and Development, and, for Trinidad and Tobago, Jamaica and Barbados, the Inter-American Development Bank of the Organisation of American States.

The provision of more jobs is largely an educational matter, and so provision for education and training has figured very largely in nationalist plans. Progress has been made in all territories. A good example is the current 15-year plan, 1968–1983, of Trinidad and Tobago, designed to spend on education $171 million in capital expenditure and $1,144 million in recurrent and aimed at extending free secondary education, in force since 1960, to 91 per cent of the age group 12–14 in junior secondary schools.

With all these heroic efforts, the unemployment problem is staggering, attaining 20 per cent in Jamaica and Puerto Rico and 15 per cent in Trinidad and Tobago, being particularly high in the age group 15–25 and higher among females than males. The result has been a steady increase in emigration. Some quarter of a million Puerto Ricans emigrated to America in the decade after 1952, the rate rising to an annual average of 40,000 since 1945. Up to mid-1962, before the tightening of British restrictions, West Indians in Britain, principally Jamaicans, numbered 300,000. From

1965 to 1968, 12,000 Trinidadians have emigrated to the United States and 7,000 to Canada.

Great strides have also been made in the fields of housing and health, to remedy past colonial deficiencies. But the backlog is so heavy that all efforts so far have merely scratched the surface and shown what could be done if financial resources permitted. Trinidad and Tobago's current efforts in the field of housing are now being assisted by a substantial loan from the Inter-American Development Bank.

And so we turn to Castro's Cuba and its distinctive effort to remove the legacy left to the West Indian people by the colonial regime.

Chapter Twenty-Eight

Castroism

The Castro Revolution in 1958 was a belated attempt to catch up with the nationalist movement in the rest of the Caribbean. Cuba presented the following picture:

75 per cent of rural dwellings were huts made from the palm tree.

The peasantry were isolated on account of the state of the roads.

There was one doctor for more than 2,000 persons in the rural areas, leading to the saying in Cuba that only cattle were vaccinated.

Only 4 per cent of the Cuban peasantry ate meat as a regular part of their diet; while 1 per cent ate fish, less than 2 per cent eggs, 3 per cent bread, 11 per cent milk; none ate green vegetables.

Over 50 per cent of Cuba's rural dwellings had no toilets of any kind, 97 per cent had no refrigeration facilities, 85 per cent had no inside running water, 91 per cent had no electricity.

More than one-third of the rural population had intestinal parasites.

In 1956 the average annual income per person among the peasantry was $91, less than one-third of the national income per person.

27 per cent of the urban children and 61 per cent of the rural children were not attending school.

Slightly over 50 per cent of the peasants could read and write; 43 per cent were completely illiterate, 44 per cent had never attended school.

82 per cent of Cuba's total land area was farm land, but only 22 per cent of that was cultivated.

Sugar accounted for nearly 90 per cent of Cuba's exports and 33 per cent of the country's national income.

American sugar companies controlled about 75 per cent of Cuba's arable land.

American participation exceeded 90 per cent in the telephone and electric services, 50 per cent in railways, and about 40 per cent in sugar production.

25 per cent of the Cuban labour force was chronically unemployed.

Few countries had a heavier overhead and such under-utilised production facilities.

Yet pre-Castro Cuba was not underdeveloped or backward in the same sense as most countries of Africa and Asia. It was, on the contrary, among the more highly developed of the Latin American countries. Cuba ranked first among the Latin American countries in the extent of railway communication and in television sets per head of population. It ranked second in private motor-cars in relation to population and in energy consumption; third in life expectancy at birth, radio sets in relation to population, and the proportion of the population (58 per cent) not employed in agriculture. It ranked fourth in electricity consumption *per capita*, telephones in relation to population, and the literacy of the population over 10 years of age (76 per cent). It was fifth among the Latin American countries in the annual income *per capita*, $353 US in 1958.

Cuba's backwardness was largely due to the fact that it was at the mercy of external forces on the world market. Sugar production fluctuated from 3.6 million tons in 1923 to 5.2 million in 1925, 3 million in 1932, 7 million in 1952, 4.7 million in 1954. The price fluctuated even more widely, from just under 12 cents per pound on the American market in 1920 to $1\frac{3}{4}$ cents in 1937 and 5 cents between 1953 and 1958. It was obviously impossible for any country to plan its economy or to develop its standard of living on the basis of such dependence on capricious world forces which it could not hope to control.

This was the Cuba governed by the dictator Batista and his army, against which Castro had launched an unsuccessful and premature attack in 1953. Castro was back in 1957. Reliable sources say that on the day of victory the whole Castro army consisted of 803 men, which together with all other groups made up a force of 1,000 to 1,500. In his speech of July 26, 1963, Castro claimed to have won the war against Batista with less than 500 soldiers. A pro-Castro French journalist has given this explanation: 'Fidel Castro's victory was no real military victory. It was primarily a moral victory of the people ... Castro did not destroy the enemy. The latter collapsed because he was rotten to the core.'

Castro's initial programme was the typical programme of Caribbean nationalists. Basing himself on the November 1956 Manifesto of his 26 July Movement, his movement was 'democratic, nationalist and dedicated to social justice'. Following his Declaration of the Sierra Maestra on July 12, 1957, he pledged political guarantees, civil rights, 'establishment of a civil service', free elections in all trade unions, distribution of barren lands with 'prior indemnification to the former owners', an intensive campaign against illiteracy, acceleration of industrialisation, and the creation of new jobs. His revolution was to be a 'a humanist revolution', as Cuban as the palm trees, which would restrict consumption in order to build factories and machinery.

The essential feature of Castro's revolution was its anti-Americanism. Castro repeated the cry familiar in Latin America for over half a century, 'Yankee Imperialism'.

The first object of attack was the sugar industry, the monoculture it encouraged, the foreign-owned latifundia on which it was erected, and the landless peasantry it created. Castro's answer was agrarian reform.

The Agrarian Reform Law was promulgated on May 17, 1959. The two major goals of this law were the replacement of the latifundia by co-operatives or private small and medium farms with diversified production, and the elimination of renting, tenancy and sharecropping by establishing the legal principle that the land belongs to those who work it. The law prohibited the ownership of more than 995 acres by either an individual or a company, by certain legal exceptions, however, the limit could be increased to 3,316 acres; further, the National Institute of Agrarian Reform was empowered to retain units of production if the interest of productivity and economic efficiency might be better served. For those not in co-operatives, the Government undertook to provide a minimum allotment of sixty-six acres.

The Agrarian Reform Law affected the relations between Cuba and the United States. The law provided for compensation on the basis of bonds issued in Cuban currency and maturing in 20 years at $4\frac{1}{2}$ per cent annually, based on assessments of the land in accordance with tax valuations that the owners had filed with the Batista regime. It was well-known that American real property had been assessed at only a fraction of its value, so the American owners threatened with expropriation faced the difficulty that any public protests against the expropriation terms would be an admission of past tax evasion.

The United States retaliation against the Agrarian Law took the form of a cut in Cuba's sugar quota in the United States market. Castro replied with an arrangement to sell 5 million tons of sugar to the Soviet Union over a 5-year period—thus continuing the infiltration of the Soviet market which had begun from 1955 during the Batista regime. The Soviet Union undertook to pay 80 per cent of the price in merchandise and 20 per cent in dollars. The price agreed upon was the world price.

President Eisenhower used the sugar quota as 'a tool of diplomacy'. Castro retaliated that he would take a 'a mill for every pound' cut from Cuba's sugar quota. As he said in his speech on June 24, 1960: 'We can lose our sugar quota and they can lose their investments. We will exchange the sugar quota for American investments.' The bonds between Cuba and the Soviet Union were tightened in 1962 when Russia agreed to take an increased supply of Cuban sugar. The deal, however, was contingent on the continued refusal of the United States to grant Cuba a sugar quota and would change if the United States again offered to buy Cuban sugar. Cuban-American tension was further aggravated by the exchange of Soviet oil for Cuban sugar, whereupon the

American oil refineries in Cuba refused to refine the Soviet oil —and were promptly nationalised.

Castro's original economic programme had, in the tradition of the West Indian nationalist movement, opposed the pronounced tendency to monoculture in Cuba's economy with emphasis on sugar, and foreign ownership of the sugar industry, and it pledged diversification of the economy principally by a programme of accelerated industrial development. In power, Castro took the decision to reduce sugar production. The combination of a bad drought and government policy led in the period 1961–1963 to a reduction of 14 per cent in the sugar area cut, 42 per cent in the cane ground, and 33 per cent in unit yield.

Then followed the Soviet-Cuban trade agreement after the abortive American invasion of April 1961. Castro came up against the basic economic fact that no other agricultural activity would give such returns as those yielded by the cultivation of sugar cane, and Guevara announced that one of the 'two fundamental errors' made by Castroism was the 'declaration of war on sugar cane'. After Castro's tour of the Soviet Union in 1963 he came back with the view that an 'international division of labour' was necessary, according to which Cuba would specialise in what it usually was best fitted for by nature—namely, agriculture.

As the price of sugar rose to the dizzy heights that reminded world observers of the 'dance of the millions' in the Cuba of 1920, Castro announced that sugar production, which totalled less than 4 million tons in 1963, would be progressively increased until it reached 10 million tons in 1970. This led to a new agrarian reform which Castro had not anticipated. Specifically the result was the expropriation of the medium-sized farmer; with all the experience of collectivisation in Russia before the Cuban Government, the balance shifted from 40–60 in favour of the private sector to 70–30 in favour of the State sector, bringing State ownership in agriculture almost to the level achieved in industry. Draper, as an American who understands this sugar question, writes:

'The new line was, in theory, not so much a clear-cut choice between agriculture and industry as a reversal of their previously-allotted roles. The old line had encouraged industry at the expense of agriculture. The new one was based on the development of agriculture as the precondition of industrialisation. In practice, however, agriculture was given such a high priority that not much was left over, at least in the foreseeable future, for industry... There have been few ironies in recent history greater than the comeback of "monoculture" in Cuba... One wonders whether a revolution was really necessary to restore sugar to the place that it had in the Cuba of the 1920s.'

The answer of one of Castro's apologists, Boorstein, to Draper is amusing: 'In achieving their 10-million-ton sugar goal, the Cuban people will be writing an epic in the annals of socialism.'

In a speech in Havana on January 25, 1964, Castro emphasised the difference between monoculture under the Americans and his own monoculture. Castro said:

'The Soviet Union did not have any sugar plantations in Cuba. It did not have any sugar mills in Cuba. It did not have any property in Cuba. The Soviet Union was not receiving foreign exchange from Cuba. The Soviet Union did not collect dividends. It did not collect interest. On the contrary, the Soviet Union was extending large loans to Cuba to allow us to cope with this situation.'

Castro's anti-Americanism was then reflected in his attack on the American-owned public utilities, principally telephones and electricity. Cubans everywhere had avenged themselves after the flight of Batista against the symbols of American domination: they smashed parking meters in Havana, severed telephone lines, and raided and looted casinos. Castro reduced electricity rates outside Havana to the Havana level, resulting in a saving of $15 million a year for Cuban consumers. Castro's Government assumed the management functions of the telephone company whilst the company continued to receive the profits. All this brought Castro enormous popularity.

A decisive stage in Castro's relations with the United States was reached in 1959 when, at the Buenos Aires Conference of the Organisation of American States, Castro proposed a $30 billion aid programme for Latin America over 10 years and the creation of a Latin American common market. His opponents, especially the United States, sneered. But two years later President Kennedy proposed his Alliance for Progress with $10 billion over 10 years, and President Johnson later pledged an additional $10 billion. In 1967 the Organisation of American States—excluding Cuba which had by then been expelled—voted unanimously at Punta del Este in Uruguay for the establishment of a Latin American common market.

The United States remained adamant in its refusal to compromise with Castro and in its failure to read the signs of Castro's popularity. Basing itself on Castro's refusal to hold the free elections he had promised, and obsessed with the rough, unorthodox justice meted out in popular trials to the Batista reactionaries, the United States ignored the fact that nearly 90 per cent of the population either favoured Castro or the Government, and only 10 per cent were definitely in opposition. More women and young people were for Castro than men and people over 25, and his following was naturally greater among the lower than among the upper classes. The following were listed, in this order, as the greatest achievements of the revolution: land reform, honest government, educational advances, and greater social justice. The Cuban Revolution is a revolution of peasants, workers, youth, Negroes and the poor.

Ignoring all this, impressed only with the number of exiles from Cuba whom Castro readily allowed to leave as there would be fewer mouths to feed, the United States launched the comedy of the Bay of Pigs invasion in April 1961. The result was a resounding victory for Castro, who, thereupon, with characteristic audacity, proceeded to aggravate the situation by placing himself squarely in the Soviet camp and declaring himself a Marxist-Leninist. As Khrushchev had prophesied at the United Nations in September 1960, the United States made Castro a Communist. As Herbert Matthews, Castro's great American adviser and friendliest critic, argues convincingly, 'Communism was not a cause of the Cuban revolution; it was a result'.

The road was clear for the missile crisis of 1962, when the Russians, at Castro's prompting, installed offensive missiles 90 miles from the American coast. Khrushchev yielded in the subsequent confrontation with Kennedy, and notwithstanding Castro's angry protests, withdrew the missiles. Castro thereupon set out to emphasise that, whilst he was economically dependent on the Soviet bloc for his sugar contract, factories, economic aid and arms, he was politically independent of it, and proceeded to develop a society allegedly Marxist-Leninist such as Moscow and Peking never dreamed of and unlike anything developed in the socialist world. On one occasion in 1967 Castro proclaimed that his aim was to give free sugar, free coffee, and free fruit to the population. He added:

'It will take a long time, but we do not believe in the materialistic concepts of capitalism or of other types of Communism in which money is the incentive. Men live for other things than money. The incentives must be to guarantee them a decent life in which they and their children are educated, cared for, housed, fed and acquire culture. They must be given dignity and in return must learn that their work is a contribution to the good of all the people and the State. This is true Marxism-Leninism as we see it, but it is not Communism as it is practised in Russia, Eastern Europe or China. We are working out our own Cuban system, to meet our problems and satisfy our people.'

Castro has maintained neutrality in the Sino-Soviet dispute, and has differed markedly and publicly from Russia's aims in Latin America: where Russia stands for trade with Latin America and Communist achievement of power by electoral and constitutional means, Castro, with his Tricontinental Solidarity Organisation, is for revolutionary action based on guerrilla warfare, with emphasis on Venezuela and Bolivia. Marxist-Leninist or not, the Cuban Revolution remains Castro's revolution, and the Communist Party has no power in Cuba.

For the rest Castro's programme is pure nationalist, comprehensible to and acceptable by any other Caribbean nationalist. Pride of place goes to his achievements in education. The fantastic situation he inherited was as follows:

Over 10,000 students aged 15 and over were in the first standard; of these approximately 9 out of 10 were in the rural areas.

About 59,000 students in the first standard were aged 12–14; 4 out of 5 of these were in the rural areas.

About 142,000 students in the first standard were aged 9–11; 8 out of 9 of these were in rural areas.

Of the total of $1\frac{1}{2}$ million students in primary schools, 58,000 were in the 6th standard; of these 1 in 5 came from the rural areas.

Insisting that what had to be done was to be done as quickly as possible and without regard to cost, Castro was able in 30 months to open more classrooms than his predecessors had opened in 30 years. In his country schools thousands of country girls between the ages of 14 and 21 learned sewing and dressmaking as well as reading, writing, arithmetic and history. At the end of the course every pupil was presented with a sewing machine of her own, on condition that she taught the others at her home in her village. In a special school in Havana domestic servants were trained to be taxi drivers. But Castro's key achievement was his literacy campaign, which unleashed 300,000 people (among them 100,000 secondary school pupils and 35,000 teachers plus many key workers and employees) to reduce the illiteracy rate to 4 per cent of the total population.

The number of illiterates was estimated at one million. Primary school teachers, secondary school students, adults were recruited and grouped into brigades. Each member was supplied with a uniform, hammock, blanket, instruction books, a teaching manual, a Cuban flag, and a paraffin lamp (in the absence of rural electricity) which became the symbol of the campaign. The test at the end of the course consisted of reading one or two short paragraphs from the basic textbook *Venceremòs* (We shall overcome), taking simple dictation, and writing a letter to Castro.

Every Caribbean nationalist would similarly have envied the road construction programme of Castro under which 600 miles of road were constructed in the first six months of the revolution, and the announcement that a sewerage and water scheme would be constructed in rural areas at a cost of $300 million. The popularity of the Castro regime was increased by its construction of rural medical centres, mobile dispensaries and people's stores, its attention to social welfare in the form of children's nurseries, homes for the aged, institutes for the handicapped, its tremendous housing programme under which houses were going up at the rate of 27 a day and 833 a month, and its conversion of exclusive American facilities under the Batista regime such as the Havana Biltmore Yacht and Country Club and the Varadero International Hotel into establishments open to the people of Cuba at minimum rates. Most important of all, unemployment has been eliminated. The *New York Times*, on April 24, 1960, summed up the position as follows: 'The nation is simply not prepared to go back to the old days.'

But a high price has been paid for these achievements and many errors have been made. Castro has been criticised as much by his friends as by his enemies, in language that would be understood in all developing countries.

The first error we can identify is what Guevara called 'planless planning'. In August 1961, the Minister of Economy, Regino Boti, pledged that in 1965 Cuba would be, in relation to its population, the most industrialised country in Latin America, and would be at the head of production *per capita* in electrical energy, steel, cement, tractors, and refining of petroleum. In May 1961, Guevara prophesied that Cuba would double its standard of living by 1965, 'if the Americans do not trouble us', and at the Punta del Este Conference credited Cuba with the following achievements by 1965: first place in America in *per capita* production of steel, cement, electrical energy, and, except for Venezuela, refining of petroleum; first place in Latin America in tractors, razors, shoes, textiles; second place in world production of metallic nickel.

By 1962 Guevara was singing a different tune:

'We failed to put the proper emphasis on the utilisation of our resources; we worked with the fixed purpose of producing substitutes for finished imported articles, without clearly seeing that these articles are made with raw materials which must be had in order to manufacture them... We began to acquire factories, but we did not think of the raw materials for them that we would have to import... Two years had been lost installing factories for a series of articles which could be bought at almost the same price as the raw materials that we needed to produce them.'

Guevara made an even more astonishing confession in his speech in Algiers on July 14, 1963. He said:

'The suggestion of having a 15 per cent increase in agricultural production was simply ridiculous... In the distribution of income, we at first gave too much emphasis to the satisfaction of social necessities, paying more equitable wages and increasing employment, without sufficiently considering the condition of the economy... The structure of our economy has still not changed after four years of revolution.'

In an article in *International Affairs* in October 1964 Guevara continued the self-criticism of the regime. He wrote:

'In its agricultural policy the Revolution represented the antithesis of what had existed during the years of dependence on imperialism and exploitation by the land-owning class. Diversification versus monoculture; full employment versus idle hands; these were the major transformations in the rural areas during those years ...

'Our first error was the way in which we carried out diversification. Instead of embarking on diversification by degrees we attempted too much at once. The sugar cane areas were reduced and the land thus made available was used for the cultivation of new crops. But this meant a general decline in agricultural production. The entire economic history of Cuba has demonstrated that no other agricultural activity would give such returns as those yielded by the cultivation of the sugar cane. At the outset of the Revolution many of us were not aware of this basic economic fact, because a fetishistic idea connected sugar with our dependence on imperialism and with the misery in the rural areas, without analysing the real causes: the relation to the uneven trade balance.

'Unfortunately, whatever measures are taken in agriculture do not become apparent until months, sometimes years, afterwards. This is particularly true as regards sugar cane production ...

'The second great mistake was, in our opinion, that of dispersing our resources over a great number of agricultural products, all in the name of diversification ...

'Only a very solid productive organisation could have resisted such rapid change. In an underdeveloped country, in particular, the structure of agriculture remains very inflexible and its organisation rests on extremely weak and subjective foundations ...

'I have spoken of certain achievements in the industrial field during the first years, but it is only just that I should also mention the errors made. Fundamentally, these were caused by a lack of precise understanding of the technological and economic elements necessary in the new industries installed during those years. Influenced by existing unemployment and by the pressure exerted by the problems in our foreign trade, we acquired a great number of factories with the dual purpose of substituting imports and providing employment for an appreciable number of urban workers. Later we found that in many of these plants the technical efficiency was insufficient when measured by international standards, and that the net result of the substitution of imports was very limited, because the necessary raw materials were not nationally produced.'

Dudley Seers has emphasised the 'number of serious miscalculations' made by Castro's regime. He is particularly critical of the fact that 'the magnitude of the task that Cuba was attempting does not seem to have been understood by the administration'. He castigated 'an overambitious attempt at detailed planning, owing to the uncritical adoption of planning methods being used in the Soviet Union and Czechoslovakia'. Whilst he berates the errors of others—for example, Brazil, with its ten motor vehicle manufacturing plants in a market which is possibly not big enough for three—he warns against uncritical acceptance of later prognostications. He writes: 'After the experience of the past two years we ought not to fall into the trap of mistaking planned for probable development. What is physically possible is not necessarily organisationally possible.'

Boorstein, a foreign Marxist sympathetic to the Castro regime, who himself worked in Cuba with the Cubans, has given us an unvarnished picture of the planlessness—what Suarez calls Castro's 'profound allergy to any form of organisation': unco-ordinated projects, inefficiency of management; 'a driving impatience to make progress rapidly which resulted in unrea-listically ambitious plans and a tendency to see things parochially'; nebulous schemes; 'the problem of financial discipline ... com-pletely ignored'; the balance-of-payments deficit; Ministries run 'like separate economic fiefs' without systematic review of their operations.

This was the background to the more systematic planning attempted in 1962. Then came the real problem, according to Boorstein—the plans were drawn up by technicians from socialist countries. Boorstein writes:

'We were deluged with models used for planning in Czechoslovakia, some of which were read to us line by line ... There was no discussion of why the different organisations were set up the way they were, what alternative forms were possible, and what advantages or disadvantages they might have. The planning models used in Czechoslovakia were presented as immutable and fully applicable everywhere ... Hardly 10 per cent of the required technicans existed in Cuba. But the absence of trained people was ignored ... But our efforts to draw the Czech technicians into a dis-cussion of Cuban circumstances did not succeed ... The lectures, translated into Spanish for Cubans, could, with minor changes, have been translated into Persian for Iranians ... In the design of the planning forms, the manual and models of Czechoslovakia—and sometimes also those of the Soviet Union—were used for guidance ... the forms came out adapted more closely to Czechoslovakia than to Cuba ... A spirit of formalism began to spread ... The style of work became bureaucratic ... the real economy and its problems became something remote.'

The second principal error pinpointed by Dumont, the well-known French economist sympathetic to the developing countries, consists in the 'socialist errors' made by Castro and his colleagues. Dumont writes:

'The adoption of so-called "superior" forms of property, leading more rapidly to communism, are, together with its underdevelopment, the essential cause of the present difficulties of Cuba. The desire for a rapid transition to a social structure defined, *a priori,* in European books of the past century without verifying whether it was adaptable either to the situation or to the mentality of the Cubans, has up to now not yielded brilliant results ... to repeat and prolong the same cycle of errors as the U.S.S.R., starting from theories abandoned in their country of origin, and when the first results have already demonstrated their danger, cannot be approved ... Cuba uselessly recommences the whole cycle of economic errors of the socialist countries ... What I saw in Cuba in 1963 exceeded my apprehensions. After constituting a powerful revelation of the principal difficulties of neocolonial capitalism, Cuba presents to us today, apart from its powerful social effort, a picture of a development effort accompanied by a series of economic difficulties and errors as a socialist regime. I had underestimated these difficulties in the establishment of socialism.'

Dumont then proceeds to make specific criticisms. His first criticism is of agriculture, emphasising time and again that socialism has been more successful in the industrial field than in agriculture, as evidenced by the massive Soviet purchases of wheat, the severe rationing in China, the agrarian difficulties in Algeria. Dumont criticises the expropriation of agricultural land pursued without any preconceived plan, according to the fantasy of the director, without examining if it was really useful and above all whether the Agrarian Reform Institute was capable of handling it. He pointed to the enormous congregation of animals on State-owned live-stock farms, which required rations that were well prepared and the assurance of a continuous supply of feeds of high quality, and which were exposed to the risk of epidemics, especially because of the insufficiency of veterinarians. Dumont emphasised that Castro's gigantic plan of 100,000 chickens a month to be produced on each of his 100 giant poultry farms from 1961 had been realised to the extent of only 25 or 30 per cent in March 1963. Castro proposed to sell these birds at 30 cents a pound, less than the cost of production, as compared with 50 cents for beef. Dumont stresses that 'the giant unit of production is not an article of Marxist faith', which merely condemns the tiny holdings as an obstacle to modern technological methods.

Bianchi, one of the Chilean economists on Dudley Seers' team which reported in 1964, goes even further. He criticised the inaccurate assessment of the need of fertiliser. He laid stress on the serious unbalanced importation of farm machinery—relatively too many tractors were purchased and too few ploughs, harrows and other complementary equipment. 'The output targets tended to express wishes rather than economic realities . . . over-estimation of output targets co-existed with underestimation of consumption requirements.'

The third principal error was the programme of excessive nationalisation. In 1953 Castro had limited himself to a pledge to nationalise the American-owned electricity and telephone under-takings. In February 1958 he had regarded nationalisation as 'at best a cumbersome instrument' which did not make the state any stronger but enfeebled private enterprise; he pledged that foreign investment would always be welcome and secure in Cuba. However, on October 13, 1960, he nationalised three million acres of United States-owned land, to be followed later by Cuban-owned land, 376 Cuban industrial and commercial enterprises including 18 distilleries, 5 breweries, 4 paint factories, 61 textile factories, 16 rice mills, 11 cinemas, and 13 depart-ment stores. Eleven days later he nationalised 166 properties owned wholly or partially by United States interests. The American Draper comments: 'Castroism has taken a far more extreme position *vis-à-vis* the "national bourgeoisie" than the Chinese Communists have ever done. In some ways Castroism is more extreme than any existing Communist tendency, and even Mao Tse-Tung might privately consider it a "leftist deviation".'

Dumont was scandalised. He considered that the basic error of the Cuban leaders, which produced multiple consequences, was 'the pronounced tendency to disregard the co-operative formula'. Did the necessary control of the strict application of rationing imply nationalisation of retail trades, textiles, garments? he asked; did it exclude the co-operative? Socialisation of restaurants and hotels, even the small ones, of small workshops and a large slice of retail trade was arguable; 'a co-operative formula would have been even more appropriate, without any possible hesitation'. On agriculture he was even more forthright. He commented:

'Agricultural co-operatives should be more carefully prepared, instead of being brutally improvised as was the case in Cuba, in the centralisation of disorder and authoritarianism. Such a progressive evolution is not directed against the Revolution; it facilitates the progress of the economy and thus makes it less difficult to establish the Revolution ... Instead of nationalising a sugar factory or a condensary, why not turn them over, under the control of the State, to the group of workers whose products are utilised by these installations? An agrarian socialism aiming firstly at development does not demand brutal collectivisation imposed from above as was the case in the U.S.S.R. in 1929.'

Charles Bettelheim, a French economist of communist persuasion, after visiting Cuba in the latter half of 1961, tried, according to Draper, to tell the Cubans that they had nationalised and centralised too much, too far and too fast. All that he earned for his pains was a violent attack from Guevara.

The fourth error, pinpointed by Bianchi, was the allocation of too many resources to social, as opposed to economic, investments, especially in agriculture—for example, the construction of new secondary roads unnecessarily wide for the traffic. Dumont criticised the housing as too lavish; it was restricted to the few, and too often involved importation of materials and furnishing which further complicated the balance of payments. Castro had to abandon his grandiose housing schemes when it appeared in May 1962 that there were 150,000 applicants for 5,000 dwellings.

Dumont attacked the volunteer system of labour to assist the agricultural economy. He found that 41,300 volunteers utilised in the coffee harvest picked an average of 1.06 boxes of berries a day against an average of 7 boxes for regular pickers and 12 boxes for a large group of workers. He condemned the subordination of technical to literary education—too many literary people, lawyers and artists, too few technicians. He advised Castro to charge for water for irrigation purposes, at least the cost of winning and distributing it. He complained: 'Everything is done in Cuba as if the country was too rich.'

Many doubts have been expressed from time to time about the cost of the literacy campaign and its success, notwithstanding the continuation courses offered by way of follow-up. Enormous quantities of basic equipment were used—2 million copies of *Venceremos*, 1 million copies of the teacher's instruction manual, hundreds of thousands of hammocks, uniforms, shirts, trousers, boots, haversacks, blankets, 145,999 paraffin lamps; in addition 104,000 pairs of spectacles were issued free to illiterate students. About half a year of Cuba's regular schooling had to be foregone.

Emphasising that the literacy campaign helped to create

enormous sympathy for the Cuban revolution, Goldenberg criticises it:

'What Cuba needed above all were technicians of all kinds and levels—and it seemed odd to close all secondary schools for eight months and to draft a considerable proportion of primary teachers into the literacy campaign. The results were doubtful. 707,000 adults were taught by more than 300,000 teachers.'

Dumont considered it too high a price to pay to disrupt the national education system and even the labour needs of the country by the illiteracy campaign to find at the end of it that certain of the peasants could, with a tutor guiding their hand, sign their name.

Finally, Dumont launched a concentrated attack on Castro's wages policy. He wrote: 'The too absolute priority accorded to labour by certain Marxists in the process of the creation of wealth frustrates or retards the adoption of such economically efficacious measures as profit and interest.' He challenged that the demand for consumer goods was increased still more by the increase of rural wages by 20 per cent between 1959 and 1961. This created an inflationary situation, which would have required a parallel increase in productivity that was not forthcoming. Each time the workers produced one dollar in products, he complained, quoting a Soviet economist, he received on an average two dollars in wages. Dumont wrote:

'I explained to Guevara the necessity of increasing the labour provided without increasing quite as quickly the number of wage earners; and I proposed that the members of co-operatives should provide voluntary labour for the construction of their houses, especially during the second half of the year, the dead season in agriculture . . . he did not sufficiently comprehend the danger of rural overconsumption . . . and its economic consequences were underestimated . . . The essential vice of the present-day State farms in Cuba is to distribute $2 in wages everytime a worker has created $1 in wealth. The principal remedy is therefore the abandonment of the *guaranteed* daily wage, and not only the reduction (relative to the price) of the wage. This could be achieved by *wages tied as closely as possible to the labour provided* as measured by norms . . . if workers were clearly advised that the Cuban State would no longer meet deficits produced by the laziness of certain workers, all would have an incentive to change their attitude. They would quickly understand the basic economic relationship and the strict connection between the productivity of their labour and their wages...From 1965 deficits should no longer be met by the State, so as to relate wages compulsorily to the real productivity of labour.'

This basic criticism of Dumont's was not met by Castro's control of wages. With absolute power in his hands as *Lider Máximo*, Castro in 1963 was able to institute labour camps and the reorganisation of the system of wages scales in Cuba, under which three out of every four Cuban workers were graded in the lowest category in which the average hourly wage was reduced from 90 cents to 75 cents. This was followed by the Law of Labour Justice of October 3, 1964, which opened an offensive against absenteeism. Nor does Seers grasp Dumont's criticism when he emphasised the egalitarian system of wages in effect in Cuba, by which the minimum wage was set at 65 pesos a month, and, according to a labour census in 1960, only 10,000 persons received more than 500 pesos a month.

What conclusions can we draw from Castroism? Dumont suggests three priorities for the future: (1) a ban on luxury imports, with heavy taxes on some luxuries—in order to leave more money available for the importation of machinery as well as to reduce the balance of payments deficit; (2) the requirement that large trading establishments dealing with imports and exports must invest in the country the larger part of all of their profits; (3) priority to productive investment (balanced between agriculture, infrastructure and industrial development) over administrative requirements. Every one of these prescriptions is commonplace in developing countries; they all figure, for example, in the 1968 budget of the People's National Movement in Trinidad and Tobago.

Seers notes that planning techniques had improved by the time of his visit. These included: (a) an investment of $99 million (U.S. dollars) in the years 1962–1965 of which 20 per cent was allotted to electricity and by which industrial output was to increase by 1.5 per cent each year; (b) by the end of 1965 work would commence on a steel mill with a capacity of 1.3 million tons to cost $150 million; (c) a motor vehicle assembly plant to cost $90 million; (d) a big ammonia plant to cost $54 million. Trinidad and Tobago has for years been investing heavily in electricity, three motor vehicle assembly plants have been started, a big ammonia plant exists, and negotiations are in progress in respect of a steel mill.

All these errors and failures add up to the warning which Herbert Matthews has recently issued:

'Taking the population of Cuba as a whole, it is arguable that Cubans have been better fed under the Revolution than before 1959 although some hundreds of thousands of Cubans are much worse fed, especially in the cities ... It does not follow that the Cuban Revolution has been a failure; at least, not yet. It will fail *in the long run* if the Cuban economy is not put on a healthy, viable basis which, among other things, means plentiful and unrationed food supplies. Cuba is still far from that in 1968.'

Castro has two lines of defence. The first is Dumont's estimate that Castro gets in foreign aid from the Soviet Union $40 *per capita* as against a little more than $2 provided by the U.S.A. to Latin America. Dumont writes:

'These $40 are equivalent to the average annual income of the poorest regions in Africa, like South Morocco, part of Algeria, the North Region of Nigeria, part of Kenya, Tanganyika, Ethiopia, etc. This allowed the Cubans to construct many factories, without giving proper thought to their localisation which was often defective.'

This explains why the Russians, like the Americans, are determined not to have another Cuba in the Western Hemisphere.

The second line of defence is stated thus by Matthews:

'One advantage of a totalitarian regime is that it can impose efficiency and mechanisation and let the workers grumble under their breath. The justifiable complaints now are that real wages are lower than before, that work norms are higher, that there is no freedom to move from job to job and place to place, and that there is precious little to spend extra money on.'

Other Caribbean countries, which have to deal with powerful labour unions that oppose mechanisation and automation because of the unemployment situation, dedicated as they are to democratic systems, cannot fall back on Castro's line of defence.

What then, of the future of Castroism? Goldenberg praises it as 'an autochthonous product of the Continent. It had not been imported from outside'. Whether Castroism can be exported, via the Tricontinental Congress, which, in attacking Latin America, attacked specifically Trinidad and Tobago, Guyana and Jamaica, whether the Andean mountain range can be made into the Sierra

Maestra of all America, as Castro said on July 26, 1960, remains to be seen. It is significant that Castro seemed unable to take advantage of the Mexican disorders in 1968.

But on one point the future is not obscure. Dumont makes two suggestions: that the socialist countries should abandon autarchy in agriculture, that is, the beet sugar industry (he should study the history of sugar some more), and that Cuba should find a larger market for its production in general in the West Indies.

But Trinidad and Tobago, producing sugar, ammonia, petroleum, garments, condensed milk and other products complementing Cuba's, could hardly be expected to surrender its independent development of its own economy in order to be a dumping ground for Cuba's products and allow Castro to be the sugar bowl of the Caribbean. The future cries out for a Caribbean Economic Community and the extension of CARIFTA to the entire area, to work out a rational system of interchange between the Caribbean territories, a common external tariff, and the establishment of regional integrated industries as far as possible owned and operated by the Caribbean people themselves in their own interest.

Chapter Twenty-Nine

The Future of the Caribbean

The Caribbean area in 1969 is one of the most unstable areas in our unstable world. A mere catalogue of the instability will suffice: the British invasion of Anguilla (resulting from its secession from the associated state of St. Kitts-Nevis-Anguilla); anti-police rioting in Montserrat; serious labour disturbances in Curaçao; political crises in Surinam; chronic labour unrest in Antigua; endemic racial tension in Jamaica; the secessionist movement in the Rupununi in Guyana; the independence movement in Guadeloupe attended by grave disturbances; the unpopular dictatorship in Haiti; the uncertainties of the democratic movement in the Dominican Republic; the United States blockade of Cuba; and the Castro support for Latin American guerrillas.

The constitutional diversity aggravates the chronic instability— the three Latin American republics of Cuba, Haiti and the Dominican Republic; the four independent Commonwealth states of Jamaica, Trinidad and Tobago, Guyana and Barbados, with Guyana soon to become a republic; associated statehood with Britain of the smaller Commonwealth islands; the departmental status of Martinique, Guadeloupe and Cayenne making them parts of metropolitan France; the peculiar status of Surinam and the

Netherlands Antilles in the tripartite kingdom of the Netherlands, which leaves defence and foreign affairs to the Netherlands; the semi-colonial status of the United States Virgin Islands; the Free Associated State relationship with the U.S.A. of Puerto Rico, which since the 1968 elections seems to be heading for statehood within the American Union.

This constitutional diversity is matched by an appalling degree of economic fragmentation—totally absurd for so small an area. Fragmentation goes to such fantastic lengths as would make the angels weep. Fragmentation is reflected both in the politically ordained economic links with different external powers and in the type of development strategy being pursued by individual territories. Thus Puerto Rico (in spite of impressive gains in industrial development and increases in *per capita* income) is being daily ever more closely integrated into the United States economy, enjoying a free flow of its goods and people into the Mainland and receiving vast inflows of both public and private Mainland capital. The traditional agricultural exports—sugar, bananas and citrus—of both the independent and non-independent Commonwealth Caribbean countries still depend on tariff preferences and even more on other forms of special protective arrangements in the United Kingdom market. The French Departments of Martinique and Guadeloupe are economically no less than constitutionally part of metropolitan France. Surinam and the Netherlands Antilles are integrated economically with Holland and the European Common Market and receive unilateral transfers of funds from these two sources. Cuba is heavily dependent for trade and credit on the U.S.S.R. and the Eastern European countries.

Not only do the past and present political links with metropolitan powers determine the pattern of trade and economic alignments and so contribute to fragmentation within the region. The economic policies pursued by the Governments—both independent and non-independent—also serve to strengthen 'vertical' ties between the individual territories and metropolitan countries and frustrate the creation of 'horizontal' ties between the countries of the region. The individual territories all vie with one another to entice metropolitan firms to establish branches and subsidiaries in the region and to attract tourists from the richer countries.

In so vying they pursue competitive rather than co-operative
strategies of economic development, competing with one another
in the granting of absurdly long tax holidays and in giving concessions such as beach rights, freehold sales of large portions of
the areas of their islands to foreign interests, and even in some
cases the right to establish casinos. Regional economic disintegra-
tion and failure to combine regional resources for production for
regional and extra-regional markets are further enhanced by the
existence of large international corporations exploiting minerals—
oil in Trinidad and Tobago, bauxite in Jamaica, Guyana, Surinam,
the Dominican Republic and Haiti. The large mineral-producing
metropolitan firms are vertically-integrated concerns, with their
lines of trade running from the individual Caribbean territory
to the metropolis rather than between the Caribbean territories.

Fragmentation is accompanied by massive dependence on the
outside world, even in the independent countries of the Commonwealth Caribbean. With the exception of Cuba (the character of
whose dependence is different from that of the others), the
politically dependent and the politically independent countries
of the Caribbean differ only in the latter's possession of formal
sovereignty. For the most part, they are all highly dependent on
the outside world—for economic aid; for large portions of the
capital annually invested in both the traditional and the new
manufacturing and tourist sectors of the economy; for sheltered
markets for their traditional primary products; and even for
emigration outlets for their surplus labour—Puerto Ricans to
U.S.A., Jamaicans to Britain, Trinidadians to Canada,
Martiniquans to France, Surinamers to Holland. The strategic
decisions affecting the economies are made outside the national
boundaries—by foreign companies and by large international
firms. The original mercantilism of the seventeenth and eighteenth
centuries has been replaced by the neo-mercantilism of the
second half of the twentieth century. Instead of the British or
European merchant firm and the absentee sugar plantation
owner, the allocation of resources in the Caribbean is now controlled by the large international corporations. This is the case
whether one looks at sugar production and refining; the international marketing of other primary products such as bananas;
shipping; banking; insurance; manufacturing industries; hotels;

minerals such as oil and bauxite; and even many of the newspapers and mass media. The locus of economic decision-making and the dynamics of economic growth continue to rest well outside the territorial boundaries of the Caribbean territories.

These extensive economic contacts with the outside world do have their positive side. The standard of living and *per capita* incomes of nearly all the Caribbean countries (with the notable exception of Haiti, which has relatively few contacts with the outside world) have been undergoing fairly impressive increases over the last two decades; and social services such as health and education have expanded to some extent. The Caribbean territories (with the exception of Haiti) do not, therefore, face the dismal levels of poverty to be found in Africa and Asia; but dissatisfaction with the standard of living and the level of social services already attained is perhaps greater than in either Africa or Asia. The close proximity to North America; contact with tourists; the high hopes expected of self-government and independence; the existence of strong trade union movements; and the large amount of emigration have fanned the flames of the revolution of rising expectations. Even more critically, deep-seated and rising unemployment, coexisting with the rising levels of *per capita* income and of expectations, aggravate the restlessness. The chronic unemployment and underemployment which emerged after slavery in the nineteenth century have in recent years been intensified by rapid population growth, inappropriate capital intensive technologies imported from abroad, and rising wage rates produced by the activities of the trade unions. Short-term solutions to the unemployment problem continue to be elusive and add to the feeling of helplessness and dependence on the outside world. In the Caribbean, it almost appears as if the growth of *per capita* income and the reduction of unemployment are not only mutually exclusive but also conflicting tendencies.

Dependence on the outside world in the Caribbean in 1969 is not only economic. It is also cultural, institutional, intellectual and psychological. Political forms and social institutions, even in the politically independent countries, were imitated rather than created, borrowed rather than relevant, reflecting the forms existing in the particular metropolitan country from which they were derived. There is still no serious indigenous intellectual life. The ideological formulations for the most part still reflect the concepts and vocabulary of nineteenth-century Europe and, more sinister, of the now almost defunct Cold War. Authentic and relevant indigenous formulations are either ignored or equated with 'subversion'. Legal systems, educational structures and administrative institutions reflect past practices which are now being hastily abandoned in the metropolitan countries where they originated. Even though both in the Commonwealth Caribbean countries and in the French Departments literature of world standard and universal validity has been produced by writers such as Lamming, Naipaul, Braithwaite (from Barbados), Walcott, Aimé Césaire and Frantz Fanon in Martinique, and even though in Trinidad and Tobago the steel band and calypso have emerged, nevertheless artistic, community and individual values are not for the most part authentic but, to borrow the language of the economist, possess a high import content, the vehicles of import being the educational system, the mass media, the films, and the tourists. V. S. Naipaul's description of West Indians as 'mimic men' is harsh, but true. Finally, psychological dependence strongly reinforces the other forms of dependence. For, in the last analysis, dependence is a state of mind. A too-long history of colonialism seems to have crippled Caribbean self-confidence and Caribbean self-reliance, and a vicious circle has been set up: psychological dependence leads to an ever-growing economic and cultural dependence on the outside world. Fragmentation is intensified in the process. And the greater degree of dependence and fragmentation further reduces local self-confidence.

The difficulties multiply. Economic uncertainties are increased by the ever-present danger of Britain joining the European Common Market, with the possibility of its abandonment of the traditional preferential position enjoyed by West Indian exports of primary products in the British market, especially sugar. With respect to these commodities, the West Indies are not free to opt for Latin America as a substitute for Britain and Europe. The Organisation of American States and the Inter-American Development Bank exclude from their purview the non-independent British islands, while Guyana, engaged in a serious boundary dispute with Venezuela, is barred from admission into the Organisation of American States and even from signing the denuclearisation treaty in respect of the Western Hemisphere.

As the Black Power movement makes headway in the United States in its fight for black dignity, there are the obvious repercussions in the Caribbean. Jamaica is seething with racial tension, black versus brown and white. The labour unrest in Antigua and the labour riots in Curaçao were both responses to Black Power propaganda. The large Indian population of Guyana, Surinam and Trinidad and Tobago adds another dimension to the racial disharmony which has already erupted in serious racial riots in Guyana. As the Hindu-Muslim disturbances continue in India, and the Protestant-Catholic disturbances in Northern Ireland, the religious diversity of the Caribbean region raises another cloud over the future. In this bleak picture the only bright spot is the apparent success in Castro's Cuba with the full integration of the black population into his society.

Youth and the students are becoming increasingly restless under the stimulus of world protest, in America, in France, in England, in Mexico and elsewhere. The situation is aggravated by the action of the Government of Jamaica in banning two Guyanese lecturers from the University of the West Indies.

The overshadowing fear and apprehension is the United States of America, which has vowed that it will not tolerate another Cuba in the Western Hemisphere. It was with this motive that the United States intervened in the Dominican Republic in 1965.

To sum up: the contemporary Caribbean is an area characterised by instability; political and economic fragmentation; constitutional diversity; economic, psychological, cultural and in some cases political dependence; large-scale unemployment and underemployment; economic uncertainty; unresolved racial tensions; potential religious conflicts; the restlessness of youth; and an all-pervading fear of the United States.

What then, is the future of the Caribbean?

Given its past history, the future of the Caribbean can only be meaningfully discussed in terms of the possibilities for the emergence of an identity for the region and its peoples. The whole history of the Caribbean so far can be viewed as a conspiracy to block the emergence of a Caribbean identity—in politics, in institutions, in economics, in culture and in values. Viewed in historical perspective, the future way forward for the peoples of the Carib-

which would impel them to start making their
be the subjects rather than the objects of history,
he playthings of other people. In this respect, the
so far been the 'outsider' in the New World. The
anada have emerged as sovereign countries with an
eir own—even though in recent years Canadians have
had   to be worried about the preservation of their own
identity in the face of massive American economic penetration.
The countries of Middle and South America (with the exception
of the Guyanas) have achieved some small measure of identity—
Mexico and Brazil more so than the others. Viewed in this light,
the present crisis in Latin America should be seen as a desire
on the part of the Latin American countries to complete the
process of realising themselves—a process which started with the
Wars of Independence against Spain in the nineteenth century.
What today appears to the inhabitants of the metropolitan
countries to be xenophobia and irrational nationalism in the
Third World is more often than not the outward manifestation
of this quest for self-realisation. To George III and his Ministry,
the leaders of the thirteen American colonies in the 1770's must
have appeared to be very bad boys indeed.

In its quest for identity and self-realisation, the Caribbean in
1969 starts with certain favourable conditions—young populations,
affected by the world-wide restlessness and idealism of youth;
relatively high rates of literacy and education; relatively high
levels of *per capita* income; and a long history of contact with
the Western World. Indeed, the great Trinidadian, J. J. Thomas,
in the course of his brilliant polemic in defence of the West
Indian peoples against the calumnies of that nineteenth-century
predecessor of Enoch Powell, James Anthony Froude, Regius
Professor of History at Oxford, wrote in 1890 of West Indians as
'apt apprentices in every conceivable department of civilised
culture'. The task now is to make the West Indian peoples cease
being 'apt apprentices' and become ready innovators 'in every
conceivable department of civilised culture'. The requirements for
this transmutation are twofold—a psychological revolution among
the Caribbean peoples themselves and metropolitan empathy with
Caribbean aspirations. This revolution and this empathy must
rest on a better insight by both the Caribbean and metropolitan

peoples of the true meaning of the Caribbean historical experience, an experience which must be set within the wider context of the evolving relations between the advanced countries and the Third World and within the framework of the history of the New World.

It is now being increasingly recognised that in the interests of world peace the relations between the advanced countries and those of the Third World must be put on a new basis. The metropolis and the periphery are not equal in economic power. There cannot therefore be true interdependence between them, as there can be between countries of equal strength. There is only a relationship of dependence. Enlightened economic relationships between centre and periphery must recognise clearly the present inequality and aim at making the periphery less rather than more dependent in the long run. The implementation of this principle will have profound consequences for the future relationship between the U.S.A. and Latin America and indeed between all the developed and all the less developed countries of the world. The Caribbean as a relatively small region with a long historical legacy of heavy dependence on the metropolis will stand to gain more than most other countries of the Third World if and when this new approach is implemented.

The history of the New World represents a still unfinished process of the creation of autonomous, viable societies with equal opportunity for all—free from domination by at first Europe and now by the U.S.A.

In 1776 the thirteen American colonies struck a blow not only for national self-determination but also for liberation of the national economy from its mercantilist shackles. The revolutionary character of the forcible severance of the thirteen colonies from their mercantilist economic past has not been fully appreciated largely because the American Revolution was a 'bourgeois' revolution which left intact—and indeed enshrined in the new Constitution—private property rights.

In the case of Canada, British mercantilism was not killed but died a natural death in the course of the development of economic liberalism in the nineteenth century. Although British investment in Canada in the form of loans was quite heavy, particularly in railways in the last few decades before World War I, it would be true to say that the year 1914 found Canada with an economy controlled by Canadians—although this was an economy heavily dependent for its foreign exchange on exports of wheat. The subjection of Canada to the new American economic imperialism happened almost overnight after World War II—between 1945 and 1955—when there was a vast inflow of direct investment by U.S. corporations into raw material and manufacturing industries.

Both in the case of Canada and the U.S.A., there was never any real feudalism. In the somewhat pretentious words of the American economic historian, W. W. Rostow, the countries of white settlement were 'born free'. Further, with the two striking exceptions of the Negroes in the U.S.A. and the French in Canada, both the U.S.A. and Canada evolved after their political independence as relatively equal and open societies.

In the case of continental Latin America, while political independence was in most cases achieved early in the nineteenth century, substantial remnants of feudalism and sharp social inequality within the societies remained. Further, even though the old mercantilist links were broken largely because of Britain's diplomacy (Canning and all that), in the late nineteenth and early twentieth centuries foreign investment flowed in to exploit raw materials and to provide the infrastructure for the export trade in both food and raw materials. A period of highly unbalanced economic growth followed, led by exports of primary products to the industrial countries. But this growth did not spread through the economy, did not stimulate other economic sectors, and did not remove the underlying economic and social inequality. Gradually in the twentieth century, the U.S. corporation increased its relative share of total foreign direct investment in Latin America and spread from the traditional raw material and mining sectors, banks and public utilities to the new industrial sector. This was created in the inter-war period under the protection of the import restrictions imposed to defend the balance of payments which had deteriorated with the collapse in prices of primary products. Unfortunately, the U.S. corporations allied themselves with the privileged landowning and business classes in the Latin American countries to block social change and broadly-based economic development. And to compound the felony, the U.S. Government increasingly tended to support and promote the interest of the

U.S. corporations in its diplomacy with the Latin American governments.

To sum up, then, one can say that the achievement of political independence by the continental Latin American countries resulted, internally, in the freezing of already rigid social and economic relationships, and, externally, in very little economic independence because of external economic domination by the U.S. corporations, aided and abetted by the dollar diplomacy of the State Department. The Alliance for Progress sought to promote internal social revolution by non-violent means. But by 1964–65 it had already failed, partly because, when the chips were down, the U.S. Government became afraid of genuine social revolution, fearing that all such revolution would be contaminated by 'communism', and also partly because any thorough-going social revolution had to affect adversely the interests of the large American corporations operating in Latin America. Thus we have the supreme paradox of a nation born in revolution taking a consistent counter-revolutionary stand in the countries in its backyard. At the time of writing, whether the surprisingly mild U.S. reaction to the recent revolution in Peru augurs a permanent change remains to be seen, as will the position she will adopt towards the even more recent Bolivian changes.

The Caribbean differs profoundly from Latin America. It remained the area where both political and economic imperialism had been most deeply entrenched in the New World. In 1958 all the Caribbean islands (and the mainland territories of the three Guianas) were colonies of the European powers, with three exceptions. (Puerto Rico, if not a colony, was certainly not politically independent). The only three independent countries were Haiti, the Dominican Republic and Cuba. Haiti was economically backward and badly misgoverned, but it managed to maintain a certain degree of cultural autonomy and even self-respect. The Dominican Republic presented the spectacle of an unholy tripartite alliance between a ruthless dictator, American business interests and the State Department. In Cuba the same alliance existed, but with the U.S. presence being even more open.

The Caribbean then in 1958 had not even begun to liberate itself from the old dispensation. But in that year and the following year—1959—respectively, two important events took place. First, a political Federation was formed in 1958 among the British territories (excluding British Guiana and British Honduras). Second, in 1959 the Cuban Revolution took place.

In 1958 it was hoped that Federation would be the instrument through which the British Caribbean colonies would achieve political independence. Since 1945 Federation had been viewed as a means of permitting the small unviable West Indian islands to group together for the purpose of achieving an independence which West Indian leaders and the United Kingdom Colonial Office alike thought they were incapable of achieving on their own as individual units. But a combination of centuries-old inter-island jealousies, inept Federal leadership and the desire of the units to continue pursuing competitive rather than complementary strategies of economic development conspired to produce an early demise of the Federation. The break-up of the Federation was however followed by the granting of political independence to the three largest islands.

The Federation of the British islands lasted only four years. And by 1966 three of the Federation's constituent units—Jamaica, Trinidad and Tobago and Barbados—together with Guyana, had become politically independent. British Honduras is now on the way to independence and the smaller units of the Leeward and Windward Islands have since achieved full internal self-government, with the United Kingdom responsible for their defence and foreign affairs. The Federal experience as well as the post-independence situation in the Commonwealth Caribbean showed that the quest for identity and solidarity among the ex-British possessions in the Caribbean had to be pursued by other means— namely, the method of regional economic collaboration and the working out of complementary rather than competitive strategies of economic development.

In 1959 Cuba, as the first Caribbean country to challenge successfully the power of the U.S.A. in the hemisphere, sought to establish a regime based on national independence and social justice, including racial equality. To this extent, Cuba is the first Caribbean country to have attempted a decisive break with the past, (if we exclude the Revolution of the 'Black Jacobins' in Haiti in the 1790's).

Since the Revolution, Cuba has got rid of the traditional curse of the Caribbean—the sugar plantation—and she has got rid of the twentieth-century bane of the Third World—economic domination by metropolitan companies. She is also the first Caribbean country to have got rid of the legacy of slavery—the obsession with race and colour. Even in this respect she has been ahead of Haiti, where, ever since Independence, the mulatto élite has been in a privileged position *vis-à-vis* the black masses. In addition, she is the first Caribbean country (leaving aside the very small tourist economies) to have got rid of unemployment. Finally, whatever her economic mistakes, she is the first Caribbean country to have mobilised the entire population in the task of national reconstruction.

The other side of the coin is that she has the distinction of being the first country to introduce the full-scale apparatus of totalitarianism into the New World—even though the New World has not previously and since been without its perhaps unique collection of nasty and brutal dictatorships.

It is now generally recognised that Cuba is making a genuine attempt to transform her economic and social structure and to achieve a genuine national identity. But it is often said that Cuba has remained a sugar monoculture and that she has changed an American for a Russian master. Both of these propositions are quite misleading, unless properly qualified. Cuba finds that her scarcest resource is foreign exchange which, as a small developing country, she can earn only by exports. Tourist earnings having been lost with the revolution, the only major foreign exchange-earner is sugar, which she must continue to export in large quantities. However, at the same time there has been proceeding a great effort at diversification—the growth of production of poultry, eggs, milk, and vegetables has been phenomenal. And, with the massive new plantings of citrus and with the vast extension of cattle-raising based on Cuba's breakthrough in developing molasses as the basis of a local stockfeed, the composition of exports in the next few years will be profoundly diversified. Moreover, Cuba is the first Caribbean country to have upset the historical pattern and to have become a major fishing nation. She has turned history on its head by sending her trawlers to catch fish off Newfoundland. In education UNESCO recognises Cuba, not only to be the most successful developing country in eliminating illiteracy, but also to be in the leading ranks in general educational development.

The accusation of Russian economic domination is superficially correct. But the essential point is that the heavy dependence on Russia is at least in principle no more than transitional and will last until Cuba removes the foreign exchange constraint to her development, which she is now attempting to do. On the other hand, in the previous situation of domination of the economy by equity investment by American corporations, the dependence on the U.S.A. was a cumulative process rather than a transitional phenomenon. While the present Russian economic domination may in principle be ultimately less deleterious in its effects than the previous American control, Cuba has illustrated the basic weakness of West Indian countries—the tendency to look for external props.

But the real tragedy of Cuba is that she has resorted to a totalitarian framework within which to profoundly transform her economy and society. This is the real point about the essentials of the political system in Cuba today. Perhaps over-simplifying, we may say that Cuba is essentially a highly nationalistic totalitarian society under a form of highly personalised rule, aiming at a complete transformation of previous economic and social structures through centralised planning and mass mobilisation. If in assessing the Cuban achievements, we think too much in terms of Marxism and Communism, we shall have missed the essence of the Cuban Revolution. (To say that Marxism is a veneer, however, is not to deny the reality of the military alliance with Russia and Cuba's consistent efforts to export revolution to Latin America.) Further, even though by all objective standards it is a totalitarian regime, there can be no doubt as to the widespread extent of popular enthusiasm and popular commitment.

The question arises as to whether there are alternative paths in the Caribbean to economic and social transformation and the achievement of a national identity other than the Cuban path.

One path that is being followed by many of the countries of the region is that initiated by Puerto Rico in its 'Operation Bootstrap'. This involves the attraction of U.S. firms to establish branches in Puerto Rico, which offers lower wages and tax holidays and which, as part of the U.S. Customs Union, has free access to the American market. This policy has been successful in that it has led to a high rate of investment, rapid industrial growth and an impressive increase in standards of living and *per capita* incomes in Puerto Rico. Massive transfers of Federal funds for Government development and social welfare activities have also contributed to raise standards of living, as have unrestricted opportunities for emigration to the U.S.A. But, in spite of these advantages, unemployment has remained at a very high level and there is still widespread poverty and much inequality. And any hope of preserving and strengthening the Puerto Rican identity has been destroyed. Puerto Rico has in fact solved its problems of economic and social transformation by incorporating itself into the U.S. economy. The recent election of a pro-Statehood Governor in that island merely reflects a recognition of a *fait accompli* by the Puerto Rican electorate. Economic growth has been achieved, but national identity lost. What shall it profit a country if it gain the whole world and lose its own soul?

Apart from the French Departments of Martinique, Guadeloupe and French Guiana and also possibly of the partner territories of the Netherlands Kingdom—Surinam and the Netherlands Antilles —there is little hope of the Puerto Rican model achieving what it has in fact achieved in Puerto Rico itself. The Commonwealth Caribbean countries are not in a Customs Union relationship with the United Kingdom, which in any case is much more distant geographically from them than is the U.S.A. from Puerto Rico. Yet, even with these limitations, the offer of fiscal incentives and other concessions (such as beach rights and extensive sales of land) to induce outside investors in industry and tourism to set up shop locally is the main strategy of development being pursued. And, apart from the technical demerits of these policy instruments from the point of view of promoting regional intergration and solving the unemployment problem, the result of such a strategy is bound to be the ultimate loss of national identity.

In 1969, with its new Third Five-Year Plan, Trinidad and Tobago adopted a third type of development model which may well be adopted by the other Commonwealth Caribbean countries —a path less revolutionary and more gradualistic, and less totalitarian and more democratic than the Cuban path, but more autonomous and ultimately self-reliant than the Puerto Rican one. It involves continued reliance on outside investment and trade with the outside world; but it also involves steady and increasing assumption of control over the commanding heights of the economy by the Government and nationals, a determined attempt to promote racial harmony and social equality, and the conscious development of a national and cultural identity.

The result of the pursuit of the Puerto Rican model of development is now clear, but only time can show how successful the Cuban and the new Trinidad and Tobago model will be. The success of the new Trinidad and Tobago strategy requires the mobilisation of the population, who will need a greater degree of self-confidence and sense of commitment. In fact, it requires the 'psychological revolution' which has been mentioned earlier—the casting off of the dependent state of mind which their history has bequeathed to the West Indian peoples. The large number of young people in the population of Trinidad and Tobago offers great hope—in fact, the only ray of hope—in this respect. The emergence of a new and more tolerant attitude on the part of the U.S.A. towards Latin American and Caribbean regimes pursuing more autonomous types of social and economic change in their respective countries will also facilitate the success of the new path being followed by Trinidad and Tobago.

Increasingly the Commonwealth Caribbean countries such as Trinidad and Tobago will become aware that the goals of greater economic independence and the development of a cultural identity will involve them in even closer ties one with another—at economic and at other levels. For the present disgraceful state of fragmentation of the Commonwealth Caribbean countries—and the opportunities thereby created for manipulation by outside powers (both from the Old and New Worlds) and outside business interests—makes it extremely difficult (although not impossible) for a single country to adopt a more independent and less 'open' strategy of development. Moreover, there are obvious limits to the scope for a more independent strategy of development in the Commonwealth Caribbean countries because of their small size.

Already, some slight beginnings have been made towards Commonwealth Caribbean integration. The Caribbean Free Trade Area is now proceeding towards more meaningful integration—the harmonisation of fiscal incentives; the establishment of a common external tariff; agreement on a common policy towards foreign investment; the establishment of regional integrated industries; and the setting up of a Regional Development Bank, primarily in order to redress economic imbalances as between the relatively more and less developed territories. Commonwealth Caribbean integration will also have to be accompanied by sustained efforts to reduce the dependence of the region in the long term on protected external markets for the traditional primary product exports —principally sugar, bananas and citrus. While in the short and medium run, the preferences and special arrangements for these commodities in the United Kingdom market must be maintained —for example, in the eventuality of the United Kingdom's entry into the European Common Market—diversification and cost reduction must be long-run objectives.

Metropolitan economic assistance can serve to promote the objective of Commonwealth Caribbean economic integration, if such assistance is directed towards unifying the region and making it ultimately more independent economically. On the other hand, metropolitan aid designed to protect metropolitan political, diplomatic or commercial interests in the region will not only be a divisive factor but will serve to perpetuate the present deep-seated patterns of dependence.

It is also an imperative of meaningful Commonwealth Caribbean integration that the Associated States should achieve some form of political Independence. For these countries can only participate meaningfully in the Commonwealth Caribbean integration movement if they have the same political status which the four independent countries now have and which British Honduras —soon to join CARIFTA—is on the way to obtaining. Here there are two options. Either the Leeward and Windward Islands must federate and secure political Independence from the United Kingdom—with guarantees of continuing budgetary and development aid from the United Kingdom over a number of years; or they must associate with one or more of the independent Commonwealth Caribbean countries. The former alternative, while clearly preferable, involves the usual West Indian difficulties of inter-island jealousies and the unwillingness of insular political leaders to have the spotlight shifted from them to the Federal leaders. Nevertheless, it should be possible to devise a form of

Federalism which leaves the maximum amount of self-determination open to the units, whilst concentrating the power of dealing with the outside world in Federal hands. In fact, this principle may have to be applied in a wider setting should the present economic integration movement in the Commonwealth Caribbean ever develop into a new attempt at political union.

For the real case for unity in Commonwealth Caribbean countries rests on the creation of a more unified front in dealing with the outside world—diplomacy, foreign trade, foreign investment and similar matters. Without such a unified front the territories will continue to be playthings of outside Governments and outside investors. To increase the 'countervailing power' of the small individual units *vis-à-vis* the strong outside Governments and outside companies requires that they should aim at nothing less than the creation of a single centre of decision-making *vis-à-vis* the outside world. Everything other than external contacts can and should be left to the individual units which should be given the maximum autonomy and power of self-determination. Herein lies the resolution of the problem which plagued the former Federation so much—the division of powers between the centre and the units.

Once the movement towards economic integration and political Independence of all the units begins to gather momentum in the Commonwealth Caribbean, it will be necessary to establish closer economic relationships with the non-Commonwealth countries—the French and the Dutch territories and the independent countries of the Dominican Republic, Haiti and Cuba, which must be reincorporated into the inter-American family. (Puerto Rico, as we have seen, seems to be now drifting slowly but surely into Statehood as part of the American Union.)

A pre-condition of closer economic ties between the French territories and the other Caribbean countries would be an ending—or at least a considerable loosening—of the close ties with metropolitan France. While at present majority sentiment in Martinique and Guadeloupe favours the retention of the close links with France, it is reasonably certain that time will show that the present arrangements do not present a final solution to the problem of these territories.

It is not possible at this stage to sketch out precisely the type of relationship which might be established between the Commonwealth and non-Commonwealth Caribbean. Suffice it to say that there is great scope for functional collaboration in respect of the production, processing and marketing of commodities such as sugar and minerals such as bauxite; for the exchange of technological and scientific knowledge; for the rationalisation of regional agriculture; and, not least, for the establishment of regional integrated industries in specific sectors, drawing their raw materials either from regional or extra-regional sources and serving both regional and non-regional markets.

Once there is true integration among all the units of the Caribbean (excluding Puerto Rico for reasons mentioned above), and once all the vestiges of political, economic, cultural and psychological dependence and of racism have been removed from the Caribbean, then and only then can the Caribbean take its true place in Latin America and the New World and put an end to the international wars and inter-regional squabbles which, from Columbus to Castro, have marked the disposition of Adam's will.

Select Bibliography

There is no bibliography of the Caribbean. However, a few bibliographical undertakings, limited in scope either to specific territories or to a specific period or to a specific subject, have been attempted.

Among these are:

J. Gazin, *Eléments de Bibliographie Générale, Méthodique et Historique de la Martinique*, Fort de France (1926?)

L. J. Ragatz, *Guide to the Study of British Caribbean History, 1763–1864*, Washington, D.C., 1930—annotated, a truly monumental work, the *vade mecum* of the student of this period

C. F. Reid, (ed.), *Bibliography of the Virgin Islands of the United States*, New York, 1941

U. Duvivier, *Bibliographie Générale et Méthodique d'Háíti*, 2 vols., Port-au-Prince, 1941

L. R. Blanchard, *Martinique, A Selected List of References*, Library of Congress, Washington, D.C., 1942

Lewis Hanke and Agustin Millares Carlo, *Cuerpo de documentos del siglo XVI sobre los derechos ae España en las Indias y las Filipinas*, Mexico, 1943

P. H. Hiss, *A Selective Guide to the English Literature on the Netherlands West Indies, with a Supplement on British Guiana*, Netherlands Information Bureau, New York, 1943

A. D. Brown, *British Possessions in the Caribbean Area, A Selected List of References*, Library of Congress, Washington, D.C., 1943

Augusto Bird, *Bibliografía Puertorriqueña, 1930–1945*, 2 vols., University of Puerto Rico, 1946–1947

516

E. Gouveia, *Study of the Historiography of the British West Indies,* Mexico, 1956

Other useful bibliographical tools, of more limited scope, however, are:

B. Sanchez Alonso, *Fuentes de la Historia Española e Hispano-americana,* 3 vols., Madrid, 1927

Handbook of Latin American Studies (annual), prepared by the Hispanic Foundation, Library of Congress

The history of the Caribbean falls logically into five broad periods, as follows:

1. The Spanish Monopoly, 1492–1655, from the Discovery to the British Conquest of Jamaica from Spain.

2. The Anglo-French Rivalry, 1656–1783, the Independence of the United States of America.

3. The Abolition of Slavery, 1784–1898, the Spanish-American War.

4. The 'American Mediterranean', 1899–1940, the acquisition by the U.S.A. of naval bases in the British West Indies.

5. The Movement for Caribbean Independence, 1940–1969.

(1) The Spanish Monopoly, 1492–1655

A. DOCUMENTARY MATERIAL

The outstanding Spanish contributions to historical research on the Caribbean are the two famous collections of documents from the Spanish archives:

J. F. Pacheco, F. de Cardenas, and L. Torres de Mendoza (eds.), *Documentos Inéditos de America. Colección de documentos inéditos relativos al descubrimiento, conquista y colonización de las posesiones españolas en America y Oceania, sacados de los archivos del reino, y muy especialmente del de Indias,* 42 vols., Madrid, 1864–1884

Documentos Inéditos de Ultramar. Colección de documentos inéditos relativos al descubrimiento, conquista y organización de las antiguas posesiones españolas de ultramar, Segunda Serie, 21 vols., Madrid, 1885–1928

It is almost impossible to obtain even individual volumes of these two series. The first series is a collection of unclassified documents; few relate specifically to the Caribbean. The most important of these are Tomo 1, Primer Número, January, 1864, which deals with Santo Domingo (the Dominican Republic) up to 1541; Tomo XXIII, Cuaderno Núm. IV, April, 1875, which contains three pertinent royal decrees; Tomo XXXI, Cuaderno

Núm. IV, 1879; and Tomo XXXVII, Cuaderno Núm. VI, 1882.
The second series was prepared with greater care. Some of the
more important volumes in the second series for Caribbean history
are the following:

Tomos, 1, 4, 6 ...	...	De la Isla de Cuba, Parts I, II, III
Tomos, 5, 9, 10	...	De los documentos legislativos, Parts I, II, III
Tomos 7, 8	... ...	De los pleitos de Colon, Parts I, II
Tomo 14	... ...	Consejo de Indias, Part IV
Tomos 22, 23, 24, 25 ...		Gobernación espiritual y temporal de las Indias, Parts III, IV, V, VI

Occasional volumes in other noteworthy documentary collections have special interest for the Caribbean. Examples are Tomo
V of the *Documentos inéditos para la historia de España*, which,
published in Madrid in 1947, includes a treatise on political
economy by Don Rodrigo Vivero in the early seventeenth
century; and two volumes in the *Colección de documentos
inéditos para la historia de Ibero-America:* Tomo VIII,
Diccionario de gobierno y legislación de Indias, edited by Don
Manuel José de Ayala, and Tomo IX, *Pasajeros a Indias*, edited
by Luis Rubio y Morena.

Other valuable documentary collections of the Spanish period
include:

Fernandez de Navarrete, *Colección de los viages y descubrimientos que
hicieron por mar los españoles desde fines del siglo XV*, Madrid
1825–1837, 5 vols.—1945 edition of Editorial Guarania, Buenos Aires.
Vol. 1 is imperative

Alejandro Tapia y Rivera, *Biblioteca Histórica de Puerto Rico, que
contiene varios documentos de los Siglos XV, XVI, XVII, y XVIII*,
Puerto Rico, 1884

Cayetano Coll y Toste, *Boletín Histórico de Puerto Rico*, 14 vols., San
Juan, 1914–1926

E. G. Bourne, *The Northmen, Columbus and Cabot, 985–1503*, New York,
1925

N. A. N. Cleven, *Readings in Hispanic American History*, Boston, 1927

Eric Williams, *Documents of West Indian History*, 1492–1655, Port-of-
Spain, 1963

Two other useful documentary collections exist for Trinidad
and Puerto Rico, going, however, far beyond the period of the
Spanish monopoly.

The Historical Society of Trinidad and Tobago has published
999 documents, the majority of them original, from various
sources, on the history of the two islands (some of the documents

deal with the nineteenth century also); while the University of Puerto Rico has made a collection, not restricted to original materials, of documents relating to Puerto Rican history. The collection, the work of the Department of History, has been published under the title of *Antologia de Lecturas de Puerto Rico*.

B. EYEWITNESS OR FIRST HAND ACCOUNTS

The Spanish period is rich in eyewitness accounts, analyses or compilations of the Conquest and its consequences, or first hand accounts, by writers who had access to the official documents.

The major works are:

P. Martir de Angleria, *Decados del Nuevo Mundo* (published in Latin), 1530—reprinted in Buenos Aires in Spanish in 1944

Bartolomé de las Casas, *Historia de las Indias*, completed in 1559, first published in 1875, and now available in an inexpensive three-volume edition by the Fondo de Cultura Económica of Mexico City, 1951

Bartolomé de las Casas, *Apologética Historia de las Indias*, Madrid, 1909 —the work was completed in the middle of the sixteenth century

Gonzalo Fernandes de Oviedo y Valdez, *Historia general y natural de las Indias, islas y tierra-firme del mar oceano*, first published between 1535 and 1557, and now available in an inexpensive 14-volume edition by Editorial Guarania of Asunción del Paraguay, 1944

José de Acosta, *Historia natural y moral de las Indias*, Seville, 1590 (Hakluyt Society, translated 1880)—also reprinted in Madrid in 1894

Lopez de Velasco, *Geografía y descripción universal de las Indias* (1571–1574), Madrid, 1894

Diego de Encinas, *Provisiones, cedulas, capitulos de ordenanzas, instrucciones, y cartas . . . tocantes al buen gobierno de las Indias*, 4 vols., Madrid, 1596—reprinted in Madrid, 1945

Antonio de Herrera, *Historia general de los hechos de los castellanos en las islas y tierra firme del mar oceano*, first published in Madrid between 1601 and 1615, and now available in an inexpensive 10-volume edition by Editorial Guarania of Asunción del Paraguay, 1945

Juan de Solorzano y Pereyra, *Politica Indiana*, 5 vols., Madrid, 1647—reprinted in Madrid, 1930

J. de Veitia Linaje, *Norte de la contratación de las Indias occidentales*, Madrid, 1672. An abridged English translation, the work of one Captain John Stevens, was published in 1702 under the title of *The Spanish Rule of Trade to the Indies*

The twentieth century reprints of many of these famous works, in Spain, Mexico and Argentina, testify to the interest of Spanish scholarship in the former Spanish colonies.

C. SECONDARY SOURCES

Useful accounts of the civilisation of the Aborigines are:

Sven Loven, *Origins of the Tainan Culture, West Indies*, Goteborg, 1935
H. de Lalung, *Les Caráibes, Un peuple étrange aujourd'hui disparu*, Paris, 1948
Salvador Canals Frau, *Préhistoire de l'Amerique*, Paris, 1953
J. Bullbrook, *Aborigines of Trinidad*, Port-of-Spain, 1960

Secondary sources constitute a vast and imposing literature which has no parallel in the non-Spanish territories.

Spain's Indian policy is treated in the following:

A. G. Helps, *The Conquerors of the New World and their Bondsmen, being a Narrative of the Principal Events which led to Negro Slavery in the West Indies and America*, London, Vol. I, 1848; Vol. II, 1852
A. G. Helps, *The Spanish Conquest in America and its Relation to the History of Slavery and the Government of Colonies*, 4 vols., London, 1855
J. A. Saco, *Historia de la esclavitud de los indios en el nuevo mundo, seguida de la historia de los repartimientos y encomiendas*—published originally in Havana in two volumes in 1883 and 1892 and republished in 1932 in the Colección de Libros Cubanos, with an introduction by Fernando Ortiz
G. Latorre, 'Del trato que tuvieron los indios por el libro VI de las Leyes de Indias,' *Boletín del Centro de Estudios Americanistas de Sevilla*, Año IX, Núm. 56 y 57, 1922
S. A. Zavala, *La encomienda indiana*, Madrid, 1935
Rodolfo Baron Castro, 'Politica racial de España en Indias,' *Revista de Indias*, VII, Núm. 26, Oct.-Dec., 1946, pp. 781–802
Lewis Hanke, *The Spanish Struggle for Justice in the Conquest of America*, University of Pennsylvania Press, 1949; the Spanish version, *La Lucha por la Justicia en la Conquista de America*, Buenos Aires, 1949, contains documents not included in the English
Lewis Hanke, *Bartolomé de las Casas, pensador politico, historiador, antropólogo*, La Habana, 1949
L. B. Simpson, *The Encomienda in New Spain*, University of California Press, 1950—contains many very valuable documents on the Caribbean
M. G. Fernandez, *Bartolomé de las Casas, Volúmen Primero. Delegado de Cisneros para la reformación de las Indias (1516–1517)*, Sevilla, 1953
Fernando Ortiz, 'La "Leyenda Negra" contra Fray Bartolomé,' *Revista Bimestre Cubana*, 1953, pp. 146–184

Economic matters, trade and navigation are developed in the following:

J. A. Saco, *Historia de la escalvitud de la raza africana en el nuevo mundo y en especial en los paises americo-hispanos*—published originally in four volumes, Vols. I and II in Paris, 1875, Vols. III and

IV in Barcelona, 1877 and 1879, and republished in the Colección de Libros Cubanos, Havaria, 1938, in four volumes, with an introduction by Fernando Ortiz

Don. J. Arias y Miranda, *Exámen crítico-histórico del influjo que tuvo en el comercio, industria y población de España su dominación en América*, Madrid, 1854

J. Piernas Hurtado, *La Casa de la Contratación de las Indias*, Madrid, 1907

G. de Artinano, *Historia del comercio con las Indias durante el dominio de los Austrias*, Barcelona, 1917

C. H. Haring, *Trade and Navigation between Spain and the Indies in the time of the Hapsburgs*, Vol. XIX of the Harvard Economic Studies, 1918—the standard work on the Spanish 'exclusive'

G. Latorre, 'Relaciones geográficas contenidas en el Archivo General de Indias,' *Boletín del Centro de Estudios Americanistas de Sevilla*, Año Vi, Núms. 23 y 24, February and March, 1919; Núms. 26 y 27, 1919; Núms. 28 y 29, 1919

D. Federico Rahola y Tremols, *Comercio de Cataluña con America en el siglo XVIII*, Barcelona, 1931

R. S. Smith, 'Spanish Antimercantilism of the Seventeenth Century: Alberto Struzzi and Diego José Dormer,' *The Journal of Political Economy*, Vol. XLVIII, February-December, 1940, pp. 401–411

E. Ibarro y Rodriguez, 'Los precedentes de la Casa de Contratación de Sevilla,' *Revista de Indias*, Año II, Núm. 3, 1941, pp. 85–97; Núm. 4, April-June, 1941, pp. 5–54; Núm. 5, June-September, 1941, pp. 5–38

A. Morales-Carrion, *Puerto Rico and the Non Hispanic Caribbean: A Study in the Decline of Spanish Exclusivism*, University of Puerto Rico Press, 1952—Puerto Rican scholarship at its best, particularly valuable for its utilisation of English and United States sources as well as Spanish

J. Pulido Rubio, *El piloto mayor, pilotos mayores, catedráticos de cosmografía y cosmógrafos de la Casa de la Contratación de Sevilla*, Sevilla, 1952

Cristobal Bermudez Plata, *La Casa de la Contratación de las Indias y el Archivo General de Indias*, Madrid, n.d.

On the political side the following monographs are indispensable:

E. G. Bourne, *Spain in America*, New York, 1904

D. Manuel Serrano y Sanz, *Origenes de la dominación española en America*, Tomo I, Madrid, 1918

S. A. Zavala, *Las instituciones jurídicas en la conquista de America*, Madrid, 1935

E. Schafer, *El Consejo Real y Supremo de las Indias; su historia, organisación y labor administrativa hasta la terminación de la Casa de Austria*, Seville, 1935—the definitive work on the Spanish 'Colonial Office'

Mario Góngora, *El Estado en el derecho indiano, época de fundación, 1492-1570,* University of Chile, 1951

Contribuciones a la historia municipal de America, Instituto Panamericano de Geografía y Historia, Mexico, D.F., 1951

C. Bayle, *Los cabildos seculares en la America Española.* Madrid, 1952

There are useful studies of Trinidad and Jamaica under Spanish rule:

Pierre-Gustave-Louis Borde, *Histoire de l'Ile de Trinidad sous le Government Espagnol,* 2 vols., Paris, 1876 and 1882

F. Morales Padrón, *Jamaica Española,* Sevilla, 1952

F. M. Padrón, 'Trinidad en el Siglo XVII,' in *Anuarios de Estudios Americanos,* Seville, 1958

F. M. Padrón, 'Descubrimiento y Papel de Trinidad en la Penetracion Continental,' in *Anuarios de Estudios Americanos,* Seville, n.d.

The work and thought of some of the eminent Spanish jurists and philosophers who argued over the rights of Spain in the New World are discussed in:

L. G. Alonso Getino, *El maestro, Fr. Francisco de Vitoria, su vida, su doctrina e influencia,* Madrid, 1930

A. Truyol Serra, *Los principios del derecho público en Francisco de Vitoria,* Madrid, 1946

A. Losada, *Juan Gines de Sepulveda, Democrates Segundo o de las justas causas de la guerra contra los indios,* Madrid, 1951

Sor M. Monica, *La gran controversia del siglo XVI acerca del dominio español en America,* Madrid, 1952

Two long articles of value for a study of Spanish Caribbean history are included in C. Vinas y Mey (ed.), *Estudios de Historia Social de España,* Madrid, 1952. These articles are:

H. Sancho de Sopranis, 'Estructura y perfil demográfico de Cadiz en el siglo XVI' (pp. 535–612)

A. Dominguez Ortiz, 'La esclavitud en España durante la edad moderna' (pp. 367–428)

The influence of the discovery and conquest of the New World in Spanish literature in the Golden Age has been receiving increasing attention in Spain. The following materials may be cited as an illustration:

R. del Arco y Garay, *La sociedad española en las obras de Cervantes,* Madrid, 1901

A. Jose Vaccaro, *La Sabiduría de Cervantes,* Buenos Aires, 1947

Jorge Campos, 'Lope de Vega y el descubrimiento colombino,' *Miscelanea Americanista,* Instituto Gonzalo Fernandez de Oviedo, Madrid, 1951, Tomo I, pp. 269–293

Higinio Capote, 'Las Indias en la poesía española del siglo de oro,' *Estudios Americanos*, Sevilla, Vol. VI, Núm. 21, Junio-Julio 1953, pp. 5–36

D. CATALOGUES OF MANUSCRIPTS

Not the least valuable feature of Spanish historical research on the Caribbean is the publication of catalogues of the immense store of manuscript material. Among the most valuable of these catalogues are the following:

'Catálogo de legajos del Archivo General de Indias,' *Boletín del Centro de Estudios Americanistas de Sevilla*, Sección Primera—Patronato; Sección Segunda— Contaduría General del Consejo de Indias, Año VI, Núms. 23 y 24, February-March, 1919; Año VI, Núm. 30, 1919; Año VIII, Núms. 40 y 41, 1921

Julian Paz, *Catálogo de documentos de America existentes en la Biblioteca Nacional*, Madrid, 1933

J. Dominguez Bordona, *Catálogo de la Biblioteca de Palacio, Tomo IX, Manuscritos de America*, Madrid, 1935

V. Vincente Vela, *Indice de la colección de documentos de Fernandez de Navarrete que posee el Museo Naval*, Madrid, 1946

Ernesto Schafer, *Indice de la colección de documentos inéditos de Indias*, Madrid, 1947

To these should be added three essays by A. Bellesteros-Beretta on Juan Bautista Muñoz, the creator of the Archivo de Indias, published in the *Revista de Indias*:

'Don Juan Bautista Muñoz: Dos facetas científicas,' II, Núm. 3, pp. 5–37

'Juan Bautista Muñoz: La creación del Archivo de Indias,' Núm. 4, pp. 55–95

'Don Juan Bautista Muñoz: La Historia del Nuevo Mundo,' III, Núm. 10, October-December 1942, pp. 589–660

E. NON-SPANISH DOCUMENTARY MATERIAL

A considerable amount of documentary material for the Spanish period is available from British sources, principally the British Government and the Hakluyt Society. The chief British Government publications are:

Calendar of State Papers, Spanish Series, 1485–1603, London, 1879–1916
Calendar of State Papers, Venetian Series, 1202–1652, London, 1871–1927

The publications of the Hakluyt Society include not only Spanish voyages to the Caribbean, in violation of the Spanish monopoly, the work of the indefatigable Irene Wright, but also two indispensable works for the African background of Caribbean history. They are:

C. Jane (ed.), *Select Documents illustrating the Four Voyages of Columbus,* 2nd Series, No. LXV., 1930

Irene A. Wright (ed.), *Spanish Documents Concerning English Voyages to the Caribbean,* 1527–1568, 2nd Series, Vol. LXII, 1928
Documents concerning English voyages to the Spanish Main, 1569–1580, 2nd Series, Vol. LXXI, 1932
Further English Voyages to Spanish America, 2nd Series, Vol. XCIX, 1951

Gomes Eannes de Azurara, *The Chronicle of the Discovery and Conquest of Guinea,* translated by C. R. Beazley and E. Prestage, London, 1896–1897

Leo Africanus, *The History and Description of Africa,* translated by John Pory, 3 vols., London, 1896

The philosophical justification of the British attack on the Spanish monopoly is to be found in the writings of Richard Hakluyt:

Richard Hakluyt, *The Principal Navigations, Voyages, Traffiques and Discoveries of the English Nation,* first published in 1589, and available in several editions

E. G. Taylor (ed.), *The Original Writings and Correspondence of the Two Richard Hakluyts,* 2 vols., Works of the Hakluyt Society, Second Series, Nos. LXXVI-LXXVII, 1935. The famous 'Discourse of Western Planting, 1584,' Hakluyt's most important work, is to be found in Vol. II, Document 46, pp. 211–326

Three other valuable documentary collections are of prime importance:

C. H. Firth, *The Narrative of General Venables,* London, 1900—contains Cromwell's 'Western Design' and Henry Whistler's account of the British Expedition which conquered Jamaica

F. G. Davenport (ed.), *European Treaties bearing on the History of the United States and its Dependencies,* 4 vols., 1917–1937 (Vol. 1 to 1648)

T. Southey, *Chronological History of the West Indies,* 3 vols., London, 1827. Vol. I covers the period 1492–1655; now available in a modern reprint

Among the more general works, the best are three studies in the Pioneer Histories, edited by Vincent Harlow:

A. P. Newton, *The European Nations in the West Indies, 1493–1688,* London, 1933

J. A. Williamson, *The Age of Drake,* London, 1946

F. A. Kirkpatrick, *The Spanish Conquistadors,* London, 1946

Volume 33 of the Harvard Classics contains accounts of the voyages of Sir Francis Drake and Sir Walter Raleigh. Thomas Gage, *The English-American, A New Survey of the West Indies,*

London, 1648, is usually credited with the inspiration of Cromwell's 'Western Design'. A Warner, *Sir Thomas Warner, Pioneer of the West Indies*, London, 1933, is a useful biography of one of the founders of the British Empire in the Caribbean. A more recent British work on this period is G. C. Smith, *Forerunners of Drake, A Study of English Trade with Spain in the Early Tudor Period*, London, 1953.

(2) The Anglo-French Rivalry, 1656–1783

The principal sources for the study of this period, documentary and secondary, are British and French, rather than Spanish, though invaluable data has been made available by the Carnegie Institution of Washington.

A. DOCUMENTARY MATERIAL

The official publications of the British Government for this period rank with those of the Spanish Government for the period 1492–1655. The most important are:

Calendar of State Papers, Colonial Series, America and West Indies, 1574–1733, 27 vols., London, 1862–1939

Journal of the Commissioners for Trade and Plantations, 1704–1782, 13 vols., London, 1920–1938

A storehouse of documentary information, including valuable translations from the Dutch and Spanish Archives, is the collection of papers published by the British Government on the occasion of the boundary dispute between Venezuela and British Guiana. Five volumes of documents were presented to Parliament and published in 1896. The titles are:

Documents and Correspondence relating to the Question of Boundary between British Guiana and Venezuela, Venezuela No. 1 (1896), C.-7972, March, 1896

Further Documents relating to the Question of Boundary between British Guiana and Venezuela, Venezuela No. 2 (1896) C.-8016

Further Documents relating to the Question of Boundary between British Guiana and Venezuela, Venezuela No. 3 (1896), C.-8106, July, 1896

Further Documents relating to the Question of Boundary between British Guiana and Venezuela, Venezuela No. 4 (1896), C.-8194, August, 1896

Sir R. Schomburgk's Reports. Further Documents relating to the Question of Boundary between British Guiana and Venezuela, Venezuela No. 5 (1896), C.-8195, August, 1896

In addition, three supplementary volumes of documents were published by the Foreign Office in 1898, with the following titles:

British Guiana Boundary. Arbitration with the United States of Venezuela:
The case on behalf of the Government of Her Britannic Majesty
The Counter-Case on behalf of the Government of Her Britannic Majesty
Appendix to the Counter Case on behalf of the Government of Her
Britannic Majesty

The Hakluyt Society has given us two major works:

V. T. Harlow, *Colonising Expeditions to the West Indies and Guiana,*
1623–1667, 2nd Series, No. LVI, 1925

C. A. Harris and J. A. J. de Villiers, *Storm Van's Gravesande. The Rise*
of British Guiana. Compiled from his Despatches, 2 vols., 2nd Series,
Nos. XXVI and XXVII, London, 1911—particularly valuable because
of the translation of Dutch archival material

The research of the student of this period is enormously facilitated by three imposing documentary collections of the Carnegie
Institution of Washington:

E. Donnan (ed.), *Documents Illustrative of the History of the Slave Trade*
to America, 1930–1931, Vol. I, The Seventeenth Century; Vol. II, the
Eighteenth Century (Vols. III and IV deal with the mainland colonies)

L. F. Stock (ed.), *Proceedings and Debates in the British Parliaments*
respecting North America, 1924–1941, 5 vols.; Vol. I, 1542–1688; Vol.
II, 1689–1702; Vol. III, 1702–1727; Vol. IV, 1728–1739; Vol. V, 1739–
1754

H. T. Catterall (ed.), *Judicial Cases concerning Negro Slavery*, 2 vols.,
1926–1927

Valuable French collections have been made, mostly by private
individuals, as follows:

Annales du Conseil Souverain de la Martinique, 2 Vols., (Paris?), 1786

Moreau de Saint-Méry, *Loix et Constitutions des Colonies Françaises de*
l'Amerique sous le Vent, 1550–1785, 6 vols., Paris, n.d., but about 1789.
This is a monumental and rare work, indispensable for any study of
the French colonies. The individual volumes cover the following periods:
Vol. I, 1550–1703; Vol. II, 1704–1721; Vol. III, 1722–1749; Vol. IV,
1750–1765; Vol. V, 1766–1779; Vol. VI, 1780–1785

V. P. Malouet, *Collection de Mémoires et Correspondances Officielles sur*
l'Administration des Colonies, et notamment sur la Guiane Française
et Hollandaise, 5 vols., Paris, 1802

P. Clément, *Lettres, Instructions et Mémoires de Colbert*, Tome I, 1650–
1661, Paris, 1861; Tome II, Paris, 1863

Volume II of Southey's *Chronological History of the West*
Indies, London, 1827, covers the period under review.

B. LOCAL HISTORIES

For this period there are a number of early histories and

historical accounts, of which some of the most important are:
(i) British

R. Ligon, *A True and Exact History of the Island of Barbados*, London, 1657—a very rare and valuable work, indispensable for the early history of the sugar industry

J. Davies, *The History of the Caribby-Islands*, London, 1666

J. Esquemeling, *History of the Buccaneers in America*, Amsterdam, 1678

J. C. Jeaffreson (ed.), *A Young Squire of the Seventeenth Century. From the Papers (A.D. 1676–1686) of Christopher Jeaffreson*, London, 1878—full of data on St. Kitts

Sir Hans Sloane, *A Voyage to the Islands Madeira, Barbados, Nieves, St. Christophers and Jamaica, with the Natural History of the Herbs and Trees, Four-footed Beasts, Fishes, Birds, Insects, Reptiles, &c., of the last of those Islands*, London, 1707

Charles Leslie, *A New and Exact Account of Jamaica*, London, 1739

G. Frere, *A Short History of Barbados, from its First Discovery and Settlement to the end of the year 1767*, London, 1768

Edward Long, *History of Jamaica*, 3 vols., London, 1774—also an indispensable work for two reasons, (a) his careful analysis of the costs and profits of a sugar plantation, (b) his attack on the capacity of Negroes whom he equated with the orang-outang rather than with the white man. The work also includes, one of the rarest of all documents, an English translation of the entire *Code Noir*

T. Atwood, *The History of the Island of Dominica containing a Description of its Situation, Extent, Climate, Mountains, Rivers, Natural Productions, &c., together with an Account of the Civil Government, Trade, Laws, Customs, and Manners of the Different Inhabitants of That Island. Its Conquest by the French, and Restoration to the British Dominions*, London, 1791—West Indians, to whom this rare book is inaccessible, will find it reprinted monthly in the *Dominica Welfare News*, beginning with the issue of October, 1949

R. C. Dallas, *The History of the Maroons*, London, 1803— an account of the Jamaica slave uprising which anticipated the Haitian revolution; it ended, however, not in an independent Negro state of Jamaica but in the recognition of a Negro *imperium in imperio*

E. W. and C. M. Andrews (eds.), *Journal of a Lady of Quality, being the Narrative of a Journey from Scotland to the West Indies, North Carolina, and Portugal, in the years 1774 to 1776*, Yale University Press, 1925

(ii) French

Père J. B. du Tertre, *Histoire Générale des Antilles habitées par les Français*, 2 vols., Paris, 1661–1667—a very rare work indeed, very valuable not only for its description of Carib civilisation but also for its account of the early hostility of the colonial planters to metropolitan mercantilism

Père Labat, *Voyages aux Isles de l'Amerique (Antilles), 1693–1705*, 2 vols., Paris, edition of 1931

Père Labat, *Mémoires des Nouveaux Voyages faits aux Iles Françaises de l'Amerique*, written at the end of the seventeenth century and published in several editions, one at The Hague in 1724—another very valuable work, with a good description of the sugar industry at the end of the seventeenth century and the importance of slave labour; his plan for the economic development of the French West Indies retarded by the complacency of the planters has a strikingly modern note

(iii) Dutch

J. D. Herlein, *Beschrijving van de Volkplanting Zuriname*, Leeuwarden, 1718

Th. Pistorius, *Korte en zakelijke beschrijvinge van de Colonie van Zuriname*, Amsterdam, 1763

Ph. Fermin, *Description générale, historique, géologique et physique de la colonie de Surinam*, Amsterdam, 1767

J. J. Hartsinck, *Beschrijving van Guyana of de Wilde Kust in Zuidd Amerika*, 2 dln., Amsterdam, 1770

Ph. Fermin, *Tableau historique et politique de l'Etat ancien et actuel de la colonie de Surinam*, Maastricht, 1778

A. Blom, *Verhandeling over de Landbouw in de Colonie Suriname*, Haarlem, 1786

Essai Historique sur la Colonie de Surinam, 2 dln., Paramaribo, 1788

J. G. Stedman, *Narrative of a five years' expedition against the Revolted Negroes of Surinam, in Guiana, on the Wild Coast of South America; from the year 1772 to 1777*, London, 1796—this is an eyewitness account of the revolt of the Bush Negroes

(iv) Spanish

Actos del Cabildo de San Juan Bautista de Puerto Rico, 1730–1750, Publicación Oficial del Gobierno del Capital, San Juan, 1949

Don Juan de Nuix y de Perfina, *Reflexiones Imparciales sobre la humanidad de los Españoles en Indias, contra los pretendidos filósofos, y políticos, para servir de luz a las historias de los señores Raynal, y Robertson*, (Madrid?), 1783

Fray Inigo Abbad y Lasierra, *Historia geográfica, civil y natural de la Isla de San Juan de Puerto Rico*, Madrid, 1788 (Puerto Rico edition of 1866)

Recopilación de Leyes de los Reynos de las Indias, mandadas imprimir y publicar por la majestad Católica del Rey Don Carlos II, Nuestro Señor, Madrid 1791—collected by order of the King, 1680–1681; reprinted by the Consejo de la Hispanidad, Madrid, 1943

C. THE MERCANTILISTS

The mercantilist literature is voluminous. The following titles may be recommended, the selection being determined in large part by a desire not to duplicate the work of Ragatz from 1763 to the end of the period under review:

Jacques Savary, *Le Parfait Négociant*, Paris, 1675

E. Littleton, *The Groans of the Plantations: or a True Account of their Grievous and Extreme Sufferings by the Heavy Impositions upon Sugar, and Other Hardships Relating more particularly to the Island of Barbados*, London, 1689

Sir Dalby Thomas, *An Historical Account of the Rise and Growth of the West India Colonies, and of the Great Advantages they are to England, in respect to Trade*, London, 1690

Charles Davenant, *Discourse on the Trade and Publick Revenues of England*, London 1698—there are other useful writings of Davenant, all of which can be found in C. Whitworth (ed.), *The Political and Commercial Works of Charles Davenant*, London, 1781

W. Wood, *A Survey of Trade*, London, 1718

The Importance of the Sugar Colonies to Great Britain, London, 1731

Some Considerations humbly offer'd upon the Bill now depending in the House of Lords, relating to the Trade between the Northern Colonies and the Sugar-Islands, London, 1732

Memorials, presented by the Deputies of the Council of Trade in France to the Royal Council in 1701, London, 1736

J. Bennett, *Two Letters and Several Calculations on the Sugar Colonies and Trade*, London, 1738

W. Perrin, *The Present State of the British and French Sugar Colonies, and our own Northern Colonies, considered*, London, 1740

J. Ashley, *Memoirs and Considerations concerning the Trade and Revenues of the British Colonies in America. With Proposals for rendering those Colonies more beneficial to Great Britain*, London, 1740–1743

M. Postlethwayt, *The National and Private Advantages of the African Trade considered*, London, 1746

J. Gee, *The Trade and Navigation of Great Britain considered*, Glasgow, 1750

M. Postlethwayt, *The Universal Dictionary of Trade and Commerce*, London, 1751 (additions and improvements to Savary des Bruslons)

M. Postlethwayt, *Great Britain's Commercial Interest explain'd and improv'd*, London, 1759

J. Campbell, *Candid and Impartial Considerations on the Nature of the Sugar Trade*, London, 1763

M. Postlethwayt, *The African Trade, the Great Pillar and Support of the British Plantation Trade in North America*, London, 1765.

C. Whitworth, *State of the Trade of Great Britain in its Imports and Exports, progressively from the year 1693–1773*, London, 1776—a very rare work, the statistical basis of mercantilist exultation over Caribbean colonies

A. M. Arnould, *De la balance du commerce et des relations commerciales extérieures de la France, dans toutes les parties du globe, particulièrement à la fin du règne de Louis XIV, et au moment de la Révolution,* Paris, 1791

The classic attacks on mercantilism, imperialism and slavery, foreshadowed by Jonathan Swift and Daniel Defoe, are the writings of the Physiocrats in France, and in England the works of Josiah Tucker and Adam Smith's *Inquiry into the Nature and Causes of the Wealth of Nations,* London. 1776 An excellent account of the British mercantilists, full of documents, going back before 1656, is K. E. Knorr, *British Colonial Theories, 1570–1850,* University of Toronto Press, 1944.

The writings of two mainland statesmen are of considerable importance for this period—Benjamin Franklin and Thomas Jefferson; the former for his essays on the expensiveness of slave labour and on the reasons why Britain should annex Canada instead of Guadeloupe in 1763, in *Works,* edited by John Bigelow, New York, 1904; the latter, especially in his *Notes on Virginia* in 1781, for his opposition to the slave trade, views on the capacity of Negroes, and demands for their repatriation to Africa.

Two of the earliest British attacks on slavery are:

Granville Sharp, *An Essay on Slavery, proving from Scripture its Inconsistency with Humanity and Religion,* Burlington, 1773
John Wesley, *Thoughts upon Slavery,* London, 1774

On the French side the classic attack on the slave system in this period is Abbé G. F. Raynal, *Histoire philosophique et politique des établissements et du commerce des européens dans les deux Indes,* Geneva, 1780; there is an English translation published in Edinburgh in 1804. The book, which has often been severely criticised (e.g., by Ragatz, in his *Guide* cited above), has a useful description of sugar technology in the period, a very valuable disquisition on slavery and on its effect on the West Indian character, and, of course, the famous passage which Toussaint Louverture is alleged to have read and re-read before he launched the revolt which ended in the abolition of Negro slavery and the proclamation of the Republic of Haiti. G. Esquer (ed.), *L'Anti-colonialisme au XVIIIe Siècle* Paris, 1951, is a collection of excerpts from Raynal's *Histoire.*

D. SECONDARY SOURCES

Among the more important secondary sources for the period 1656–1783 the following may be cited:

(i) British

J. Britton, *Graphical and Literary Illustrations of Fonthill Abbey, Wiltshire; with Heraldical and Genealogical Notices of the Beckford Family*, London, 1823—Beckford was the leading absentee West Indian planter of the eighteenth century

V. L. Oliver, *The History of the Island of Antigua, One of the Leeward Caribbees in the West Indies, from the First Settlement in 1635 to the Present Time*, 2 vols., London, 1894

F. W. Pitman, *The Development of the British West Indies, 1700–1763*, New Haven, 1917—a veritable gold mine

J. E. Gillespie, *The Influence of Oversea Expansion on England to 1700*, New York, 1920

C. S. S. Higham, *The Development of the Leeward Islands under the Restoration, 1660–1688*, Cambridge University Press, 1921

L. M. Penson, 'The London West India Interest in the Eighteenth Century,' *English Historical Review*, July, 1921

L. M. Penson, *The Colonial Agents of the British West Indies*, London, 1924

J. B. Botsford, *English Society in the Eighteenth Century as influenced from Overseas*, New York, 1924

J. F. Rees, 'The Phases of British Commercial Policy in the Eighteenth Century,' *Economica*, June, 1925

R. M. Howard (ed.), *Records and Letters of the Family of the Longs of Longville, Jamaica, and Hampton Lodge, Surrey*, London, 1925

J. A. Williamson, *The Caribbee Islands under the Proprietary Patents*, Oxford University Press, 1926

V. T. Harlow, *A History of Barbados, 1625–1685*, Oxford University Press, 1926

V. B. Phillips, 'An Antigua Plantation, 1769–1818,' *The North Carolina Historical Review*, Vol. III, July, 1926

F. W. Pitman, *The West India Absentee Planter as a British Colonial Type*, Proceedings of the Pacific Coast Branch of the American Historical Association, 1927

L. J. Ragatz, *The Fall of the Planter Class in the British Caribbean 1763–1833*, New York, 1928—monumental and of equal value for the subsequent period of this essay

L. J. Ragatz, *Absentee Landlordism in the British Caribbean, 1750–1833*, London, n.d.

C. W. Taussig, *Rum, Romance and Rebellion*, New York, 1928

V. T. Harlow, *Christopher Codrington, 1688–1710*, Oxford University Press, 1928

E. F. Gay, 'Letters from a Sugar Plantation in Nevis, 1723–1732,' *Journal of Economic and Business History*, November, 1928

Cambridge History of the British Empire, Vol. I, The Old Empire, from the Beginnings to 1783, Cambridge University Press, 1929

A. M. Whitson, *The Constitutional Development of Jamaica*, Manchester University Press, 1929

A. M. Whitson, 'The outlook of the Continental American Colonies on the British West Indies, 1760–1775', *Political Science Quarterly*, March, 1930

F. W. Pitman, 'The Settlement and Financing of British West India Plantations in the Eighteenth Century,' in *Essays in Colonial History by Students of Charles McLean Andrews*, Yale University Press, 1931, pp. 252–283—*multum in parvo*

G. L. Beer, *The Old Colonial System, 1660–1754*, New York, 1933

R. Pares, *War and Trade in the West Indies, 1739–1763*, Oxford University Press, 1936—an imposing study

F. Cundall, *The Governors of Jamaica in the Seventeenth Century*, London, 1936

F. Cundall, *The Governors of Jamaica in the First Half of the Eighteenth Century*, London, 1937

C. M. Mac Innes, *Bristol. A Gateway of Empire*, Bristol, 1939

A. G. Price, *White Settlers in the Tropics*, New York, 1939

W. Sypher, *Guinea's Captive Kings: British Anti-Slavery Literature of the XVIIIth Century*, University of North Carolina Press, 1942—an indispensable work

Eric Williams, *Capitalism and Slavery*, University of North Carolina Press, 1944—of value also for the subsequent period treated in this essay; London, 1964

R. Pares, *A West India Fortune*, London, 1950—an excellent account of a single family in Nevis

R. Lowe, *The Codrington Correspondence*, 1743–1851, London, 1951

F. Armytage, *The Free Port System in the British West Indies, A Study in Commercial Policy, 1766–1822*, London, 1953

D. P. Mannix, *Black Cargoes, A History of the Atlantic Slave Trade*, London, 1962

B. Martin and M. Spurrell (eds.), *The Journal of a Slave Trader, John Newton (1750–1754)*, London, 1962

J. Pope-Hennessy, *Sins of the Fathers: A Study of the Atlantic Slave Traders 1441–1807*, London, 1967

(ii) French

S. Daney, *Histoire de la Martinique, depuis la Colonisation jusqu'en 1815*, 4 vols., Paris, 1846–1847

J. Ballet, *La Guadeloupe, Renseignements sur l'Historie, La Flore, La Faune, La Géologie, La Minéralogie, L'Agriculture, Le Commerce, L'Industrie, La Législation, L'Administration*, Vol. I, three parts, 1625–1715; Vol. II, 1715–1774; Vol. III, no dates.

Select Bibliography   533

L. Peytraud, *L'esclavage aux Antilles Françaises avant 1789*, Paris, 1897

Pierre de Vaissière, *Saint Domingue: la société et la vie créoles sous l'ancien régime, 1629-1789*, Paris, 1909

R. P. Jameson, *Montesquieu et l'esclavage*, Paris, 1911

G. Lerat, *Etude sur les origines, le développement et l'avenir des raffineries nantaises*, Paris, 1911

S. L. Mims, *Colbert's West India Policy*, Yale University Press, 1912—a classic

F. P. Renant, *Le Pacte de Famille et l'Amérique, La Politique Coloniale Franco—Espagnole de 1760 à 1792*, Paris, 1922

H. See, *Le grand commerce maritime et le système colonial dans leurs relations avec l'évolution du capitalisme*, Paris, 1925

L. Vignols, *Les Antilles Françaises sous l'ancien régime. Aspects économiques et sociaux, 1626-1774*, Paris 1928

J. Saintoyant, *La colonisation française sous l'ancien régime*, 2 vols., Paris, 1928

P. Jeulin, *L'évolution du Port de Nantes. Organisation et traffic depuis les origines*, Paris, 1929

P. Dieudonné Rinchon, *La Traite et L'Esclavage des Congolais par les Européens*, Brussels, 1929—a valuable Belgian study

Gaston-Martin, *L'Ere des Négriers* (1714–1774), Paris, 1932—the classic account of the French slave trading metropolis, Nantes

A. Martineau and L.-Ph. May, *Trois Siècles d'Histoire Antillaise, Martinique et Guadeloupe, de 1635 à Nos Jours*, Paris, 1935

S. Denis, *Nos Antilles*, Paris, 1935—contains several invaluable documents on the 'exclusive'

C. A. Banbuck, *Histoire politique, économique et sociale de la Martinique*, Paris, 1935—well-documented

P. Dieudonné Rinchon, *La Trafic Négrier, d'après les livres de commerce du Capitaine Gantois, Pierre-Ignace-Lievin van Alstein*, Brussels, 1938—another valuable Belgian analysis

Hervé du Halgouet, *Nantes, ses relations commerciales avec les Iles d'Amérique au XVIIIe siècle*, Rennes, 1939

Hervé du Halgouet, *Au temps de Saint-Domingue et de la Martinique, d'apres la correspondance des trafiquants maritimes*, Rennes, 1941

E. D. Seeber, *The Anti-Slavery Movement in French Literature of the Eighteenth Century*, Johns Hopkins University Press, 1937

N. M. Crouse, *The French Struggle for the West Indies*, 1665–1713, New York, 1943

M. G. Demeaux, *Memorial d'Une Famille du Havre. Les Fondateurs: Choses et Gens du XVIIIe Siècle en France et à Saint-Domingue*, Le Havre, 1948

A. Ducasse, *Les Négriers, ou le Trafic des Esclaves*, Paris, 1948

H. Robert, 'Le Commerce rochelais au XVIIIe Siècle,' *Bulletin de la Société des Antiquaires de l'Ouest et des Musées de Poitiers*, 3° ET 4° trimestres de 1949, pp. 135–177

M. G. Demeaux, *Mémorial d'une Famille du Havre. Stanislas Foache, Négociant de Saint-Domingue, 1737–1806*, Paris, 1951

J.-C. Nardin, *La Mise en Valeur de L'Ile de Tabago* (1763–1783), Paris, 1969

Special mention must be made of the work of G. Debien of the Institut Français d'Archéologie Orientale in Cairo. He specialises in the history of Saint-Domingue and has produced an imposing series of books and articles entitled *Notes d'Histoire Coloniale*, of which the following are relevant to the period under review:

I. *Une plantation de Saint-Domingue: la sucrerie Galbaud du Fort (1692–1802)*, Cairo, 1941

II. *Le peuplement des Antilles au XVIIe Siècle. Les engagés partis de La Rochelle (1683–1715)*, Cairo, 1942

VI. 'Comptes, profits, esclaves et travaux de deux sucreries de Saint-Domingue (1774–1798),' *Revue de la Société d'Histoire et de Géographie d'Haïti*, Vol. 15, No. 55, Octobre, 1944, pp. 1–62; Vol. 16, No. 56, Janvier, 1945, pp. 1–52

VII. 'A Saint-Domingue avec deux jeunes économes de plantation (1774–1788),' *Revue de la Société d'Histoire et de Géographie d'Haïti*, Vol. 16, No. 58, Juillet, 1945, pp. 1–80

VIII. *Gouverneurs, magistrats et colons. L'opposition parlementaire et coloniale à Saint-Domingue (1763–1769)*, Port-au-Prince, 1946

XIII. 'L'esprit d'indépendance chez les colons de Saint-Domingue au XVIIIe siècle,' *Revue de la Société d'Histoire et de Géographie d'Haïti*, Vol. 17, No. 63, Octobre, 1946, pp. 1–46

XIV. 'Aux origines de quelques plantations des quartiers de Léogane et du Cul-de-Sac (1680–1715)' *Revue de la Société d'Histoire et de Géographie d'Haïti*, Vol. 18, No. 64, Janvier, 1947, pp. 11–78

XV. 'Les Travaux d'Histoire sur Saint-Domingue de 1938 à 1946, Essai de Mise au Point,' *Revue d'Histoire des Colonies*, 1947, pp. 31–86

XX. 'Travaux d'Histoire sur Saint-Domingue, Chronique Bibliographique (1946–1950),' *Revue d'Historie des Colonies*, 1950, pp. 282–330

XXVIII. 'Aux débuts d'une grande Plantation à Saint-Domingue (1685–1714),' *Revue de la Porte Océane*, Septembre et Octobre, 1953

XXIX. 'Colons, marchands et engagés à Nantes au XVIIe siècle,' *Revue de la Porte Océane*, Décembre, 1953, Janvier et Février, 1954, pp. 1–54

There is also Debien's *Un Colon sur sa Plantation*, University of Dakar, 1959

(iii) Dutch

The definitive work on Surinam is R. van Lier, *Samenleving in een Grensgebied. Een Sociaal-historische studie van de maat-*

schappij in Suriname, 'S-Gravenhage, 1949. Other useful works are:

J. J. Reese, *De Suikerhandel van Amsterdam,* Vol. I to 1813, Vol. II to 1894, The Hague, 1908 and 1911

F. O. Dentz, *De kolonisatie van de Portugeesche Joodsche natie in Suriname en de geschiedenis van de Joden Savanne,* Amsterdam, 1927

C. Douglas, *En blik in het verleden van Suriname; beknopt verhaal omtrent gebeurtenissen met de slaven en toestanden en Suriname gedurende de jaren 1630–1863,* Paramaribo 1930

D. van der Sterre, *Zeer Aenmerkelijke Reysen Gedaan door Jan Erasmus Rayning,* Amsterdam, 1937

F. O. Dentz, *Cornelis van Aerssen van Sommelsdijk; een belangweppende figuure nit de geschiedenis van Suriname,* Amsterdam, 1938

W. R. Menkman, *De Geschiedenis van de West-Indische Campagnie,* Amsterdam, 1947

A. J. C. Kraft, *Historie en oude families van de Nederlandse Antillen, het Antilliaanse patriciaat,* 'S-Gravenhage, 1951

(iv) Danish

Of considerable value for a study of the eighteenth century is W. Westergaard, *The Danish West Indies under Company Rule (1671–1754),* New York, 1917. An interesting Spanish account of Danish expansion is M. Gutierrez de Arce, *La Colonización Danesa en las Islas Virgenes, Estudio historico-jurídico,* Escuela de Estudios Hispano Americanos, Universidad de Sevilla, Sevilla, 1945.

(3) The Abolition of Slavery, 1784–1898

The period is distinguished, in the bibliographical field, by two major characteristics: the reports of British commissions of inquiry and a scholastic productivity in Cuba, both contemporary and modern, more reminiscent of a metropolitan than a colonial country.

A. THE BRITISH WEST INDIES

(i) Commissions of Inquiry

The most important of the large number of reports of official Commissions of Inquiry are the following:

Report of the Committee of the Lords of the Privy Council for all matters relating to Trade and Foreign Plantations, 1788—an absolutely indispensable work for a comparison of the British and French colonies of the period

Report on the Commercial State of the West India Colonies, 1807

Statements, Calculations and Explanations submitted to the Board of

elative to the Commercial, Financial and Political State of the West India Colonies, since the 19th May, 1830

)f the Select Committee appointed to inquire into the Commercial of the West India Colonies, 1831–1832

of the Select Committee on the Extinction of Slavery throughout the British Dominions, 1832

Report of the Select Committee on Negro Apprenticeship, 1836

Accounts of Slave Compensation Claims, 1838

Papers relative to the West Indies, 1841–1842, Jamaica-Barbados, 1842

Papers relative to the West Indies. Antigua, Trinidad, St. Lucia, Grenada, 1841–1842, 1842

Report from the Select Committee on West India Colonies, 1842

Immigration of Labourers into the West Indian Colonies and the Mauritius, Part II, August 26, 1846

Reports* of a House of Commons Committee on Sugar and Coffee Plantations, 1847–1848

Sugar Growing Colonies, Part III, Trinidad, 1853

Report of the Royal Commission of Inquiry to enquire into the Disturbances in Jamaica, 1865

Papers relating to the Disturbances in Jamaica, Part I, 1866

Papers relative to the Affairs of Jamaica, February, 1866

Papers laid before the Royal Commission of Inquiry by Governor Eyre (Jamaica), June, 1866

Further correspondence relative to the Affairs of Jamaica, August 10, 1866

Report upon the state of Education in the Island of Trinidad, by Patrick Joseph Keenan, Esq., Dublin, 1869

Report of the Commission of Enquiry into the Condition of Indian Immigrants, British Guiana, 1870

Papers relating to the Late Disturbances in Barbados, C.—1539, 1876

Further Papers relating to the Late Disturbances in Barbados, C.—1559, 1876

Further Papers relating to the Late Disturbances in Barbados, C.—1679, 1876

India (Coolie Emigration), Return to an Address of the House of Lords, dated 20th July, 1877, London, February 6, 1878

Correspondence relating to the Financial Arrangements for Indian Coolie Immigration into Jamaica, C.—2437, 1879

Papers relative to the Condition of Indian Immigrants in Grenada, C.—2249, 1879

O. W. Warner, *Report on the Condition of Indian Immigrants and the Working of the New Immigration Law in Grenada, C.—2602, 1880*

Report of the Royal Commission appointed in December, 1882, to inquire into the Public Revenues, Expenditure, Debts, and Liabilities of the Islands of Jamaica, Grenada, St. Vincent, Tobago, and St. Lucia, and

* Eight Reports were published.

the Leeward Islands, C.—3840, 1884

Report to the Board of Trade entitled 'Progress of the Sugar Trade,' by T. H. Farrer, August 7, 1884

Report of the Royal Commission to consider and report as to the Proposed Franchise and Division of the Colony into Electoral Districts, Trinidad, 1889

Tobago Métairie Commission, 1890

Report on the Administration of Justice in the Colony, with Proceedings, Notes of Evidence and Documents, Trinidad, 15th June, 1892

Surgeon-Major D. W. D. Comins, *Note on Emigration from the East Indies to St. Lucia,* Calcutta, 1893

Surgeon-Major D. W. D. Comins, *Note on Emigration from the East Indies to Jamaica,* Calcutta, 1893

Report of the Royal Commission (appointed in September, 1893) to enquire into the Condition and Affairs of the Island of Dominica, C.—7477, 1893

Railway Enquiry Commission, Trinidad, 1894

Roads Enquiry Commission, Trinidad, 1894

Report of the West India Royal Commission, with Subsidiary Report by D. Morris, C. 8655, 8657, 8667, 8669, London, 1897, including:—

  Appendix C., Vol. I, Part I, *Minutes of Proceedings, Reports of Evidence, and Copies of Certain Documents received in London*

  Appendix C., Vol. II, Parts II-V. *Evidence in British Guiana, Barbados, Trinidad and Tobago*

  Appendix C., Vol. III, Parts VI-XIII, *Grenada, St. Lucia, St. Vincent, Domica, Monserrat, Antigua, St. Kitts-Nevis, Jamaica*

Correspondence relating to the Sugar Industry in the West Indies, February, 1897

Correspondence relating to the Re-adjustment of the Finances of the Borough of Port-of-Spain, Trinidad, 1898

(ii) Documentary Collections

The above reports contain a number of essential documents for this period. Other documentary collections include:

K. N. Bell and W. P. Morrell, *Select Documents on British Colonial Policy, 1830–1860,* Oxford, 1928

H. S. Commager (ed.), *Documents of American History,* 4th Edition, New York, 1948—contains some valuable United States documents

Alice R. Stewart, 'Documents on Canadian-West Indian Relations, 1883–1885,' *Caribbean Historical Review, No. II,* December, 1951, pp. 100–133

Eric Williams (ed.), *Documents on British West Indian History, 1807–1833* (Select Documents from the Public Record Office, London, England, relating to the Colonies of Barbados, British Guiana, Jamaica and Trinidad), Historical Society of Trinidad and Tobago (in collaboration with Social Science Research Centre, University of Puerto Rico), Port-of-Spain, Trinidad, 1952

V. T. Harlow and F. Madden (eds.), *British Colonial Developments, 1774–1834, Select Documents,* Oxford University Press, 1953

Eric Williams (ed.), *The British West Indies at Westminster. Extracts from the Debates in the British Parliament, Part I, 1789–1823* Historical Society of Trinidad and Tobago, Port-of-Spain, Trinidad, 1954

(iii) Memoirs of British Statesmen

Invaluable data on the British West Indies in the period of the abolition of slavery are to be found in the printed correspondence of a number of British statesmen. The most important of these are the following:

C. W. Vane, Marquess of Londonderry (ed.), *Correspondence, Despatches and Other Papers of Viscount Castlereagh,* London, 1848–1853

The Journal and Correspondence of William, Lord Auckland, London, 1861

Duke of Wellington (ed.), *Despatches, Correspondence and Memoranda of Field Marshal Arthur, Duke of Wellington,* London, 1867–1880

T. Walrond (ed.), *Letters and Journals of James, Eighth Earl of Elgin,* London, 1872—contains a few letters on Jamaica of which Elgin was Governor in the forties

E. J. Stapleton (ed.), *Some Official Correspondence of George Canning,* London, 1887

The Manuscripts of J. B. Fortescue, Esq., preserved at Dropmore, Historical Manuscripts Commission, 13th Report, Appendix, Part III; 14th Report, Appendix, Part IV, London, 1892–1927

Report on the Manuscripts of Earl Bathurst, Historical Manuscripts Commission, London, 1923

Unfortunately for the student the correspondence of several other important statesmen has not been printed. Thus for William Pitt one must go to the Public Record Office for the *Chatham Papers;* for the Earl of Liverpool, William Huskisson, William Wyndham and for the Minutes of the Society for the Abolition of the Slave Trade to the Additional Manuscripts in the British Museum. The *Auckland Papers* in the same collection should also be used to supplement the *Journal* referred to above.

In this category one might include also *The Dispatches and Letters of Vice-Admiral Lord Viscount Nelson, with notes by Sir Nicholas Harris Nicholas,* Vol. I, 1777–1794, London, 1845, which shows how the West Indian planters reacted to their saviour, whom they have honoured in Barbados and Antigua, when, after defeating the French naval enemy, he turned his guns on the free trader undermining the British 'exclusive'.

(iv) The Abolitionists

A considerable quantity of data is available. The following works are indispensable:

R. I. and S. Wilberforce, *The Life of William Wilberforce*, London, 1838

R. I. and S. Wilberforce, *Correspondence of William Wilberforce*, London, 1840

A. M. Wilberforce, *The Private Papers of William Wilberforce*, London, 1897

T. Clarkson, *An Essay on the Slavery and Commerce of the Human Species*, London, 1786

T. Clarkson, *Essay on the Impolicy of the African Slave Trade*, London, 1788

T. Clarkson, *History of the Rise, Progress and Accomplishment of the Abolition of the Slave Trade*, Philadelphia, 1808 (London edition of 1839)

J. Ramsay, *Essay on the Treatment and Conversion of African Slaves in the British Sugar Colonies*, London, 1784

J. Ramsay, *An Inquiry into the Effects of putting a stop to the African Slave Trade*, London, 1784

J. Ramsay, *A Ms. Vol. entirely in his own hand, mainly concerned with his activities towards the Abolition of the Slave Trade*, 1787—a copy of this rare work is in the Library of Rhodes House, Oxford

J. Ramsay, *Objections to the Abolition of the Slave Trade, with Answers*, London, 1788

J. Stephen, *The Slavery of the British West India Colonies delineated*, 2 vols., London, 1824–1830

J. Stephen, *England enslaved by her own Slave Colonies*, London, 1826

C. E. Stephen, *The Right Honourable Sir James Stephen. Letters with Bibliographical notes*, London (?), 1906—privately printed

Sir G. Stephen, *Anti-Slavery Recollections*, London, 1854

Z. Macaulay, *East and West India Sugar; or a refutation of the Claims of the West Indian Colonists to a protecting duty on East India Sugar*, London, 1823

T. F. Buxton, *The African Slave Trade*, London, 1839

C. Buxton, *Memoirs of Sir Thomas Fowell Buxton*, London, 1848

R. R. Madden, *A Twelve Months Residence in the West Indies*, London, 1834

D. Turnbull, *The Jamaica Movement, for promoting the Enforcement of the Slave Trade Treaties, and the Suppression of the Slave Trade*, London, 1850

Prince Hoare, *Memoirs of Granville Sharp, composed from his own Manuscripts*, London, 1820

J. Jeremie, *Four Esays in Colonial Slavery*, London, 1831

W. Roscoe, *A General View of the African Slave Trade demonstrating its Injustice and Impolicy*, London, 1788

W. Roscoe, *Manifesto against African Slavery, issued by the Liverpool Anti-Slavery Society*, Liverpool, 1830 (?)
H. Richard, *Memoirs of Joseph Sturge*, London, 1864

Among more modern works on the abolitionists and the abolitionist movement the following may be cited:

Viscountess Knutsford, *Life and Letters of Zachary Macaulay*, London, 1900
R. Coupland, *Wilberforce*, Oxford, 1923
F. J. Klingberg, *The Anti-Slavery Movement in England*, Newhaven, 1926 —a United States view
R. Coupland, *The British Anti-Slavery Movement*, London, 1933
N. B. Lewis, *The Abolitionist Movement in Sheffield, 1823–1833: With Letters from Southey, Wordsworth and others. From the Original Papers in the John Rylands Library*, Manchester, 1934
C. M. Mac Innes, *England and Slavery*, London, 1934
C. Booth, *Zachary Macaulay*, London, 1934
E. L. Griggs, *Thomas Clarkson, Friend of Slaves*, London, 1936
Sir G. Mac Munn, *Slavery through the Ages*, London, 1938
R. K. Nuermberger, *The Free Produce Movement, A Quaker Protest againts Slavery*, Durham, N.C., 1943
G. R. Mellor, *British Imperial Trusteeship, 1783–1850*, London, 1951—the idealist conception of history
Paul Knaplund, *James Stephen and the British Colonial System, 1813–1847*, University of Wisconsin Press, Madison, 1953
Britain and the Suppression of Slavery, Central Office of Information, London, December, 1953

In connection with the abolition movement and the work of the abolitionists, there are five important accounts of the British West Indies after emancipation, three of them hostile and two sympathetic, which are essential for any analysis of British West Indian history in the nineteenth century. These accounts are as follows:

Thomas Carlyle, *An Occasional Discourse on the Nigger Question*, London, 1848—the classic vilification of the West Indian Negro
Anthony Trollope, *The West Indies and the Spanish Main*, London, 1860
W. Sewell, *The Ordeal of Free Labour in the British West Indies*, New York, 1861—a sympathetic account of the British West Indian peasantry after emancipation when compared with Carlyle's 'niggerphobia', Trollope's taking the British people 'a-Trolloping' and Froude's 'Froudacity'
Charles Kingsley, *At Last: A Christmas in the West Indies*, New York, 1871—very important not only for its graphic picture of life in Trinidad but also for its sympathetic treatment of the problem of the small

farmer in his conflict with the plantation economy based on publicly subsidised Indian immigration

J. A. Froude, *The English in the West Indies, or the Bow of Ulysses,* London, 1887

(v) Local Histories

The following titles are among the more important for the period:

Bryan Edwards, *The History, Civil and Commercial, of the British Colonies in the West Indies,* London, 1793

John Poyer, *The History of Barbados, from the First Discovery of the Island, in the year 1605, till the Accession of Lord Seaforth, 1801,* London, 1808

Sir R. Schomburgk, *History of Barbados, comprising a Geographical and Statistical Description of the Island, a Sketch of the Historical Events since the Settlement, and an Account of its Geology and Natural Productions,* London, 1848

C. Shephard, *Historical Account of the Island of Saint Vincent,* London, 1831

E. L. Joseph, *History of Trinidad,* Trinidad, n.d.

L. A. A. de Verteuil, *Trinidad: Its Geography, Natural Resources, Administration, Present Condition, and Prospects,* London, 1884 edition

L. W. Fraser, *History of Trinidad;* from the first period from 1781 to 1813, Vol. I, Trinidad, 1891; from 1814 to 1839, Vol. II, Trinidad, 1896

J. N. Brierly, *Trinidad then and now,* Trinidad, 1912

G. W. Bridges, *The Annals of Jamaica,* London, 1828

W. J. Gardiner, *History of Jamaica, from its Discovery by Christopher Columbus to the year 1872,* London, 1909

W. F. Finlason, *A History of the Jamaica Case,* London, n.d.—a defence of Governor Eyre's conduct in the Jamaica Rebellion of 1865

Lord Olivier, *The Myth of Governor Eyre,* London, 1933—an attack on Eyre

H. G. Dalton, *History of British Guiana, comprising a General Description of the Colony, a Narration of some of the Principal Events from the Earliest Years of its Discovery to the Present Time, together with an Account of its Climate, Geology, Staple Products and Natural History,* 2 Vols., London, 1855

D. Morris, *The Colony of British Honduras, Its Resources and Prospects,* London, 1883

J. Rodway, *History of British Guiana, from the year 1688 to the Present Time,* 3 vols., Georgetown, Vol. I, 1891, Vol. II, 1893, Vol. III, 1894

Sir C. Clementi, *The Chinese in British Guiana,* Georgetown, 1915

A. R. F. Webber, *A Centenary History of British Guiana,* Georgetown, 1931

Sir C. Clementi, *A Constitutional History of British Guiana,* London, 1937

Dwarka Nath, *A History of Indians in British Guiana,* Edinburgh, 1950

Sir J. A. Burdon (ed.), *Archives of British Honduras*, London, 1931–1935; Vol. I, from the earliest date to A.D. 1800; Vol. II, A.D. 1801 to A.D. 1840; Vol. III, A.D. 1841 to A.D. 1884

C. S. Salmon, *The Caribbean Confederation. A Plan for the Union of the Fifteen British West Indian Colonies*, London, n.d.

Special mention should be made of the series of original works dealing with all phases of life in British Guiana republished by the *Daily Chronicle* of British Guiana. This represents an interest in local history which has no parallel in the British West Indies. Among the several volumes issued the following may be indicated as of special value:

H. Bolingbroke, *A Voyage to the Demerary, with an account of the Settlements there and on the Berbice and Essequibo*, London, 1806 (No. 1 of the Guiana edition)

G. Pinckard, *Letters from Guiana*, London, 1796–1797, (No. 5 of the Guiana edition)

Sir G. William des Voeux, *Experiences of a Demerara Magistrate*, (No. 11 of the Guiana edition)

Sir R. Schomburgk, *Travels in British Guiana during the years 1840–1844*, Leipzig, 1847 (No. 17 of the Guiana Edition, Georgetown, 1953)

Of the original works included in this series, reference may be made to P. Rahomon, *Centenary History of the Indians in British Guiana, 1838–1938* (No. 10 of the Guiana Edition, Georgetown, n.d.)

(vi) Church histories

Of very special significance for this period of British West Indian history are the monographs by or on famous missionaries or about the churches in general. These include:

J. M. Phillippo, *Jamaica: Its Past and Present State*, London, 1843

J. H. Hinton, *Memoir of William Knibb, Missionary in Jamaica*, London, 1847

E. A. Wallbridge, *The Demerara Martyr, Memoirs of the Rev. John Smith*, London, 1848 (republished as No. 6 of the *Daily Chronicle's* Guiana Edition)

W. F. Burchell, *Memoir of Thomas Burchell, Twenty-two Years a Missionary in Jamaica*, London, 1849

W. Moister, *Memorials of Missionary Labours in Western Africa and the West Indies*, London, 1850

E. B. Underhill, *The Tragedy of Morant Bay. A Narrative of the Disturbances in the Island of Jamaica in 1865*, London, 1895

K. G. Grant, *My Missionary Memories*, Halifax, 1923—an account of work among the East Indians of Trinidad

To this list one might add the following general accounts:

T. Coke, *A History of the West Indies, containing the Natural, Civil, and Ecclesiastical History of each Island: with an account of the Missions instituted in those islands, from the commencement of their civilization; but more especially of the Missions which have been established in that Archipelago by the Society late in connexion with the Rev. John Wesley,* 3 vols., Liverpool, 1808

A. Caldecott, *The Church in the West Indies,* London, 1898

H. P. Thomson, *Into All Lands, The History of the Society for the Propagation of the Gospel in Foreign Parts, 1701–1950,* London, 1951— contains a few chapters on the West Indies

(vii) General Accounts

The historical material on the slave trade includes a valuable collection of data on Liverpool, the capital of the British slave trade, which is very important for British West Indian history. Some titles are:

J. Wallace, *A General and Descriptive History of the Ancient and Present State of the Town of Liverpool ... together with a Circumstantial Account of the True Causes of its extensive African Trade,* Liverpool, 1795

H. Smithers, *Liverpool, Its Commerce, Statistics and Institutions.* Liverpool 1825

T. Baines, *History of the Commerce and Town of Liverpool,* Liverpool 1852

G. Williams, *History of the Liverpool Privateers with an Account of the Liverpool Slave Trade,* Liverpool, 1897

R. Muir, *A History of Liverpool,* London, 1907

The question of West Indian slavery, the West Indian monopoly and the competition of sugar from India gave rise to a voluminous literature from which the following selections may be recommended:

G. Chalmers, *Opinions on Interesting Subjects of Public Law and Commercial Policy arising from American Independence,* London, 1784

J. Allen, *Considerations on the Present State of the Intercourse between His Majesty's Sugar Colonies and the Dominions of the United States of America,* London, 1784

Lord Sheffield, *Observations on the Project for abolishing the Slave Trade,* London, 1790

W. Fox, *Address to the People of Great Britain on the Propriety of abstaining from West India Sugar and Rum,* London, 1791

The Right in the West India Merchants to a Double Monopoly of the Sugar-Market of Great Britain, and the expedience of all Monopolies, examined, London, n.d.

A Report of the Proceedings of the Committee of Sugar Refiners, for the purpose of effecting a reduction in the high prices of sugar, by lowering the bounty of refined sugar exported, and correcting the evils of the West India Monopoly, London, 1792

H. Brougham, *An Inquiry into the Colonial Policy of the European Powers*, Edinburgh, 1803

J. A. Waller, *A Voyage in the West Indies*, London, 1820

Letters to William Wilberforce, M.P., *recommending the Encouragement of the Cultivation of Sugar in our Dominions in the East Indies as the Natural and Certain Means of effecting the Total and General Abolition of the Slave Trade*, Liverpool, 1822

T. Fletcher, *Letters in Vindication of the Rights of the British West India Colonies*, Liverpool, 1822

Memorandum on the Relative Importance of the West and East Indies to Great Britain, London, 1823

T. Roughley, *The Jamaica Planter's Guide; or, a System of planting and managing a Sugar Estate, or Other Plantations in that Island, and throughout the British West Indies in general*, London, 1823

J. B. Seely, *A Few Hints to the West Indians on their Present Claims to Exclusive Favour and Protection at the expense of the East India Interests*, London, 1823

J. Cropper, *A Letter addressed to the Liverpool Society for Promoting the Abolition of Slavery, on the Injurious Effects of High Prices of Produce, and the Beneficial Effects of Low Prices, on the Condition of Slaves*, Liverpool, 1823

J. Cropper, *Relief for West India Distress, showing the Inefficiency of Protecting Duties on East India Sugar, and pointing out other Modes of Certain Relief*, London, 1823

J. Cropper, *The Support of Slavery investigated*, Liverpool, 1824

Correspondence between John Gladstone, M.P., *and James Cropper on the Present State of Slavery in the British West Indies and in the United States of America, and on the Importation of Sugar from the British Settlements in India*, Liverpool, 1824

Report of the Committee of the Society for the Mitigation and Gradual Abolition of Slavery throughout the British Dominions, London, 1824

J. Taylor, *Negro Emancipation and West India Independence, the True Interest of Great Britain*, Liverpool, 1824

East India Sugar, or an Inquiry respecting the Means of improving the Quality and reducing the Cost of Sugar raised by Free Labour in the East Indies, London, 1824

W. Naish, *Reasons for using East India Sugar*, London, 1828

M. G. Lewis, *Journal of a West India Proprietor, kept during a Residence in the Island of Jamaica*, London, 1834

E. Stanley, *Claims and Resources of the West Indian Colonies. A letter to the Rt. Hon. W. E. Gladstone*, M.P., London, 1850

H. Hume, *The Life of Edward John Eyre, Late Governor of Jamaica*, London, 1867

J. Murch, *Memoir of Robert Hibbert, Esquire*, Bath, 1874

*   *   *

The early threat of the beet sugar industry in Great Britain to British West Indian economy will be found in W. Crookes, *On the Manufacture of Beet-Root Sugar in England and Ireland*, London, 1870. To this should be added two monumental modern studies: H. C. Prinsen Geerligs, *The World's Cane Sugar Industry, Past and Present*, Manchester, 1912; N. Deerr, *The History of Sugar*, 2 vols., London, 1949–1950.

The following are the more important modern monographs dealing with the abolition of slavery and its aftermath:

W. L. Mathieson, *British Slavery and Its Abolition, 1823–1838*, London, 1926

L. J. Ragatz, *Statistics for the Study of British Caribbean Economic History, 1763–1833*, London, 1927

J. B. Dow, *Slave Ships and Slaving*, Salem, 1927

H. Merivale, *Lectures on Colonization and Colonies, delivered before the University of Oxford in 1839, 1840 and 1841*, Oxford University Press, 1928 edition

R. L. Schuyler, *Parliament and the British Empire*, New York, 1929

W. L. Mathieson, *British Slave Emancipation, 1838–1849*, London, 1932

H. T. Manning, *British Colonial Government after the American Revolution*, New Haven, 1923

H. A. Wyndham, *The Atlantic and Slavery*, Oxford University Press, 1935

W. L. Burn, *Emancipation and Apprenticeship in the British West Indies*, London, 1937—a scholarly monograph and the definitive work on apprenticeship

M. Steen, *The Sun is my Undoing*, New York, 1941—a well-informed historical novel

A. Mackenzie-Grieve, *The Last Years of the English Slave Trade*, London, 1941

W. L. Burn, *The British West Indies*, London, 1951

F. M. Henriques, *Family and Colour in Jamaica*, London, 1953

H. Craig, *The Legislative Council of Trinidad and Tobago*, London, 1953

P. D. Curtin, *Two Jamaicas, 1830–1865: The Role of Ideas in a Tropical Colony*, Cambridge, U.S.A. 1955

R. T. Smith, *The Negro Family in British Guiana*, London, 1956

B. Hamilton, *Barbados and the Confederation Question 1871–1885*, London, 1956

Eric Williams, 'The Historical Background of Race Relations in the Caribbean,' in *Miscelanea de Estudios dedicados al Dr. Fernando Ortiz*, Vol. III, Habana, 1957

D. Hall, *Free Jamaica, 1838–1865: An Economic History*, New Haven, 1959

D. Guérin, *The West Indies and their Future*, London, 1961

G. Eisner, *Jamaica, 1830–1930: A Study of Economic Growth*, Manchester, 1961

V. Murga Sans, *Historia Documental de Puerto Rico*, Vol. 1, Tomo I and II, Rio Piedras, 1957; Vol. III, Rio Piedras, 1961

L. C. Monclova, *Historia de Puerto Rico (Siglo XIX)*, Tomo I (1808–1868), Rio Piedras, 1958; Tomo II (1875–1885), 1957; Tomo III (1885–1898), 1962

B. Semmel, *Jamaican Blood and Victorian Conscience*, Boston, 1963

H. Mitchell, *Europe in the Caribbean*, Edinburgh, 1963

Eric Williams, *History of the People of Trinidad and Tobago*, London, 1964

E. Gouveia, *Slave Society in the British Leeward Islands at the end of the Eighteenth Century*, New Haven, 1965

Eric Williams, *British Historians and the West Indies*, London, 1966

H. Hoetnik, *Two Variants in Caribbean Race Relations*, London, 1967

D. Wood, *Trinidad in Transition, The Years after Slavery*, London, 1968

R. W. Beachey, *The British West Indies Sugar Industry in the late 19th Century*, Oxford, 1957

E. I. Mendes (ed.), *Crónicas de Puerto Rico*, I (1493–1797), II (1809–1955), San Juan, 1957

B. THE FRENCH WEST INDIES

The paucity of data for the French West Indies in the period under review, whether official reports or documents or scholarly monographs, is in striking contrast to the material available for the British West Indies. There is only one redeeming feature in this situation: what there is is quite good.

The best of the contemporary material is as follows:

Bryan Edwards, *An Historical Survey of the French Colony in the Island of St. Domingo*, London, 1797

Moreau de Saint-Méry, *Description topographique, physique, civile, politique et historique de la partie Française de l'isle Saint-Domingue, avec des observations...sur sa population, sur le caractère et les moeurs de ses...habitants, sur son climat, sa culture...*2 vols., Philadelphia, 1797–1798

Moreau de Saint-Méry, *A Description of the Spanish part of the Island of St. Domingo*, Philadelphia, 1798

P. de Lacroix, *Mémoires pour servir à l'Histoire de la Révolution de Saint-Domingue*, Paris, 1819

P.-Ch. de St. Amant, *Des Colonies; particulièrement de la Guyane Française, en 1821*, Paris, 1822

A. de Tocqueville, *Rapport fait au nom de la Commission chargée d'examiner la proposition de M. de Tracy, relative aux Esclaves des Colonies*, Paris, 1839

A. G. de Cassagnac, *Voyage aux Antilles*, Paris, 1842

A. Moreau de Jonnès, *Recherches statistiques sur l'esclavage colonial*, Paris, 1842

Commission instituée, par décision royale du 26 mai 1840, pour l'examen des questions relatives à l'esclavage et à la constitution politique des colonies. Rapport fait au ministre secretaire d'état de la Marine et des Colonies, Paris, March 1843

Note sur la Fondation d'une Nouvelle Colonie dans la Guyane Française, Paris, 1844

A. Cochin, *L'Abolition de l'Esclavage,* Paris, 1861—this valuable work, by the Clarkson of France, covers not only the French, but also the British, Danish and Dutch territories in the Caribbean

T. Huc, *La Martinique, Etudes sur certaines questions coloniales,* Paris, 1877

Sir John Fortescue, *History of the British Army,* Vol. IV, Parts I and II, London, 1906—an invaluable account of the British effort to capture St. Domingue which throws much light on the political aspect of the question

P. Roussier (ed.), *General Leclerc, Lettres,* Paris, 1937

Victor Schoelcher, *Esclavage et Colonisation,* Paris, 1948—this collection of excerpts from the voluminous writings of the great French abolitionist, the Las Casas of the Negro, is absolutely indispensable

Some excellent monographs of modern scholarship are available. The best are:

L. Deschamps, *Les Colonies pendant La Revolution,* Paris, 1898

P. Boissonade, *Saint-Domingue à la Veille de la Révolution et la Question de la Représentation aux Etats-Généraux,* Paris, 1906

A. Nemours, *Histoire Miltaire de la Guerre d'Indépendance de Saint-Domingue,* 2 vols., Paris, 1915 and 1928—the point of view of a Haitian General

J. Saintoyant, *La Colonisation Française pendant La Revolution (1789–1799),* 2 vols., Paris, 1930—an admirable study

J. Saintoyant, *La Colonisation Française pendant la période napoléonienne (1799–1815),* Paris, 1931

Gaston-Martin, *La Doctrine Coloniale de la France en 1789,* Cahiers de la Revolution Française, No. III, Paris, 1935

C. L. R. James, *The Black Jacobins. Toussaint Louverture and the San Domingo Revolution,* London, 1936—this is the best account of the Haitian revolution, written by a Trinidadian Trotskyite, and corrects the errors of T. Lothrop Stoddard, *The French Revolution in San Domingo,* Boston, 1914

H. Lemery, *La Revolution Française à la Martinique,* Paris, 1936

Gaston-Martin, *Histoire de l'Esclavage dans les Colonies Françaises,* Paris, 1948—a curiously disappointing book for those who have grown to associate the author with the standard of scholarship achieved in *L'Ere des Négriers*

P. Grunebaum-Ballin, *Henri Gregorire, 1789–1831,* Paris, 1948

S. Alexis, *The Black Liberator. The Life of Toussaint Louverture,* London, 1949

A. Lacroix, *Les Derniers Négriers,* Paris, 1952

J. Rennard, *Documents Inédits à l'occasion du Tricentenaire des Antilles, Guadeloupe, 1635–1935,* Basse Terre, 1935

Aimé Césaire, *Toussaint Louverture,* Paris, 1962

H. Bangou, *La Guadeloupe, 1492–1848,* Paris, 1962; *1848–1939,* Paris, 1963

French sources are, however, particularly valuable for the nineteenth century conflict between cane sugar and beet sugar, especially as that conflict was fought out in the arena of the French metropolitan market. Some excellent monographs are available, of which the following may be cited:

Chambre des Députés, *Rapport fait au nom de la Commission chargée d'examiner le projet de loi sur les Sucres,* 1837

T. Lestiboudois, *Des Colonies Sucrières et des Sucrières Indigènes,* Lille, 1839—a treatise read to the Royal Society of Science, Agriculture and Arts of Lille

T. Dehay, *Les Colonies et la Métropole, le Sucre Exotique et le Sucre Indigène,* Paris, 1839

C. Meriau, *Histoire de l'Industrie Sucrière dans la Région du Nord. Ses Commencements, ses Progrès, son Etat actuel, ses Rapports avec l'Agriculture,* Lille, 1891

J. Helot, *Le Sucre de Betterave en France de 1800 à 1900,* Cambrai, 1900

A. A. Hesse, *L'Industrie Sucrière en France et les Premières Tentatives de Législation Internationale (1864–1877),* Paris, 1909

Some of Debien's work falls in the period now under consideration. Under the general heading of *Notes d'Histoire Coloniale,* they are:

III. *Autour de l'Expédition de Saint-Domingue: les espoirs d'une famille d'anciens planteurs (1801–1804),* Port-au-Prince, 1942

IV. *Le plan et les débuts d'une caféière à Saint-Domingue: La plantation la Merveillère aux Anses-à-Pitre (1789–1792),* Port-au-Prince, 1943

XVII. *Réfugiés de Saint-Domingue aux Etats-Unis,* Port-au-Prince, 1948–1951

XVIII. *Gens de Couleur et Colons de Saint-Domingue devant la Constituante (1789–1790),* Montreal, 1951

XXXII. 'Les projets d'un ancien planteur cotonnier de Saint-Domingue (1814),' *Revue d'histoire des colonies,* 1er trimestre, 1954, pp. 83–102

C. HAITI

Among the studies on the Republic of Haiti in the nineteenth century the following may be mentioned:

M. Saint-Amand, *Histoire des Révolutions d'Haiti,* Paris, 1860

J. L. Janvier, *Les Constitutions d'Haiti (1801–1885),* Paris, 1886

J. N. Léger, *Haiti, Her History and Her Detractors,* New York, 1907

D. THE SPANISH TERRITORIES

(i) Cuba

Nineteenth century Cuba produced more great men than the rest of the Caribbean territories combined throughout their entire history—José Martí, Luz y Caballero, Arango y Parreño, Saco, Bachiller y Morales, Máximo Gomez, Céspedes, Maceo, Juan Gualberto Gómez, Plácido, statesmen, philosophers, humanists, generals, politicians and poets. Twentieth century Cuba has produced Fernando Ortiz, jurist, sociologist, anthropologist, historian and humanist, the greatest scholar in the Caribbean. The wealth of material available on Cuban history and development in the period under review is accordingly so considerable that, in a summary of this nature and scope, one can do no more than attempt a selection of the best of the printed material. The following works can safely be recommended as indispensable:

Gonzalo de Quesada y Miranda (ed.), *Obras Completas de Martí*, 74 vols., La Habana, 1936–1949. This can usefully be supplemented by the *Archivo Jose Martí*, published by the Ministry of Education, of which 18 volumes have appeared to date

Centón Epistolario de Domingo del Monte, Academia de La Historia, La Habana, 1923–1938. The five volumes cover the years 1822–1843

J. A. Saco, *Colección de papeles científicos, históricos, políticos y de otros ramos sobre la Isla de Cuba*, 2 vols., Paris, 1858

J. A. Saco, *Contra la Anexión*, Vols. VI-VII of Colección de Libros Cubanos, La Habana

D. Figarola-Caneda, *José Antonio Saco, Documentos para su vida*, La Habana, 1921

F. de Armas y Céspedes, *De la Esclavitud en Cuba*, Madrid, 1866

José A. Fernandez de Castro, *Medio Siglo de Historia Colonial de Cuba (1823–1879)*, La Habana, 1923

Escritos de Domingo del Monte, Vols. XII-XIII of Colección de Libros Cubanos, La Habana, 1929

Emilio Roig de Leuchsenring, *Cuadernos de Historia Habanera*, Municipio de la Habana, 1936–1939. Among the brochures issued are studies of Maximo Gomez, Emilio Hostos, Aldama, Bachiller y Morales, Arango y Parreño, Morales Lemus, and Juan Francisco Manzano, the slave poet

Juan Gualberto Gómez, *Su labor patriótica y sociológica*, the first volume of a tribute by the Club Atenas of La Habana, 1934

Joaquin Llaverias (ed.), *Boletín del Archivo Nacional*—a mine of documentary information

Alejandro de Humboldt, *Ensayo político sobre la Isla de Cuba*, Vols. XVI-XVII of Colección de Libros Cubanos, La Habana, 1930

J. G. Cantero, *Los Ingenios de Cuba*, La Habana, 1857

J. de la Pezuela, *Diccionario geográfico, estadístico, histórico de la Isla de Cuba*, 4 vols., Madrid, 1863

H. H. S. Aimes, *A History of Slavery in Cuba, 1511 to 1868*, New York, 1907—deals mainly with the nineteenth century

R. R. Madden, *The Island of Cuba: Its Resources, Progress, and Prospects, considered in relation especially to the Influence of its Prosperity on the Interests of the British West India Colonies*, London, 1849

D. Turnbull: *Travels in the West. Cuba; with notices of Porto Rico and the Slave Trade*, London, 1840

R. M. de Labra, *La Abolición de la Esclavitud en las Antillas Españolas*, Madrid, 1869

R. M. de Labra, *La Abolición de la Esclavitud en el Orden Económico*, Madrid, 1873

D. Miguel de Cardenas y Chavez, *Observaciones sobre el principal artículo de la industria agricola cubana*, Memorias de la Sociedad Patriotica de la Habana, 1840, Vol. X

R. Jameson, *Letters from the Havana during the year 1820*, London, 1821

La Cuestión de la Esclavitud en 1871, Propaganda Anti-esclavista, Vol. I, Sociedad Abolicionista Espanola, Madrid, 1871

D. F. Rosillo y Alquier, *Noticia de los ingenios y datos sobre la producción azucarera de la Isla de Cuba*, La Habana, 1873

A. Abbot, *Letters written in the Interior of Cuba, February-May, 1828*, Boston, 1829

R. de la Sagra, *Historia física, económico-politica, intelectual y moral de la Isla de Cuba*, Paris, 1861

V. Queipo, *Cuba, ses ressources, son administration, sa population au point de vue de la colonisation européenne et de l'émancipation progressive des esclaves*, Paris, 1861

Don Urbano Feyjoo Sotomayor, *Immigración de trabajadores españoles. Documentos y memorial escrita sobre esta materia*, La Habana, 1853

Reglamento para la introduccion de trabajadores chinos en la Isla de Cuba, La Habana, August 4, 1860

Dictamen de la Comisión sobre immigración de colonos libres asiáticos en las islas de Cuba y Puerto-Rico, leido en la Sesion general de la 'Sociedad Economica Matritense el dia 26 de Noviembre de 1870, Madrid, 1870

A. Bachiller y Morales, *Los Negros*, Barcelona, n.d.

J. Ferrer de Couto: *Los Negros en sus diversos estados y condiciones*, New York, 1864

R. M. de Labra, *La brutalidad de los negros*, Madrid, 1876

El proletario en España y el Negro en Cuba, La Habana, 1866

J. M. Sanroma, *La esclavitud en Cuba*, Madrid, 1872

Emilio Castelar, *Los crímenes de la esclavitud*, Madrid, 1873

Emilio Castelar, *Discurso contra la esclavitud, en la Asamblea Constituyente*, Madrid, 1870

J. Suarez Argudín, *Proyecto sobre inmigración africana*, La Habana, 1856

F. Figuera, *Estudios sobre la Isla de Cuba. La Cuestión Social*, Madrid, 1866

Un habanero, *Representacion a la Reina de Espana, sobre la abolición de la esclavitud en las Islas de Cuba y Puerto Rico*, Philadelphia, 1862

The Everett Letters on Cuba, Boston, 1897

The best of the more modern works are:

Fernando Ortiz, *Hampa Afrocubana*, Havana, 1915

Ramiro Guerra y Sánchez, *Azúcar y Población en las Antillas*, La Habana, 1935. A classic of Cuban 'philosophy', this is an indispensable book not only for Cuban but indeed for Caribbean historical analysis. Available in an English translation, *Sugar and Society in the Caribbean*, New Haven, 1964

J. Weiss y Sánchez, *La Arquitectura Cubana Colonial* La Habana, 1936

Herminio Portel Vila, *Historia de Cuba en sus relaciones con los Estados Unidos y Espana*, La Habana, Tomo I (1512–1853), 1938; tomo II (1853–1878), 1939; Tomo III (1878–1899), 1939—a standard work

Fernando Ortiz, *Contrapunteo cubano del tabaco y el azúcar*, La Habana, 1940. An English translation of this classic by Harriet de Onis, under the title of *Cuban Counterpoint: Tobacco and Sugar*, can unhesitatingly be recommended. Its literary merits are enhanced by very valuable documents, including a few gems on the development of the sugar industry

Ramiro Guerra y Sánchez, *Guerra de los diez años, 1868–1878*, La Habana, 1950

Eric Williams, 'The Negro Slave Trade in Anglo-Spanish Relations,' *Caribbean Historical Review*, No. I, December, 1950, pp. 22–45

Elias Entralgo, *La Liberación Etnica Cubana*, La Habana, 1953—a remarkable and comprehensive analysis of Cuban philosophy on and practice in race relations which has no counterpart elsewhere in the Caribbean

(ii) Puerto Rico

There is a limited quantity of very valuable material available for the development of Puerto Rico in the nineteenth century. The following documents and studies may be highly recommended:

G. D. Flinter, *Examen del estado actual de los esclavos de la Isla de Porto Rico bajo el gobierno español*, New York, 1832

Los Diputados Americanos en las Cortes Españolas, 1872–1873, Madrid, 1880—a very rare book but absolutely indispensable, including speeches of Sanroma, Facundo Cintron, de Labra and Alvarez Peralta which would do credit to any legislature

L. M. Diaz Soler, *Historia de la Esclavitud Negra en Puerto Rico*

(1493–1890), Madrid, *n.d.*—a valuable addition to the extensive literature on Caribbean slavery

(iii) Santo Domingo

The information on Santo Domingo (Dominican Republic) in the
nineteenth century is limited. The following may be recommended:

Documentos históricos procedentes del Archivo de Indias, Secretario de
   Estado de Relaciones Exteriores, Dominican Republic, 5 vols., 1924,
   1928–1929

Report of the Commission of Inquiry to Santo Domingo, Washington,
   D.C., 1871—regarding the proposal for United States annexation

S. Hazard, *Santo Domingo, Past and Present, with a glance at Haiti,*
   New York, 1873

W. R. Tansil, *Diplomatic Relations between the United States and the
   Dominican Republic, 1874–1899,* Washington, D.C., 1951

E. THE DANISH TERRITORIES

The resurgence of scholarly interest in the Caribbean in recent
years is nowhere better exemplified than by the publication of
Vore Gamle Tropekolonier (Our Former Tropical Colonies) in
Denmark. Edited by the Director of the National Museum, Dr.
Johannes Brudsted, Vol. II of this monumental study covers the
Danish Virgin Islands in four major periods: up to 1755, 1755–
1848, 1848–1880, 1880–1917. Vol. I (the volumes are not sold
separately) deals with the East Indies and Danish Guinea, and
will therefore, be of some value also for West Indian history.

Other essential sources on the former Danish colonies are as
follows:

J. P. Nissen, *Reminiscences of a 46 years' Residence in the Island of St.
   Thomas, in the West Indies,* Nazareth, Pa., 1838

E. Heilbuth, *Denmark and Saint Croix, in their Mutual Relations,*
   Buffalo, 1845—an English translation of a work published in Copenhagen in 1841 attacking Danish mercantilism

J. P. Knox, *A Historical Account of St. Thomas,* New York, 1852—
   contains a few very valuable documents including the Labour Act after
   emancipation which was the cause of a serious insurrection in 1878

C. E. Taylor, *Leaflets from the Danish West Indies,* London, 1888—
   among the important documents included are eye-witness accounts of
   the slave revolt of 1848 which led to emancipation and the royal
   proclamations regarding the abortive efforts to sell the islands to the
   United States in 1867 (An interesting United States view of the abortive
   transaction will be found in J. Parton, *The Danish Islands: Are we
   bound in honour to pay for them,* Boston, 1869)

H. Lawaetz, *Peter v Scholten, Vestindiske Tidsbilleder fra den sidste
   Generalguvernors dage,* Kobenhavn, 1940—a biography of the Governor

General who emancipated the slaves on his own initiative without prior instructions from the metropolitan government

A. A. Campbell, *St. Thomas Negroes—A Study of Personality and Culture*, American Psychological Association, Inc., Psychological Monographs, Vol. 55, No. 5, Northwestern University, 1943—an indispensable work, richly documented.

The *St. Croix Agricultural Reporter* contains two valuable articles on the economy of the Virgin Islands—'The Sugar Estates in St. Croix,' No. 1, April, 1851; 'Removal of Population after Emancipation,' No. 5, April, 1952. The general decline of the slave economy before emancipation is statistically presented in *Statistics regarding landed properties in the Island of St. Croix from 1816 to 1857 with a table showing the quantity of sugar shipped from 1835 to 1840 and from 1835 to 1840 and from 1850 to 1857*, St. Croix, 1859. *The Proceedings of the Colonial Council of St. Croix* contain English accounts of the insurrection of 1878. The question of immigration is treated in *Terms on which Agricultural Labourers from British or Dutch West India Islands will be engaged for the Island of St. Croix*, 1867.

F. THE NETHERLANDS TERRITORIES

In addition to the definitive work of van Lier previously cited, other necessary sources for this period of Netherlands Caribbean history are as follows:

Schets van een Ontwerp tot Behoud van Suriname. Met Planteekeningen, 's Gravenhage, 1847—contains excellent statistics on the plantation economy of Surinam

Rapport der Staatscommissie, benoemd bij Koninklijk bestent van 29 November, 1853, No 66, tot het voorstellen van maatregelen ten aanzien van de slaven in de Nederlandsche Kolonien, 's Gravenhage, 1855–1856: two reports of the government commission of inquiry on the abolition of slavery. The first report (1855) deals with Surinam; the second (1866) with the Netherlands Antilles. Both are indispensable

C. J. M. de Klerk, *De Immigratie der Hindostanen in Suriname*, Amsterdam, 1953—a well documented account of Indian immigration into Surinam

L. L. E. Rens, *The Historical and Social Background of Surinam Negro-English*, Amsterdam, 1953—a very interesting and well documented study

De West-Indische Gids, Emancipatienummer, June, 1953, 's-Gravenhage, 1953—a series of articles with English summaries, containing valuable documents and an invaluable bibliography

(4) The 'American Mediterranean', 1899–1940

A. OFFICIAL REPORTS
(a) British Islands:

Report of the Sugar Commission, 1929
Report of the Trinidad Disturbances Commission, 1937
Report of the Closer Union Commission, 1933
Report of a Commission appointed to consider Problems of Secondary and Primary Education in Trinidad etc., 1931–32
Report of a visit to certain West Indian colonies and to British Guiana (Major Wood), 1921
Labour Conditions in the West Indies, 1937
Recommendations of the West India Royal Commission, 1938–1939

These reports, by commissioners sent out from England, should be supplemented by the reports of various local commissions of which the most useful are:

Reports on nutrition in the various colonies
Report of the Barbados Disturbances Commission, 1937
Report of Select Committee of the Legislative Council on Restriction of Hours of Labour, Trinidad, 1926
Report of the British Guiana Franchise Commission, 1934
Report of the Economic Investigation Committee, British Guiana, 1930
Report of the Small Farmers Committee, British Guiana, 1930
Commission of Inquiry into Labour Conditions, St. Lucia, 1937—Interim and Final Reports on the Sugar Industry
Report by Minimum Wage Advisory Board in regard to ... Agricultural Labourers, St. Lucia, 1936
Report of a Commission to enquire into the Economic Condition of various classes of wage-earners in the Colony, Grenada, 1938
Report on the Agricultural Conditions of Dominica, 1925
Report of the Unemployment Commission, Jamaica, 1936
Report of the Commissioners appointed to enquire into and report on the Labour Disputes ... British Guiana, 1935
Report of the Labour Disturbances Commission, Trinidad, 1934
Report of the Jamaica Banana Commission, 1936

These reports, local and imperial, lay bare the conditions of the British West Indies; their number and their repetition of the same themes illustrate the inertia and indifference of governments not representative of the majority of the inhabitants.

(b) American Islands:

Annual Reports of the Governor, Department of Education, Commissioner of Labor in Puerto Rico

Health and Socio-Economic Studies in Puerto Rico:

1. *On a Sugar Cane Plantation*
2. *In the Coffee, Fruit and Tobacco Regions*

3. *Physical Measurements of Agricultural Workers*
4. *Physical Impairments of Adult Life Among Agricultural Workers*
5. *Health Work in the Rural Areas of Puerto Rico*

Five invaluable scientific studies.

E. A. Bird: *Report on the Sugar Industry in Relation to the Social and Economic System of Puerto Rico*, 1937
Report of the Puerto Rico Policy Commission (Chardon Report), 1934
E. W. Zimmermann: *Staff Report to the Interdepartmental Committee on Puerto Rico*, 1940

These three reports represent official investigations of conditions in Puerto Rico. Their recommendations have been as usual ignored.

(c) Independent Islands:
Annual Reports of the American Fiscal Representative in Haiti and Dominican Republic.

B. BOOKS
B. W. and J. W. Diffie, *Porto Rico, a Broken Pledge,* New York, 1931
L. H. Jenks, *Our Cuban Colony,* New York, 1928
M. M. Knight, *The Americans in Santo Domingo,* New York, 1928

These three studies in American imperialism are of the greatest value today, as illustrating the inconsistency of dollar diplomacy with the policy of the good neighbour.

Foreign Policy Association, *Problems of the New Cuba,* New York, 1935. Full of useful information
A. Calder-Marshall, *Glory Dead,* London, 1939. A sympathetic description of conditions in Trinidad and its people
K. Pringle, *Waters of the West,* London, 1938. Includes a good chapter on Jamaica
O. P. Starkey, *The Economic Geography of Barbados,* New York, 1939. A superficial book which does not live up to the pretentiousness of its title, but which includes some useful tables
W. M. Macmillan, *Warning from the West Indies,* London, 1938. A good description by a South African Liberal professor, with conclusions typical of the academic liberal.
A. Arredondo, *El Negro en Cuba,* La Habana, 1939. Useful for readers of Spanish
The European Possessions in the Caribbean Area, American Geographical Society, 1941. A good compilation of facts and figures
C. L. Jones, *et al, The United States and the Caribbean,* Chicago, 1929
V. S. Clarke, (ed.), *Porto Rico and Its Problems,* Washington, D.C., 1930
D. G. Munro, *The United States and the Caribbean Area,* Boston, 1934
Lord Olivier, *Jamaica, The Blessed Island,* London, 1936
J. F. Dalton, *Sugar, A Case Study of Goverment Control,* New York, 1937

A. P. Gayer, *et al, The Sugar Economy of Puerto Rico*, New York, 1938

U. S. Department of Labour, *Welfare of Families of Sugar-Beet Laborors*, Washington, D.C., 1939

W. H. Callcott, *The Caribbean Policy of the United States 1890–1920*, Baltimore, 1942

S. W. Mintz, *Worker in the Cane, A Puerto Rican Life History*, New Haven, 1960

D. G. Munro, *Intervention and Dollar Diplomacy in the Caribbean, 1900–1921*, Princeton, 1964

Eric Williams, *Education in the British West Indies*, Port-of-Spain, 1951; New York, 1968

Eric Williams, *The Negro in the Caribbean*, Washington, D.C., 1942; being reprinted New York

C. PAMPHLETS

The West Indies Today, published by the International African Service Bureau of London. Presents the case of progressive British colonials

A. A. Lewis, *Labour in the West Indies*, London, 1939

R. Picó, *Studies in the Economic Geography of Puerto Rico*, Rio Piedras, 1937. A collection of three good studies by a member of the Faculty of the University of Puerto Rico

E. B. Hill and S. L. Descartes, *An Economic Background for Agricultural Research in Puerto Rico*, Rio Piedras, 1939. Contains useful data

C. L. R. James, *The Case for West Indian Self Government*, London, 1933.

M. Dartigue, *Conditions Rurales en Haiti*, Port-au-Prince, 1938. A very good analysis of Haitian agriculture.

Foreign Policy Reports (Foreign Policy Association, New York):

E. K. James, *Puerto Rico at the Crossroads*, Oct. 15, 1937

L. H. Evans, *Unrest in the Virgin Islands*, March 27, 1935

C. A. Thomson, *Dictatorship in the Dominican Republic*, April 15, 1936

A. R. Elliott, *European Colonies in the Western Hemisphere*, August 15, 1940

H. J. Trueblood, *The Havana Conference of 1940*, Sept. 15, 1940

D. ARTICLES

G. Simpson, 'Haitian Peasant Economy' *Journal of Negro History* October 1940

Price Mars, 'Social Castes and Social Problems in Haiti' *Inter-American Quarterly*, July 1940. A discussion of Haitian society by Haiti's outstanding man of letters

R. Picó, 'Puerto Rico, Economic Sore Spot' *Inter-American Quarterly*, April 1940. A good article, by one of the foremost intellectual opponents of the large plantation

W. A. Roberts, 'Future of the British Caribbean' *Survey Graphic*, April 1941

V. P. Tschebotareff, 'New Problems for the British West Indies' *Inter-American Quarterly*, July 1941

Eric Williams, 'The Negro in the British West Indies' *The Negro in the Americas,* Graduate School, Howard University, 1940

(5) The Movement for Caribbean Independence 1940–1969

H. S. Perloff, *Puerto Rico's Economic Future, A Study in Planned Development,* Chicago, 1950

L. Nelson, *Rural Cuba,* Minneapolis, 1950

Colonial Office, *Plan for a British Caribbean Federation agreed by the Conference held in London in April 1953,* London, 1953, Cmmd. 8895

Colonial Office, *Plan for a British Caribbean Federation:* (1) *Report of the Fiscal Commissioner,* Cmmd. 9618, (2) *Report of the Judicial Commissioner,* Cmmd. 9620, (3) *Report of the Civil Service Commissioner,* Cmmd. 9619

M. Leiris, *Contacts de Civilisations en Martinique et en Guadeloupe,* Paris, 1955

D. Guérin, *Les Antilles Décolonisées,* Paris, 1956

Colonial Office, *Report by the Conference on British Caribbean Federation held in London in February 1956,* London, Cmmd. 9733

Colonial Office, *Report of the Chaguaramas Joint Commission,* London, 1958

Economics of Nationhood, Port-of-Spain, 1959

R. F. Smith, *The United States and Cuba,* New York, 1960

F. Castro, *La Revolución Cubana,* Buenos Aires, 1960

G. E. Cumper (ed.), *The Economy of the West Indies,* Kingston, 1960

M. Ayearst, *The British West Indies, the Search for Self-Government,* London, 1960

M. M. Tumin, *Social Class and Social Change in Puerto Rico,* Princeton, 1961

J. H. Adhin, *Development Planning in Surinam in Historical Perspective,* Leyden, 1961

C. Julien, *La Révolution Cubaine,* Paris, 1961

Les Antilles et la Guyane à l'heure de la Décolonisation, Congrès des 22 et 23 avril, 1961, Paris, 1961

M. Klass, *East Indians in Trinidad, A Study of Cultural Persistence,* New York, 1961

Présence Africaine, *Antilles-Guyane,* Revue Culturelle du Monde Noir, 3e Trimestre, 1962

R. T. Smith, *British Guiana,* Oxford, 1962

I. L. Vivas, *Historia de Puerto Rico,* New York, 1962

F. Draper, *Castro's Revolution, Myths and Realities,* New York, 1962

P. Vilar *et al, Eveil aux Amériques, Cuba,* Paris, 1962

L. Sauvage, *Autopsie du Castrisme,* Paris, 1962

R. Scheer and M. Zeitlin, *Cuba, An American Tragedy,* New York, 1963

G. K. Lewis, *Puerto Rico, Freedom and Power in the Caribbean,* New York, 1963

R. Dumont, *Cuba, Socialisme et Développement,* Paris, 1964

D. Seers, (ed.), *Cuba, The Economic and Social Revolution,* Chapel Hill, N.C., 1964

H. Johnson, *The Bay of Pigs,* New York, 1964

J. A. Diaz, (ed.), *Cuba; Geopolítica y Pensamiento Económico,* Miami, 1964

M. G. Smith, *The Plural Society in the British West Indies,* Berkeley, 1965

F. and S. Andic, *Fiscal Survey of the French Caribbean,* Rio Piedras, P.R., 1965

B. Goldenberg, *The Cuban Revolution and Latin America,* London, 1965

F. Draper, *Castroism, Theory and Practice,* New York 1965

W. G. Demas, *The Economics of Development in Small Countries, with special reference to the Caribbean,* Montreal, 1965

Report of the United States-Puerto Rico Commission of the Status of Puerto Rico, Washington, D.C., 1966

R. D. Crassweller, *Trujillo: The Life and Times of a Caribbean Dictator,* New York, 1966

T. Szulc, *Dominican Diary,* New York, 1966

J. B. Martin, *Overtaken by Events, The Dominican Crisis from the Fall of Trujillo to the Civil War,* New York, 1966

J. Bosch, *The Unfinished Experiment, Democracy in the Dominican Republic,* London, 1966

C. Jagan, *The West on Trial, My Fight for Guyana's Freedom,* London, 1966

A. Suarez, *Cuba: Castroism and Communism, 1959–1966,* Cambridge, Mass., 1967

J-P. O. Gingras, *Duvalier, Caribbean Cyclone: The History of Haiti and its Present Government,* New York, 1967

J. Plank, (ed.), *Cuba and the United States,* New York, 1967

H. Brewster and C. Thomas, *Dynamics of West Indian Economic Integration,* Mona, Jamaica, 1967

Ministry of Overseas Development, *Report of the Tripartite Economic Survey of the Eastern Caribbean,* London, 1967

P. A. Perez Cabral, *La Communidad Mulata,* El caso socio-político de la República Dominicán, Caracas, 1967

R. W. Logan, *Haiti and the Dominican Republic,* Oxford, 1968

J. Yglesias, *In the Fist of the Revolution, Life in Castro's Cuba,* London, 1968

E. Boorstein, *The Economic Transformation of Cuba, A First-Hand Account,* New York, 1968

I. Oxaal, *Black Intellectuals come to Power, The Rise of Creole Nationalism in Trinidad and Tobago,* Cambridge, Mass., 1968

J. Mordecai, *West Indies: The Federal Negotiations,* London, 1968

G. K. Lewis, *Growth of the Modern West Indies,* London, 1968

C. O'Loughlin, *Economic and Political Change in the Leeward and Windward Islands,* New Haven, 1968

H. L. Matthews, *Castro, A Political Biography,* London, 1969

L. Huberman and P. M. Sweezy, *Socialism in Cuba,* New York, 1969

R. Dumont with M. Mazoyer, *Développement et Socialisme,* Paris, 1969

Eric Williams, *Inward Hunger, The Education of a Prime Minister,* London, 1969

R. Dumont, *Cuba est-il socialiste?* Paris, 1970.

Index